Second Canadian Edition

Macroeconomics

DOUGLAS CURTIS
Trent University

IAN IRVINE
Concordia University

DAVID BEGG
Imperial College Business School, London

McGraw-Hill
Ryerson
Connect. Learn. Succeed.™

The McGraw·Hill Companies

Macroeconomics
Second Canadian Edition

ISBN-13: 978-0-07-096955-1
ISBN-10: 0-07-096955-8

1 2 3 4 5 6 7 8 9 10 WCD 1 9 8 7 6 5 4 3 2 1 0

Printed and bound in the United States of America.

Vice President and Editor-in-Chief: *Joanna Cotton*
Executive Sponsoring Editor: *Leanna MacLean*
Sponsoring Editors: *Bruce McIntosh, James Booty*
Executive Marketing Manager: *Joy Armitage Taylor*
Developmental Editors: *Daphne Scriabin, Andria Fogarty*
Permissions Editor: *Amy Rydzanicz*
Editorial Associate: *Stephanie Hess*
Senior Supervising Editor: *Joanne Limebeer*
Copy Editor: *Imogen Brian*
Production Coordinator: *Lena Keating*
Cover Design: *Liz Harasymczuk*
Cover Image: © *Anton Sokolov/Shutterstock.com*
Interior Design: *Liz Harasymczuk*
Composition: *Aptara, Inc.*
Printer: *Worldcolor*

Library and Archives Canada Cataloguing in Publication Data

Curtis, D. C. A. (Douglas Charles Amos), 1942-
Macroeconomics / Douglas Curtis, Ian Irvine, David Begg. — 2nd Canadian ed.

Includes index.
ISBN 978-0-07-096955-1

1. Macroeconomics—Textbooks. I. Irvine, Ian Joseph, 1949-
II. Begg, David K. H III. Title.

HB172.5.C85 2010 339 C2009-905343-8

About the Authors

Douglas Curtis is a specialist in macroeconomics. He is the author of twenty research papers on fiscal policy, monetary policy, and economic growth and structural change. He has also prepared research reports for Canadian industry and government agencies and authored numerous working papers. He completed his PhD at McGill University, and has held visiting appointments at the University of Cambridge and the University of York in the United Kingdom. His current research interests are monetary and fiscal policy rules, and the relationship between economic growth and structural change. He is Professor Emeritus of Economics at Trent University in Peterborough, Ontario, and Sessional Adjunct Professor at Queen's University in Kingston, Ontario.

Ian Irvine is a specialist in microeconomics and public economics. He is the author of almost thirty research papers in the fields of taxation, health economics, microeconomics, and economic inequality. He completed his PhD at the University of Western Ontario, and has been a visiting lecturer at the London School of Economics, the University of Sydney, the University of Colorado, University College Dublin, and the Economic and Social Research Institute. His current research interests are in tobacco use and taxation, Canada's Employment Insurance and Welfare systems, and crime. He has done numerous studies for the Government of Canada, and is currently a Professor of Economics at Concordia University in Montreal.

David Begg is Principal of the Tanaka Business School at Imperial College London. He has been a Research Fellow of the Centre for Economic Policy Research (a network of leading European economists) since its inception in 1984. David's research focuses mainly on monetary policy, exchange rates, monetary union, and economic transition. He is a Research Fellow of the Centre for Economic Policy Research. He co-authored several of the CEPR annual reports in the series he helped found: *Monitoring the European Central Bank,* and *Monitoring European Integration*. The 1997 MEI Report, *EMU: Getting the Endgame Right,* changed the policy that the European Union adopted to launch the euro in 1999. He was also founding Managing Editor of *Economic Policy,* now an official journal of the European Economic Association.

Brief Contents

Contents

PART 3 AGGREGATE EXPENDITURE AND OUTPUT 117

Chapter 6 Output, Aggregate Expenditure, and Aggregate Demand 118

Chapter 7 Government, Fiscal Policy, and Real GDP 147

PART 4 FINANCIAL MARKETS AND ECONOMIC ACTIVITY 179

Chapter 8 Money, Banking, and the Money Supply 180

Preface

The second Canadian editions of Curtis, Irvine, Begg: *Microeconomics* and *Macroeconomics* continue the focus, philosophy, and pedagogy of the first editions. They build on the fresh approach to Canadian content, organization, and writing of the first editions.

In writing the second Canadian editions, we have been well guided and encouraged by the many comments, criticisms, and suggestions received from adopters and reviewers of the first editions, and from reviewers of drafts of the second editions. We are grateful to them.

These second Canadian editions continue to emphasize policy issues and the use of core analytical tools and economic models that first year students should master. The books are focused and compact. We concentrate on the core topics and institutions important to students in a Canadian introductory course. There are no appendices or "afterthought" chapters. If important material is challenging, it is still included in the main body of the text; it is not relegated elsewhere for a limited audience.

The results are introductory *Microeconomics* and *Macroeconomics* books of just fifteen chapters each, four of which—three introductory and an international trade chapter—are common to both.

CONTENT

Macroeconomics, Second Canadian Edition, provides complete, concise coverage of introductory macroeconomic theory and policy. It examines the Canadian economy as an economic system, and embeds current Canadian institutions and approaches to monetary policy and fiscal policy within that system. Particular attention is given to the recent structure, performance, and evolution of the Canadian economy, and to the current targets and instruments of Canadian monetary and fiscal policy.

These are exciting and challenging times in which to study macroeconomics. The importance of our focus on short-run macroeconomic performance, analysis, and policy is confirmed by the remarkable recession of 2008–2009, and the previous recessions of the early 1980s and 1990s. To that end, the text develops the analysis of macroeconomic institutions, performance, and policies in ways that help students understand and evaluate critically the news media coverage and broader public discussion of:

- Recessions and recoveries, unemployment and inflation, and conditions in financial markets—topics of ongoing reporting, discussion, and debate.
- Monetary and fiscal policy announcements and discussions focused on inflation targets, interest rate settings, budget balances, tax rates, expenditures, and public debt targets as these affect economic performance.
- Exports, imports, international capital flows, foreign exchange rates, and the importance of the international sector of the Canadian economy.
- Economic growth, productivity growth, and the importance of productivity growth for standards of living in Canada and other countries.

The Aggregate Demand and Supply model is introduced early and used to help students understand these topics by tying them together within a consistent analytical framework. The analysis builds on a study of short-run business cycle fluctuations in output and employment, under constant price conditions. The balance of payments, exchange rate policy, and monetary and fiscal policy under different exchange rate systems complete the short-run open economy model.

This model is then extended to longer term issues of inflation and monetary policy in short and long run equilibrium and the adjustment from short to long run equilibrium. Theories to explain growth in potential output, per capita output, and standards of living flow naturally from this analysis.

The treatment of monetary and fiscal policy is modern and up-to-date and includes an analysis of Canadian performance and policy responses to the recession of 2008–2009:

- Canadian monetary policy is examined in terms of inflation targets, interest rate policy instruments, and current Bank of Canada operating techniques, including the potential for quantitative or credit easing.
- Canadian fiscal policy is examined in terms of output stabilization, deficit and debt control targets, the government's budget function, and the effect of the shift to fiscal stimulus in 2009 on budget balances and the public debt.

Numerical examples, diagrams, and basic algebra are used in combination to illustrate and explain economic relationships. This approach gives students an important variety of ways to learn about the consumption function; aggregate expenditure; government budgets; the money supply; financial asset prices, yields, and interest rates; Okun's Law; the Philips curve; and other key relationships in the economy. Canadian and selected international data are used to provide real world examples and comparisons.

STRUCTURE

The chapters in the second Canadian edition of *Macroeconomics* have been revised and sequenced in a smooth, cumulative development of introductory macroeconomic theory and policy.

PART 1 **Chapter 1** (Economics and the Economy), **Chapter 2** (The Tools of Economic Analysis), and **Chapter 3** (Demand, Supply, and the Classical Marketplace) provide the conventional tool kit, covering the nature of economics, models, data and diagrams, and basic supply and demand.

PART 2 provides an introduction to Canadian macroeconomics that differs from the usual approach by building the AD/AS model explicitly on the system of national accounts. Aggregate demand is defined in terms of the major expenditure components of the accounts. The income side of national accounts identifies the major labour cost, profit, and indirect tax components of aggregate supply and the price level.

Chapter 4 (Measuring National Economic Activity and Performance) develops a basic national accounts system to define and measure economic activity and performance. Data from the Canadian system of national accounts illustrate recent economic structure and conditions in Canada, and provide comparisons with economic performance in other countries.

Chapter 5 (Output, Business Cycles, and Employment) bases the AD/AS model on the output, expenditure, and income approaches in national accounts. It then uses AD/AS to illustrate nominal and real GDP, and to introduce business cycle analysis. Students see the main performance and policy issues—like recessions and recoveries and unemployment, and the economic model—at the start of their study of introductory macroeconomics. Subsequent chapters elaborate on and analyze these issues.

PART 3 starts the detail of model building on the real expenditure side of the economy. Aggregate demand is constructed in the conventional way, based on autonomous expenditures and multipliers. The material is developed using careful explanations of numerical examples, diagrams, and basic algebra. Up-to-date Canadian data are used to show the empirical dimensions of each expenditure component.

Chapter 6 (Output, Aggregate Expenditure, and Aggregate Demand) has been revised to cover expenditure and income in the market or private sector of the aggregate economy. Consumption, saving, investment, exports, and imports under constant prices explain the equilibrium level of real expenditure, the multiplier, the position of the AD curve, and the equilibrium level of real GDP when the AS curve is horizontal. Covering consumption, investment and net exports in this consistent, integrated way recognizes the importance of each of these expenditure sectors in the Canadian economy.

Chapter 7 (Government Fiscal Policy and Real GDP) has been revised to focus specifically on the government sector. (The coverage of net exports in Chapter 7 of the first edition has been integrated into the revised Chapter 6). The government sector is studied in terms of a government budget function that includes net tax revenue and expenditure. Fiscal policy tools and objectives, the effects of policy programs and economic activity on budget balances, and the link between the budget balance and the public debt are discussed in terms of the budget function. This provides the context for discussing the effects of fiscal policy on equilibrium real GDP and AD.

In PART 4, to reflect the increased importance of financial markets and monetary policy in current work in macroeconomics, more emphasis is placed on the financial sector and monetary policy than is found in existing texts. Students take a keen interest in financial markets, the key role financial markets play in the modern economy, their potential to disrupt the economy as in the financial crisis of 2008–2009, and the broad media coverage of these topics.

Chapter 8 (Money, Banking, and the Money Supply) uses a conventional approach to money, banking, and the money supply to establish the importance of the monetary base, public cash holdings, and bank behaviour to the supply side of the money market.

The development of the demand for money balances in **Chapter 9** (Financial Markets, Interest Rates, Foreign Exchange Rates, and Aggregate Demand) goes somewhat beyond the conventional approach. It is based on an introduction to financial asset prices and yields, and portfolio choices. The discussion has been revised and extended to cover both domestic money markets and foreign exchange markets and the foreign exchange rate. This approach is of particular importance to understanding the link between monetary policy and aggregate demand. Students find this material of particular interest and of current empirical relevance.

Chapter 10 (Central Banking and Monetary Policy) takes the modern approach to monetary policy. It uses simple monetary policy "rules" to explain current monetary policy. This approach is the key to understanding the Bank of Canada's monetary policy, which is based on an inflation target and interest rate setting under flexible exchange rates. The discussion of the tools of monetary policy has been revised and extended to cover "quantitative easing" and "credit easing."

PART 5 has been restructured and revised, based on suggestions from reviewers, to complete the short run, fixed equilibrium price model AD/AS before introducing either inflation or economic growth. To that end, Chapter 12 integrates the open economy material of first edition Chapters 14 and 16 into a single chapter. It extends the policy analysis of Chapter 11 by linking the effectiveness of monetary and fiscal policy to foreign exchange rates and exchange rate policy. Chapter 13 (revised from first edition Chapter 12) then brings inflation into the AD/AS model (dropping the assumption of a constant equilibrium price level used in the preceding chapters) to examine equilibrium performance and policy in terms of short run and long run equilibrium real GDP and *inflation*. Economic growth is now covered in Chapter 14 in Part 6.

Chapter 11 (Monetary and Fiscal Policy in the Short Run) examines the short-run effects of fiscal and monetary policies and the recent evolution of Canadian macroeconomic policy. It concludes with an empirical examination of recent Canadian macroeconomic performance and policy.

Chapter 12 (The Balance of Payments, Exchange Rates, and Monetary and Fiscal Policy) discusses the balance of payments and exchange rates. The approach to exchange rates makes explicit the link between the foreign exchange market and the flows of funds recorded in the balance of payments, a link many existing texts ignore. The importance of the policy choice between fixed or flexible exchange rates for the effectiveness of monetary and fiscal policy is examined. Recent Canadian experience with flexible rates and inflation targeting are topics of particular interest.

Chapter 13 (Aggregate Supply, Inflation, and Adjustments to Shocks) introduces inflation in wages and prices to the short-run AS/AD model, and gives monetary policy an inflation target. Short-run output gaps cause changes in inflation rates to adjust the economy to potential output. The Bank of Canada's current approach to monetary policy fits neatly within this framework.

PART 6 is revised to cover growth theory and international trade theory, topics covered in Chapters 13 and 16 of the first edition.

Chapter 14 (Economic Growth) studies growth in potential output and an examination of the sources and importance of productivity growth. Growth accounting, neoclassical growth models, and endogenous growth theory are examined.

Chapter 15 (International Trade) examines the net export components of aggregate demand in more detail. It starts with the data on recent trading patterns and a discussion of the issues raised by international trade. The theory of comparative advantage is used to explain exports, imports, and the gains from international trade. Trade protectionism arising from tariffs, quotas, and subsidies is evaluated. The current institutions and multilateral agreements governing international trade are discussed.

LEARNING SOLUTIONS

To provide guidance and insights throughout the text, we include a number of proven pedagogical aids, including:

Part Openers/Chapter Openers set the scene for the areas of study in the chapters that follow.

PART 1

Introduction

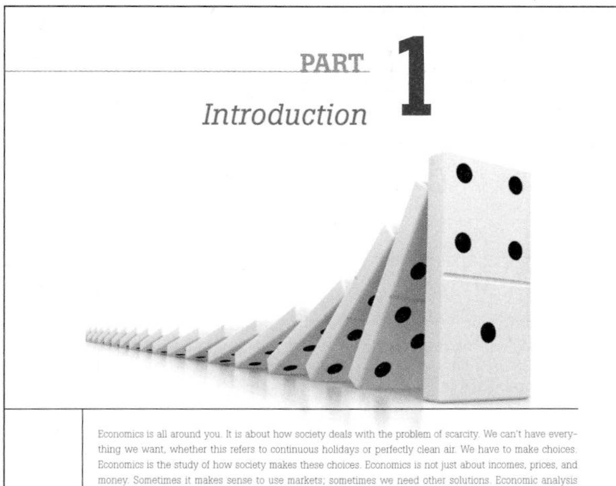

Economics is all around you. It is about how society deals with the problem of scarcity. We can't have everything we want, whether this refers to continuous holidays or perfectly clean air. We have to make choices. Economics is the study of how society makes these choices. Economics is not just about incomes, prices, and money. Sometimes it makes sense to use markets; sometimes we need other solutions. Economic analysis helps us decide when to leave things to the markets and when to override the market.

Chapter 1 introduces the central issues of choice and scarcity, the role of the marketplace, and the impact of belief systems in our discipline. Chapter 2 introduces the economist's analytical tool kit, and then examines how the combination of theory, models, and data permits us to make valid inferences on behaviour. Chapter 3 introduces the basic supply and demand model that is used to study price and output determination in individual markets. It provides an example of a simple economic model, and also the method of analysis used in economics.

Chapter 1: *Economics and the Economy*
Chapter 2: *The Tools of Economic Analysis*
Chapter 3: *Demand, Supply, and the Classical Marketplace*

Learning Outcomes identify the primary topics to be covered in the following pages, and highlight what should be understood when the chapter has been completed.

CHAPTER 3

Demand, Supply, and the Classical Marketplace

LEARNING OUTCOMES

By the end of this chapter you should understand:

1. The market
2. Demand, supply, and equilibrium; concepts
3. Demand and supply curves; equilibrium solutions
4. Behind the demand curve
5. Shifts in the demand curve
6. Behind the supply curve
7. Shifts in the supply curve
8. Simultaneous shifts in supply and demand
9. Free and managed markets
10. From individuals to markets
11. How markets answer the what, how, and for whom

Application Boxes contain current and practical examples to highlight the application of the concepts to economics in the real world. These boxes also provide further and more in-depth discussions of key models and theories to expand on the core concepts in the book.

APPLICATION BOX 2.4

Nobel Laureates: Economists, Statisticians, Sociologists, and Psychologists

The discipline of Economics is not an island unto itself. It has influenced other disciplines and has learned from other disciplines.

The first winners of the Economics Prize in Memory of Alfred Nobel in 1969 were Ragnar Frisch and Jan Tinbergen. Frisch's PhD was in mathematical statistics, while Tinbergen's was in Physics. Frisch brought his validating and testing skills to the study of economic data, while Tinbergen built differential-equations-based economic models using the methods of physics.

Gary Becker, of the University of Chicago, won that prize in 1992. His interest in bringing the rigour of economics to the analysis of social issues such as crime, divorce, drug use, the family, and human capital resulted in him being appointed to a joint position in Economics and prohibition "was a confession that the U.S. experiment in banning drinking had failed dismally. It was not an expression of support for heavy drinking or alcoholism." Becker's solution for the drug problem in the modern era is the same as his solution would have been for prohibition—legalize, tax, protect minors, cut out organized crime's supply monopoly, and free up police to pursue criminal activity of a more serious nature.

Daniel Kahneman of Princeton University was a winner of the Prize in 2002. He was trained as a psychologist, obtaining his PhD in Berkeley. His work on decision theory was path breaking, and when he began to publish his work in the Economics journals, decision theory in Economics received a tremendous boost. The re-

Summary Boxes appear where it is useful to emphasize and summarize key chapter content.

SUMMARY BOX **The Algebra of Income Determination**

We have used diagrams and numerical examples to show the determination of national income in a model of an economy that does not have a government. Two things determine equilibrium income: autonomous expenditures and a multiplier. The following example shows the same thing, but in a general model.

Consumption:	$C = C_0 + cY$
Investment:	$I = I_0$
Exports:	$X = X_0$
Imports:	$Z = Z_0 + zY$

We have used the lower case letters c and z for the marginal propensities to consume and import. They measure the changes in consumption and imports that would be caused, or induced, by a change in national income. The subscript $_0$ indicates the initial values of autonomous expenditures.

Figures and Tables are presented in a simple and clear design. The use of colour will help students to interpret and absorb key economic data and concepts. Captions explain what is being demonstrated.

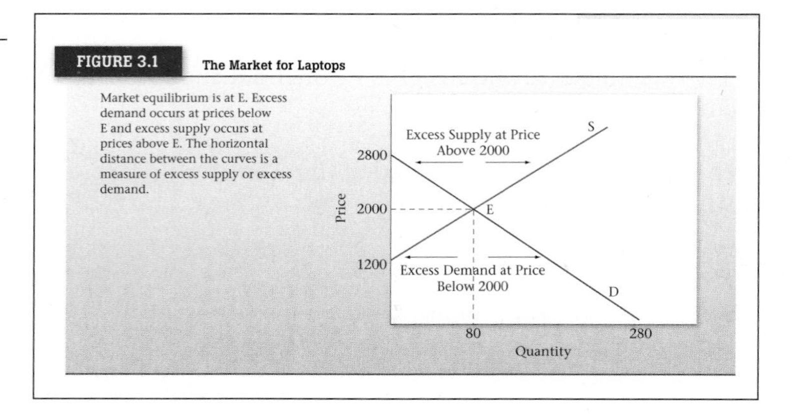

"Next"—a paragraph linking the current chapter with the material to come in the next chapter—appears before the end-of-chapter summary.

Next

Now that we have described the essentials of economics and our philosophy of economics, we must develop an analytical toolkit. Economics is a social science, and so it uses the scientific method. Let's explore this method.

End-of-Chapter Summaries review and reinforce the main topics covered in each chapter.

SUMMARY

- **Demand** defines a relationship between price and quantity on the part of buyers. Other things being equal, the lower the price the higher will be the quantity demanded; demand curves slope downward. **Quantity demanded** is the particular amount demanded at a given price.
- **Supply** defines a relationship between price and quantity on the part of suppliers. Other things being equal, the higher the price, the higher is the quantity supplied; supply curves slope upward. **Quantity supplied** is the particular amount supplied at a given price.
- The **market clears**, or **is in equilibrium**, when the price equates the quantity supplied and the quantity demanded. At this point supply and demand curves intersect. At prices below the equilibrium there is an **excess demand**, and at prices above the equilibrium an **excess supply**. In a **free market**, deviations from the equilibrium tend to be self-correcting. When trades take place at prices other than the equilibrium price, the **short side dominates**.
- **Along a given demand curve**, the **other things assumed constant** can be categorized as other prices, incomes, tastes, networks, expectations, and the scale of the market. Changes in these influences **shift the demand curve**.
- An increase in the price of a **substitute good or service** (or decrease in the price of a **complement**) will raise the quantity demanded at every price.
- An increase in consumer income will increase demand if it is a **normal good** and decrease demand if it is an **inferior good**.
- **Along a given supply curve**, the **other things assumed constant** are technology, input costs, the prices of other commodities, expectations, and the number of suppliers. A **technological innovation** lowers the supply curve; that is, it enables producers to supply any quantity at a lower price.
- **Comparative statics** compares the equilibrium that emerges in a market with an original equilibrium that is disturbed. Changes in the factors

www.mcgrawhillconnect.ca

Key Terms appear in boldface within the text where the term first appears, with the explanation provided in the margin and summarized at the end of each chapter.

KEY TERMS

Demand 40
Supply 40
Quantity demanded 41
Quantity supplied 41
Equilibrium price 41
Excess supply 41
Excess demand 41
Short side 42
Demand curve 42
Supply curve 42
Complementary goods 44
Substitute goods 44
Inferior good 45
Normal good 45
Comparative static analysis 49
Price controls 54
Quotas 54
Market demand curve 58

KEY EQUATIONS AND RELATIONS

Equations

The price level $P = \frac{W}{Y} + \frac{BI + CCA}{Y} + \frac{T_{IN}}{Y}$	(5.1)	p. 99
The output gap $= Y - Y_P$	(5.2)	p. 104
The output gap $= \frac{Y - Y_P}{Y_P} \times 100\%$	(5.2a)	p. 104
Unemployment rate $u = \frac{\text{Labour force} - \text{number of people employed}}{\text{labour force}}$	(5.3)	p. 107
Natural unemployment $u_n = \frac{\text{Labour force} - \text{equilibrium employment}}{\text{Labour force}} \times 100\%$	(5.4)	p. 107
Change in unemployment rate $= \Delta u = -\frac{1}{2}(\text{growth rate of } Y - \text{growth rate of } Y_P)$	(5.5)	p. 107

Relations

Aggregate demand AD: $\Delta P \rightarrow \Delta$ interest rates $+ \Delta$ domestic/foreign prices
$+ \Delta$ real financial wealth $\rightarrow \Delta$ expenditure and real output, $(\Delta Y/\Delta P) < 0$
Aggregate supply AS: Δ real output $\rightarrow \Delta$ costs of production $\rightarrow \Delta P$, $(\Delta P/\Delta Y) > 0$

Equilibrium real GDP and price: AD = AS

Output gaps $(Y \neq Y_P)$: Fluctuations in AD or AS $\rightarrow$ business cycles in Y $\rightarrow$ output gaps

Key Equations and Relations are serially numbered. Linear equations are explicitly solved in the textual development.

REVIEW QUESTIONS

Review Questions and answers are included in Connect at www.mcgrawhillconnect.ca.

1. An economy has 100 workers. Each one can produce four cakes or three shirts, regardless of the number of other individuals producing each good. You are going to draw the PPF for this economy, with cakes on the vertical axis and shirts on the horizontal axis.
   a. How many cakes can be produced in this economy when all the workers are cooking? This answer is the point on the vertical axis where the PPF intersects it.
   b. How many shirts can be produced in this economy when all the workers are sewing? This answer is the point on the horizontal axis where the PPF intersects it.
   c. Join these points with a straight line; this is the PPF.
   d. Label the inefficient and unattainable regions on the diagram.
2. In the table below are listed a series of points that define a production possibility frontier for thinkpods and ipads.
   a. Plot these points to scale, on graph paper if it helps.
   b. Suppose there is technological change so that at every output level of thinkpods the economy can produce 20 percent more ipads. Compute the co-ordinates for the new economy and plot the new PPF.

Review Questions located at the end of each chapter encourage students to review and apply the knowledge acquired from each chapter. Text material tied into the Review Questions is indicated by a question-mark and the corresponding question numbers in the margin of the text.

COMPREHENSIVE LEARNING AND TEACHING PACKAGE

We have developed a variety of high-quality supplements for both teaching and learning to accompany this text.

FOR THE STUDENT

Connect

Developed in partnership with Youthography, a Canadian youth research company, and hundreds of students from across Canada, McGraw-Hill Connect™ embraces diverse study behaviours and preferences to maximize active learning and engagement.

With McGraw-Hill Connect™, written by Carol Lau, Concordia University, students complete pre- and post-diagnostic assessments that identify knowledge gaps and point them to concepts they need to learn. McGraw-Hill Connect™ provides students the option to work through recommended learning exercises and create their own personalized study plan using multiple sources of content, including a searchable e-book, multiple-choice and true/false quizzes, Internet questions, a searchable glossary, graphing questions, algorithmic questions, chapter-by-chapter learning goals, interactivities, personal notes, Review Questions and answers, flashcards, and more. Using the copy, paste, highlight, and sticky note features, students collect, organize, and customize their study plan content to optimize learning outcomes. Visit www.mcgrawhillconnect.ca.

Lyryx

Lyryx Assessment for Economics is a leading-edge online assessment program designed to support both students and instructors. The assessment takes the form of homework assignments called Labs. These Labs offer algorithmically generated and automatically graded assignments. Students get instant grades and instant feedback—no need to wait until the next class to find out how well they did! Grades are instantly recorded in a grade book that the student can view.

Students are motivated to do their labs for two reasons: first because it can be tied to assessment, and second, because they can try the lab as many times as they wish prior to the due date with only their best grade being recorded.

Instructors know from experience that if students are doing their economics homework, they will be successful in the course. Recent research regarding the use of Lyryx has shown that when labs are tied to assessment, even if worth only a small percentage of the total grade of the course, students WILL do their homework—and MORE THAN ONCE! Visit http://lyryx.com.

FOR THE INSTRUCTOR

Connect

McGraw-Hill Connect™ assessment activities don't stop with students! There is material for instructors to leverage as well, including a personalized teaching plan from which instructors can choose a variety of quizzes to use in class, assign as homework, or add to exams. They can edit existing questions and add new ones; track individual student performance—by question, assignment, or in relation to the class overall—with detailed grade reports; integrate grade reports easily with Learning Management Systems such as WebCT and Blackboard; and much more. Instructors can also browse or search teaching resources and text-specific supplements and organize them into customizable categories. All the teaching resources are now located in one convenient place, on a password-protected Web site for instructors. The downloadable instructor supplements include the Instructor's Manual, a computerized Test Bank, and PowerPoint® Presentations.

- **Instructor's Manual** Prepared by Douglas Curtis, Trent and Queen's Universities, this tool contains brief chapter outlines, introductions, examples, teaching tips, and answers to the end-of-chapter Review Questions.
- **Computerized Test Bank** Prepared by Rashid Khan, McMaster University, the Test Bank contains extensive multiple-choice questions and problems for exams.
- **Microsoft® PowerPoint® Presentations** Prepared by David Gray, University of Ottawa, these slides offer visual presentations that may be edited and manipulated to fit a particular course format. The slides contain useful outlines, summaries, and exhibits from the text.

In addition, content cartridges are available for the course management systems **WebCT** and **Blackboard.** These platforms provide instructors with user-friendly, flexible teaching tools. Please contact your local McGraw-Hill Ryerson *i*Learning Sales Specialist for details.

McGraw-Hill Connect™—helping instructors and students Connect, Learn, Succeed! Visit www.mcgrawhillconnect.ca.

Lyryx

The goal of Lyryx Assessment for Economics is for instructors to use the labs for course marks instead of creating and marking their own assignments, saving instructors and teaching assistants valuable time which they can use to help students directly. After registering their courses with Lyryx, instructors can create labs of their choice by selecting problems from our bank of questions, and set a deadline for each one of these labs. The content, marking, and feedback of the problems has been developed and implemented with the help of experienced instructors in economics. Instructors have access to all their students' marks and can view their labs. At any time, the instructors can download the class grades for their own programs.

Please contact your *i*Learning Sales Specialist for additional information on the Lyryx Assessment Economics system. Visit http://lyryx.com.

Σ-STAT

Σ-STAT is an educational resource designed by Statistics Canada and made available to Canadian educational institutions. Using 450,000 current CANSIM (Canadian Socio-economic Information Management System) Time Series and the most recent—as well as historical—census data, Σ-STAT lets you bring data to life in colourful graphs and maps. Access to Σ-STAT is made available to purchasers of this book by special agreement between McGraw-Hill Ryerson and Statistics Canada.

SUPERIOR SERVICE

Service takes on a whole new meaning with McGraw-Hill Ryerson and *Microeconomics* and *Macroeconomics*. More than just bringing you the textbook, we have consistently raised the bar in terms of innovation and educational research—both in economics and in education in general. These investments in learning and the education community have helped us understand the needs of students and educators across the country and allowed us to foster the growth of truly innovative, integrated learning.

Your **Integrated Learning Sales Specialist** is a McGraw-Hill Ryerson representative who has the experience, product knowledge, training, and support to help you assess and integrate any of the above-noted products, technology, and services into your course for optimum teaching and learning performance. Whether it's using our test bank software, helping your students improve their grades, or putting your entire course online, your *i*Learning Sales Specialist is there to help you do it. Contact your local *i*Learning Sales Specialist to learn how to maximize all of McGraw-Hill Ryerson's resources.

***i*Learning Services Program** McGraw-Hill Ryerson offers a unique *i*Services package designed for Canadian faculty. Our mission is to equip providers of higher education with superior tools and resources required for excellence in teaching. For additional information, please visit http://www.mcgrawhill.ca/highereducation/services.

McGraw-Hill Ryerson National Teaching and Learning Conference Series The educational environment continually changes, and McGraw-Hill Ryerson continues to be committed to helping instructors acquire the skills they need to succeed in this new milieu. Our innovative McGraw-Hill Ryerson National Teaching and Learning Conference Series brings faculty together from across Canada with 3M Teaching Excellence award winners to share teaching and learning best practices in a collaborative and stimulating environment. Pre-conference workshops on general topics, such as teaching large classes and technology integration, are also offered. McGraw-Hill Ryerson will also work with instructors at their institution to customize workshops that best suit the needs of faculty.

ACKNOWLEDGEMENTS

We would like to thank the many reviewers whose useful and constructive suggestions have made the end-product so different and so much better than the earlier drafts.

Ugurhan Berkok, Queen's University
Janice Compton, University of Manitoba
Nick Debiparshad, Vanier College
Livio DiMatteo, Lakehead University
Kieran Furlong, York University
Robert Gateman, University of British Columbia
Eric Kam, Ryerson University
Stephen Kosempel, University of Guelph
Carol Lau, Concordia University
Brian VanBlarcom, Acadia University
Jane Waples, Memorial University
Andrew Wong, University of Alberta

David Desjardins, of John Abbott College, has been especially helpful with the technical feedback.

We are indebted to the team of people at McGraw-Hill Ryerson whose efforts and dedication guided us through this project:

Leanna MacLean, Executive Sponsoring Editor
Bruce McIntosh and James Booty, Sponsoring Editors
Joy Armitage Taylor, Executive Marketing Manager
Daphne Scriabin and Andria Fogarty, Developmental Editors
Joanne Limebeer, Senior Supervising Editor
Imogen Brian, Copy Editor
Stephanie Hess, Editorial Associate

We owe special thanks to Bruce McIntosh and James Booty who provided invaluable advice and encouragement much of the way, to Daphne Scriabin and Andria Fogarty for their help with the timely preparation and submission of the manuscript, and to our families who lived with our preoccupation with this project.

Douglas Curtis
Ian Irvine
David Begg

PART 1
Introduction

Economics is all around you. It is about how society deals with the problem of scarcity. We can't have everything we want, whether this refers to continuous holidays or perfectly clean air. We have to make choices. Economics is the study of how society makes these choices. Economics is not just about incomes, prices, and money. Sometimes it makes sense to use markets; sometimes we need other solutions. Economic analysis helps us decide when to leave things to the markets and when to override the market.

Chapter 1 introduces the central issues of choice and scarcity, the role of the marketplace, and the impact of belief systems in our discipline. Chapter 2 introduces the economist's analytical tool kit, and then examines how the combination of theory, models, and data permits us to make valid inferences on behaviour. Chapter 3 introduces the basic supply and demand model that is used to study price and output determination in individual markets. It provides an example of a simple economic model, and also the method of analysis used in economics.

Chapter 1: *Economics and the Economy*
Chapter 2: *The Tools of Economic Analysis*
Chapter 3: *Demand, Supply, and the Classical Marketplace*

CHAPTER 1

Economics and the Economy

LEARNING OUTCOMES

By the end of this chapter you should understand:

1. Resource allocation and scarcity: the what, how, and for whom to produce
2. Dynamic aspects of resource allocation
3. Production possibilities and opportunity cost
4. The roles of markets and governments in the allocation problem
5. Positive and normative economics
6. The economist's belief system
7. Micro and macro economics

The key economic problem for society is to reconcile the conflict between our virtually endless desire for goods and services, on the one hand, and the limited resources in our economy or on our planet that are available to satisfy those desires, on the other hand. By desires, or needs, we mean more than just consumer products; we mean the need for public health, the need to educate our population, the need for investment in our economy. **Economics** is therefore frequently described as the study of how society decides to allocate scarce resources in determining *what, how,* and *for whom to produce.*

Economics is the study of how society decides to allocate scarce resources in determining what, how, and for whom to produce goods and services.

Economics investigates how scarce resources are allocated between competing claims upon their use. Although economics is about human behaviour, we call it a science. This reflects the method of analysis rather than the subject matter. Economists develop theories of human behaviour and test them against the facts, using data. At the same time, economics is concerned with very immediate *social issues* within the national economy: Should health care spending get priority over education? Should we enhance welfare payments to single parents or provide more money for job and skills training? Since economics is concerned with societal issues, we call it a *social science.*

There are also *dynamic aspects* to the resource allocation problem: We attempt to understand why some economies grow and others stagnate; why some economies have high saving rates that turn into investment, capital, and growth and others do not; why some are successful in achieving stable long-term growth, while others go through periods of boom, bust, and uncertainty. There is a time dimension to all of these resource allocation questions.

If any social science in today's world is to be useful, it must furnish us with a way of analyzing, understanding, and diagnosing the major challenges of the era. Today's challenges are as great as those faced by previous generations, even though we have more wealth and knowledge than ever before. Climate change, in the form of global warming caused by the emission of greenhouse gases, could change the planet radically. Continued population growth may put enormous pressures on our water supply and hence on our ability to feed the planet's poor. And the worldwide economic meltdown that began in 2008 as a result of low interest rates, unjustifiable mortgage contracts, and poor incentives for corporate employees raises profound questions about the appropriate roles of government, the central bank, and regulation in the financial sector. We will address these concerns in depth in this book, and we will see that while the price system has undeniably played a role in what has gone wrong, it can play an equally important role in setting the system straight again.

1.1 Resource Allocation

EXPLORING THE WHAT, HOW, AND FOR WHOM

It is frequently easier to learn by studying examples than by studying definitions. In an effort to understand the resource allocation problem, let us analyze the evolution of the international oil market during the last three decades.

Oil is an essential ingredient for every developed economy. It provides fuel for transport, heating, and manufacture. It is a raw material in plastics and synthetic fabrics. Until 1973 the use of oil had increased steadily. It was cheap and abundant. OPEC, the Organization of Petroleum Exporting Countries, became active in 1973, and organized a production cutback by its members. Oil became scarce, and its price tripled because users could not easily adjust to making do with less in the immediate term. Making oil scarce was very profitable for OPEC.

Figure 1.1 shows the price of oil, adjusted for inflation, through to mid-2009. Even though the price tripled again in 1979, Figure 1.1 indicates that, in the 1980s, markets found a way to overcome the shortage that had been created. Given time, the higher prices induced consumers to use less, and some producers to sell more. The high prices subsided several years later in response to changes in demand behaviour. But oil prices (and the price of other energy sources, such as natural gas and coal) began a steep climb in the early years of the new millennium. Prompted by sustained growth, and hence demand, in the world economy—particularly Asia, crude oil hit an all-time high in June 2008, before going on a roller-coaster ride induced by the worldwide economic recession and uncertainties regarding the future.[1] Throughout this period of rising

[1] The extent to which speculation was a driver of energy prices in 2008 is still subject to a great deal of debate.

FIGURE 1.1 Price of Oil Adjusted for Inflation in 2000 U.S. Dollars

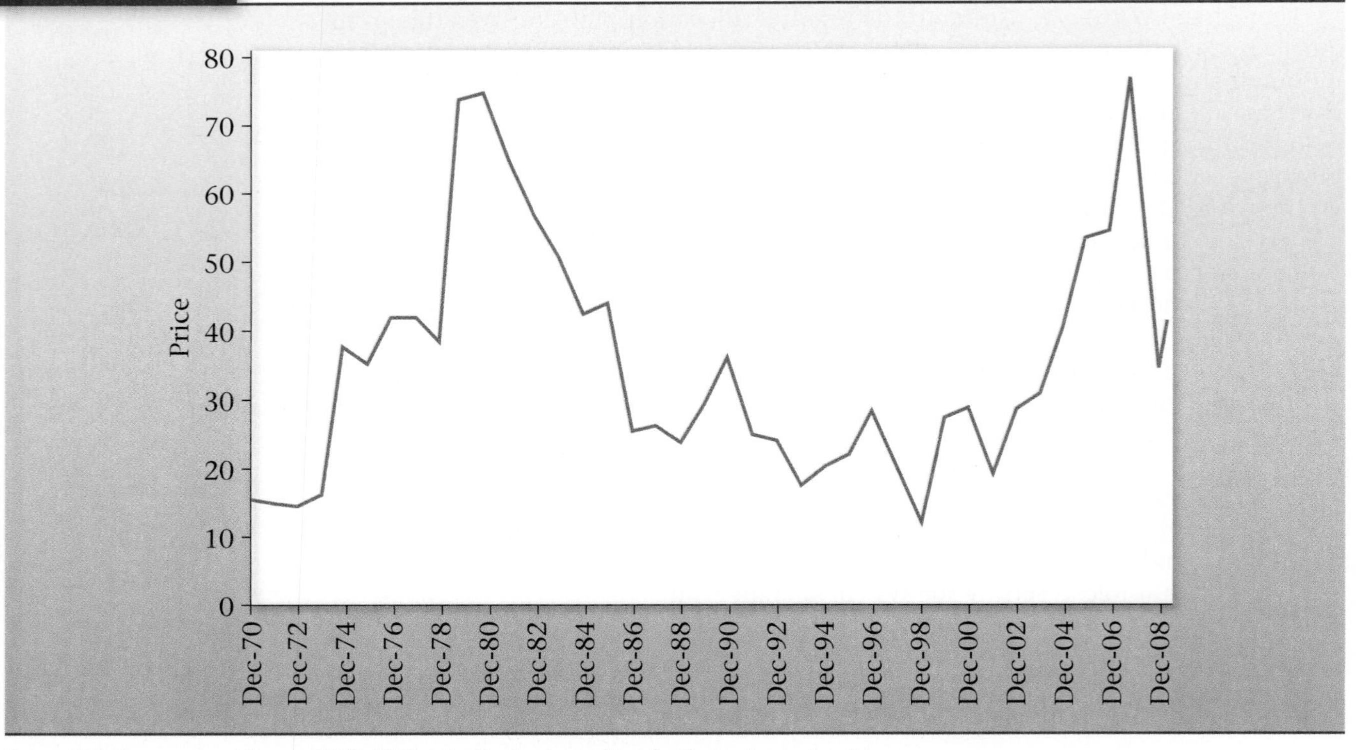

Source: U.S. Department of Energy (DOE), 2009, http://tonto.eia.gov/dnav/pet/pet_pri_spt_s1_m.htm.

prices, the world economy reacted by researching and developing alternative energy sources such as solar, wind, and geothermal, in addition to investing further in quasi-conventional sources such as Alberta's tar sands. The elevated price of conventional energy induced the economy's actors to consume less of it, to seek new alternatives, and to make a return on investing. Such responses reflect the way economies determine what, how, and for whom to produce.

Consider first the *how*. When the price of oil jumps, firms cut their use of oil-based products. Airlines order more fuel-efficient aircraft; chemical firms develop substitutes for petroleum inputs. Higher prices force the economy to produce in a way that uses less oil. The economy becomes less energy intensive, and more energy efficient.

What goods are produced as a consequence? Consumers may switch to gas and electricity, or solar, wind, biofuel, and geothermal alternatives. This substitution to alternative products encourages their further development.

The *for whom* question has a clear answer in this example. OPEC oil revenues climbed dramatically in 1973, in 1980, and again in the new millennium. Of course, some of this increased revenue going to the oil exporting economies was spent on goods and services supplied from the oil-importing economies. Consequently, the oil exporting economies were able to consume more goods and services in total as a result of their more valuable energy exports.

While the first two price increases had a very negative impact on Canada, by the time the third hit Canada had become a major producer and net exporter of oil, natural gas, and coal, and so benefited from the higher price of energy.

APPLICATION BOX 1.1

World Poverty and Development Aid: The Players and Philosophies

Jeff Sachs is Director of the Earth Institute at Columbia University; he has also been Director of the U.N. Millennium Project and special advisor to the Secretary-General of the United Nations. He holds a PhD in Economics from Harvard. The goal of the Millennium Project is to reduce extreme world poverty to half of its 2000 level by the year 2015. He is a passionate advocate of debt reduction for less developed economies, and for an increase in aid to these economies so that they can get on a self-sustaining development path or "ladder." His ideas are developed in *Ending World Poverty* and *Common Wealth: Economics for a Crowded Planet.* The fight against poverty is supported by many entertainment figures and entrepreneurs turned philanthropists: U2 singer Bono is an ardent supporter of Jeff Sachs; singer Bob Geldoff was instrumental in the original Live Aid concert in July 1985 for famine victims in Ethiopia, and a major figure in the twenty-year anniversary Live 8 concerts for famine in 2005. Founder of Microsoft, Bill Gates, is head of the Gates Foundation, the largest charitable foundation in the world. Warren Buffet and George Soros, extraordinarily successful investors have also given billions to this cause.

But not all economists are convinced that direct aid is the way to help poor economies develop. William Easterly, of New York University, argues in his book *The White Man's Burden,* that trillions of aid dollars have seen little return in the post-war era, as a result of bad management.

Contemporary efforts to channel aid frequently work through non-governmental-organizations (NGOs) and financial institutions that lend to small borrowers, in order to ensure that most of the money gets to where it is intended and needed. The Nobel Peace prize was awarded to economist Mohammed Yunus in 2006 in recognition of his work in setting up microcredit in Bangladesh for small borrowers in the 1970s. Microcredit has grown to such an extent that Forbes Magazine ranked the world's top 50 microcredit institutions in December 2007. Among the best known is KIVA: www.kiva.org.

1.2 Dynamic Resource Allocation

Perhaps the greatest challenge to economics and economists in the modern world is to promote policies that enable the less developed economies to grow and climb out of their misery. Low life expectancy, malnutrition, and ethnic conflict reflect the impoverished state of local human existence in a world that has the knowledge and ability to provide a satisfying standard of health and well-being globally. The World Bank is an excellent source of information on how world income is divided between high and low income economies[2]. Despite dramatic economic growth in India and China, almost two billion people (nearly one-third of the world's population) still live on only $2 per day, making for an annual income of less than one thousand dollars—not even half of what most Canadian households spend on gasoline. About four fifths of world income accrues to just one fifth of the world's population, and the poorest two fifths of the world's population generate perhaps five percent of all income.

In contrast, Canada's income per person is among the highest in the world. Why? On one level this reflects how goods are produced. Developed economies have much

[2] World Development Report 2009. World Bank. www.worldbank.org/wdr2009.

more capital and equipment than less-developed economies. In addition, they are also endowed with much more *human capital*—a highly educated labour force. But while it is easy to say this, it is more difficult to explain *why*. For example, comparing Argentina and Canada, both economies are well endowed with natural resources, and had the same living standards in the early years of the twentieth century. Yet today Canada has an income per person that is several times that of Argentina. Clearly, economic policy has played a role. Policy in Argentina has been poor relative to policy in Canada.

Similar differences abound: Why are Korea, Japan, and Hong Kong so prosperous compared with their neighbours? Of most recent interest are China and India: Why have they broken through the development barrier and been growing by several percent each year since the early nineties?

High-growth economies are usually characterized by two key patterns. First, they allocate a large share of their resources to improving their capital stock—they save and invest. China currently saves about one-quarter of its income. The Asian "miracle economies" of the post-war period have also had high saving and investment rates. In resource allocation terms, *people decided to allocate away from present consumption and towards investment so that future consumption could be higher.* Not only do they invest in physical capital, they also invest in education. Today, virtually every child in China is literate and attends school. This is not yet so in India, and is very far from being the case in Africa.

The second component of this dynamic problem is the fostering of institutions and property rights. The Soviet Union in the 1950s was able to allocate a large share of its income to investment goods, and its economy was successful for almost two decades. But it eventually hit a development wall, *because it did not provide incentives to its workers and did not ensure property rights.*

The most important development in understanding growth and dynamics in the modern era is the recognition of the role played by institutions. The study of institutions in economic growth is usually referred to as *political economy*, as opposed to just economics. Simply put, if individuals are not guaranteed that they will reap the rewards of their efforts and be granted title to what they have purchased, they will not undertake investment or commit resources to producing goods and services.

Some of the world's poverty and inequality can be understood best in these terms. Poor policies in Argentina have meant that investment by individuals and entrepreneurs has been insufficient. The lack of property rights in the less-developed world, frequently coinciding with the presence of "war lords," dictators, and communist governments, has meant that insufficient resources have been devoted to the future in the form of investment.

1.3 Scarcity and the Competing Use of Resources

THE ECONOMY'S PRODUCTION POSSIBILITIES

The **production possibility frontier (PPF)** shows, for each output of one good, the maximum amount of the other that can be produced with given resources and a given state of technology.

The production possibilities of an economy are many and varied, because resources can be put to different uses. If the economy's resources—its labour and capital—are being less than fully utilized, the economy's potential is not being exploited. This can be illustrated simply, as in Figure 1.2, where we depict a hypothetical two-dimensional set of possibilities. The **production possibility frontier (PPF)** shows, for each output of one good, the maximum amount of the other that can be produced with given resources and a given state of technology.

FIGURE 1.2 **The Production Possibility Frontier**

The PPF defines the production possibilities of the economy. Points above are unattainable, and points inside do not fully utilize the economy's resources. The slope of the frontier defines the rate at which one output can be transformed into the other. For example, from point B a reduction in peacekeepers of 300 implies that these resources can be used to provide 250 additional doctors. But from point C an additional 250 doctors requires that we sacrifice 600 peacekeepers.

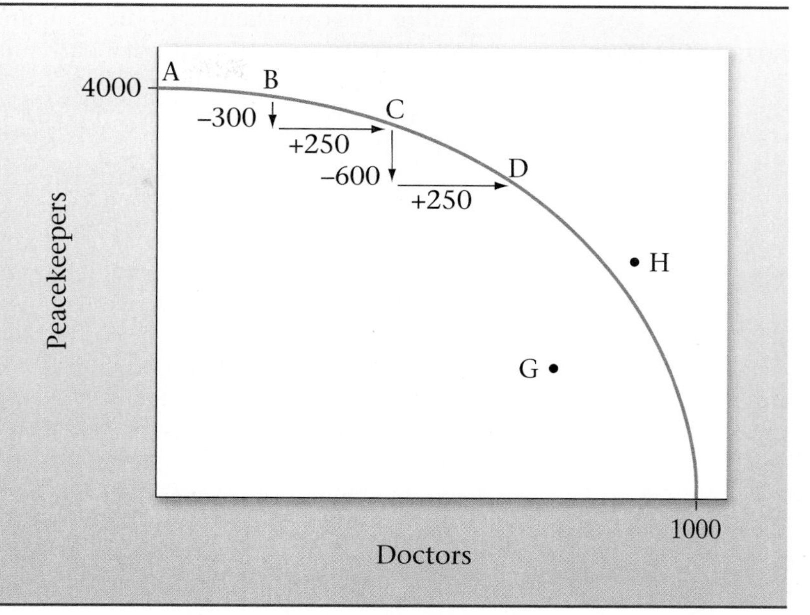

On the horizontal axis we have health (number of doctors), and on the vertical axis we have peacekeeping (number of peacekeepers). This trade-off is actually a very real one for Canadians in the new millennium. With an aging population, the nation's system of health care requires new doctors, nurses, and equipment. At the same time, Canada is being called upon to supply peacekeepers in the international arena by the United Nations and NATO—the North Atlantic Treaty Organization.

The PPF defines the trade-offs. It does not solve our problem of resource scarcity, but it defines the options clearly. In this economy the PPF indicates that, if we were to devote all of our resources to producing health, we could produce 1000 doctors per annum. But we could alternatively supply 4000 peacekeepers. These are the intercept points on the axes. The PPF is not necessarily a straight line, and we have drawn it here with a concave form.

First, note that, by definition, any point inside the frontier, such as G, does not exhaust the economy's productive capacity. The frontier is essentially a constraint; we cannot go beyond it because the economy's productive capacity is limited. But all points along the frontier, such as A, B, C, or D are attainable. At point B we are producing a certain combination of doctors and peacekeepers. If it is decided that we need an additional 250 doctors, the PPF indicates that 300 peacekeepers must be sacrificed. Point C defines such a combination. This trade-off is called an **opportunity cost**, and defines the amount of other goods or services that must be sacrificed to obtain more of the first one. In our everyday life we define costs in money terms. The PPF indicates that the real value of money is the quantity of products it can buy.

The **opportunity cost** is the quantity of other goods or services that must be sacrificed to get an increment in the first good.

Every point along the PPF is termed an efficient point. Points such as G are not efficient because the productive capacity of the economy is not being fully used. In contrast, points such as H are not attainable. **Efficient production** fully utilizes the economy's resources.

Production efficiency means that the economy's resources are being fully utilized.

Since both doctors and peacekeepers are desirable, we make a choice as to the combination that will best reflect social preferences. Will the choice be towards the intercept on the horizontal axis, indicating a preference for more health, or a point nearer the vertical axis, indicating a preference for more peacekeeping? These are *political choices*, and in this case the role of the economist is to point out the consequences of political action: to describe the cost of a particular action in terms of the opportunities that will be forfeited as a consequence.

Review Question 1

We have drawn the PPF with a concave shape—it bulges out from the origin. In principle, we could have drawn it as a straight line, or even with a convex shape, where it would be "sucked in" towards the origin. The different possible shapes tell us about the opportunity costs. In the example in Figure 1.2, the concave shape indicates that the opportunity cost changes as we move around the frontier. At point B 300 peacekeeping years must be traded to obtain 250 additional doctors; but at point C 400 peacekeepers would have to be sacrificed to obtain a further 250 doctors. The trade-off rate is different. In contrast, if the PPF were a straight line, the opportunity cost would always be the same—to get more of one good we would give up the same amount of the other good, *regardless of the point on the PPF.*

We have also taken a very particular set of options here. In Canada these goods are not traded in the marketplace in the traditional sense; for the most part, government supplies them both. Yet the economist still plays a role in this process.

Consider instead an example involving the trade-off between autos and plasma-screen televisions. These goods are traded freely in the marketplace, and the government plays very little role in choosing how many of each to produce. How does society as a whole make a decision on how many of each of these goods to consume and produce? In developed economies the most important process determining the what, how, and for whom to produce is the marketplace.

While we tend to think of production in terms of "goods," we should not forget that most of the "output" in developed economies comes in the form of "services." Goods are physical commodities such as steel, Nintendo games, textbooks, or buildings. Services are activities such as concerts, home-delivered newspapers, education, or psychological counselling. In Canada, about 3 percent of the value of all output produced each year is in the form of agricultural production, less than 30 percent in the form of goods, and a whopping 70 percent in the form of services.

EXPANDING THE PRODUCTION POSSIBILITIES

Today's economy produces twice the level of output that it produced in the late 1970s. We have, in other words, *expanded our production possibilities*. How has this been achieved, and how can it be represented in our abstract construct, the PPF? Canada's economy has grown for several reasons. First, we have more capital in the economy, coupled with more people working. This greater productive capability shifts the PPF outwards, meaning that we have the potential to produce more goods and services. In the second instance, we have experienced technological improvements in the way we produce goods and services and in the goods and services themselves. As obvious examples, windows in new houses and offices are more energy efficient, and we can produce a greater standard of living or more output for the same energy consumption. Or, computing has become so efficient and inexpensive that commercial output has increased dramatically while requiring relatively modest additional outlays. Furthermore the quality of Canada's stock of human capital has increased—people are now more educated and skilled than they were three decades ago. Just as more labour and capital push out the production possibilities, so too do technological improvement and higher-level skills.

Review Questions 2 and 3

OPPORTUNITY COST AND COMPARATIVE ADVANTAGE AS GUIDING PRINCIPLES

While we have developed the concept of opportunity cost in the context of the economy's production capabilities, the idea permeates the whole discipline. Individuals face opportunity costs at every turn: In deciding to go to the hockey game tonight, you will either have to forgo a concert tomorrow night, or else you will have to forgo some leisure at the weekend in order to generate additional income for the hockey game ticket. Indeed, there is no such thing as a free lunch, or a free hockey game.

Review Questions 4 and 5

Opportunity costs play a determining role in markets. It is precisely because different individuals and organizations have different opportunity costs that they enter into exchange agreements. If you are a skilled plumber and an unskilled gardener, while your neighbour is a skilled gardener and an unskilled plumber, then you and your neighbour have not only different capabilities, you also have different opportunity costs, and *you could gain by trading your skills*. Here's why. Fixing a leaking pipe has a low opportunity cost for you; you can do it quickly. But pruning your apple trees will be costly because you must first learn how to avoid killing your tree and this may require many hours. Your neighbour has exactly the same problem, with the tasks in reverse positions. In a sensible world you would fix your own pipes *and* your neighbour's pipes, and she would ensure the health of the apple trees in both backyards.

If you reflect upon this "sensible" solution—one that involves each of you achieving your objectives while minimizing the time input—you will quickly realize that it resembles the solution provided by the marketplace. You may not have a gardener as a neighbour, so you buy the services of a gardener in the marketplace. Likewise, your immediate neighbour may not need a leaking pipe repaired, but many others in your neighbourhood do, so you sell your service to them. You each specialize in the performance of specific tasks as a result of having different opportunity costs or different efficiencies. A numerical version of this exchange process is illustrated in Table 1.1. Penelope, the plumber, requires two hours to repair a water supply; Gordon, her neighbour the gardener, requires four hours to perform the same task. On the gardening front, Gordon can prune his trees in two hours, while Penelope requires three hours. If each individual does their own plumbing job and prunes their own trees, a total of eleven hours of work will be required (column iv). But, if instead they each specialize, Penelope can do both plumbing jobs in four hours, and Gordon can also do both garden jobs in four hours, for a total of eight hours (column v). By specializing they jointly save three hours of work time.

Review Questions 6 and 7

TABLE 1.1 **Hours Required to Perform Plumbing and Gardening Tasks**

i	ii	iii	iv	v
	Plumbing Repair	Garden Maintenance	Total Hours Without Specialization	Total Hours With Specialization
Penelope the plumber	2	3	5	4
Gordon the gardener	4	2	6	4
			Total = 11	Total = 8

In the foregoing example we could say that Gordon has an advantage in providing gardening services, and Penelope has an advantage in providing plumbing services. The term **comparative advantage** is frequently used in the context of international trade, and signifies that gains can flow from trade as a result of economies being endowed differently or having different relative efficiencies in producing goods and services. In the preceding example, gains flow as a result of individuals trading a service that they can supply advantageously. This principle can also explain much of what we observe in the global economy. For example, research, development and design tend to be carried out in Europe and North America on account of their being knowledge-based economies, while fabrication and assembly are often done in less developed economies where lower-skill labour costs less. In Chapter 15, which develops the theory of international trade, we will delve into this issue more deeply, and also explore how the concept of comparative advantage differs from that of absolute advantage.

Comparative advantage signifies an ability to supply a product at a lower relative cost than a competitor.

1.4 The Role of the Market

Markets bring together buyers and sellers of goods and services. In some cases, as in an auto dealership, buyers and sellers meet physically. In others, such as a stock market, business can be conducted remotely by computer or through a broker. A **market** is a process by which households' decisions on consumption, firms' decisions on production and sales, and workers' decisions on working hours are all reconciled by the adjustment of prices.

Markets are institutions that bring together buyers and sellers of goods and services.

Review Question 8

Price adjustment is the key to ensuring that scarce resources are used to supply the goods and services that society wants. Let us return to our oil example. Supplying oil from the Middle East oil wells is not an expensive proposition. The oil is still abundant and easy to extract. But in Canada's tar sands in Northern Alberta oil is mixed with sand and grit and is anything but easy to get to market. Why then have tens of billions of dollars been invested there by companies such as Syncrude, Suncor, and Western Oil, and why are vast expenditures on the planning board for the next decade?

This is a textbook case of resources following a perceived high-value use. For three decades the world has worried about its future oil resources and supplies. When the conventional sources of oil in the Middle East become depleted, how will we be able to run our transport fleet, heat our homes, and power industry? The prospect of a depleting oil supply has made investors aware that the price of oil would at some point have to rise significantly to reflect this shortage. The dizzying pace of growth in India and China, which account for one third of the world's population, has drawn this date closer. Extracting oil from the tar sands is expensive, but, if the price for the end product is sufficiently high, not only can the elevated costs be covered but profits can also result.

The response of the economy has been to devote resources to oil production. The high price in the marketplace, and the anticipated continued high price, have signalled to investors that they should move productive resources to where they can yield a profit. But the high price of energy has stimulated more than just investment in traditional energies. It has promoted massive investment in the development of wind, solar, biofuel, and geothermal power. In summary, the market has directed resources to where they are valued.

THE COMMAND ECONOMY

In a **command economy**, a government planning office decides what, how, and for whom goods and services will be produced.

How would resources be allocated if markets did not exist? In a **command economy**, a government planning office decides what is to be produced, how it is produced, and for whom.

Such planning is very complicated, and even the most centrally planned economies, like North Korea, Cuba, and the former Soviet Union, cannot plan every last detail of a firm's or a household's economic decisions. Instead, the state may own land and production facilities, determine who works where and for how many hours, and make only the most important production decisions. But even this is an enormous task. Just imagine the complexity of running a small city that includes several businesses, many households, and publicly supplied services. Then multiply this task by a large number to imagine the complexity associated with running a complete economy. In most economies this myriad of decisions is decentralized and made by independent individuals and firms.

THE INVISIBLE HAND

A **free market** is one in which governments do not intervene, and do not regulate unduly. The idea that it is possible for individual economic actors, pursuing their own interests without direction, to solve the what, how, and for whom problem dates back to at least Adam Smith, who developed his ideas in *The Wealth of Nations* (1776). He argued that individuals pursuing their own interest would be led by an "**invisible hand**" to do things that are not only in their own interests, but also broadly in the interests of society as a whole. The central idea is that, if a good or service is valued highly, the market in which the good is traded will likely reflect that value in the form of a high price. This in turn should induce additional supply, as we saw above in the energy example. This "signalling" aspect of the marketplace makes it a valuable institution. High prices signify that buyers value the product highly, and since high prices should encourage the owners of the economy's resources to direct those resources to where they can earn a high return, this means that resources will go towards producing products that are valued; and conversely if prices are low. Prices that can move freely are thus important for resource allocation.

A **free market** is one in which governments do not intervene significantly.

The **invisible hand** is the assertion that the individual pursuit of self-interest within free markets will allocate resources efficiently from society's viewpoint.

In contrast, if the government were to set a maximum permissible price for goods that are highly valued in the marketplace, the economy's producers would not have the incentive to direct resources to such products. Shortages, rationing, and "black markets" could result.

The invisible hand may work well in most markets, but there are many where it does not. The government may then be able to improve on the invisible hand in the task of allocating scarce resources.

THE MIXED ECONOMY

Between the extremes of the centrally planned market and completely free markets lies the mixed economy. In a **mixed economy** the government and the private sector jointly solve economic problems. The government influences decisions through taxation, subsidies, transfers, and the provision of particular services. It also regulates the extent to which individuals may pursue their own interest. In the mixed economy the government does not adopt the "let it be" philosophy; hence, the expression *laissez faire* is frequently used to denote the unhindered market.

A **mixed economy** is one where goods and services are supplied by both the private sector and the government.

Virtually all economies fall into this mixed category, and the main difference lies simply in the degree to which government is involved. For example, Scandinavian economies have a greater role for government than North American economies. Before the fall of the Berlin Wall in 1989, Hungary had a significant private sector, but East Germany did not. At the present time many economies in Eastern Europe and Asia are radically changing the balance between government and the private sector, in favour of the latter.

APPLICATION BOX 1.2

Incentives—Both Good and Bad—Are Everywhere

During 1989–1991 the Soviet bloc abandoned Marxist central planning and began the (painful) transition to a market economy. A decade earlier China began the same process. While neither economy at present replicates a typical Western economy, Russia and China are vastly different from what they were prior to their transformation. Three key problems had plagued their economies: information overload, bad incentives, and insufficient competition.

We no longer doubt the role of incentives in promoting economic growth. After all, would a whole workforce go to work each day if it were not paid? Would we invest if we did not reap some rewards?

Because incentives are so powerful, it is important to recognize that bad incentives can damage the economy just as good incentives can enrich it. Stock options in "new-economy" firms may encourage employees to defer rewards and work particularly hard for the success of their company. But bad incentives can wreak havoc also. We will see in the following chapters that poor incentives lay behind much of the damage caused to the world economy by the "sub-prime" mortgage crisis and subsequent bank failures, that inappropriate incentives to produce ethanol from corn contributed to substantial price increases in world grain prices, and that a failure to implement an effective worldwide policy against carbon emissions up to 2009 has led to higher emission levels than would otherwise have occurred. As a consequence, hundreds of billions of dollars were lent to economically insecure borrowers who bought houses in a rising market. Millions of such borrowers subsequently defaulted on their mortgages when economic conditions turned sour. The lending companies were left with houses that were declining in value and many went bankrupt.

A second example of poor incentives that wrought havoc was the U.S. government's decision under the second Bush presidency to provide subsidies for the production of fuel from corn—ethanol. The incentives were so "successful" that corn was redirected from the food market to the fuel market. This redirection had a powerful impact on the world price of food in the years 2007 and 2008. Millions worldwide saw their living standards and nutrition levels fall.

1.5 Positive and Normative Economics

Positive economics studies objective or scientific explanations of how the economy functions.

Normative economics offers recommendations that incorporate value judgements.

Positive economics studies objective or scientific explanations of how the economy functions. Its aim is to understand and generate predictions about how the economy may respond to changes and policy initiatives. In this effort economists strive to act as detached scientists, regardless of political sympathies or ethical code. Personal judgements and preferences are (ideally) kept apart. In this particular sense, economics is similar to the natural sciences such as physics or biology.

In contrast, **normative economics** offers recommendations based partly on value judgements. While economists of different political persuasions can agree that raising the income tax rate would lead to a general reduction in the number of hours worked, they may yet differ in their views on the advisability of such a rise. One may believe that the additional revenue that may come in to government coffers is not worth the disincentives to work; another may think that, if such monies can be redistributed to benefit the needy or provide valuable infrastructure, the negative impact on the workers paying the income tax is worth it.

Review Question 9

Competent research can frequently resolve differences that arise in positive economics—not so in normative economics. For example, if we claim that "the elderly have high medical bills, and the government should cover all of the bills," we are making both a positive and a normative statement. The first part is positive, and its truth is easily established. The latter part is normative, and individuals of different beliefs may reasonably differ. Some people may believe that the money would be better spent on the environment and that the aged should cover at least part of their own medical costs. Economics cannot be used to show that one of these views is correct and the other false. They are based on value judgements, and are motivated by a concern for **equity**. Equity is a vital guiding principle in the formation of policy and is frequently, though not always, seen as being in competition with the drive for economic growth. Equity is driven primarily by normative considerations. Virtually no economist would disagree with the assertion that a government should implement policies that improve the lot of the poor and dispossessed—but to what degree?

Economic equity is concerned with the distribution of well-being among members of the economy.

Most economists hold normative views, sometimes very strongly. They frequently see their role as not just to analyze economic issues from a positive perspective, but also to champion their normative cause in addition. Conservative economists see a smaller role for government than left-leaning economists. A scrupulous economist will distinguish her positive from her normative analysis.

Review Question 10

1.6 An Economist's Credo

Having distinguished between positive and normative economics, it is important to set out a set of beliefs that are subscribed to by a broad spectrum of economists. So let us enumerate some of these.

- **Incentives Matter.** A key element in markets is that prices determine behaviour. If the price of business class seats on Air Canada flights is reduced, then we expect that some passengers will respond by moving from economy to business class. Economists believe strongly that the price mechanism influences behaviour, and therefore favour the use of price incentives in the marketplace and public policy more generally. Environmental economists, for example, frequently advocate the use of tradable pollution permits—a type of permission slip that can be traded (at a price) between users—or carbon taxes on the emission of greenhouse gases such as carbon dioxide.

  In saying that economists believe in incentives, we are not proposing that human beings are purely mercenary; people have many motivations: a sense of public duty, kindness, noblesse oblige, etc. Acting out of a sense of self-interest does not imply that people are immoral or have no sense of altruism. It is just a recognition of one important motivating factor in an individual's life.

Review Question 11

- **Markets and Trade Play a Key Role in Improving Economic Well-Being.** Before the arrival of Man Friday, Robinson Crusoe had to hunt, cook, make fire, and sustain shelter. The arrival of Man Friday enabled Crusoe to specialize in the tasks where he was relatively more productive. More generally, trade creates benefits for the trading parties. For example, Canada has not the appropriate climate for growing coffee beans, and Colombia has not the terrain for wheat. If Canada had to be self-sufficient, we might have to grow coffee beans in green-houses—a costly proposition. But with trade we can simply exchange some of our wheat for Colombian coffee. Similar benefits arise for the Colombians.

APPLICATION BOX 1.3

The Development of Markets

The development of markets in less developed economies was viewed as essential by many development economists in the 1980s. The focus on "freeing up" productive resources from the hand of the state was a central idea in what became known as the Washington Consensus. This emphasis represented a turning point in development philosophy; away from believing in the efficacy of the mega project, protectionism, and state-led development. While the latter approach rarely produced the desired result due to the missing incentives, the Washington Consensus did not produce the hoped-for results either. This was because the supposed "free markets" were not always accompanied by property rights or enforceable contracts, and markets and contracts do not work well in a legal vacuum. Such "free markets" have been described by Oxford economist Marcel Fafchamps as "flea markets."

Development economists have, as a consequence, refocused their thinking. First, they now emphasize micro-level development: education and health, which we call *human capital*, are seen as being essential to economic success. Such capital is as important as the physical capital going into roads, sewage treatment, and other infrastructure needs. Second, and consistent with this approach, micro finance now plays a central role—in the form of loans, to groups or individuals, that can finance small projects or investments. Third, the development of a meaningful set of legal institutions is as important as setting up a market place: of what value are markets if the fruits of work and investment are plundered by crooks? Not surprisingly, economists have found a high correlation between economic growth and wealth on the one hand and the rule of law on the other. The consequence on the world stage is fascinating: numerous "economic" development projects now focus upon training jurists, police officers, and bureaucrats in the rule of law!

These same benefits from specialization can be reaped in the domestic market, or even in the home—we sometimes observe that one spouse always cuts the grass and the other does most of the cooking.

A frequent complaint against globalization is that it does not benefit the poor. For example, workers in the Philippines may earn only a few dollars per day manufacturing clothing for Western markets. What these voices are really trying to say is that, in their opinion, most of the gains from trade go to the Western consumers, and a lesser part to the Asian worker.

Globalization does not always involve free access to markets. Among the greatest impediments to development in poor economies are the barriers the rich nations have effectively erected to exports of food from these economies, in the form of the subsidies that the rich countries give to their own producers of specific foods. These subsidies are so high in many cases that they make it "profitable" for Europeans to export food at a price that is below the cost of production. This in turn prevents the low-income economies from competing in these markets internationally. The sugar market is a good example. Not only is effective competition lessened, barriers to produce from less-developed economies deter farmers in these countries from investing in soil and irrigation because the returns are too low.

- **Property Rights Are Vital to Development.** The incorporation of institutional structure into the economist's lexicon of thought is one of the most important

APPLICATION BOX 1.4

Public Policy: Kyoto, Greenhouse Gases, and Global Warming

The Kyoto Protocol, developed in December 1997, committed signatory countries to reducing the emissions of several types of greenhouse gases (GHGs) from their 1990 levels by the year 2012. Canada committed itself to a 6 percent reduction, but will miss that target by a wide margin. By 2008 Canada had increased its emissions by one quarter above its 1990 levels, despite reducing the GHG "intensity" of GDP—the amount of GHGs emitted per unit of output produced.

Greenhouse gases are created primarily from burning fossil fuels and, when sufficiently concentrated in the earth's atmosphere, can prevent heat from escaping, thereby leading to global warming. The consequences of global warming could be severe, and are discussed at length in the Stern Review published in the UK in October, 2007, and in several reports of the IPCC—the Intergovernmental Panel on Climate Change.

The challenge of controlling and reducing these gases is considerable. Primarily this is because we collectively face a choice known as the "tragedy of the commons": Individual economies, in reducing their own emissions, do not themselves appropriate more than a fraction of the climatic or environmental gains from the costs they incur. The benefits from GHG reductions in one economy are spread around the world. There is thus a natural tendency for individual economies to prefer that other economies take measures to reduce emissions; hence the need for a global accord to attack the problem. A second challenge relates to the fact that developed economies, such as Canada, emit vastly more pollutants per person than developing economies do. Developing economies therefore tend to claim that it is the responsibility of the rich economies to take strong measures to reduce their GHG levels before telling the developing economies how they should behave.

The Stern Review proposed that emissions could be reduced without sacrificing an undue amount of economic growth if controls were adopted in the near term. One tool for reducing emissions is a carbon tax—a levy imposed on activities that produce GHGs. The second instrument is a system of pollution permits that could be traded among polluters, perhaps even internationally, in a market. By restricting the number of permits, the permitted level of pollution could meet a given target.

developments in the discipline in the last two decades. This is particularly true in the field of growth and development economics.

For example, the excessive rigidity in the Soviet Union from the late 1960s resulted from the lack of property rights, incentives, and markets. By the late 1980s, the USSR had reached a point of internal decline on account of its stultifying structure. As a further example, the tragedy of the great famines in China in 1959 and 1960, when twenty million people died of starvation, sprang from the communal structure of land ownership.

- **Public Policy Can Improve Well-Being.** Traditionally, economists have thought of governments as directing what was called "the great trade-off" (between equity and efficiency). This expression suggests that governments have a dual impact on the economy: On the one hand, *taxation* discourages work and entrepreneurship; on the other, government-supplied *services* provide benefits. Thus, while workers and investors lose from taxation, specific groups, and perhaps the public at large, gain. Where we draw the line in this redistributive role for government is a normative issue.

While we do not question the existence of a trade-off in most taxing and redistributive activities, it is vital to recognize that there are many areas where the free market breaks down and where the government can step in to improve upon unregulated market activity. For example, we have no markets for pollution, or exhaust fumes, or lead particles in the air. In the case of such *missing markets*, or *market failures*, when the government taxes these particles and pollution activities it not only generates tax revenue for positive uses, but also reduces harmful activities. The trade-off between equity and efficiency is radically changed.

Review Question 12

- **Marginalist thinking** characterizes economic analysis. When studying whether or not to install a dam on a river, the engineer will develop the blueprint of what is required. But the economist will play a role in deciding whether the costs of the dam are less than its benefits. In doing his analysis, the economist must decide not only whether or not the dam should be built, but also *the right size for the dam*: How many square kilometres of land should be flooded? How many cubic metres of water should the reservoir hold? This is an example of marginalist thinking. It is not sufficient to think in "all or nothing" terms.

  A student, having finished her bachelor degree, contemplates graduate school, but she should not simply examine the benefits and costs of doing her doctorate. She should consider the costs and benefits of each of a diploma, a master's degree, a doctorate, and even post-doctoral studies. In applying for a student loan, she should not think "shall I go into debt, or stay debt-free?" She should think instead of *how much* debt to take on, and this involves a range of possibilities. Economists dislike the all-or-nothing approach, something that is frequently called a "corner solution" in the discipline's jargon. Perhaps the economist's approach to decision making is one reason why some of them like calculus: Differential calculus examines in a systematic way the impact of a small change in one variable on the value of another.

1.7 Micro and Macro Economics

Economists, like most analysts, tend to specialize in a particular branch of their discipline. Labour economics deals with jobs and wages, urban economics with land use and transportation, and so forth. However, we need not classify branches of economics by their subject area. We can also classify them by the approach or method of analysis used. The division into microeconomics and macroeconomics cuts across the subject boundaries. **Microeconomics** offers a detailed treatment of individual decisions at both the household level and the level of the firm.

Microeconomics analyzes individual decisions at the household and firm level.

For example, we can study why individuals use bicycles or cars, and how producers decide upon which to produce and at what price. We can then aggregate the decisions of individual agents and examine the markets in which they participate. The challenge in all of economic science is to devise judicious simplifications about behaviour so as to keep our analysis manageable, without letting it become unproductively simple at the same time. This makes economics an art as well as a science.

Microeconomics generally assumes the economy is operating with its resources fully utilized. It may ignore interactions with other sectors of the economy in order to preserve simplicity. We sometimes refer to microeconomic analysis as being a *partial equilibrium* analysis in nature, in that it tends not to delve into the neighbouring impacts of its conclusions. For example, in analyzing the impact of a plant closure as a result of industry or firm consolidation, microeconomics might not concern itself with the impact of such a closure on the local real-estate market.

Macroeconomics studies the whole economy. Macroeconomists rarely worry about the division of vehicles into cars, SUVs, and trucks. They are mainly concerned with the fluctuations and growth rate in the level of the total national economy. In contrast to microeconomists, they try to understand why the economy might *not* operate on the production possibility frontier for substantial periods of time but, instead, experience recessions when output falls inside the production possibilities frontier (or economic booms or price inflation). These business cycles raise important questions for the design of macroeconomic policy, especially fiscal and monetary policy. Macroeconomists are also vitally concerned with the factors that promote growth in the economy's production possibilities.

Macroeconomics is the study of the behaviour and performance of the whole economy as a system, and the total output of goods and services.

Because macroeconomics refers to the whole economy, and fluctuations in national economic conditions, it tends to get more coverage in the media than microeconomic issues. For example, trends in interest rates are important for virtually every sector of the economy. The degree of unemployment, economy-wide, is a barometer of the economy's health. The rate at which prices increase—inflation—is of vital interest to participants in financial markets.

While good policy is vital to an economy's health, it must be recognized that governments cannot magically correct shocks that hit an economy. For example, energy price increases reduce the standard of living in economies that import energy. There is little or nothing a government can do that will offset the fact that energy importing economies must give more of their own goods and services to energy exporting economies following an energy price increase.

Review Question 13

Next

Now that we have described the essentials of economics and our philosophy of economics, we must develop an analytical toolkit. Economics is a social science, and so it uses the scientific method. Let's explore this method.

SUMMARY

- **Economics analyzes what, how, and for whom society produces.** The key economic problem is to reconcile wants with the limited availability of resources.
- **The allocation of resources to competing needs is also a dynamic problem.** How much to save and invest will determine the rate of economic growth.
- The **production possibility frontier** (PPF) shows the combinations of outputs that can be produced by an economy using all of its resources.
- The **opportunity cost** of a good is the quantity of other goods that must be forgone to produce an additional unit of the good in question. It is defined by the slope of the PPF. **Production efficiency** requires that the economy produce at a point on the PPF. Points inside the PPF do not fully utilize the economy's resources, while points outside are not attainable.
- Economies rely heavily on **markets** to allocate resources. The concept of **comparative advantage** is central to determining who produces specific goods and services, and where they are produced. The market resolves production and consumption decisions through price adjustments.
- In a **command economy**, a central planner makes resource allocation decisions. Few such economies exist in the modern world.

- A **free market economy** has no significant government intervention. Resources are allocated in accordance with the pursuit of self-interest and prices. Adam Smith called this process the **invisible hand.**
- Modern Western economies are all **mixed economies.** These economies, to varying degrees, rely on a combination of markets and government control and intervention.
- **Positive economics** studies how economies function. **Normative economics** recommends particular policy measures, based on both scientific investigation and value judgements. A wide degree of agreement characterizes positive economics, but not normative economics.
- Economists have a set of **guiding beliefs**, or a **credo** that distinguishes them from their fellow social scientists: They believe in incentives, the value of trade and markets, property rights, positive policy, and marginalist thinking.
- **Microeconomics** offers a detailed analysis of particular activities and markets in the economy. **Macroeconomics** focuses upon the interactions of different sectors and variables in the economy at large.

KEY TERMS

REVIEW QUESTIONS

Review Questions and answers are included in Connect at www.mcgrawhillconnect.ca.

1. An economy has 100 workers. Each one can produce four cakes or three shirts, regardless of the number of other individuals producing each good. You are going to draw the PPF for this economy, with cakes on the vertical axis and shirts on the horizontal axis.
   a. How many cakes can be produced in this economy when all the workers are cooking? This answer is the point on the vertical axis where the PPF intersects it.
   b. How many shirts can be produced in this economy when all the workers are sewing? This answer is the point on the horizontal axis where the PPF intersects it.
   c. Join these points with a straight line; this is the PPF.
   d. Label the inefficient and unattainable regions on the diagram.
2. In the table below are listed a series of points that define a production possibility frontier for thinkpods and ipads.
   a. Plot these points to scale, on graph paper if it helps.
   b. Suppose there is technological change so that at every output level of thinkpods the economy can produce 20 percent more ipads. Compute the co-ordinates for the new economy and plot the new PPF.

Thinkpods	1000	900	800	700	600	500	400	300	200	100	0
ipads	0	1600	2500	3300	4000	4600	5100	5500	5750	5900	6000

3. Using the PPF that you have graphed using the data in question 2, indicate if the following points lie inside or outside the PPF:

Thinkpods	720	480
ipads	3000	4800

4. Most Canadians think that free health care is a right for every citizen. Do you agree? If there is unlimited free health care, would such a program have any impact on other government programs?

5. The federal government's program of Employment Insurance (EI) has become less generous and more difficult to access since the early 1990s.
   a. How do you think this has impacted the number of individuals who are currently drawing EI benefits?
   b. Can you explain your answer by using the principle of opportunity cost?
   c. Do you think that individuals who lose their jobs should have open-ended income support through EI?

6. You and your partner are highly efficient people. You can earn $50 per hour in the workplace; your partner can earn $60 per hour. If there is no domestic cleaning service in your area, which of you should do the housework, assuming that you are equally efficient at housework? Why?

7. Louis and Carrie Anne are students who have set up a summer business in their neighbourhood. They cut lawns and clean cars. Louis is particularly efficient at cutting the grass—he requires one hour to do a typical lawn, while Carrie Anne needs one and one half hours. In contrast, Carrie Anne can wash a car in half an hour, while Louis requires three quarters of an hour.
   a. If they decide to specialize in the tasks, who should cut grass and who should wash cars?
   b. If they each work an eight-hour day, how many lawns can they cut and how many cars can they wash if they specialize in performing the work?

8. Markets are evolving all the time. Google, the search engine company, went public in 2004. This means that the original shareholders sold some of their shares in the company to the public in order to bring in more investment. The novelty here was that the shares were sold by auction: The highest bidders got the shares. Why do you think this form of market was used rather than the traditional one in which a fixed price was set for the shares and the shares were allocated on a "first-come, first-served" basis?

9. Which of the following statements are positive, and which are normative?
   a. Total production in the economy increased by less than 3 percent last year.
   b. Because of the relatively slow growth in the economy's output, the government should cut taxes.
   c. Income per person is higher in Alberta than in New Brunswick.
   d. The most recent opinion polls in New Brunswick and Alberta indicate that New Brunswick residents are happier than Albertans.

10. In deciding whether you are a political supporter of the left, the centre, or the right in Canadian politics, write down a set of stances that you favour on economic policy issues. Having done this, ask yourself if, in the past, you have voted in accordance with your normative views on the economy.

11. When British Columbia Ferries ordered new boats, it had to decide whether to give the building job to a builder registered in British Columbia, or to open up the bidding and tender process to builders from all across Canada, or from all over the world. From your knowledge of markets, how would you have advised BC's premier to decide how to allocate the contract?

12. In Canada you can draw your Canada (or Quebec) pension plan when you attain the age of 60, or any year thereafter until 69, at which point you can

postpone it no longer. For each year that you postpone taking the pension, the government pays you more per month when you actually draw your pension. If you continue to work, you would earn more per month. If you were 60 years of age, how would you go about deciding whether to retire or not?

13. Which of the following statements pertain to macroeconomics and which to microeconomics?
    a. Inflation in 2003 was lower than in 2002.
    b. *Dell* computers are cheaper than *Hewlett-Packard* computers.
    c. Unemployment in Quebec is higher than in Ontario.
    d. The recent rise in interest rates will likely be accompanied by a change in the unemployment rate.

14. *Internet* Go to the World Bank Web site at www.worldbank.org and search for information on infant mortality in each region. This is a good indicator of how health systems are progressing in different economies. You will find that such mortality rates have diminished radically in Asia and North Africa, but not in most of Africa.

15. *Internet* Markets come in many different forms. Auctions are one form of market. Go to your favourite search engine and type in the following: "English auction"; "Dutch auction"; "sealed bid auction"; and "eBay." See if you can figure out the differences between these various auction types.

CHAPTER 2

The Tools of Economic Analysis

LEARNING OUTCOMES

By the end of this chapter you should understand:

1. Theories, models, and reality
2. Data and data types
3. Index numbers
4. Models and data
5. Testing, accepting, and rejecting theories
6. The Canadian data hunt
7. Criticisms of economists

It is more fun to play tennis if you know how to serve, and cutting trees is easier if you can handle a chainsaw. Every activity or academic discipline has a basic set of tools. Tools may be tangible, like the chainsaw or tennis racquet, or intangible, like the ability to serve or to scamper up a tree. This chapter is about the tools of the economics trade.

2.1 Models and Theories

A **theory** is a logical view of how the world and its parts work.

Models or theories are frameworks we use to organize how we think about a problem. A **theory** is a logical view of how the world and its parts work, and is frequently formulated on the basis of observation. For example, if global warming is observed to follow increased levels of economic activity, we might theorize that greenhouse gases (created as a result of the economic activity) influence temperatures in a specific

A **model** is a formalization of the essential elements of a theory and is a deliberate simplification of reality.

manner. A **model** is a formalization of the essential elements of a theory. A model simplifies, by omitting some details of the real world in order to concentrate on essentials. As an example of an economic model, suppose we theorize that a household's expenditure depends on its many defining characteristics. An economic model might specify that wealth, income, and household size determine household expenditures, while the model might ignore other, less important traits, such as the household's neighbourhood, its religious beliefs, or its state of health. The model reduces and simplifies the theory to manageable dimensions. From such a reduced picture of reality we develop an analysis of how an economy and its components work.

An economist uses a model as a tourist uses a map. Any city map misses out some detail—traffic lights and speed bumps, for example. But with careful study you can get a good idea of the best route to take. Economists are not alone in this approach. Meteorologists, physicists, and genetic scientists operate similarly. Meteorologists disregard weather conditions in South Africa when predicting tomorrow's conditions in Winnipeg. Genetic scientists, in examining evolution, concentrate on the interactions of limited subsets of genes that they believe are the most important. Even with huge computers, all of these scientists build *models* that concentrate on the essentials.

As a final word on theories and models: despite the subtle difference between the two, economists frequently use the terms interchangeably!

2.2 Data

Data are pieces of evidence about behaviour.

Data are pieces of evidence about behaviour. The data, or facts, interact with models in two ways. First, they help us *quantify* theoretical relationships. Knowing that the Don Valley Parkway is congested does not tell us how slow our trip to downtown Toronto will be. To choose the best route downtown we need to ascertain the *degree of congestion*—the data. A model is useful because it suggests which facts are most valuable.

Second, the data help us to test our models or theories. For example, if sunspots or baggy pants were found to be correlated with economic expansion, would we consider these events a coincidence or a key to understanding economic growth? The facts frequently alert us to the need to ponder causal relationships, but we can decide only with the help of logical reasoning.

While the more frequent wearing of loose clothing in the past may have been associated with economic growth because they both occurred at the same time (correlation), one could not argue on a logical basis that this behaviour *causes* good economic times. Therefore, the past association of these variables should be considered as no more than a coincidence. *Without a logical underpinning,* the empirical connection will break down sooner or later. Science should always attempt to distinguish between causation and correlation.

The blending of models and data is subtle. The data alert us to logical relationships that we might have overlooked. And theory must always be checked against the facts. But only logical reasoning can guide an intelligent assessment of what evidence has relevance. A theory that has been supported by data for a long period is called a **behavioural law.**

A **behavioural law** is a sensible theoretical relationship that has been supported by data for a long period of time.

We now turn to the representation of economic data; then we show how an economist might develop a theoretical model of an economic relationship; and subsequently we discuss how data are used to test theory.

TABLE 2.1 **House Prices and Price Indexes**

1	2	3	4	5
Date (month of January)	Price of Houses in North Vancouver	House Price Index	Consumer Price Index	Real House Price Index
1999	330,000	100.0	100.00	100.00
2000	345,000	104.55	101.29	103.21
2001	350,000	106.06	104.63	101.37
2002	360,000	109.09	105.49	103.41
2003	395,000	119.70	108.61	110.21
2004	434,000	131.52	110.01	119.55
2005	477,000	144.55	112.81	128.13
2006	580,000	175.76	114.32	153.75
2007	630,000	190.91	117.33	162.71
2008	710,000	215.15	118.62	181.38
2009	605,000	183.33	120.56	152.07

Source: Prices for North Vancouver houses come from Royal Le Page and the CPI is obtained from Statistics Canada, CANSIM II, Series V41692930.

TIME-SERIES DATA

A **time series** is a sequence of measurements at different points in time.

Data come in several forms. One form is **time-series**, which reflects a sequence of measurements at different points in time. Table 2.1 reports the values for several price series. Such information may also be presented in charts or graphs. Figure 2.1 plots the data from column 2, and each point represents the data observed for a specific time period. The horizontal axis reflects time, the vertical axis price in dollars. The data here are in annual form—one observation per year. We could, alternatively, have presented them in quarterly, monthly, or even weekly form. The frequency we use depends on the purpose: If we are interested in the longer-term trend in house prices, then the annual form suffices. In contrast, financial economists, who study the behaviour of stock prices, might not be content with daily or even hourly prices; they may need prices minute-by-minute. Such data are called *high-frequency* data, whereas annual data are *low-frequency* data.

Charts and diagrams must be interpreted with care. It is easy to be misled by changes made to the scale on the axes. To illustrate this, the data from column 2 of Table 2.1 are plotted in Figures 2.1a and 2.1b, but with a change in the scale of the vertical axis. The greater *apparent* slope in panel a might easily be interpreted to mean that prices increased more steeply than suggested in panel b. While a careful reading of the axes reveals that this is not so, the use of different scales can mislead the unaware viewer. Advertisers are masters of the art.

CROSS-SECTION DATA

Cross-section data record the behaviour of economic variables across different individuals or groups at a point in time.

In contrast to time-series data, **cross-section data** record the behaviour of economic variables across different individuals or groups at a point in time. Table 2.2 contains a cross-section of unemployment rates for several economies. For the year 2002 we have a snapshot of the economies at a point in time, likewise for 2003 through 2007. This table therefore contains **repeated cross-sections**.

Review Question
1

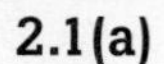

FIGURE 2.1 **North Vancouver House Prices 1999–2009 in Thousands of Dollars**

2.1(a)

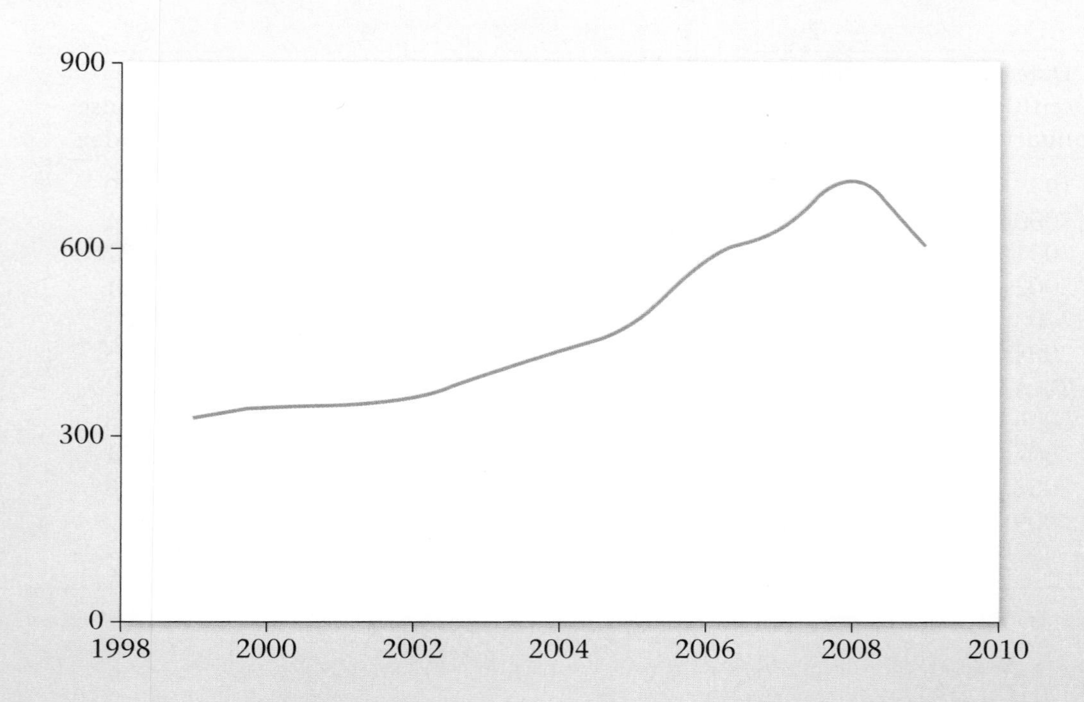

2.1(b)

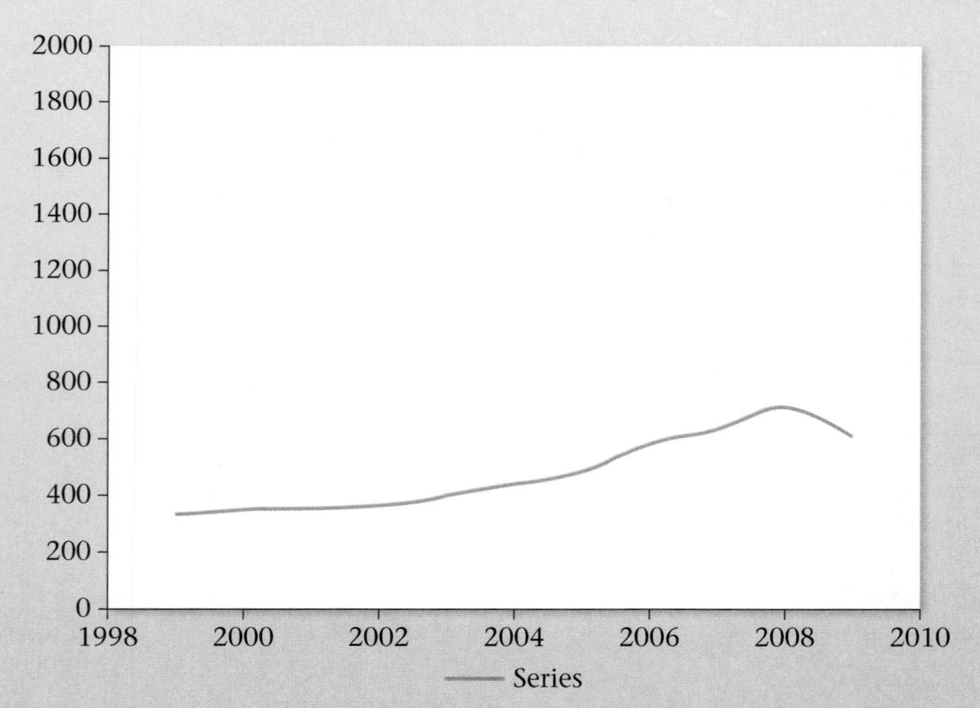

The information in Figures 2.1(a) and 2.1(b) is identical despite the initial visual impression. The different impression is achieved by changing the scale of the vertical axis. Graphical representations carry meaning only in the context of a clearly labelled scale on each axis.

TABLE 2.2 **Unemployment by Country (%)**

	Canada	U.S.	Japan	Germany	France	U.K.	Ireland
2002	7.7	5.8	5.4	8.2	8.9	5.1	4.3
2003	7.6	6.0	5.3	9.1	9.5	4.9	4.6
2004	7.2	5.5	4.7	9.5	9.6	4.7	4.5
2005	6.8	5.1	4.4	10.6	9.3	4.8	4.3
2006	6.3	4.6	4.1	9.8	9.2	5.3	4.4
2007	6.0	4.6	3.9	8.4	8.3	NA	4.4

Source: Harmonised Unemployment Rates and Levels (HURs) under Labour Force Statistics (MEI), Labour, OECD. Stat Extracts, http://stats.oecd.org.

Finally, **longitudinal data** follow the same individuals or particular components of the economy over time. Surveys which involve a follow-up of the same households who are initially surveyed are of this type.

Longitudinal data follow the same individuals or units over time.

2.3 Index Numbers

It is important in economic analysis to discuss and interpret data in a meaningful manner. Index numbers help us greatly in doing this. The key characteristics of indexes are that they are *not dependent upon the units of measurement of the data in question, and they are interpretable easily with reference to a given base value.* To illustrate, let us change the price data in column 2 of Table 2.1 into index number form.

An **index number** expresses data relative to a given base value.

The first step is to choose a reference point. This could be any one of the periods; we will simply take the first period as the reference point and *set the price value equal to 100 in that year.* The value of 100 is chosen in order to make comparisons simple. To transform \$330,000 into 100 we multiply the base period dollar value by 100 and **divide** by the price level in the base year.

$$\text{Base year index value} = \$330{,}000 \times (100\ /\ \$330{,}000) = 100$$

Applying the same ratio to every element in column 2 yields column 3, which is now in index number form. For example, the January 2003 value is:

$$\text{Index value in 2003} = \$395{,}000 \times (100\ /\ \$330{,}000) = 119.7$$

Each value in the index is interpreted relative to the value of 100, the price in January 1999. The beauty of this column lies first in its *ease of interpretation.* For example, by 2003 the price increased to 119.7 points relative to a value of 100. This yields an immediate interpretation: The index has increased by 19.7 points *per hundred* or *percent.* While it is particularly easy to compute a percentage change in a data series when the base value is 100, it is not necessary that the reference point have a value of 100. By definition, a **percentage change** is given by the change in values relative to the initial value, multiplied by 100. For example, the percentage change in the price from 2006 to 2007 is: $(630{,}000 - 580{,}000)/580{,}000 \times 100 = 8.6$ percent.

Percentage change = (difference in values)/ base value × 100.

Furthermore, index numbers enable us to make *comparisons with the price patterns for other goods* much more easily. If we had constructed a price index for cell phones, which also had a base value of 100 in 1999, we could make immediate comparisons without having to compare one set of numbers defined in dollars with another defined in tens of thousands of dollars. In short, index numbers simplify the interpretation of data.

INDEX NUMBERS AS AVERAGES

Index numbers have even wider uses than those we have just described. Suppose you are interested in the price trends for fuels in Canada during the last decade. You know that this group includes coal, natural gas, and oil, but you suspect that these components have not all been rising in price at the same rate. You also know that, while these fuels are critical to the economy, some play a bigger role than others, and therefore should be given more importance, or weight, in a general fuel price index. In fact, the official price index for these fuels is a *weighted average of the component price indexes*. The fuels that are more important get a heavier weighting in the overall index. For example, if oil accounts for 60 percent of fuel use, natural gas for 25 percent, and coal for 15 percent, the price index for fuel could be computed as follows:

Review Questions 2 and 3

$$\text{Fuel price index} = \text{oil index} \times 0.6 + \text{natural gas index} \times 0.25 + \text{coal index} \times 0.15$$

To illustrate this, Figure 2.2 presents the price trends for these three fuels. The data come from Statistics Canada's CANSIM database. In addition, the overall fuel price index is plotted. It is frequently the case that components do not display similar patterns, and in this instance the composite index follows oil most closely, reflecting the fact that oil has the largest weight.

FIGURE 2.2 **Price Index for Mineral Fuels, Canada**

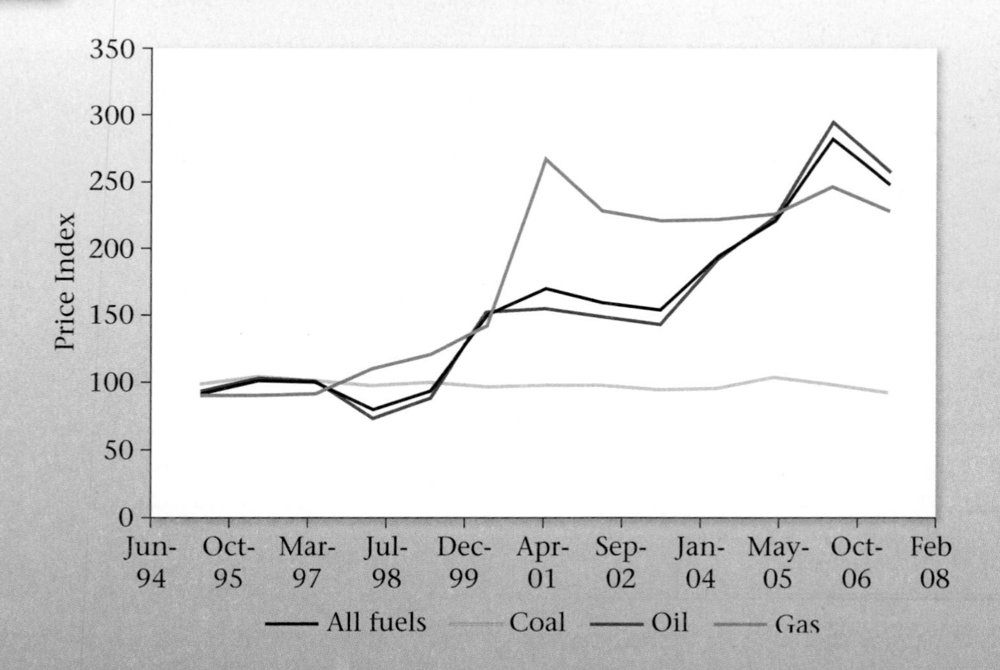

The dark line is a price index for mineral fuels. It is a weighted average of the coal, oil, and natural gas prices, whose indexes are illustrated by the other three trend lines.

Source: CANSIM Table 330–0006.

THE CONSUMER PRICE INDEX

The **consumer price index (CPI)** is the most widely quoted price index in the economy. It measures the average price level in the economy and yields the average rate at which goods and services change in price—**inflation** if prices increase, **deflation** if prices decline. It is constructed in the same logical fashion as the fuel index described above. First, surveyors record individual price changes, and then weights are assigned that reflect the importance of the various items in the budgets of households. Accordingly, if the price of a good that accounts for a large share of household budgets increases, this is reflected more strongly in the CPI than if an increase is recorded in a less important item.

Other frequently cited indexes are the index of wages in manufacturing, and the S&P/TSX—a weighted index of the Toronto Stock Exchange prices. The procedure by which the index numbers are computed is essentially the same in all cases.

The **consumer price index** measures the average price level in the economy and yields the average rate at which all consumer goods and services change in price.

The **inflation rate** is the percentage increase in the consumer price index.

The **deflation rate** is the percentage decrease in the consumer price index.

NOMINAL AND REAL VARIABLES

The CPI is useful both as an indicator of how much prices change in the aggregate, and also as an indicator of *relative price* changes. Column 4 of Table 2.1 provides the Vancouver CPI with the same base year as the North Vancouver house price index. Note how the two indexes move very differently over time. The price of housing has increased considerably *relative to the overall level of prices* in the local economy, as measured by the CPI: Housing has experienced a *relative price increase*, or a **real price index**. This real increase is to be distinguished from the **nominal price** index, which is measured without reference to overall prices. The real price index for housing (or any other specific product) is obtained by dividing its specific price index by the CPI.

The **real price index** for a product is its nominal price index divided by the consumer price index, scaled by 100.

The **nominal price index** reflects the dollar price of a good or service, without reference to the consumer price index.

$$\text{Real house price index} = (\text{nominal house price index/CPI}) \times 100$$

The resulting index is given in column 5 of Table 2.1. This index has a simple interpretation: It tells us by how much the price of Vancouver houses has changed relative to the general level of prices for goods and services. For example, between 1999 and 2004 the number 119.55 in column 5 for the year 2004 indicates that housing increased in price by 19.55 percent *relative to prices in general.*

Review Question 4

Here is a further simple example: The price of a Volkswagen Beetle in 1970 was about $3000; today it retails for about $30,000. Does this mean that the *real price* has risen tenfold? The answer is no, because the CPI also rose in the meantime.

The distinction between nominal and real variables applies to all variables *measured in monetary units*. It does not apply to units measured in physical terms: 3000 bicycles manufactured per year are still 3000 bicycles, even if the price level has changed.

QUALITY AND TECHNOLOGICAL CHANGE

Advances in technology and production methods have led to a reduction in even the nominal prices of many goods. Televisions, audio equipment, computers, telecommunications equipment, and domestic appliances have displayed this pattern for some decades. For example, the modern VW Beetle has independent suspension, disc brakes, stereo sound, and interior luxury. The 1970 Beetle was a reliable entry-level car, but not much more. An appropriate correction for such quality changes would likely indicate that the *real quality-adjusted price* of the Beetle has declined.

APPLICATION BOX 2.1

Hyperinflation

In 1918, the Allied victors demanded that Germany make reparations for the damage done during the First World War. By 1922, in economic ruin, Germany suspended reparation payments. In 1923, French and Belgian troops occupied the Ruhr coalfields. German workers went on strike, and the government rolled the printing presses to get the money to pay its workers. Prices subsequently spiralled out of control, and monthly inflation reached the equivalent of one million percent annually.

For at least a decade, Zimbabwe experienced an inflation rate of several hundred percent each year, reaching a rate of thousands in several years. It also has had an unemployment rate of one-half of the labour force. Economists dubbed President Mugabe's brand of policy "Mugonomics," because it addressed the symptoms rather than the causes of economic collapse. Shortages and money printing made Zimbabwe's currency virtually useless. When the leader of the political opposition, Mr. Tsvangirai, was arrested in 2003, several people were needed to carry the boxes of bail money that was demanded.

Many quality improvements are genuinely enormous. The Boskin Commission in the United States reported in 1995 that the CPI overstated inflation by about one percentage point at that time, in part due to the underestimation of quality change. Government statistical agencies worldwide now measure quality change more accurately.

MEASURING CHANGE IN ECONOMIC VARIABLES

To conclude: Index numbers provide a very useful basis for measuring change in economic data. Economists are particularly interested in *percentage changes* in variables over time. Such percentages are what we term *unit-free measures*. They are more intuitive than dollar changes or quantity changes. For example, if the minister of finance decrees that federal expenditures must increase by no more than 4 percent annually, this is much more comprehensible to the average voter than if he or she states that they must rise by no more than $2 billion per year. Likewise, it is easier for voters to assess economic performance when growth is presented in percentage rather than dollar terms.

2.4 Economic Models and Analysis

Let us now investigate the interplay between models and data by means of the following example. Health Canada wants to understand how to reduce the number of cigarettes smoked in Canada. It therefore needs an economic model, or a logical description of the way the population behaves. It needs to understand how smokers make their decisions and how non-smokers might be influenced in their "stay away" practices.

Health Canada first must define the influences on quantity consumed. Economists always consider that price is an important factor; psychologists might tell us that peer pressure among youth is important; marketing specialists might propose that messages, or health warnings on packages, would be useful; doctors might tell us that subsidizing

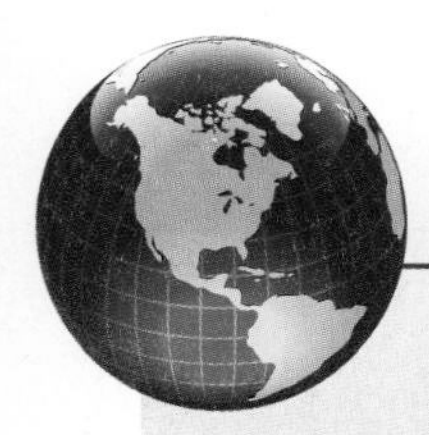

APPLICATION BOX 2.2

Moore's Law

In 1965, George Moore discovered regularity in the increasingly efficient production of computer chips. This has since come to be known as *Moore's Law*. As the Research Director of a semiconductor company, the future founder of *Intel Corporation* observed at that early date that, with the arrival of each new generation of chips, which were less than two years apart on average, the capacity (the number of transistors per chip) doubled. The chips are the essential component in the computer's microprocessor. In essence, this represented a productivity increase of about 35 percent per year! Astonishingly, his 1965 observation is still accurate today. The 1971 logic chip had 2300 transistors, the Pentium 4 released in 2000 had 42 million, and present-day chips have hundreds of millions!

the "patch" would induce smokers to try quitting. If we write these influences down, we have the elements of a model:

$$\text{Smoking} = f(\text{price of cigarettes, peer pressure, messages, price of the "patch"})$$

The notation $f(\ldots)$ means that the variable on the left-hand side of the equation is *a function of* the variables inside the parentheses. This equation is, therefore, an economic model that links behaviour to its main determinants.

EVIDENCE

To support or reject the above model, we need to confront it with data. Unlike some experimental sciences, economics is a social science; therefore we rarely have data that come from laboratory experiments. Most of our research uses data collected over periods of time during which many relevant factors change simultaneously. A basic challenge in testing is how to disentangle the separate influences of these changing factors.

Review Question 5

Table 2.3 contains data on the sale of cigarettes in Canada and a real price index of tobacco where 1996 is the base year; that is, where the price index takes a value of 100. Figure 2.3 shows the associated **scatter diagram** for the data up to 2005. The vertical axis measures the real price index, the horizontal axis billions of cigarette sales. The scatter is a series of points, each one defining a pair of corresponding values. A clear negative relationship between the two variables is evident in the scatter diagram: As the price index increases, the quantity of sales declines. This suggests that a behavioural relationship may exist between the two variables, but doesn't necessarily mean that one causes the other.

A **scatter diagram** plots pairs of values simultaneously observed for two variables.

FITTING LINES THROUGH THE SCATTER PLOT

A line through the scatter of points in Figure 2.3 shows the average relationship between price and sales. A challenge is to define the line that most accurately characterizes the relationship. This task is the job of **econometricians**, who practise **econometrics**. Econometrics is the science of examining and quantifying relationships between economic variables. It attempts to determine the separate influences of each variable, in an environment where many things move simultaneously.

Econometrics is the science of examining and quantifying relationships between economic variables.

TABLE 2.3 Tobacco Sales and Prices, Canada 1996 to 2006

Year	Sales (billions of cigarettes)	Real Price Index
1996	47.1	100.0
1997	45.5	101.7
1998	45.6	106.6
1999	45.1	108.5
2000	43.4	108.7
2001	42.3	133.6
2002	38.2	168.4
2003	36.1	181.7
2004	34.4	184.3
2005	32.8	185.3
2006	21.9	190.9

Source: Statistics Canada, CANSIM Series, V1548 for sales; V735584 and V735319 for cigarette prices.

A **regression line** represents the average relationship between two variables in a scatter diagram.

In two dimensions, the line drawn through the scatter is chosen to minimize the sum of distances (or distances squared) between the line and the various points. It is called a **regression line**, or a trend line if the data are in time-series form. Computer algorithms that do this are plentiful, and fortunately computers can work in many dimensions in order to capture the influences of *all* the variables in addition to price that we believe influence tobacco sales.

FIGURE 2.3 Price and Quantity of Cigarettes, Canada 1996–2005

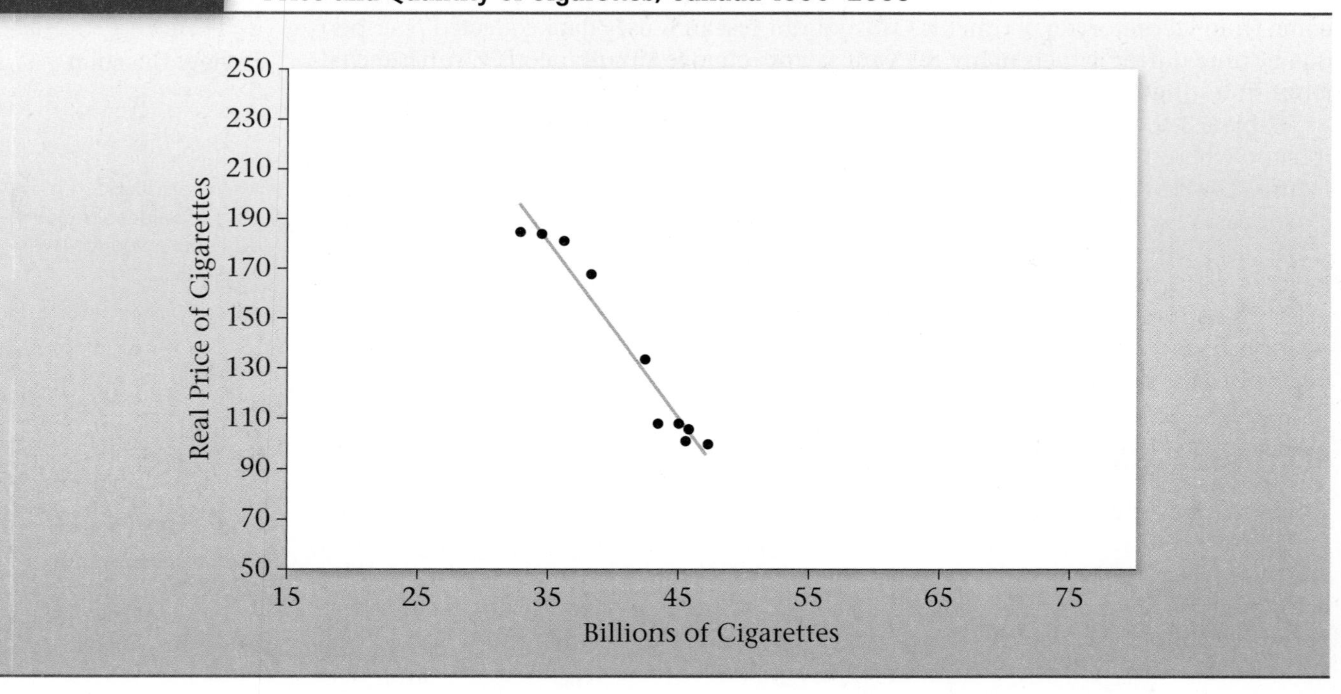

FIGURE 2.4 **A Negative Linear Relationship**

A straight line is defined totally by two values: the intercept, which is where the line meets the vertical axis, and the slope, which is measured by the ratio of the vertical distance over the horizontal distance for any segment of the function. Functions which are upward sloping define positive relationships, and functions that are downward sloping define negative relationships.

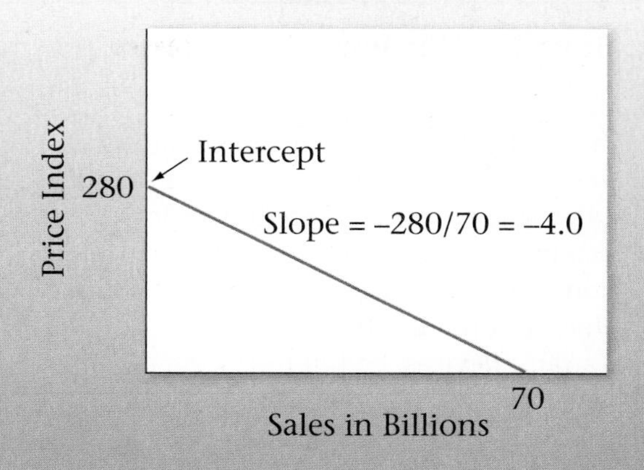

INTERPRETING LINEAR RELATIONSHIPS

For diagrams to be useful, we must be able to understand them. Figure 2.4 is somewhat similar to Figure 2.3: The regression line has been projected to intersect each axis, and we find that it meets the axes at a horizontal value of 70 and a vertical value of 280. When the function is a straight line, two pieces of information fully describe the relationship: the **intercept** and the **slope**. The intercept is the height of the line when the variable on the horizontal axis has a zero value—in Figure 2.4 it has a value of 280.

The **intercept** is the height of the line when the variable on the horizontal axis has a zero value.

The slope of the line indicates the amount by which the variable on the vertical axis increases in response to a change in the value of the variable on the horizontal axis. Since this is a straight line, the slope is constant throughout. It is measured as the ratio of the vertical distance divided by the horizontal distance for any segment of the line. In this example, that ratio is given by 280/70 = 4.0. It is also negative, since an increase in one variable is correlated with a decrease in the other.

The **slope** of the line is the ratio of the vertical distance divided by the horizontal distance for any segment of the line.

We can now define a linear equation for this regression line:

$$P = 280 - 4Q$$

where P is price and Q is sales quantity. To verify that this indeed represents the line, remember that the (vertical) intercept reflects the value of P when Q is zero. In this equation a zero value of Q yields:

$$P = 280 - 4 \times 0 = 280$$

Second, the number 4 is the slope. It goes with the value of variable Q, indicating that, for every unit change in Q, price changes by four units. Since there is a negative sign governing the term, a unit increase in Q results in a four-unit *decline* in P. In geometric terms, the line is downward, or negatively sloped.

It is worth repeating that this line is an *average* representation of the relationship between price and quantity; it does not go through every point in the scatter diagram. For any price that is fed into the equation, we obtain a corresponding quantity, or any quantity value that is fed into the equation yields a corresponding price. The prediction therefore always lies on the line, whereas the actual value seldom does.

APPLICATION BOX 2.3

Statistics for Policy Making

Data are an integral part of policy making in the public domain. A good example of this is in the area of driver policy. Road fatalities have fallen dramatically in recent decades in Canada, in large measure due to the introduction of safety measures such as speed limits, blood-alcohol limits, seat belt laws, child-restraint devices, and so forth. Safety policies are directed particularly strongly towards youth: They have a lower blood-alcohol limit, a smaller number of permitted demerit points before losing their licence, a required period of learning (driver permit), and so forth. While fatalities among youth have fallen in line with fatalities across the age spectrum, they are still higher than for other age groups. The figure below presents data on fatalities per licensed driver by age group in Canada for 2006. Note the strong *non-linear pattern* to the data—fatalities decline quickly, then level off and again increase for the oldest age group.

In response to these data, drivers are now required to re-pass a driving test in most provinces once they attain a certain age—usually 80, because the data indicate that fatalities increase as drivers reach their senior years.

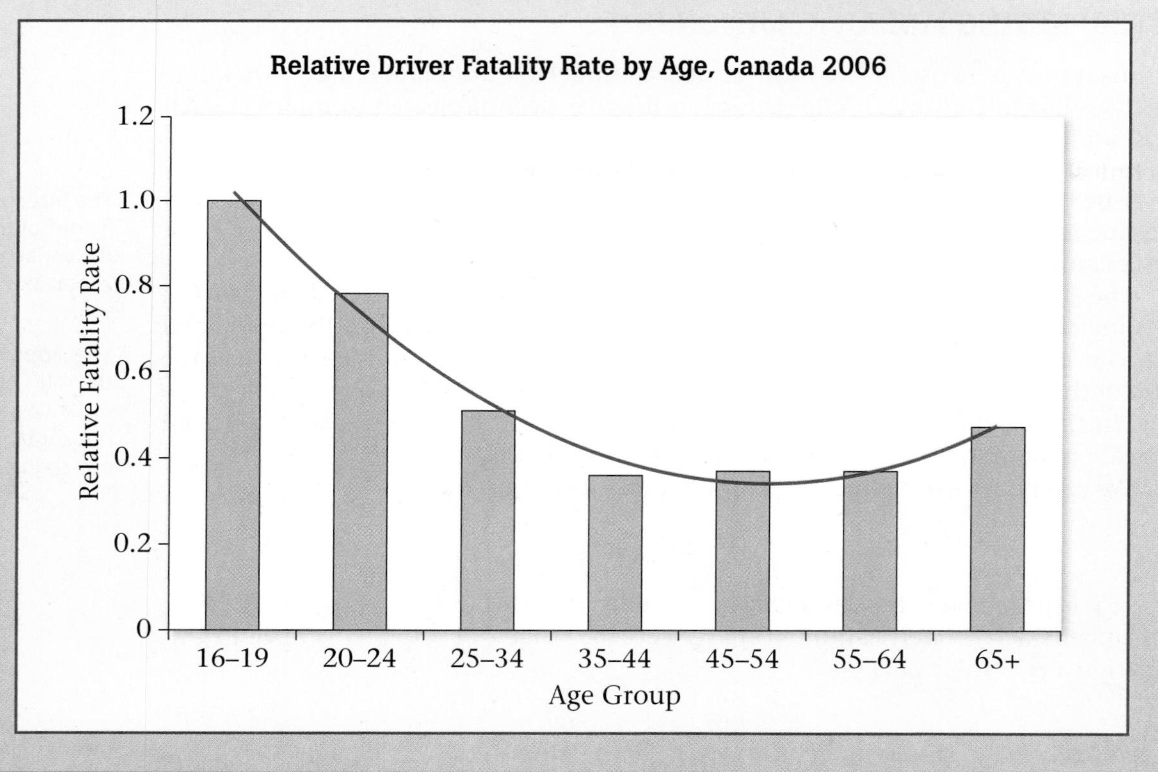

Source: www.tc.gc.ca, search for "Canadian Motor Vehicle Traffic Collision Stats, 2006."

When the predictions and the actual values are very close to one another, i.e., where the scatter is closely concentrated around the regression line, we say that the line is a *good fit*.

Economic relationships need not be linear; we could imagine fitting a slightly curved function through the data linking tobacco sales to prices. Such a curved function might result in the points being slightly closer to such a line on average. But to

Review Questions 6 and 7

maintain simplicity we will work with linear functions and lines throughout. Furthermore, economic relationships are not unchanging. Had we constructed a scatter plot for earlier or later years in Figure 2.3, the slope and intercepts of the regression line might well have been different.

Review Question 8

VISUAL THOUGHT

The scatter plot presented above is one example of how we use visual tools in analyzing economic issues. The price indexes in Figure 2.2 are another, as is the production possibility frontier in discussed in Chapter 1. We will see in Chapter 3 and subsequent chapters that the graphical presentation of an idea or economic model greatly facilitates the analysis of economic behaviour and economic theories.

2.5 Theories and Evidence: Accepting and Rejecting Theories

Economists analyze a problem in three distinct phases. First, a phenomenon is observed and a theory is formulated. By reasoning or by an inspection of the data, we propose that a certain relationship exists—for example, that tobacco prices and tobacco sales move in opposite directions. Second, we develop a model to capture the essence of the phenomenon: By thinking about the factors that influence demand, we can identify ingredients in addition to price that should go into an econometric model. In technical terminology, we formulate a hypothesis or belief. Third, the predictions of the theory are tested by examining the data econometrically in all its generality—that is, by estimating the quantitative relationships between the variable whose behaviour we are seeking to explain and its proposed influences.

Having done this, suppose that our theory and the data seem compatible. Then we *do not reject* the theory. If the theory and data are not compatible, however, we do not accept the theory and start again. But if the data do not reject the theory this does not guarantee that we have found the *only* correct model. There may be an alternative model lurking in the background that we have not managed to conceive, and it might be equally or *more* compatible with the data.

As a general rule, the more we confront our model with data, the more robust it becomes if new data sets do not reject it. For example, a particular model might be applied to data from a series of economies to see how well it stands up. As we stated earlier, relationships that stand repeated testing are sometimes called economic or behavioural laws.

2.6 The Great Canadian Data Hunt

The most comprehensive source of data for Canadian economists is to be found in the CANSIM database, which is managed by Statistics Canada. CANSIM stands for Canadian Socio-economic Information Management System. It can be accessed through libraries, or by students who have a university or college library number. Access is obtained by going to your library Web site, and by clicking on "databases" in the menu bar and following the obvious choices. There are two versions: one is called CHASS; the other is called E-STAT. The second is more user-friendly because it enables the user to search by subject matter. The data bank contains about 27 million series! Explore it.

2.7 Popular Criticisms of Economics and Economists

If you have some nagging doubts about the economist's tool kit or methodology, you are not alone in the world. Let's look at some popular criticisms of economics and economists.

No two economists ever agree: You need to distinguish between positive and normative economics. Even if all economists agree on how the world works (positive economics), there remains scope for disagreement on recommendations based on different value judgements or *norms*. Many disagreements are of this type. For example, the political left tends to favour more supportive welfare, higher unemployment insurance payments, higher minimum wages, and more redistributive taxation, while the political right stresses the importance of market incentives, self-reliance, minimal government intervention and lower taxes. Economic analysis can inform, but cannot resolve such opposing viewpoints. An economic analyst might have much to say about the impact of minimum wages on unemployment rates, but this may not be sufficient to sway a voter who votes according to her ethical beliefs.

Furthermore, there exist many disagreements in the domain of positive economics itself. Economics is not an experimental science, and different data sets frequently point in different directions when it comes to testing theories. Using data for long time periods and from different economies does indeed help to discriminate between different theories, but not always.

It is also incorrect to think there are not similar disagreements among physicists or doctors or engineers. Most people do not claim to know too much about physics, so physicists are somewhat immune from this criticism. But few individuals would confess ignorance of every area in economics.

Models in economics are too simple to be considered realistic: A model is a deliberate simplification of reality. Good models simplify without distorting. The test of a good model is not how simple it is, but how much of observed behaviour it can explain.

Sometimes we get a long way with a simple model. On other occasions the underlying behaviour is too complex to be adequately captured by a simple model. But economists are criticized much less today than some decades ago for their modelling approach to the discipline. Among social scientists, economists were among the first to introduce the rigour of mathematical analysis. Such an approach often necessitates a "stripped-down" version of reality. In the current era we see political scientists and sociologists adopting similar analytical approaches and tools.

People are not as mercenary as economists portray them to be: Economists believe that much of the behaviour they study is influenced by monetary incentives. But this does not mean that incentives alone matter. At the same time as other social scientists have been adopting the methods of economists, economics has been learning a great deal from those disciplines also, particularly behavioural psychology. For example, our economic models of crime used to focus predominantly on incentives and deterrents. Now we realize the importance of stigma and peer influences. As another example, we now know that tobacco price/tax changes influence young smokers in two distinct ways: first as a result of the product's being more expensive, and second through the peer impact that results from fewer friends smoking because of the higher price. The willingness of economists to recognize the importance of insights from other disciplines, coupled with success in integrating these insights into their theoretical and econometric models, has been one of the most important developments in economics in recent decades.

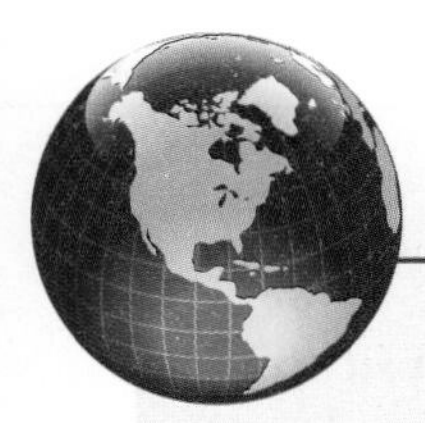

APPLICATION BOX 2.4

Nobel Laureates: Economists, Statisticians, Sociologists, and Psychologists

The discipline of Economics is not an island unto itself. It has influenced other disciplines and has learned from other disciplines.

The first winners of the Economics Prize in Memory of Alfred Nobel in 1969 were Ragnar Frisch and Jan Tinbergen. Frisch's PhD was in mathematical statistics, while Tinbergen's was in Physics. Frisch brought his validating and testing skills to the study of economic data, while Tinbergen built differential-equations-based economic models using the methods of physics.

Gary Becker, of the University of Chicago, won that prize in 1992. His interest in bringing the rigour of economics to the analysis of social issues such as crime, divorce, drug use, the family, and human capital resulted in him being appointed to a joint position in Economics and Sociology in 1983. The use of economic analysis in this way was ground breaking. He argued, for example, that the prohibition of alcohol in the 1920s gave the U.S. Al Capone, gangsters, crime, and smuggling from Canada; but it failed to stop its citizens from drinking. The end of prohibition "was a confession that the U.S. experiment in banning drinking had failed dismally. It was not an expression of support for heavy drinking or alcoholism." Becker's solution for the drug problem in the modern era is the same as his solution would have been for prohibition—legalize, tax, protect minors, cut out organized crime's supply monopoly, and free up police to pursue criminal activity of a more serious nature.

Daniel Kahneman of Princeton University was a winner of the Prize in 2002. He was trained as a psychologist, obtaining his PhD in Berkeley. His work on decision theory was path breaking, and when he began to publish his work in the Economics journals, decision theory in Economics received a tremendous boost. The result was that many economists began to think in new ways and were able to develop a more profound understanding of incentives. Among his many contributions were the development of what are called prospect theory and reflection theory.

Actions of human beings cannot be reduced to scientific laws: Physicists accept that individual molecules behave randomly, but that we can still construct and test theories based on their *average behaviour.* Economists take the same view of people. While we cannot explain every human action, random differences tend to cancel out. If behaviour shows no systematic tendencies, there is little to discuss; observing the past is of no value and there is no guide to the future. Not only is this view unhelpful; it is not supported by the data. The economic theories that survive are those that are consistently compatible with the data. Even in the face of some random and inexplicable actions, human behaviour has a large systematic, or predictable, component.

Next

We have now developed, admittedly in an elementary way, the tools of economic analysis. We proceed to examine the behaviour of particular markets and the economic actors who take part in them using these tools. Since much of behaviour is determined by supply and demand conditions, and, given that markets are all-important, the study of these is a good place to begin.

SUMMARY

- There is a continuous interplay between theory, models, and data in the study of economic relationships. A **theory** is a logical view of how the world or its components work. A **model** is a simplified framework that enables us to organize how we might validate a theory or formulate a solution to a problem.
- **Data**, or facts, are essential for two reasons: They suggest relationships that we should aim to explain, and they allow us to test hypotheses and to quantify effects.
- A **behavioural law** is a meaningful theoretical relationship that has been validated repeatedly by data.
- Tables present data in a form that is easy to understand. **Time-series data** are values of a given variable at different points in time. **Cross-section data** refer to data gathered at a given point in time for different individuals or groups. **Longitudinal data** follow the same individuals or agents through time.
- **Index numbers** express data values relative to a given base value. Many index numbers incorporate averages of other variables. The **consumer price index** measures the average price level in the economy and yields the average rate at which all consumer goods and services change in price. It assigns heavier **weights** to items that account for a larger share of expenditure.
- The **percentage change** in a variable is defined as the change in that variable relative to its base value, scaled by 100. The percentage change in the retail price index is the **inflation rate** or **deflation rate**, depending upon whether prices increase or decrease.
- **Nominal price variables** measure values at prices ruling when the variable is measured. **Real price variables** adjust the nominal price level to account for changes in the economy's overall price level.
- **Quality change** is a dominant characteristic of many goods and services we buy today. When correctly integrated into the consumer price index, measured inflation may be reduced.
- **Scatter diagrams** show the relationship between two variables plotted in a diagram. By fitting a **regression line** through these points, we summarize the average relationship between the two.
- **Econometrics** is the science of developing and understanding the precise relationships between variables. It uses computers, allowing it to handle large blocks of data with many variables. When a scatter diagram is closely concentrated around a regression line we say that the model fits the data well.
- **A straight-line equation** is completely characterized by an intercept and a slope.
- **Figures and charts** that are based on data are often used in building a model. They describe relationships between two variables, holding other things equal. If we wish to change one or some of these other influences, the position of our two-dimensional functional relationship will generally shift.
- Econometric relationships may be **non-linear and subject to change**.
- To understand how the economy works **we need theories and facts**. Theory is needed to sort out the data—there are too many facts for the facts alone to describe the workings of an economy. Conversely, theory without facts is just theory, not a validated understanding of the world we live in.
- **Economists are subject to criticism** on account of their methodology, but much less so today than in earlier eras. Other disciplines have taken on the methodology of economists, and economists are learning much from behavioural scientists.

KEY TERMS

Theory *21*
Model *22*
Data *22*
Behavioural law *22*
Time series *23*
Cross-section data *23*
Longitudinal data *25*
Index number *25*
Percentage change *25*
Consumer price index *27*
Inflation and deflation *27*
Real price index *27*
Nominal price index *27*
Scatter diagram *29*
Econometrics *29*
Regression line *30*
Intercept *31*
Slope *31*

REVIEW QUESTIONS

Review Questions and answers are included in Connect at www.mcgrawhillconnect.ca.

1. The research department of the Royal Canadian Mounted Police wants to study whether the crime rate in a particular province is related to the unemployment rate in the province.
   a. As an analyst, what steps would you take in this research?
   b. What data series would you require?
   c. What "other things being equal" problems would you keep in mind?

2. The table below gives unemployment rates for big cities and the rest of the country. Two-thirds of the population lives in the big cities, and one-third in other areas. Construct a national unemployment index, using the year 2000 as the base.

	Unemployment (%)	
Year	**Big Cities**	**Other Areas**
1997	7	10
1998	6	9
1999	5	8
2000	4	8
2001	6	9

3. The prices in the table below are for three components in a typical consumer's budget: transportation, rent, and food. You must construct an aggregate price index based on these three components on the assumption that rent accounts for 55 percent of the weight in this index, food for 35 percent, and transport for 10 percent. You should start by computing an index for each component, using year 1 as the base period.

	Year 1	Year 2	Year 3	Year 4	Year 5
Transport $	70	70	75	75	75
Rent $	1000	1000	1100	1120	1150
Food $	600	620	610	640	660

4. The price of carrots per kilogram is given in the table below for several years, as is the corresponding CPI.
   a. Compute a nominal price index for carrots using 2000 as the base period.
   b. Recompute the CPI using 2000 as the base year.
   c. Construct a real price index for carrots.

	2000	2002	2004	2006	2008	2010
Nominal carrot price $	2.60	2.90	3.30	3.30	3.10	3.00
CPI	110	112	115	117	120	124

5. The following table shows hypothetical consumption spending by households and income of households in billions of dollars.
   a. Plot the scatter diagram with consumption on the vertical axis and income on the horizontal axis.
   b. Fit a line through these points.
   c. Does the line indicate that these two variables are related to each other?

Year	Income	Consumption
2002	476	434
2003	482	447
2004	495	454
2005	505	471
2006	525	489
2007	539	509
2008	550	530
2009	567	548

6. Using the data from the preceding question, compute the percentage change in consumption and the percentage change in income for each pair of adjoining years between 2002 and 2009.

7. You are told that the relationship between two variables, X and Y, has the form $Y = 10 + 2X$. By trying different values for X you can obtain the corresponding predicted value for Y (e.g., if $X = 3$, then $Y = 10 + 2 \times 3 = 16$). For values of X between 0 and 12, compute the matching value of Y and plot the relationship.

8. Perform the same exercise as in the preceding question, but use the formula Y = 10 – 0.5X. What do you notice about the slope of the relationship?

9. For the data below, plot a scatter diagram with variable Y on the vertical axis and variable X on the horizontal axis.
   a. Is the relationship between the variables positive or negative?
   b. Do you think that a linear or non-linear line better describes the relationship?

Y	40	33	29	56	81	19	20
X	5	7	9	3	1	11	10

10. Using the data in question 5, construct a scatter diagram using Excel, or any other spreadsheet program you know. Then see if you can fit a trend line through the scatter diagram. To do this you may need to click on "help" and type "trendline" into the search box.

11. *Internet* You are considering buying a house and you want to find out what mortgage rates are. You are also interested in discovering whether they have moved up or down in the last couple of years. Finally, you would like to know the difference between the mortgage rate that is renewed in one year and the rate that is fixed for five years. To answer all of these questions you can go to the Bank of Canada Web site at www.bankofcanada.ca. Search the "interest rate" and "rates and statistics" segments of the site.

12. *Internet* Your father has just retired, and you and he are discussing the salary you might earn upon graduating with an economics degree. Your father proudly tells you that he earned $30,000 as a starting salary in 1990. Of course, prices have changed since then, and salaries reflect this. So you are wondering if this was a good or not-so-good salary. To find out the equivalent salary at today's prices you could go again to the Bank of Canada web site, and retrieve some information on the CPI between 1980 and the present time. What would your father's salary be at the present time in order for it to have the same real value?

13. CANSIM Go to Statistics Canada's CANSIM database through your school library. Using what Statistics Canada calls its "user-friendly" interface, see if you can find a data series on the CPI for Canada since 1995. Can you get this in monthly form?

CHAPTER 3

Demand, Supply, and the Classical Marketplace

LEARNING OUTCOMES

By the end of this chapter you should understand:

1. The market
2. Demand, supply, and equilibrium; concepts
3. Demand and supply curves; equilibrium solutions
4. Behind the demand curve
5. Shifts in the demand curve
6. Behind the supply curve
7. Shifts in the supply curve
8. Simultaneous shifts in supply and demand
9. Free and managed markets
10. From individuals to markets
11. How markets answer the what, how, and for whom

How does society decide upon what, how, and for whom to produce? Modern economies rely heavily on markets and prices to allocate resources to competing uses. In the marketplace, the interplay of demand, which is the behaviour of buyers, and supply, which is the behaviour of sellers, determines the quantity of goods and services produced, and the prices at which they are traded. Not all resources are allocated through the market mechanism. Schooling and health care are allocated in Canada primarily by government decree. But even here the market plays a role: Universities and some colleges charge fees, and most individuals must pay for their pharmaceuticals.

3.1 The Market

In Chapter 1 we described a market as a set of arrangements whereby buyers and sellers exchange goods and services. Stores and fruit stalls physically bring the players together. A stock exchange involves intermediaries (brokers) who act on behalf of clients; it also invites electronic participation by the buyers and sellers directly. In supermarkets, sellers choose the price and allow customers to determine whether or not to buy. In contrast, auctions permit buyers to bid.

Although superficially different, these markets perform the same economic function: They determine prices which ensure that the quantity people wish to buy equals the quantity people wish to sell. Price and quantity cannot be considered separately. If the market price of a Lexus is a multiple of the price of a Hyundai, the quantities sold of each will differ. Prices, therefore, influence the economic choices of what, how, and for whom to produce. To understand this process more fully, we need to *model* a typical market. The essentials are demand and supply.

3.2 Demand, Supply, and Equilibrium

Demand is the quantity of a good or service that buyers wish to purchase at each possible price, with all other influences on demand remaining unchanged.

Supply is the quantity of a good or service that sellers are willing to sell at each possible price, with all other influences on supply remaining unchanged.

Demand is the quantity of a good or service that buyers wish to purchase at each conceivable price, with all other influences on demand remaining unchanged. It is not a particular quantity, such as three mugs of coffee or two cell phones, but rather a full description of the quantity of a good or service that buyers would purchase at various prices.

As an example, the first column of Table 3.1 shows the price of laptop computers. The second column shows the quantity that would be purchased each month by students living in Utown at these prices. It is therefore a demand schedule.

Supply is the quantity of a good or service that sellers are willing to sell at each possible price, with all other influences on supply remaining unchanged. Again, it is not a particular quantity, but a complete description of the quantity that sellers would want to sell at each price. Such a supply schedule is defined in the third column of the table. It is assumed that no supplier can make a profit (on account of their costs) unless the price is at least $1600, and therefore a zero quantity is supplied below that price. The higher price is more lucrative, and therefore induces a greater quantity supplied, perhaps by attracting more suppliers.

TABLE 3.1 Monthly Demand and Supply of Laptops in Utown

Price ($)	Demand	Supply	Excess Demand/Supply
800	200	0	
1200	160	0	Excess demand
1600	120	40	
1800	100	60	
2000	80	80	Equilibrium
2200	60	100	
2400	40	120	Excess supply
2800	0	160	

Note the distinction between *demand* and **quantity demanded**. Demand describes the behaviour of buyers at every price, whereas quantity demanded describes behaviour at a particular price. The same distinction applies to *supply* and **quantity supplied**.

Quantity demanded refers to the amount purchased at a particular price.

Quantity supplied refers to the amount supplied at a particular price.

In everyday language we may say that the demand for hockey tickets exceeds their supply when some people do not get into the arena. As economists we must be more precise: *At the price charged for tickets*, the quantity demanded exceeds the quantity supplied. A higher ticket price would reduce the *quantity demanded*. Yet the higher price would not change *demand*, because demand refers to the whole schedule of possible quantities demanded at different prices.

OTHER THINGS BEING EQUAL—*CETERIS PARIBUS*

The demand and supply schedules are constructed on the assumption that, when the price changes, other influences on supply and demand remain the same. We use the expression *other things being equal*, or its Latin counterpart *ceteris paribus*, to describe this constancy of other influences. For example, we assume on the demand side that the prices of other goods remain constant, that tastes and incomes are unchanging, that the size of the market is given, and so forth. On the supply side we assume, for example, that there is no technological change in production methods.

THE EQUILIBRIUM PRICE

We will keep other things constant for the moment, and combine the behaviours of buyers and sellers to model the market. At low prices, the data in Table 3.1 indicate that the quantity demanded exceeds the quantity supplied. The opposite occurs when the price is high. At some intermediate price, where the quantity demanded equals the quantity supplied, equilibrium is established. The **equilibrium price** equates demand and supply—it clears the market.

The **equilibrium price** clears the market. It is the price at which the quantity demanded equals the quantity supplied.

In Table 3.1 the equilibrium price is $2000, and the equilibrium quantity is 80 computers per month. At higher prices there is an **excess supply**—suppliers wish to sell more than buyers wish to buy. Conversely, at lower prices there is an **excess demand**. Only at the equilibrium price is the quantity supplied equal to the quantity demanded.

Excess supply exists when the quantity supplied exceeds the quantity demanded at the going price.

Excess demand exists when the quantity demanded exceeds the quantity supplied at the going price.

Does the market automatically reach equilibrium? To answer this question, suppose initially that the sellers choose a price of $2800. Here suppliers would like to supply 160 laptops, but there are no buyers—a situation of extreme excess supply. At the price of $2400 the excess supply is reduced to 80, because both the quantity demanded is now higher at 40 units, and the quantity supplied is lower at 120. But excess supply means that there are suppliers willing to supply at a lower price, and this willingness exerts continual downward pressure on any price above the price that equates demand and supply.

At prices below the equilibrium there is an excess demand. In this situation, suppliers could force the price upward, knowing that buyers will continue to buy at a price at which the suppliers are willing to sell. Such upward pressure would continue until the excess demand is eliminated.

In general then, at prices above the equilibrium price excess supply exerts downward pressure on price, and below the equilibrium excess demand exerts upward pressure on price. This process implies that the participants in the market have information on the various elements that make up the marketplace.

Note that if sales do take place at prices above or below the equilibrium price the quantity traded always corresponds to the short side of the market: At high prices the quantity demanded is less than supply, and it is the quantity demanded that is traded because buyers will not buy the amount suppliers would like to supply. At low prices the quantity demanded exceeds quantity supplied, and it is the amount that suppliers are willing to sell that is traded. In sum, when trading takes place at prices other than the equilibrium price it is always the lesser of the quantity demanded or supplied that is traded. Hence we say that at non equilibrium prices the **short side** dominates. We will return to this in a series of examples later in this chapter.

The **short side** dominates, at prices other than the equilibrium price.

THE CLASSICAL MARKETPLACE

Before progressing to a graphical analysis, it is important to note a characteristic of this type of example: It is assumed that the supply side of the market captures all of the costs associated with producing the good. For example, if electricity were the good being traded and this electricity were produced using a polluting, coal-burning power plant that inflicted costs on society at large, then the supply curve would not reflect the full costs of production. Stated another way, the private costs of production would not reflect the total costs of production. For the moment the assumption is that no such additional costs are associated with the markets we analyze.

3.3 Demand and Supply Curves

The **demand curve** shows the relation between price and quantity demanded, holding other things constant.

The **supply curve** shows the relation between price and quantity supplied, holding other things constant.

The **demand curve** shows the relation between price and quantity demanded, holding other things constant. Figure 3.1 measures price on the vertical axis and quantity on the horizontal axis. The curve D represents the data from the first two columns of Table 3.1. Each combination of price and quantity demanded lies on the curve. In this case the curve is *linear*—it is a straight line, and it has a negative slope, reflecting the fact that buyers wish to purchase more at lower prices.

The **supply curve** shows the relation between price and quantity supplied, holding other things constant. The supply curve S in Figure 3.1 is based on the data from columns 1 and 3 in Table 3.1. It, too, is linear, but has a positive slope indicating that suppliers wish to supply more at higher prices.

The demand and supply curves intersect at point E, corresponding to a price of $2000 which, as illustrated above, is the equilibrium price for this market. At any price below the equilibrium price of $2000 the horizontal distance between the supply and demand curves represents excess demand, because demand exceeds supply. Conversely, at any price above $2000 there is an excess supply that is again measured by the horizontal distance between the two curves. Market forces tend to eliminate excess demand and excess supply.

COMPUTING THE MARKET EQUILIBRIUM

It is not difficult to represent the supply and demand functions underlying Table 3.1 in their mathematical form:

$$\text{Demand: } P = 2800 - 10Q \qquad \text{Supply: } P = 1200 + 10Q$$

In the previous chapter we stated that a straight line is represented completely by the intercept and slope. Let us first verify that these equations do, indeed, represent

FIGURE 3.1 **The Market for Laptops**

Market equilibrium is at E. Excess demand occurs at prices below E and excess supply occurs at prices above E. The horizontal distance between the curves is a measure of excess supply or excess demand.

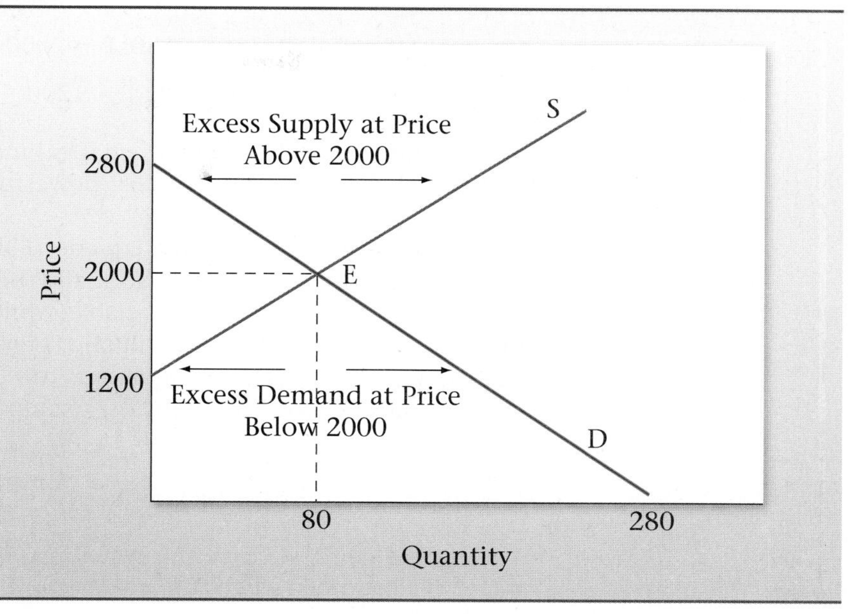

the data in Table 3.1. On the demand side, we see that a zero quantity is demanded at a price of \$2800, and this is therefore the intercept with the price (vertical) axis. To see this just set $Q = 0$ in the demand equation. As for the slope, each unit change in quantity demanded is associated with a \$10 change in price. For instance, when the price is increased by \$400, the quantity demanded declines by 40 units. In reverse, if the price is lowered by \$200, the quantity demanded increases by 20 units. Since the price is on the vertical axis, it follows that the slope is given by $-200/20 = -10$. It is negative because an increase in quantity demanded is associated with a decrease in price.

On the supply side, column 3 in Table 3.1 indicates that at a quantity of zero the price is \$1200. Therefore, 1200 is the price intercept. As for the slope, each change in quantity is associated with a change in price in the ratio of 10 to 1. For instance, each twenty-unit change in quantity supplied is associated again with a \$200 change in price. Consequently, the slope is given by $200/20 = 10$. In this case the slope is positive, since both the price and quantity move in the same direction.

We have now obtained the two defining characteristics of the demand and supply curves, which enable us to write them as above. Next we must find where they intersect—the market equilibrium. Since, at their intersection point, the price on the demand curve equals the price on the supply curve, and the quantity demanded equals the quantity supplied, this unique price-quantity combination is obtained by equating the two curves:

$$2800 - 10Q = 1200 + 10Q, \textit{ i.e. } 2800 - 1200 = 10Q + 10Q, \text{ or } 1600 = 20Q$$

$$\text{Therefore } Q = 1600/20 = 80$$

The *equilibrium solution* for Q is therefore 80 units. What about an equilibrium price? It is obtained by inserting the equilibrium Q value into *either the supply or the demand function*. *Either* function can be used because, where Q = 80, the supply and demand functions intersect—they have equal P values:

$$\text{Demand price at } Q = 80\text{: } P = 2800 - 10 \times 80 = 2800 - 800 = 2000$$

$$\text{Supply price at } Q = 80\text{: } P = 1200 + 10 \times 80 = 1200 + 800 = 2000$$

We have just solved a mathematical model of a particular market. It was not so difficult, but the method is very powerful and we will use it many times in the text.

In the demand and supply equations above the price appeared on the left hand side and quantity on the right. Normally this format implies a causation running from the right to the left hand side variable, while in economic markets we normally think of the quantity demanded and supplied depending upon the price in the market place. But the supply and demand equations can be rearranged so that quantity appears on the left and price on the right. For example the demand equation can be rewritten as follows:

$$P = 2800 - 10Q \text{ implies } 10Q = 2800 - P \text{ or } Q = 280 - P/10.$$

Review Question 1

Writing the demand curve this way illustrates that the quantity intercept is 280—the quantity demanded when the price becomes zero. The supply curve can be rearranged similarly.

3.4 Behind the Demand Curve

The demand curve depicts the relationship between quantity and price, holding other things constant. These other things fall into several broad categories: the prices of related goods; consumer incomes; consumer tastes; and expectations about the future. Before proceeding, note that, for the moment, we are dealing with *market* demand rather than demand by one *individual*. The relationship between the two is developed in section 10 of the chapter.

THE PRICES OF RELATED GOODS

How has the arrival of high-speed Internet, and its declining price, affected the demand for laptops? Internet access and computers are called complementary goods in economics: They go together. A more formal definition of complements relates the quantity purchased of one good or service to price changes in the other. Specifically, if a price reduction for one good *increases* the demand for a second good, the second good is a **complement** to the first.

Complementary goods: If a price reduction for one good increases the demand for a second good, the second good is a complement to the first.

Substitute goods: If a price reduction for one good reduces the demand for a second good, the second good is a substitute for the first.

In contrast, when the behaviour runs in the opposite direction, the goods are substitutes. If a price reduction for one good *reduces* the demand for a second good, the second good is a **substitute** for the first.

Substitutes for the laptop are desktop computers, hand-held electronic devices that mimic some laptop functions, audio-recording devices that enable students to record lectures, or laptops that students can borrow on a daily basis from the media centre in their library. If the price for any one of these items were to increase, we would expect the demand for laptops to increase *at any price* for laptops. In graphical terms, the demand curve *shifts* in response to changes in the prices of other goods. For example, a reduction in the price of high-speed Internet service will shift the demand outward or upward, because more laptops will be purchased at any price[1]

CONSUMER INCOMES

When incomes rise, the demand for most goods increases. Given this, the demand curve will shift outward if student incomes increase. Here we are referring to total income, and this can increase as a result of a greater population.

Most goods are demanded in greater quantity in response to higher incomes at any given price. But there are exceptions. For example, public transit demand may decline at any price when household incomes rise, because some individuals move to cars. Or the demand for laundromats may decline in response to higher incomes, as households purchase more of their own consumer durables. We use the term **inferior good** to define these cases: An inferior good is one whose demand declines in response to increasing incomes, whereas a **normal good** experiences an increase in demand in response to rising incomes.

An **inferior good** is one whose demand falls in response to higher incomes.

A **normal good** is one whose demand increases in response to higher incomes.

There is a further sense in which consumer incomes influence demand, and this relates to how the incomes are *distributed* in the economy. In our discussion above we stated that higher total incomes shift demand curves outwards when goods are normal. But think of the difference in the demand for laptops between Greece and Saudi Arabia. These economies have roughly the same average income, but incomes are distributed more unequally in Saudi Arabia. Saudi Arabia does not have a large middle class that can afford laptops, despite the huge wealth held by the elite. In contrast, Greece has a relatively larger middle class that can afford such goods. Consequently, the *distribution of income* can be an important determinant of the demand for many commodities and services.

TASTES AND NETWORKS

While demand functions are drawn on the assumption that tastes are constant, in an evolving world they are not. We are all subject to peer pressure, the fashion industry, marketing, and a desire to maintain our image. If the fashion industry dictates that lapels or long skirts are *de rigueur* for the coming season, some fashion-conscious individuals will discard a large segment of their wardrobe, even though the clothes may be in perfectly good condition: Their demand is influenced by the dictates of current fashion.

Networks are increasingly important in the modern era. Why do we all use and, more importantly, purchase WinZip to compress computer files when there are literally dozens of free compression packages available on the Internet? The answer is that, for whatever reason, *other people* use WinZip; we are all part of a network. Your professor would certainly be frustrated if students submitted assignments that were each zipped using a different compression package. She would not want to download dozens of different software packages in order to unzip and read all the student assignments. Consequently, the extent to which some goods and services are used by others can influence demand.

---

[1] We can say either that the demand curve shifts outward or upward. 'Outward' denotes the view that buyers wish to purchase more at any price, whereas 'upward' denotes that buyers are willing to pay more for any given quantity. Similar terminology applies to the supply side: an inward or upward shift indicates *less* will be supplied at any price, or that any given quantity requires a higher price.

EXPECTATIONS

In 2005, Google stocks quadrupled in value, while General Motors stock plummeted and its bonds were demoted to junk status. Why did investors drive these stock prices so hard? It was not because Google was making billions in 2005, nor because GM was doing so much worse than in 2004. Rather, it was because investors believed that the *future* was bright for Google and dim for GM. The expectation that Google profits would increase, but that GM's profits might not, increased the demand for Google shares on the stock market, and this increase in demand resulted in a higher price. History vindicated the market participants in these cases.

Of course, individuals frequently make poor guesses about the future. For example, ticket scalpers at sports events may overestimate demand and set the street price for their tickets too high, with the result that they are left with unsold tickets; or the buyers of "tech" company stocks in the late '90s overestimated the future profits of such companies, and paid too high a price for their stocks.

3.5 Shifts in the Demand Curve

The demand curve we saw in Figure 3.1 is drawn for a given level of other prices, incomes, tastes, and expectations. Movements along the demand curve reflect solely the impact of different prices for the good in question, holding other influences constant. But changes in any of these other factors will change the position of the demand curve.

Figure 3.2 illustrates a shift in the demand curve. This shift could result from a rise in student incomes that increases the quantity demanded *at every price*. That more students can now afford a laptop at any price is illustrated by a shift in the demand curve from D to D^1. With supply conditions unchanged, there is a new equilibrium at E^1, indicating a greater quantity of purchases accompanied by a higher price. The new demand curve reflects a *change in demand*, as opposed to a *change in the quantity demanded*.

Review Question 2

FIGURE 3.2 **Shifts in the Demand Curve**

Initially the market equilibrium is at E^0. When incomes are higher, or when the prices of substitutes are higher, demand increases to D^1. At the price P^0 excess demand develops and the price adjusts upward to P^1 at the new equilibrium E^1.

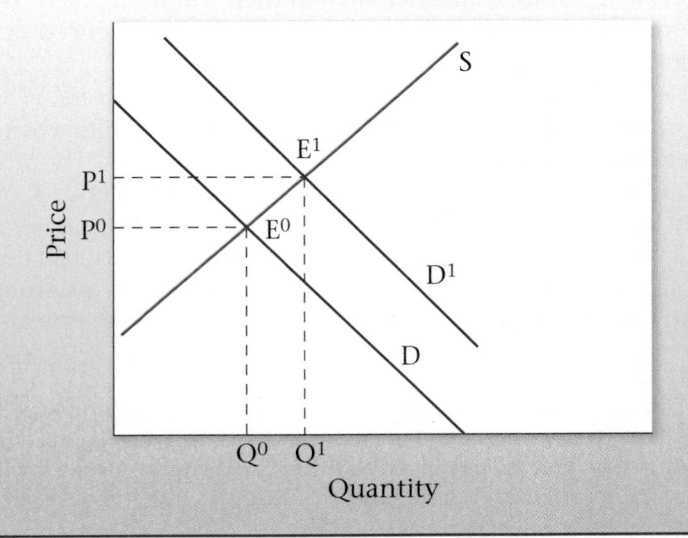

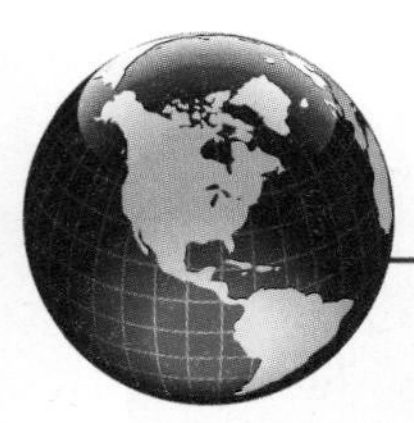

APPLICATION BOX 3.1

Crop Prices—Strong Demand Shifts

In the middle of its second mandate, the Bush Administration decided to encourage the production of ethanol—a fuel that is cleaner than gasoline and less polluting. The policy set a production target of 6 billion gallons for 2007 (from a base of 1 billion in 2000) and 35 billion for 2017.

The principal input in ethanol production in both the U.S. and Canada is corn. Corn is used primarily as animal feed, and secondarily as a sweetener and a food for humans. The target was to be met with the help of a subsidy to ethanol producers and a tariff on imported ethanol (Brazil is a major producer of sugar-cane based ethanol).

The impact on corn prices was immediate, as can be seen from the figure below. From a farm-gate price of $2 per bushel in 2005, the price reached the $4 range two years later, despite an increase in U.S. production of almost 20 percent.

In addition to the U.S. initiative, the world demand for grains has increased on account of growing demand in India and China. Rising incomes in these economies mean that their citizens are demanding more grain and more meat—which requires grain as an input.

The wider impact of these developments has been that the prices of virtually all grains increased in tandem with corn. For example, the prices of sorghum and barley increased in line with corn, partly because of a switch in land use towards corn—the crop that initially drove up prices. Corn was seen as more profitable, less acreage was allocated to other grains, and the supply of these other grains fell.

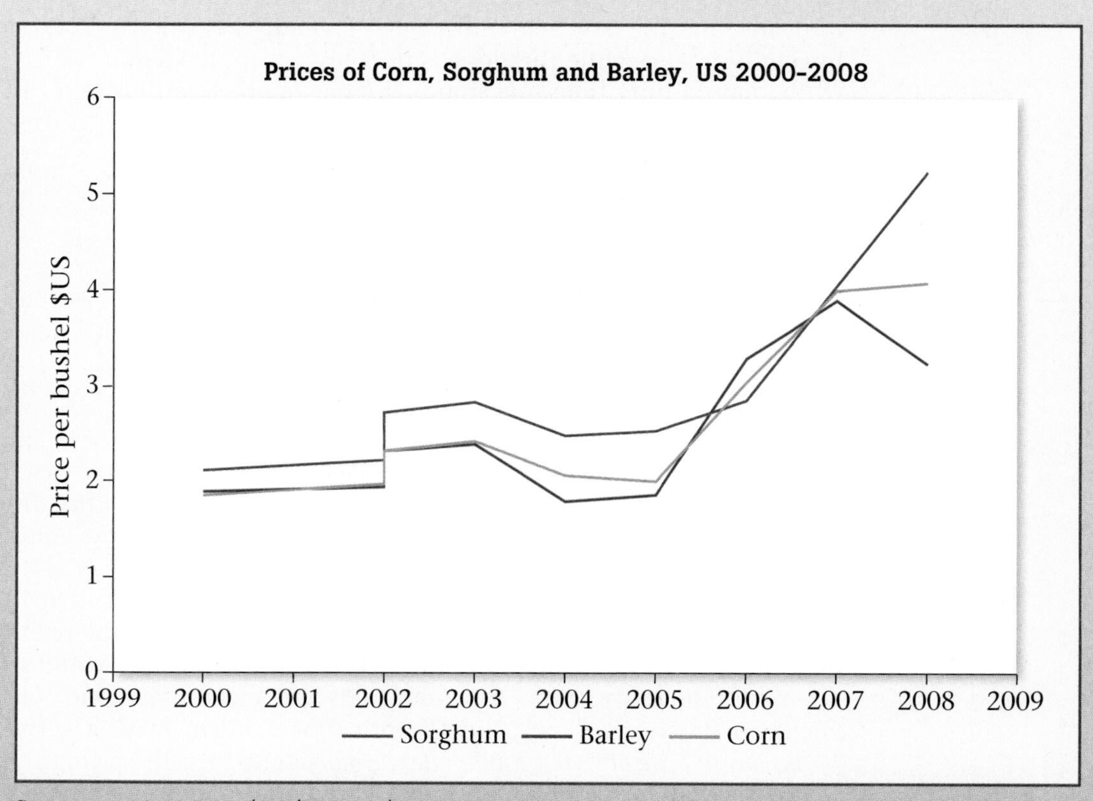

Source: www.ers.usda.gov/data/feedgrain/StandardReports

APPLICATION BOX 3.1 *continued*

While producers and producing nations benefited from the price rise, consumers—particularly those on low incomes and those in less developed economies—experienced a dramatic increase in their basic living costs. Visit the site of the United Nations' *Food and Agricultural Organization* for an assessment.

In terms of supply and demand shifts, the demand side has dominated. The ethanol drive, combined with secular growth for food, means that the demand for grains has shifted outward faster than the supply has.

A similar impact would be caused by an increase in the price of substitutes. Suppose that the media centre in the school library decides to implement a fee for borrowing laptops. More students would now feel it worthwhile to purchase their own. In contrast, if students expect some new technological breakthrough in operating systems, they may postpone their purchase for the moment, and this would be reflected in a inward shift of the demand curve: At any price fewer will be purchased.

How are such changes reflected in our *economic model*? Let us say that market research quantifies the degree to which the demand curve shifts: Market analysis indicates that the new demand curve is given by $P = 3200 - 10Q$. Note that the intercept is greater while the slope is unchanged, so the demand curve shifts outward while maintaining the same slope. The new market equilibrium can be established by solving for the intersection of the new demand curve with the existing supply curve. Let us do it.

$$\text{Demand: } P = 3200 - 10Q \qquad \text{Supply: } P = 1200 + 10Q$$

Equating the two yields:

$$3200 - 10Q = 1200 + 10Q \text{ or } 3200 - 1200 = 10Q + 10Q \text{ or } 2000 = 20Q$$

$$\text{Therefore } Q = 2000/20 = 100$$

One hundred laptops are now traded, rather than 80. The new equilibrium price is obtained as before, by estimating the price at which 100 computers will be supplied or demanded. Inserting $Q = 100$ in either the supply or demand function yields a value of \$2200. As a result of the demand increase, therefore, both the equilibrium quantity traded and the equilibrium price in the market increase.

We may well ask why so much emphasis in our diagrams and analysis is placed on the relationship between *price* and quantity, rather than on the relationship between quantity and its other determinants. The answer is that we could indeed draw diagrams with quantity on the horizontal axis and a measure of one of these other influences on the vertical axis. But the price mechanism plays a very important role. *Variations in price are what equilibrate the market.* By focusing primarily upon the price, we see the self-correcting mechanism by which the market reacts to excess supply or excess demand.

In addition, this analysis illustrates the method of **comparative statics**—examining the impact of changing one of the other things that are assumed constant in the supply and demand diagrams.

Comparative static analysis compares an initial equilibrium with a new equilibrium, where the difference is due to a change in one of the other things that lie behind the supply and demand curves.

The analysis is *comparative* because it compares the old and new equilibria. It is *static* because it compares *only* the initial and new equilibria, not the path between the two. In Figure 3.2 we explain the difference between the points E^0 and E^1 by indicating that there has been a change in incomes or in the price of a substitute good. We do not attempt to analyze the details of this move or the exact path from E^0 to E^1. That is the subject matter of dynamic analysis.

3.6 Behind the Supply Curve

To date we have drawn supply curves with an upward slope. Is this a reasonable representation of supply in view of what is frequently observed in markets? We suggested in the preceding sections that the various producers of a particular good or service may have different levels of efficiency. If so, only the more efficient producers can make a profit at a low price, whereas at higher prices more producers or suppliers enter the market—producers who may not be as lean and efficient as those who can survive in a lower-price environment. This view of the world yields an upward-sloping supply curve, although there are other perspectives on the supply curve's slope.

Frequently producers simply choose a price and let buyers purchase as much as they want at that price. Monopolists, who are sole suppliers, normally act in this way. Thus we do not encounter a supply curve for a Windows® operating system, or Microsoft Office®. Microsoft sets a price, and buyers purchase as many as they desire at that price. In yet other situations supply is *fixed*. This happens in auctions, and bidders at the auction simply determine the price to be paid. Regardless of the type of market we encounter, however, it is safe to assume that supply curves, where they exist, do not slope downward. So, for the moment, we adopt the stance that supply curves exist and that they are generally upward sloping.

Next, we examine those other influences that underlie supply curves. Technology, input costs, the prices of competing goods, expectations and the number of suppliers are the most important.

TECHNOLOGY

A technological advance may involve an idea that allows more output to be produced with the same inputs, or an equal output with fewer inputs. A good example is *just-in-time* technology. Until the 1970s, auto manufacturers kept large stocks of components in their production facilities, but developments in communications and computers at this time made it possible for manufacturers to link directly with their input suppliers. Nowadays assembly plants place their order for, say, seat delivery to their local seat supplier well ahead of time. The seats swing into the assembly area hours or minutes before assembly—just in time. The result is that the assembler reduces his seat inventory (an input) and thereby reduces production cost.

Such a technology-induced cost saving is represented by moving the supply curve downward or outward: The supplier is willing to supply the same quantity at a lower price because of the technological innovation. Or, saying the same thing slightly differently, suppliers will supply more at a given price than before. This is but one example of how "supply chains" are evolving in the modern globalized world. Computer assemblers such as Dell and Hewlett-Packard are prime examples of the same developments.

INPUT COSTS

Input costs can vary independently of technology. For example, a wage negotiation that grants workers an increase well ahead of the general inflation rate will increase the cost of production. This is reflected in a leftward, or upward, supply shift. Any quantity is now priced higher; alternatively, suppliers are willing to supply less at the going price.

Government regulation is a type of cost. Increased safety may raise costs, while at the same time generating benefits in the form of better health and reduced accidents and absenteeism.

As a further example, suppose the government decrees that power-generating companies must provide a certain percentage of their power using wind-driven turbines. Since such turbines are not yet as efficient as more conventional power sources, the electricity they generate comes at a higher cost.

Review Question 3

COMPETING PRODUCTS

If competing products improve in quality or fall in price, a supplier may be forced to follow suit. Hewlett-Packard and Dell are constantly watching each other's pricing policies. If Dell brings out a new generation of computers at a lower price, Hewlett-Packard will likely lower its prices in turn—which is to say that Hewlett-Packard's supply curve will shift downward.

THE NUMBER OF SUPPLIERS AND EXPECTATIONS

As a general rule, the greater the number of suppliers, the greater will be the total supply of a good. We will see in later chapters, when comparing markets in which there are many suppliers with markets where there are very few, that the quantity supplied will reflect these different environments.

In the modern era of rapid technological change, expectations are an important determinant of supply. New products arrive in the marketplace almost continuously. If entrepreneurs believe that certain products are here to stay they expect that profits will be made in the future. New suppliers enter the marketplace and thereby increase supply—more will be supplied at any given price.

3.7 Shifts in the Supply Curve

Whenever technology changes, or the costs of production change, or the prices of competing products adjust, then one of our *ceteris paribus* assumptions is violated. Such changes are generally reflected by shifting the supply curve. Figure 3.3 illustrates the

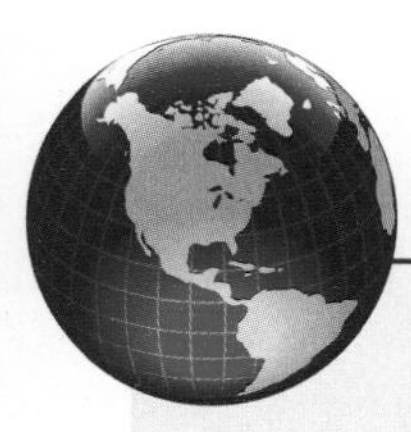

APPLICATION BOX 3.2

Technology-Driven Price Declines in the Price of Light—Strong Supply Shifts

While news media tend to focus on price increases, technological developments have had a truly staggering impact on price declines for some goods and services. William Nordhaus of Yale University is an expert on measuring the impact of technological change. In a recent piece of research he examined the trend in the real price of lighting. Originally, light was provided by whale oil and gas lamps and these sources of lumens (our scientific measure of the amount of light produced) were costly. In his research, Professor Nordhaus pieced together evidence on the actual historic cost of light produced at various times, going all the way back to 1800. His results were staggering: He found that light in 1800 cost about 100 times more than in 1900, and light in 2000 cost a fraction of its cost in 1900. A rough calculation suggests that light was five hundred times more expensive at the start of this 200-year period than at the end.

In terms of supply and demand analysis, light has been subject to very substantial downward supply shifts. Despite the long-term growth in demand, the technologically induced supply changes have been the dominant factor in its price determination.

For further information, visit Professor Nordhaus's Web site in the Department of Economics at Yale University.

impact of the arrival of just-in-time technology. The supply curve shifts downward/outward, reflecting the ability of suppliers to supply the same output at a reduced price. The resulting new equilibrium price is lower, since production costs have fallen. At this reduced price more cars are purchased.

Review Questions 4, 5, and 6

FIGURE 3.3 **Shifts in the Supply Curve**

Initially the equilibrium is at E^0. A technological innovation, or a fall in the price of an input, shifts the supply curve to S^1. At the price P^0 excess supply develops and this exerts downward pressure on the price until a new equilibrium is established at E^1. The new equilibrium results in a lower price and more of the good being traded.

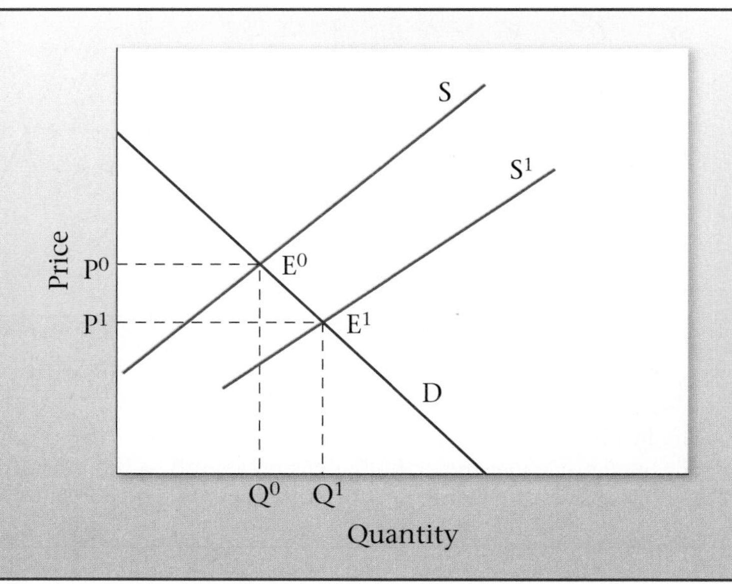

3.8 Simultaneous Shifts in Supply and Demand: Applications

Review Question 7

In the real world, demand and supply frequently shift at the same time. We present three very real such cases in Figures 3.4 through 3.6.

Case 1: Expectations and the Price of Cars

The price of gasoline began its most recent ascent in 2004. Once consumers became convinced that higher prices were not just a temporary blip on the radar, they decided in essence that the future costs of running their gas guzzlers was going to be much higher than they previously thought. Two things happened. First, owners of big cars put them on the market in greater numbers; the supply of second-hand "guzzlers" shifted outward on account of a different set of expectations. In addition, potential second-hand buyers also decided that they would purchase fewer big vehicles and, instead, buy more fuel-efficient vehicles. This meant that the demand for large second-hand cars shifted downward. The combined impact of an increase in supply and a decrease in demand sent the price downward. This is illustrated in Figure 3.4. Note that while the price must unequivocally fall in this market, the actual quantity traded may increase or decrease.

FIGURE 3.4 **Expectations and the Price of Large Second-Hand Cars**

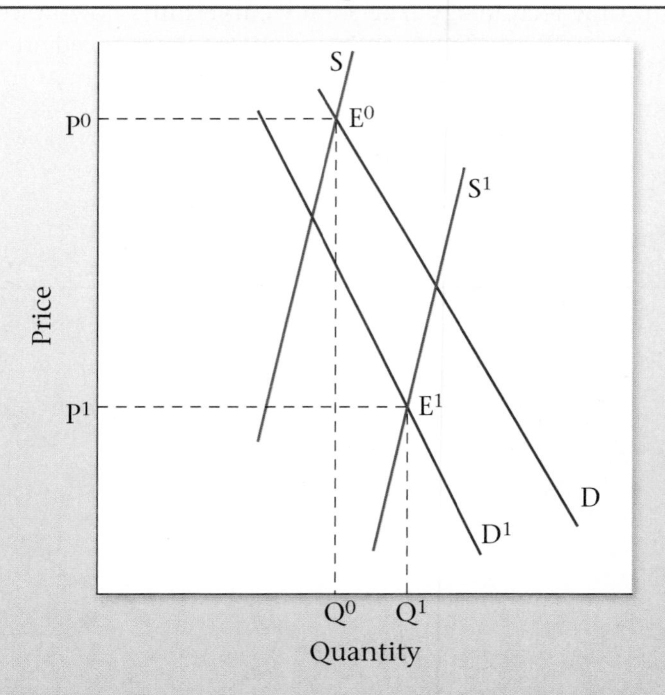

The initial equilibrium is at E^0. Supply shifts from S to S^1 as more individuals wish to sell their large cars. But buyers also fear future higher gas prices and so their demand shifts down to D^1. The price decreases to P^1 at the new equilibrium E^1.

Case 2: Alberta Beef Market: The Power of One

In May 2003 a shudder went through the Canadian beef market: One cow in Alberta was diagnosed with bovine spongiform encephalopathy ("mad cow" disease). As a result, Canadian consumers became very anxious about purchasing beef, and decreased their demand. At the same time, the U.S. imposed a ban on the sales of such beef in the United States. Consequently, suppliers redirected that beef onto the Canadian market; the supply of beef in the domestic market increased.

This one sick cow had a dramatic impact on the Alberta beef market. Prices fell by more than one-third in the space of four months because of a downward shift in demand and an outward shift in supply to the domestic market, as illustrated in Figure 3.5. A frequent sight was one of Albertans in grocery store parking lots purchasing beef priced at rock-bottom prices direct from the producers. In contrast, the price of pork and poultry remained almost unchanged.

Case 3: A Housing Market

Figure 3.6 contains two data points, each reflecting a market equilibrium. One (E_{1997}) defines the number of houses traded in 1997 and the average price of those houses; the other (E_{2002}) reflects the same information for 2002. These are two actual data points for the small community of Montreal West.

FIGURE 3.5 **Alberta Beef: The Power of One**

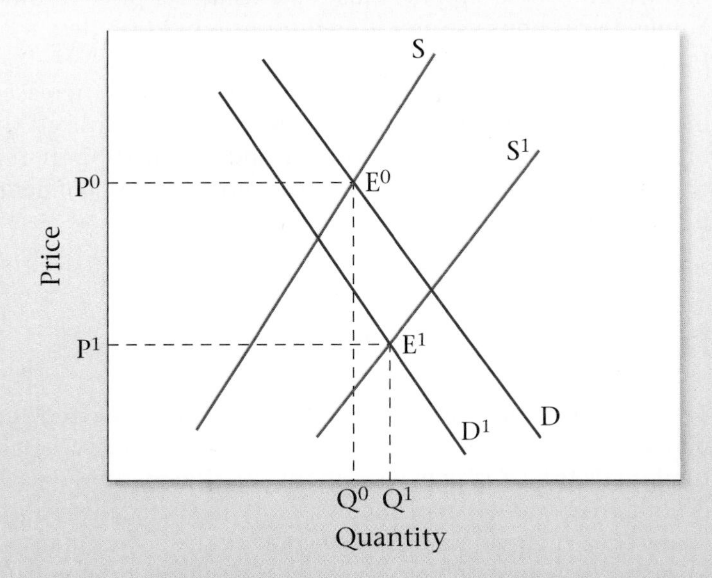

The initial equilibrium price P^0 is disturbed by a ban on Alberta beef sales in the U.S. This beef supply is redirected to the Canadian market therefore the Canadian supply curve shifts outwards from S to S^1. In addition, fears about disease reduce demand from D to D^1. The price declines from P^0 to P^1 as a result of these twin shifts.

FIGURE 3.6 **A Model of the Housing Market**

The vertical supply curves denote a fixed number of houses being supplied to the market each year. Demand was stronger in 2002 than in 1997 on account of both higher incomes and lower mortgage rates. Thus the higher price in 2002 is due to both a reduction in the supply of houses coming onto the market and an increase in demand.

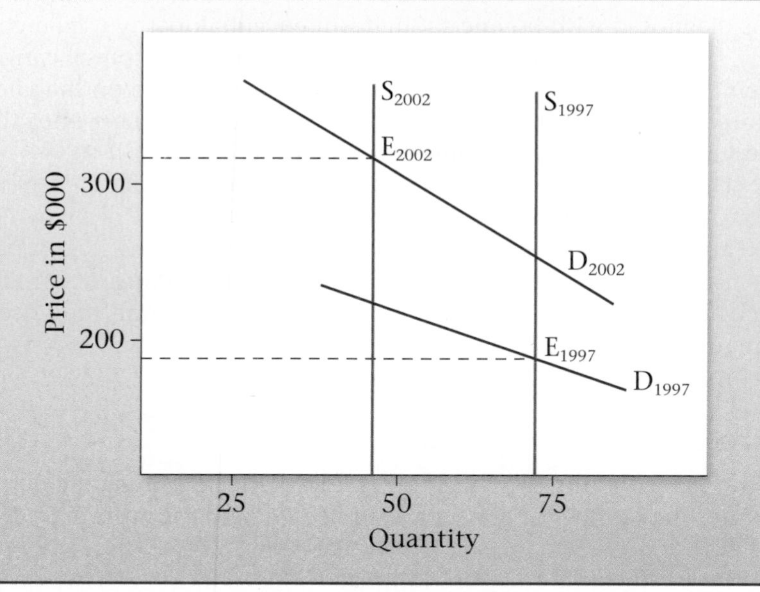

On the supply side we have inserted two vertical supply curves. Such vertical curves mean that a fixed number of homeowners decide to put their homes on the market, and these suppliers just take whatever price results in the market. In this example, fewer houses were offered for sale in 2002 (less than 50) than in 1997 (more than 70).

During this time period household incomes increased substantially and, also, mortgage rates fell. Both of these developments shifted the demand curve upward: buyers were willing to pay more for housing in 2002 than in 1997.

The higher price in 2002 was therefore due to *both* demand and supply side shifts in the marketplace.

3.9 Free Markets and Managed Markets

The freely functioning markets that we have developed certainly do not describe all markets. For example, minimum wages characterize the labour market, most agricultural markets have supply restrictions, apartments are subject to rent controls, and blood is not a freely traded market commodity in Canada. In short, price controls and quotas characterize many markets. **Price controls** are government rules or laws that inhibit the formation of market-determined prices. **Quotas** are physical restrictions on output.

Price controls are government rules or laws that inhibit the formation of market-determined prices.

Quotas are physical restrictions on output.

Price controls come in the form of either *floors* or *ceilings*. Ceilings make it illegal for suppliers to charge more than a specific price. Limits on apartment rents are one form of ceiling. In wartime, price controls are frequently imposed on foodstuffs, in conjunction with rationing, to ensure that access is not determined by who has the most income. The problem with price ceilings, however, is that they leave demand unsatisfied, and therefore they must be accompanied by some other allocation mechanism. Consider the example in Figure 3.7.

FIGURE 3.7 **The Effect of a Price Ceiling**

The free market equilibrium occurs at E^0. A price ceiling at P^c succeeds in holding down the price but leads to excess demand E^cB, because Q^c is the quantity actually traded. A price ceiling above P^0 is irrelevant since the free market equilibrium E^0 can still be attained.

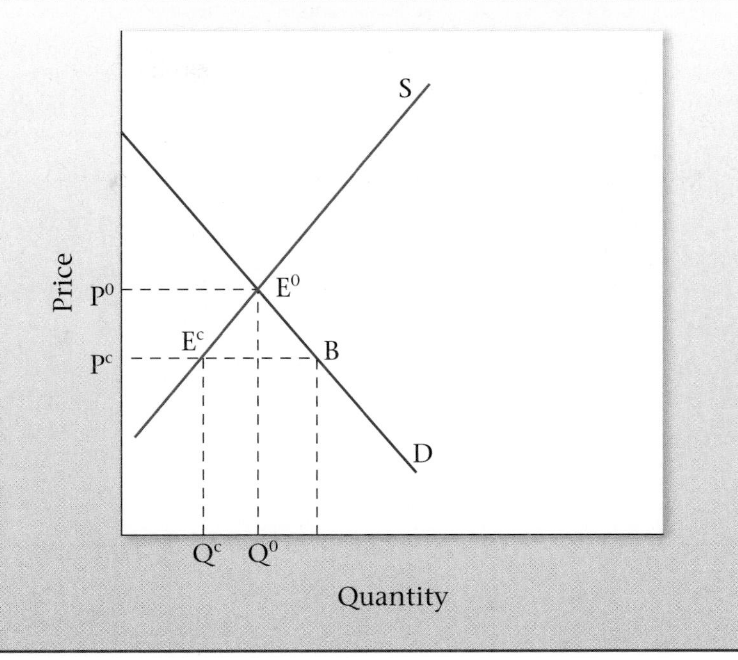

PRICE CEILINGS AS RENT CONTROLS

Consider an environment where, for some reason—perhaps a sudden and unanticipated growth in population—rents increase. Let the resulting equilibrium be defined by the point E^0 in Figure 3.7. If the government were to decide that this is an unfair price because it places hardships on low- and middle-income households, it might impose a price limit, or ceiling, of P^c. The problem with such a limit is, of course, that excess demand results: Individuals want to rent more apartments than are available in the city. In a free market the price would adjust upward to eliminate the excess demand, but in this controlled environment it cannot. So some other way of allocating the available supply between demanders must evolve.

Review Question 8

In reality, most apartments are allocated to those households already occupying them. But what happens when such a resident household decides to purchase a home or move to another city? It holds a valuable asset, since the price/rent it is paying is less than the market price. Rather than give this surplus value to another family, it might decide to sublet at a price above what it currently pays. While this might be illegal, the family knows that there is excess demand and therefore such a solution is possible. A variation on this outcome is for an incoming tenant to pay money, sometimes directly to an existing tenant or to the building superintendent, or possibly to a real estate broker who will "buy out" existing tenants. This is sometimes called "key money."

Rent controls are widely studied in economics, and the consequences are well understood: Landlords tend not to repair or maintain their rental units and so the residential stock deteriorates. Builders realize that more money is to be made in building condominium units, or in converting rental units to condominiums. The frequent consequence is a *reduction* in supply and a reduced quality. Market forces are hard to circumvent because, as we emphasized in Chapter 1, economic players react to the incentives they face.

FIGURE 3.8 **Price Floor/Minimum Wage**

In a free market the equilibrium wage and number of hours worked are defined by E^0. A minimum wage equal to P^f raises the hourly wage, but reduces the hours of work demanded from Q^0 to Q^f. Consequently the amount E^fC represents the excess supply at P^f, since Q^f is the amount actually traded.

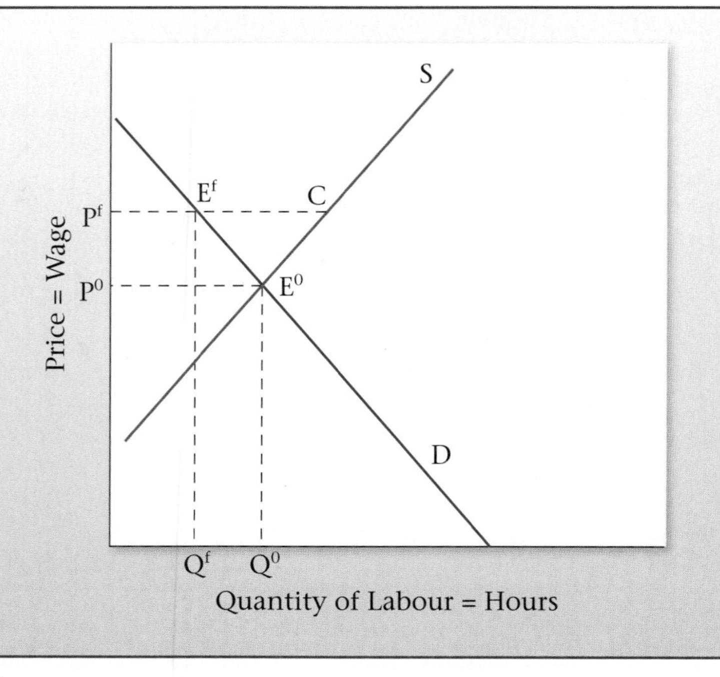

PRICE FLOORS

Review Question 9

An effective price floor sets the price *above* the market-clearing price. A minimum wage is the most widespread example in the Canadian economy. Provinces each set their own minimum, and it is seen as a way of protecting the well-being of low-skill workers. Such a floor is illustrated in Figure 3.8. The free-market equilibrium is again E^0, but the effective market outcome is the combination of price and quantity corresponding to the point E^f at the price floor, P^f. In this instance, there is excess supply equal to the amount E^fC.

Note that there is a similarity between the outcomes defined in the floor and ceiling cases: The quantity actually traded is *the lesser of the supply quantity and demand quantity at the going price: the short side dominates.*

QUOTAS

A quota represents the right to supply a specified quantity of a good to the market. It is another method of keeping prices higher than the free-market equilibrium price. As an alternative to imposing a price floor, the government can generate a high price by restricting supply. Agricultural markets abound with examples. In these markets, farmers can supply only what they are permitted by the quota they hold, and there is usually a market for these quotas. For example, in several Canadian provinces it currently costs in the region of $30,000 to purchase a quota granting the right to sell the milk of one cow. The cost of purchasing quotas can thus easily outstrip the cost of a farm and herd. Canadian cheese importers must pay for the right to import cheese from abroad. Restrictions also apply to poultry and other meat markets. The impact of all of these restrictions is to raise the domestic price above the free market price.

In Figure 3.9, the free-market equilibrium is at E^0. In order to raise the price above P^0, the government restricts supply to Q^q by granting quotas, which permit producers to supply a limited amount of the good in question. This supply is purchased at the price P^q.

APPLICATION BOX 3.3

Labour Markets and Laws in Ireland and France

In November 2005 an explosion of anger and violence hit Paris and other French cities as thousands of young French citizens protested about their exclusion from mainstream society and their inability to find jobs in a labour market that had a 10 percent unemployment rate. These youth were, for the most part, second-generation citizens whose parents had migrated from North and West Africa.

At the same time, young Poles, Czechs, and Romanians were migrating in their thousands to a much smaller labour market at the edge of Europe that had a 3.8 percent unemployment rate—Ireland. An enormous chasm separated these labour markets. In Ireland workers could be laid off very easily and there were fewer government controls in the market. Employers bore only a small responsibility for the longer-term employment status of workers and, as a consequence, were unafraid to hire foreign workers about whom they knew relatively little.

In contrast, French law demanded more protection of workers: It was difficult for employers to lay off a worker; workers were entitled to more sick leave, and employer social security payments on behalf of workers were higher. This deterred French employers from hiring individuals whom they did not know. In particular, employers were less willing to hire members of a minority than members of the established "mainstream"—they discriminated. The sons and daughters of immigrants, even though citizens of France, suffered most from this "protective" legislation—this is the "law of unintended consequences."

FIGURE 3.9 **The Effect of a Quota**

The government decides that the equilibrium price P^0 is too low to support agricultural suppliers. It decides to boost the price by reducing supply from the equilibrium Q^0 to Q^q. It achieves this by requiring producers to have a production quota. This is equivalent to fixing supply at S^q.

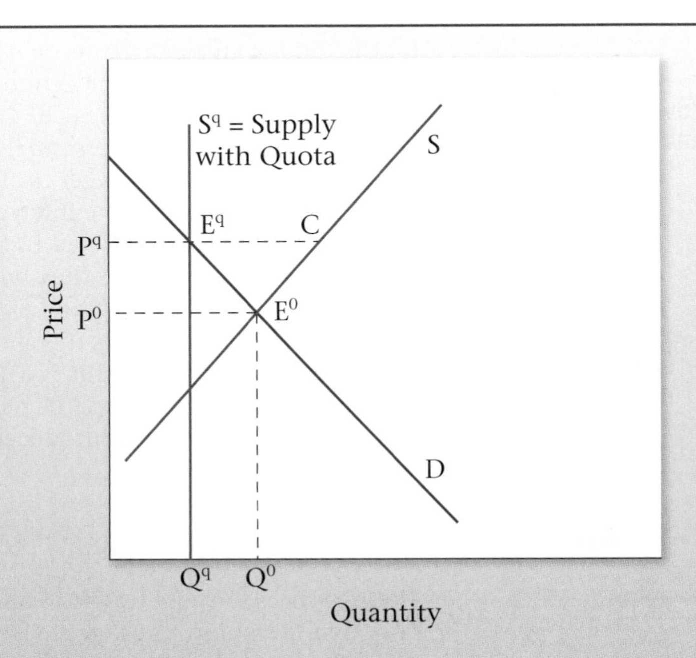

FIGURE 3.10 **Summing Individual Demands**

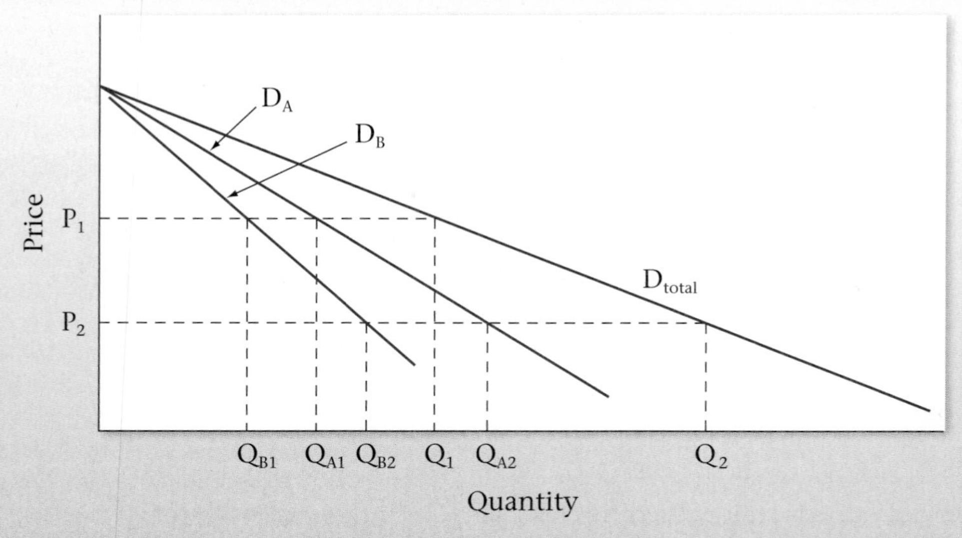

At a price P_1 individual A purchases Q_{A1} and individual B purchases Q_{B1}. The total, or market, demand is the sum of these individual demands at this price and equals Q_1. Similarly, at the price P_2 individual demands are summed to yield Q_2. Since the points Q_1 and Q_2 define the total demand of the market participants it follows that the market demand is the horizontal summation of the individual demand curves.

3.10 Summing Individual Decisions

Markets are made up of many individual participants on the demand and supply side. The supply and demand functions that we have worked with in this chapter are those for the total of all participants on each side of the market. But how do we arrive at such market functions when the economy is composed of individuals? We can illustrate how, with the help of Figure 3.10.

Review Questions 10 and 11

To concentrate on the essentials, imagine that there are just two buyers of gasoline in the economy. A has a bigger car than B, so his demand is greater. To simplify, let the two demands have the same intercept on the vertical axis. The curves D_A and D_B indicate how much gasoline A and B, respectively, will buy at each price. The market demand indicates how much they buy *together* at any price. Accordingly, at P_1, A and B purchase the quantities Q_{A1} and Q_{B1} respectively. At a price P_2, they purchase Q_{A2} and Q_{B2}. The **market demand** is therefore the horizontal sum of the individual demands at these prices. In the figure this is defined by D_{total}.

The **market demand curve** is obtained by summing individual demand curves horizontally.

On the supply side, the same relationship generally holds. Market supply curves are the horizontal sums of the producer supply curves in an industry.

3.11 What, How, and For Whom

The free market is one way for society to solve the basic economic questions of what, how, and for whom to produce. This chapter has illustrated how the market allocates scarce resources among competing uses.

APPLICATION BOX 3.4

Futures Markets

Futures markets involve participants who agree to trade a good or service at some point in the future at a price agreed upon today. Futures markets have grown dramatically in recent decades. A sense of their scope can be obtained by visiting the *Chicago Mercantile Exchange*, at www.cme.com, or the *Chicago Board of Trade*, at www.CBOT.com. Agricultural products and currencies are particularly important elements.

The reason such markets have evolved is that they reduce risk, and participants are willing to pay a premium for this. Here are two examples.

(i) A farmer, uncertain about weather conditions and yield in the coming growing season, faces uncertainty about the price he will obtain for his harvest. If he can agree upon a price with a buyer in the springtime, before sowing his crop, the farmer may prefer a price that is slightly lower that his estimate of the likely price in the fall. He is willing to pay a premium for certainty.

(ii) A Canadian manufacturer will sell a product to a European buyer one year from now. The buyer will pay her an agreed price, denominated in euros, and she will then exchange these euros for Canadian dollars. In order to be certain about how many dollars she will get for her product, the manufacturer may enter into an agreement with a currency dealer to supply her with dollars one year from now in exchange for euros at a price or rate that they agree upon today.

These markets are particularly important where prices are *subject to volatility*. Such volatility signifies uncertainty, and most individuals prefer to avoid uncertainty where possible, even if it means paying a premium to do so.

The market decides *how much* of a good or service should be supplied by finding the price at which quantity demanded equals quantity supplied.

The market determines *for whom* the goods and services are produced—for those buyers willing to pay at least the equilibrium price for the good. The market also tells us *who* is producing—those producers who are willing and able to supply at the existing price.

The market determines *what* goods and services are produced. While nature endows us with resources, people engage in costly supply activities only if they are rewarded. The supply curve specifies how much the producers must be paid in order to induce supply, and the demand curve specifies the value that buyers place on any product.

DISTRIBUTIONAL CONCERNS

Society may not like the answers that the market provides. Even if prices for goods, services, and inputs to production are completely flexible, free markets do not allocate food and shelter in such a way as to remove hunger or hardship. Markets provide these goods to individuals willing to pay the going price. Society usually decides that the poor should get more food and shelter than the market would dictate, and governments therefore intervene. A major question of policy is whether governments should transfer money to the poor and encourage them to participate in markets, or whether the government should intervene directly in the market by limiting prices or influencing supply.

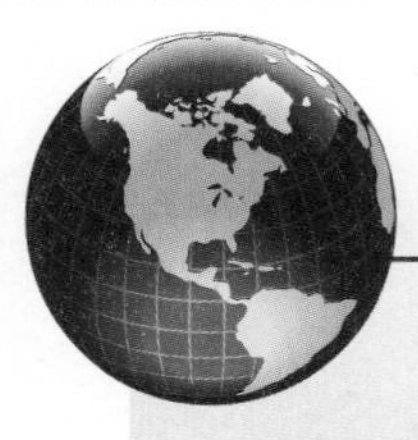

APPLICATION BOX 3.5

Price Controls in Canada—the Pharmaceuticals Sector

Canadian households consider themselves fortunate in having lower-priced pharmaceutical products than U.S. households have. In Canada we have the Patented Medicine Prices Review Board (PMPRB), which is an independent quasi-judicial body whose role is to ensure that prices charged by manufacturers for patented medicines are not excessive. The PMPRB regulates the price of each patented drug product sold in Canada.

Recent reports from the PMPRB show that drug prices in the *generic* prescription drug market segment tend to be *higher* in Canada than in most other countries. In the *patented* and non-patented branded prescription drug segments, Canada also tends to have relatively high prices. But the United States, where such products are as much as 200 percent higher than in Canada, has by far the highest prices.

MACROECONOMICS AND MICROECONOMICS

Macroeconomics studies the multitude of markets for goods and services, factors of production, and financial assets that make up the entire country's economy. An economic disturbance like the 2008/2009 crisis in financial markets, or a shift in the demand for exports, or a sharp change in energy and commodity prices, can push the macroeconomy away from equilibrium at full employment. Across the economy, prices and wages in some markets may be *rigid and slow to adjust*. As a result, the forces of excess supply and excess demand act more slowly and require a longer adjustment period to restore individual markets to equilibrium.

A decline in demand in an important sector of the economy, like the residential housing sector, has effects that spread across other markets in the economy. Production and employment decline across several sectors of the economy. If these impacts are widespread and persistent, the economy moves into recession. It operates at less than full employment and inside its production possibilities frontier: Some individuals who would be willing to work at current wage rates cannot find employment. Some producers who would be willing to produce and sell more at current prices cannot find buyers for their output. Plant and machinery don't operate at capacity. Society loses and standards of living suffer because not all resources are being used.

Over time, wages and prices begin to respond to these recessionary conditions. Even markets with rigid prices slowly begin to adjust and output and employment begin to rise. The economy embarks on a recovery phase, adjusting to the economic conditions created by the initial disturbance. With sufficient time these adjustments return the economy to full employment and the production possibilities frontier.

At other times the economy may be pushed temporarily *outside* its production possibilities frontier. High demand raises output levels above the designed capacity of producers' plants and pushes costs of production up. Shortages of labour with appropriate skills and experience exert upward pressure on wage rates and costs. The economy experiences inflationary pressure. If this level of economic activity persists, prices and wages will rise at increasing rates. Financial conditions will tighten, raising the costs of financing expenditure. Those on fixed money incomes will suffer losses in their living standards and purchasing power. Competitiveness in international markets will deteriorate. Businesses and households generally will begin to devote more time and effort to protecting themselves against the costs of inflation.

As a result, demand for output will decline as will output, moving the economy back to full employment.

Because these adjustments involve many markets with different degrees of price flexibility, they take time. The economy experiences cycles in levels of total output and employment. For periods of several months, or even years, prices and outputs deviate from their long-run equilibrium values. These cycles are fluctuations from periods of recession to periods of boom and inflationary pressure. Macroeconomics studies the causes and consequences of these business fluctuations, and the roles government fiscal and monetary policies can play to stabilize output and inflation.

Next

We have now covered some key aspects of economic analysis, the economist's tool kit, and a simple market supply and demand model for a single product or service. Our next task is to examine the performance of the economy as a complete system at the national level. We start this study of *macroeconomics* in Chapter 4 by looking at the main indicators of macroeconomic activity and the recent macroeconomic performance of the Canadian economy.

SUMMARY

- **Demand** defines a relationship between price and quantity on the part of buyers. Other things being equal, the lower the price the higher will be the quantity demanded; demand curves slope downward. **Quantity demanded** is the particular amount demanded at a given price.
- **Supply** defines a relationship between price and quantity on the part of suppliers. Other things being equal, the higher the price, the higher is the quantity supplied; supply curves slope upward. **Quantity supplied** is the particular amount supplied at a given price.
- The **market clears**, or **is in equilibrium**, when the price equates the quantity supplied and the quantity demanded. At this point supply and demand curves intersect. At prices below the equilibrium there is an **excess demand**, and at prices above the equilibrium an **excess supply**. In a **free market**, deviations from the equilibrium tend to be self-correcting. When trades take place at prices other than the equilibrium price, the **short side dominates**.
- **Along a given demand curve**, the **other things assumed constant** can be categorized as other prices, incomes, tastes, networks, expectations, and the scale of the market. Changes in these influences **shift the demand curve**.
- An increase in the price of a **substitute good or service** (or decrease in the price of a **complement**) will raise the quantity demanded at every price.
- An increase in consumer income will increase demand if it is a **normal good** and decrease demand if it is an **inferior good**.
- **Along a given supply curve**, the **other things assumed constant** are technology, input costs, the prices of other commodities, expectations, and the number of suppliers. A **technological innovation** lowers the supply curve; that is, it enables producers to supply any quantity at a lower price.
- **Comparative statics** compares the equilibrium that emerges in a market with an original equilibrium that is disturbed. Changes in the factors

behind the demand or supply curves shift these curves and result in a new market equilibrium. In real-world markets **simultaneous shifts** in supply and demand curves are frequent.

- **Managed markets** can involve **price ceilings, price floors, and quotas**. To be effective, a floor must be set above the free-market price, and a ceiling below that price. Quotas achieve higher prices by limiting supply. The marketplace will react to the excess supply or demand that follow from these controls.
- **The marketplace** provides one solution to the *what, how, and for whom* questions.
- **Macroeconomics** studies the multitude of markets that make up the entire country. If prices are rigid or slow to adjust in some of these markets, changes in economic conditions cause business cycles in output and employment. The time it takes to adjust to these disturbances creates the opportunity for monetary and fiscal policy to stabilize economic activity.

KEY TERMS

REVIEW QUESTIONS

Review Questions and answers are included in Connect at www.mcgrawhillconnect.ca.

1. Supply and demand data for concerts are shown below.

	Price					
	$20	$24	$28	$32	$36	$40
Demand Quantity	10	9	8	7	6	5
Supply Quantity	1	3	5	7	9	11

   a. Plot the supply and demand curves to scale and establish the equilibrium price and quantity.
   b. What is the excess supply or demand when price is (i) $24, (ii) $36?
   c. Describe the market adjustments in price induced by these prices.
   d. The functions underlying the example in the table are linear and can be represented as $P = 18 + 2Q$ (supply) and $P = 60 - 4Q$ (demand). Solve the two equations for the equilibrium price and quantity values.

2. Illustrate the effect on the demand for *Air Canada* flights between Halifax and Montreal as a result of:
   a. increasing the annual government subsidy to *Via Rail*.
   b. improving the Trans-Canada highway between the two cities.
   c. the arrival of a new budget airline on the scene.

3. Suppose farm workers in California are successful in obtaining a substantial wage increase. Illustrate the effect of this on the price of lettuce in the Canadian winter using a supply and demand diagram.

4. The (former) Government of Canada was planning to decriminalize the use of marijuana. Illustrate by means of supply and demand analysis how the existing equilibrium in this market at the time would likely have developed under the new law.

5. A new scourge in U.S. high schools is the widespread use of chewing tobacco. A recent survey indicates that 15 percent of males in upper grades now use it—a figure not far below the use rate for cigarettes. Apparently this development came about in response to the widespread implementation by schools of regulations that forbade smoking on and around school property. Draw a supply/demand equilibrium for each of the cigarette and chewing tobacco markets before and after the introduction of the regulations.

6. In question 1, suppose there is a simultaneous shift in supply and demand caused by an improvement in technology and a surge in incomes. The technological improvement is represented by a lower supply curve: $P = 10 + 2Q$. The higher incomes boost demand to $P = 76 - 4Q$.
   a. Draw the new supply and demand curves on a diagram and compare them with the pre-change curves.
   b. Equate the new supply and demand functions and solve for the new equilibrium price and quantity.

7. The market for labour can be described by two linear equations. Demand is given by $P = 150 - (1/6)Q$, and supply is given by $P = 50 + (1/3)Q$. P is the wage.
   a. Graph the functions and find the equilibrium price and quantity by equating demand and supply.
   b. Suppose a price ceiling is established by the government in this market at a price of $100. This price is below the equilibrium price that you have obtained in part a. Calculate the amount that would be demanded and supplied and then calculate the excess demand.

8. In the preceding question, suppose that the supply and demand functions describe an agricultural market rather than a labour market, and the government implements a *price floor* of $125. This is greater than the equilibrium price.
   a. Estimate the quantity supplied and the quantity demanded at this price, and calculate the excess supply.
   b. Suppose the government instead chose to maintain a price of $125 by implementing a system of quotas. What quantity of quotas should the government make available?

9. Consider Figure 3.10 (page 59), which aggregated two individual demand curves to obtain a market demand curve. Instead of the assumption that each individual demand curve intersects the vertical axis at the same point, see if you can derive the market demand when D_A not only lies everywhere to the right of D_B, but where D_A intersects the vertical axis above the intercept for D_B.

10. Let us say that the two demand curves corresponding to Figure 3.10 are given by $P = 42 - (1/3)Q$ and $P = 42 - (1/2)Q$.
    a. Draw these demands to scale and carefully label the intercepts on both the price axis and quantity axis.
    b. Determine how much would be purchased at prices $10, $20, and $30.

11. Consider a market with two suppliers whose supply functions are given by $P = 12 + 0.5Q$ and $P = 12 + 1.5Q$. Draw these supplies to scale and estimate the total quantity supplied by the two suppliers at prices of $15 and $21.

12. The market demand curve in question 10 can be represented by the equation $P = 42 - Q/5$, and the market supply curve in question 11 can be represented by $P = 12 + Q/3$. Find the equilibrium price and quantity in the market.

13. *Internet* Go to Statistics Canada's CANSIM database and find the price of wheat or corn for the most recent five-year period.

14. *Internet* Go to the Web site of the Canadian Real Estate Association at www.crea.ca. Click on their statistics bar. Now compare the price of housing in each province across Canada. You will see dramatic differences. Identify these differences and, with the help of a supply and demand diagram, see if you can explain them.

15. *Internet* Go to the Web site of the Chicago Board of Trade at www.CBOT.com and see if you can find out the price of corn or wheat that will be delivered six months from now.

16. *Internet* Go to the Statistics Canada Web site: www.statcan.gc.ca/menu-en.htm. In the "Latest Indicators" box, click on "Gross Domestic Product." Describe the pattern of changes you see in the time series plot of "Final demand and GDP."

PART 2

Introduction to Macroeconomics

The two chapters in this part of the text introduce macroeconomic concepts and models. They explain the measurement of macroeconomic activity and performance, and introduce the aggregate demand and supply model used to explain national output, prices, employment, and business cycle fluctuations in economic activity.

CHAPTER 4

Measuring National Economic Activity and Performance

LEARNING OUTCOMES

By the end of this chapter you should understand:

1. Three main indicators of macroeconomic activity and performance
2. Canadian economic performance
3. National accounting measures of the economy
4. Nominal and real GDP and the GDP deflator
5. Per capita real GDP

Macroeconomic performance and policy dominated the media, political debates, and public discussion in 2008 and 2009. A financial crisis originating in the American financial and housing markets had deep and profound impacts on U.S. banks and households. Major financial institutions collapsed on an international scale. Output and employment fell sharply and continuously in the midst of the most dramatic recession since the 1980s. Recession spread quickly and widely to other countries through international capital markets and financial flows, trade flows, commodity prices, and exchange rates. The crisis triggered unprecedented government intervention in U.S and European financial markets and calls for large and innovative changes in both monetary and fiscal policy stimulus. The media reported widely and pessimistically on the prospects for a deep and prolonged slump in national economies.

Macroeconomic theory and models emerged from an earlier major financial collapse and crisis followed by the depression years of the 1930s. Macroeconomics studies the national economy as a system. It starts with carefully developed measures of the economy's total output of goods and services, and expenditures on current output by households, businesses, national governments, and residents of other countries. Expenditures generate incomes for households and businesses and, through taxation, revenues for governments. Money, banking, financial markets, and foreign exchange markets play key roles in financing these expenditure flows. Macroeconomics explains the ways in which different parts of the economy interact to determine outputs, incomes, prices, and employment in the whole economy.

The links between macroeconomic performance and policy have dominated media discussions in recent years. Newspapers, radio news reports, and the TV news have reported extensively on financial market turmoil, output growth, predictions of prolonged recession or rapid recovery, jobs lost, the unemployment rate, prices, and risks of inflation or deflation. These are all measures of economic activity at the national level. The media also report on budget surpluses or deficits; the central bank's decisions to set interest rates; and exchange rates and equity markets like the S&P/TSX, and Dow Jones Industrial Average.

To understand how these different dimensions of economic activity and economic conditions are tied together we need a framework that recognizes how they are related and how they interact. Macroeconomics provides that framework, based on a consistent and comprehensive system of definitions for the measurement of economic activity in the national economy.

4.1 Three Main Indicators of Macroeconomic Activity

Output, price, and employment are three main indicators of macroeconomic activity and performance. Output is a measure of the total quantity of goods and services produced in the economy. It is also a measure of the incomes generated by that production. Price or the price level in macroeconomics is the weighted average of the market prices of all final goods and services produced. The price level reflects the costs of production in the economy. Employment is a measure of the number of jobs involved in the production of goods and services, or, in more refined terms, the number of hours of labour input required to produce the economy's output.

Real gross domestic product (real GDP) measures output and income. Real GDP is the quantity of final goods and service produced in the economy in a specific time period, say, one year, measured in the market prices of a base year, 2002, for example. (It may also be called GDP in constant 2002 dollars.) As we will see later in this chapter, the production of goods and services generates incomes equal to the value of those goods and services. As a result, real GDP is also the real income in the economy and the quantity of goods and services the economy can afford to buy.

Real GDP measures the quantity of final goods and services produced by the economy in a specified time period and the real incomes generated by that production.

When we look at the economy over time we see that real GDP changes from year to year. Because we measure real GDP in the prices of a base year, the changes we see in real GDP are the result of changes in the quantities of goods and services produced and not the result of changes in prices. This distinction is important. Increased quantities of goods and services provide for increased standards of living in the economy. Increases in prices do not. As a result, we define **economic growth** as an increase in real GDP, and the **rate of economic growth** is the annual percentage change in real GDP. The rate of growth in real GDP is calculated as follows:

Economic growth is an increase in real GDP.

The **rate of growth** in real GDP is the annual percentage change in real GDP.

$$\text{Rate of growth of real GDP} = \frac{\text{Real GDP}_{\text{year 2}} - \text{Real GDP}_{\text{year 1}}}{\text{Real GDP}_{\text{year 1}}} \times 100 \qquad (4.1)$$

Recent measures of real GDP in Canada provide an example of economic growth and the calculation of the rate of economic growth. In the year 2006, real GDP in

Canada measured in 2002 dollars was $1,282 billion. In 2005, real GDP in 2002 dollars was $1,248 billion. Using these data:

$$\text{Rate of growth of real GDP in 2006} = \frac{\$1282 - \$1248}{\$1248} \times 100 = 2.7\%$$

Similarly, real GDP in 2007 was $1,311 billion, which means that the rate of growth in 2007 was 2.3 percent. We will examine GDP growth rates over longer time periods in the next section of this chapter.

The **price level** in the economy is a measure of the average prices of all goods and services produced.

A **price index** is a measure of the price level in one year compared with prices in a base year.

The **Consumer Price Index (CPI)** compares the cost of living in one year to the cost of living in a base year.

Inflation is a persistent rise in the general price level.

The **inflation rate** is the annual percentage change in the price level.

The **price level** in the economy is a measure of the weighted average of prices of a wide variety of goods and services. Section 2.3 in Chapter 2 explained how a **price index** is constructed and used to provide a measure of prices in one year compared with prices in a base year. The **Consumer Price Index (CPI)**, for example, compares the cost of a fixed basket of goods and services bought by the typical household at a specific time with the cost of that same basket of goods and services in the base year. It is the most widely used indicator of prices in Canada and is often referred to as the "cost of living."

Application Box 4.1 shows the recent data in the Consumer Price Index in Canada. Today, the base year for the consumer price index is 2002, and the base year value of the index is set at 100. In 2006 Statistics Canada reported a CPI of 109.1. That means the cost of the basket of goods and services in 2006 was 9.1 percent higher than it was in 2002. Prices and the cost of living increased over the four-year period. At the end of 2007 the CPI was 111.5. Prices had increased again. **Inflation** is defined as a persistent rise in the general price level as indicated by these increases in the price index over time. The **inflation rate** is the annual rate of change, as a percentage, in the price level.

The inflation rate is calculated using the same method used for calculating the growth rate in real GDP. For example:

$$\textbf{Inflation rate for 2006} = \frac{\text{CPI}_{2006} - \text{CPI}_{2005}}{\text{CPI}_{2005}} \times 100 \qquad (4.2)$$

Statistics Canada reported the 2007 CPI at 111.5 and the 2006 CPI at 109.1. The inflation rate for 2007 was:

$$\text{Inflation rate for 2007} = \frac{111.5 - 109.1}{109.1} \times 100 = 2.2\%$$

Employment is the number of adults employed full-time and part-time and self-employed.

Unemployment is the number of adults not working but actively looking for work.

The **labour force** is those adults employed plus those not employed but actively looking for work.

The **participation rate** is the percent of the population that is either working or unemployed.

Statistics Canada collects and publishes information on the Canadian labour market. It uses a monthly Labour Force Survey of approximately 50,000 Canadian individuals 15 years of age or over living in the provinces of Canada, excluding full-time members of the armed forces, those persons living on Indian reserves, and those in institutions such as penal institutions, hospitals, and nursing homes. The survey provides the data used to estimate the size of the labour force, employment, and unemployment.

Employment is defined as the number of adults (15 years of age and older) employed full-time and part-time and self-employed. **Unemployment** covers those not working but available for and seeking work. The civilian **labour force** is those adults who are employed plus those not employed but actively looking for jobs. Based on these concepts, and data on the surveyed population, Statistics Canada reports three key labour market indicators, namely: the participation rate, the unemployment rate, and the employment rate.

The **participation rate** is the proportion of the surveyed population that is either working or unemployed. It measures the size of the labour force relative to the surveyed population. The participation rate changes as people become more optimistic about

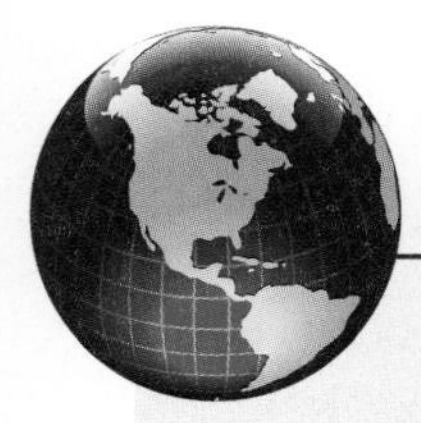

APPLICATION BOX 4.1

The Consumer Price Index

The Consumer Price Index (CPI) is an indicator of the changes in prices of consumer goods and services in Canada. It compares the cost of a *fixed basket* of goods and services in a particular year with the cost of that basket in the year chosen as the *base year*. Since the basket is fixed, the index reflects changes in prices.

Statistics Canada uses a fixed basket classified under eight consumer expenditure categories. The weight or importance of each category is based on its share of expenditure as determined by consumer expenditure surveys. By visiting the Statistics Canada Web site, www.statcan.gc.ca, and selecting Consumer Price Index in the *Latest Indicators* table on the right side of the home page, you can scroll down to a table showing the components of the CPI.

The time base or base year of the index is the year in which the index is given a value of 100. The cost of the same basket of goods and services in the prices in any other year is compared with its cost in base year prices. The ratio of the two costs multiplied by 100 gives the CPI in that year.

Recent values of the Canadian CPI on the base 2002 = 100 reported by Statistics Canada are:

Year	2003	2004	2005	2006	2007
CPI	102.8	104.7	107.0	109.1	111.5

Source: Statistics Canada, CANSIM Database, Series V41690914.

finding employment, or discouraged by periods without employment. Discouraged workers want to work but are no longer looking for work because they believe suitable work is not available. As a result they are excluded from the measurement of the labour force and reduce the participation rate. Changes in the participation rate change the size of the labour force even if the population is constant.

$$\textbf{Participation Rate} = \frac{\textbf{Labour force}}{\textbf{Population 15 + yrs}} \times 100 \qquad \textbf{(4.3)}$$

In Canada in September 2008 Statistics Canada reported the population 15 years and older was 27.013 million persons and the labour force was 18.326 million persons. These data give:

$$\text{Participation Rate in 2008} = \frac{18.326}{27.013} \times 100 = 67.8\%$$

The **unemployment rate** is the number of unemployed persons as a percentage of the labour force. However, because the size of the labour force depends on the participation rate, the choices people make about looking for work, the unemployment rate will rise if people become more optimistic about job prospects and begin to look for work, increasing the participation rate and the labour force. On the other hand, the unemployment rate will decline if some people become discouraged and give up looking for work, reducing the participation rate and the labour force.

The **unemployment rate** is the percentage of the total labour force that is not employed but is actively looking for employment.

The unemployment rate is calculated as follows:

$$\textbf{Unemployment rate} = \frac{\textbf{Labour force} - \textbf{Employed}}{\textbf{Labour force}} \times 100 \qquad \textbf{(4.4)}$$

Statistics Canada reported labour force participation rate of 67.8 percent, a labour force of 18.326 million persons in September 2008 and total employment of 17.206 million persons. In that month, 1.119 million persons were unemployed and the unemployment rate was:

$$\text{Unemployment rate September 2008} = \frac{18.326 - 17.206}{18.326} \times 100 = 6.1\%$$

Cyclical unemployment would be eliminated by higher levels of economic activity.

Structural unemployment comes from labour market structures and institutions.

The **natural unemployment rate** reflects structural unemployment.

The **employment rate** is the percent of the population 15 years of age and over that is employed.

Unemployment as measured by the broad unemployment rate has two important components. **Cyclical unemployment** is unemployment that would be eliminated by a higher level of economic activity without putting increased pressure on wage rates and inflation. **Structural unemployment** reflects institutions and conditions in the labour market. It is regarded as the "full employment" level of unemployment, and the corresponding unemployment rate is defined as the **natural unemployment rate**. In recent years in Canada, estimates of structural unemployment suggest a natural unemployment rate of about 6.0 percent. An unemployment rate persistently below 6.0 percent would create inflationary pressure in the labour market and the economy.

The **employment rate** is the percentage of the population 15 years of age and over that is employed. Employment rates provide a different perspective on labour market conditions because they are not affected by changes in the participation rate, which can change unemployment rates. If some people become discouraged and stop looking for work the labour force and the unemployment rate decline, but the employment rate is unchanged. The employment rate is calculated as:

$$\textbf{Employment Rate} = \frac{\textbf{Employment}}{\textbf{Population 15 yrs+}} \times 100 \qquad \textbf{(4.5)}$$

In September 2008 the population 15 years of age and over was 27.013 million and employment was 17.206 million and the employment rate was:

$$\text{Employment Rate in September 2008} = \frac{17.206}{27.013} \times 100 = 63.7\%$$

The employment rate was lower than the participation rate because some members of the labour force were unemployed.

Table 4.1 gives recent data on the Canadian labour force and labour market conditions using these concepts.

TABLE 4.1 The Canadian Labour Market, September 2008 (Thousands of persons)

1) Non-institutional population 15+ yrs.	27,013
2) Labour force	18,326
3) Employment	17,206
4) Unemployment [(2) − (3)]	1,120
	(Percent)
5) Participation rate [(2)/(1)] × 100	67.8
6) Employment rate [(3)/(1)] × 100	63.7
7) Unemployment rate [(4)/(2)] × 100	6.1

Source: Statistics Canada, CANSIM Series V2062809, V2062810, V2062811, V2062814, V2062815, V2062816, V2062817.

Almost every day the media discuss some aspects of economic growth, inflation, and employment. These issues often play large roles in elections and discussions of economic policy. In the chapters that follow, we will study causes of changes in output, income, prices and inflation, and employment and unemployment. As a background to that work, consider recent Canadian economic performance.

Review Questions 1 and 2

4.2 Canadian Economic Performance

Table 4.2 provides a summary of economic growth, inflation, and unemployment in Canada from 1980 to 2008, and a comparison with the United States economy. Over this period, real GDP in Canada grew at a rate of 2.5 to 3 percent per year, with higher growth in the 1980s than in more recent years. Growth in the United States economy was stronger than in Canada in the 1990s, but not as strong in the following decade. Inflation rates declined in both countries over this same time period. The fall in inflation rates in Canada from the 1980s to the 1990s was much larger than that in the United States, although both countries have experienced similar inflation rates in recent years. Unemployment rates in Canada were high in the 1980s and 1990s compared with recent years and compared with unemployment rates in the United States. In broad terms, we see growth in real GDP over the past 25 years, but not steady growth, with lower inflation rates and lower unemployment rates, particularly in recent years.

Figures 4.1 to 4.3 provide a more detailed look at real GDP growth, inflation, and unemployment in Canada from 1980 to 2008. They show the trends and annual variations in these measures of economic performance that lie behind the longer-term averages in Table 4.2. Understanding the causes of these short-term fluctuations in economic performance, and the economic policy questions they raise, are major reasons for studying macroeconomics.

TABLE 4.2 **Real GDP Growth, Inflation, and Unemployment 1980 to 2008 (Annual Average)**

	Canada %	United States %
Real GDP growth rate		
1980s	3.0	3.0
1990s	2.5	3.0
2000–2008	2.9	2.5
Inflation rate		
1980s	6.5	5.6
1990s	2.2	3.0
2000–2008	2.3	2.8
Unemployment rate		
1980s	9.4	7.3
1990s	9.5	5.8
2000–2008	7.0	5.0

Sources: Statistics Canada, CANSIM Series: V1992067,V41690914 V735319, V2062815; and U.S. Department of Commerce, Bureau of Economic Analysis Series GDPCA, and Bureau of Labor Statistics, U.S. Department of Labor, Occupational Outlook Handbook, 2008–09 Edition, Computer Software Engineers, at http://www.bls.gov/oco/ocos267.htm (visited January 21, 2009).

FIGURE 4.1 **Real GDP and Growth of Real GDP in Canada**

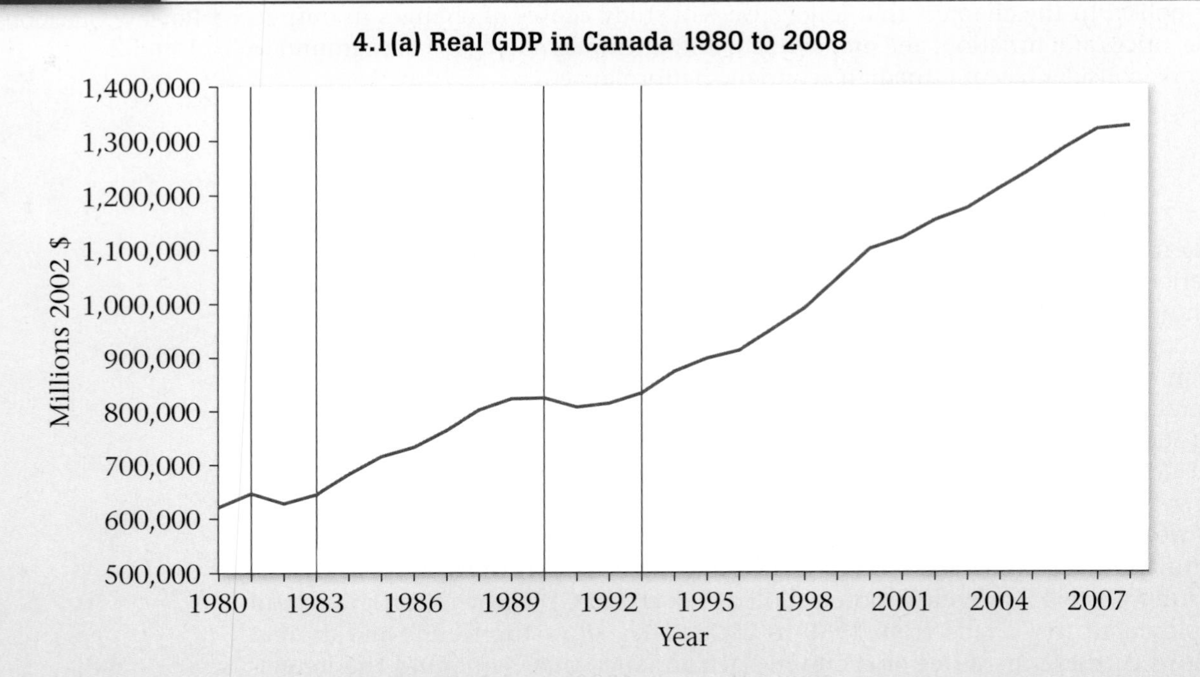

Total output produced and total real income is measured by real GDP in each year, Figure 4.1(a) shows the strong upward trend in output over the period 1980 to 2008. However, the economy did suffer recessions in the early 1980s and the early 1990s, time periods marked by the solid vertical lines. The economy has grown over time, but it has not grown smoothly.

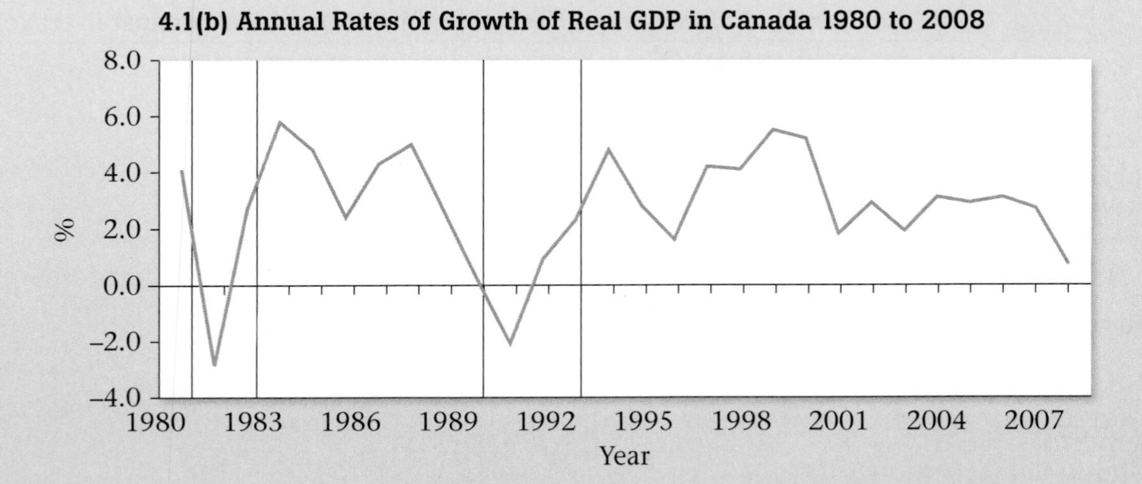

Figure 4.1(b) shows the annual growth rates in real GDP that lie behind the trend we see in Figure 4.1(a). Growth rates fluctuate from year to year. 1984 and 1999 were years of high growth, in excess of 5 percent. By contrast, 1982 and 1991 were recession years with negative growth. Real GDP became smaller in those years than in the preceding years.

Source: Statistics Canada, CANSIM Series V1992067.

Figure 4.1(a) shows the substantial growth in real GDP over the 1980–2008 period. It also shows that growth was not steady. We see two periods, the early 1980s and the early 1990s in which real GDP actually declined. These were times of **recession**. By contrast, after 1994 real GDP grew consistently year by year until 2009, the start of another recession.

A **recession** is a decline in economic activity, often defined as two consecutive quarters of negative growth in real GDP.

Figure 4.1(b) shows the considerable fluctuations in real GDP annual growth rates and the negative growth rates that mark recessions. Even the continuous growth after 1994 was not steady. Annual growth rates ranged from about 5.5 percent in 1999 to 1.8 percent in 2001. We study macroeconomics to find explanations for the causes and effects of these fluctuations in economic activity.

The decade averages of inflation rates in Table 4.2 (page 71) also hide the volatility of annual inflation rates in Canada. Figure 4.2 shows annual inflation rates in Canada since 1961. This longer time frame gives us an interesting look at the rise and fall in Canadian inflation. It also raises questions about the causes and effects of the strong rise in inflation rates in the 1960s and 1970s, and the sharp drops in inflation rates in the early 1980s and early 1990s. Our recent experience with low and stable inflation rates is quite different from past experience. We will examine the role that macroeconomic policy played in these changes in inflation rates.

Fluctuations in growth rates and inflation rates are also accompanied by fluctuations in unemployment rates. Annual unemployment rates plotted in Figure 4.3 have fluctuated between 6 percent and 12 percent. Although employment in the economy has grown over time, the annual unemployment rates show that job creation has at times fallen short of the growth in the labour force, pushing unemployment rates up. The periods of recession in the early 1980s, the early 1990s, and 2009 caused sharp

FIGURE 4.2 **Annual Inflation Rates in Canada 1961 to 2008**

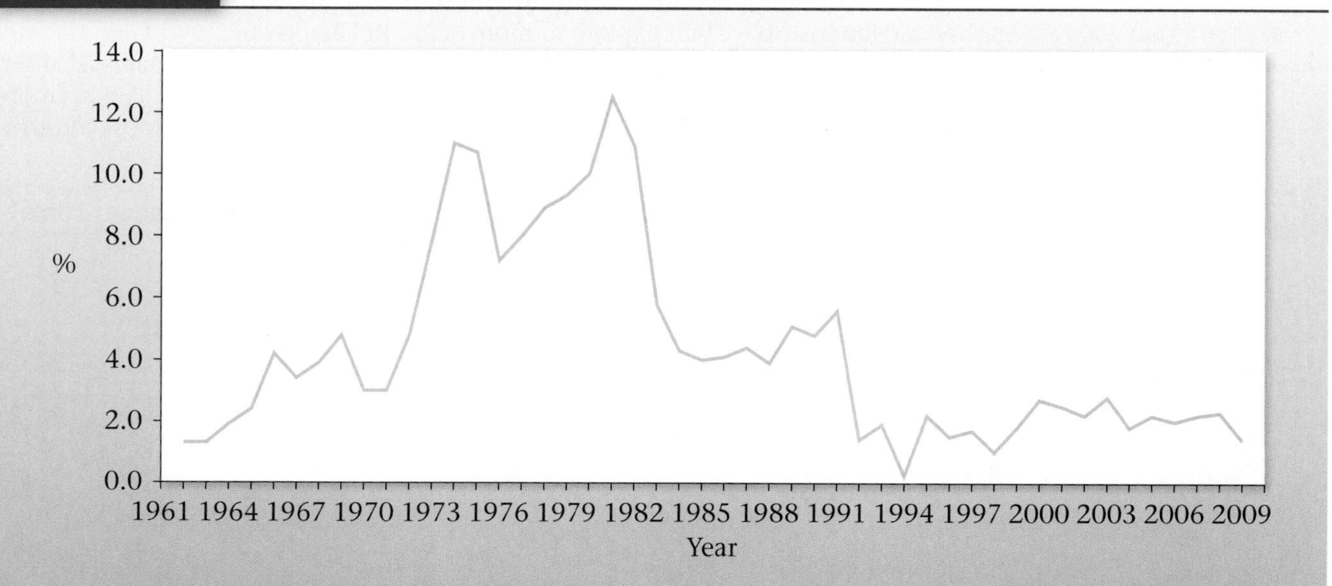

The inflation rate is the annual percent change in the Consumer Price Index. This figure shows the strong rise in inflation in Canada in the 1960s and 1970s, the sharp drop in inflation in the 1980s and again in 1990s, In later chapters we will discuss the importance of monetary policy for this experience with inflation.

Source: Statistics Canada, CANSIM Series V41690973.

FIGURE 4.3 **Annual Unemployment Rates in Canada 1980 to 2008**

The unemployment rate is the number of persons without work but actively looking for work as a percent of the total labour force. Annual unemployment rates in Canada have fluctuated over the1980–2008 period in the range of 6 percent to 12 percent. The high unemployment rates in 1983 and 1993 coincide roughly in time with the negative growth rates in real GDP and recessions we see in Figure 4.1. The subsequent decline from those highs coincides with high growth rates in real GDP.

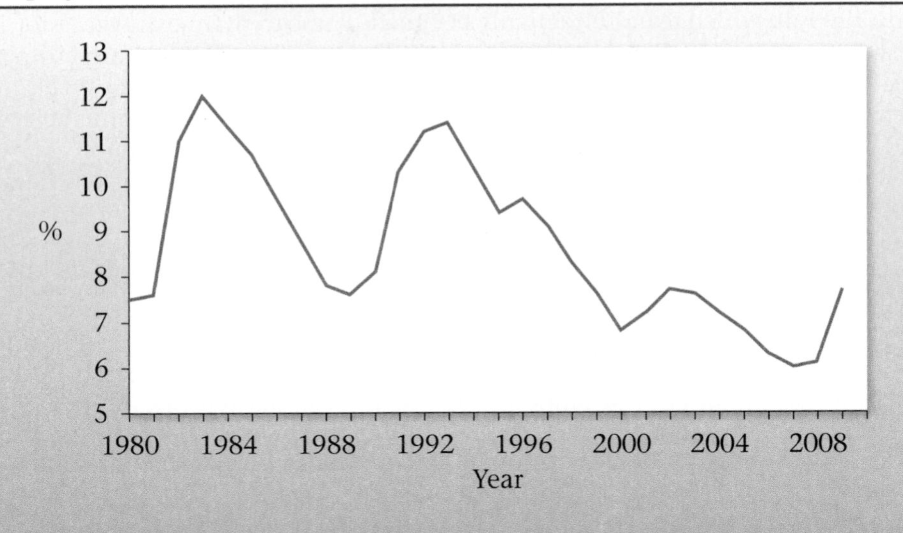

Source: Statistics Canada, CANSIM Series V2062815.

rises in unemployment rates. At other times, strong real GDP growth and job creation have lowered the unemployment rate. The falling unemployment rates from 1993 to 2000 coincided in time with the continuous growth in real GDP we saw in Figure 4.1. This gives us an example of the way growth in real GDP and employment are tied together; a relationship we will explore in more detail in Chapter 5.

Table 4.3 provides an international perspective on unemployment rates. It shows that measured unemployment rates differ quite widely among countries. Furthermore, unemployment rates change over time in different ways across countries. Most countries

TABLE 4.3 **Unemployment Rates in Selected Countries, 1990 to 2007 (Percentage of Labour Force)**

Country	1990	1995	2000	2007
Canada	8.1	9.5	6.8	6.7
United States	5.6	5.6	4.0	5.0
Japan	2.1	3.2	4.7	4.0
India	—	2.2	4.3	—
China	2.5	2.9	3.1	4.2
Belgium	7.2	9.3	7.0	7.9
France	9.0	11.6	10.0	9.1
Italy	11.0	11.3	10.5	6.4
Netherlands	7.5	7.1	3.3	3.8
Sweden	1.6	7.7	4.7	5.3

Source: International Labour Office, ILO LABORSTA, http://laborsta.ilo.org.

experienced lower unemployment over the later 1990s and the first part of the current decade. Japan was an exception. It experienced a persistent recession and rising unemployment rates until the middle of the current decade. High unemployment rates in some European countries also indicate difficult economic conditions and perhaps different economic policies.

Macroeconomics studies the causes of differences in the performance of the total economy over time and across countries. We start by looking in more detail at the way outputs and incomes in the total economy are measured and linked.

4.3 National Accounting Measures of the Economy

The economy is made up of millions of individual households, businesses, and government departments. The individual decisions made by these economic units determine the economy's total spending, output, and income. The **circular flow diagram** shows the relationship between spending, output, and income. National accounts provide a framework for the definitions and measurement of spending, output, and incomes.

The **circular flow diagram** shows how real resources and money payments flow between households and businesses.

We start with the simplest of economies. There are only households and businesses; no government and no trade with other countries. Households own the factors of production: labour, land, capital, and entrepreneurship. Businesses use these factors of production to produce outputs of goods and services. Businesses pay households for the factor services they use and recover these costs by selling their output to the households.

Figure 4.4 shows the circular flow of inputs to production, outputs of goods and services, costs of the inputs to production, and receipts from sales. The upper half of the diagram, above the horizontal dotted line, shows the outputs of goods and services supplied by business to households in return for household expenditures on those goods and services. The lower half of the diagram shows the factor services of labour, land capital, and entrepreneurship supplied by households to business in exchange for the factor incomes: wages, rent, interest, and profit.

The figure also suggests an alternative way to look at activity in the aggregate economy. The inner loop in the diagram shows the *flows of real resources* between households and businesses. Households provide factor services to business and get goods and services in return. In modern economies this exchange of factor services for goods and services is facilitated by the use of money as a means of payment. The outer loop in the diagram illustrates the *flows of money payments* made by business to buy factor services, and by households to buy goods and services produced by business. Business pays wages, rent, interest, and profits to households and finances those costs with their receipts from sales to households. To keep the example simple, we assume that households spend all the income they receive from the business sector on goods and services produced by the business sector.

Figure 4.4 suggests four ways to measure economic activity in an economy, namely:

a. the output of goods and services at market prices,
b. the total expenditure on goods and services at market prices,
c. the inputs to the production of goods and services costed at market prices,
d. the incomes received by households for providing factor inputs to production.

The four ovals in the diagram show these four alternative but equal measurements.

FIGURE 4.4 **The Circular Flow between Households and Businesses**

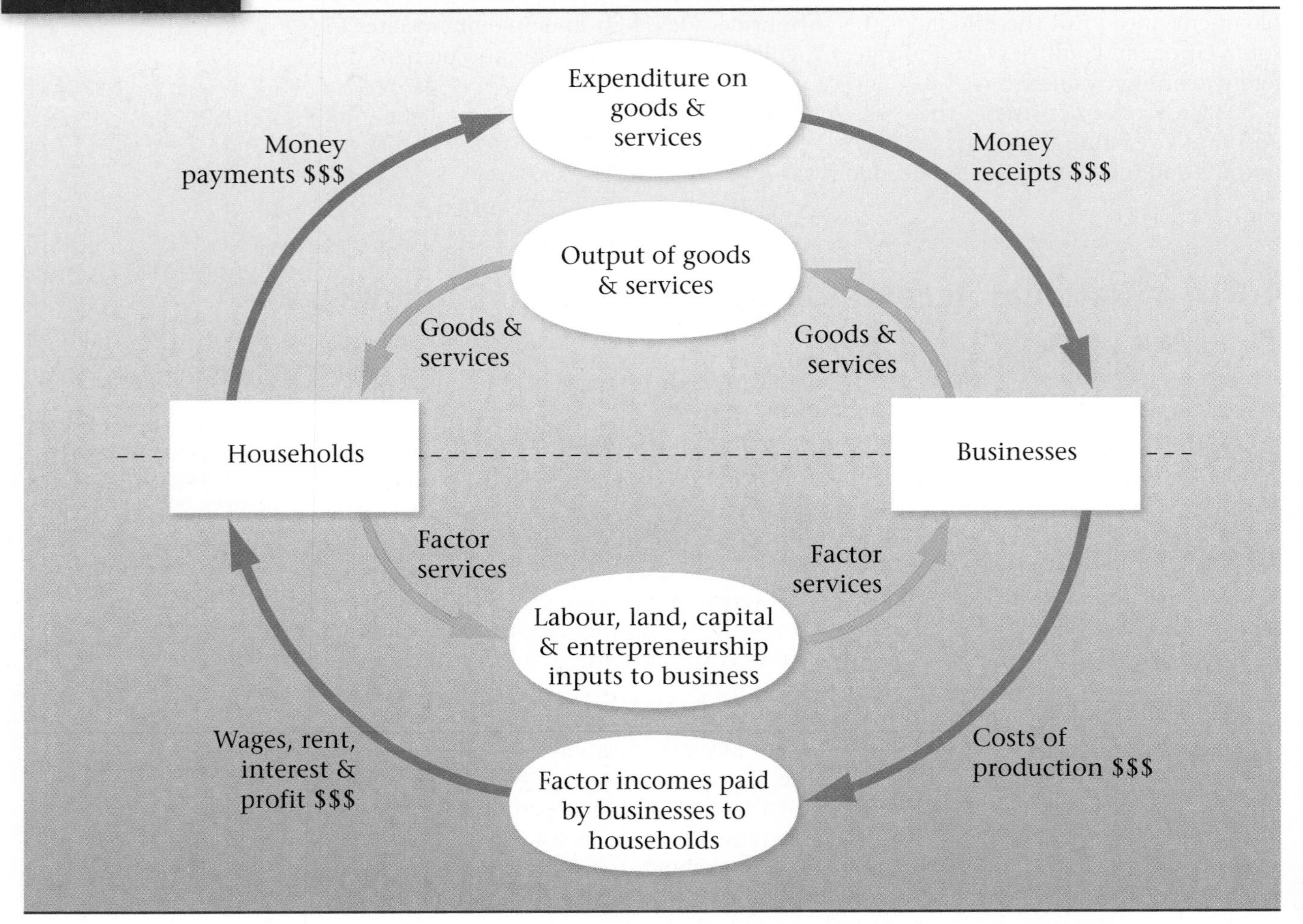

As a result, we get the same measure of total economic activity whether we use the market value of output, total spending on that output, inputs to production, or the factor incomes received by households in return for those inputs.

This circular flow model is kept very simple to illustrate the basic principle:

$$\text{Market value of output} \equiv \text{total expenditure} \equiv \text{market value of factor services} \equiv \text{Household income}$$

But what happens if households don't spend all their income, as we have assumed? What happens if businesses cannot sell all their output? What happens if businesses sell some of their output to other businesses and not to households? The next section answers these questions. When we have found the answers to our questions, our conclusion will be unchanged: The four ways to measure total activity in the economy give, by definition, the same answer.

While the principle illustrated by the circular flow is sound, the economy in Figure 4.4 is too simple. It does not allow households to save or businesses to invest. It leaves out government expenditures and taxes, and transactions between households and businesses with the rest of the world. Including those aspects of economic activity will make our model more complex, and we will need a comprehensive system of national income accounts to describe and measure it.

MEASURING GDP

Nominal GDP is measured using market prices and a specific time period. It is not possible to add up the final physical outputs of many different businesses and arrive at a meaningful result. Instead we let current market prices determine the money values of these different outputs. Then the total market value can be found by adding up the money values. Nominal GDP is the market value at current prices of all final goods and services.

Furthermore, the outputs of goods and services occur over time, not all at once. They flow over time and must be measured relative to time. GDP measured over three-month and one-year time periods is reported as quarterly GDP and annual GDP. Annual nominal GDP for any year is the value of the final goods produced in that year at the prices of that year.

In Canada, Statistics Canada uses the Canadian System of National Accounts (CSNA) to measure GDP. This framework is based on the circular flow concept we have discussed, but is applied to the complexity of the actual economy.

Although we defined and discussed *real GDP,* measured at prices of a base year, earlier in this chapter, national accounting measures **nominal GDP** at current prices. The CSNA produces three measurements of nominal GDP:

Nominal GDP measures the output of final goods and services, the money incomes generated by the production of that output, and expenditure on the sale of that output in a specific time period.

1. *Output-based GDP* is the sum of value added (output less the cost of goods and services purchased from other businesses) by all industries in Canada.
2. *Income-based GDP* records the earnings generated by the production of goods and services, and
3. *Expenditure-based GDP* is equal to expenditure on final goods and services produced.

These three alternative measures of GDP provide importantly different perspectives on the level of national economic activity. The output and income measures describe the *supply side* of the economy in terms of goods and services produced, and costs of production. The expenditure measure of GDP describes the *demand side* of the economy.

OUTPUT-BASED GDP

To measure output in the economy, and the contribution of particular businesses or industries to that output, we use the **value-added** approach to GDP. Value added measures the *net* output of each industry. To find the value added (net output) of a particular business or industry, the costs of the goods and services purchased from other businesses and industries are deducted from the value of the final product. National, or all-industry GDP, is then the sum of GDP by industry.

Value added is the difference between the market value of the output of the business and the cost of inputs purchased from other businesses.

This method recognizes that businesses buy inputs to production from other businesses as well as from households. Automakers like General Motors and Honda buy parts and components like tires and windshields from other businesses, and include the costs of those inputs in the prices of the finished cars they sell. They also buy services like accounting, advertising, and transportation from service producers. Similarly, pizza makers buy cheese and pepperoni from cheese factories and meat processors. If we were to add up the outputs of auto parts manufacturers, cheese makers, meat processors, pizza makers, General Motors, and Honda in our measurement of nominal GDP, we would overstate GDP by *double counting*. The cheese would be counted once at the cheese factory and again in the pizza. The same applies to the tires and windshields of the new cars. To avoid double counting, we could use value added, the increase in the value of goods and services as measured by the difference between market value of output and the cost of **intermediate inputs** bought from other businesses. Or we could count only the outputs sold to *final* users. Notice that total GDP by our definition measures the output of **final goods and services.**

Intermediate inputs are services, materials, and components purchased from other businesses and used in the production of final goods.

Final goods and services are purchased by the ultimate user.

Consider a simple example. A coffee shop sells 100 cups of coffee an hour at a price, before tax, of $1.50. To make 100 cups of coffee the shop uses 2 kilos of ground coffee costing $10.00 per kilo, 25 litres of pure spring water costing $0.40 a litre, and electricity and dairy products costing, in total $20. The coffee shop's sales per hour are $150 using inputs costing $50. Its value added is $150 − $50 = $100. As we will see shortly, this value added, or $100, covers the labour costs, rent, interest expenses, and management costs of the business, for producing 100 cups of coffee an hour.

Table 4.4 shows the industrial structure of output in Canada in July 2008, based on the percentage shares of selected industries in Canadian GDP. Industry outputs are measured by value added. The data illustrate the importance of service-producing industries to economic activity in Canada. This industrial structure is typical of today's high-income economies and raises many interesting questions about the relationship between economic structure, performance, and growth. However, when our main interest is in the total level of economic activity rather than its industrial structure, the expenditure-based and income-based measures of GDP are used.

Review Questions 3 and 4

TABLE 4.4 **Outputs of Selected Industries in GDP: Canada, July 2008 (Percentage shares)**

All industries	**100.0**
Goods-producing industries	29.5
Service-producing industries	70.5
Agriculture, forestry, fishing, etc.	2.1
Mining, oil, and gas extraction	4.6
Construction	6.0
Manufacturing	14.4
Wholesale and retail trade	11.8
Transportation	4.6
Finance, insurance, and real estate	19.3
Professional and educational service	9.7
Health and social assistance	6.4
Public administration	5.6
All other	15.5

Source: Statistics Canada, CANSIM Table 379-0027 and author's calculations.

THE EXPENDITURE-BASED GDP

The expenditure-based measurement of nominal GDP adds up the market value of all the final goods and services produced and bought in a given time period, say one year. The national accounts classify this *final expenditure* into five main categories: consumption, investment, government expenditure, exports, and imports. This classification system is useful for our study of macroeconomic activity for two reasons. First, the classification scheme covers final expenditure in the economy completely; nothing is omitted. Second, the categories represent expenditure decisions made for different reasons in different parts of the economy. Understanding expenditure decisions is key to the work that lies ahead. Defining the *expenditure* categories is the first step.

Consumption expenditure is expenditure by the household sector on currently produced final goods and services in one year. It includes expenditures on food, clothing, housing, home appliances, transportation, entertainment, personal services, financial services, and so forth. The total of these expenditures is aggregate consumption. We will use **C** to indicate these household expenditures.

Consumption expenditure (C) is spending by households on currently produced final goods and services.

Investment is expenditure by the business sector on currently produced final goods and services to be used in the future production of goods and services. Investment adds to the *buildings, machinery, and inventories* that business uses for the production of goods and services. This is the country's capital stock. It was included in our discussion of the factors of production and factor incomes. By national accounts conventions, investment also includes expenditure on newly constructed residential housing, another component of the nation's capital stock, one that produces housing services.

Investment (I) is expenditure by business on currently produced final goods and services.

The investment defined here is *gross investment*. It does not take account of the decline or *depreciation* of the capital stock through wear and tear and obsolescence. Net investment is gross investment minus depreciation. *Net investment* measures the change in capital stock from one year to the next. Notice that net investment will be smaller than gross investment and could even be negative if the current level of investment expenditure is not enough to cover the depreciation of the capital stock. The key concept for our work is gross investment expenditure by business on currently produced final goods and services. We will use **I** to indicate this expenditure.

Government expenditure is the purchase of currently produced final goods and services by the government sector of the economy. It includes the wages and salaries of government employees and the military, and thus the government-provided services like health care, education, the courts, foreign embassies, and national defence. Governments also spend on office equipment, buildings, roads, and military equipment. This public sector capital stock is also used to provide government services to the economy. We use **G** to indicate government expenditure on final goods and services.

Government expenditure (G) is government spending on currently produced final goods and services.

Governments also make payments to households and business that are not expenditure directly on current final output. These include payments made under government programs like Old Age Security, Employment Insurance Benefits, and Social Assistance, as well as the interest payments the government makes to holders of government bonds. These are *transfer payments* that do not require the provision of any goods or services in return. They are not included in GDP because there is no corresponding output. We will see in later chapters that government taxes and transfer payments redistribute existing income and spending power away from those taxed and towards those receiving transfer payments.

Exports and **Imports** measure the expenditures arising from international trade in goods and services. Our **exports** are the result of expenditures by residents of other countries on the final goods and services produced in this country. These expenditures provide incomes to domestic factors of production. Our **imports** are our expenditures on goods and services produced in other countries. They do not give rise to incomes for

Exports (X) are purchases of our domestic goods and services by residents of other countries.

Imports (Z) are our purchases of goods and services produced by other countries.

domestic factors of production. However, some part of household consumption expenditures, business investment expenditures, and government expenditures are for goods and services produced in other countries. Furthermore, many of our exports of goods and services have imports included in them; for example, the new cars we assemble in Ontario and sell in the United States have components made in other countries. We could subtract the import component separately from the other expenditure categories and measure only expenditure on domestically produced final goods and services, but it is easier to continue to measure that final expenditure in total and then subtract imports from that total.

Net exports (NX) is the difference between exports and imports.

The effect of international trade on domestic incomes is the result of the difference between exports and imports. **Net exports**, exports minus imports, measures this effect. We will use X to represent exports, Z to represent imports, and NX (= X − Z) to represent net exports.

Gross domestic product measured by the expenditure approach is the sum of expenditures by households, businesses, governments, and residents of other countries on domestically produced final goods and services. Using the expenditure categories and notation we have discussed gives:

$$\text{GDP} = \text{consumption} + \text{investment} + \text{government expenditure} + \text{exports} - \text{imports},$$

or

Review Questions 5 and 6

$$\text{GDP} = C + I + G + X - Z \quad (4.6)$$

This approach to the measurement of GDP corresponds to the output and expenditure in the upper part of Figure 4.4 (page 76). The left-hand columns of Table 4.5 show Canadian GDP in 2008 measured by the expenditure approach.

TABLE 4.5 **Canadian National Accounts, 2008 ($ billion at current prices)**

Expenditure Measures		Income Measures	
At market price:		Income source:	
C by households	893.0	Employment income	827.0
G by government	365.6	Profit and business income	323.1
I by industry	310.6	Investment income	79.7
X exports	559.8	Net domestic income	1229.8
Z imports	−534.1		
Statistical discrepancy	7.6	Capital consumption	206.1
		GDP at basic prices	**1435.9**
		Net indirect taxes	166.6
GDP at Market Prices	**1602.5**	**GDP at Market Prices**	**1602.5**
Net foreign property income	−14.7	Net foreign property income	−14.7
GNP	1587.8	GNI	1587.8

Source: Based on Statistics Canada, CANSIM Tables 380-0001 and 380-0002, and author's calculations.

THE INCOME-BASED GDP

The income-based measurement of nominal GDP follows from the lower part of the circular flow diagram in Figure 4.4. By the national accounts definition, expenditures are equal to incomes. National accounts classify incomes roughly in terms of the factors of production used to produce the goods and services in the economy in a year or a quarter of a year. Other costs and taxes are then added to include all the things that enter into the final market prices of goods and services. We begin our measurement of the income-based GDP by defining each of these income sources and components of price.

Employment income is the income earned by labour from its contribution to the production of goods and services. It includes the wages and salaries paid by businesses to employees. It also includes supplementary income, the costs of benefits like pensions, employment insurance premiums, supplemental health care, and dental insurance plans. This is the total cost of the labour services supplied by households to businesses. It reflects the money wage rates and salaries multiplied by total employment. We will use the **W** to represent total employment income.

Employment income (W) is the sum of all wages, salaries, and benefits paid to labour.

Profit and business income is the sum of the profits of corporations before tax, and the incomes and rents earned by unincorporated business, which include many small owner-operated businesses, professional practices, and farm operations. It measures the costs of management and entrepreneurship, and the cost of owners' labour and capital used in the production of goods and services. **Interest and investment income** includes interest income earned on bank deposits, holdings of corporate bonds, and other incomes from financial assets, excluding government bonds. We can think of it as income coming from the use of capital in the production process. We will sum up profit, business income, and investment income and use **BI**, for **business and investment income**, to represent this type of income.

Profit and business income is the sum of corporate profit and small business income.

Interest and investment income is income earned from financial assets.

Business and investment income (BI) is the sum of profit, interest, investment, and business income.

Adding together the incomes earned by labour, by businesses, and by holders of investment assets gives the total of incomes earned by the factor inputs to the production of goods and services in the domestic economy. This total is called **Net Domestic Income (NDI)** at factor cost.

Net Domestic Income (NDI) is the total income earned by factors of production.

$$\text{Net Domestic Income} = \text{employment income} + \text{profit and business income} + \text{interest and investment income}$$

$$\text{NDI} = \text{W} + \text{BI} \quad (4.7)$$

Canadian Net Domestic Income for the year 2008 is reported in the right-hand side of Table 4.5. It is the sum of the three factor incomes reported in the lines above Net Domestic Income.

Factor incomes are the largest part of the income flow resulting from the production of goods and services, but they do not cover all the components of the market prices by which expenditures are measured. Two things are missing. The first is an allowance for the depreciation of the capital stock used for production. The second is the effect of taxes and government subsidies. We include both of these to measure GDP by the income approach.

We can think of depreciation as using up the capital stock. Even with expenditures on repair and maintenance, the reliability and productive capacity of the capital stock declines over time. The ability of business to produce goods and services declines with it. A car or a bicycle depreciates and loses its reliability in the same way. Business recognizes "consumption" of the capital stock as a cost of production over and above the factor cost. As with factor costs, businesses cover depreciation and the replacement costs of capital with part of the revenue received from sales of goods and services.

Capital Consumption Allowance (CCA) measures depreciation of the capital stock.

GDP at basic price = Net Domestic Income + Capital Consumption Allowance.

Net indirect taxes (T_{IN}) are sales and excise taxes minus subsidies.

GDP at market price = Net Domestic Income + Capital Consumption Allowance + Net Indirect Tax.

Review Question 7

National accounts take depreciation into account by including a **Capital Consumption Allowance** (CCA) in the measurement of the income.

Adding the Capital Consumption Allowance to Net Domestic Income gives **GDP at basic price**. That is the price before indirect tax or subsidy.

$$\text{GDP at basic price} = \text{NDI} + \text{CCA} \tag{4.8}$$

Net indirect taxes (T_{IN}) are the sales and excise taxes imposed by government on products and services, or on expenditure more generally, minus the subsidies governments give to some production. The GST, provincial retail sales taxes, taxes on liquor and tobacco products, and gasoline taxes are all indirect taxes. You pay if you buy. Sellers of these products collect the tax revenue for the government and remit it to the government. As a result, the expenditures on goods and services at market price exceed production cost and generate a flow of income to the government in addition to the flow of income going to business and households.

Subsidies are payments made by governments to producers to cover some of the costs of production. A producer who receives such a payment does not have to recover all factor and depreciation costs from the market price of the product. As a result, the market price is less than the full cost. Subsidies are subtracted from indirect taxes to give the net effect. GDP at basic price plus net indirect tax equals **GDP at market price**, measured by the income approach.

$$\text{GDP at market price} = \text{NDI} + \text{CCA} + T_{IN} \tag{4.9}$$

The right-hand side of Table 4.5 (page 80) shows GDP at market prices measured by this income approach, which is illustrated by the lower loops in Figure 4.4 (page 76).

Although the economy we have discussed in terms of national accounts is more complex than the simple economy of the circular flow, the basic principle remains. The final output of the economy is, by definition, equal to the sum of expenditures on final goods and services at market price and the flows of income to households, business, and government. GDP is the same by either approach if we measure correctly.

Figure 4.5 shows a more extensive circular flow diagram for the economy. It includes the basic national accounting measures we have discussed, including the government sector and international trade, exports and imports, and uses the notation of the national accounts variables. We will model this economy in Chapters 6 and 7.

As you examine Figure 4.5, you will see that it includes three concepts we have not yet discussed. In the upper half of the diagram, which shows expenditure flows, the household sector may *save* some of its income, as indicated by S in the circle to the left. The government sector may also *save* or *borrow*. This depends on whether the difference between tax revenues T and expenditures G, as indicated by the circle (T − G), is in a surplus, $(T - G) > 0$, or in a deficit, $(T - G) < 0$. Adding these concepts does not change the basic principle that GDP as measured by the expenditure approach is equal to $C + I + G + X - Z$. We will examine them carefully as we study expenditure decisions in Chapter 6 and government budgets in Chapter 7.

The third new concept included in Figure 4.5 is the *net direct tax* that governments impose on incomes, T_{DN}. You will see this in the lower part of the diagram, which illustrates the income approach to measuring GDP. Direct taxes based on household and business incomes are sources of revenue to the government, in addition to the *net indirect taxes* on expenditures on goods and services we discussed earlier. Net direct taxes do not interfere with our measurement of GDP by the income approach, but we will see that they are important to expenditure decisions by households. In the lower part of

FIGURE 4.5 **The Circular Flow with Government and International Trade**

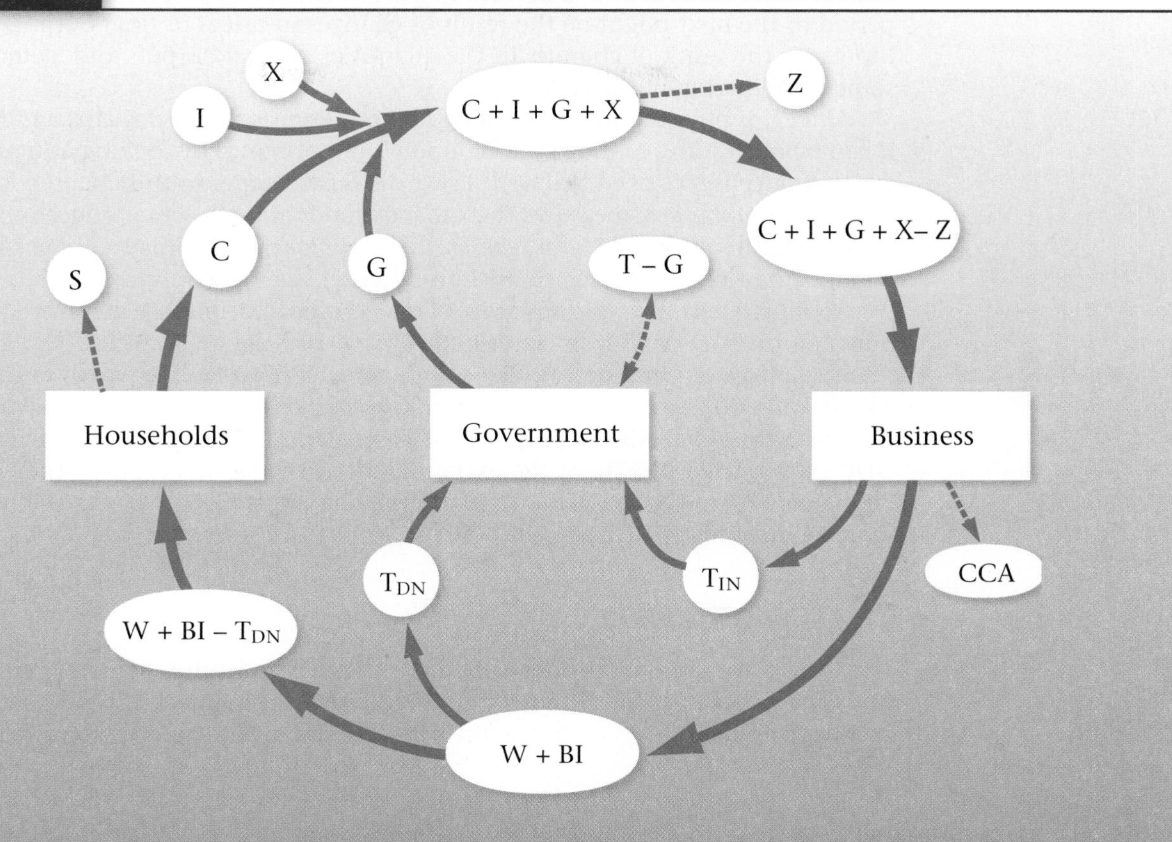

This figure extends the circular flow diagram by including the government and international sectors. Expenditures include government expenditure (G) and net exports (X − Z). Businesses make factor payments to households. Government imposes direct tax (T_{DN}) on those incomes and collects net indirect tax on expenditures. GDP at market price, PY, is equal to P × (C + I + G + NX) and W + BI + CCA + T_{IN}.

the diagram, Net Domestic Income (W + BI) plus capital consumption (CCA) and net indirect tax (T_{IN}) gives GDP = W + BI + CCA + T_{IN}.

The economy in Figure 4.5 is clearly more complex and realistic than the simple two-sector model we started with. Macroeconomic theory and models capture the linkages among the elements in the diagram. They explain how this economic system works to determine GDP, business cycle fluctuations in GDP, inflation, and employment.

4.4 Nominal and Real GDP and the GDP Deflator

We have discussed *real GDP* briefly in the beginning of this chapter, and then nominal GDP in some detail. Now we need to look carefully at both concepts and the relationship between them, which is the GDP deflator.

Nominal GDP measures output and incomes based on *current market prices* for goods and services and factors of production. As a result, changes in nominal GDP from one period to the next might be the result of changes in prices of final outputs and factor inputs, or the result of changes in the quantities of final outputs and factor inputs, or some combination of the two.

Since it is physical quantities of goods and services that yield satisfaction or utility, it can be misleading to judge the economy's performance by looking at nominal GDP. For that purpose we need real GDP, as we discussed earlier in this chapter. *Real GDP, or GDP in constant prices*, measures the value of goods and services produced in any given year using the *prices of a base year*. In this way, real GDP adjusts changes in GDP for changes in prices by measuring GDP in different years in constant prices.

To illustrate this important point, Table 4.6 shows a simple economy. In this economy nominal GDP rises from $29,000 to $87,000 between 1990 and 2008, a 200 percent increase measured in current prices. If we take 1990 as the base year, we can measure *real GDP* in 2008 by valuing output quantities in 2008 using 1990 prices. This gives real GDP in 2008 of $45,500 in prices of the base year. The rise of about 57 percent in real GDP gives a truer picture of the extra quantity of goods available in the economy in 2008 compared with 1980. It eliminates the change in GDP that was the result of the increase in prices by 91.2 percent between 1990 and 2008.

THE GDP DEFLATOR

The Canadian economy is obviously more complex than this economy. We have seen that GDP includes expenditures by households, governments, businesses, and residents of other countries who supply us with imports and buy our exports. To convert nominal

TABLE 4.6 **Nominal and Real GDP**

		1990	2008	Change (%)
Quantity	blue jeans (pairs)	1000	1500	
	hamburgers	2000	4000	
Price in $	blue jeans	25	50	
	hamburgers	2	3	
Value in current $	blue jeans	25,000	75,000	
	hamburgers	4,000	12,000	
Nominal GDP		**29,000**	**87,000**	**200**
Value in 1990 $	blue jeans	25,000	37,500	
	hamburgers	4,000	8,000	
Real GDP		**29,000**	**45,500**	**56.9**
GDP deflator		**100.0**	**191.2**	**91.2**

GDP to real GDP we need to use an index that includes what is happening to the prices of all these different goods and services. This index is called the **GDP deflator**.

The **GDP deflator** is an index of current prices relative to base year prices.

If we have data for both nominal and real GDP, we can calculate the GDP deflator as the ratio of nominal GDP to real GDP expressed as an index with a value of 100 in the base year.

$$\textbf{GDP deflator} = \frac{\textbf{Nominal GDP}}{\textbf{Real GDP}} \times 100 \qquad (4.10)$$

The GDP deflator differs from the consumer price index (CPI) used earlier to measure inflation. First, the CPI is based on a "representative basket" of goods and services that consumers buy, while the GDP deflator covers all the goods and services included in national accounts. Second, the CPI is constructed on the base of a fixed quantity that changes in market value as prices change. The GDP deflator, by contrast, is built on the base year prices, and measures the value of a changing flow of goods and services in those base year prices. In other words the current GDP deflator "deflates" the dollar value of current 2008 output to what it would be in 2002 prices, while the CPI measures the increase in the cost of the "basket" of consumer goods and services.

But why does the GDP deflator change over time? The data on nominal and real GDP do not provide an explanation. From our earlier discussion of the national income accounting framework, we can see that *costs of production* and *net indirect taxes* determine the general level of market prices measured by the GDP deflator. Nominal GDP measured by the income approach is reported in Table 4.5 (page 80). It is the sum of incomes paid to factor inputs to production, plus depreciation allowances and net indirect taxes. These components of nominal GDP are the costs of production, gross profits, and taxes that are built into the market prices of the goods and services. We can write:

$$\begin{aligned}\text{Nominal GDP} \equiv\ & \text{employment income} + \text{profit, business, and investment income} \\ & + \text{capital consumption allowance} + \text{net indirect taxes}\end{aligned}$$

or

$$\textbf{Nominal GDP} \equiv \mathbf{W + BI + CCA + T_{IN}} \qquad (4.11)$$

Alternatively, using the expenditure approach as illustrated in Table 4.5, using Y to denote *real* GDP and P for the weight average price level we have:

$$\textbf{Nominal GDP} \equiv \mathbf{P \times Y \equiv P \times (C + I + G + X - Z)} \qquad (4.12)$$

Our national accounting framework and procedures tell us that nominal GDP will be the same whether measured by the income approach or the expenditure approach. This means we can define the general price level as:

$$\mathbf{P = \frac{W}{Y} + \frac{BI + CCA}{Y} + \frac{T_{IN}}{Y}} \qquad (4.13)$$

This shows us that the general price level in the economy is equal to the sum of:

i) labour cost per unit of output, W/Y,

ii) gross business income per unit of output, (BI + CCA)/Y, and

iii) net indirect tax per unit of output T_{IN}/Y.

Changes in any one of these three components of the price level must change *both* price and nominal GDP, whether we measure nominal GDP by the income or the expenditure approach. The GDP deflator is an index of this price level in any particular year relative to a chosen base year.

This same framework gives *real income*, the purchasing power of money income in terms of final goods and services.

$$\textbf{Real income} = Y = \frac{W + BI + CCA + T_{IN}}{P} \qquad (4.14)$$

We know that $Y = (C + I + G + X - Z)$ is the real output of goods and services in the economy. Now we can see as well that *real output* measured by the expenditure approach is equal to *real income* as measured by the income approach. These relationships provide the basis for a simple economic model of the economy in the next section. But first, look at the importance of the distinction between real and nominal GDP.

Table 4.7 gives Canadian data over the period 1987 to 2008. Nominal GDP rose from $513 billion in 1987 to $1602.5 billion in 2008. Without knowing what happened to prices of goods and services in general, we cannot judge what happened to the quantity of output over that period. To answer this question we use the GDP deflator to convert nominal GDP to real GDP in the prices of the base year 2002 as follows:

Review Questions 8 and 9

$$\textbf{Real GDP} = \frac{\textbf{Nominal GDP}}{\textbf{GDP deflator}} \times 100 \qquad (4.15)$$

For example, in 2008, nominal GDP was $1602.5 billion and the GDP deflator (2002 = 100) was 120.9. Real GDP measured in constant 2002 dollars was then:

$$\text{Real GDP}_{2008} = \frac{\$1{,}602.5}{120.9} \times 100 = 1325.5 \text{ in 2002 dollars}$$

When converted to constant dollars, the change in real GDP is much smaller than the change in nominal GDP. Over the 1987–2008 period, real GDP increased by 88.8 percent compared to a 212 percent increase in nominal GDP. On average, prices in 2008 were 65 percent higher than in 1987. Clearly, it is important to distinguish between nominal and real GDP.

TABLE 4.7 **Canadian Nominal and Real GDP, 1987 to 2008**

	1987	1994	2001	2008
Nominal GDP (billion current $)	513	771	1,108	1,602.5
GDP deflator (2002 = 100)	73.1	88.2	98.9	120.9
Real GDP (billion 2002 $)	702	944	1120	1325.5

Source: Statistics Canada, CANSIM Series V1 and V1992067.

4.5 Per Capita Real GDP

Real GDP is a simple measure of the total real income and output of an economy. The percentage change in real GDP we saw in Figure 4.1 (page 72) shows how fast the economy is growing. But we are also interested in what is happening to the *standard of living* in the economy and how it changes over time. For a given real GDP, the larger the population, the smaller is the quantity of goods and services per person. To get a simple measure of the standard of living enjoyed by a person in the economy it is better to look at **per capita real GDP**, which adjusts for population. Whether or not growth in total GDP improves standards of living depends also on what is happening to the size of the population. To find per capita real GDP for a country, which is real GDP per person, we simply divide real GDP by population.

Per capita real GDP is real GDP per person.

$$\textbf{Per capita real GDP} = \frac{\textbf{Real GDP}}{\textbf{Population}} \tag{4.16}$$

Figure 4.6 shows the growth in per capita real GDP in Canada over the 1980–2008 period. Two important aspects of the economy's behaviour are clear in the graph. First, the standard of living as measured by per capita real GDP has increased from 1980 to 2008 by about 50 percent. Second, this increase has not been smooth and steady. In the early 1980s and early 1990s—periods of recession and slow growth in real GDP—per capita real GDP declined. These recessions reduced the standard of living of the average Canadian. In more recent times, since about 1995, the growth in per capita real GDP has been more stable if not always positive and consistent, until the onset of recession in 2008.

Review Question 10

We saw earlier in the chapter that growth in total GDP, unemployment rates, and inflation rates have also been more stable recently than in earlier years. Recessions and fluctuations in economic growth cause changes in standards of living. It is the work of macroeconomics to discover the causes of fluctuations in economic performance and to ask how government policy might reduce those fluctuations to protect standards of living.

LIMITATIONS OF GDP

Because we use GDP to measure the output and income of an economy, the coverage should be as comprehensive as possible. We should also recognize that the composition of GDP and the distribution of income are important to a country's standard of living.

In practice, we encounter several problems when including all production in GDP. First, some output production causes noise, pollution, and congestion, which do not contribute to economic welfare. Current national and international concern about greenhouse gases and global warming is a clear and obvious example of the issues involved. We should adjust GDP for these costs to evaluate standards of living more accurately. This is sensible but difficult to do. Recent policy changes by governments to impose carbon taxes on fuels and fuel efficiency targets for automobiles aim to reduce some greenhouse gases. But most such nuisance goods are not traded through markets, so it is hard to quantify their output or decide how to value their costs to society.

Similarly, many valuable goods and services are excluded from GDP because they are not marketed and therefore are hard to measure. These include the home cleaning, maintenance, and improvements households carry out for themselves, and any unreported jobs and incomes in the economy. Deducting nuisance outputs and adding the

FIGURE 4.6 **Per Capita Real GDP in Canada 1980 to 2008**

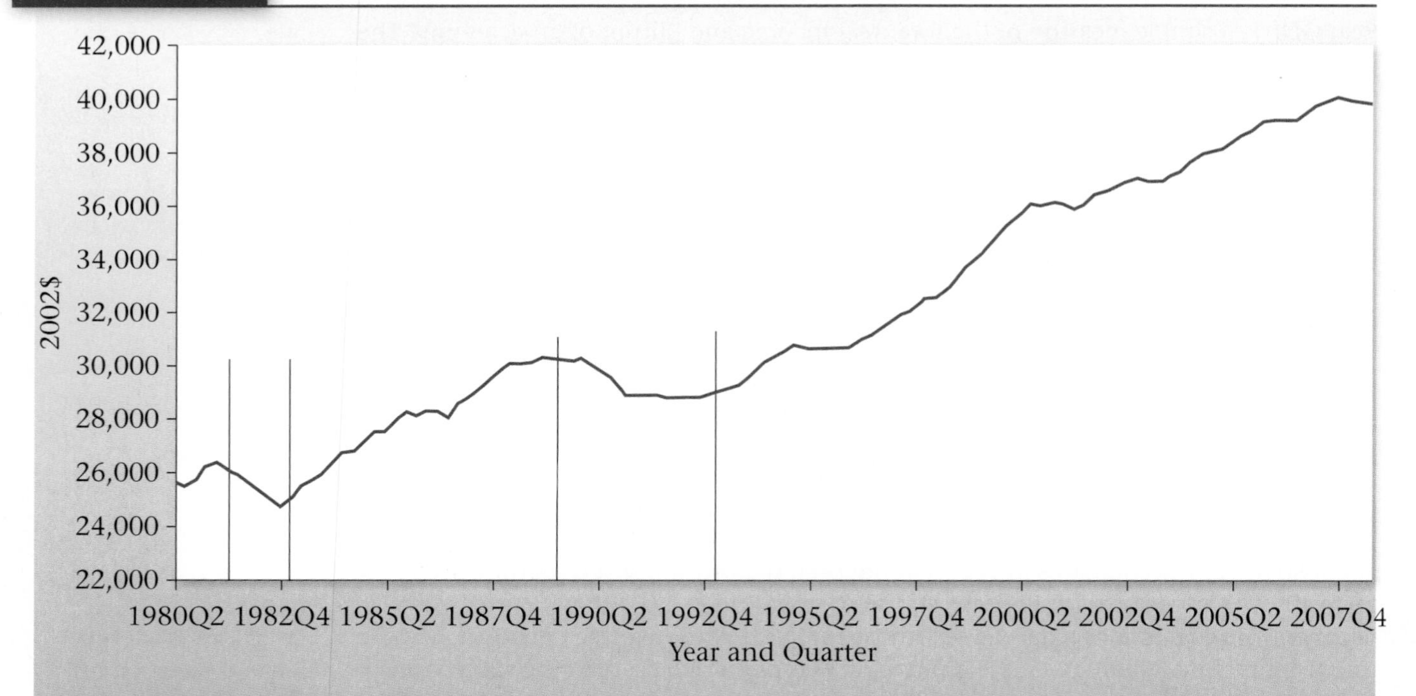

Over the 1980–2007 period per capita real GDP has grown strongly, raising the standard of living of the average Canadian. This growth has not been steady or consistent. In some years, particularly in the early 1980s and 1990s, per capita real GDP declined, and standards of living were reduced by recessions and high unemployment. After a brief pause at the start of the current decade, growth in per captia real GDP continued until 2008 when the slow down resulted in a drop in per capita real GDP.

Source: Statistics Canada, CANSIM Series V1 and V1992067.

value of unreported and non-marketed incomes would make GDP a more accurate measure of the economy's production of goods and services.

Furthermore, high GDP and even high per capita GDP are not necessarily good measures of economic well-being. The composition of that output also affects standards of living. Health care services are likely to have different effects than military expenditures. The United Nations prepares an annual Human Development Index (HDI) to provide a more comprehensive measure of a country's achievements. The HDI provides a summary measure based on life expectancy, adult literacy, and real GDP per capita.

Table 4.8 shows HDIs for the top twelve countries in 2005, according to the *Human Development Report, 2007/2008*. The last column in the table is of particular interest. It shows that some countries enjoy a higher standard of living relative to others even though their per capita GDP is lower. The inclusion of life expectancy and literacy as indicators of development moves Iceland, the Scandinavian countries, Australia, and Canada up in the development rankings. By contrast, the United States, despite having the highest per capita GDP, ranks twelfth as a result of lower life expectancy and education indexes. Per capita real GDP is not the only indicator of standard of living.

Do these limitations of GDP matter for our study of macroeconomics? Probably not. We will be examining changes in real GDP from year to year, for the most part. As

TABLE 4.8 **Top Twelve Countries Based on the 2005 Human Development Index**

Country	Life Expectancy Index	Education Index	GDP Index	HDI Index	HDI Rank Minus GDP[1]
1. Iceland	0.94	0.98	0.99	0.968	4
2. Norway	0.91	0.99	1.00	0.968	1
3. Australia	0.93	0.99	0.96	0.962	13
4. Canada	0.92	0.99	0.97	0.961	6
5. Ireland	0.89	0.99	0.99	0.959	−1
6. Sweden	0.93	0.98	0.97	0.956	7
7. Switzerland	0.94	0.95	0.98	0.955	−1
8. Japan	0.95	0.95	0.96	0.953	9
9. Netherlands	0.90	0.99	0.97	0.953	3
10. France	0.92	0.98	0.95	0.952	8
11. Finland	0.90	0.99	0.96	0.952	3
12. United States	0.88	0.97	1.00	0.951	−10

[1] A positive value indicates a country HDI rank higher than its per capita GDP rank.

Source: Human Development Report 2007–2008, Table 1, p. 229. New York: United Nations Development Programme, /hdr.undp.org/en/reports/global/hdr2007-2008/.

long as the importance of nuisance and non-marketed outputs, life expectancy, and literacy do not change dramatically in that time frame, changes in measured real GDP will provide good measures of changes in economic activity and performance. Changes in per capita real GDP will also provide measures of changes in standards of living.

Review Question 11

Next

In this chapter we have looked at indicators of macroeconomic activity and performance, and the measurement of macroeconomic activity using the national accounts. We have not examined the conditions that determine the level of economic activity and fluctuations in that level. An economic model is required for that work. In the next chapter we start to build a simple macroeconomic model.

SUMMARY

- **Macroeconomics** studies the whole national economy as a system. It examines expenditure decisions by households, businesses, and governments, and the total flows of goods and services produced and incomes earned.
- **Real Gross Domestic Product** (GDP), prices and **inflation rates**, and employment and **unemployment rates** are indicators of macroeconomic activity and performance.
- **Fluctuations** in the growth rate of real GDP, in inflation rates, and in unemployment rates are important aspects of recent economic performance in Canada.

- The expenditures by households, production of goods and services by businesses, and the incomes that result are illustrated by the **circular flow** of real resources and money payments.
- The **national accounts** provide a framework for the measurement of the output of the economy and the incomes earned in the economy.
- **Nominal GDP** measures the output of final goods and services at market prices in the economy, and the money incomes earned by the factors of production.
- **Real GDP** measures the output of final goods and services produced, and incomes earned at constant prices.
- The **GDP deflator** is a measure of the price level for all final goods and services in the economy.
- **Real GDP** and **per capita real GDP** are crude measures of national and individual welfare. They ignore non-market activities, the composition of output, and the distribution of income among industries and households.

KEY TERMS

Real GDP *67*
Economic growth *67*
Rate of growth *67*
Price level *68*
Price index *68*
Consumer Price Index (CPI) *68*
Inflation *68*
Inflation rate *68*
Employment *68*
Unemployment *68*
Labour force *68*
Participation rate *68*
Unemployment rate *69*
Cyclical unemployment *70*
Structural unemployment *70*
Natural unemployment *70*
Employment rate *70*
Recession *73*
Circular flow diagram *75*
Nominal GDP *77*
Value added *77*
Intermediate inputs *78*
Final goods and services *78*
Consumption expenditure (C) *79*
Investment (I) *79*
Government expenditure (G) *79*
Exports (X) *79*
Imports (Z) *79*
Net exports (NX) *80*
Employment income (W) *81*
Profit and business income *81*
Interest and investment income *81*
Business and investment income (BI) *81*
Net Domestic Income *81*
Capital consumption allowance (CCA) *82*
GDP at basic price *82*
Net indirect taxes (T_{IN}) *82*
GDP at market price *82*
GDP deflator *85*
Per capita real GDP *87*

KEY EQUATIONS AND RELATIONS

Equations

$$\text{Rate of growth of real GDP} = \frac{\text{Real GDP}_{\text{year 2}} - \text{Real GDP}_{\text{year 1}}}{\text{Real GDP}_{\text{year 1}}} \times 100$$ **(4.1)** p. 67

$$\text{Inflation rate for 2008} = \frac{\text{CPI}_{2008} - \text{CPI}_{2007}}{\text{CPI}_{2007}} \times 100$$ **(4.2)** p. 68

$\text{Participation Rate} = \frac{\text{Labour force}}{\text{Population 15+ yrs}} \times 100$	**(4.3)**	p. 69
$\text{Unemployment rate} = \frac{\text{Labour force} - \text{Employed}}{\text{Labour force}} \times 100$	**(4.4)**	p. 69
$\text{Employment Rate} = \frac{\text{Employment}}{\text{Population 15 yrs+}} \times 100$	**(4.5)**	p. 70
Gross Domestic Product: $GDP = C + I + G + NX$	**(4.6)**	p. 80
Net Domestic Income: $NDI = W + BI$	**(4.7)**	p. 81
GDP at basic price $= NDI + CCA$	**(4.8)**	p. 82
GDP at market price $= NDI + CCA + T_{IN}$	**(4.9)**	p. 82
$\text{GDP deflator} = \frac{\text{Nominal GDP}}{\text{Real GDP}} \times 100$	**(4.10)**	p. 85
$\text{Nominal GDP} = W + BI + CCA + T_{IN}$	**(4.11)**	p. 85
$\text{Nominal GDP} \equiv P \times Y \equiv P(C + I + G + NX)$	**(4.12)**	p. 85
Price level: $P = \frac{W}{Y} + \frac{BI + CCA}{Y} + \frac{T_{IN}}{Y}$	**(4.13)**	p. 85
Real income: $Y = \frac{W + BI + CCA + T_{IN}}{P}$	**(4.14)**	p. 86
$\text{Real GDP} = \frac{\text{Nominal GDP}}{\text{GDP deflator}} \times 100$	**(4.15)**	p. 86
$\text{Per capital real GDP} = \frac{\text{Real GDP}}{\text{Population}}$	**(4.16)**	p. 87

Relations

National accounts: Measures of current national output and income

National accounts: Total expenditure ≡ market value of output ≡ total income

National accounts: Current income not spent → current output not sold

Change in nominal GDP: Δ nominal GDP ≈ Δ real GDP + ΔP

Change in real GDP: Δ real GDP = Δ quantity of final goods and services produced

Change in P: $\Delta P = \Delta$ general price level (weighted average for all final goods and services)

Change in standard of living: Δ real GDP per capita → Δ standard of living

REVIEW QUESTIONS

Review Questions and answers are included in Connect at www.mcgrawhillconnect.ca.

1. You have the following annual data for an economy:

Year	Real GDP (2002 $)	Consumer Price Index (2002 = 100)	Labour Force (000)	Employment (000)
2006	1282	109.1	17,593	16,537
2007	1307	111.9	17,857	16,696
2008	1288	138.9	18,125	16,856

   a. What was the rate of growth of real GDP from 2006 to 2007, and 2007 to 2008?
   b. What was the rate of inflation in 2007 and in 2008?
   c. What were the rates of growth of the labour force and employment from 2006 to 2007, and 2007 to 2008?
   d. What happened to the unemployment rate between 2006 and 2007, and between 2007 and 2008?

2. Suppose the economy represented by the table in question 1 above had a population of 27.885 thousand in 2008.
   a. What were the participation and employment rates in the economy in those years?
   b. Suppose a mild recession in that year discouraged some *unemployed* workers and they stop looking for work. As a result the participation rate fell to 64.5 per cent. How would the unemployment rate and the employment rate be affected? Why?

3. If brewers buy barley and hops from agricultural producers, natural gas to fire their brew kettles from gas companies, and bottles from glass manufacturers, as in the following table, what is the value added of the brewing industry?

   If brewers also wholesale some of their output to pubs, is that output counted in GDP? Explain your answer.

Costs (Millions of Current $) of:			
Brewery Retail Sales	Barley and Hops	Natural Gas	Bottles
1000	350	125	150

4. The economy has two main types of industry. One produces services and the other produces goods. The services industries produce services for households and businesses with a total market value of $10,000. The goods industries produce goods for the use of both households and businesses with a total market value of $5000. The service industries spend $1000 on computers and paper and envelopes supplied by the goods industries. The goods industries spend $1000 to buy financial, insurance, advertising, and custodial supplies from the service industries. Explain how you measure nominal GDP in this economy and the value of output you find.

5. Suppose you are given the following data on incomes and expenditures for the economy of Westland, in current prices for factors of production and outputs.

Consumption expenditures	2500
Employment income	2800
Government expenditure	800
Net indirect taxes	150
Exports	1200
Business income	700
Capital consumption allowance	200
Investment expenditure	600
Imports	1100
Investment income	150

   a. What is the value of nominal GDP measured by expenditures?
   b. What is net domestic income?
   c. What is the value of nominal GDP measured by the income approach?

6. Suppose GDP is $2000, consumption expenditure is $1700, government expenditure is $50, and net exports are $40.
   a. What is business investment expenditure?
   b. If exports are $350, what are imports?
   c. If the capital consumption allowance for depreciation is $130 and net indirect taxes are $100, what is net domestic income?
   d. In this example, net exports are positive. Could they be negative?

7. a. Using the data in Table 4.5 (page 80), calculate the percentage share of each of the major expenditure components in GDP. What is the largest component?
   b. Similarly, calculate the shares of the different factor incomes in net domestic income and in GDP. What is the largest income share in each case?

8. Suppose you have the following measure of income-based nominal GDP.

   $PY = W + BI + CCA + T_{IN}$
   $PY = 600 + 200 + 100 + 100 = 1000$

   Now an increase in the average wage rate in the economy increases employment income by 5 percent without any change in total employment or real GDP.
   a. What effect would this increase in employment income have on costs of production?
   b. If business raised prices to pass on these changed costs to buyers, how much would prices change, as measured by the GDP deflator?

9. Suppose business and investment income is 20 percent of nominal GDP. A rise in profit margins in industry increases business and investment income by 5 percent, without any change in output. What effect would this have on prices as measured by the GDP deflator?

10. Consider the information about a hypothetical economy in the table below:
    a. Calculate the growth (percentage change) in nominal GDP from 2007 to 2008.
    b. What was real GDP in 2007 and 2008? How much did real GDP grow?
    c. If changes in the standard of living can be measured by changes in real per capita GDP, did growth in nominal and real GDP raise the standard of living in this economy from 2007 to 2008?
    d. Explain the reasons for the change in standard of living that you have found.

Year	Nominal GDP (Billion $)	GDP Deflator (2000 = 100)	Population (Millions)
2007	750	104.0	25.0
2008	825	112.0	30.0

11. *Internet* Visit the United Nations Development Program (UNDP) Web site, and consult the latest *Human Development Report* (hdr.undp.org/en/reports/global/hdr2007–2008). How does Canada's ranking by the HDI index compare with its ranking based on per capita real GDP?

12. *Internet* Visit the Statistics Canada Web site, www.statcan.gc.ca, and examine the latest data on unemployment, inflation, and growth in real GDP by industry. Following the links in the "Latest Indicators" box on the right-hand side of the home page, write a brief note on Statistics Canada's explanations of the latest changes in these indicators.

13. *Internet* The Canadian Economy Online Web site provided by the Government of Canada, canadianeconomy.gc.ca/, provides a link that reports provincial and territorial economic indicators. Using the latest data reported on that link, examine the differences in unemployment and inflation across provinces. Write a brief note on the range of unemployment and inflation rates across provinces, and the relationship, if any that you see between provincial unemployment rates and inflation rates.

CHAPTER 5

Output, Business Cycles, and Employment

LEARNING OUTCOMES

By the end of this chapter you should understand:

1. Short-run aggregate demand and supply
2. Equilibrium output and potential output
3. Business cycles and output gaps
4. Okun's Law: Output gaps and unemployment rates
5. Adjustments to output gaps
6. The role of macroeconomic policy

Macroeconomic analysis has important time dimensions. In the long run, over periods of several years and decades, real GDP in most industrial economies grows and per capita real GDP grows as well, raising standards of living. We have seen the data for Canada on this long-run performance in Chapter 4. We have also seen that growth rates fluctuate over short time periods of a few months or a few years. At some times real output declines and at other times it grows very rapidly. Economists describe these short-run fluctuations as business cycles, using the words recession, recovery, boom, and slump to describe different stages of the business cycle. These words are also part of the everyday language of the news media, which often engages in a debate over current economic conditions as they foretell continuing stability, a recession, or recovery from a recession. The financial crises and recession of 2008–2009 is the most recent example.

The aggregate demand and aggregate supply model is the workhorse of macroeconomics. It illustrates the determination of real GDP and the GDP deflator, and changes in those measures of output and prices. In this chapter we introduce an aggregate demand and supply model and use it to illustrate the causes and effects of business cycle fluctuations in real output and prices. This provides the framework for most of what comes later, the development of the economic theory on which aggregate demand and supply are based.

5.1 A Short-Run Aggregate Demand and Aggregate Supply Model

The **short run** in macroeconomics is defined by assuming a specific set of conditions in the economy. These are:

1. There are constant prices for factors of production, especially money wage rates for labour.
2. The supply of labour, the stock of capital, and the state of technology are fixed.

In the **short run**, factor prices, supplies of factors of production, and technology are fixed by assumption.

In the short run, changes in output cause changes in the employment of labour and in the use of plant and equipment, but these changes are not sustainable over longer time periods. Furthermore, because supplies of factor inputs and technology are fixed, there is no growth in real GDP. We leave that topic for a later chapter.

The national accounts we studied in Chapter 4 describe and measure economic activity in terms of aggregate expenditures, outputs, and incomes. But they do not explain the level of economic activity and prices or the reasons for changes in output and prices from time to time. For that we need an analytical framework that looks at cause and effect. An **aggregate demand (AD)** and **aggregate supply (AS) model** is such an analytical framework. It helps us to understand the conditions that determine output and prices, and changes in output and prices over time.

An **AD/AS model** is a framework used to explain the behaviour of real output and prices in the national economy.

The short-run AD/AS model is closely related to the national accounts framework. Aggregate demand is the relationship between aggregate expenditure on final goods and services and the general price level. Real GDP by the expenditure approach measures this expenditure at the price level given by the GDP deflator. Aggregate supply is the relationship between the output of goods and services produced by business and the general price level. Real GDP by the income approach measures this output, and the corresponding real incomes. The price level is again the GDP deflator. National accounts tell us that, by definition, these *measured* outputs and incomes are equal. AD and AS use the national accounts framework to describe *expenditure plans, output, and prices*.

This distinction between measured and planned expenditure and output is important. Planned expenditure is the current output households and businesses would want to buy at different levels of income and price. Output is what businesses actually produce. They may not be the same.

Figure 5.1 gives us a first look at output, real income, and prices for the year 2008 from Table 4.7 (page 86), using an aggregate demand and aggregate supply diagram. The price level as measured by the GDP deflator is measured on the vertical axis. Real output and income are measured on the horizontal axis. The point of intersection of the AD and AS lines shows that real output by the expenditure approach is equal to real income by the income approach at the price level 120.9, as required by national accounts. However, we need to explain the aggregate demand and aggregate supply relationships indicated by the slopes and positions of the AD and AS lines in the diagram before we use the model to study output and prices.

Aggregate Demand (AD) is **planned aggregate expenditure** on final goods and services (C + I + G + NX) at different price levels when all other conditions are constant. We will examine this relationship in detail in the chapters that follow. The relationship between planned aggregate expenditure and the general price level is negative. A higher price level reduces the expenditures planned by households, businesses, and residents of other countries. Lower price levels increase those expenditure plans.

Aggregate Demand is **planned aggregate expenditure** on final goods and services at different price levels, all other conditions remaining constant.

FIGURE 5.1 **The Aggregate Demand and Supply Model**

The intersection of the AD and AS lines shows real output measured by the output approach (AD) equal to real income measured by the income approach (AS) at the price level given by the GDP deflator.

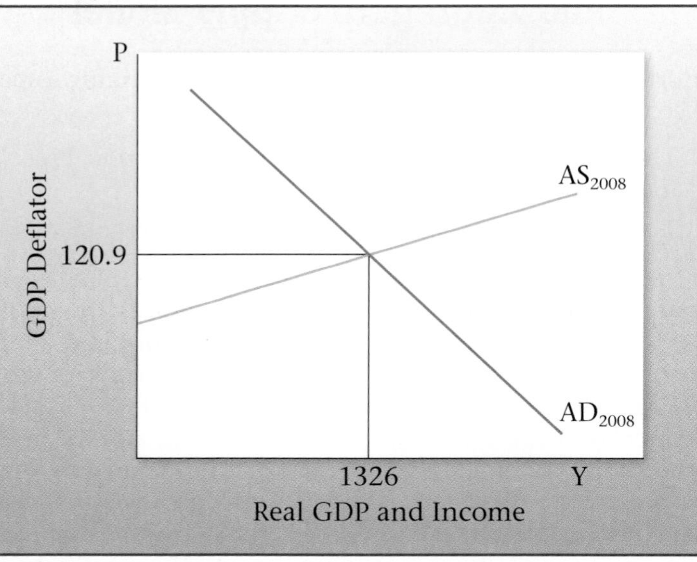

Aggregate Supply is the output of final goods and services businesses would produce at different price levels, all other conditions held constant.

Aggregate Supply (AS) is the output of final goods and services business produces at different price levels when other conditions are constant. As Figure 5.1 suggests, the relationship between the volume of goods and services produced and the price level is positive. Prices and output rise or fall together. We will examine this relationship in more detail below and in later chapters.

AGGREGATE DEMAND

It is important to recognize the difference between aggregate demand and the market demand for an individual product. In our discussion of the market for an individual product in Chapter 3, demand is based on the assumptions that incomes and prices of other products are constant. Then a rise in the price of the product makes the product more expensive relative to income and relative to other products. As a result, people buy less of the product. Alternatively, if price falls people buy more.

The link between the *general* price level and aggregate demand is different. We cannot assume constant incomes and prices of other products. In the aggregate economy a rise in the GDP deflator raises money incomes by an equal amount. A 10 percent rise in the general price level is also a 10 percent rise in money incomes. Changes in the price level do not make goods and services either more or less affordable, *in terms of incomes*. There is no incentive to change aggregate expenditure.

Furthermore, if prices of individual goods and services do not rise or fall in the same proportion as the general price level, the distribution of aggregate expenditure among goods and services may change without a change in aggregate expenditure. If, for example, the general price level is pushed up because oil and commodity prices rise, and expenditure on those products rises in the short run because there are no alternatives, expenditures on other goods and services fall. Aggregate expenditure is unchanged.

As a result, we cannot explain the negative relationship between the general price level and aggregate expenditure as we would explain demand for an individual good or service. Nor can we simply add up all the demands for individual products and services to get aggregate demand. The assumptions of constant incomes and other product prices that underlie market demand do not hold in the aggregate. Different explanations are needed.

The negative relationship between planned aggregate expenditure and the general price level rests on three effects that arise from a change in the general price level. These are:

1. the interest rate effect,
2. the substitution effect, and
3. the wealth effect.

The **interest rate** effect comes from changes in interest rates and asset prices in financial markets caused by changes in the general price level for goods and services. As we will see in later chapters, interest rates are determined in financial markets by the demand for and the supply of financial assets, including money balances. A rise in the general price level increases the size of the money balances that households, businesses, and governments need to pay their expenses. This increase in the demand for money balances raises interest rates, which are the costs of borrowing. Interest rates on household lines of credit, mortgages, business bank loans, and other means of financing expenditure rise, increasing the cost of expenditures.

The **interest rate effect** is the change in expenditures when interest rates change.

An increase in interest rates also lowers the foreign exchange rate, the prices of imports, and the profitability of exports. As a result, some expenditure plans are reduced and others postponed. These interest rate effects make an important link in the negative relationship between price levels and planned aggregate expenditure.

The **substitution effect** changes the net export component of planned aggregate expenditure. Planned expenditures on exports and imports are based in part on the prices of domestic goods and services relative to foreign goods and services. A rise in the domestic price level increases the price of domestic output both in the home market and in foreign markets. The fall in the exchange rate coming from the interest rate effect reinforces this change in relative prices. Domestic goods become more expensive relative to foreign goods and services. Some households and businesses at home and abroad react to the change in relative price by substituting foreign goods and services for domestic goods and services. Imports rise and exports fall, lowering net exports and aggregate expenditure on domestic goods and services.

The **substitution effect** is the change in net exports when relative national prices change.

The **wealth effect** reduces aggregate expenditures by households and businesses when the general level of prices rises, and increases aggregate expenditure when prices fall. Households and businesses hold money balances like bank deposits as a part of their financial wealth. They use those balances to pay for routine purchases, to cover routine expenses, and as reserves against unpredictable expenses. As a student, you might have a bank balance at the start of term that you expect will cover your expenses for the term, perhaps with a bit left over in case you need to fix your computer.

The **wealth effect** is the change in planned consumption when household wealth changes.

The purchasing power of money balances at any point in time depends on the general price level. A rise in the price level reduces the quantity of goods and services that can be purchased with a fixed number of dollars. A fall in the price level increases the quantity. In other words, price changes cause changes in real financial wealth. Changes in real financial wealth change the quantities of goods and services households and businesses can buy with their fixed money balances. As a result, the *wealth effect* of a change in the general price level changes aggregate expenditure. It explains part of the negative relationship between price and aggregate expenditure in the aggregate demand curve.

In Figure 5.2, the negatively sloped AD line shows planned aggregate expenditures at different price levels, on the assumption that anything other than price that might

FIGURE 5.2 **The Aggregate Demand Curve**

The **AD** curve shows planned aggregate expenditures at different prices. At point **A** the price P_0 results in planned aggregate expenditure Y_0. A fall in price from P_0 to P_1 would result in an increase in planned aggregate expenditure to Y_1.

The wealth, substitution, and interest rate effects of price changes *cause movements along* the AD curve.

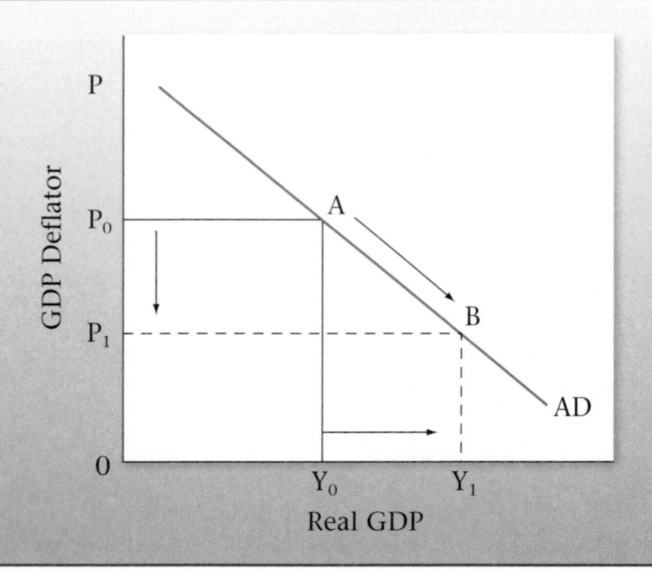

Review Question 1

affect expenditure plans is held constant. A change in price level causes a movement along the AD curve resulting from the interest rate, substitution, and wealth effects. If the price level falls from P_0 to P_1, the movement along AD from A to B shows the negative relationship between planned aggregate expenditure and price. A rise in price would reduce planned expenditure as shown by moving up the AD curve.

The negative slope of the AD curve illustrates the way price changes affect planned aggregate expenditures. The *position of the curve* depends on all the conditions other than price that affect aggregate expenditure plans. We study these other conditions in detail in later chapters.

AGGREGATE SUPPLY

Aggregate Supply (AS) is the output of final goods and services businesses would produce at different price levels. The aggregate supply curve is based on the following key assumptions:

1. Prices of the factors of production—the money wage rates for labour in particular—are constant.
2. The stock of capital equipment—the buildings and equipment used in the production process—and the technology of production are constant.
3. The rates of indirect taxation imposed by governments are held constant.
4. The prices of key raw material inputs, which are determined in international markets like the market for crude oil, are constant.

With these conditions, there is a positive relationship between the output of final goods and services businesses would produce and the general price level.

From national accounts we know that the costs of production include labour costs, business and investment income, and depreciation. Market prices depend on these *costs per unit of output* plus the net indirect taxes imposed by governments. Aggregate supply is the positive relationship between quantities of final goods and services businesses are willing to produce and prices. Higher outputs of final goods and services and higher prices go together.

We can explain the aggregate supply relationship between outputs and prices using the national accounts framework. As we saw earlier, prices measured by the GDP deflator reflect factor costs of production and indirect taxes as follows:

P = labour costs per unit + business income and deprecation per unit + net indirect tax per unit,

$$P = \frac{W}{Y} + \frac{BI + CCA}{Y} + \frac{T_{IN}}{Y} \quad (5.1)$$

Changes in prices are the result of:

1. Changes in labour cost per unit of output, or
2. Changes in business and investment income (profit) plus capital consumption per unit of output, or
3. Changes in net indirect taxes per unit of output, or some combination of these three components.

We start by assuming constant net indirect taxes, which are determined by government policy, and constant capital consumption to concentrate on two factor costs, namely labour costs and business profits.

The relationship between aggregate output, these costs, and prices reflects two different market conditions on the supply side of the economy. In some markets, particularly those for commodities and standardized products, supply and demand in international markets establish price. Producers of those products are price takers. They decide how much to produce and sell based on market price. Many raw material markets are like this, including those for agricultural products, forestry products, base metals, and crude oil.

When the market price changes, these producers change their output. A rise in product price with constant factor prices offers an increase in business profit per unit of output, (BI/Y) and an opportunity to increase total profit by producing and selling more. As output increases, marginal and average labour costs (W/Y) rise, even with constant wage rates, because labour productivity (output per worker) diminishes. Total labour costs, W, rise faster than output, Y. With a higher price it is profitable to expand output until marginal costs have risen to the new price level. (For students who have studied Microeconomics, producers in this part of the economy behave as if the market were perfectly competitive.)

A fall in price reduces profitability and output. Prices fall relative to costs of production. Producers reduce output and employment, reducing labour costs as revenues have fallen, until costs have fallen sufficiently to make up for lower prices. These output and employment decisions in response to price changes are part of the reason for a positive relationship between aggregate output and price.

In other parts of the economy, producers are price setters. Major manufacturing and service industries like auto producers, banks, and cell phone companies face market conditions that are different from those of commodity producers. They set prices based on costs of production and profit targets, and supply the number of cars or bank services or cell phone accounts that are in demand at those prices. If increased demand and output push up their labour costs (W/Y), as will happen if labour productivity declines as output expands, they raise prices to cover their increased costs. Alternatively, if low demand and price competition have squeezed profits, increased demand may result in increased prices to restore profit margins, raising business income per unit of output (BI/Y). Producer price-setting behaviour in this part of the economy also gives a positive aggregate supply relationship between real output and price. Producers are willing to produce more if they can raise prices to cover their increased production costs. If demand falls and sales fall, causing an unwanted build up of inventories of finished goods, some producers may cut profit margins and prices. Price cuts and sales incentives in the new car market illustrate this relationship between prices and output in a market for manufactured products.

The upward-sloping aggregate supply curve shows the positive relationship between the aggregate output of real goods and services that producers are willing to produce and the price level. The aggregate supply curve in Figure 5.3 is drawn based on the assumptions that money wage rates, net indirect taxes, and all other conditions except price that might affect output decisions are constant. As we will see in later chapters, money wage rates and productivity are the most important of these conditions. They determine the *position* of the AS curve. The positive *slope* of the AS curve shows how changes in aggregate output and price are linked through changes in cost per unit when output changes.

In Figure 5.3, if price were P_2 the AS curve shows that business would be willing to produce aggregate output Y_2, which would generate an equal flow of real income. A rise in aggregate output from Y_2 to Y_3 would mean a rise in price to P_3 to meet the increased costs and profits associated with output at this level. Changes in output or price, holding all other conditions constant, move the economy along the AS curve. Moving from point C to point D in the diagram shows this relationship.

On the other hand, a change in any of the conditions assumed to be constant will shift the entire AS curve. A rise in money wage rates, for example, would increase labour costs per unit of output (W/Y) at every level of output. The AS curve would shift up vertically as prices rose to cover the increased unit labour costs. Alternatively, a cut in indirect taxes like the GST would lower indirect taxes per unit of output and shift

FIGURE 5.3 **The Aggregate Supply Curve**

The AS curve shows aggregate output at different prices as measured by real GDP. At C the price P_2 results in aggregate output Y_2. A rise in price from P_2 to P_3 would accompany an increase in output to Y_3, moving along the AS curve.

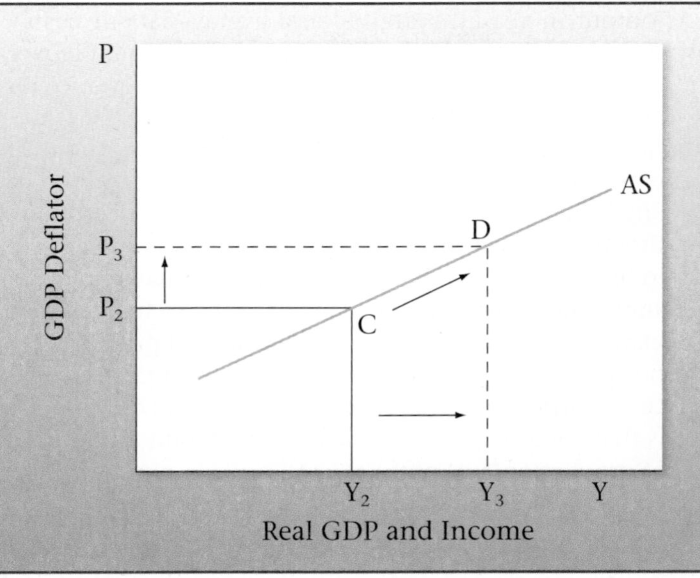

the AS curve down. Producers would continue to sell at the same *basic* price but final market price to buyers would be lower by the reduced indirect tax.

Review Question 2

EQUILIBRIUM REAL GDP AND PRICE

Aggregate demand and aggregate supply together determine equilibrium real GDP and the general price level. Aggregate demand is planned aggregate expenditure at different prices. Aggregate supply is aggregate output at different prices. The circular flow diagram and national accounts show how aggregate expenditure provides the flow of revenue business needs to cover its costs of production, and that those costs of production are income flows to households. When planned aggregate expenditure is equal to output, we have equilibrium real GDP. The revenues businesses receive from aggregate expenditure are just what they require to cover their costs, including expected profit. As long as conditions affecting expenditure and output plans are constant, business has no incentive to change output. This *equilibrium* between aggregate expenditure, outputs, and income and the general price level is illustrated by the intersection of the AD and AS curves.

Equilibrium real GDP and price mean planned expenditure equals current output and provides business revenues that cover costs including expected profit.

Figure 5.4 takes us back to Figure 5.1. *Equilibrium* real GDP and price are shown by the intersection of AD and AS at point A with P = 120.9 and Y = 1326.

It helps us to understand what equilibrium means if we consider what would happen if the economy were not at point A in the diagram. Suppose, for example, business produced output and paid costs greater than $ 1326, as would be the case at point B on the AS curve. Output would be Y_0, but planned expenditure at Y_1 would be less than business needs to cover its costs. Aggregate demand is lower than expected, output Y_1Y_0 is not sold. Costs of production are not recovered and *unwanted inventories build up.* In response, business would cut output, moving back to point A. Alternatively, if output were less than $ 1326, higher demand and *unwanted reductions in inventories* would provide strong incentives to increase output. Market conditions push the economy to equilibrium, the point where AD equals AS.

FIGURE 5.4 **Equilibrium Real GDP and Price**

The intersection of AD and AS gives equilibrium real GDP and price at point A. At any other real GDP, such as either Y_1 or Y_0, AD and AS would not be equal and *unwanted changes in business inventories* would lead business to change output in the direction needed to reach equilibrium.

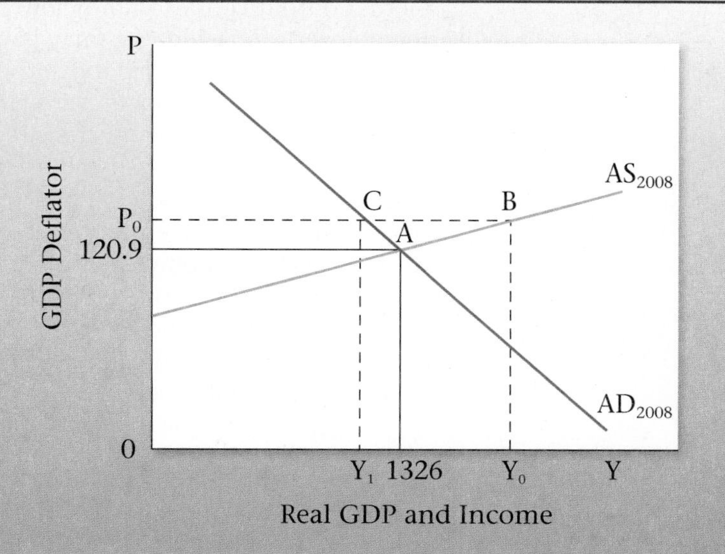

The equilibrium determined by aggregate demand and aggregate supply at point A is the result of the economic conditions at a moment in time, and the expenditure and output decisions in the economy. It is a short-run equilibrium. The aggregate supply curve is based on the assumption that money wage rates, other factor prices, capital stock and technology are constant. However, any change in the conditions that affect expenditure and output plans would change the AD and AS curves and lead to a new short-run equilibrium real GDP and price.

Review Questions 3 and 4

5.2 Equilibrium Output and Potential Output

Potential output is the output the economy can produce on an ongoing basis with current labour capital and technology without putting continuous upward pressure on prices.

Short-run equilibrium real GDP is determined by AD and AS conditions. Fluctuations in real GDP and price are a result of short-run changes in economic conditions. To evaluate the economy's performance and understand how it behaves over time, we need a benchmark. **Potential output** is the output the economy can produce on an ongoing basis using the current labour force, capital, and technology without putting continuous upward pressure on the price level or the inflation rate.

In the short run, the labour force, the capital stock, and technology are fixed by assumption. Potential output is the economy's output based on "full employment" of these inputs, but it is not the maximum output an economy can conceivably make. For short periods of time we could make more by using labour for longer hours and factories for extra production shifts. Just as a marathon runner can sprint from time to time but cannot sustain the sprint over the whole race, the economy can operate for short time periods at levels of output above potential. Potential output is the output the economy can produce on a sustained basis.

When the economy is at potential output, every worker wanting a job at the equilibrium wage rate can find a job, and every machine that can be profitably used at the equilibrium cost for capital is in use. Thus, potential output includes an allowance for "equilibrium unemployment" or structural unemployment and some excess capacity. Some people, who would work at higher wage rates, do not want to work at the equilibrium wage rate. Moreover, in a constantly changing economy, some people are joining the labour force, others are leaving, and still others are temporarily between jobs. Today, Canadian potential output means an unemployment rate of about 6 to 7 percent.

Actual output can also fall below potential output. Workers who want jobs may be unemployed, and producers may have idle plant and equipment or excess capacity. The unemployment rate rises above the 6 to 7 percent "full employment" rate. A key issue in macroeconomics is the way differences between actual output and potential output affect unemployment rates, wage rates, and inflation rates. These effects are important to how the economy adjusts equilibrium output to potential output, as we will see later in this chapter.

The distinction between equilibrium output and potential output is very important to our study of the economy. In the short run, AD and AS determine equilibrium output. Potential output is determined by the size of the labour force, the stock of capital, and the state of technology. The general level of prices and short-run aggregate demand and supply conditions do not affect potential output.

Figure 5.5 illustrates potential real GDP (Y_p) with a vertical line. Changes in price from P_0 to P_1, for example, have no effect on Y_p. Changes in the supply of labour, the stock of capital, or the state of technology would increase the economy's potential output and shift the Y_P line horizontally to the right or left.

Figure 5.6 shows actual real GDP each year in Canada over the period from 1975 to 2007 compared with estimates of potential GDP. Actual and potential GDP had strong

FIGURE 5.5 Potential GDP

Potential GDP (Y_P) is the real output the economy could produce on a sustained basis without putting pressure on costs and prices. Y_P is not affected by changes in the price level.

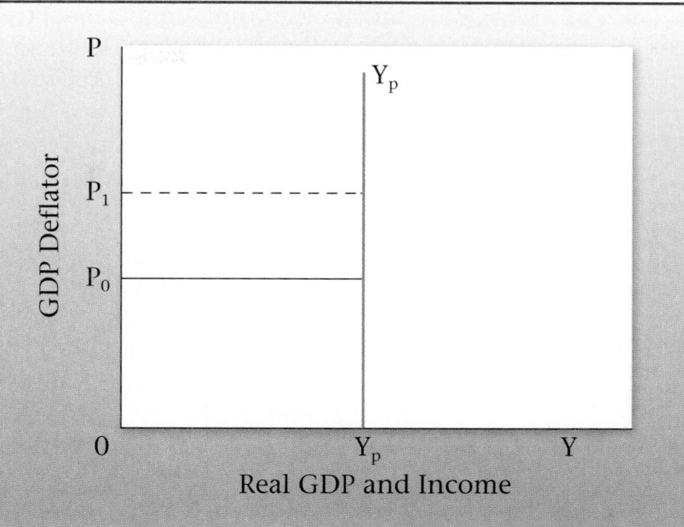

FIGURE 5.6 Potential and Actual Real GDP in Canada 1975 to 2007

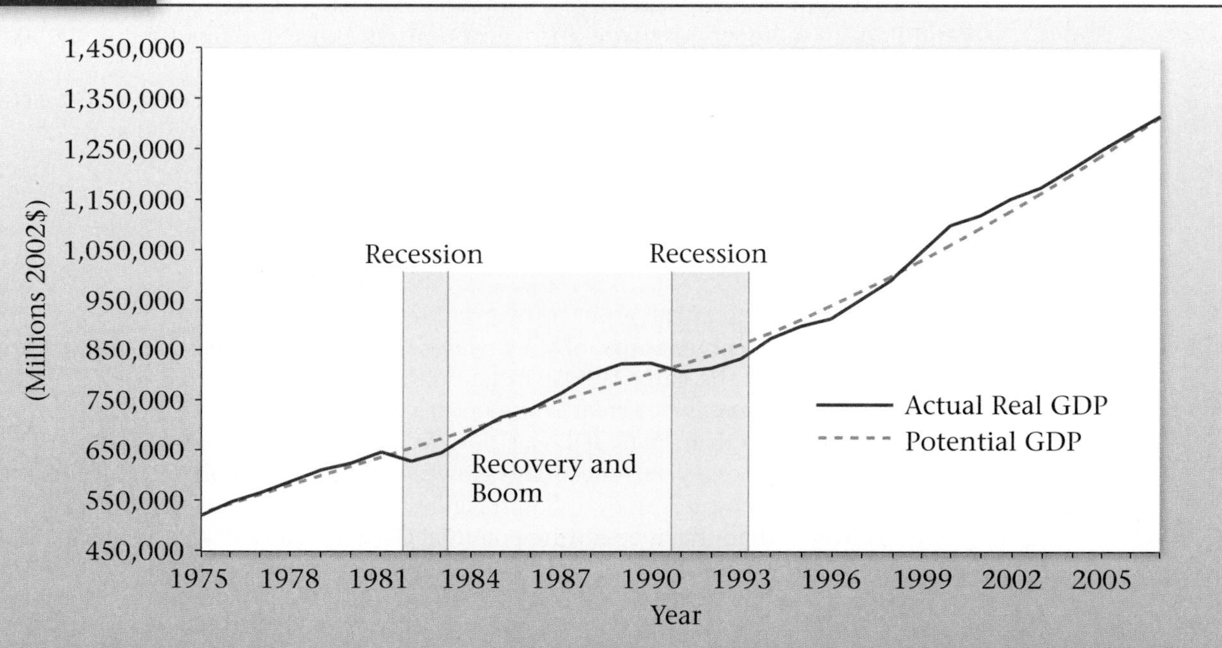

Potential GDP in any year is the real output the economy could produce using the existing labour force, stock of capital equipment, and available technology, if all markets were in equilibrium. Potential output grows over time as the labour force and capital stock grow and technology improves. Actual real GDP fluctuates around potential GDP as a result of short-run variations in aggregate demand and supply. The recession of 1981 created a recessionary gap. The subsequent recovery and boom from 1983 to 1989 eliminated the recessionary gap and resulted in an inflationary gap. The recession and recovery of the 1990s illustrates another more prolonged business cycle.

Sources: Real GDP, Statistics Canada, CANSIM Series V3860085. Potential GDP calculated using H-P Filter.

upward trends, reflecting the underlying growth in labour force, the stock of capital, and improved technology. However, sometimes actual GDP was lower than potential, and at other times higher, as the growth in actual GDP fluctuated around the growth in potential GDP. These fluctuations in actual GDP relative to potential GDP were the result of fluctuations in short-run AD and AS conditions.

Review Questions 5 and 6

5.3 Business Cycles and Output Gaps

The **business cycle** is the short-term fluctuation of actual real GDP.

Output gaps are the differences between actual and potential output.

Figure 5.6 shows us that actual real GDP does not grow smoothly. In some years GDP grows very rapidly, and in other years it actually falls. The smooth growth of potential GDP we see in Figure 5.6 was the trend path of output with the short-run fluctuations smoothed out. Actual output fluctuates about this measure of potential output. These up and down fluctuations in the growth of real GDP are described as **business cycles** in economic activity.

Business cycles cause differences between actual and potential GDP. **Output gaps** measure these differences. In a short-run aggregate demand and supply model with a constant potential output, the gap is:

$$\textbf{Output Gap} = Y - Y_P \qquad (5.2)$$

In an economy that grows over time the absolute output gap $Y - Y_P$ is usually normalized by measuring it relative to potential output. This recognizes that a gap of $10 million is a more serious matter in an economy with a potential output of $1,000 million than in an economy with a potential output of $5,000 million.

Figure 5.7 plots the Bank of Canada's estimates of the differences between actual and potential GDP for Canada for each year from 1982 to 2008, expressed as a percentage of potential GDP, calculated as:

$$\textbf{Output gap}(\%) = \frac{Y - Y_P}{Y_P} \times 100 \qquad (5.2a)$$

When we look at the growth in actual real GDP and potential GDP in Canada in the 1980s, we see an example of the business cycle and the output gaps it creates. Real GDP declined in the early 1980s, and actual GDP fell below potential GDP in Figure 5.6. This was a *recession*. It created the negative output gap in Figure 5.7 in 1982.

By 1983 growth in real GDP was positive again as the economy entered a *recovery* phase of the business cycle. Indeed, this growth was strong enough and lasted long enough to eliminate the output gap by 1985. In Figure 5.6 we see that the line plotting actual real GDP is steeper than the line plotting potential GDP. Actual GDP rose above potential GDP in the late 1980s, and the economy entered a *boom* phase of the business cycle. Actual GDP was then greater than potential GDP during the late 1980s and the output gap was positive until a recession in 1990 produced another more persistent output gap. Similarly, the slowdown in growth in late 2008 that marked the beginning of the 2008–2009 recession created a negative output gap starting in the fourth quarter of 2008.

An **inflationary gap** is a measure of the amount by which actual GDP is greater than potential GDP.

A **recessionary gap** is a measure of the amount by which actual GDP is less, than potential GDP.

Output gaps describe and measure these short-run economic conditions, and indicate the strength or weakness of the economy's performance. High growth rates in the boom phase of the cycle create positive output gaps, which are called **inflationary gaps** because they put upward pressure on costs and prices. Low or negative growth rates that result in negative output gaps and rising unemployment rate are called **recessionary gaps**. They put downward pressure on costs and prices. As economic conditions change over time, business cycle fluctuations move the economy through

APPLICATION BOX 5.1

Measuring Output Gap

The Bank of Canada offers the following description of the importance and measurement of the output gap:

"THE OUTPUT GAP is the difference between the economy's actual output and the level of output it can achieve with existing labour, capital, and technology without putting sustained upward pressure on inflation.

"The output gap is also referred to as spare capacity or excess capacity. The gap is positive when actual output exceeds the economy's potential, and negative when actual output is below potential. A positive gap is also referred to as excess demand, and a negative gap is referred to as excess supply."

However, while the output gap is clearly defined in terms of economic theory and simple to illustrate in a diagram, there is no consensus on its measurement. The Bank of Canada notes:

"Both the level of potential output and the output gap are estimates, and therefore there is major uncertainty in their calculation.

"This uncertainty may be larger now because the estimated output gap is relatively small, and the economy seems to have undergone significant changes in the 1990s. As a result the Bank now places increased weight on a range of indicators to assess the degree of pressure on the economy's production capacity."

Nevertheless, the potential output and output gaps are very important to our study of the economy's performance.

Source: *BACKGROUNDERS: The Output Gap*, http://www.bankofcanada.ca/en/backgrounders/bg-p5.html. Bank of Canada, 2009.

FIGURE 5.7 **The Output Gap in Canada 1982 to 2008**

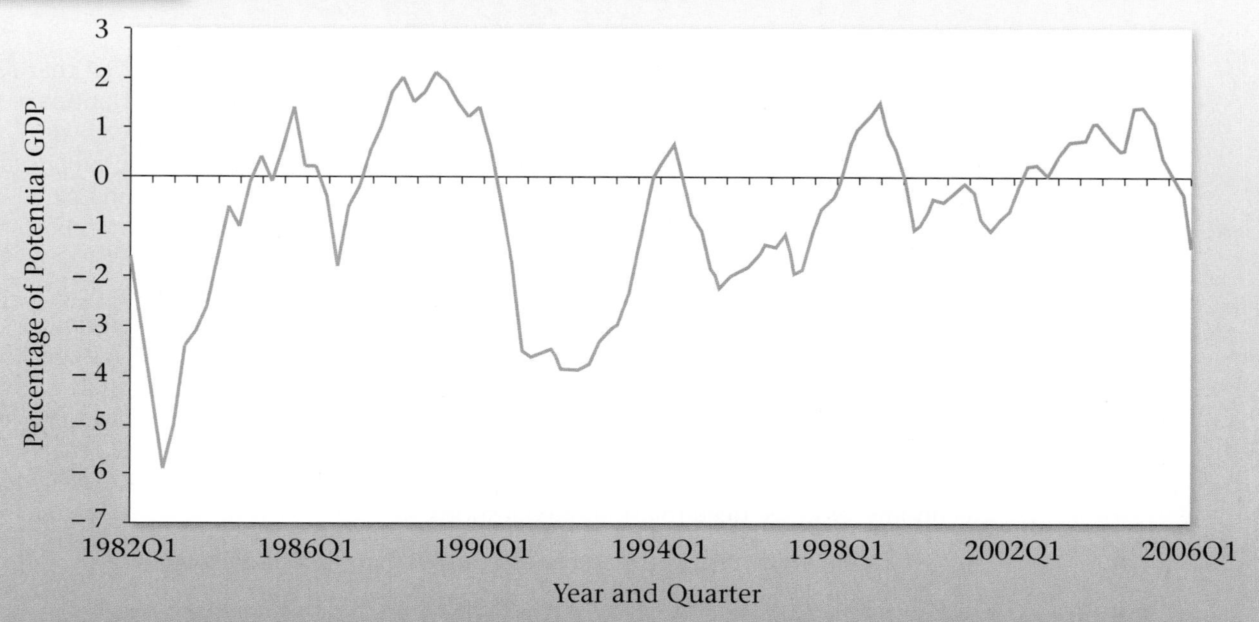

The output gap measures the difference between actual real GDP and potential GDP as a percentage of potential GDP. When output gaps are negative, as in the early 1980s and most of the 1990s, the economy is operating below potential. There is a recessionary gap. Positive output gaps are inflationary gaps.

Source: "Indicators of Capacity and Inflation Pressures for Canada." Bank of Canada, 2009.

FIGURE 5.8 Output Gaps

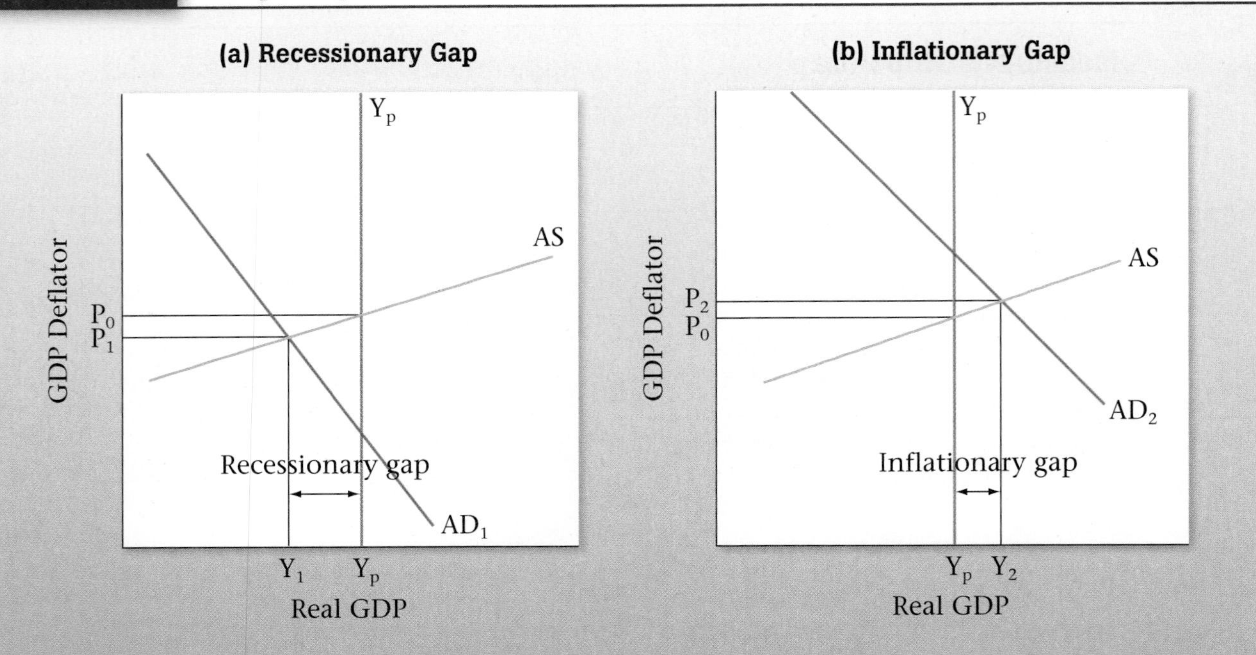

AD_1 in panel (a) is not strong enough to give equilibrium real GDP at Y_P. The result is a recessionary GDP gap in the amount $Y_1 - Y_P < 0$. By contrast, stronger AD_2 in panel (b) gives equilibrium real GDP greater than potential output and an inflationary GDP gap $Y_2 - Y_P > 0$. In each case, short-run AD and AS determine equilibrium real GDP, which may be different from potential GDP. The output gaps measure the differences.

recessionary and inflationary gaps. However, you will notice in Figure 5.7 that recessionary gaps in Canada have been deeper and more persistent than inflationary gaps over the past 25 years.

We can show output gaps in diagrams using the aggregate demand and supply curves and the potential output line. Figure 5.8 provides an example. The left-hand panel illustrates a recessionary gap. The right-hand panel shows an inflationary gap. In both cases the aggregate supply curve crosses the potential output line at price level P_0, the price level consistent with equilibrium at potential output at the assumed factor prices.

The AD and AS model provides a basic explanation of the differences we see between actual real GDP and potential real GDP. Short-run AD and AS conditions determine equilibrium real GDP, which may be either greater or less than potential GDP. Furthermore, the business cycles are the results of changes in the short-run AD and AS conditions.

Review Questions 7, 8, 9 and 10

We have made an important first step in our study of the performance of the macro economy. Now we need to ask more questions:

- What is the relationship between output gaps and unemployment?
- How would the economy react to a persistent output gap?
- Why do short-run AD and AS conditions change from time to time?

The first two questions are considered in the remainder of this chapter. The third question is much larger. Chapter 6 starts to examine it in detail.

5.4 Output Gaps and Unemployment Rates

The unemployment rate is measured and reported monthly. In Chapter 4 we used it as one measure of macroeconomic performance, and noted how it changed from year to year. The unemployment rate measures the difference between the number of people employed and the number of people in the labour force, expressed as a percentage of the labour force, as we saw in Chapter 4. If the letter **u** indicates the unemployment rate,

$$u = \frac{\textbf{Labour force} - \textbf{number of people employed}}{\textbf{Labour force}} \times 100 \qquad (5.3)$$

The **equilibrium** or **natural unemployment rate** is the unemployment rate when the economy is at potential output and the labour market is in equilibrium. Although this is full employment, the unemployment rate will not be zero. Some people are between jobs and some are looking for work but not willing to work at current wage rates. When the economy is at potential output, Y_P, we will use $\mathbf{u_n}$ to indicate the equilibrium or natural unemployment rate.

The **equilibrium** or **natural unemployment rate** is the unemployment rate when the economy is at potential output Y_P.

$$u_n = \frac{\textbf{Labour force} - \textbf{equilibrium employment}}{\textbf{Labour force}} \times 100 \qquad (5.4)$$

Potential GDP, actual real GDP, and unemployment rates are tied together. The linkage between them is often summarized by a relationship known as **Okun's Law**. According to this "law," when the growth rate of actual real GDP is faster than the growth rate of potential GDP, the unemployment rate falls. Conversely, when real GDP grows more slowly than potential GDP, the unemployment rate increases. This negative relationship between growth rates in real GDP and changes in the unemployment rate is one of the most consistent empirical regularities in macroeconomics.

Okun's Law: Changes in unemployment rates result from differences between the growth rate of Y and the growth rate of Y_P.

A numerical example and a diagram show this relationship. The basic relationship suggested by Okun is:

$$\textbf{Change in unemployment rate} = \Delta u = -\frac{1}{2}\,(\textbf{growth rate of } Y - \textbf{growth rate of } Y_P) \quad (5.5)$$

A change in the unemployment rate that is one-half the difference between the growth rates is used here as an illustration. A link of this size is roughly correct for the Canadian and United States economies. When the growth rate of actual real GDP is greater than that of potential GDP during the recovery and boom phases of the business cycle, the unemployment rate falls by half the difference, and vice versa. For example, if the growth rate in potential output is 3 percent but actual output grows by 4 percent, the unemployment rate will fall by 0.5 percentage points.

Looking back, Figure 5.6 shows differences in the growth rates of Y and Y_P, roughly approximated by differences in the slopes of the two lines plotted in the diagram. The recessions of the early 1980s and 1990s and subsequent recoveries provide the clearest examples of these growth rate differences, first negative and then positive. Figure 4.3 showed the changes in unemployment rates during these same time periods, and more recent years. Higher growth in real GDP then potential GDP after the mid 1990s produced a persistent decline in unemployment rates.

APPLICATION BOX 5.2

Okun's Law in Canada

Over the years from 1976 to 2007, the real GDP in the Canadian economy grew at an average annual rate of 2.9 percent. In the same period, the unemployment rates for the core labour force—men aged 25 years and over—were as low as 4.3 percent in 1976 and as high as 10.4 percent in 1992.

The annual data for the unemployment rate, and the difference between the actual and the average growth of real GDP, are plotted in a scatter diagram to illustrate the negative relationship described by Okun's Law. The regression line drawn in the diagram has a slope of –0.42. This slope shows that an increase in the growth rate of real GDP by 1 percentage point lowered the unemployment rate by 0.42 percentage points on average in this time period in Canada. By the same argument, a decrease in the growth rate resulted in an increase in the unemployment rate.

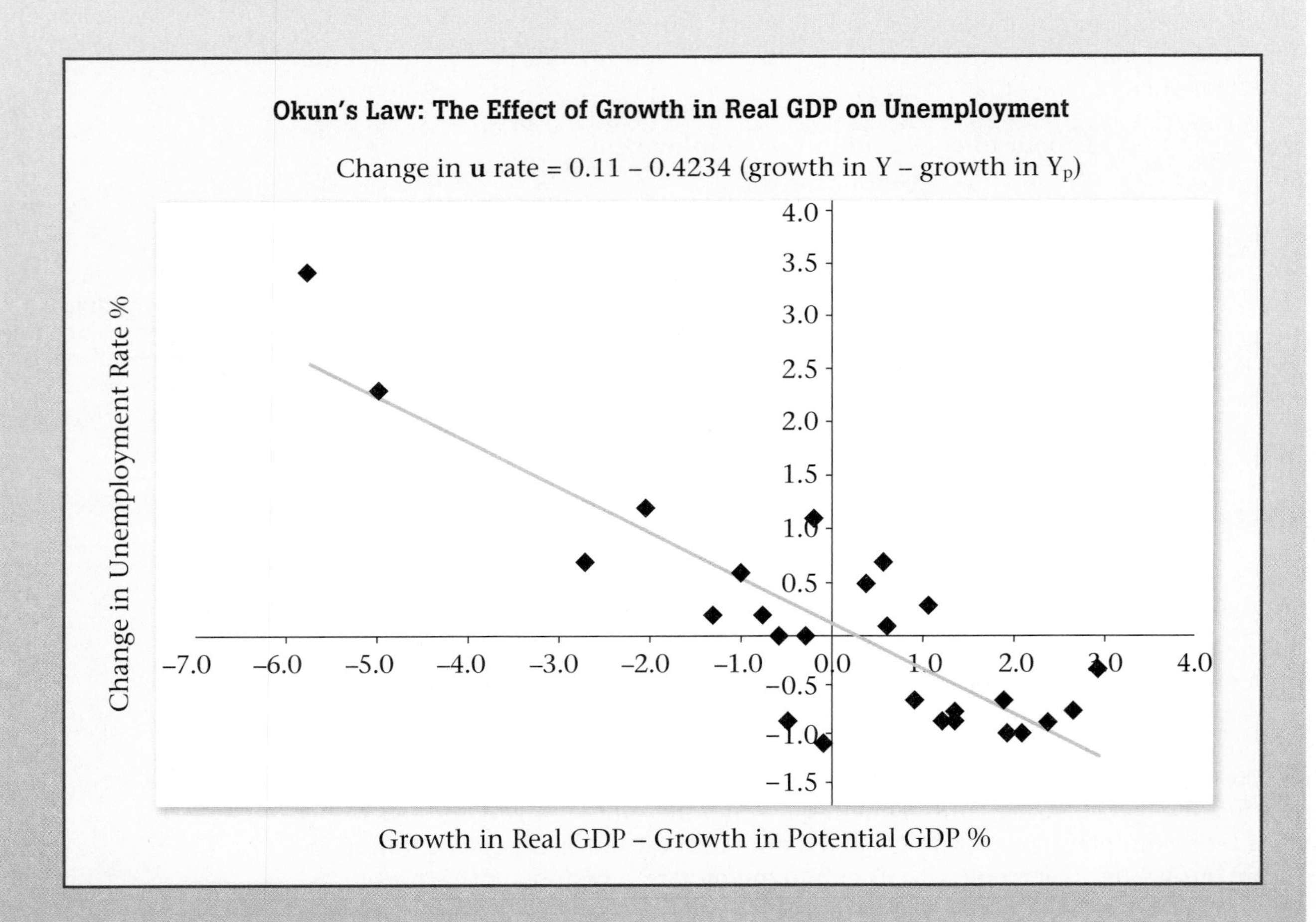

Source: Statistics Canada, CANSIM Series V2170281 and V3860085.

FIGURE 5.9 **Okun's Law**

Growth rates in real GDP are measured on the vertical axis. Changes in the unemployment rate are measured on the horizontal axis. The line ABC shows the relationship described by Okun's law. When the growth rate of real GDP (gY) is equal to the growth rate of potential GDP (gY_P), the unemployment rate does not change. $\Delta u = 0$ at point B. At point A the growth rate of actual real GDP (gY_1) is higher than the growth rate of potential output (gY_P), the demand for labour inputs is growing faster than the labour force, and the unemployment rate falls. Point C shows the opposite condition and result.

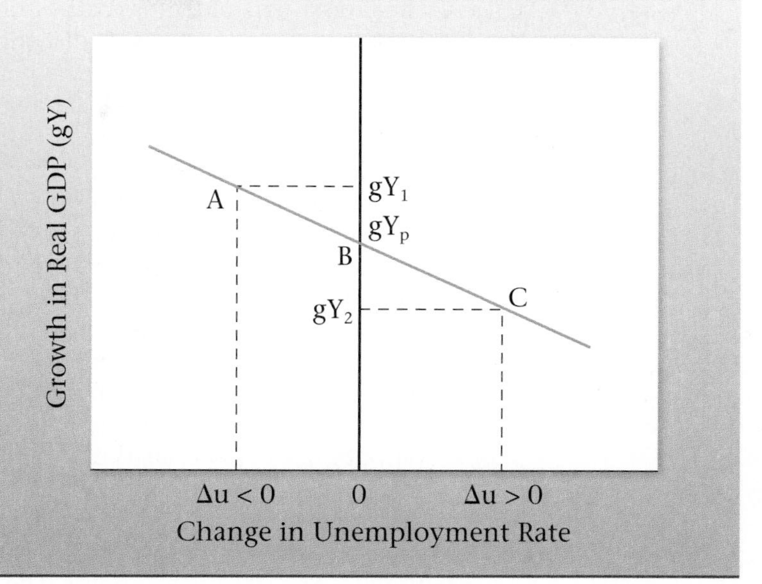

Figure 5.9 shows this relationship in a simple diagram. Growth rates of real GDP (gY) are measured on the vertical axis. Changes in the unemployment rate (Δu), either positive or negative, are measured on the horizontal axis. The negatively sloped line labeled A B C illustrates Okun's Law. At point B the growth rates of actual and potential GDP are equal, and there is no change in the unemployment rate. At point A, growth in actual GDP is higher than growth in potential GDP, and the unemployment rate declines. Point C shows the opposite case, with unemployment rising as a result of slow growth in actual GDP.

Now we can see that output gaps occur when the growth rate in real GDP differs from the growth rate of potential output during the business cycle. Okun's Law shows us that those output gaps also result in changes in the employment and unemployment rates. When growth in real output is slow or negative, recessionary output gaps and rising unemployment rates follow. Recoveries and booms, when growth in output is rapid, close the recessionary gaps and may go on to produce inflationary gaps. Unemployment rates fall during these periods. Stable unemployment rates mean the economy is growing over time at the same rate as the growth in potential output based on growth in the labour force, growth in capital stock, and improvements in productivity. It may also mean that the economy is growing along the potential output growth path if the unemployment rate is equal to the natural rate.

Review Question 11

5.5 Adjustments to Output Gaps

Potential output is real GDP when all markets are in equilibrium. Output gaps indicate disequilibria in some markets. If we leave the short run and drop the assumption that factor prices are constant, we can ask:

How does the economy react to persistent output gaps?

The answer to this question depends on the *flexibility of wage rates and prices.*

Okun's Law suggests that the labour market is one of the markets not in equilibrium when there is an output gap. We also know from national accounts that labour costs are the largest part of factor costs of production, and labour costs per unit of output are the largest part of prices. If disequilibria in the labour market—which means unemployment rates not equal to the natural rate—result in changes in money wage rates, persistent output gaps will change wage rates and other factor prices and costs. Changes in costs will change prices, shifting the short-run AS curve. The economy has an adjustment mechanism that tries to eliminate output gaps over time.

The effects of output gaps on factor prices and factor costs are the source of adjustment to output gaps. The recession phase of the business cycle creates recessionary gaps. Demands for factor inputs to production are low, and there is downward pressure on factor prices. The boom phase of the cycle creates inflationary gaps. Demands for factor inputs are high and there is upward pressure on factor prices. If factor prices, especially money wage rates for labour, are *flexible over time*, output gaps cause changes in factor prices, in factor costs, and in short-run aggregate supply conditions.

Figure 5.10 illustrates the changes in real output as the economy adjusts over time to output gaps. In panel (a), the high unemployment of a recessionary gap at Y_0 lowers wage rates and other factor prices. You will recall that the curve AS_0 in the diagram is drawn on the assumption that factor costs are fixed. A change in factor costs changes the entire AS curve. In this case it shifts down to AS_0'. With lower costs, producers are willing to produce and sell at lower prices. The change in factor costs and AS conditions continues, moving the economy along the AD curve until the recessionary gap is eliminated and output is at Y_P.

Review Question 12

FIGURE 5.10 **Adjustments to Eliminate Output Gaps**

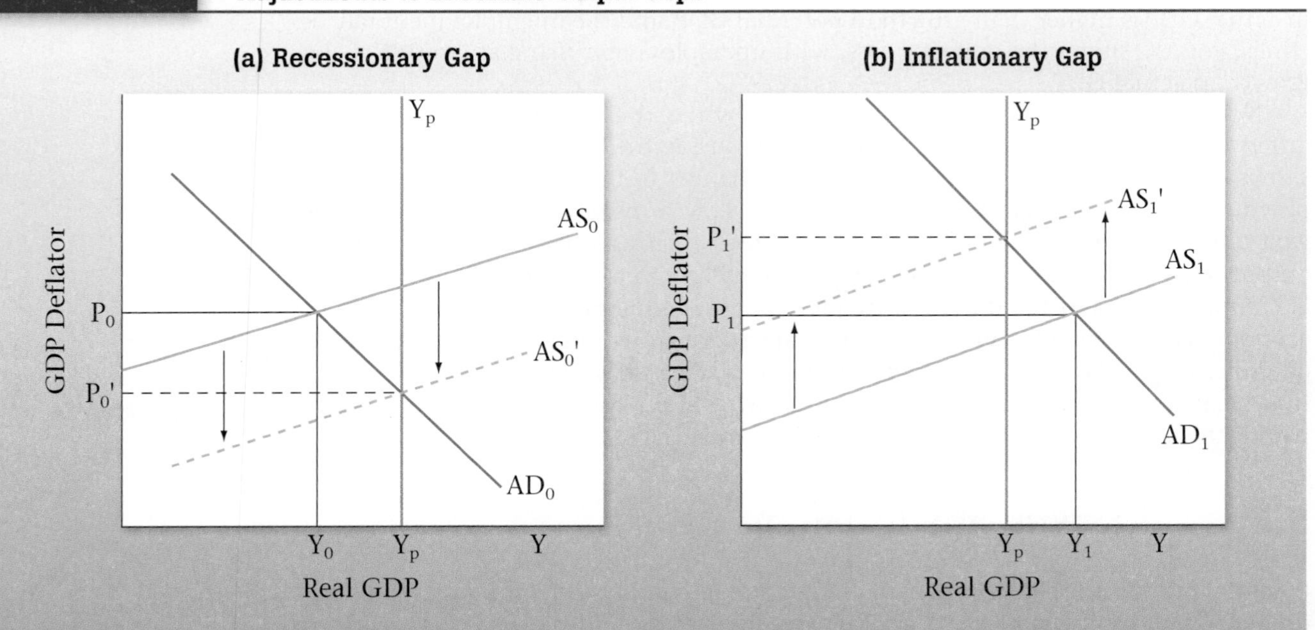

In panel (a) a recessionary gap results in lower wage rates and other factor prices. AS shifts down and equilibrium output increases to eliminate the gap. In panel (b) an inflationary gap raises factor prices and costs. AS shifts up and equilibrium output falls to eliminate the gap.

Panel (b) in Figure 5.10 shows adjustment to an inflationary gap. Rising factor prices and costs shift the AS curve up to AS_1'. Producers need higher prices to cover the higher production costs. Upward pressure on costs and prices continues, shifting AS up and moving the economy back along the AD curve until Y is in equilibrium at Y_P and the inflationary gap is eliminated.

5.6 The Role of Macroeconomic Policy

In Chapter 4, performance of the economy was evaluated based on the standard of living, or real GDP per capita, it provided. Recessionary gaps reduce the standard of living in the economy by reducing employment, real GDP, and per capita real GDP.

Inflationary gaps reduce standards of living in more subtle ways. They push up the price level, raising the cost of living. But the rise in the cost of living affects different people in different ways. Those on fixed money incomes suffer a reduction in their standards of living. People holding their wealth in fixed price financial assets like bank deposits and bonds suffer a loss in their real wealth. On the other hand, inflation reduces the real value of debt, whether it is mortgage debt used to finance the purchase of a house, or a student loan used to finance education. The money repaid in the future has a lower purchasing power than the money borrowed. In these and other ways, the costs of inflation are distributed unevenly in the economy, making decisions about employment, household expenditure, and investment more difficult.

Using Figure 5.10, we have described the self-adjusting mechanism within the AD/AS model that could eliminate output gaps and move the economy to equilibrium at potential output. We have also seen, in Figure 5.7 (page 105), that output gaps have been persistent in the Canadian economy despite the possibility that flexible wages and prices might automatically eliminate gaps. These observations raise two questions:

- Why are output gaps, especially recessionary gaps, persistent?
- Can government policy work to eliminate output gaps?

To answer the first question, we need to think about the *flexibility* or *rigidity of wages and prices*. The economy's reaction to output gaps takes time, because wage rates and prices are sticky and slow to adjust to changed economic circumstances.

In the modern economy, wage rates for labour are often fixed by contract or custom for finite periods of time. Labour contracts often set wage rates for periods of several years. Even without explicit contracts, employers are unlikely to change the wages they pay on an hour-by-hour or day-to-day basis. Custom may suggest an annual adjustment. Minimum wage laws prevent cuts in the lowest wage rates. These institutional arrangements mean that the money wage rates paid to labour adjust slowly to changes in economic conditions. Cuts to money wage rates are particularly difficult and controversial, although they have occurred in particular industries, like the airline industry and the auto industry under very difficult market conditions. The macroeconomic adjustment process calls for a change in the average money wage rate across the entire economy. That is a more complex process.

Contracts and custom also affect the speed of price adjustment to economic conditions. Producers in many cases have supply contracts with their customers that fix prices for a finite time period. Sellers may be reluctant to change prices frequently, in part because they are uncertain about how their competitors will react to their price changes, and in part to avoid alienating their customers. Retailers often issue catalogues in which prices are fixed for a specified period. The result is slow price adjustment to changing economic conditions in many parts of the economy.

Nevertheless, if the economy experiences a persistent output gap, that gap will lead eventually to changes in factor prices, costs, and market prices for goods and services. Indeed, the adjustment to inflationary gaps may come more quickly than to recessionary gaps because it is easier to raise money wage rates than to cut them. The important policy question is: When wages and prices are sticky, should government wait for the self-adjustment process to work, accepting the costs of high unemployment or rising inflation that it produces? This was a very serious and widely debated question in late 2008 in the face of a growing international recession and a serious international financial market crisis.

Fiscal policy: government expenditure and tax changes designed to influence AD.

Monetary policy: changes in interest rates and money supply designed to influence AD.

Government has policies it can use to reduce or eliminate output gaps. In Chapter 7 we will examine **fiscal policy**, the government expenditures and tax policy that establish the government's budget and its effect on aggregate demand. Government can use its fiscal policy to change the AD curve and eliminate an output gap without waiting for the economy to adjust itself. Chapters 9 and 10 discuss **monetary policy**, actions by the monetary authorities designed to change aggregate demand and eliminate output gaps by changing interest rates, money supply, and the availability of credit. Both fiscal and monetary policy work to change aggregate demand and eliminate output gaps, which reduce the standard of living the national economy provides for its citizens.

Review Questions 13 and 14

Next

In Chapter 6 we study the expenditure decisions by households and business that determine the consumption, investment, export, and import components of aggregate demand.

SUMMARY

- The **Aggregate Demand and Supply** model provides a framework for our study of the operation of the economy.
- **Aggregate Demand** is the negative relationship between planned aggregate expenditure on final goods and services and the price level, assuming money supply, interest rates, exchange rates, and all other conditions in the economy are constant.
- **Aggregate Supply** is the positive relationship between outputs of goods and services and the price level, assuming factor prices, capital stock, and technology are constant.
- **Short-Run Equilibrium Real GDP and Price** are determined by the equality of short-run Aggregate Demand and Aggregate Supply, illustrated by the intersection of the AD and AS curves.
- **Potential Output** is the output the economy can produce on an ongoing basis with given labour, capital, and technology without putting persistent upward pressure on prices or inflation rates. The corresponding unemployment rate is called the natural unemployment rate.

- **Business Cycles** are the short-run fluctuations of actual real GDP around Potential Output caused by short-run changes in Aggregate Demand and Supply.
- **Output Gaps** are the differences between actual real GDP and Potential GDP that occur during business cycles.
- **Okun's Law** makes a link between output gaps and unemployment rates. Negative output gaps cause unemployment rates that are higher than the natural unemployment rate.
- **Inflationary Gaps and Recessionary Gaps** are the terms used to describe positive and negative output gaps based on the effects the gaps have on factor prices.
- **Actual output adjusts to Potential Output** over time *if factor input and final output prices are flexible* and changes in prices shift the Aggregate Supply curve to equilibrium with Aggregate Demand at Y_P.
- **Fiscal and monetary policy** are tools governments and monetary authorities can use to speed up the economy's adjustment to output gaps.

KEY TERMS

Short run *95*
AD/AS model *95*
Aggregate Demand *95*
Planned aggregate expenditure *95*
Aggregate Supply *96*
Interest rate effect *97*
Substitution effect *97*
Wealth effect *97*
Equilibrium real GDP and price *101*
Potential output *102*
Business cycle *104*
Output gaps *104*
Inflationary gap *104*
Recessionary gap *104*
Equilibrium or natural unemployment rate *107*
Okun's Law *107*
Fiscal policy *112*
Monetary policy *112*

KEY EQUATIONS AND RELATIONS

Equations

The price level $P = \frac{W}{Y} + \frac{BI + CCA}{Y} + \frac{T_{IN}}{Y}$ **(5.1)** p. 99

The output gap $= Y - Y_P$ **(5.2)** p. 104

The output gap $= \frac{Y - Y_P}{Y_P} \times 100\%$ **(5.2a)** p. 104

Unemployment rate $u = \frac{\text{Labour force} - \text{number of people employed}}{\text{labour force}}$ **(5.3)** p. 107

Natural unemployment $u_n = \frac{\text{Labour force} - \text{equilibrium employment}}{\text{Labour force}} \times 100\%$ **(5.4)** p. 107

Change in unemployment rate $= \Delta u = -\frac{1}{2}(\text{growth rate of } Y - \text{growth rate of } Y_P)$ **(5.5)** p. 107

Relations

Aggregate demand AD: $\Delta P \rightarrow \Delta$ interest rates + Δ domestic/foreign prices + Δ real financial wealth $\rightarrow \Delta$ expenditure and real output, $(\Delta Y/\Delta P) < 0$

Aggregate supply AS: Δ real output $\rightarrow \Delta$ costs of production $\rightarrow \Delta P$, $(\Delta P/\Delta Y) > 0$

Equilibrium real GDP and price: AD = AS

Output gaps ($Y \neq Y_P$): Fluctuations in AD or AS $\rightarrow$ business cycles in Y $\rightarrow$ output gaps

Okun's Law: Output gaps $\rightarrow \Delta$ employment and unemployment, $Y < Y_P \rightarrow u > u_n$, $Y > Y_P \rightarrow u < u_n$

Adjustments to output gaps: Output gaps $\rightarrow \Delta$ wage rates $\rightarrow \Delta$ production costs $\rightarrow \Delta AS$, $Y \rightarrow Y_P$

REVIEW QUESTIONS

Review Questions and answers are included in Connect at www.mcgrawhillconnect.ca.

1. Define the Aggregate Demand curve. Explain the reasons for the negative relationship between real GDP and the price level that is described by the AD curve.

2. Define the Aggregate Supply curve. Explain the reasons why the Aggregate supply curve is upward sloping from left to right when we draw it in a diagram.

3. Suppose we have the following information for an economy:
   a. Plot the AD and AS curves in a carefully labelled diagram.
   b. What are the short-run equilibrium values of real GDP and the price level?

GDP Deflator	Planned Aggregate Expenditure	Planned Aggregate Output
90	550	150
100	500	300
110	450	450
120	400	600
130	350	750

4. Suppose research has uncovered the following aggregate demand and supply functions for an economy:
   AD: $Y = 2000 - 12P$
   AS: $P = 100 + 0.25Y$
   a. What are the short-run equilibrium values for real GDP and the price level?
   b. In a carefully labelled diagram, not necessarily to scale, draw the AD and AS functions to illustrate the short-run equilibrium real GDP and price. What are the intercepts of AD and AS with the axes in your diagram?
   c. Suppose a fall in demand for new houses reduced the investment component aggregate expenditure, and reduced AD at each price level by 100. Illustrate this change in AD in the diagram you have drawn for part b and describe the change in equilibrium real GDP and price that would result.

5. Explain what we mean by potential output (GDP). Explain why potential GDP does not depend on the price level. Is it possible that real GDP might be larger or smaller than potential GDP?

6. Potential GDP is determined by the size of the labour force, the stock of capital, and the state of technology used in the production process. If the labour force grows over time, and research and development lead to improvements in technology, what would happen to potential GDP? Use a diagram to illustrate potential GDP both before and after the growth in labour force and the improvement in technology.

7. Suppose we learn that potential output is 500 for the economy in question 3.
   a. Add a line to your diagram for question 3 to illustrate potential GDP.
   b. Does your diagram show an output gap for this economy?
   c. What is the size of any output gap you see in the diagram?
   d. If there is an output gap, is it an inflationary gap or a recessionary gap? Explain why.

8. What are the implications of differences between actual and potential GDP for the unemployment rate and the rate of utilization of factories and machinery?

9. Consider an economy described by the following:
   AD: $Y = 2250 - 10P$
   AS: $P = 125 + 0.1Y$
   a. What are the short-run equilibrium values for real GDP and the price level?
   b. Assume potential output is 500 and draw an AD/AS/Y_P diagram to show the initial short-run equilibrium real GDP, price level, and potential output.
   c. Now changes in international market conditions drive up prices for crude oil and base metals. Increased production costs driven by these higher input prices raise the general price level by five at every level of output. Write the equation of the new AS curve. What are the new short-run equilibrium real GDP and price level?
   d. Draw the new AS curve in your diagram for b. Is there now an output gap? If so what kind of gap and what size is the gap?

10. Suppose we have the following data for an economy:

Year	Potential Output (billions 02$)	Real GDP (billions 02$)
2003	1,038	1,017
2004	1,069	1,030
2005	1,101	1,101
2006	1,134	1,160
2007	1,168	1,139
2008	1,203	1,130
2009	1,240	1,187
2010	1,277	1,163

Calculate the output gap as a percent of potential output for each year in this economy. Plot the output gap in a time series diagram. Describe the timing of the phases of any business cycles you see in your plot of the output gap.

11. Okun's Law says that differences between the growth rate in potential output and the growth rate in real GDP change the unemployment rate as follows:

$$\Delta u = -\frac{1}{2}\,(gY - gY_p)$$

Based on the data in the table, calculate the annual growth rates of potential output and real GDP. If the unemployment rate in 2005 were 7.0 percent, what unemployment rate would Okun's Law predict for the years 2006, 2007, and 2008?

12. a. Construct an Aggregate Demand and Aggregate Supply diagram that shows an economy in short-run equilibrium with an inflationary gap.
    b. Explain what a persistent inflationary gap means for wage rates and other factor prices when there is enough time for factor prices to adjust.

c. In your diagram, show the effects of any change in factor prices on Aggregate Demand and Aggregate Supply conditions and on short-run equilibrium real output and price.
d. What equilibrium real output and price would you expect, based on your diagram, once factor prices have adjusted and the unemployment is at the natural rate?

13. *Internet* Visit the Bank of Canada's Web site at www.bankofcanada.ca and, using the link to "Indicators of Capacity and Inflationary Pressures," record the data provided for the output gap and the unemployment rate. Describe the relationship you see between changes in the output gap and the unemployment rate.

14. *Internet* Visit the Bank of Canada's Web site and follow the links through "Monetary Policy" to "Inflation." What are the costs of inflation and the benefits of low inflation, according to the Bank?

PART 3

Aggregate Expenditure and Output

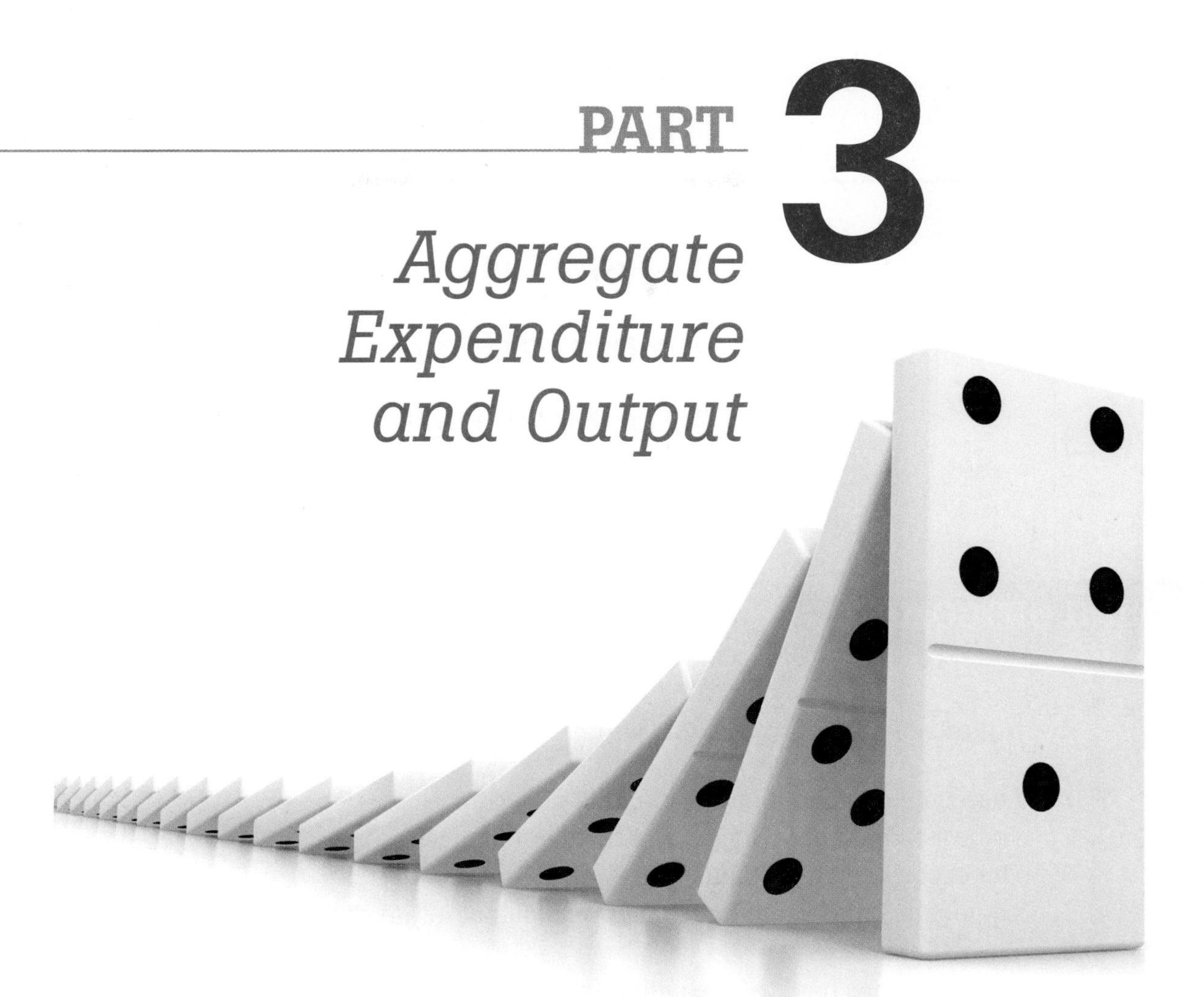

The two chapters in this part of the text examine aggregate expenditure. They explain the position of the aggregate demand function. They also show how aggregate demand determines output and incomes in the short run when factor prices and output prices are constant.

CHAPTER 6

Output, Aggregate Expenditure, and Aggregate Demand

LEARNING OUTCOMES

By the end of this chapter you should understand:

1. Aggregate demand and output in the short run
2. The consumption, saving, and investment functions
3. The export and import functions
4. Aggregate expenditure and equilibrium output in the short run
5. The multiplier
6. Leakages, injections, and equilibrium output
7. Equilibrium output and aggregate demand

In Chapter 5 we saw that real output and employment are sometimes smaller, and at other times larger, than potential output Y_P. According to our aggregate demand and aggregate supply model, short-run changes in AD and AS conditions cause these fluctuations in output. But why do AD and AS conditions fluctuate? To answer this question, we begin with a simple short-run model of the economy.

6.1 Aggregate Demand and Output in the Short Run

We concentrate first on the private market sector. Assume there are households and businesses in our simple economy, but no government. The households and businesses buy domestically produced and imported goods and services. Businesses also sell some output in export markets to residents of other countries. This model will help us to understand the mechanics that determine real output and employment and the main causes of fluctuations in real GDP. Chapter 7 will add a government sector and introduce fiscal policy. These additions will begin to make the model more realistic, but the internal mechanics will be the same. Understanding how this simple model works is key to understanding how the actual economy works.

This initial *short run* model has a number of crucial properties:

- All prices and wages are fixed at a given level.
- At these prices and wages, businesses produce the output that is demanded and labour accepts opportunities to work.
- Interest rates and foreign exchange rates are fixed because at this stage we ignore the financial sector.

Holding prices constant makes it unnecessary to analyze the supply side of the economy in detail. Total output is demand-determined. Figure 6.1 illustrates these conditions and the expenditure function we will develop.

FIGURE 6.1 **Aggregate Demand, Expenditure, and Output When Price is Constant**

When the price level is constant at P_0, the AS curve is a horizontal line and short-run equilibrium real GDP is determined by the *position* of the AD curve and its intersection with AS at point E. The upper diagram illustrates these AD/AS conditions.

The lower diagram illustrates the relationship between planned aggregate expenditure (on the vertical axis) and real GDP and Income (on the horizontal axis). The diagram shows that planned Aggregate Expenditure (AE) is positively related to real income and output. It also shows that when planned aggregate expenditure is equal to real GDP, as it is at point E', the economy is in short-run equilibrium. This short-run equilibrium level of planned expenditure at the price P_0 determines the position of the AD curve.

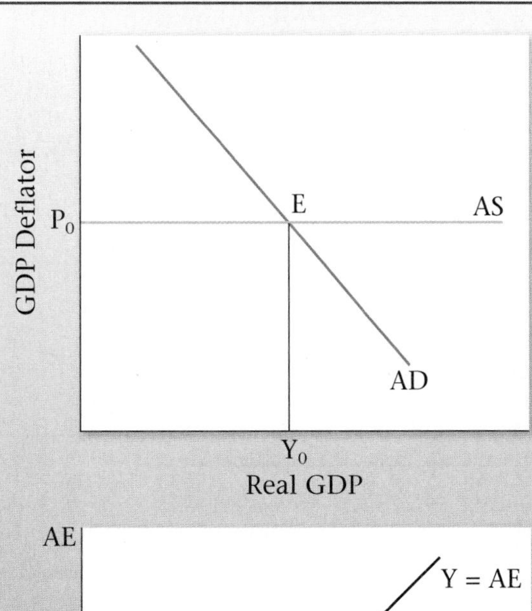

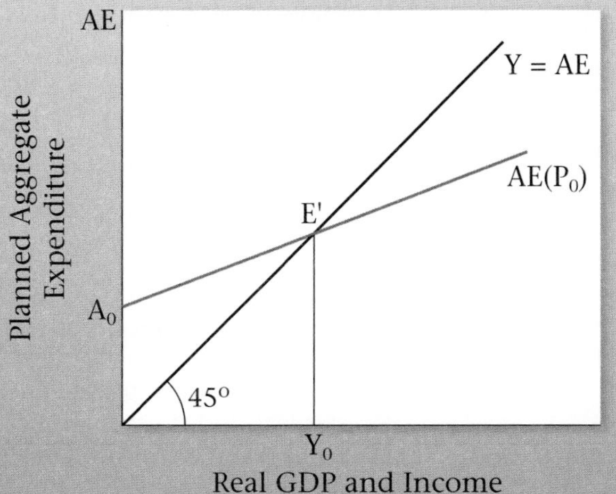

The horizontal AS curve in the upper part of Figure 6.1 shows that the price level is fixed at P_0, as we have assumed. As a result, the equilibrium real GDP in this example is determined by the *position* of the AD curve. Changes in the position of the AD curve would cause changes in real output and real income, and corresponding changes in employment. But what determines the position of the AD curve? Those things, *other than price,* that establish expenditure. Understanding these factors is the focus of this and the next several chapters.

The lower part of Figure 6.1 offers the first answer. It shows the relationship between planned aggregate expenditure and *income* when the price level is fixed. It also shows that, if the aggregate expenditure function (AE) has the right position and slope, there is a level of output at which planned expenditure and output are equal. This equality between planned expenditure and output determines the position of the AD curve. We begin our study of the interactions of expenditure, output, and income under simple conditions in this chapter. The relationships in the lower part of Figure 6.1 are the starting point.

Later we will introduce financial markets and relax the assumption that prices, wages, interest rates, and exchange rates are fixed. Not only do we want to study inflation; we also want to examine how quickly market forces acting through changes in prices and wages can eliminate unemployment and spare capacity and move the economy to potential output. We had a first look at that process in Chapter 5, and will examine it in detail in Chapter 13.

6.2 Consumption, Saving, and Investment

Chapter 4 introduced the circular flow of income payments between households and business. Business pays incomes to households to buy factor inputs. Households use income to buy the output of business, providing business revenue. Business revenue is ultimately returned to households as factor incomes. We now build a simple model of this interaction between households and business.

Aggregate expenditure (AE) is the sum of planned expenditure in the economy.

Aggregate expenditure is the sum of planned consumption expenditure by households, investment expenditure by business, and expenditure by residents of other countries on exports of domestic output, minus the imports contained in all these planned expenditures on goods and services. Using **AE** to denote aggregate expenditure, **C** for consumption expenditure, **I** for investment expenditure, **X** for exports, and **Z** for imports,

$$AE = C + I + X - Z \quad (6.1)$$

Consumption expenditures, investment expenditures, and expenditures on exports of domestic output and imported goods and services are made by different groups and depend on different things. To establish the underlying sources of aggregate expenditure we examine each of its components in more detail.

CONSUMPTION EXPENDITURE

Disposable income is income net of taxes and transfers.

Households buy goods and services ranging from food to cars, to movie tickets to Internet services and downloads of music and video. These consumption purchases account for about 90 percent of disposable income. **Disposable income** is the income households receive from business, plus transfer payments received from governments, minus direct taxes paid to governments. It is the net income households can either spend or save.

FIGURE 6.2 **The Consumption Function in Canada 1961 to 2007**

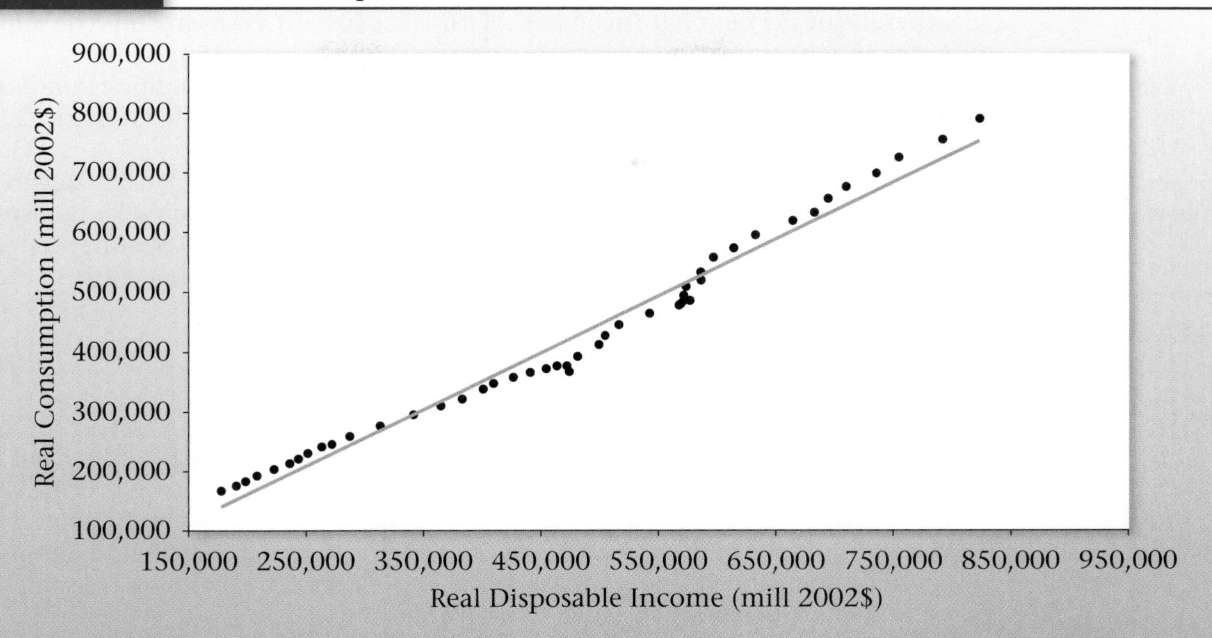

A scatter diagram of annual data illustrates the relationship between real disposable income and real consumption expenditure in Canada. We know from Chapter 4 that consumption expenditure is the largest component of real GDP measured by the expenditure approach. The slope of the line drawn in the diagram, which passes close to the data points, tell us that a $1 increase in real disposable income results in an increase in real consumption expenditure of about $0.90.

Source: Statistics Canada, CANSIM II, Series V3860062, V498186, and V1997738.

With no government, disposable income is simply the income households receive from business firms. Given its disposable income, each household decides how much to spend and how much to save. Deciding one decides the other. Some families save part of their disposable income; others spend more and borrow. Many things affect consumption and saving decisions. We will examine some of these in later chapters. To get started, one simplification takes us a long way. We assume that *aggregate* consumption expenditure rises with *aggregate* disposable income.

Figure 6.2 shows annual data for real consumption expenditure and real disposable income in Canada. Because the scatter of points lies close to a line summarizing this relationship, our simplification is helpful. Nevertheless, the points do not lie exactly along the line. Our simplification omits some other influences on consumption expenditure that we take up later.

This positive relationship between disposable income and consumption expenditure we see in Figure 6.2 is called the **consumption function**.

The **consumption function** explains consumption expenditure at each level of disposable income.

The consumption function tells us how disposable income Y and consumption expenditure C are related. If C_0 is a positive constant, and c is a positive fraction between zero and one,

$$C = C_0 + cY \qquad (6.2)$$

Our model has no government, no transfer payments, and no taxes. Personal disposable income equals national income. Equation 6.2 then relates consumption expenditure to national income Y. With c a constant fraction, the consumption function is a straight line.

Autonomous expenditure is expenditure not related to current income.

The intercept is C_0. We call this *autonomous* consumption expenditure. **Autonomous expenditure** is not related to current income. Households wish to consume C_0 based on things other than income, even if income Y is zero.

The **marginal propensity to consume (MPC)** is the change in consumption expenditure caused by a change in income.

Induced expenditure is expenditure determined by national income.

The slope of the consumption function is the **marginal propensity to consume.** The marginal propensity to consume is the fraction of each extra dollar of disposable income that households wish to spend on consumption. It determines the change in consumption expenditure *caused by* a change in income. We call this **induced expenditure**, and write,

$$\Delta C/\Delta Y = MPC$$

Table 6.1 and Figure 6.3 illustrate these relationships. Autonomous consumption expenditure, $C_0 = 20$ in the numerical example, determines vertical intercept of the function in the diagram. The marginal propensity to consume, $c = 0.8$, is the slope of the function. You can see in the table that an increase in income by 50 induces an increase in consumption expenditure by 40, which is 0.8×50. A change in autonomous consumption expenditure would shift the entire function, changing consumption at every level of income.

SAVING

Saving is income not consumed. Figure 6.3(a) and Equation 6.2 imply that when income Y is zero, saving is $-C_0$. Households are dissaving, borrowing, or running down their assets.

The **marginal propensity to save (MPS)** is the change in saving caused by a change in income.

Since a fraction c of each dollar of extra income is consumed, a fraction $(1 - c)$ of each extra dollar of income is saved. The **marginal propensity to save** ($MPS = \Delta S/\Delta Y$) is $(1 - c)$. Since an extra dollar of income leads either to extra planned

TABLE 6.1 **The Consumption Function: A Numerical Example**

The consumption function: $C = C_0 + cY$
For example: $C = 20 + 0.8Y$

Y	C	ΔC/ΔY	S = Y − C	ΔS/ΔY
0	20	—	−20	—
50	60	0.8	−10	0.2
100	100	0.8	0	0.2
150	140	0.8	10	0.2
200	180	0.8	20	0.2

FIGURE 6.3 **The Consumption Function**

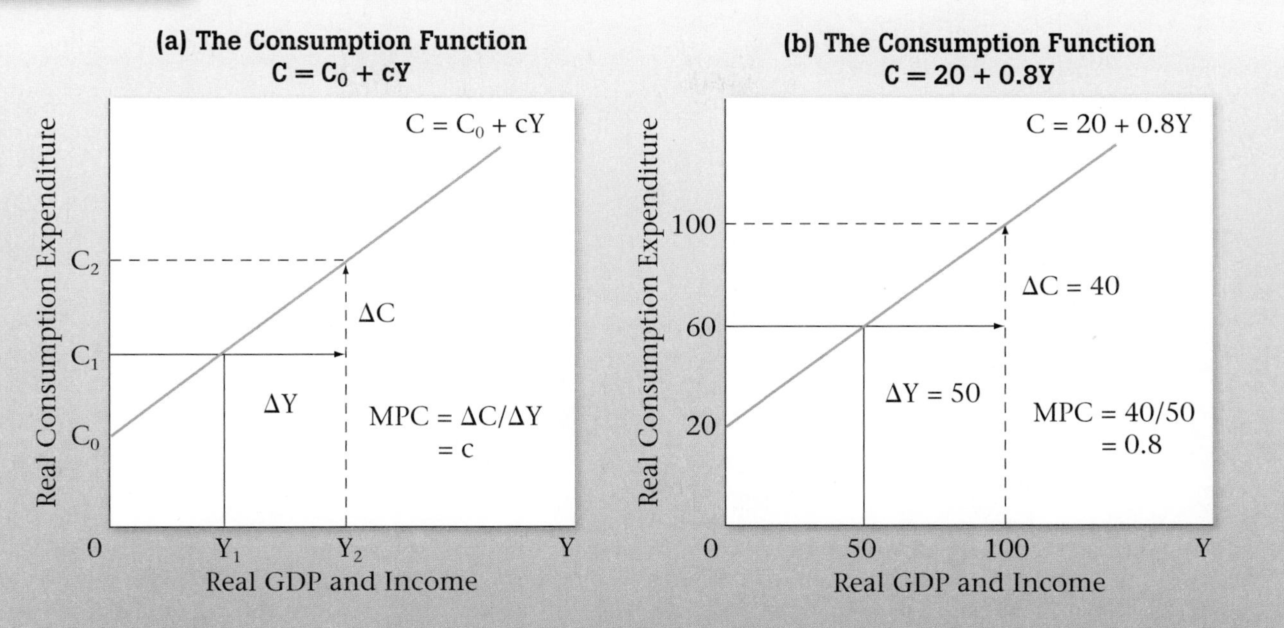

The consumption function shows aggregate consumption expenditure at each real national income. When income is zero, autonomous consumption is C_0 in panel (a) or 20 in panel (b), where the consumption function intersects the vertical axis. At higher income Y_1 consumption is higher at C_1, moving along the consumption function. The marginal propensity to consume is the change in consumption expenditure caused by a change in income. In the diagrams it is the slope of the line $\Delta C/\Delta Y$: c in panel (a) or 0.8 in panel (b).

consumption or extra planned saving, MPC + MPS = 1. Figure 6.4 shows the **saving function** corresponding to the consumption function in Figure 6.3.

The **saving function** shows planned saving at each level of income.

Note that, using Equation 6.2 and the definition $Y \equiv C + S$, and $S = Y - C$ so the saving function shown in Figure 6.4. It must be

$$S = -C_0 + (1 - c)Y \qquad (6.3)$$

Adding Equations 6.2 and 6.3, the left-hand side gives planned consumption plus planned saving, and the right-hand side gives income, Y, as it should. Planned saving is the part of income not planned to be spent on consumption.

When using diagrams, we make an important distinction between events that move the economy along the consumption and saving functions as opposed to events that shift the consumption and saving functions. A change in income causes a *movement along* the consumption and saving functions, and changes in consumption expenditure and saving are determined by the MPC and the MPS. These are changes in expenditure and saving plans *induced* by changes in income. Any change other than a change in income that changes consumption and saving at every income level causes a *shift* in the consumption and saving functions. These changes in expenditure and saving plans are *autonomous*, caused by something other than changes in income. They might be caused

FIGURE 6.4 **The Saving Function**

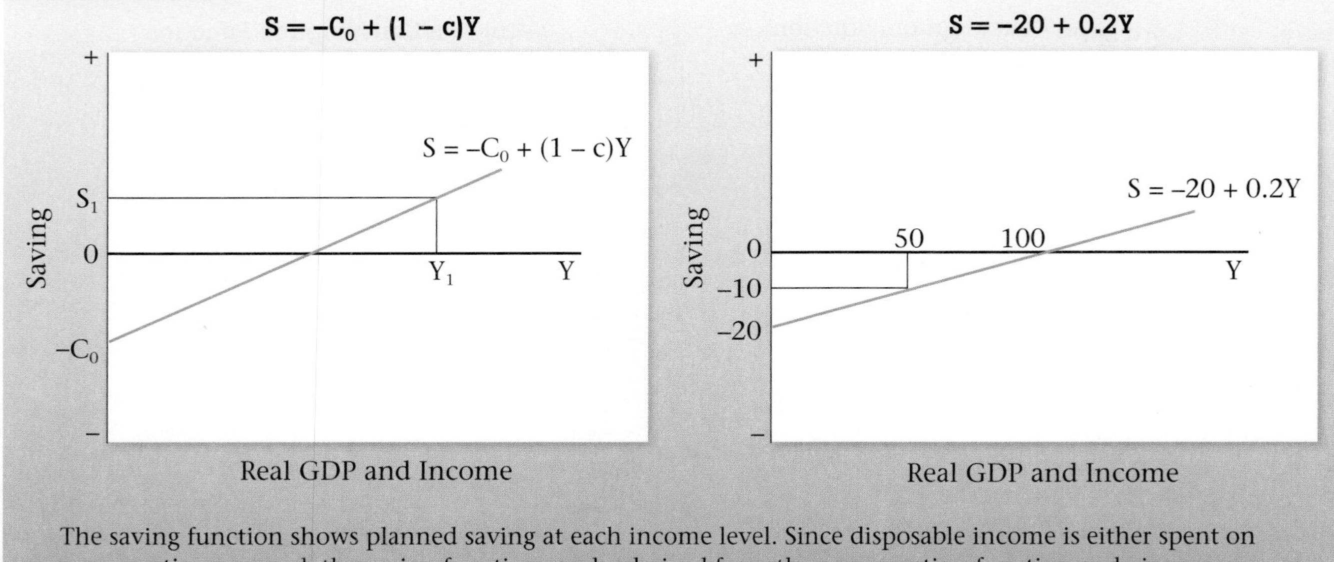

The saving function shows planned saving at each income level. Since disposable income is either spent on consumption or saved, the saving function can be derived from the consumption function and vice versa. The saving functions in this diagram are derived from the consumption functions in Table 6.1 and Figure 6.3

Review Questions 1 and 2

by changes in confidence and expectations about the future state of the economy; by changes in household financial wealth, interest rates, and house prices; by changes in demographics; or by changes in government policy.

We also identify a limited number of changes in the economy that will change the slopes of the consumption and saving functions. These events are of special interest because, as we will see shortly, the slope of the consumption function—and the household expenditure behaviour it describes—is one key to our understanding of fluctuations in real output.

Consumption expenditure plays a special role in our model because it is the largest and most stable component of expenditure.

INVESTMENT EXPENDITURE

Income is the key determinant of household consumption or spending plans as described by the consumption function. What about the factors determining investment decisions by business firms?

Investment expenditure (I) is business expenditure on current output to add to physical capital (factories and machinery) and to inventories.

Investment expenditure (I) is planned additions by business to their stock of fixed capital (factories and machinery) and to inventories. Business capacity to produce goods and services depends on the numbers and sizes of factories and machinery they operate and the technology embodied in that capital. Inventories of raw materials, component inputs, and final goods for sale allow firms to maintain a steady flow of output and supply of goods to customers. Firms' investment expenditure on fixed capital depends chiefly on their current *expectations* about how fast the demand for their output will increase and the *expected profitability* of higher future output. Sometimes output is high and rising; sometimes it is high and falling. Since there is no close connection between the current *level* of output and firms' expectations about

FIGURE 6.5 **The Investment Function**

Planned investment expenditure by business is *autonomous*, independent of national income. In the diagram it is shown as a horizontal line. With the assumption that the interest rate i_0 is constant, investment is equal to I_0 at every income level. Planned investment expenditure is the new plant and equipment and new level of inventories business thinks will be required for the production of future levels of output. Any change in business expectations of future output, or in the interest rate, will change planned investment and *shift the I line vertically* in the diagram.

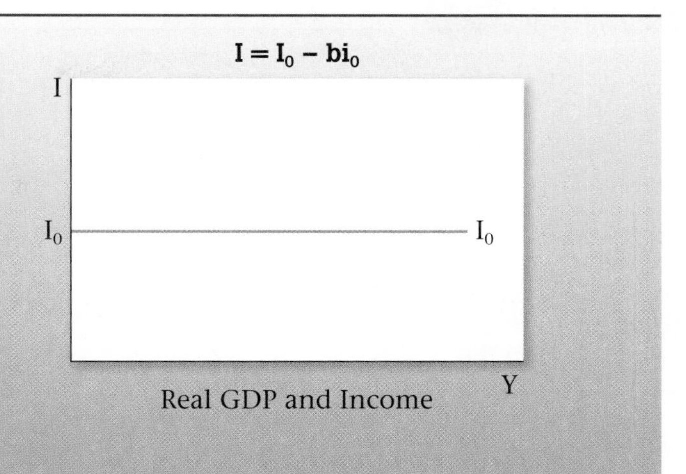

how demand for their output is going to *change*, we make a simple assumption that investment expenditure is autonomous. Planned investment I is independent of current output and income.

However, the interest rates determined by conditions in financial markets do affect investment decisions. For the moment we are assuming interest rates are constant. But it will be important to understand that interest rates are the *cost of financing* investment expenditure and of carrying inventories.

Higher interest rates reduce investment expenditure and lower interest rates raise investment expenditure. After we study financial markets and interest rates in Chapter 9 we will drop the assumption of constant interest rates and bring interest rates into the investment decision.

For now, with interest rates constant at i_0, we can write the investment function as

$$I = I_0 - bi_0 \qquad (6.4)$$

Figure 6.5 shows this investment function. For a given level of interest rates and business expectations about future markets and profits, it is a horizontal line that intersects the vertical axis at I_0. Any change in business firms' expectations about future markets or the interest rate or any other conditions that cause a change in their investment plans would *shift* the investment line in Figure 6.5 up or down, but leave its slope unchanged at zero.

Investment, unlike consumption, is a volatile component of expenditure. Changes in business expectations about future markets and profits happen frequently. New technologies and products, like hybrid automobiles, "clean" diesel engines, biofuels, LED televisions, advanced medical diagnostic processes, and "green" building products lead to the investment in factories to produce these products and the infrastructure to use them. Investment expenditures increase. A sudden uncertainty about safety reduces demand for plastic products in food and beverage packaging. Investment in new capacity to produce these products drops and a search for new packaging begins. Increased gasoline prices reduce the demand for large cars and trucks, leading some auto manufacturers to close plants and cut investment spending. More recently, sharp drops in prices for conventional energy and difficult financial market conditions have led to the postponement and cancellation of large investments in both conventional and

FIGURE 6.6 **Annual Percentage Change in Real Consumption, Investment, and Exports: Canada 1987 to 2008**

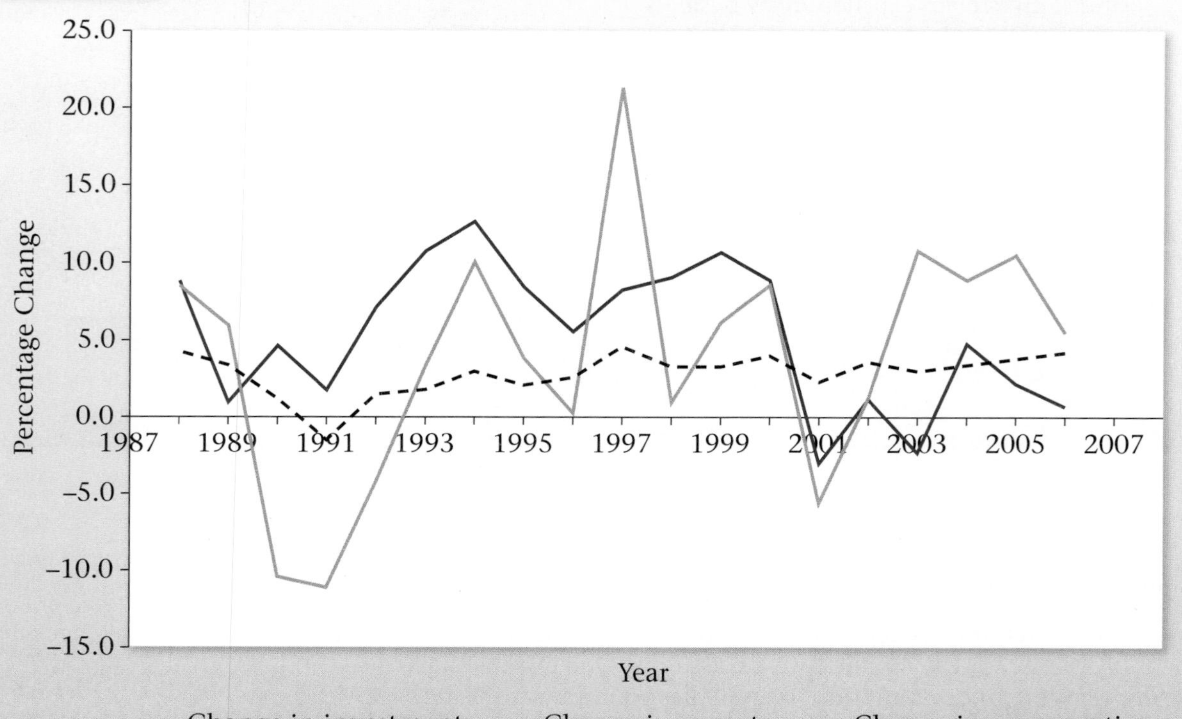

A plot of the annual percent changes in consumption, investment, and exports shows the greater volatility of expenditure on investment and exports compared to consumption.

Source: Statistics Canada, CANSIM Series V1992115, V1992053, V1992056, V1992060, V1992067 and author's calculations.

alternative energy projects. Fluctuations in investment in Canada caused by these factors are illustrated in Figure 6.6.

6.3 The Export and Import Functions

Exports, X, are domestic goods and services sold to residents of other countries.

Imports, Z, are goods and services bought from other countries.

Net exports, NX, measure the difference between exports and imports.

Our **exports**, X, are the goods and services produced at home but sold to residents of other countries. Our **imports**, Z, are goods and services produced in other countries but bought by domestic residents. Exports and imports each amounted to between 30 and 40 percent of GDP in 2008. **Net exports**, $NX = X - Z$, is the difference between exports and imports, which is the net effect of international trade on aggregate expenditure.

Canada is a very open economy. In the United States, by comparison, exports and imports make up only 10 to 15 percent of GDP. International trade is much more important to aggregate expenditure in Canada and most European countries than in a very large country with diverse regions like the United States, which trades mostly internally.

Exports are a part of *autonomous* aggregate expenditure. Canadian exports are not determined by Canadian national income. Instead they depend on income levels in other countries, price levels here and in those countries, and the foreign exchange rate. The **foreign exchange rate** is the domestic currency price of a unit of foreign currency. This is the price people pay to buy the U.S. dollars they want to cover travel costs in the U.S. It is also the amount of Canadian dollar revenue a Canadian exporter receives for each $1.00U.S. of exports sales to U.S. buyers. In early 2008 our exchange rate, the Canadian dollar price of the United States dollar, was $0.995Cdn for $1.00U.S.

The **foreign exchange rate** is the domestic currency price of foreign currency.

With our assumption that prices and exchange rates are constant, the price competitiveness and profitability of Canadian exports is fixed. Changes in national incomes in export markets will cause changes in our exports. A recession in the United States, for example, reduces demand for Canadian exports of raw materials, energy, and manufactured goods like automobiles, as was the case in 2008 and 2009. Previously, strong growth in U.S. real GDP created strong demand for Canadian exports. Canadian exports to other parts of the world, such as China and India, are driven by GDP and GDP growth in those countries.

However, as we will see in later chapters, changes in economic and financial conditions change exchange rates. The competitiveness and profitability of exports change as a result. In Canada between 2002 and 2007 the exchange rate fell, lowering the Canadian dollar price of the United States dollar from $1.58Cdn to $0.98Cdn for $1.00U.S. A U.S. dollar of sales revenue from exports that provided $1.58 in Canadian dollar revenue in 2002 brought just $0.98 in Canadian dollar revenue in 2007. In the earlier period, 1995 to 2001, the rise in the exchange rate made Canadian exports very competitive and profitable, supporting strong export growth. Subsequently, the fall in the exchange rate caused a difficult market and competitive conditions for manufactured exports.

For now, assuming exchange rates are constant and letting X_0 be autonomous exports, the export function is

$$X = X_0 \tag{6.5}$$

Exports, like investment, can be a volatile component of aggregate expenditure. Changes in economic conditions in other countries, changes in tastes and preferences across countries, changes in trade policies, and the emergence of new national competitors in world markets all impact on the demand for domestic exports. To illustrate this volatility in exports and in investment, Figure 6.6 shows the year-to-year changes in investment, exports, and consumption expenditures in Canada from 1987 to 2008. You can see how changes in investment and exports were much larger than those in consumption. This volatility in investment and exports appears as up and down shifts in the functions in Figures 6.5 and 6.7.

Imports are part of domestic expenditure. Like consumption expenditure, imports rise when national income rises and fall when national income falls. Goods and services bought by households and business are a mix of domestic output and imports. Exports of goods and services embody imported components and services. Some imports are *autonomous*; that is, independent of current income. Changes in autonomous consumption, investment, and exports include changes in autonomous imports. Some changes in imports are *induced* by changes in income through the **marginal propensity to import** (MPZ). The MPZ is a positive fraction, reflecting the fact that a rise in income causes an increase in induced expenditure, including induced imports.

The **marginal propensity to import (MPZ)** is the change in imports caused by a change in national income.

Imports also depend on domestic and foreign prices and the foreign exchange rate. The recent fall in the Canada–United States exchange rate resulted in strong increases in cross-border shopping and travel by Canadian residents. In earlier years the high

FIGURE 6.7 **Exports and Imports**

Exports are autonomous at X = 100. Imports increase from an autonomous level of 40 as income increases, according to the marginal propensity to import z = 0.20, the slope of the import function. At income levels less than 300, exports exceed imports and the net effect of international trade on aggregate expenditure is positive. Above income of 300 the net effect is negative as higher incomes have caused a rise in imports to levels greater than exports.

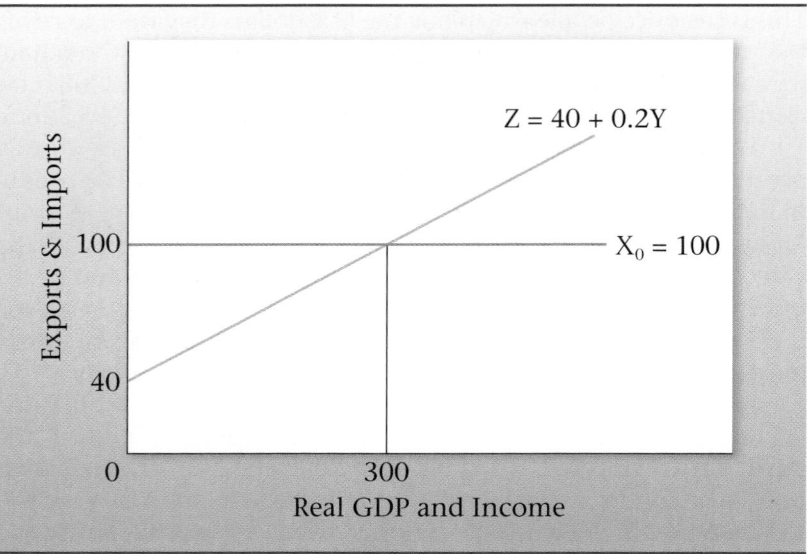

exchange rate raised prices of imports to Canada. Higher costs in Canadian dollars for U.S. goods, travel, and tourist services reduced cross-border travel by Canadians and imports from the United States.

Using $\mathbf{Z_0}$ for autonomous imports and **z** for the marginal propensity to import ($\Delta Z/\Delta Y$), and assuming constant exchange rates, the import function is

$$Z = Z_0 + zY \tag{6.6}$$

Figure 6.7 shows expenditure on exports and imports at different levels of national income. Assume for purposes of illustration that $X_0 = 100$. The export function with a vertical intercept of 100 is a horizontal line because exports are autonomous. Autonomous imports are $Z_0 = 40$ when national income is zero, and rise as national income rises. The slope of the import function is the marginal propensity to import (MPZ) with z = 0.2. A change in national income of $1 changes imports by $0.20.

The difference between exports and imports at each level of national income is the net export level. At low income levels, imports are low and net exports are positive. At higher income levels, higher imports result in negative net exports. The marginal propensities to import and consume play very important roles in the operation of the economy through the induced changes in aggregate expenditure they generate.

6.4 Aggregate Expenditure and Equilibrium Output in the Short Run

The **aggregate expenditure function (AE)** is the relationship between planned expenditure in the total economy and real national income or GDP.

Aggregate expenditure is the amount firms and households *plan to spend* on currently produced final goods and services at each level of national income. The **aggregate expenditure function** (AE) is the relationship between planned expenditure in the total economy and real national income or GDP. Table 6.2 and Figure 6.8 together show the aggregate expenditure function in terms of numerical examples and diagrams.

TABLE 6.2 **The Aggregate Expenditure Function: A Numerical Example**

Consumption function:	$C = 20 + 0.8Y$
Investment function:	$I = 20$
Export function:	$X = 50$
Import function:	$Z = 10 + 0.2Y$
Aggregate expenditure:	$AE = C + I + X - Z = 80 + 0.6Y$

Y	C	I	X	Z	AE = C + I + X − Z
0	20	20	50	10	80
100	100	20	50	30	140
150	140	20	50	40	170
200	180	20	50	50	200
250	220	20	50	60	230

Aggregate expenditure AE, as defined above and earlier in Equation 6.1 on page 120, is:

$$AE = C + I + X - Z \tag{6.1}$$

In Table 6.2 and Figure 6.8, the *aggregate expenditure function* is derived using this equation. Aggregate expenditure is different at different income levels because of induced expenditure on consumption and imports. Aggregate expenditure changes by $(c - z)$ times any change in income. ($\Delta AE = \Delta C - \Delta Z = c\Delta Y - z\Delta Y$). In the Figure the vertical intercept of AE is the sum of autonomous expenditure. The slope of AE is $(c - z)$, the marginal propensity to consume minus the marginal propensity to import.

Many things other than income influence autonomous expenditure. It is not fixed, but it is independent of income. The AE function separates the change in expenditure directly induced by changes in income from changes caused by other sources. All other sources of changes in aggregate expenditure are shown as *shifts* of the AE line. If firms get more optimistic about future demand and invest more, autonomous expenditure rises. The new AE line that results is parallel to, but higher than, the old AE line. Similarly, a change in exports shifts the AE line up or down without changing its slope as exports either increase or decrease.

EQUILIBRIUM OUTPUT

Output is said to be in **short-run equilibrium** when planned aggregate expenditure (AE) equals the current output of goods and services (Y). Spending plans are not frustrated by a shortage of goods and services. Nor do business firms make more output than they can sell. In short-run equilibrium, output equals the total of goods and services that households, businesses, and residents of other countries want to buy. Real GDP is determined by aggregate expenditure.

Short-run equilibrium output: Aggregate expenditure equals current output.

Figure 6.9 shows income on the horizontal axis and aggregate spending on the vertical axis. It also includes a 45° line labelled $Y = AE$, along which quantities measured on the horizontal axis (Y) and vertical axis (AE) are equal. This 45° line has a slope of 1.

The AE function in Figure 6.9 starts from a positive intercept on the vertical axis to show autonomous aggregate expenditure, and has a slope which is less than one and

FIGURE 6.8 **Aggregate Expenditure**

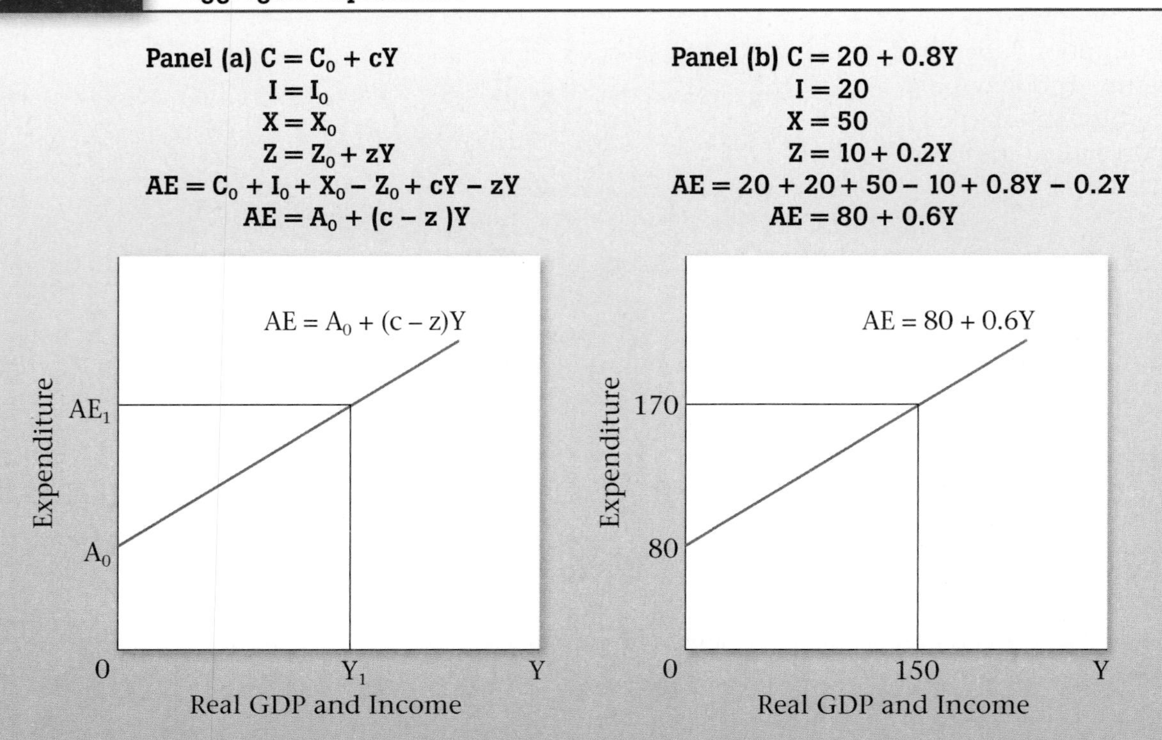

Aggregate expenditure is planned expenditure by households on consumption, business on investment, residents of other countries on exports minus domestic expenditure on imports. Parts of these expenditures are *autonomous*, independent of the level of income. The vertical intercepts of the AE lines at A_0 and 80 in the diagrams illustrate this expenditure. Some of consumption and imports is also *induced* expenditure, which depends on income and changes when income changes. The slopes of the AE lines reflect this induced expenditure. In the diagram of panel (b) autonomous expenditure is 80. Induced expenditure, based on the marginal propensity to consume minus the marginal propensity to import, is $(0.6) \times 150 = 90$. Aggregate expenditure is $AE = 170$ at $Y = 150$.

equal to $(c - z)$. This positive intercept and slope less than 1 means that the AE line crosses the 45° line at E. On the 45° line, the value of output (and income) on the horizontal axis equals the value of expenditure on the vertical axis, as required by the national accounts framework. Since E is the only point on the AE line also on the 45° line, it is the only point at which output and *planned* expenditure are equal. It is the equilibrium point.

Figure 6.9 shows equilibrium output at E. Firms produce Y_e. That output is equal to income. At income Y_e, the AE function tells us the demand for goods and services is $AE_e = Y_e$. At E, planned expenditure on currently produced final goods and services is exactly equal to the output of current goods and services produced by business.

At any other output, output is not equal to aggregate expenditure. Suppose, in the diagram, that output and incomes are only Y_1. Aggregate expenditure at D exceeds actual output as measured at B. There is excess demand. Aggregate spending plans cannot be realized at this output level. Consumption and export plans will be realized only if business fails to meet its investment plans as a result of an *unplanned fall in inventories* of goods.

Figure 6.9 shows that, for all outputs below the equilibrium output Y_e, aggregate expenditure exceeds income and output. The AE line lies above the 45° line along

FIGURE 6.9 **The 45° Diagram and Equilibrium Output**

The 45° line reflects any value on the horizontal axis onto the same value on the vertical axis. The point E at which the AE line crosses the 45° line is the only point at which aggregate expenditure is equal to output and income. Hence E is the *equilibrium* point, at which *planned* expenditure equals actual output and income.

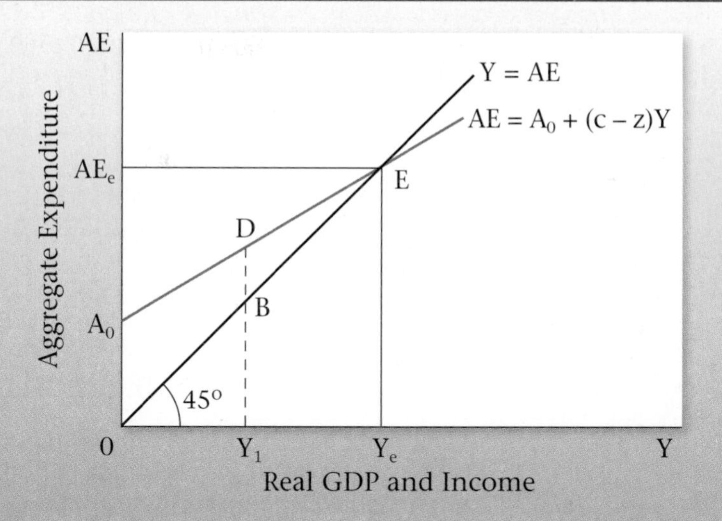

which expenditure and output are equal. Conversely, at all outputs above the equilibrium output Y_e aggregate expenditure is less than output. Businesses have unwanted and *unplanned increases in inventories* of unsold goods.

We can also find equilibrium output using the consumption function (equation 6.2), the investment function (equation 6.4), the export function (equation 6.5), the import function equation 6.6), and the equilibrium condition Y = AE. We have:

$$AE = C + I + X - Z \quad (6.1)$$
$$C = C_0 + cY \quad (6.2)$$
$$I = I_0 \quad (6.4)$$
$$X = X_0 \quad (6.5)$$
$$Z = Z_0 + zY \quad (6.6)$$

Using the equilibrium condition Y = AE and solving for Y gives:

$$Y = C + I + X - Z$$
$$Y = C_0 + cY + I_0 + X_0 - Z_0 - zY$$
$$Y - cY + zY = C_0 + I_0 + X_0 = Z_0$$
$$Y(1 - c + z) = C_0 + I_0 + X_0 - Z_0$$
$$Y_e = \frac{(C_0 + I_0 + X_0 - Z_0)}{(1 - c + z)} = \frac{A_0}{1 - c + z} \quad (6.7)$$

This is the equilibrium output Y_e we found using the diagram in Figure 6.9. From the numerical example in Table 6.2 we have:

$$C = 20 + 0.8Y$$
$$I = 20$$
$$X = 50$$
$$Z = 10 + 0.2Y$$
$$AE = 20 + 0.8Y + 20 + 50 - 10 - 0.2Y$$
$$AE = 80 + 0.6Y$$

Using the equilibrium condition Y = AE and solving for Y gives:

$$Y = 80 + 0.6Y$$
$$Y - 0.6Y = 80$$
$$Y = \frac{80}{(1 - 0.6)}$$
$$Y_e = 200$$

Review Questions 3 and 4

When we look back at Table 6.2 (page 129), we do see that aggregate expenditure and income are equal when income is 200. You can construct a diagram like Figure 6.9 using the numerical values for aggregate expenditure in Table 6.2 and a 45° line to show equilibrium $Y_e = 200$.

ADJUSTMENT TOWARDS EQUILIBRIUM

Unplanned changes in business inventories cause adjustments in output that move the economy to equilibrium output. Suppose in Figure 6.9 the economy begins with an output Y_1, below equilibrium output Y_e. Aggregate expenditure is greater than output Y_1. If firms have inventories from previous production, they can sell more than they have produced by running down inventories for a while. Note that this fall in inventories is unplanned. Planned changes in inventories are already included in planned investment and aggregate expenditure.

If firms cannot meet planned aggregate expenditure by unplanned inventory reductions, they must turn away customers. Either response—unplanned inventory reductions or turning away customers—is a signal to firms that aggregate expenditure is greater than current output, markets are strong, and output and sales can be increased profitably. Hence, at *any* output below Y_e, aggregate expenditure exceeds output and firms get signals from unwanted inventory reductions to raise output.

Conversely, if output is initially above the equilibrium level, Figure 6.9 shows that output will exceed aggregate expenditure. Producers cannot sell all their current output. *Unplanned and unwanted additions to inventories* result, and firms respond by cutting output. In recent years, North American auto producers found demand for their cars and trucks was less than they expected. Inventories of new cars and trucks built up on factory and dealer lots. Producers responded by lowering production to try to reduce excess inventory. In general terms, when the economy is producing more than current aggregate expenditure, unwanted inventories build up and output is cut back.

Review Questions 5 and 6

Hence, when output is below the equilibrium level, firms raise output. When output is above the equilibrium level, firms reduce output. At the equilibrium output Y_e, firms sell their current output and there are no unplanned changes to their inventories. Firms have no incentive to change output.

EQUILIBRIUM OUTPUT AND EMPLOYMENT

In the examples of short-run equilibrium we have discussed, output is at Y_e with output equal to planned expenditure. Firms sell all they produce, and households and firms buy all they plan to buy. But it is important to note that nothing guarantees that equilibrium output Y_e is the level of potential output Y_P. When wages and prices are fixed, the economy can end up at a short-run equilibrium below potential output with no forces present to move output to potential output. Furthermore, we know that, when output is below potential output, employment is less than full and the unemployment rate u is higher than the natural rate u_n. The economy is in recession and *by our current assumptions* neither price flexibility nor government policy action can affect these conditions.

6.5 The Multiplier: Changes in Aggregate Expenditure and Equilibrium Output

In our model the slope of the AE line depends on the marginal propensity to consume and the marginal propensity to import. For any given MPC and MPZ, the level of autonomous expenditure ($C_0 + I_0 + X_0 - Z_0$) determines the height of the AE line. Recall that autonomous expenditure is expenditure that is not related to national income.

Changes in autonomous expenditure cause parallel vertical shifts in the AE function. Investment expenditure depends chiefly on firms' current expectations about future demand for their output and future profits. These expectations about the size and strength of future markets can fluctuate significantly, influenced by current pessimism or optimism about the future. We saw this volatility in investment in Figure 6.6. Similarly, changes in conditions in export markets change exports and changes in consumer confidence change autonomous consumption expenditure.

Suppose firms become very optimistic about future demand for their output. They want to expand their factories and add new equipment to meet this future demand. Planned investment rises. If other components of aggregate expenditure are unaffected, AE will be higher at each income than before. Figure 6.10 shows this upward shift in AE to AE_1. Before we go into detail, think about what is likely to happen to output. It will rise, but by how much?

FIGURE 6.10 **The Effect of a Rise in Investment Expenditure**

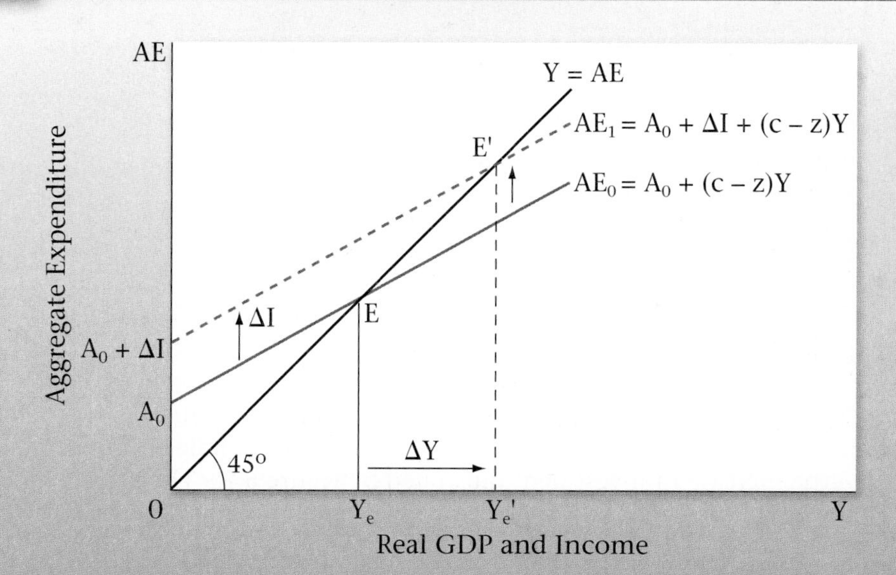

When investment rises, the AE line shifts up from AE_0 to AE_1, the amount of the rise in investment, ΔI. Equilibrium income rises by a larger amount, from Y_e to Y_e'.

When investment rises, firms increase output, increasing their payments for factor inputs to production. Households have higher income and increase their consumption expenditure ($c\Delta Y$) and imports ($z\Delta Y$). Firms increase output again to meet this increased demand, further increasing household incomes. Consumption and imports rise further. What brings this process of rising output and income to an end?

Figure 6.10 shows that an upward shift in the AE function increases equilibrium income by a finite amount, but by a larger amount than the vertical rise in the AE line. This is because $(c - z)$, the slope of AE, is less than unity, giving the AE line a lower slope than the 45° line. Households increase their expenditure when incomes rise, but they increase expenditure by less than the rise in income. Equilibrium moves from E to E'. Equilibrium output rises more than the original rise in investment, $\Delta Y_e > \Delta I$, but does not rise without limit.

We can also show the change in equilibrium output caused by a rise in autonomous investment expenditure using the simple algebra we used earlier. As before, start with:

Consumption:	$C = 20 + 0.8Y$
Investment:	$I = 20$
Exports:	$X = 50$
Imports:	$Z = 10 + 0.2Y$
Aggregate expenditure:	$AE = C + I + X - Z$
	$AE = 80 + 0.6Y$

Then, equilibrium requires output (Y) equal to aggregate expenditure (AE):

$$Y = 80 + 0.6Y$$
$$(1 - 0.6)Y = 80$$
$$Y = \frac{80}{(1 - 0.6)}$$
$$Y = 200$$

Now suppose investment increases to $I = 30$ and AE increases to

$$AE = 90 + 0.6Y$$

Equilibrium still requires output (Y) equal to aggregate expenditure (AE), but now:

$$Y = 90 + 0.6Y$$
$$(1 - 0.6)Y = 90$$
$$Y = \frac{90}{(1 - 0.6)}$$
$$Y = 225$$

A rise in autonomous investment expenditure by 10 has increased equilibrium output and income by 25, from 200 to 225. This is an algebraic example of the effect of the increase in investment illustrated by Figure 6.10. The algebra gives us the equilibrium output under two different levels of autonomous investment expenditure. But it does not show us the adjustment process.

Table 6.3 gives an illustration of the process starting with the numerical values from Table 6.2 (page 129).

If the original investment demand is $I = 20$, the first row of Table 6.3 shows the original equilibrium output is 200, since consumption is $180 = (20 + 160)$ and

TABLE 6.3 **Adjustment to a Rise in Investment Expenditure**

	Y	I	C = 20 + 0.8Y	X	Z = 10 + 0.2Y	AE	Y − AE	Unplanned Inventory Change	Output
Step 1	200	20	180	50	50	200	0	zero	constant
Step 2	200	30	180	50	50	210	−10	falling	rising
Step 3	210	30	188	50	52	216	−6	falling	rising
Step 4	216	30	192.8	50	54	222	−2.8	falling	rising
New Equilibrium	225	30	200	50	55	225	0	zero	constant

investment expenditure is 20, exports are 50, and imports are 50 = (10 + 40). Thus, aggregate expenditure just equals actual output. There is no unplanned change in inventories.

In Step 2, investment rises by 10 to 30. Firms did not expect aggregate expenditure to change and still produce 200. Output falls short of aggregate expenditure by 10. Firms have produced less than current aggregate expenditure, resulting in an unplanned fall in inventories of 10. Firms increase output to 210, their observed level of expenditure, so this inventory change won't happen again.

Step 3 shows firms making 210, the level of planned expenditure in Step 2. But when firms raise output, income rises. Step 3 shows that consumption expenditure rises from 180 to 188. Since the MPC is 0.8, a rise in income by 10 causes a rise in consumption expenditure by 8. However, some of this rise in consumption was imports, which rose by 2 when income rose by 10. The induced rise in expenditure means that output of 210 still falls short of aggregate expenditure, which is now 216. Again inventories fall below planned levels and again firms respond by raising output, this time from 210 to 216.

At Step 4, firms make enough to meet expenditure at Step 3. Output is 216, but again higher income induces a further rise in expenditure. Output still falls short of aggregate expenditure. The process keeps going, through many steps, until it reaches the new equilibrium, an output of 225. Output and income rise by 25, consumption expenditure has risen by 20, imports by 5, and investment expenditure is higher by 10. Output again equals aggregate expenditure.

How long it takes for the economy to reach the new equilibrium depends on how well firms figure out what is going on. If they keep setting output targets to meet the level of demand in the previous periods, it will take a long time to adjust. Smart firms may notice that, period after period, they are underproducing and unable to maintain planned levels of inventory. They would anticipate that demand is still rising and raise output more quickly than Table 6.3 suggests.

Why does a rise of 10 in investment expenditure cause a rise of 25 in equilibrium output? Higher investment expenditure induces a rise in output and income that induces a further rise in consumption expenditure. Total expenditure rises by more than the original rise in investment, but the process does not spiral out of control. Equilibrium output is 225.

The **multiplier** $(\Delta Y/\Delta A)$ is the ratio of the change in equilibrium income Y to the change in autonomous expenditure A that caused it.

The **multiplier** is a concept used to define the change in equilibrium output and income caused by a change in autonomous expenditure. If A is autonomous expenditure:

$$\textbf{The multiplier} = \frac{\Delta Y}{\Delta A} \tag{6.8}$$

In our example, the initial change in autonomous expenditure $\Delta I = \Delta A$ is 10, and the final change in equilibrium output ΔY is 25. The multiplier is $\Delta Y/\Delta A = 25/10 = 2.5$. That is why in Figure 6.10, a small upward shift in the AE line leads to a much larger increase in equilibrium output and income.

THE SIZE OF THE MULTIPLIER

The multiplier is a number that tells us how much equilibrium output changes as a result of a change in autonomous expenditure. The multiplier is bigger than 1 because a change in autonomous expenditure sets off further changes in induced expenditure. The marginal propensities to consume and import determine the induced expenditure.

The size of the multiplier depends on the sizes of the marginal propensities to consume and import. The initial effect of a unit rise in autonomous investment expenditure is to raise output and income by one unit. If the (MPC – MPZ) is large, this rise in income causes a large rise in induced expenditure, and the multiplier is large. If the (MPC – MPZ) is small, a given change in autonomous expenditure and output induces only small changes in expenditure, and the multiplier is small.

To find the multiplier, add all the increases in aggregate expenditure and output from each step in Table 6.3, based on $c = 0.8$ and $z = 0.2$ as follows:

$$\text{Multiplier} = 1 + (0.8 - 0.2) + (0.8 - 0.2)^2 + (0.8 - 0.2)^3 + (0.8 - 0.2)^4 + \ldots\ldots\ldots$$

The dots at the end mean we keep adding terms such as $(0.8 - 0.2)^5$ and so on. The right-hand side of the equation is a geometric series. Each term is $(0.8 - 0.2)$ times the previous term. Fortunately, mathematicians have shown that there is a general formula for the sum of all terms in such a series, which gives:

$$\text{Multiplier} = \frac{1}{[1 - (0.8 - 0.2)]} = \frac{1}{(1 - 0.6)}$$

The formula applies whatever the (constant) values of c and z, the marginal propensities to consume and import, as follows:

$$\textbf{Multiplier} = \frac{1}{(1 - c + z)} \tag{6.9}$$

For the particular values of $c = 0.8$ and $z = 0.2$, equation 6.9 confirms that the multiplier is, $\frac{1}{(1 - 0.6)}$, which is $\frac{1}{0.4} = 2.5$. Hence, a rise in investment expenditure by 10 causes a rise in equilibrium output by 25, as we know from Table 6.3. Similarly, the multiplier allows us to predict that a fall in investment expenditure by 10 would lower equilibrium output and income by 25, if $c = 0.8$ and $z = 0.2$. Indeed, you will probably have guessed this from Equation 6.9. Equilibrium output is simply autonomous expenditure multiplied by the multiplier!

In more general terms, because $MPC - MPZ = c - z$ is the slope of the AE function, we can write:

$$\textbf{Multiplier} = \frac{1}{(1 - \textbf{slope of AE})} \tag{6.10}$$

Review Questions 7, 8, 9, and 10

In the model we have here, the slope of AE is MPC − MPZ, but this formula for the multiplier will still be useful when we introduce the tax system in the government sector in Chapter 7.

6.6 Leakages and Injections and Equilibrium Output

Equilibrium output equals planned expenditure on consumption, investment, and exports net of imports. This also means that planned investment and exports equal planned saving and imports. If:

$$Y = C + I + X - Z, \text{ then}$$
$$Y - C + Z = I + X$$

From equation 6.3, $Y - C = S$, and thus,

$$S + Z = I + X \tag{6.11}$$

This condition holds only when aggregate expenditure is at the right level to achieve equilibrium.

Savings and imports are leakages from the expenditure stream that do not pass current income on to business through expenditure on current output. On the other hand, autonomous investment and exports are injections into expenditure and a flow of funds to business that is independent of current income. When these injections just offset the leakages, aggregate expenditure equals output and the economy is in equilibrium.

In modern economies, business managers make investment decisions and residents of other countries make decisions about expenditure on domestic exports. Household expenditure plans depend on their income. Since planned saving and imports depend on income but planned investment and exports do not, equation 6.11 means that output and income adjust to establish equilibrium by making savings and import plans by households (leakages) equal to the investment plans of firms and export plans of non-residents (injections). Figure 6.11 illustrates this equilibrium condition.

From the consumption and import functions we know that planned saving equals income minus consumption, and imports are partly autonomous and partly dependent on income through the marginal propensity to import:

$$S = -C_0 + (1 - c)Y$$
$$Z = Z_0 + zY,$$

Then:

$$S + Z = Z_0 - C_0 + (1 - c + z)Y,$$

and equilibrium income is:

$$Y = \frac{C_0 + I_0 + X_0 - Z_0}{1 - c + z},$$

the same equilibrium as $Y = C + I + X - Z$.

The saving plus import function has a negative intercept and a slope of $[(1 - c) + z]$, equal to the sum of marginal propensities to save and import. Changes in output move the economy along the $S + Z$ function. Firms adjust output in reaction to unwanted changes in their inventories until planned saving and imports equal planned investment plus exports. Y^e in the diagram is at equilibrium.

FIGURE 6.11 **At Equilibrium Planned Leakages Equal Planned Injections**

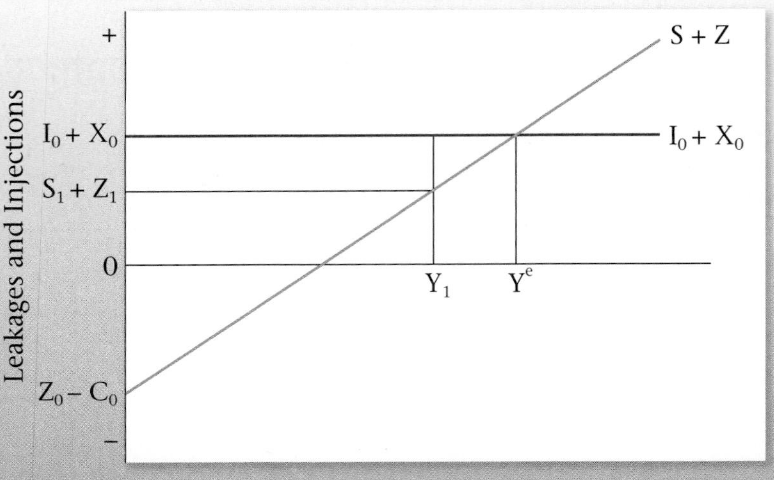

At equilibrium Y^e, planned saving plus imports equal planned investment plus exports.

The numerical example we used before illustrates the same equilibrium by this alternative approach.

Consumption:	$C = 20 + 0.8Y$
Saving:	$Y - C = S = -20 + 0.2Y$
Investment:	$I = 20$
Exports;	$X = 50$
Imports:	$Z = 10 + 0.2Y$

Then for equilibrium:

$$S + Z = I + X$$
$$-20 + 0.2Y + 10 + 0.2Y = 20 + 50$$
$$0.4Y = 80$$
$$Y = 200$$

When $Y = 200$, planned saving is 20, planned imports are 50, planned investment is 20, and planned exports are 50, giving: $S + Z = I + X$.

In Figure 6.11 we can see that if income at Y_1 is less than equilibrium at Y^e, households want to save and import less than business and residents of other countries want to buy for investment and export. Firms cannot actually add more or less of current output to their capital through investment than households and export buyers leave after they meet their expenditure plans. As a result, the difference between $S_1 + Z_1$ and $I_0 + X_0$ measures the unplanned decline in business inventories at Y_1. This provides the signal to firms to increase output, moving toward equilibrium at Y^e.

Review Questions 11, 12, 13 and 14

6.7 Equilibrium Output and Aggregate Demand

Our objective in this chapter was to build a simple model to help us understand the short-run fluctuations we see in real GDP. We now have such a model. It is built on the assumption that wages, prices, interest rates, and exchange rates are constant, on the important distinction between *autonomous* and *induced* expenditures, and on the equilibrium condition that output is equal to planned aggregate expenditure.

This model shows that fluctuations in autonomous expenditures multiplied by the multiplier cause fluctuations in output, income, and employment.

In our model, investment and exports are the main sources of fluctuations in autonomous expenditures. The marginal propensities to consume and import describe the changes in aggregate expenditure caused by changes in income. These induced expenditures are the source of the multiplier. When business changes its investment plans in response to predictions and expectations about future markets and profits, or exports change in response to international trade conditions, the multiplier translates these changes into larger changes or fluctuations in income and employment.

In Chapter 5 and at the beginning of this chapter, we used an Aggregate Demand and Aggregate Supply model to explain business cycle fluctuations. In this chapter we have developed a basic explanation for the *shifts in AD* that cause changes in real output. Figure 6.12 shows how this works.

FIGURE 6.12 **Equilibrium Output and Aggregate Demand**

Equilibrium output in panel (a) determines the position of the AD curve in panel (b).

Any change in autonomous expenditure (ΔA) causes a larger increase in equilibrium output (ΔY) based on the multiplier, as shown by Y_e to Y'_e in panel (a). This increase in equilibrium Y in panel (a) is an increase in AD in panel (b).

As a result, ΔA causes a *horizontal shift* in AD in panel (b) equal to the ΔY determined in panel (a), namely by ΔA and the multiplier.

With price constant at P_0, equilibrium real GDP increases from Y_e to Y'_e in panel (b)

Fluctuations in autonomous expenditure cause fluctuations in AD and real GDP.

(a) Equilibrium Y = AE

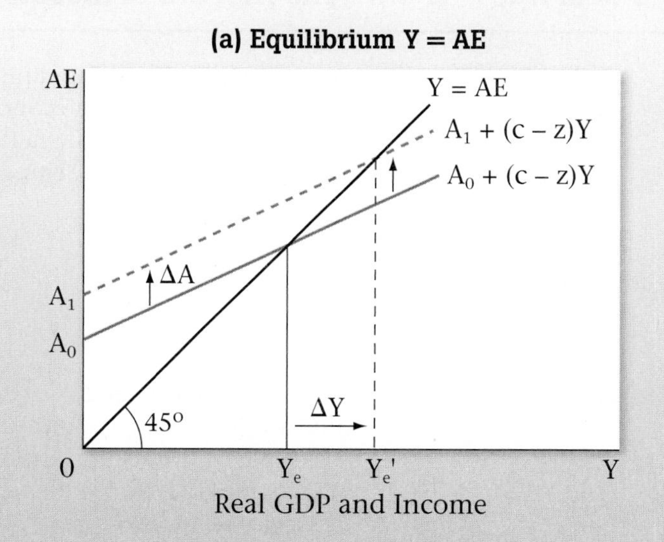

(b) Equilibrium AD = AS

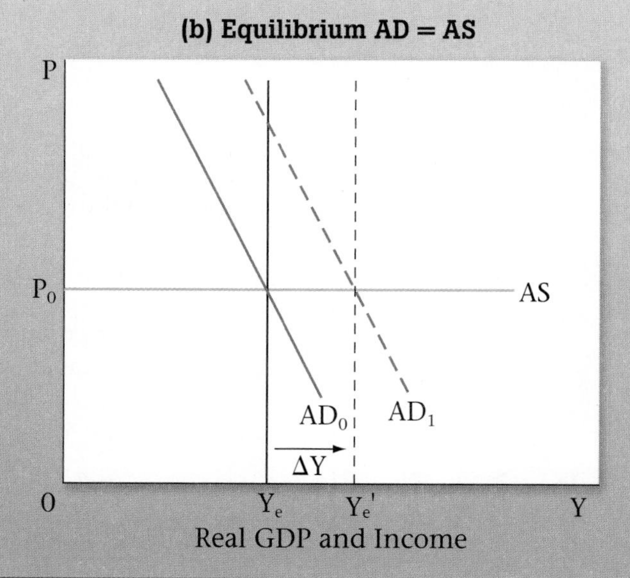

In panel (a), equilibrium output Y_e is determined by autonomous aggregate expenditure $A_0 = C_0 + I_0 + X_0 - Z_0$ and the multiplier from MPC − MPZ = c − z. The horizontal aggregate supply curve AS in panel (b) captures the assumption that prices are constant. The position of the aggregate demand AD_0 in panel (b) is determined by equilibrium in panel (a). AD_0 gives the same equilibrium output Y_e at the price level P_0 as in panel (a). In general terms, the level of autonomous expenditure and the multiplier set the position of the AD curve.

Changes in autonomous expenditure shift the AD curve. If autonomous expenditure increased from A_0 to A_1 as shown in panel (a), equilibrium output would increase to Y'_e. The change in equilibrium output would be ($\Delta A \times$ multiplier). The AD curve would shift to the right to AD_1 as a result of the increase in autonomous expenditure. The size of the horizontal shift would be ($\Delta A \times$ multiplier).

SUMMARY BOX The Algebra of Income Determination

We have used diagrams and numerical examples to show the determination of national income in a model of an economy that does not have a government. Two things determine equilibrium income: autonomous expenditures and a multiplier. The following example shows the same thing, but in a general model.

Consumption:	$C = C_0 + cY$
Investment:	$I = I_0$
Exports:	$X = X_0$
Imports:	$Z = Z_0 + zY$

We have used the lower case letters c and z for the marginal propensities to consume and import. They measure the changes in consumption and imports that would be caused, or induced, by a change in national income. The subscript $_0$ indicates the initial values of autonomous expenditures.

Aggregate expenditure is:

$$AE = C + I + X - Z, \text{ which by substitution is}$$
$$AE = C_0 + cY + I_0 + X_0 - Z_0 - zY \text{ or}$$
$$AE = C_0 + I_0 + X_0 - Z_0 + cY - zY$$

We can reduce this expression to its two key components, autonomous and induced expenditures, by writing:

$$AE = A_0 + (c - z)\,Y, \text{ letting } A_0 = C_0 + I_0 + X_0 - Z_0$$

If this aggregate expenditure function were drawn in a diagram, A_0 would be its intercept on the vertical axis and c − z would be its slope.

National income and output are in equilibrium when national income and planned aggregate expenditure are equal. This is the condition:

$$Y = AE$$

Using this condition and solving for Y_e, we have

$$Y = A_0 + (c - z)Y$$
$$Y - (c - z)Y = A_0$$
$$Y(1 - c + z) = A_0$$
$$Y_e = \frac{A_0}{(1 - c + z)} = \frac{A_0}{(1 - \text{slope of AE})}$$

Equilibrium national income is determined by the total autonomous expenditure in the economy, A_0, multiplied by the multiplier $\frac{1}{(1 - \text{slope of AE})}$, which is based on the changes in expenditure induced by changes in national income.

Changes in equilibrium national income come mainly from changes in autonomous expenditures A, multiplied by the multiplier. The multiplier is based on the stable predictable relationship we see between consumption and import expenditures and national income.

Next

This model provides an important first insight into the sources of business cycles in the economy. However, it is a pure private household/private business sector economy. Autonomous consumption, investment, exports and imports, and the multiplier drive real GDP and income and fluctuations in those measures of economic activity. There is no government, and thus no way for government policy to affect real output and employment. There is no financial sector to explain the interest rates and foreign exchange rates that affect expenditure decisions, and thus no monetary policy. In the next few chapters we extend our discussion of aggregate expenditure and aggregate demand to include the government sector and financial sectors, as well as fiscal and monetary policy. The framework becomes a bit more complicated and realistic, but the basic mechanics are still those we have developed in this chapter.

SUMMARY

- **Aggregate demand** determines real output and national income in the short run when prices are constant.
- Equilibrium between **aggregate expenditure** and output determines aggregate demand.
- **Aggregate expenditure** (AE) is planned spending on goods and services. The AE function shows aggregate expenditure at each level of income and output.
- This chapter assumes an economy without a government sector. It concentrates on the **consumption expenditure (C)** by households, the **investment expenditure (I)** by business (planned additions to plant, equipment, and inventories), exports of goods and service to foreign countries (X), and imports of goods and services from those countries (Z). We assume wages, prices, interest rates, and exchange rates are constant.
- Consumption expenditure is closely though not perfectly related to **disposable income**. Without a government sector, there are no taxes or transfer payments. Disposable income is equal to national income.
- **Autonomous consumption** expenditure is planned consumption, even at zero income. The **marginal**

propensity to consume is the change in planned consumption expenditure caused by a change in income ($MPC = \Delta C/\Delta Y$). The MPC is positive but less than unity.

- The **marginal propensity to save** is the change in planned saving caused by a change in income ($MPS = \Delta S/\Delta Y$). Since income must be either spent or saved, $\mathbf{MPC + MPS = 1}$.
- Investment and exports are **autonomous expenditures.** Business's plans to add to their factories, machinery, and inventories lead to investment expenditure. Demand from residents of other countries for domestic goods and services lead to exports.
- **Imports** are that part of consumption, investment, and exports supplied by goods and services produced in other countries. A change in national income causes a change in imports according to the **marginal propensity to import, ($MPZ = \Delta Z/\Delta Y$).**
- For given prices and wages, the economy is in **equilibrium** when output equals planned spending or aggregate expenditure **($Y = AE$)**. Equivalently, the economy is in equilibrium when leakages equal injections **($S + Z = I + X$)**.
- **Equilibrium output** and income does *not* mean that output equals potential output. Equilibrium output might be either lower or higher than potential output.
- Because we assume that prices and wages are fixed, **equilibrium output is determined by aggregate expenditure and aggregate demand.** Firms and workers supply the output and labour services that are demanded.
- **Adjustment to equilibrium** is a response to unplanned changes in inventories. When aggregate expenditure exceeds actual output, there is an **unplanned fall in inventories.** Unplanned decreases in inventory are a signal to producers to increase output. Similarly, **unplanned increases in inventories** mean output is greater than aggregate expenditure. Producers will reduce output.
- Starting from an equilibrium income, an **increase in autonomous expenditure** causes an increase in output and income. The initial increase in income to meet the increased autonomous expenditure leads to further increases in consumption expenditure through the MPC, and imports through the MPZ.
- **The multiplier** determines the change in equilibrium income caused by a change in autonomous expenditure (multiplier $= \Delta Y/\Delta A$). In the model of this chapter, the multiplier is determined by the MPC and the MPZ [multiplier $= 1/(1 - MPC + MPZ)$] $=$ **$1/(1 -$ slope of AE$)$**. The multiplier is greater than 1 because the MPC and MPZ are positive fractions and the MPC is larger than the MPZ.
- The **equilibrium output** determined by the equality of aggregate expenditure and output determines the **position of the AD** curve in the AD/AS model. Changes in equilibrium output caused by **changes in autonomous expenditure and the multiplier shift the AD curve** horizontally.

KEY TERMS

Aggregate expenditure (AE) *120*
Disposable income *120*
Consumption function *121*
Autonomous expenditure *122*
Marginal propensity to consume (MPC) *122*
Induced expenditure *122*
Marginal propensity to save (MPS) *122*
Saving function *123*
Investment expenditure *124*
Exports (X) *126*
Imports (Z) *126*
Net exports (NX) *126*
Foreign exchange rate *127*
Marginal propensity to import (MPZ) *127*
Aggregate expenditure function (AE) *128*
Short-run equilibrium output *129*
Multiplier ($\Delta Y/\Delta A$) *136*

KEY EQUATIONS AND RELATIONS

Equations

Aggregate expenditure: $AE = C + I + X - Z$	**(6.1)**	p. 120
Consumption function: $C = C_0 + cY$	**(6.2)**	p. 121
Saving function: $S = -C_0 + (1 - c)Y$	**(6.3)**	p. 123
Investment expenditure: $I = I_0 - bi_0$	**(6.4)**	p. 125
Exports: $X = X_0$	**(6.5)**	p. 127
Import function: $Z = Z_0 + zY$	**(6.6)**	p. 128
Equilibrium real GDP: $Y_e = \frac{C_0 + I_0 + X_0 - Z_0}{(1 - c + z)}$	**(6.7)**	p. 131
The multiplier $= \frac{\Delta Y}{\Delta A}$	**(6.8)**	p. 136
The multiplier $= \frac{1}{(1 - c + z)}$	**(6.9)**	p. 136
The multiplier $= \frac{1}{(1 - \text{slope of AE})}$	**(6.10)**	p. 136
Equilibrium real GDP: $S + Z = I + X$	**(6.11)**	p. 137

Relations

Equilibrium real GDP: Aggregate expenditure, AE, determines equilibrium real GDP.
$AE = C + I + X - Z.$
If $AE\uparrow \rightarrow Y\uparrow$. If $AE\downarrow \rightarrow Y\downarrow$.

The marginal propensity to consume: $\Delta Y \rightarrow \Delta C$. If $Y\uparrow \rightarrow C\uparrow$. If $Y\downarrow \rightarrow C\downarrow$.

$$0 < \frac{\Delta C}{\Delta Y} < 1 \rightarrow \text{slope of the C function.}$$

The marginal propensity to save: $\Delta Y \rightarrow \Delta S$. If $Y\uparrow \rightarrow S\uparrow$. If $Y\downarrow \rightarrow S\downarrow$.

$$0 < \frac{\Delta S}{\Delta Y} < 1 \rightarrow \text{slope of saving function.}$$

The marginal propensity to import: $\Delta Y \rightarrow \Delta Z$. If $Y\uparrow \rightarrow Z\uparrow$ If $Y\downarrow \rightarrow Z\downarrow$

$$0 < \frac{\Delta Z}{\Delta Y} < 1 \rightarrow \text{slope of Z function.}$$

Autonomous expenditure (A): A is independent of current national income and output.
$A_0 = C_0 + I_0 + X_0 - Z_0$

The multiplier: $\Delta A \rightarrow \Delta$ equilibrium $Y > \Delta A$. $\frac{\Delta Y}{\Delta A} = \frac{1}{1 - \text{slope AE}}$

Changes in equilibrium real GDP: $\Delta A \rightarrow \Delta Y$. By the multiplier $\Delta Y > \Delta A$.

Changes in equilibrium real GDP shift Aggregate Demand: $\Delta A \rightarrow \Delta Y = \Delta AD$ at P_0.

REVIEW QUESTIONS

Review Questions and answers are included in Connect at www.mcgrawhillconnect.ca.

1. Suppose that in an economy with no government the consumption function is: C = 50 + 0.75Y.
   a. Draw a diagram showing the consumption function, and indicate the level of consumption expenditure when income is 150.
   b. In this same diagram, show what would happen to consumption expenditure if income increased to 200.
   c. Write the equation for the saving function and draw the saving function in a diagram.
   d. In this diagram show what would happen to savings if income increased from 200 to 250.

2. a. Suppose the media predicts a deep and persistent economic recession. Households expect their future income and employment prospects to fall. They cut back on expenditure, reducing autonomous expenditure from 50 to 30. How would the consumption and saving functions you have drawn in your diagrams for question (1) be different?
   b. Faced with economic uncertainty and a possible recession, households also reduce the amount by which they are willing to spend out of any increase in income. What effect would this have on the marginal propensities to consume and save, and the consumption and savings functions you have drawn?

3. The consumption function is C = 50 + 0.75Y and investment is I = 50, exports are X = 25, and the import function is Z = 20 + 0.25Y.
   a. Write the equation for the aggregate expenditure function for this economy.
   b. Draw a diagram showing the aggregate expenditure function AE. What is the intercept of this function on the vertical axis? What type of expenditure does this intercept measure?
   c. What is the slope of the AE function, and what does the slope measure?

4. Output and income are in equilibrium when planned expenditures C + I + X − Z are equal to national income, in other words, Y = AE.
   a. Suppose the consumption function is C = 100 + 0.8Y, investment is 25, exports are 30, and imports are Z = 10 + 0.05Y. Draw a diagram showing the aggregate expenditure function.
   b. In your diagram, draw the 45° line that shows all points at which national income and aggregate expenditures are equal (Y = AE).
   c. Using your diagram, a numerical example, or an algebraic solution, find equilibrium output and income in this example and show it in the diagram.

5. The following diagram shows the aggregate expenditure schedule for the economy and the equilibrium condition on the 45° line.
   a. Suppose output is 0G. What is the level of planned aggregate expenditure? Is planned expenditure greater or less than output?
   b. What is the size of the unplanned change in inventories at output 0G?
   c. How will business firms respond to this situation?
   d. What is the equilibrium income and expenditure?
   e. Suppose output is at 0J: Is there an unplanned change in inventories? If so, by how much?

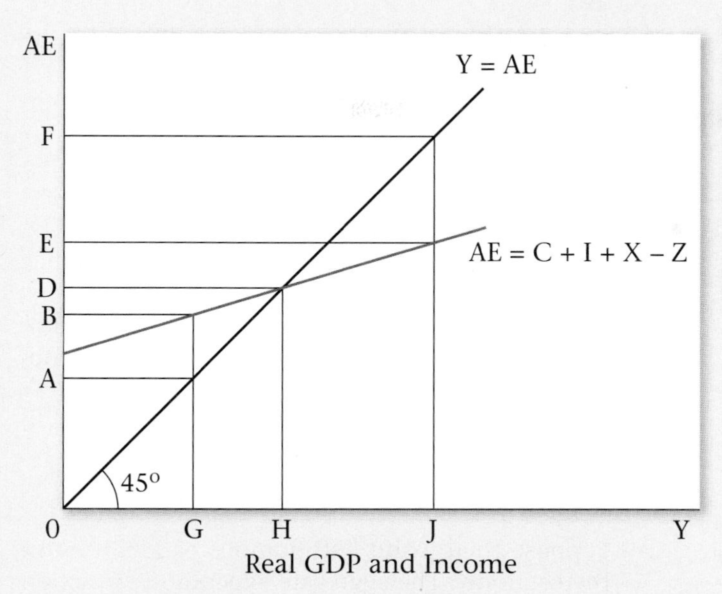

6. What part of actual investment is not included in aggregate expenditure? Explain why.

7. The following diagram shows an economy that initially has an aggregate expenditure function AK.
   a. What is the initial equilibrium real GDP?
   b. Suppose there is an increase in the marginal propensity to import. What is the new aggregate expenditure function?
   c. What is the new equilibrium real GDP and income?
   d. Suppose, instead, the marginal propensity to consume has increased. What is the new aggregate expenditure function? What is the new equilibrium real GDP and income?

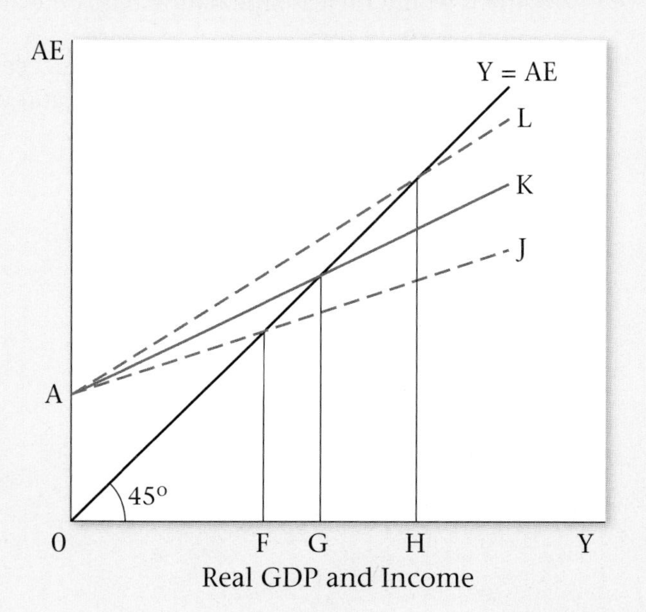

8. The distinction between autonomous and induced expenditure is important for the determination of equilibrium real GDP. Assume that the marginal propensity to consume is 0.90, the marginal propensity to import is 0.10 and autonomous aggregate expenditure is zero.
   a. What is the equation for the aggregate expenditure function under these assumptions?
   b. Draw the aggregate expenditure function in an income-expenditure 45° line diagram.
   c. What is the equilibrium level of real GDP illustrated by your diagram?
   d. Explain why this is the equilibrium level of real GDP.

9. Suppose the marginal propensities to consume and import are 0.75 and 0.25, as in question 3. Starting from equilibrium, planned investment increases by 10.
   a. By how much and in what direction does equilibrium income change?
   b. How much of that change in equilibrium income is the result of the change in consumption expenditure?
   c. How would your answers to (b) differ if the marginal propensity to consume were 0.85 rather than 0.75?
   d. Define the multiplier and explain how it is used in our macroeconomic analysis.

10. Research by a team of expert economists has uncovered the consumption and import functions and produced a forecast of planned investment and exports for the economy of Wonderland as reported below.

Real GDP Y	Consumption C	Investment I	Exports X	Imports Z
0	100	100	75	25
800	820	100	75	145
900	910	100	75	160
1000	1000	100	75	175
1100	1090	100	75	190
1200	1180	100	75	205

a. What equilibrium real GDP would Wonderland produce?
b. What are the marginal propensities to consume and import in Wonderland?
c. What is the size of the multiplier?
d. If actual GDP were 900, what difference between planned and actual investment would result? Why?
e. If planned investment increased by 50 to 150, what would happen to equilibrium income?

11. Planned investment is 100, exports are 50, saving is $S = -25 + 0.2Y$, and imports are $Z = 25 + 0.3Y$.
   a. Draw a diagram showing the initial equilibrium level of income.
   b. Now households decide to increase their saving at every level of income, but do not change their marginal propensity to save. What happens to equilibrium income and to household saving?
   c. In a diagram, show the effect of increased thriftiness by households on equilibrium real GDP, investment, saving, and imports.

12. In Figure 6.2 (page 121) the consumption function for Canada has a slope of about 0.90. Suppose that there is no government to tax income and make transfers to households, and that the marginal propensity to import is 0.30. A survey of Canadian businesses found that current pessimism about a recession and falling demand for output had cut business plans to spend on new factories and equipment by $100. What changes in Canadian real GDP, consumption, and imports would you predict? What change in the unemployment rate, if any, would you predict?

13. Recall the important distinction between *autonomous* and *induced* aggregate expenditure. Research reveals the follow planned expenditure in the economy: $C = 250$, $I = 75$, $X = 30$, $Z = 55$.
   a. What is the aggregate expenditure function in this economy?
   b. Draw the aggregate expenditure function in a 45° line diagram.
   c. What is the equilibrium level of real GDP?
   d. Suppose exports increased by 20. What change in real GDP, if any, would you predict?
   e. What change in induced aggregate expenditure would be caused by the change in autonomous exports?
   f. What is the size of the multiplier you used in predicting the effect of increased exports on equilibrium GDP?

14. Suppose there is no autonomous expenditure in the economy. The aggregate expenditure function is $AE = 0.75Y$.
   a. Draw the aggregate expenditure function and the 45° line in a diagram.
   b. What is the equilibrium level of real output and income?
   c. How would you explain your answer to (b)?

15. *Common fallacies*: Why are these statements wrong?
   a. Lower output leads to lower incomes and lower spending and still lower output. The economy could spiral down forever.
   b. If people are prepared to save, more investment would increase the national income and output would rise.
   c. For business investment plans to succeed, households must reduce consumption and increase saving.

CHAPTER 7

Government, Fiscal Policy, and Real GDP

LEARNING OUTCOMES

By the end of this chapter you should understand:

1. The government sector of the Canadian economy
2. How the government sector is included in the circular flow
3. Government expenditure, taxes, and equilibrium real GDP
4. The government's budget function and budget balance
5. Fiscal policy and the government's budget balances
6. Automatic and discretionary fiscal policy
7. The public debt and the government's budget balance
8. Government, aggregate demand, and equilibrium output

In most industrial countries, the government directly buys about 20 percent of national output and spends about the same again on transfer payments. Government spending is financed mainly by taxes. In this chapter, we extend our model to include the government sector. This adds an important new dimension to our model, namely fiscal policy. A government can use its taxing and spending powers to manage aggregate demand and reduce business cycle fluctuations in real GDP and employment.

In late 2008 and early 2009 strong recessionary conditions led to an international call for fiscal stimulus. Many countries, including Canada, introduced substantial increases in government expenditures and reductions in tax rates to offset broad-based declines in aggregate demand. This was an important revival of fiscal policy.

However, over time, governments must also manage their budgets in ways that control the size of their debt relative to GDP. Until very recently, Canadian governments have been more concerned about government budget surpluses, deficits, and debt than about demand management when designing fiscal policy.

We start with a brief look at the data on the size of the government sector in Canada.

7.1 Government in Canada

The total government sector in Canada includes the federal, provincial, and municipal governments, as well as hospitals, in Canada. Table 7.1 shows total outlays by the government sector in 2007. These totalled $579 billion. Of this total, 59 percent was expenditure on the goods and services that provided government services to Canadians. The remaining 41 percent was transfer payments to persons, business, and non-residents, and interest paid on the outstanding public debt.

Table 7.2 shows a comparison of the sizes of the government sectors relative to GDP in the G7 group of industrial countries (Canada, the United States, Japan, the United Kingdom, Germany, France, and Italy) in 2006. The expenditures by Canada's government sector—the combined federal, provincial, and local governments—on goods, services, and transfers (Old Age Security, Employment Insurance, and Social Assistance) were just under 40 percent of GDP. This is about average for the G7 countries, although you will notice that some spend quite a bit more and others less than this average. The differences reflect national political choices about the role the government sector plays in the economy.

In 2006, Canada was unique among G7 countries in terms of its government sector budget balance. We operated with a budget surplus (revenues were greater than expenditures), while all other countries had budget deficits. Our budget surplus was the latest in a series of annual government-sector budget surpluses over the period from 1997 to 2006. These budget surpluses reduced the outstanding public debt.

The right-hand column of the table shows the ratios of public debt to GDP in G7 countries. Canada's public debt, the total bonds issued by governments to finance past government deficits, has been declining in recent years as a result of government budget surpluses. At the same time, GDP has been growing. By 2006, the debt ratio in Canada was substantially lower than the average for G7 countries. Debt ratio reduction has been one objective of federal government budget policy in Canada in recent years.

TABLE 7.1 **The Component Breakdown of Government Outlays in Canada 2007**

Total Outlay (Billion $)	Goods & Services %	Transfers Persons %	Transfers Business %	Transfers Non Residents %	Interest on Public debt %
579	59.2	26.4	2.6	0.8	11.0

Source: Fiscal Reference Tables 2008, Table 33, Finance Canada, 2008. Reproduced with the permission of the Minister of Public Works and Government Services Canada, 2009.

TABLE 7.2 **The General Government Sector in G7 Countries 2006**

	Total Revenues % of GDP	Expenditures on Goods, Services, and Transfers % of GDP	Budget Balance % of GDP	Net Public Debt Ratio % of GDP
Canada	**40.3**	**39.5**	**+ 0.8**	**26.6**
United States	34.1	36.4	− 2.3	36.0
Japan	33.9	36.3	− 2.4	85.4
United Kingdom	42.2	45.1	− 2.9	39.7
Germany	43.9	45.6	− 1.7	51.9
France	51.2	53.7	− 2.6	42.5
Italy	45.6	50.1	− 4.5	94.6
G7 average	38.1	40.4	− 2.3	50.0

Source: Fiscal Reference Tables 2007, Table 46, Finance Canada, 2007. Reproduced with the permission of the Minister of Public Works and Government Services Canada, 2009.

7.2 Government and the Circular Flow

As we saw in Chapter 4, government spending on goods and services, **G**, adds directly to aggregate expenditure. The government also withdraws income from the circular flow through direct taxes on factor incomes, T_d, and net indirect taxes, T_{IN}, on expenditure. It returns part of this to the income flow through transfer payments, which affect aggregate expenditure only by their effects on other expenditure components, mainly consumption.

The management of government revenues and expenditures has implications beyond simply adding to aggregate expenditures. It opens the possibility that the government may make its tax and expenditure decisions with the aim of changing aggregate expenditure, aggregate demand, output, and employment. Budget changes can be directed at the elimination of recessionary gaps, for example, to stabilize the economy at potential output. *Fiscal policy* is this use of government taxing and spending power to change output and employment. We will examine it in more detail after we look at the government's budget.

The government's budget statement in Table 7.3 shows the Government of Canada's expenditures and revenues for the year 2007. The federal government's direct expenditures on goods and services (G) cover a variety of things: general government services, support for research innovation establishments, transportation and communication facilities, the justice system, and national defence. The larger parts of its expenditures are the transfers to persons, like the Old Age Security and Employment Insurance Benefits, and transfers to the other levels of government. Transfers to persons are a part of disposable income and enter the circular flow through consumption expenditure. Transfers to provincial governments support provincial government expenditures on health and education, which we capture in G for the total government sector.

TABLE 7.3 The Federal Government Budget in Canada 2007

Revenue	$ Billion	Expenditure	$ Billion
Direct taxes		Goods and services	53.5
On persons	118.4		
On corporations	36.7	Transfers to persons	79.8
On non-residents	6.9	Transfers to provincial	
Contributions to social		and local governments	57.5
insurance plans	17.5		
Indirect taxes	48.8	Interest on public debt	31.5
Investment income	9.4	Subsidies and assistance	1.9
Capital consumption	3.6	Other	18.7
Other	12.2		
Total	253.5	Total	242.9
Budget balance, surplus (+) or deficit (−) +10.6			

Sources: Adapted from Statistics Canada, CANSIM Table 380-0007, and *Bank of Canada Banking and Financial Statistics*, March 2008. Bank of Canada, 2009.

The main sources of revenue are the direct taxes on personal income and corporate profits. Contributions to social insurance plans are the employment insurance premiums and the public pension plan (CPP and QPP) contributions made by employers and employees. Indirect taxes include the GST and specific taxes like those on tobacco, alcohol, and gasoline. We will see how direct taxes, including contributions to social insurance programs, reduce national income to disposable income.

Indirect taxes affect the final prices paid for goods and services, the difference between basic price and market price, as we saw in national accounts. Their effects will emerge later when we discuss prices and aggregate supply in Chapter 13.

7.3 Government Expenditure, Taxes, and Equilibrium Real GDP

Since it is time-consuming to keep distinguishing between market prices and basic prices as we did in Chapter 4, we will assume that all taxes are direct taxes. With no indirect taxes, measurement at market prices and basic prices coincide. We continue to assume fixed wages, prices, interest rates, and exchange rates.

Government expenditure (G) is government spending on currently produced goods and services.

Aggregate expenditure AE is now consumption expenditure C, investment expenditure I, and **government expenditure** G on goods and services, including the public services provided to households and business at zero price, valued at cost, plus exports X minus imports Z. Direct taxes and transfer payments do not enter directly into aggregate expenditure. Thus we have:

$$AE = C + I + G + X - Z \tag{7.1}$$

In the short run, government expenditure G does not vary automatically with output and income. We assume G is fixed, or at least autonomous and independent of income. It reflects government policy decisions on how many hospitals to build, how many teachers to hire, and how large the armed forces should be. This means we now have five autonomous components of aggregate expenditure independent of current output and income: the autonomous consumption expenditure C_0, investment expenditure I, exports X, autonomous imports Z_0, and government expenditure G.

We illustrate autonomous government expenditure in the same way we did with other autonomous expenditures, using a simple equation. For a specific level of government expenditure:

$$G = G_0 \tag{7.2}$$

In a diagram with income on the horizontal axis and government expenditure on the vertical axis, we would draw a horizontal line intersecting the vertical axis at G_0. Any change in government expenditure would shift this line up or down in a parallel way.

The government also levies taxes and pays out transfer payments. The difference between taxes collected and transfers paid is **net taxes** (NT), the revenue collected by government from households.

Net taxes ($NT = T_d - T_r$) are taxes minus transfer payments.

With no indirect taxes, net taxes NT are simply direct taxes T_d minus transfer payments T_r. Net taxes reduce disposable income—the amount available to households for spending or saving—relative to national income. Thus, if **t** is the *net tax rate*, the total revenue from net taxes is:

$$NT = tY \tag{7.3}$$

For simplicity, we assume that net taxes are proportional to national income. If **YD is disposable income**, Y national income and output, and NT net taxes,

Disposable income (YD) is national income minus net taxes.

$$YD = Y - NT = Y - tY = (1 - t)Y \tag{7.4}$$

Suppose taxes net of transfers are about 15 percent of national income. We can think of the net tax rate as 0.15. If national income Y rises by $1, net tax revenue will rise by $0.15, so household disposable income will increase by only $0.85.

Household planned consumption expenditure is still determined largely by household disposable income. For simplicity, suppose, as before, the marginal propensity to consume out of disposable income is 0.8. The consumption function is as before:

$$C = 20 + 0.8\ YD$$

With a net tax rate t, equation 7.4 says disposable income is only (1 − t) times national income. Thus, to relate consumption expenditure to national income:

$$C = 20 + 0.8(1 - t)Y$$

A change in national income of $1 changes consumption expenditure by only 0.8 times (1 − t) of a dollar. If the net tax rate is 0.15, consumption expenditure changes by only $1 × (0.8 × 0.85) = $0.68. Each extra dollar of national income increases disposable income by $0.85, out of which households plan to spend 68 cents and save 17 cents. Figure 7.1 illustrates.

Clearly, spending $0.68 of each extra dollar of national income implies a flatter consumption function, when plotted against national income, than spending $0.80

FIGURE 7.1 **Net Taxes and Consumption**

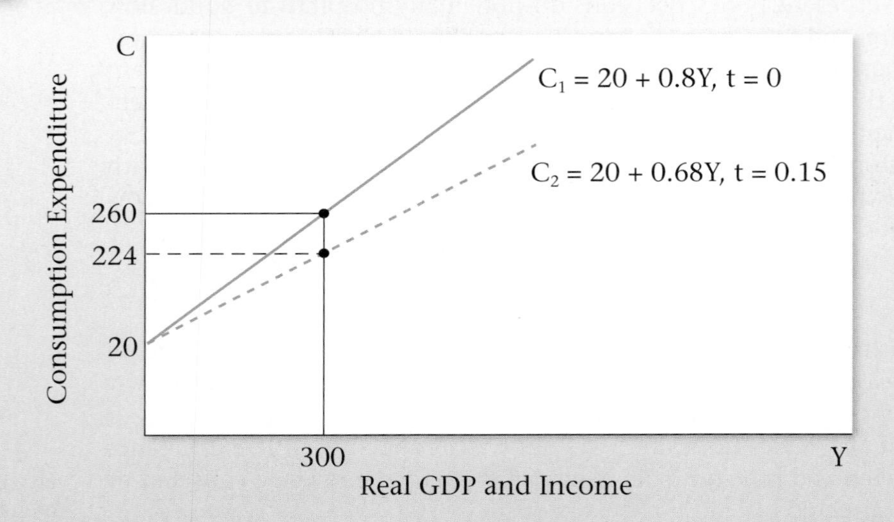

A numerical example:

(a) $C = 20 + 0.8YD$
$NT = 0$
$YD = Y$

$C = 20 + 0.8Y$

Y	NT	YD	C	S
100	0	100	100	0
300	0	300	260	40
500	0	500	420	80

(b) $C = 20 + 0.8YD$
$NT = 0.15Y$
$YD = (1 - 0.15)Y$
$C = 20 + 0.8(1 - 0.15)Y$
$C = 20 + 0.68Y$

Y	NT	YD	C	S
100	15	85	88	−3
300	45	255	224	31
500	75	425	360	65

In the absence of taxation, in example (a), national income Y and disposable income YD are the same. The consumption function C_1 shows how much households wish to consume at each level of national income, based on the numerical example. With a proportional net tax rate of 0.15, households still consume $0.80 of each dollar of disposable income. Since, as example (b) shows, YD is now only 0.85 of Y and households consume only $0.8 \times 0.85 = 0.68$ of each extra dollar of national income, the effect of net taxes is to rotate the consumption function from C_1 to C_2. The slope of the consumption function is reduced. A comparison of the numbers in examples (a) and (b) shows the effects of the tax rate at each income level. These numerical effects are also shown in the diagram.

of each extra dollar of national income. The marginal tax rate t lowers disposable income at every level of national income and as a result lowers *induced* consumption expenditure. In a diagram the net tax rate *lowers the slope of the consumption function*.

Aggregate expenditure and equilibrium output do not depend on whether the leakage is through saving (as when the MPC is low) or through imports or through taxes [as when the MPC multiplied by $(1 - t)$ is low]. Either way, the leakage prevents income from being recycled as expenditure on the output of producers.

If MPC is the marginal propensity to consume out of disposable income, and there is a proportional tax rate t, then the slope of the consumption function, the *marginal propensity to consume out of national income*, is given by:

$$\frac{\Delta C}{\Delta Y} = MPC \times (1 - t) = c(1 - t) \tag{7.5}$$

Government taxes and expenditure affect equilibrium national income and output and the position of the AD curve. To show this we start with an example in which investment expenditure is I_0, exports are X_0, imports are $Z_0 + zY$, and the consumption function in terms of disposable income is $C = C_0 + cYD$.

With the addition of government expenditure and taxes, aggregate expenditure equilibrium real GDP still determines *equilibrium real GDP*. The aggregate expenditure equation is:

$$AE = C + I + G + X - Z \tag{7.1}$$

Equilibrium real GDP is:

$$Y = C + I + G + X - Z \tag{7.6}$$

Then $\quad Y = C_0 + c(1 - t)Y + I_0 + G_0 + X_0 - Z_0 - zY$, and

$$Y = \frac{C_0 + I_0 + G_0 + X_0 - Z_0}{1 - c(1 - t) + z}$$

As before, equilibrium real GDP equals autonomous aggregate expenditure multiplied by the multiplier. With government added there is a new autonomous expenditure component G_0 and a new factor $(1 - t)$ in the multiplier, which lowers the slope of the AE function and the size of the multiplier.

THE EFFECT OF NET TAXES ON EQUILIBRIUM OUTPUT

Suppose that initially government spending is zero. Figure 7.2 illustrates. A rise in the net rate from zero to $t > 0$ makes the consumption function pivot downwards from C_1 to C_2, as we saw in Figure 7.1. We get AE by adding investment and exports to the consumption function and subtracting imports. Hence, the rise in the net tax rate, which lowers the slope of the consumption function, causes a lowering of the slope of aggregate expenditure from AE to AE' in Figure 7.2. As a result, AE equals output at a lower output level. The aggregate expenditure function now crosses the 45° line at E', not E. Equilibrium output and income fall. Panel (b) in Table 7.4 illustrates this effect of the increased net tax rate on equilibrium.

Raising the net tax rate reduces equilibrium output because it lowers the slope of the AE function and the size of the multiplier. You will recall from Chapter 6 that the multiplier comes from the induced expenditure that is driven by autonomous expenditure. In the absence of net taxes, the slope of the AE function is $MPC - MPZ = c - z$, and the multiplier is $1/[1 - (c - z)] = 1/(1 - \text{slope of AE})$. A net tax rate $t > 0$, or a change, $\Delta t > 0$, lowers the slope of the consumption function, lowers the slope of AE, lowers the multiplier, lowers equilibrium output, and lowers aggregate demand. A cut in t, $\Delta t < 0$, has the opposite effect.

FIGURE 7.2 The Effect of a Higher Net Tax Rate

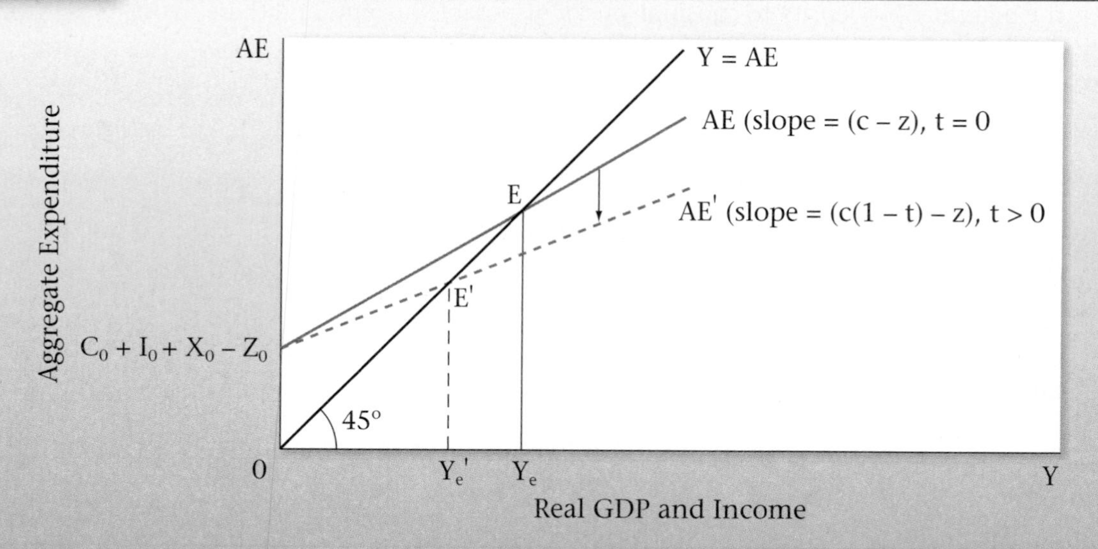

An increase in the tax rate on income or a reduction in transfer payments like employment insurance benefits, will increase the net tax rate, $\Delta t > 0$. The slope of the aggregate expenditure function is reduced. With constant autonomous expenditure, equilibrium output falls from Y_e to Y_e' because the multiplier is reduced.

TABLE 7.4 The Effects of Net Taxes on Equilibrium GDP

(a) Equilibrium with no net taxes (NT = 0)

$Y = C + I + X - Z$
$C = 20 + 0.8Y$
$I = 20$
$X = 50$
$Z = 10 + 0.2Y$

Y	C	I	X	Z	AE
100	100	20	50	30	140
150	140	20	50	40	170
200	180	20	50	50	200
250	220	20	50	60	230

(b) Equilibrium with net taxes at 12.5%(t = 0.125)

$Y = C + I + X - Z$
$C = 20 + 0.8(1 - 0.125)Y$
$I = 20$
$X = 50$
$Z = 10 + 0.2Y$
$NT = 0.125Y$

Y	NT	YD	C	I	X	Z	AE
120	15	105	104	20	50	34	140
140	17.5	122.5	118	20	50	38	150
160	20	140	132	20	50	42	160
180	22.5	157.5	146	20	50	46	170

Panel (a) begins the illustration with an economy that does not have a government sector. Autonomous expenditure of 80 and the multiplier of 2.5 gives equilibrium income $Y_e = 200$.

Panel (b) adds a government sector that imposes a net tax rate of 12.5% giving t = 0.125. Autonomous expenditure is still 80 but the net tax rate lowers the slope of AE from 0.6 to 0.5, lowering the multiplier from 2.5 to 2.0. The new equilibrium income is $Y_e' = 160$.

THE EFFECTS OF GOVERNMENT EXPENDITURE AND TAXATION

Suppose the economy begins with no government and equilibrium output of 200. Assume autonomous consumption, investment, and exports minus imports combined are (20 + 20 + 50 − 10) = 80. With a marginal propensity to consume out of disposable income of 0.80 and marginal propensity to import of 0.20, aggregate expenditure is (80 × multiplier) = 80/[1 − (0.8 − 0.2)] = 80 × 2.5 = 200, which is equal to output. Panel (a) of Table 7.4 shows this equilibrium.

Now introduce new autonomous expenditure G = 25 from the government, taking total autonomous expenditure to 105. Also introduce a net tax rate t = 0.125. The marginal propensity to consume out of national income (MPC) falls from 0.8 to 0.7, [0.8 × (1 − 0.125)], and the multiplier falls from 2.5 to 1/(1 − (0.70 − 0.20) = 1/0.5 = 2.0. Multiplying autonomous expenditure of 105 by 2.0 gives equilibrium output of 210, higher than the original equilibrium output of 200. Panel (b) in Table 7.5 and Figure 7.3(b) illustrate this result.

Review Questions 1, 2, and 3

THE BALANCED CHANGE IN GOVERNMENT REVENUE AND EXPENDITURE

Starting from equilibrium GDP, Y = 210 as in Panel (b) of Table 7.4, suppose an increase in government expenditure is financed by an equal increase in net tax revenue. In Panel (c) of Table 7.5, ΔG = ΔNT; that is, equal increases in autonomous expenditure and autonomous net tax revenue. The economy began in equilibrium with output of 210. The proportional tax rate of 0.125 is unchanged but a new autonomous tax raises initial tax revenue by 10 at every level of GDP, precisely the amount of the increase in government expenditure.

This balanced increase in spending and tax revenue does not leave expenditure and output unchanged. Panel (c) of Table 7.5 shows that a balanced increase in the government budget of 10 increases equilibrium GDP by 4, from 210 to 214. This happens because the balanced change in the budget shifts income from households, with a marginal propensity to consume of less than one (0.8), to the government, with a marginal propensity to spend equal to one. Autonomous consumption is reduced by ΔC = 0.8 × (−10) = −8 by the autonomous tax of 10. Autonomous government expenditure is increased by ΔG = +10. The net increase in autonomous expenditure of 2, multiplied by the multiplier of 2.0, gives the change in equilibrium GDP, ΔY = 4, from 210 to 214.

Review Question 4

THE MULTIPLIER REVISITED

The multiplier relates changes in equilibrium national income to the changes in autonomous expenditures that cause them. The formula in Chapter 6 still applies.

$$\text{The multiplier} = \frac{1}{1 - \text{slope of Aggregate Expenditure}}$$

Without government and taxes, disposable income and national income are the same, and when the marginal propensity to import is included, the multiplier is:

$$\frac{\Delta Y}{\Delta A} = \frac{1}{1 - MPC + MPZ} = \frac{1}{1 - c + z}$$

With government and taxes proportional to income, the slope of the AE function is reduced.

$$\frac{\Delta AE}{\Delta Y} = MPC \times (1 - t) - MPZ = c(1 - t) - z$$

TABLE 7.5 **The Effects of Government Expenditure and Taxes on Equilibrium GDP**

(a) Equilibrium with No Government (G = 0) and No Net Taxes (NT = 0)

$Y = C + I + X - Z$
$C = 20 + 0.8Y$
$I = 20$
$X = 50$
$Z = 10 + 0.2Y$

Y	C	I	X	Z	AE
100	100	20	50	30	140
150	140	20	50	40	170
200	180	20	50	50	200

(b) Equilibrium with Government (G = 25) and Net Taxes (NT = 0.125Y)

$Y = C + I + G + X - Z$
$C = 20 + 0.8(1 - 0.125)Y$
$I = 20$
$G = 25$
$X = 50$
$Z = 10 + 0.2Y$
$NT = 0.125Y$

Y	NT	YD	C	I	G	X	Z	AE
190	23.75	166.25	153	20	25	50	48	200
200	25	175	160	20	25	50	50	205
210	26.25	183.75	167	20	25	50	52	210
220	27.5	192.5	174	20	25	50	54	215

(c) A Balanced Change in Government Expenditure and Net Taxes: $\Delta G = \Delta NT = 10$

$Y = C + I + G + X - Z$
$C = 20 + 0.8(Y - 10 - 0.125Y)$
$I = 20$
$G = 25 + \Delta G = 35$
$X = 50$
$Z = 10 + 0.2Y$
$NT = 0.125Y + \Delta NT = 10 + 0.125Y$

Y	NT	YD	C	I	G	X	Z	AE
190	33.75	156.25	145	20	35	50	48	202
200	35	165	152	20	35	50	50	207
210	36.25	173.75	159	20	35	50	52	212
214	36.75	177.25	161.8	20	35	50	52.8	214

Panel (a) begins with equilibrium in an economy without taxes or government expenditure. Autonomous expenditure is 80, the multiplier is 2.5 and equilibrium GDP is Y = 200.

Panel (b) introduces government expenditure of G = 25 and net tax revenue NT = 0.125Y. Government expenditure increases autonomous expenditure to 105 while net taxes reduce induced expenditure and the multiplier to 2.0. Equilibrium GDP is Y = 210. This combination of increased government expenditure and taxes has a small positive effect on equilibrium.

Panel (c) introduces a "balanced change" in the government budget by increasing government expenditure by $\Delta G = 10$ and introducing an autonomous net tax increase of $\Delta NT = 10$. The net effect is an increase in autonomous expenditure by $\Delta A = \Delta G - c\Delta NT = 10 - 8 = 2$. The multiplier is unchanged at 2.0. Equilibrium GDP increases by 4 to Y = 214.

FIGURE 7.3 Government Expenditure, Taxes, and Equilibrium GDP

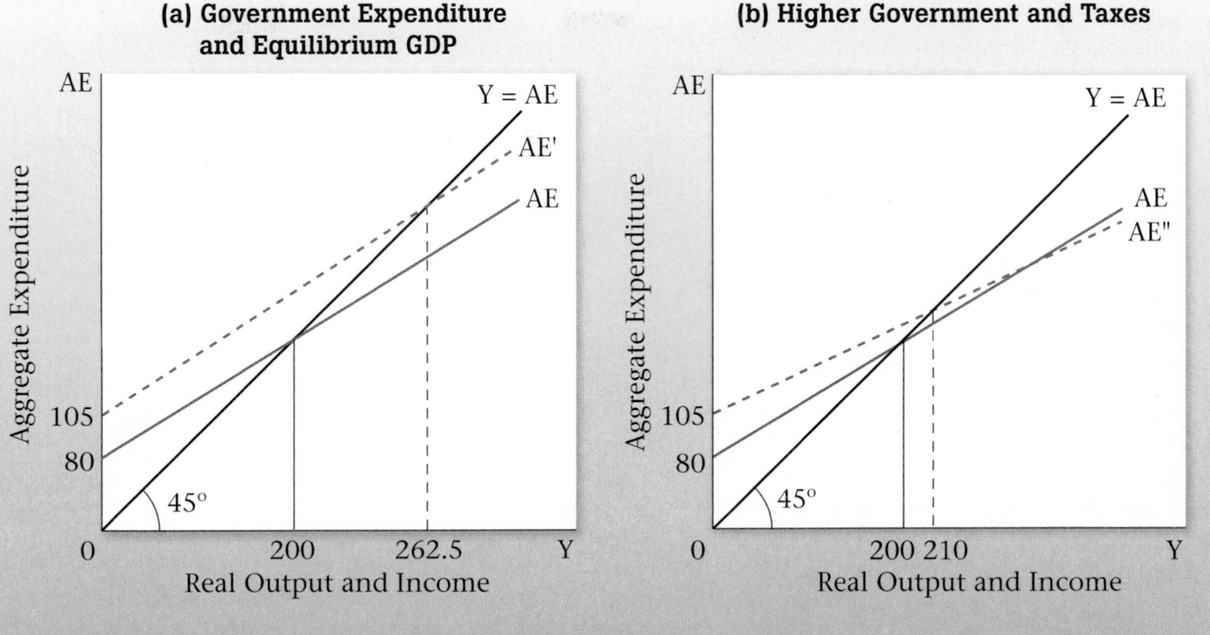

Panel (a) Beginning from equilibrium at 200, adding G = 25 shifts AE up to AE'. The new equilibrium is 265, an increase equal to ΔG × multiplier (25 × 2.5 = 62.5).

Panel (b) Beginning from equilibrium at 200, government expenditure increases as in panel (a), ΔG = 25, and the net tax rate rises from zero to t = 0.125. The new tax rate lowers the slope of AE and lowers the multiplier from 2.5 to 2.0. As a result the new equilibrium income is 210. Panel (b) in Table 7.4 gives a numerical example of this equilibrium income.

The multiplier is smaller as a result, namely:

$$\frac{\Delta Y}{\Delta A} = \frac{1}{1 - c(1 - t) + z}$$

Table 7.5 provides numerical examples of these multipliers.

Now that we have seen that government expenditure and net tax taxes have effects on aggregate expenditure and equilibrium income, it is time to examine the effects of government budgets on AE, AD, and real GDP. The government implements fiscal policy through its budget.

7.4 The Government's Budget and Budget Balance

A budget is the revenue and spending plan of an individual, a company, or a government. The **government budget** describes what goods and services the government will buy during the coming year, what transfer payments it will make, and how it will pay for them. Most spending is financed by taxes, but some revenue comes from charges for services. When revenues and spending are equal, the budget is balanced. When revenues exceed spending, there is a budget surplus. When revenues fall short of

The **government budget** reports government revenues and expenditures.

FIGURE 7.4 **A Government Budget**

The budget balance equals revenue minus total government spending, or net taxes minus government purchases of goods and services. This diagram shows *one budget or fiscal plan*. Government purchases are shown as constant, independent of income at $G_0 = 200$. Net tax revenue is based on the tax rate $t_0 = 0.2$ set by the government and the level of income. Tax revenue rises when income rises and falls if income falls. Thus, if income levels are low, the budget is in deficit; at high income levels the budget is in surplus.

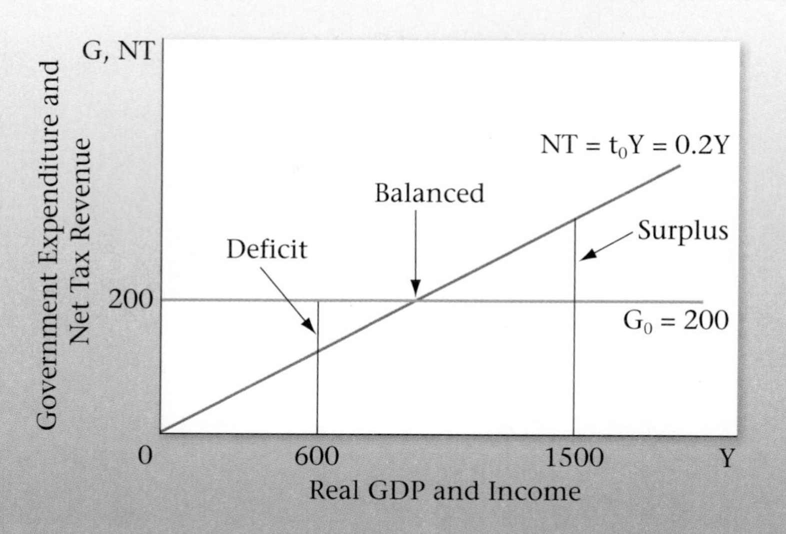

spending, there is a budget deficit. Continuing to use G for government expenditure on goods and services, and NT for net tax revenue or taxes minus transfer payments (ignoring other sources of revenue, for simplicity),

$$\textbf{Government budget balance: } BB = NT - G$$

$$BB = tY - G \tag{7.7}$$

The government budget balance is the difference between revenues and expenditures. Figure 7.4 shows government purchases G and net tax revenue $NT = tY$ in relation to real GDP and income. We assume G is fixed at 200. With a net tax rate of $t = 0.20$, net tax revenue is 0.2Y. The tax function has a positive slope. Taxes are zero when income is zero, 100 when income is 500, and 200 when income is 1000. At incomes and outputs below 1000, NT is less than G and the budget balance is a deficit, $BB < 0$. At income and output of 1000, it is balanced, $BB = 0$. At any output and income above 1000, the budget balance shows a surplus, $BB > 0$. Thus, for any fiscal plan like the *fiscal plan* that sets $G = 200$ and $t = 0.20$, the budget balance depends on the level of output and income.

The budget balance, whether deficit, surplus, or zero, is determined by three things:

- the net tax rate t set by the government,
- the level of expenditure G set by the government, and
- the level of output Y determined by AE and AD.

We can summarize the relationship between national income and the government's budget balance in a way we will find useful for discussing fiscal policy. Table 7.6 shows the numbers in more detail, and Figure 7.5 shows **the budget function** that gives the budget balance for this fiscal program at different incomes.

The **budget function** gives the budget balance at each level of income.

TABLE 7.6 **Real GDP, Income, and the Government Budget Balance**

The fiscal program is:

$G_0 = 200$
$NT = t_0Y = 0.2Y$
$BB_0 = 0.2Y - 200$

National Income	Net Tax Revenue	Government Expenditure	Budget Balance
0	0	200	−200
200	40	200	−160
600	120	200	− 80
1000	200	200	0
1400	280	200	+ 80
1800	360	200	+160

FIGURE 7.5 **The Government Budget Function**

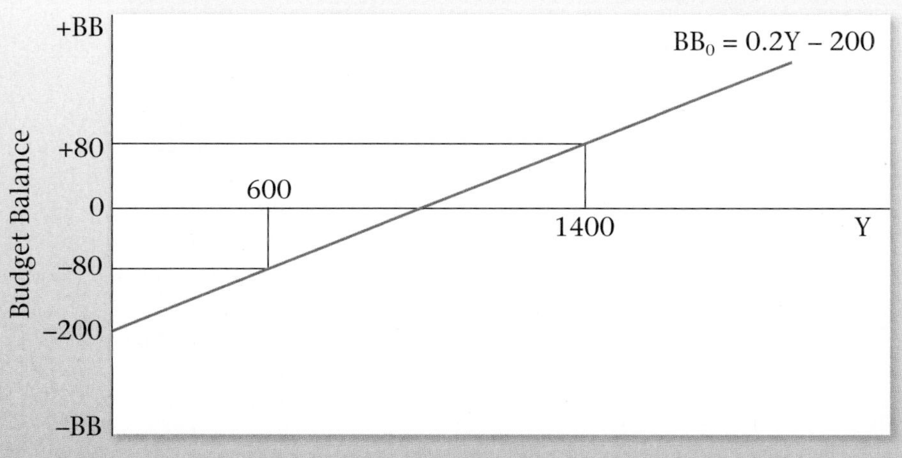

The fiscal program G = 200 and NT = 0.2Y is illustrated by the budget function:

$$BB = 0.2Y - 200$$

The position of the function, its vertical intercept, is determined by autonomous government expenditure, 200 in this *fiscal program*. The slope of the budget function is the net tax rate 0.20 in this fiscal program. The budget balance depends on the level of national income. This program would run deficits at incomes below 1000 and surpluses at incomes above 1000. Different fiscal programs, different G, or different t, or different G and t, would give budget functions with different positions and slopes.

The Minister of Finance sets the fiscal program by setting the net tax rate and level of planned government expenditure in a budget statement presented to parliament. A budget function shows us the different budget balances for one fiscal policy program at different levels of national income.

Once that fiscal program is set, the budget function is set, but the budget balance is not. The budget balance depends on the performance of the economy in terms of national income. In presenting the budget, the minister gives a forecast of the budget balance based on a forecast of national income. If the income forecast is wrong, the budget program will result in either a larger or smaller budget balance than initially predicted. In recent years in Canada, federal government budget surpluses have consistently exceeded predictions, while many provincial government budget balances have been smaller than predicted. These experiences illustrate clearly the difficulty in making accurate income forecasts and the important effects income levels have on the actual government budget balances.

Review Questions 5 and 6

Finally, notice that because a budget function describes one fiscal plan, any change in the fiscal plan will change the BB line to show a new budget function.

LEAKAGES AND INJECTIONS AND THE BUDGET

By national accounting definitions, actual leakages from the circular flow always equal actual injections to the circular flow. Payments cannot vanish into thin air. Our model now has three leakages from the income flow—savings by households, imports, and net taxes paid to government—and three injections—investment expenditure by business, exports, and government expenditure on goods and services. Thus, *actual* savings plus *actual* imports plus *actual* net taxes always equal *actual* investment expenditure plus *actual* exports plus *actual* government expenditure.

In the last chapter we saw that, when the economy is not in equilibrium, actual saving and investment differ from planned saving and investment. Firms have unplanned changes in inventories, and households may be forced to make unplanned saving if planned expenditure exceeds actual output.

The economy is in equilibrium when all quantities demanded, which make up planned aggregate expenditure, equal actual output. Planned saving S, imports Z, and net taxes NT are uses of current income that are not demands for current output. For planned expenditure to be equal to output, these leakages must be offset by planned investment expenditure, exports and government expenditure. As a result, in equilibrium, planned leakages and planned injections are equal.

$$S + Z + NT = I + X + G \tag{7.8}$$

Equation 7.8 implies that if planned saving was equal to planned investment, $(S = I)$ the government's budget balance would have to be offset by the difference between exports and imports

$$NT - G = X - Z \tag{7.9}$$

If the government has a budget surplus net exports will be positive. On the other hand a government budget deficit will be matched by negative net exports, a trade deficit. This relationship is usually described as the "twin deficits" although there may also be twin surpluses.

Recent observations on government sector budget balances are broadly illustrative of this relationship. Table 7.7 provides data on government budget balances and net

TABLE 7.7 **Total Government Budget Balances and Net Exports: Canada and the United States**

	(Billions of dollars in national currencies) Annual Average 1997–2008	2006	2008
Canada			
Budget balance	11.7	19.4	1.2
Net exports	42.4	35.7	37.0
United States			
Budget balance	−135	−171	−581
Net exports	−470	−755	−710

Sources: Banking and Financial Statistics, Bank of Canada, 2009; and Fiscal Reference Tables, 2008, Finance Canada, 2008. Reproduced with the permission of the Minister of Public Works and Government Services Canada, 2009; and Federal Reserve Bank of St. Louis, FRED database; and author's calculations.

exports in Canada and the United States in recent years. In Canada, surpluses in the total government sector budget balances and positive net exports have been consistent over the 1997 to 2008 period, although not of equal magnitude. The implication from Equation 7.8 is that saving, S, has been less than investment, I.

The experience in the United States has been the opposite of that in Canada. In the U.S, on average over the 1997–2008 period, the government budget has been in deficit and net exports have been negative.

The annual data show the effects of more recent changes in economic circumstances and policies in both countries. In Canada the government budget balance fell in 2006, partly as a result of budget policy and partly as a result of declining economic growth rates. Net exports increased in the same period as a result of rising energy and commodity prices, and slowdown in import growth as GDP growth rates declined.

Changes in the United States were more dramatic. The government budget deficit increased substantially, and net exports increased somewhat. These developments reflected the ongoing costs of U.S. involvement in wars in Iraq and Afghanistan, tax cuts introduced as part of budget policy, and growing imports from China and other Asian countries. However they predate the substantial fiscal actions taken in response to the financial crisis and recession of late 2008 and the decline in U.S. imports as GDP growth declined.

7.5 Fiscal Policy and Government Budget Balances

Fiscal policy is the government's use of its taxes and spending powers to affect aggregate expenditure and equilibrium real GDP. One of the main objectives of fiscal policy is to stabilize output by managing aggregate demand, keeping output close to potential output, and reducing the size and duration of business cycle fluctuations. This requires changes in the government's expenditure plans and tax policy to offset changes in autonomous consumption, investment, and exports that would otherwise push the economy away from equilibrium at potential output. In 2008

Fiscal policy is government use of its taxes and spending to affect real output.

and 2009, for example, the international financial crisis and its effects on expenditures led to calls for fiscal stimulus at national levels and through international coordination.

Figure 7.6 illustrates the use of fiscal policy to eliminate output gaps. In the diagram on the left, the economy has a recessionary gap at $Y_0 < Y_P$ because aggregate expenditure is not high enough to give equilibrium at Y_P. Government can intervene to raise AE to AE_1 by increasing government expenditures or by lowering the net tax rate or a combination of the two. In this case, the government chooses to increase G. Working through the multiplier, the increase in G moves the economy to equilibrium at potential output.

The right-hand diagram in Figure 7.6 shows a fiscal policy response to an inflationary gap. Again the government can choose between changing expenditures and changing the tax rate. In this example, an increase in the net tax rate reduces the slope of AE and moves the economy to equilibrium at Y_P.

Fiscal policy makes changes in net tax rates and government spending that are intended to change aggregate expenditure and aggregate demand and stabilize equilibrium output at potential output. These changes also change the government's budget function. An important question we need to consider is if the observed budget balance—whether surplus, balanced, or deficit—is a good measure of the government's policy intention or fiscal stance.

FIGURE 7.6 **Fiscal Policies to Eliminate Recessionary and Inflationary Gaps**

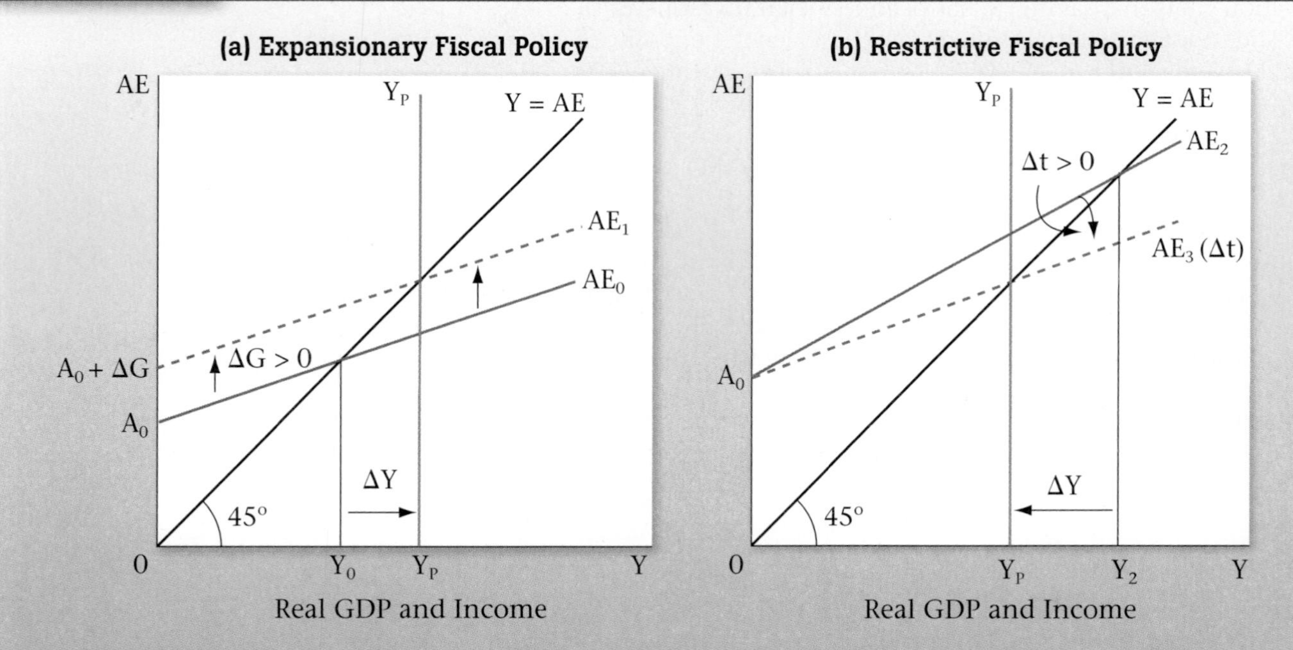

The diagrams show fiscal policy used to eliminate output gaps. The government can choose to implement fiscal policy using either its spending or its taxing power.

In (a) an expansionary fiscal policy increases government expenditure $\Delta G > 0$, increases AE, and eliminates a recessionary gap. In (b) an increase in the net tax rate $\Delta t > 0$ reduces the slope of AE, reduces the multiplier, and eliminates a recessionary gap.

Does the budget balance show whether fiscal policy is *expansionary*, aiming to raise national income, or *contractionary*, trying to reduce national income?

In itself, the budget balance may be a poor measure of the government's fiscal stance, because the budget balance can change for reasons unconnected to fiscal policy. Even if G and t are unaltered, a fall in investment or exports will reduce national income and output. In turn, this reduces net tax revenue and reduces the budget balance. Indeed, any change in non-government autonomous expenditure changes equilibrium income, net tax revenue, and the government's budget balance.

For given levels of government expenditure and tax rates, the budget function shows us that the budget balance is smaller in recessions, when national income is low, than in booms, when income is high. Suppose autonomous aggregate expenditure and demand fall suddenly. The budget may go into deficit. Someone looking only at that deficit might conclude that fiscal policy had shifted toward expansion with an increase in expenditure or a cut in the net tax rate, and no further fiscal stimulus was needed. That might be wrong. The deficit may be caused by the recession, not by a change in policy.

Canadian experience provides a good example. The Minister of Finance in his budget of February 2008, provided a fiscal plan based on a projected rate of growth in nominal GDP in 2008 of 3.5 percent and in 2009 of 4.3 percent. Under this plan and these growth rates, the projected budget surplus for the fiscal year 2008–2009 was $2.3 billion. However, the financial crisis in the U.S. and the U.S. recession that developed in the last quarter of 2008 along with the drop in energy and commodities prices undermined the Minister's GDP growth projections. By the time of his Economic and Financial Statement of November 2008 he was projecting much smaller budget surpluses of $0.8 billion in fiscal 2008–2009 and $0.1 billion in fiscal 2009–2010. In terms of the budget function in Figure 7.5, the economy had moved to the left and down the budget function.

Review Question 7

THE STRUCTURAL BUDGET BALANCE

The **structural budget balance (SBB)** is the budget balance at potential output.

To use a budget balance as an indicator of fiscal stance, we calculate the **structural budget balance (SBB)**. This is an estimate of what the budget balance would be if the economy were operating at potential output. By evaluating the budget at a fixed level of income, namely potential GDP, the structural budget balance does not change as a result of business cycle fluctuations in output. In terms of the budget function we used above, the structural balance is:

$$SBB = tY_P - G \tag{7.10}$$

Notice that this structural budget function differs from the general budget function of Equation 7.8 by calculating net tax revenue at Y_P rather than at any Y.

Using the previous numerical example, suppose government expenditure is 200 and the tax rate is 0.20. As in Figure 7.5, the budget balance is a deficit at any income below 1000 and a surplus at any income above 1000. If, given other components of aggregate expenditure, the equilibrium output is 800, the actual budget balance will be a deficit. Net tax revenue will be $NT = 0.2 \times 800 = 160$. With government expenditure of $G = 200$, $BB = 160 - 200 = -40$.

Conversely, suppose equilibrium output is 1200. With a tax rate of 0.20 and government expenditure of 200, the budget balance would be a surplus of 40. The important point of these examples is that we cannot tell the stance of fiscal policy, or a change in the stance of fiscal policy, by looking at the actual budget balance. We need to look at a structural budget balance, calculated at potential income that is not changed by business fluctuations in actual output around potential output.

Changes in the government's *fiscal policy program* change the structural budget balance and shift the budget function. An increase in government expenditure on goods and services, for example, would *shift the BB* line in Figure 7.7 down and lower the structural budget balance. The AE line would shift up and increase equilibrium income and aggregate demand. This would be an expansionary fiscal policy.

A change in the net tax rate would also change the structural budget balance and the budget line BB in the diagram. In this case, the slope of the line would increase with an increase in the tax rate or fall with a cut in the tax rate. In either case it would be the change in the structural budget balance that would tell us that fiscal policy had changed and whether the change would increase or reduce aggregate expenditure.

Figure 7.7 shows the difference between actual and structural budget balances for one fiscal policy program and budget. Application Box 7.1 shows why this measure of the budget balance is important to understanding recent Canadian fiscal stance and policy changes.

FIGURE 7.7 **The Actual and the Structural or Cyclically Adjusted Budget Balance**

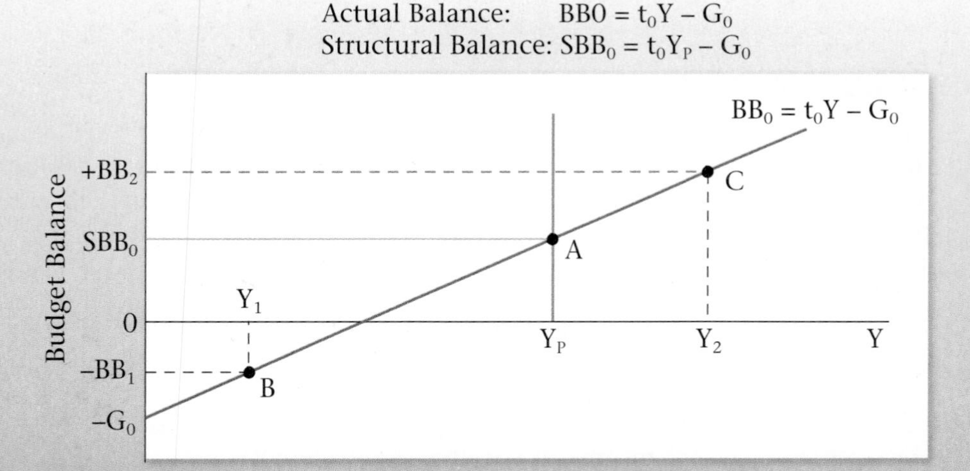

The *structural budget balance* shows what the budget balance for a fiscal program would be if output were at potential output, Y_P. The budget function BB_0 is one such program based on the net tax rate t_0 and government expenditure G_0. Point A in the diagram shows the budget balance for this program at the level of potential output Y_P. This is the structural budget balance SBB_0. The fiscal program and the *actual* national income Y together determine the *actual* budget balance. Points B and C show that this same fiscal program could produce a budget deficit or a larger surplus if the economy were not operating at Y_P.

APPLICATION BOX 7.1

A Better Measure of Fiscal Stance

Recent Canadian experience shows the importance of using the structural or cyclically adjusted budget balance as a measure of fiscal stance. Consider the following data on the federal government's budget balances, reported as a percentage of GDP to allow for the growth in the economy over time:

Year	Actual Balance (% GDP)	Structural Balance
1998	+ 0.8	+ 1.3
2000	+ 1.9	+ 1.3
2002	+ 0.8	+ 0.9
2004	+ 0.6	+ 0.9
2006	+ 0.6	+ 0.6

Source: Fiscal Reference Tables 2007, Table 46, Finance Canada, 2008. Reproduced with the permission of the Minister of Public Works and Government Services Canada, 2009.

We see the government's *actual* budget surplus increased between the years 1998 and 2000 by 1.1 percent of GDP (about $11.3 billion). If we were looking simply at the actual balance, we might conclude that the government must have cut its expenditures or increased taxes, or some combination of the two. Either of these budget changes would reduce aggregate expenditure and output. From the actual budget numbers, it looks as though the government's fiscal policy shifted to restrict aggregate expenditure.

Now look at the structural balance, the balance measured at potential output. It did not change, staying at +1.3 percent in both years. This means that any changes in the fiscal program between 1998 and 2000 were neutral as far as their effect on aggregate expenditure was concerned, not restrictive as the actual balance suggested. A diagram will help us sort out the different measures of fiscal stance we see in the numbers.

The budget function in the diagram shows the fiscal programs of two years, 1998 and 2000. In both years, the structural budget balance, which is measured at potential output Y_p, was a surplus of 1.3 percent of Y_p. This is point A on the budget function. In 1998, the actual balance was a surplus of 0.8, smaller than the structural budget surplus. This means that actual output must have been lower than potential output in that year. Point B shows this. By contrast, in 2000 the actual budget surplus of 1.9 percent was larger than the structural surplus of 1.3 percent. Actual output was greater than potential output as at point C. Now we see that changes in the actual budget were caused by fluctuations in actual output relative to potential output, not by changes in government's fiscal policy program. Using the structural budget balance gives us this better measure of the government's fiscal stance.

Now, if you look at the budget balances for 2002 and 2004, you should be able to say what has happened to the fiscal stance from 2000 to 2002 and 2004, and what has happened to actual output compared with potential output. The change in the structural balance indicates the change in the fiscal policy program. Differences between actual and structural balances indicate differences between actual and potential output. On this basis the economy was at potential output in 2006 when actual and structural balances were equal.

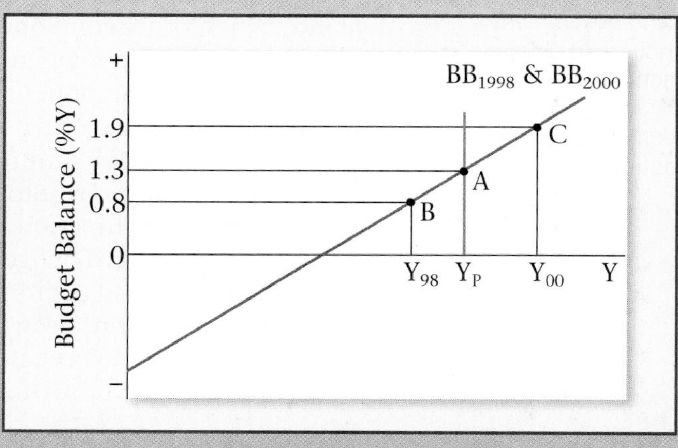

7.6 Automatic and Discretionary Fiscal Policy

Automatic stabilizers reduce fluctuations in GDP caused by autonomous expenditure shocks.

Table 7.4 (page 154) showed that a higher net tax rate **t** reduces the multiplier. Suppose investment expenditure falls by 100. The larger the multiplier, the larger is the fall in aggregate expenditure, aggregate demand, and equilibrium output. A high net tax rate reduces the multiplier, and dampens the effect of shocks to autonomous expenditure on aggregate demand and output. A high net tax rate is a good **automatic stabilizer**. It reduces the size of fluctuations in real GDP caused by fluctuations in autonomous expenditure.

Income taxes and transfers, such as unemployment benefits, are important automatic stabilizers. At given net tax rates, a fall in national income, output, and employment raises payments of unemployment benefits and reduces tax collections. Both effects mean that disposable income changes by less than the change in national income. The slope of the aggregate expenditure function $[c(1 - t) - z]$ is lower, and so is the multiplier. Conversely, in a boom, net tax revenues rise and disposable income rises by less than the rise in national income, which helps dampen the boom.

Automatic stabilizers have a great advantage. They are built into the budget program by setting the net tax rate, and work automatically. Nobody has to decide whether there has been a shift in autonomous expenditure to which policy should respond. By reducing the sensitivity of the economy to expenditure shocks, automatic stabilizers reduce output and employment fluctuations.

All leakages are automatic stabilizers. A higher marginal propensity to save and lower marginal propensity to consume reduce the multiplier. Similarly a higher marginal propensity to import reduces the multiplier and dampens output fluctuations.

However, automatic stabilizers only serve to moderate the fluctuations in real GDP caused by fluctuations in autonomous expenditure. They do not offset those autonomous expenditure disturbances. There is no automatic change in autonomous government expenditure or tax rates. Those changes come from discretionary fiscal policy.

ACTIVE OR DISCRETIONARY FISCAL POLICY

Discretionary fiscal policies change net tax rates and government expenditure to offset autonomous expenditure shocks and stabilize aggregate expenditure and output.

Although automatic fiscal stabilizers are always at work, governments can also use **discretionary fiscal policies** to change government spending or tax rates to offset autonomous expenditure shocks and stabilize aggregate expenditure and aggregate demand. When other components of aggregate expenditure are abnormally low, the government can boost expenditure by cutting taxes, raising its own expenditure, or both. When other components of aggregate expenditure are abnormally high, the government raises taxes or cuts its expenditures.

The budget function and the structural budget balance we discussed earlier provide a good illustration of automatic and discretionary fiscal policy. Figure 7.8 shows a government budget function $BB_0 = t_0Y - G_0$ and a structural budget balance SBB_0 at potential output Y_P. This budget function represents a fiscal program designed by the Minister of Finance and approved by parliament.

Automatic stabilization is a part of this program. It comes from the *slope of the budget function*, the net tax rate t_0 in this case. Any fluctuation in income Y, for example, down to Y_1 or up to Y_2, during a business cycle, *moves the economy along the*

Automatic and Discretionary Fiscal Policy

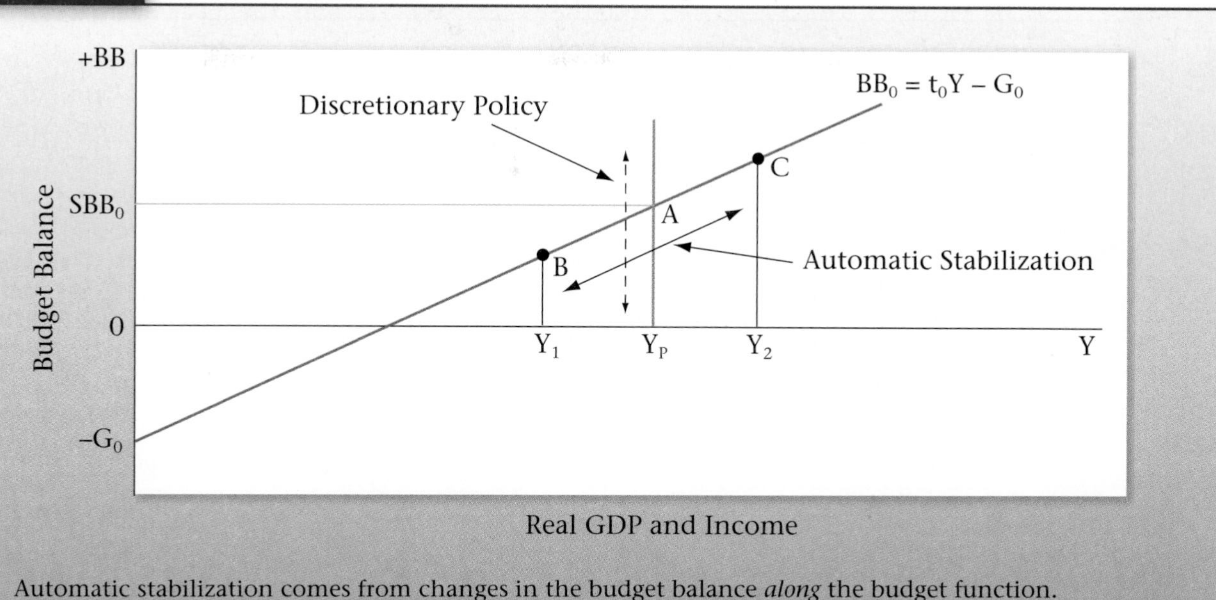

Automatic stabilization comes from changes in the budget balance *along* the budget function. Discretionary fiscal policy *shifts* the budget function and changes the SBB.

budget function. The effect of the budget change is stabilizing. A larger net tax rate would mean larger automatic changes in the budget balance in response to changes in income and more automatic stabilization.

Discretionary fiscal policy is a change in t or in G, or in both t and G, that *shifts the budget function* and may also change its slope. The Minister of Finance brings in a new budget with a new program of taxes and expenditures. In the simple case of a change in G, for example, more expenditure on health care, the budget function in Figure 7.8 would *shift* down. We see this change in discretionary policy as a change in the structural budget balance. That is why we use the structural budget balance as an indicator of fiscal stance. To stimulate the economy in times of recession, the Minister of Finance would introduce a new budget program that reduced the structural budget balance.

When we use the budget function to show fiscal policy changes, we can also consider more complex programs that change both the slope of the function and the structural balance.

By now you should be asking two questions. First, can fiscal policy stabilize aggregate demand completely and eliminate business cycles? Surely, by maintaining aggregate expenditure at its full employment level, the government could eliminate booms and slumps altogether? Second, why are governments reluctant to expand aggregate expenditure and demand to a level that would completely eliminate unemployment? Application Box 7.2 provides some of the answers.

Review Questions 8, 9 and 10

APPLICATION BOX 7.2

The Limits of Fiscal Policy

Why can't aggregate expenditure and demand shocks be fully offset by fiscal policy?

1. Time lags: It takes time to spot that aggregate expenditure has changed. It may take six months to get reliable statistics on output. Then it takes time to change discretionary fiscal policy. Long-term spending plans on hospitals or national defence cannot be changed overnight. And, once policy is changed, it takes time to work through the multiplier process and have its full effect.

2. Uncertainty: The government faces two problems. First, it is unsure of key magnitudes such as the multiplier. It only has estimates based on past data. Mistaken estimates lead to incorrect decisions about the extent of fiscal change needed. Second, since fiscal policy takes time to work, the government has to forecast the level that expenditure will reach by the time fiscal policy has its full effect. If investment is low today but about to rise sharply, a fiscal expansion may not be needed. Mistakes in forecasting non-governmental expenditure, such as investment or exports, lead to incorrect decisions about fiscal policy changes currently required.

3. Expectations: Household and business reactions to fiscal policy change depend on expectations about future policy. Tax cuts or expenditure programs that are seen as temporary will not lead to increased consumption and investment expenditures. The same applies to temporary tax increases or expenditure cuts. Household and business sector expectations about future fiscal and budget policy may come from budget changes that are explicitly temporary. They may also come, in part, from an understanding that increased budget deficits, for example, cannot be sustained. Future tax increases and expenditure cuts will be required. If households and businesses do not respond to fiscal policy changes because they think they are temporary, expenditure and output effects will be weak.

4. Induced effects on autonomous expenditure: Our model treats investment expenditure and part of consumption expenditure as autonomous of income, independent of income and, more importantly, of government fiscal policy. This is only a simplification. Changes in fiscal policy may lead to offsetting changes in other components of autonomous expenditure. If estimates of these induced effects, coming from changes in interest rates and exchange rates, are wrong, fiscal policy changes have unexpected results. We study these possibilities in more detail as we extend our model in later chapters.

7.7 The Public Debt and the Budget Balance

Budget balances and outstanding debt are closely related. A student's debt at the time of graduation is the sum of her budget balances during years of study. In any year in which her income is less than her expenses, she finances the difference by borrowing. In another year, if income is greater than expenses, she can repay some previous borrowing. In the end, the sum of borrowings minus the sum of repayments is her outstanding student debt (loan). This debt is a result of borrowing to finance investment in education.

The **public debt (PD)** is the outstanding stock of government bonds issued to finance government budget deficits.

Similarly, the outstanding **public debt (PD)** at any point in time is simply the sum of past government budget balances. Governments borrow to finance budget deficits by selling government bonds to households and businesses. Budget surpluses reduce the government's financing requirements. Some bonds previously issued mature without being refinanced. In simple terms, the budget balance in any year changes the outstanding public debt by an equal amount but with the opposite sign. A positive balance, a surplus

(BB > 0), reduces the public debt (ΔPD < 0). A negative balance, a deficit (BB < 0), increases the public debt (ΔPD > 0). Using PD to represent the outstanding public debt, we can express the link between the public debt and the government's budget balance as:

$$\Delta PD = -BB \quad (7.11)$$

Figure 7.9 shows the relationship between the government budget balance and the public debt based on Canadian data for the 1983–2007 period. Recognizing that growth in the economy makes absolute numbers for deficits and debt hard to evaluate, the budget balance and the public debt are presented as percentages of nominal GDP. The effects of budget balances on the public debt are illustrated clearly in the diagrams.

In recent years the Government of Canada has had budget surpluses, but things were different a few years ago. Large budget deficits, averaging more than 5 percent of GDP, were the norm in the 1980s and early 1990s. As a result, the outstanding federal government public debt soared from 38 percent of GDP in 1983 to 68 percent of GDP in

FIGURE 7.9 **Canadian Federal Government Budget Balances and Debt Ratios 1983–2007**

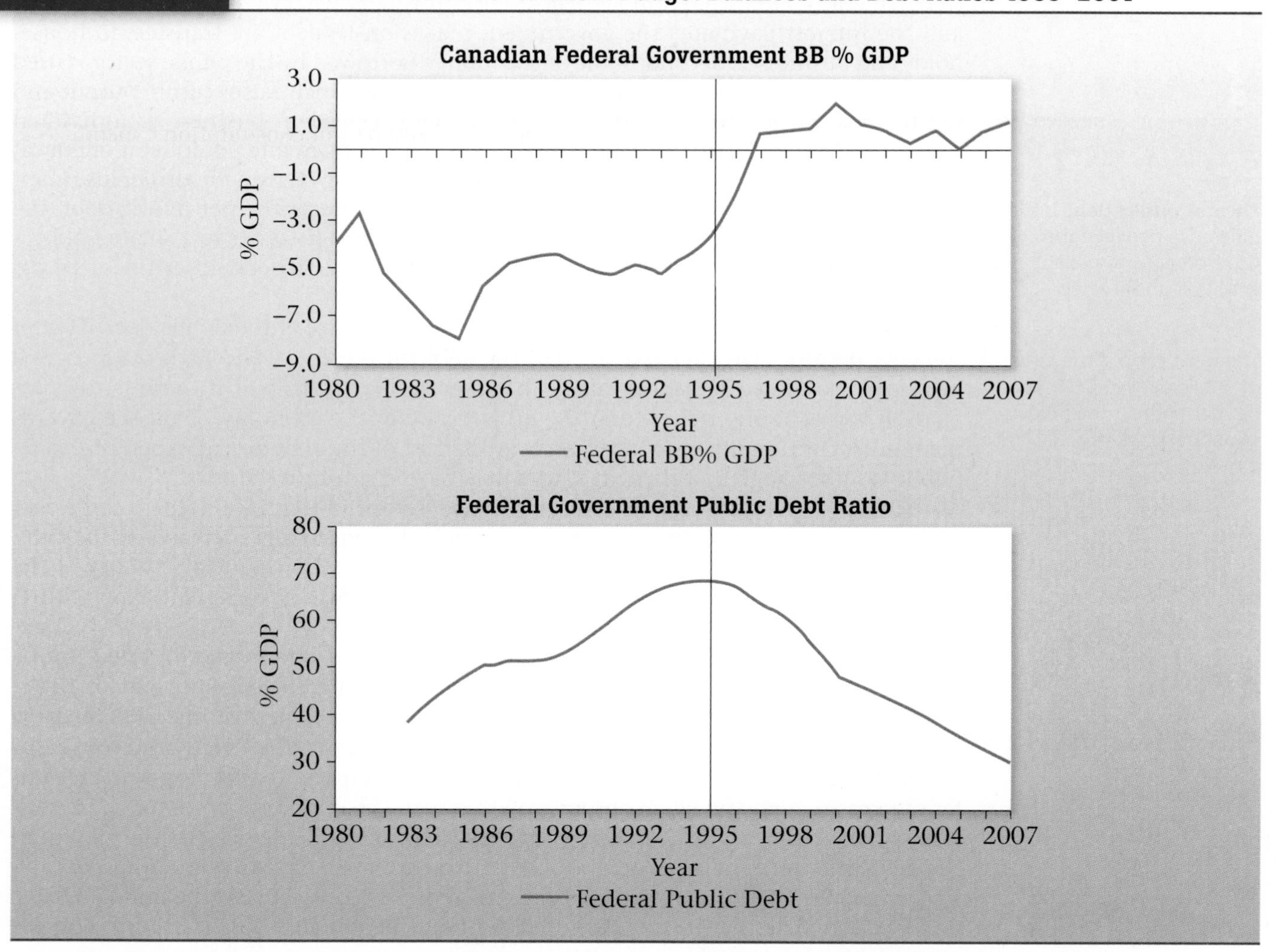

Source: Fiscal Reference Tables 2008, Tables 15 and 46, Finance Canada, 2008. Reproduced with the permission of the Minister of Public Works and Government Services Canada, 2009; *Banking and Financial Statistics,* Table H1, November 2008. Bank of Canada, 2009.

1996. The cost of the interest payments the government had to make to the holders of its bonds increased from $3.9 billion to $42.4 billion. These costs accounted for almost 30 percent of budgetary expenses in 1995. As a result, Canadian fiscal and budgetary policy focused much more on deficit and debt control than on income stabilization.

The results of this focus on debt control were budget surpluses that averaged about 0.8 percent from 1995 to 2007. These surpluses lowered the public debt in absolute terms and, combined with the growth in GDP, lowered the outstanding public debt from 68 percent of GDP to 29 percent of GDP.

Although cumulative deficits can raise the public debt dramatically, it is not the absolute value of the outstanding debt that should be of interest or concern. If, at the same time as the debt is rising, the economy is growing and tax revenues are rising as a result of a growing tax base, the government may be able to service a growing debt without having to raise taxes. The ratio of public debt to GDP is then the appropriate measure of the debt situation. A rise in the outstanding debt is not in itself a source of concern. However, the government cannot allow the debt ratio to rise without limit.

Nevertheless, concerns about the debt may be overstated for three reasons. First, Canadian citizens own much of it, about 90 percent in 2007, according to the Department of Finance, *Fiscal Reference Tables*. It is debt we owe ourselves as a nation, and the interest payments the government makes on its debt are transfers to households and businesses. Second, some of the money borrowed by the public sector is used to finance investment in physical and human capital, which raises future output and tax revenue to help service and pay off the debt. A prudent business or individual sometimes borrows to finance profitable investment in plant and equipment or education. A prudent government may do the same. Third, the government also holds financial assets on which it earns investment income. This reduces the **net public debt**, the difference between the government's gross total debt and its assets to a smaller obligation than the total debt measurement suggests. In 2007 the federal government's gross debt was $706 billion and the net debt was $524 billion.

The **net public debt** is the difference between the government's total debt and its financial assets.

When should a sensible economist worry about the size of the public debt? First, if the debt becomes large relative to GDP, the **debt ratio** is high, and high tax rates will be needed to meet the debt burden. This is particularly difficult if the interest rates paid on the debt are higher than the growth rate of the economy. Then the government must continually raise taxes to cover the cost of the debt, or cut expenditures on public services. High and rising tax rates may have disincentive effects.

The **debt ratio** is the ratio of public debt to GDP. The net debt ratio is the ratio of net public debt to GDP.

Second, if the government cannot raise taxes beyond a certain point, a large debt and large interest payments may cause large deficits and further increases in the debt, to the point where financial markets lose confidence in the financial stability of the government. It becomes necessary to print money to cover government expenditure. That is how hyperinflations start.

By 2007, the Government of Canada's net debt to GDP ratio had declined from a peak of 70.5 percent in 1995 to 34.2 percent. Table 7.8 shows the large rise and fall of the debt ratio over the period since 1970. We have also seen, in Table 7.1 (page 148), the large range of general government debt ratios across the G7 countries. There is no consensus on what is the right debt ratio, but high debt ratios are especially worrying when real interest rates are high and when output growth is low. The important point for our discussion of fiscal policy in this and later chapters is that, at times, the size and the growth in the debt ratio limit the government's use of fiscal policy to expand equilibrium output. This was indeed the case in Canada from the mid-1980s until at least the mid-1990s.

This completes our introduction to the government budget, fiscal policy, aggregate expenditure, and the economy. We have seen two ways in which the government sector affects aggregate expenditure and output. Government expenditure is a part of

TABLE 7.8 Government of Canada Net Debt Ratio: Selected Years 1970 to 2007

(% GDP)						
1970	1975	1980	1985	1990	1995	2007
21.4	16.4	24.6	44.5	55.7	70.5	34.2

Sources: The Canadian Financial Services sector, http://www.fin.gc.toc.2005/fact-cfss-eng.asp, Finance Canada, 2005. Reproduced with the permission of the Minister of Public Works and Government Services Canada, 2009.

autonomous aggregate expenditure. It affects the position of the AE function, equilibrium output, and the aggregate demand curve. The net tax rate is a leakage from the income expenditure flow. It affects induced expenditure, the slope of the AE function, the size of the multiplier, equilibrium output, and the AD curve. Government expenditure and the net tax rate are *policy levers* the government can use to influence aggregate expenditure and output. The net tax rate provides some automatic stabilization by reducing the size of the multiplier. Changes in the net tax rate or government expenditure are discretionary fiscal policy tools. In later chapters we will study in more detail how the government might use fiscal policy to stabilize the economy and control the public debt.

Review Questions 11, 12, 13 and 14

SUMMARY BOX The Algebra of Income Determination

We have used diagrams and numerical examples to show the determination of national income in an open economy based on autonomous expenditures and a multiplier. The following example shows the same thing, but in a general model.

Consumption	$C = C_0 + cYD$, where $YD = Y - NT$
Investment	$I = I_0$
Government expenditure	$G = G_0$
Net taxes	$NT = tY$
Exports	$X = X_0$
Imports	$Z = X_0 + zY$

The lower case letters c, t, and z indicate induced relationships, and the subscript $_0$ indicates initial values for autonomous expenditures.

Aggregate expenditure is:

$$AE = C + I + G + X - Z, \text{ which, by substitution, is}$$
$$AE = C_0 + c(1 - t)Y + I_0 + G_0 + X_0 - Z_0 - zY, \text{ or}$$
$$AE = C_0 + I_0 + G_0 + X_0 - Z_0 + [c(1 - t) - z]Y$$

We can reduce this expression to its two key components, autonomous and induced expenditures, by writing:

$$AE = A_0 + [c(1 - t) - z]Y, \text{ letting } A_0 = C_0 + I_0 + G_0 + X_0 - Z_0$$

If this aggregate expenditure function were drawn in a diagram, A_0 would be its intercept on the vertical axis, and $[c(1 - t) - z]$ would be its slope.

continued

continued

National income and output are in equilibrium when national income and planned aggregate expenditure are equal. This is the condition:

$$Y = AE$$

Using this condition and solving for Y_e we have:

$$Y = A_0 + [c(1 - t) - z]Y$$
$$Y - [c(1 - t) - z]Y = A_0$$
$$Y[1 - c(1 - t) + z] = A_0$$
$$Y_e = \frac{A_0}{1 - c(1 - t) + z}$$

Equilibrium national income is determined by the total autonomous expenditure in the economy, A_0, multiplied by the multiplier, $Y_e = \frac{A_0}{1 - c(1 - t) + z}$, which is based on the changes in expenditure induced by changes in national income.

Changes in equilibrium national income come mainly from changes in autonomous expenditures A, multiplied by the multiplier. The multiplier itself might also change if households changed their expenditure behaviour relative to national income or in terms of domestic and imported goods. The net tax rate t in the multiplier is a fiscal policy tool that adds automatic stability to the economy in addition to raising revenues to finance the G component of A.

The Multiplier in Canada

Based on the importance of exports and imports in GDP, we know that Canada is a small open economy. What, then, is the size of the multiplier in Canada? A simple statistical estimate, using Statistics Canada annual data for real GDP and consumption expenditures, gives a Canadian marginal propensity to consume out of national income $MPC(1 - t) = 0.54$, and marginal propensity to import $MPZ = 0.34$. Using these estimates, we get a multiplier for Canada:

$$\frac{\Delta Y}{\Delta A} = \frac{1}{(1 - 0.54 + 0.34)} = \frac{1}{1 - 0.2} = 1.25$$

If you recall, in Chapter 6 we had an estimate of the Canadian marginal propensity to consume out of disposable income of $MPC = 0.88$. In the absence of the net tax rate and the marginal propensity to import, an $MPC = 0.88$ would mean a multiplier of about 8.33. The difference between the multipliers 1.25 and 8.33 shows clearly the automatic stabilization that results from the net tax rate and marginal propensity to import.

7.8 Government, Aggregate Demand, and Equilibrium Output

Our objective in this chapter was to extend the model of Chapter 6 to include a government sector and fiscal policy. To do this we continued to assume that *wages, prices, interest rates, and foreign exchange rates are constant*. We also continued to make the important distinction between *autonomous* expenditure and *induced* expenditure, which leads to the existence of a multiplier. The equilibrium condition is still output and income equal to planned expenditure. Even though the model is more complex, it still shows us that fluctuations in autonomous expenditures, multiplied by the multiplier, cause fluctuations in output, income, and employment.

In our model, there are five sources of fluctuation in autonomous expenditures. In addition to the autonomous parts of consumption and imports the model includes autonomous investment, exports and government expenditures. The link between changes in national income and the induced changes in consumption expenditure is also more complex. As a result, the multiplier is determined by the marginal propensity to consume (MPC), the net tax rate (t), and the marginal propensity to import (MPZ). The net tax rate and the marginal propensity to import are sources of leakage from the income stream, in addition to the marginal propensity to save. They reduce the size of the multiplier.

Nevertheless, changes in autonomous expenditures are still the sources of business cycles. If business changes planned investment expenditure in response to changed expectations about future markets, or if changes in economic conditions in other countries change exports or imports, the multiplier translates these changes into larger changes or fluctuations in income and employment. Government expenditure plans and net tax rates are fiscal policy tools that could be used to moderate or offset these fluctuations through a combination of automatic and discretionary fiscal policy.

Figure 7.10 shows the relationship between equilibrium income and output, and the link between changes in aggregate expenditure, aggregate demand, and equilibrium income.

FIGURE 7.10 **Aggregate Expenditure, Aggregate Demand and Equilibrium Output**

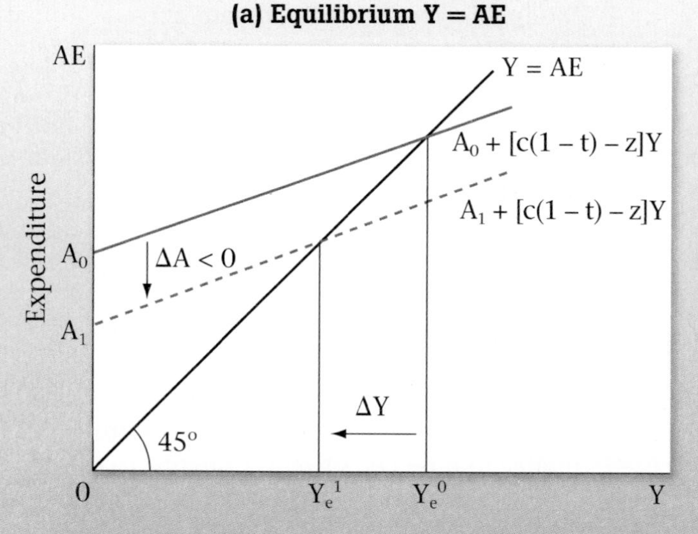

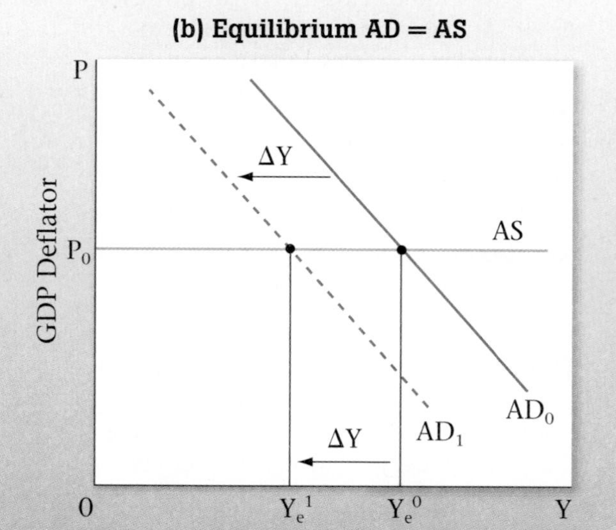

Autonomous expenditure $A_0 = C_0 + I_0 + G_0 + X_0 - Z_0$

$$\text{Slope of AE} = \frac{\Delta AE}{\Delta Y} = [c(1-t) - z]$$

$$\text{Multiplier} = \frac{\Delta Y}{\Delta A} = \frac{1}{1 - \text{slope AE}} = \frac{1}{1 - c(1-t) + z}$$

Equilibrium expenditure and output in panel (a) determine the *position* of the AD curve in panel (b). A change in autonomous expenditure ΔA causes a larger change in equilibrium income ΔY based on the multiplier. As a result, ΔA causes a horizontal shift in AD in panel (b) equal to (ΔA × multiplier). Fluctuations in AD and output, which we see as business cycles, are caused by fluctuations in autonomous expenditure.

Next

Now we have assembled the full aggregate demand side of our model, including all the sectors of the economy identified by the national accounts framework. However, we have not said anything yet about money, financial markets, interest rates, foreign exchange rates, or monetary policy. The three chapters in the next part of the text, Chapters 8, 9, and 10, examine money, financial markets, and the impacts of money and financial markets on aggregate demand. Those institutions in the economy create the opportunity for a central bank, like the Bank of Canada, to use monetary policy to change money supply and interest rates. Monetary policy, like fiscal policy, aims to manage aggregate demand to reduce business cycle fluctuations in output, employment, and prices.

SUMMARY

- The **government** buys about 20 percent of national output to provide public services, and levies taxes (net of transfers) to finance its purchases.
- The government can use **fiscal policy** to stabilize or offset business cycle fluctuations and reduce inflationary and recessionary gaps.
- **Government expenditure on goods and services** is an *autonomous* part of aggregate expenditure and raises aggregate demand and equilibrium national income.
- **Net taxes** reduce the change in consumption caused by a change in national income, *reduce the slope of the AE function, and reduce the multiplier.*
- **The government budget balance** is a deficit (surplus) if government expenditure is larger (smaller) than tax revenue. Higher government spending reduces the budget balance. A higher tax rate raises it.
- **Fiscal policy** is the government's use of its taxing and spending powers to offset business cycle fluctuations in aggregate demand, output, and employment.
- The **structural budget balance** is the budget balance measured as if the economy were at potential output.
- Changes in the structural budget balance are indicators of changes in **discretionary fiscal policy**.
- **Automatic stabilizers** reduce fluctuations in real GDP by *reducing the multiplier.* Leakages from the income/expenditure stream act as automatic stabilizers.
- The government may also use **discretionary fiscal policy, changes to structural budget balance**, to eliminate output gaps and stabilize output. In practice, fiscal policy cannot stabilize output perfectly.
- Budget deficits add to the **public debt**. Budget surpluses reduce the public debt. If citizens of the country own most of the debt, interest payments are merely transfers within the economy. However, the national debt may be a burden if the **debt ratio** is large, or the government is unwilling or unable to raise taxes to meet interest payments on the debt.
- **Budget deficits** are not necessarily bad. Particularly in a recession, a move to cut the deficit may move output further away from potential output.

KEY TERMS

Government expenditure (G) *150*
Net taxes ($NT = T_d - T_r$) *151*
Disposable income (YD) *151*
Government budget *157*
Budget function *158*
Fiscal policy *161*
Structural budget balance (SBB) *163*
Automatic stabilizer *166*
Discretionary fiscal policies *166*
Public debt (PD) *168*
Net public debt *170*
Debt ratio *170*

KEY EQUATIONS AND RELATIONS

Equations

Agregate expenditure: $AE = C + I + G + X - Z$	(7.1)	p. 150
Autonomous government expenditure: $G = G_0$	(7.2)	p. 151
Net tax revenue: $NT = tY$	(7.3)	p. 151
Disposable income: $YD = Y - NT = Y - tY = (1 - t)Y$	(7.4)	p. 151
MPC out of national income: $\frac{\Delta C}{\Delta Y} = MPC \times (1 - t) = c(1 - t)$	(7.5)	p. 153
Equilibrium real GDP: $Y = AE = C + I + G + X - Z$	(7.6)	p. 153
Government budget balance: $BB = tY - G$	(7.7)	p. 158
Equilibrium condition: $S + Z + NT = I + X + G$	(7.8)	p. 160
$NT - G = X - Z$	(7.9)	p. 160
Structural budget balance: $SBB = tY_P - G$	(7.10)	p. 163
Change in the public debt: $\Delta PD = -BB$	(7.11)	p. 169

Relations

Equilibrium real GDP: Aggregate expenditure, AE, determines equilibrium real GDP.

$$Y = AE = C + I + G + X - Z. \uparrow AE \rightarrow \uparrow Y, \downarrow AE \rightarrow \downarrow Y$$

Slope of AE: Slope of AE is determined by the MPC, the net tax rate t, and the MPZ.

$$\text{Slope } AE = MPC \times (1 - t) - MPZ$$

Autonomous expenditure with government and net exports: $A_0 = C_0 + I_0 + G_0 + X_0 - Z_0$

Multiplier with government and net exports: $\Delta A \rightarrow \Delta$ equilibrium $Y > \Delta A$

$$\frac{\Delta Y}{\Delta A} = \frac{1}{1 - [MPC \times (1 - t) - MPZ]}$$

Changes in equilibrium real GDP: $\Delta A \rightarrow \Delta Y$, By the multiplier $\Delta Y > \Delta A$

REVIEW QUESTIONS

Review Questions and answers are included in Connect at www.mcgrawhillconnect.ca.

1. Suppose a government is established in a country where none previously existed. The government spends 100, financed by borrowing, to provide public services. If autonomous consumption, investment, and exports minus imports are 200 and the marginal propensity to consume MPC = 0.75, and the MPZ = 0.15, what are the equilibrium real GDP values before and after the government is established?

2. If the government expenditure in question 1 were financed by imposing a net tax rate on income of t = 0.10:
   a. Calculate and compare the slopes of the AE functions in questions 1 and 2.
   b. Calculate and compare the multipliers in questions 1 and 2.
   c. What is the equilibrium real GDP in question 2 compared to question 1?

3. Equilibrium income in an economy is 1000, consumption expenditure is 800, investment is 80, imports are 15, exports are 35, the marginal propensity to consume is 0.9, the marginal propensity to import is 0.10, and there are no taxes.
   a. What is G?
   b. Investment rises by 50. What are the new equilibrium levels of C, I, G, and Y?
   c. What is the size of the multiplier?
   d. If further research shows that potential income Y_p = 1300, how much must G rise to make actual output equal potential output?

4. How would you explain to someone who has not had the pleasure of studying economics that an equal increase in taxes and government spending will change equilibrium real GDP?

5. If government expenditure is 100 and the net tax rate is t = 0.20:
   a. Complete the following table:

Y	NT = tY	G	BB = NT − G
100			
200			
300			
400			
500			
600			
700			

   b. In a diagram with national income Y on the horizontal axis and government revenue and expenditure on the vertical axis, draw the government expenditure and net tax functions. Explain the intercept on the vertical axis, and the slope you have given to the NT and G functions in your diagram.
   c. Suppose the government cuts the tax rate to t = 0.15. Repeat parts a) and b) with this new tax rate.

6. Draw diagrams to illustrate the initial equilibrium national income, the effect of the increase in government expenditure on equilibrium national income, and the government's budget functions and balances before and after the increase in government expenditure.

7. Suppose the government raises its revenue by a net tax of 25 percent on income, t = 0.25, the marginal propensity to consume out of disposable income is 0.8 and the marginal propensity to import is z = 0.15.
   a. What is the slope of the AE function? What is the size of the multiplier?
   b. Autonomous expenditure by the non-government sectors ($C_0 + I_0 + X_0 - Z_0$) is 300 and government expenditure is 400. What is the equilibrium income and output? What is the government's budget balance?
   c. The government increases its expenditures by 100 to provide additional funding for national defence. What is the effect on equilibrium income and output? What is the effect on the government's budget balance?

8. An economy is in equilibrium at a real GDP of 750, but current estimates put potential output at $Y_P = 850$.
   a. Is there an inflationary or a recessionary gap, and, if there is either, what is its size?
   b. Research suggests that the MPC is 0.75, the MPZ is 0.10, and the net tax rate is 0.20. If there is a gap, what change in government expenditure would eliminate the gap?
   c. If the government preferred to change its net tax rate to eliminate the gap, and not change government expenditure, what new tax rate would be required to eliminate the gap?

9. a. What is the government's structural budget balance, and why might it differ from the actual budget balance?
   b. Draw a diagram that shows the government's budget balance relative to national income. Explain briefly the vertical intercept of the budget function and its slope.
   c. Using your diagram from b), show the structural budget balance and a situation in which the actual balance is different from the structural balance.
   d. Based on this diagram, show and explain the difference between the budget effects of automatic stabilization and discretionary fiscal policy.

10. Suppose the Minister of Finance, in presenting the government's budget to Parliament, forecasts a budget surplus of $5 billion at the end of the budget year. Then, when it comes to the end of the fiscal year, the Minister reports to Parliament that the actual budget surplus has turned out to be $10 billion. How might the Minister explain this difference between the forecast and actual budget balance? You might use a diagram to illustrate your explanantion.

11. Looking back to question 7, suppose the government had an outstanding public debt of 1000 at the start of that question.
   a. What was the initial debt to GDP or debt to national income ratio?
   b. What was the size of the outstanding public debt after the increase in government expenditure, assuming the economy has reached its new equilibrium national income in one year?
   c. What is the debt ratio after the increase in government expenditure and equilibrium income?
   d. Did the increased government expenditure and its effects on the budget balance and debt ratio create problems for future fiscal policy?

12. In recent years Canadian governments have posted budget surpluses that allowed room for reduced tax rates on incomes.
   a. Use a diagram to illustrate the effect a reduction in the net tax rate would have on the government's budget function.
   b. What effect would the cut in the tax rate have on the government's structural budget balance? Does this change indicate an expansionary or restrictive policy change?
   c. What effect would the cut in the tax rate have on the automatic stabilization provided by the government's budget function? Why?

13. Define the public debt and explain briefly how it is related to past government budget deficits and surpluses.

14. In the first half of 2008 the Canadian economy was operating at potential output, according to

the Bank of Canada's estimate of the output gap. Then a slowdown in growth opened a small but growing recessionary gap. The federal government budget of February 2008 projected a small surplus for the year of about $2.3 billion, revised to $0.2 billion in the November Fiscal Update. In December 2008, Statistics Canada reported a decline in Canadian exports that stretched back to the last quarter of 2007. By that time the consensus forecast for the Canadian economy predicted a recession and called for fiscal stimulus.

a. Could the federal government provide fiscal stimulus without creating a deficit in its budget?
b. Do you think a government in this situation should provide sufficient stimulus to offset declining exports even if it means running a budget deficit?
c. Explain and defend your answers.

15. *Common fallacies* Why are these statements wrong?
    a. If the Minister of Finance raised tax revenues and expenditures by equal amounts, the change in the budget would have no effect on aggregate expenditure or equilibrium income.
    b. Government policy should balance exports and imports and ensure that the government and private sector spend less than they earn.

16. *Internet* Visit the Department of Finance Web site and examine Tables 32 and 33 of the *Fiscal Reference Tables 2006* (www.fin.gc.ca/toc/2006/frt06_-eng.asp). Describe the changes you observe in the main sources of government revenue, and the main categories of government expenditure, in the past 20 years.

PART 4

Financial Markets and Economic Activity

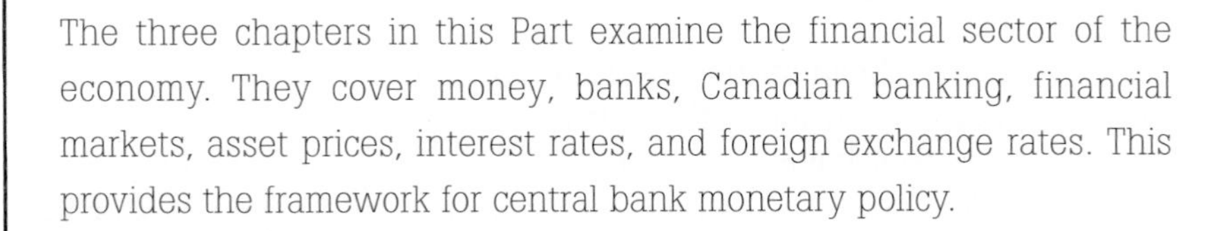

The three chapters in this Part examine the financial sector of the economy. They cover money, banks, Canadian banking, financial markets, asset prices, interest rates, and foreign exchange rates. This provides the framework for central bank monetary policy.

CHAPTER 8

Money, Banking, and the Money Supply

LEARNING OUTCOMES

By the end of this chapter you should understand:

1. Money and the functions of money
2. Modern banking in Canada
3. Competition among banks
4. How banks create money
5. The monetary base, the money multiplier, and the money supply
6. Different measures of the money supply in Canada

Many different things have been money. Dog's teeth in the Admiralty Islands, seashells in parts of Africa, gold in the nineteenth century—all are examples of money. You can see the variety of things that have been used as money in Canada by looking at James Powell's *A History of the Canadian Dollar,* which is available on the Bank of Canada's Web site, www.bankofcanada.ca/en/publication/pub_res.html#books. Silver and gold coins from many countries, and playing cards, were our money in the seventeenth and eighteenth centuries. The British pound sterling, the Spanish silver dollar, and the U.S. dollar were the main moneys in Canada in the nineteenth century, followed by paper currencies issued by banks and by the government since the late nineteenth century.

It is not the commodity used as money that matters, but the social convention that it is accepted without question as a means of payment. In this chapter we study how society uses money to make it easier for everyone to buy and sell goods and services and economize on the use of scarce resources. We examine the structure and operation of the banking system that provides our money, the factors that determine the size of the money supply in the economy, and the different measures of money supply in Canada. Then, in Chapter 9, we will build money and financial markets into our model of output, income, and employment.

8.1 Money and the Functions of Money

Although the crucial feature of money is its *general acceptance as a means of payment* or medium of exchange, money has three other functions. It serves as a unit of account, a store of value, and a standard of deferred payment.

THE MEDIUM OF EXCHANGE

Money is the **medium of exchange** used to make payments.

Money, the **medium of exchange**, is used on one side of almost every exchange. Workers exchange labour services for money. Students buy university courses with money. More generally, people and businesses buy or sell goods and services for money. We accept money, not to consume it directly, but to use it subsequently to buy things we do wish to consume. Money is the medium through which people exchange goods and services.

A **barter economy** has no medium of exchange. Goods trade directly for goods.

To see how society benefits from a medium of exchange, imagine an economy without money, a **barter economy**. In a barter economy the seller and buyer of any good or service *each* must want something the other has to offer. Each person is simultaneously a buyer and a seller. To see a film, you must swap a good or service that the theatre manager wants. There has to be a double coincidence of wants. The buyer must have what the seller wants at the same time as the seller has what the buyer wants.

Furthermore, in a barter economy each good or service has a "price" in terms of its exchange value for every other good or service, rather than just one "money price." If the economy is simple, with exchanges of very few goods and services, the number of prices is small. With three goods, the number of relative prices is three. As the economy becomes more complex, with more goods and services, the number of prices increases dramatically. In general terms, the number of prices in the barter economy is $[n \times (n - 1)/2]$, where n is the number of goods. If there are 10 goods, there are 45 prices. If there are 20 goods, there are 190 prices $[20 \times (20 - 1)/2]$.

As a result, trading is very expensive in a barter economy. People spend a lot of time and effort finding others with whom to make mutually satisfactory trades at acceptable exchange ratios. The use of money—any commodity generally accepted in payment for goods, services, and debts—makes trading much simpler and more efficient. It eliminates the "double coincidence of wants" problem. If oranges are money in the example above, you can buy or sell pizza and coffee for oranges. If there are 20 goods, using one as money reduces the number of prices from 190 to 20. The time, effort, and information involved in trading goods and services are reduced dramatically. Society can use its resources to enjoy more leisure or produce more goods and services, making everyone better off.

OTHER FUNCTIONS OF MONEY

A **unit of account** is the unit in which prices are quoted and accounts are kept.

Money also serves as a **unit of account**. In Canada prices are quoted in Canadian dollars, in Britain in pounds sterling, in much of Europe in euros, in the United States in U.S. dollars. It is convenient to use the same units for the medium of exchange and the unit of account. However, there are exceptions. During the German hyperinflation of 1922–1923, when prices in marks changed very quickly, German shopkeepers found it more convenient to use U.S. dollars as the unit of account. Prices were quoted in U.S. dollars but payments were made in marks, the German medium of exchange. Historically, in Canada, during the time of the fur trade, books were kept in "currency" but actual currency never changed hands in the barter of trade goods for furs.

A **store of value** carries purchasing power forward in time for future purchases.

To be accepted as a medium of exchange, money *must be* a **store of value**. Nobody will accept money in payment for goods supplied today if money is worthless when they try to buy goods and services with it later. But money is not the only store of value. Houses, stamp collections, interest-bearing bank deposits, and government bonds and other financial assets all serve as stores of value. Since money pays little or no interest and its real purchasing power is eroded by inflation, there are better ways to store value, but people still choose to hold some of their wealth as money. This choice to hold money balances is very important to the effects money balances have on financial markets and aggregate expenditure. We will examine it in detail in the next chapter.

Review Question 1

Finally, money is a *standard of deferred payment* or unit of account over time. When you borrow, the student loan you will repay in the future is measured in dollars. This is not an essential function of money the way the store of value function is. Canadian citizens can get bank loans that specify in U.S. dollars the amount to be repaid in the future. Thus, the key feature of money is its use as a medium of exchange. For this it must act as a store of value. And it is usually, although not invariably, convenient to make money the unit of account and standard of deferred payment as well.

DIFFERENT KINDS OF MONEY

In prisoner-of-war camps, cigarettes were money. In the nineteenth century, money was mainly gold and silver coins. These are examples of *commodity money*, ordinary goods with industrial uses (gold) or consumption uses (cigarettes), which also serve as a medium of exchange. To use commodity money, society must either cut back on the other uses of that commodity or devote scarce resources to additional production of the commodity. There are cheaper ways for society to make money.

The money we use today is the product of a long and continuing evolution in the financial services industry. This evolution is a testament to the ingenuity of people and society seeking to reduce the costs and increase the volume of trade in goods and services.

Historically, there were no banks. Money was a commodity. Gold and silver bullion are two commodities that came to be used extensively because of their relative scarcity and durability. Concerns about the purity of these metals and the inconvenience of weighing out small quantities to make payments led to coinage. The minting of gold and silver coins by heads of state offered a solution to these problems. The monarch certified the purity and quantity of the metal in the coin by having his or her likeness stamped into the metal.

Unfortunately, coinage did not completely solve the concerns about the quantity and quality of gold and silver money. The quantity of gold in a coin could be reduced by clipping its edges, or by rubbing the surfaces of the coin to wear some of the metal away. "Sweating" coins by placing them in a leather bag and shaking them was one technique used to remove some of their precious metal. The edge designs, millings, or facets that we still see on coins today were introduced to combat clipping, and wear on the heads and tails stamped into coins provided evidence of sweating. Coins that were worn or clipped were not accepted at full value in exchange for goods and services.

A second difficulty with precious metal coinage came from the sovereign who controlled the minting process. Adding a little base metal to the gold or silver being minted resulted in coins with less precious metal content than their face value certified. A little of the precious metal was withheld and could be used to mint more coin, which was, in effect, free money for the sovereign. This "debasing" of the coinage was a serious problem at times and, like clipping and sweating, reduced the acceptability of precious metal coinage as money.

The emergence of banks and paper money was a response to the problems with gold and silver commodity money. The first banks were goldsmiths who used gold in the production of jewellery and ornaments. They were accustomed to buying and selling gold bullion, and holding stocks of gold bullion. It was a natural extension of their business to offer to hold gold for safekeeping. Those who stored their gold with goldsmiths were given paper claims or receipts (IOUs), which were convertible back into gold on demand.

When people began to use gold receipts to make payments, gold receipts became a means of payment. They were **token money**, representing a fixed amount of the precious metal. Goldsmiths became bankers when they realized that not all their customers would show up at the same time and want their gold back. The convertibility of gold receipts made them acceptable as a medium of exchange. Gold merchants could make loans by issuing more gold receipts than they had gold in their storage vaults. They only needed gold holdings equal to a fraction of the gold receipts they had issued, as long as people used the receipts as a medium of exchange.

Token money is a convertible claim on a commodity money.

Banks as we know them grew out of this acceptance by society of credit (IOU) money as a medium of exchange. Banks began to accept customer deposits of token money and to issue their own bank notes (credits) as receipts. People liked the convenience and safety of storing some of their wealth with banks. As society became more comfortable with banks and confident in the safety of banks, bank deposits, which could be transferred by cheque, became widely accepted as the medium of exchange. Bank notes and deposits were no longer convertible into gold or commodity money, but they were convertible into **legal tender**. Governments established central banks to control the supply of legal tender, bank notes, or cash. Bank notes now serve as both a medium of exchange and as the **reserves** banks hold to ensure the convertibility of their customers' deposits.

Legal tender is the money that by law must be accepted as a means of payment.

Bank reserves are the cash held by the bank to meet possible withdrawals by depositors.

Unlike other financial institutions, such as pension funds and insurance companies, the key aspect of banks is that some of their liabilities are used as the medium of exchange; cheques and debit cards allow their deposits to be used as money to make payments. Bank deposits are credit money.

In Canada today, as in most industrial countries, we use a combination of **fiat money** and **credit money**. Fiat money, in contrast to commodity or token money is money that the government has declared to be legal tender. Coins and paper bank notes are fiat money in Canada. If you look carefully at a $5, $10, or $20 Bank of Canada bill you will find the statement: "This note is legal tender." By law it must be accepted as a means of payment for goods and services bought or debts repaid.

Fiat money is the money the government has declared as legal tender.

Credit money is the debt of a private business or individual.

Our fiat money is supplemented by credit money. A bank deposit is credit money, and is redeemable in fiat money on demand, or in the case of some savings and time deposits, after a short waiting period. Furthermore, the bank is obliged to pay when your cheque is presented, or when you use your debit card. Bank deposits are a medium of exchange because they are generally accepted as a means of payment, even though they are not legal tender. The sum of bank deposits and fiat money in circulation outside the banks at any time is the stock of medium of exchange and the economy's **money supply**.

The **money supply** is the stock of medium of exchange in circulation.

8.2 Modern Banking in Canada

In Canada today, and in other industrial countries, the banking system is made up of a *central bank* and a number of *commercial banks* and other deposit-taking institutions called *near banks*. Table 8.1 illustrates the structure of the banking industry in Canada. The industry is defined broadly to include deposit-taking institutions, not just those that operate under the federal Bank Act.

APPLICATION BOX 8.1

Travellers' Tales

The following contrast between a monetary and a barter economy is taken from the World Bank, *World Development Report*, 1989.

Life Without Money

"Some years since, Mademoiselle Zelie gave a concert in the Society Islands in exchange for a third part of the receipts. When counted, her share was found to consist of 3 pigs, 23 turkeys, 44 chickens, 5000 cocoa nuts, besides considerable quantities of bananas, lemons, and oranges .... as Mademoiselle could not consume any considerable portion of the receipts herself it became necessary in the meantime to feed the pigs and poultry with the fruit." W. S. Jevons (1898)

Marco Polo Discovers Paper Money

"In this city of Kanbula [Beijing] is the mint of the Great Khan, who may truly be said to possess the secret of the alchemists, as he has the art of producing money......

"He causes the bark to be stripped from mulberry trees..... made into paper..... cut into pieces of money of different sizes. The act of counterfeiting is punished as a capital offence. This paper currency is circulated in every part of the Great Khan's domain. All his subjects receive it without hesitation because they can dispose of it again in the purchase of merchandise they may require." *The Travels of Marco Polo*, Book II

A **financial intermediary** is a business that specializes in bringing borrowers and lenders together.

Banks are **financial intermediaries**. They borrow money from the public, crediting them with a deposit. The deposit is a liability of the bank. It is money owed to depositors. The money raised from depositors provides the funds to support the bank loans made to businesses, households, and governments.

Banks are not the only financial intermediaries. Box 8.2 describes the broader financial services industry in Canada, and identifies the major institutions involved. The crucial feature of banks for our work is that some of their liabilities are used as a means of payment. Those bank deposits are a part of the money supply in the economy.

TABLE 8.1 The Canadian Banking System in 2008

Banking institutions:	Number	Assets (bill $)
Central bank:		
The Bank of Canada	1	77
Number of chartered banks:		
Schedule I domestic banks	22	
Schedule II foreign bank subsidiaries	24	
Schedule III foreign bank branches	25	
Total	71	2787
Number of near banks:		
Credit unions and caisses populaires	1000	197
Non-bank trust and mortgage companies	35	18

Source: Bank of Canada Banking and Financial Statistics, December 2008, Tables B2, C3, C4, D1, D2. Bank of Canada, 2009.

APPLICATION BOX 8.2

Banks and Other Financial Services Institutions in Canada

The banks that accept and issue the deposits we use as money are a key part of the larger financial services industry in Canada. Trust companies, credit unions, caisses populaires, insurance companies, securities dealers, mutual fund companies, and independent financial advisors all play a role in this industry. But banks hold more than 70 percent of the assets in the financial services sector, and the six largest Canadian banks account for over 90 percent of the assets of the banking industry. Trust companies, credit unions, and caisses populaires also accept deposits that are used as money, but those deposits are a small fraction of the total of deposit money. As a result, bank deposits are the focus of our discussion of money in Canada. You will recognize the names of the big banks among the top ten financial services companies in Canada listed in the table below.

The banks and other financial services companies provide important *financial intermediation* services to their customers: governments, businesses, and the general public. You will recall from Chapter 6 that equilibrium national income means that planned saving is equal to planned investment. In the more complex economy of Chapter 7, we saw that total planned leakages from the income stream will equal total planned injections into the stream. But planned leakages are the result of decisions that are different from the decisions that result in planned injections. We need some mechanism to bring these two sets of decisions together. That is what financial intermediaries and financial markets do.

The Top 10 Financial Services Companies in Canada by Asset Size, 2007

Company	Total assets[1] ($ billions)
Royal Bank of Canada	612
TD Financial Group	429
Bank of Nova Scotia	416
Bank of Montreal	368
Manulife Financial Corporation[2]	352
Canadian Imperial Bank of Commerce	348
Sun Life Financial Inc.[2]	187
Mouvement des caisses Desjardins[3]	144
Great-West Lifeco	118
National Bank of Canada	113

[1] Includes both domestic and foreign assets.
[2] Including segregated fund assets.
[3] Mouvement des caisses Desjardins consists of a network of Desjardins' caisses populaires, which are individual financial co-operatives owned by their members, and a network of subsidiaries grouped in Desjardins-Laurentian Financial Corporation. While the caisses populaires are independent institutions, because of the close partnership between caisses and subsidiaries, Desjardins is often portrayed as a single financial institution.

Sources: The Canadian Financial Services Sector, http://www.fin.gc.ca/toc/2005/fact-cfss-eng.asp, Finance Canada, 2005. Reproduced with the permission of the Minister of Public Works and Government Services Canada, 2009; and 'Top 150 Banks Worldwide Ranked by Asset Size,' *The Banker: A Financial Times Publication*, July 2009, http://www.thebanker.com/cp/57/T1000_25_Tier1&TotalAssets.gif.

The **Bank of Canada** is Canada's central bank.

The **Bank of Canada** is Canada's central bank. It is the source of the bank notes used to make payments and held as cash reserves by commercial banks. Established by the government in 1935, it has the responsibility to regulate the national money supply and support the operation of financial markets. The Bank's power to meet these responsibilities comes from its monopoly on the issuance of bank notes.

The Bank of Canada also is the provider of:

- Banking services for the commercial banks in the system
- Banking services for the federal government
- Lender-of-last-resort facilities in times of reserve shortfalls

Commercial banks hold some of their reserves as deposits in the Bank of Canada, and make payments among themselves using their Bank of Canada deposits. These interbank payments arise from wire transfers, direct deposits, pre-authorized debits, bill payments, point-of-sale debits, and online payments made by bank customers. For example, cheques written by customers at one bank, say Scotiabank, but paid to and deposited by customers of the Royal Bank result in transfers of deposits between these banks. To settle these transfers, Scotiabank must pay the Royal Bank. Funds held by Scotiabank on deposit in the Bank of Canada are used for this purpose. They are called "settlement balances." In 2007, the Canadian Payments Association, which coordinates this clearing of interbank transactions, handled more than 1.09 billion cheques and 3.29 billion point-of-sale debits.

The government holds some deposits in the Bank of Canada. Government receipts, like income tax payments payable to the Receiver General, are deposited in government accounts in the Bank of Canada. Government payments like Old Age Security, Employment Insurance benefits, bond interest, and income tax refunds are paid with government cheques or transfers drawn on its Bank of Canada account. Government funds over and above those needed to make regular payments are held on deposit in the commercial banks, and earn interest income for the government.

The key difference between a central bank and the commercial banks in the banking system is the profit motive. Central banks *do not* pursue profits. Their operations focus on the management of the cash reserves available to the public and the banks. The supply of cash reserves affects the behaviour of other banks and financial markets more generally. This is the monetary policy role of the central bank. We will examine it in detail in Chapter 10.

Commercial banks, on the other hand, are profit-oriented businesses. They operate, as we will see shortly, to maximize the profit they earn for their owners. To this end, they offer banking services to the public. Using the notes and deposits issued by the Bank of Canada as reserves, they issue bank deposits to their customers—which are widely used as the medium of exchange—and they make loans to finance purchases made by businesses and households.

Table 8.1 showed the private sector commercial banks classified according to the provisions of the Bank Act, an act of parliament that regulates banking. The Act sets out both the conditions required to establish a banking business and the operating regulations. Large Canadian-owned retail banks such as BMO Bank of Montreal, CIBC, RBC Royal Bank, Scotiabank, TD Bank Financial Group, and fifteen others operate as Schedule I banks under the *Bank Act*. The *Bank Act* also provides for foreign-owned banks and branches of foreign-owned banks under Schedules II and III. Schedule I banks are commonly referred to as "the chartered banks." You will find a full list of Canadian banks at the Canadian Bankers Association Web site, www.cba.ca.

Review Question 2

TABLE 8.2 **Balance Sheet of Canadian Chartered Banks, February 2008**

Assets	$ billion	Liabilities	$ billion
Canadian dollars:		Canadian dollars:	
Cash	5.3	Personal savings deposits	494.7
Government of Canada securities	134.6	Demand deposits	180.6
Personal and business loans	574.5	Non-personal term deposits	366.3
Mortgages	489.0	Government of Canada deposits	2.7
Other financial securities	238.6	Other liabilities	529.2
Other assets	280.9	Shareholders' equity	116.1
	238.3		
Foreign currency assets	959.8	Foreign currency liabilities	993.1
Total assets	2682.7	Total liabilities and shareholders' equity	2682.7

Source: Bank of Canada Banking and Financial Statistics, April 2008, Tables C3 and C4. Bank of Canada, 2009. Figures have been rounded.

To illustrate the business of these banks, Table 8.2 shows the consolidated balance sheet of Canadian chartered banks in February 2008. In the table we see that the banks held small cash balances as reserves against their deposit liabilities. Their other Canadian assets were mainly loans to households and businesses, including mortgage loans, and their holdings of financial securities. Because cash and many of their financial securities have high **liquidity**, banks can lend long and still have cash and funds available if depositors withdraw their money.

Liquidity is the cheapness, speed, and certainty with which asset values can be converted into cash.

However, many loans to businesses and households are quite illiquid. The bank cannot easily get its money back in a hurry. This is not really a cause for concern when people and businesses have confidence in the banks and make widespread use of bank deposits as money. Payments and receipts are both in bank deposit form, which are cleared quickly and efficiently through the cheque-clearing and transfer facilities. Banks need only small cash balances to cover the net clearings and net public demand for cash. In Table 8.2, the banks are holding only $5.3 billion against deposit liabilities of $1044.3 billion.

The liabilities of the chartered banks include the savings, demand, and term deposits issued to customers. Some savings deposits and all demand deposits have chequing privileges. Some other savings deposits do not permit chequing and may require notice before funds can be withdrawn. These deposit accounts and the term deposits have fixed withdrawal dates; they pay a higher rate of interest to the deposit holder. Different types of bank deposits are the money we use as a medium of exchange and a store of value.

Canadian banks also carry on important international banking operations, as do banks in many other countries. We see this business recorded on the balance sheet as foreign currency assets and liabilities. The foreign currency assets are mainly loans to customers and holdings of foreign financial securities. Foreign currency deposits of customers are the main foreign currency liabilities. These foreign currency operations are similar to the banks' domestic currency operations. The banks provide loan financing to customers needing foreign currency to make payments in other countries, and they provide deposit facilities for customers using foreign currency for international transactions.

8.3 Bank Competition and Co-operation

Competition and co-operation are important to the efficient operation of the banking system. Banks compete among themselves for customer deposits and customer loans. Some of the competition for deposits is based on the location, convenience, and quality of bank branches, some on the offers of service packages including personal financial advice and wealth management, and some on the interest rates offered on deposit balances. If you watch TV, you are probably aware that ING Bank would like to pay you a relatively high interest rate and will make no service charges if you will put some of your funds on deposit with them. Success in attracting deposits is very important to size and growth of a bank's business.

Credit-worthy customers willing to borrow funds are equally important to a bank's operations. Interest income earned on customer loans is the major source of bank revenue. As a result, banks compete in the personal and business loan markets, using both the terms of loans and the interest rates charged on loans to attract borrowers. The market for mortgage funds is one of the most competitive areas of bank operations. Mortgage rates and terms are advertised widely in the media and in displays in bank offices and even in supermarkets.

Despite this competition for deposits and loans, the banking system depends on the co-operation among banks that makes deposits the medium of exchange. Co-operation in the cheque-clearing system and the debit card *Interac* system are two important examples of banks working jointly to provide the payments system. A cheque book or a debit card is not very useful if it can make payments only to other people or businesses that do business with the bank you use. Joint interests in *VISA* and *MASTERCARD* are a second important part of inter-bank co-operation that makes these cards widely acceptable as a source of credit.

There are also important areas of bank co-operation on the lending side of their operations. It often happens that businesses and industries have projects that need more financing than any one bank can or wants to provide. However, several banks might agree to provide funding jointly, increasing their lending capacity and spreading the risks associated with the project among them.

These dimensions of competition and co-operation among banks, and their contribution to the efficient functioning of the money and financial sector of the economy, appear regularly in the debate over bank mergers in Canada.

BANKING OPERATIONS AND PROFITS

A commercial bank is a profit-oriented business. Its profits come from the difference between what it costs it to raise funds and the revenues it earns from lending. To bring deposits in, the bank offers customers a range of banking services, including safekeeping, record keeping, access to banking offices or bank machines, chequing, Internet banking and debit card facilities, and interest income on some types of deposits. Service charges or fees cover the costs of some of these services. The interest payments to depositors are the main net cost of funds to the bank.

To be profitable, banks have to find ways to lend, at acceptable levels of risk, the funds they have attracted from depositors. Table 8.2 shows how banks lend their money. In Canadian dollars, most is lent to households and businesses at interest rates established for different types of personal, business, and mortgage lending. Some is used to buy government securities and other financial assets, usually with a short time to maturity. These assets pay a lower rate of interest than loans, but they are more liquid and provide the banks with funds if people decide to withdraw a lot of money from their deposit accounts. Notice that the banks also hold some cash, on which no interest is earned, to cover the day-to-day clearing balances that come from the withdrawals, deposits, and transfers made by their customers.

Bank profits come from the difference or spread between the interest cost of raising funds from depositors and the interest income earned on bank assets. If, for example, the banks pay, on average, 4 percent on their deposit liabilities of all types and earn, on average, 6 percent on their assets of all types, their **net interest income** would be 2 percent. To take actual examples, the *Scotiabank Annual Report* for 2007 reports net interest income of 1.89 percent of average assets in 2007, while the *Royal Bank of Canada Annual Report* for 2007 reports 1.30 percent. In both cases, the net interest income was lower than the previous year as competitive pressures narrowed the spread and interest rates in general declined. The key to profitability is choosing the right mix of high-quality (low-risk) loans and investments while at the same time controlling the costs of raising funds.

Net interest income is the excess loan interest earned over deposit interest paid.

A bank uses its specialist expertise to acquire a diversified portfolio of investments. Without the existence of banks, depositors would have neither the time nor the expertise to decide which loans and investments to make. Table 8.2 shows that Canadian banks held only $5.3 billion in cash and $1044.3 billion in savings demand and term deposits. Their cash reserve assets were about 0.51 percent of their total deposits. The skill in running a bank entails being able to judge just how much must be held in liquid assets, including cash, and how much can be lent out in less liquid forms that earn higher interest income. The profit motive pushes the bank toward riskier, higher interest paying assets and higher net interest income. Banker's risk, the risk that customers will withdraw their deposits and demand cash, pushes the bank toward holding higher cash balances. But cash balances earn no interest income and reduce the bank's net interest income.

8.4 How Banks Create Money

Banks *create money* when they increase their deposit liabilities to pay for the loans they make to customers, or for the financial securities they buy. The public uses the deposit liabilities of the banks as money to make payments or to hold as a store of wealth. The banks' ability to create money comes from the willingness of the public to use bank deposits, the liabilities of the bank, as money. Thus, four key conditions that give banks the ability to create money are:

1. The non-bank public has confidence in banks and is willing to hold and use bank deposits as money.
2. The non-bank public is willing to borrow from the banks to finance expenditure or asset purchases.
3. The banks are willing to operate with cash reserves equal to some small fraction of their deposit liabilities.
4. The banks are willing to accept the risks involved in lending to the non-bank public.

If any of these is absent, the banks cannot create money, although they may provide safekeeping services.

The first condition is described and defined by the **currency ratio** (cr). That is the ratio of cash balances to the bank deposits that members of the non-bank public

The **currency ratio (cr)** is the ratio of cash balances to deposit balances.

wish to hold. The banks hold the cash in the economy not held by the non-bank public. Banks acquire cash by offering customers deposit services, as we have discussed above. If the non-bank public holds all its money as cash, the banks cannot acquire the cash reserves they need to cover their deposit liabilities. There is no banking industry.

$$\text{cr} = \frac{\text{non-bank public cash holdings}}{\text{non-bank public bank deposits}}$$

The **reserve ratio (rr)** is the ratio of cash reserves to deposit liabilities held by banks.

The third condition required for the banks to create money is a bank reserve ratio that is less than one. The **reserve ratio (rr)** is the ratio of cash on hand to deposit liabilities that banks choose to hold. We defined this ratio earlier as:

$$\text{rr} = \frac{\text{reserve assets}}{\text{deposit liabilities}}$$

Cash holdings are reserve assets. If banks choose to hold reserves equal to their deposit liabilities, rr = 1 and the banks cannot create deposits. They are simple safety deposit boxes.

To see how banks can and do create deposits, we start with a very simple case. Let's assume banks use a reserve ratio of 10 percent (rr = 0.10), and the public decides it does not wish to hold any cash balances (cr = 0). Suppose initially the non-bank public has wealth of $1000 held in cash, before they decide to switch to bank deposit money. This cash is a private sector asset. It is a liability of the central bank or government, which issued it, but not a liability of the private banks. The first part of Table 8.3 uses simple balance sheets to show this cash as an asset of the non-bank private sector.

Now people pay this $1000 of cash into the banks by opening bank deposit accounts. Banks get assets of $1000 in cash and issue deposit liabilities of $1000. These deposits are

TABLE 8.3 **How the Banking System Creates Money**

Banks				Non-Bank Private Sector			
Assets		Liabilities		Assets		Liabilities	
1. Initial position							
Cash	0	Deposits	0	Cash	$1000	Bank loans	0
2. People deposit their cash in the banks.							
Cash	$1000	Deposits	$1000	Cash	0	Bank loans	0
				Deposits	$1000		
3. Banks make loans of $9000 and create $9000 in new deposits for customers.							
Cash	$1000	Deposits	$10,000	Cash	0	Bank loans	$9000
Loans	$9000			Deposits	$10,000		

money the banks owe to their depositors. If banks were simply safety deposit boxes or storerooms, they would hold cash assets equal to their deposit liabilities. Their reserve ratio would be 100 percent of deposits, making rr = 1.0. Table 8.3 would end with part 2.

However, if the public uses bank deposits as money, the banks don't need all deposits to be fully covered by cash reserves. It is unlikely that all depositors will show up at the same time and demand cash for their deposits. Recognizing this, the banks decide that reserves equal to 10 percent (rr = 0.10) of deposits will cover all net customer demands for cash. In this case, the banks have excess reserves equal to 90 percent of their deposit liabilities or, initially $900.

The banks use their excess reserves to expand their lending. Each bank makes new loans equal to its excess reserves. It pays for those loans by creating an equal amount of deposits. In our example, all banks combined create $9000 of loans. In part 3 of Table 8.3, we see loans of $9000, as assets on the banks' balance sheets, and $9000 of new deposits to customers, against which they can write cheques. The deposits of $9000 are a liability on the banks' balance sheets. Because the public uses bank deposits as money, the banks can buy new loans by creating new deposits.

Now the banks have $10,000 total deposits—the original $1000 when cash was deposited, plus the new $9000 created by making new loans—and $10,000 of total assets, comprising $9000 in loans and $1000 in cash in the vaults. The reserve ratio is 10 percent in part 3 of Table 8.3 (rr = $1000 cash/$10,000 deposits = 0.10 or 10%).

It does not even matter whether the 10 percent reserve ratio is imposed by law or is merely smart profit-maximizing behaviour by the banks that balances risk and reward. The risk is the possibility of being caught short of cash; the reward is the net interest income earned.

How did banks create money? Originally, there was $1000 of cash in circulation. That was the money supply. When paid into bank vaults, it went out of circulation as a medium of exchange. But the public got $1000 of bank deposits against which cheques could be written. The money supply, cash in circulation plus bank deposits, was still $1000. Then the banks created deposits *not* fully backed by cash reserves. Now the public had $10,000 of deposits against which to write cheques. The money supply rose from $1000 to $10,000. *The public was willing to use bank deposits as money and the banks were willing to lend.* This allowed the banks to create money by making loans based on their fractional reserve ratio.

If the currency ratio is not zero the example is a bit more complex. The banks are still able to create deposits but the extent of the deposit creation is limited by the public's withdrawal of currency to maintain the currency ratio as deposits increase. A rise in the currency ratio could be a result of a fall in public confidence in the banks in times of financial problems like those in the autumn of 2008. Bank deposits and lending capacity would be reduced as a result.

Suppose the reserve ratio rr = 0.10 as above but now the currency ratio is also cr = 0.10 rather than zero. To keep the numbers simple, assume the public initially holds $1100 in cash and no deposits. Then people open bank accounts and deposit $1000, but continue to hold $100, to satisfy their currency ratio of 10 percent. Table 8.4 illustrates the results for bank lending, deposit creation, and the money supply.

In this example the banks respond to the receipt of new cash from depositors as they did before. In part 2 they expand their lending by the amount of the excess reserves created by the new deposits. However, as bank loans and deposits expand, the non-bank public withdraws cash equal to 10 percent of the newly created deposits, in order to maintain their 10 percent currency ratio as illustrated in part 3. This cash drain reduces but does not immediately eliminate the excess reserve position of the banks and their capacity to make additional loans.

TABLE 8.4 How the Currency Ratio Limits the Banking System's Deposit Creation

Banks				Non-Bank Private Sector			
Assets		Liabilities		Assets		Liabilities	
1. Initial position							
Cash	0	Deposits	0	Cash	1100	Bank loans	0
2. People deposit cash in the banks							
Cash	1000	Deposits	1000	Cash	100	Bank loans	0
				Deposits	1000		
3. Banks make loans equal to excess reserves of $900 (rr = 0.10)							
Cash	1000	Deposits	1900	Cash	100	Bank loans	900
Loans	900			Deposits	1900		
4. People withdraw $81.81 cash to maintain their currency ratio (cr = 0.10)							
Cash	918.18	Deposits	1818.19	Cash	181.81	Bank loans	900
Loans	900			Deposits	1818.19		
5. Banks make loans equal to excess reserves $736.36 (rr = 0.10)							
Cash	918.18	Deposits	2554.55	Cash	181.81	Bank loans	1636.36
Loans	1636.36			Deposits	2554.55		
6. People withdraw $66.95 cash to maintain their currency ratio (cr = 0.10)							
Cash	851.23	Deposits	2487.6	Cash	248.76	Bank loans	1636.36
Loans	1636.36			Deposits	2487.60		
7. Banks and non-bank private sector adjusted to reserve and currency ratios							
Cash	500	Deposits	5000	Cash	500	Bank loans	4500
Loans	4500			Deposits	5000		

Banks continue to expand lending and create new deposits as long as they are in an excess reserve position and can find creditworthy borrowers. The non-bank public withdraws cash as their deposits increase and maintains their currency ratio. The adjustment continues until the banks have expanded lending and deposits enough to restore their desired reserve ratio. This expansion is limited, compared to that illustrated in Table 8.3, by the loss of cash reserves that the banks experience through the currency drain that maintains the non-bank public's desired currency ratio.

Currency ratio and the cash drains they create have important implications. If banks can promote public confidence and make deposits more convenient as a means of payment, through debit cards for example, and reduce the public's need for cash, their lending capacity is increased relative to a given stock of cash in the economy. On the other hand, if the public has growing concerns about the stability of banks and the safety of bank deposits, they hold more cash and withdraw cash in larger proportion to an increase in bank deposits and lending. The lending and deposit creation of the banks is reduced accordingly.

Usually currency ratios are thought to be quite stable with some consistent variation that reflects seasonal changes in expenditure. However, in late 2007 and continuing into 2008 the currency ratio increased as financial difficulties in assets markets raised concerns about the financial stability of some banks. Customers showed some reluctance to maintain their bank deposits and in some cases withdrew funds. As a result, the banks found it more difficult and costly to raise funds through deposits to support their lending operations. Even with central bank support for bank liquidity, interest rates on bank mortgage lending remained high and the willingness of banks to lend was reduced.

Review Questions 3 and 4

FINANCIAL PANICS

Everybody knows that the banks create money by making loans based on their fractional reserve ratio. Usually people don't mind. But if people believe that a bank has lent too much and would be unable to meet depositors' claims for cash, there would be a *run on the bank* and a **financial panic**. If the bank cannot repay all depositors, you try to get your money out first while the bank can still pay. Since everyone does the same thing, they ensure that the bank is unable to pay. It holds cash equal to a small percentage of its deposit liabilities and will be unable to liquidate its loans in time to meet the demands for cash.

In a **financial panic,** people lose confidence in banks and rush to withdraw cash.

The experience of the Northern Rock Bank in the U.K. starting in the summer of 2007 is a recent example of a financial panic and its consequences. Northern Rock was one of Britain's largest mortgage lenders. It financed its lending with sales of **commercial paper** to banks and other financial institutions, as well as a relatively small amount of deposits from savers. The crisis in the U.S. sub-prime mortgage market and confidence in mortgage-backed commercial paper led banks and other money market participants to stop lending money to Northern Rock through purchases of its paper. The risks involved were unknown. News of this collapse in its major source of funds triggered a loss of confidence among depositors and the first run on deposits in a British bank in about 140 years.

Commercial papers are short term 30-day and 60-day notes designed to pay the buyers interest generated by bundled accounts receivable and loans of different types during the term to maturity.

Despite substantial support from the Bank of England and government assurances that deposits were safe, depositors continued to withdraw funds and sales of commercial paper collapsed, as did the value of the bank's shares on the stock market. In the end, the government, unable to find a suitable private buyer, nationalized the bank in order to prevent a bank failure that might spread to other financial institutions.

Fortunately, financial panics involving depositor runs on the bank are rare, particularly in Canada. A key reason for this, which we discuss in the next chapter, is that the central bank, the Bank of Canada, and other national central banks, will lend cash to banks in temporary difficulties. Furthermore, deposit insurance plans like the Canadian Deposit Insurance Corporation, CIDC, cover individual bank deposits up to $100,000 against default. Knowledge of these institutional arrangements helps prevent a self-fulfilling stampede to withdraw deposits before the bank runs out of cash.

However, recent experience shows how financial crises can arise in other ways. Northern Rock was the first casualty of the crisis in the U.S. sub-prime mortgage market and real estate sector. Once portfolio mangers realized that it was difficult if not impossible to evaluate the risks of commercial paper, financial institutions were in difficulties if they held those paper assets or relied on selling them to raise funds. Several large financial institutions in the United States required government rescue or failed. The plight of famous names like Bear Sterns, Countrywide Financial, Fannie May, and Freddie Mac became headline news.

The crisis was not limited to the U.S. financial sector. Banks in Iceland could no longer sell new commercial paper to refinance their maturing paper and were taken over by the government. In late 2008 the large Swiss bank USB announced a bailout agreement with the Swiss National Bank to stabilize its financial position after continued difficulties based on its holdings of commercial paper and dating back to 2007. Other European lenders, including Bradford & Bingley in the U.K., and Fortis in Belgium and Luxembourg have been rescued by their governments.

Banks in Canada were not immune to the financial difficulties created by the collapse of the commercial paper markets. All the major chartered banks were holding some of the commercial paper that contributed to the market collapse in 2008. They were forced to accept that without a market these assets had no value and funds tied up in them were lost. Fortunately, Canadian banks relied more heavily on strong retail depositor bases as sources of funds. The banks remained financially strong even after their commercial paper losses, and public confidence in the banks did not collapse. No Canadian bank failed or required a government bailout. By way of contrast, the U.S. Federal Deposit Insurance Corporation listed 25 U.S. bank failures in 2008, compared to three in 2007, and none in 2006.

Review Questions 5 and 6

8.5 The Monetary Base and the Money Multiplier

The cash reserves of the chartered or commercial banks are a small fraction of total bank deposits. Deposit money created by banks is by far the largest part of the money supply in modern economies. You have mastered the basics, but now we examine the mechanics of bank deposits and money supply in a bit more detail.

Banks' deposits depend on the cash reserves of the banks. To complete our analysis of how the money supply is determined, we need to examine two things:

1. The first is the source of the cash in the economy.
2. The second is the amount of that cash that is deposited in the banking system, rather than held as cash balances by the public.

As we discussed earlier, the original source of bank reserves was gold, which people deposited in banks for safekeeping and convenience. Bank notes and deposits in those days were convertible into gold. Today, in developed countries, central banks are the source of bank reserves. The central bank, the Bank of Canada in Canada, controls the issue of token money in the form of Bank of Canada notes. These are the $5, $10, $20, $50, and $100 bank notes you can withdraw from the bank when you wish to covert some of your bank balance to cash. Bank reserves are the banks' holdings of these central bank notes in their vaults and bank machines. Our bank deposits are now convertible into Bank of Canada notes, not gold. The central bank has the responsibility to manage the supply of cash in the economy. We will examine the details of central bank operations in Chapter 10.

The **monetary base** or stock of **high-powered money (H)** is the notes and coins in circulation plus the cash held by the banks.

The cash the central bank provides to the economy is called the **monetary base** or the stock of **high-powered money (H)**. It is the legal tender into which bank deposits can be converted. It is the ultimate means of payment in transactions and the settlement of debts. Notes and coins in circulation and held by the banking system are the main part of the high-powered money issued by the central bank. As we discussed earlier, the commercial banks hold small settlement balances in the central bank to make inter-bank payments arising from cheque clearings.

How much of this monetary base is held by banks as cash reserves? In our simple example of deposit creation in Table 8.3, we assumed the public deposited all its cash with the banks. This was only a simplification. Everyone carries some cash around. We don't write cheques or use debit cards for small purchases like bus fare and coffee. Cash is more convenient.

There are other reasons why people hold cash. Some people don't trust banks. They keep their savings under the bed or in the cookie jar. Some people hold cash to make illegal or tax-evading transactions in the "underground economy." As a result, the non-bank public holds some of the high-powered money provided by the central bank, and some is held in the banks as reserves for deposits.

Our main interest is the relationship between the money supply in the economy, the total of cash in circulation plus bank deposits, and the monetary base created by the central bank. Using our earlier discussion of the fractional reserve ratio in the banking system, we can define a **money multiplier**. The money multiplier provides the link between the high-powered money supplied by the central bank and the money supply in the economy. It also predicts the change in money supply that would result from a change in the monetary base, the quantity of high-powered money supplied by the central bank.

The **money multiplier** is the change in the money supply caused by a change in the monetary base or stock of high-powered money.

$$\text{Money supply} = \text{money multiplier} \times \text{monetary base}$$

$$\text{Money multiplier} = \frac{\Delta\text{money supply}}{\Delta\text{monetary base}}$$

The value of the money multiplier depends on two key ratios:

1. **rr**, the banks' ratio of cash reserves to total deposits, and
2. **cr**, the non-bank public's ratio of cash balances to bank deposits.

Banks' ratio of cash reserves to total deposits determines how much they can expand lending and create bank deposits based on their reserve holdings. The *lower* the reserve ratio, the more deposits banks can create against given cash reserves, and the *larger* is the multiplier. We saw this relationship earlier in our discussion of Table 8.3.

Similarly, the lower the non-bank public's ratio of cash to bank deposits, the larger is the share of the monetary base held by the banks. When the banks hold more monetary base, they can create more bank deposits. The lower the non-bank public's currency ratio, the larger are bank holdings of monetary base and the larger the money supply for any given monetary base.

THE MONEY MULTIPLIER

Suppose banks wish to hold cash reserves R equal to a fraction rr of their deposits D.

$$R = rrD \tag{8.1}$$

The non-bank sector also wishes to hold some money as cash to pay for small purchases. If cash holdings outside the banks, C, are also a fraction cr of deposits, we can write:

$$C = crD \tag{8.2}$$

As a result, the monetary base, or supply of high-powered money, H, is held either as cash in bank vaults and automatic banking machines or as cash in business cash registers and safes and cash in peoples' wallets, purses, or cookie jars. This means from equations (8.1) and (8.2) that:

$$\mathbf{H = (rr + cr)D} \tag{8.3}$$

The money supply, M, is the sum of cash in circulation outside the banks and bank deposits. This gives us:

$$M = C + D, \text{ and}$$

$$\mathbf{M = (1 + cr)D} \tag{8.4}$$

By dividing equation (8.4) by (8.3), we can find the money multiplier, the ratio of M to H:

$$\frac{\Delta M}{\Delta H} = \frac{(1 + cr)}{(rr + cr)} \tag{8.5}$$

which will be greater than 1 as long as rr is less than 1.

If, for example, banks want to hold cash reserves equal to 5 percent, and the non-bank public wants to hold cash equal to 10 percent of their holdings of bank deposits, the money multiplier will be:

$$\frac{\Delta M}{\Delta H} = \frac{(1 + 0.1)}{(0.05 + 0.1)} = \frac{1.1}{0.15} = 7.33$$

The money multiplier tells us how much the money supply in the economy would change as a result of a change in the monetary base. In this example, a $1 change in the monetary base results in a change in the money supply equal to $7.33.

We can see from the way we have found the money multiplier that it depends on the decisions made by the banks in terms of their reserve holdings, and the decisions made by the public in terms of their use of cash rather than bank deposits as money. If you experiment with different values for rr and cr, you will see how the money multiplier would change if these ratios were to change.

HOW BIG IS THE MONEY MULTIPLIER?

Now that we have a formula for the money multiplier, we can ask: What is the size of the multiplier in Canada? Based on data from *Bank of Canada Banking and Financial Statistics*, April 2008, Tables B1, C3, and C4, on average, in the first two months of 2008, Canadian banks held cash reserves of $5.4 billion against liquid savings and demand deposits of $494.3 billion, giving a reserve ratio rr = 1.09%. The private sector held cash balances of $47.3 billion, giving a currency ratio cr = 9.6% Then, using equation (8.5) gives a money multiplier:

$$\frac{\Delta M}{\Delta H} = \frac{(1 + 0.096)}{(0.0109 + 0.096)} = \frac{1.096}{0.107} = 10.24$$

Each $100 change in monetary base would change the money supply by about $1024.

It is important to remember that a fall in either the banks' cash reserve ratio or the private sector's ratio of currency to bank deposits raises the money multiplier. For a given monetary base the money supply rises. A rise in either or both these ratios reduces the money multiplier and the money supply.

What determines the reserve ratio desired by banks? It is a matter of choice and economic behaviour. The higher the interest rate spread between loans and deposits, the more the banks wish to lend and the more they risk a low ratio of cash reserves to deposits. Conversely, the more unpredictable are withdrawals from deposits, or the fewer lending opportunities banks have for liquid loans, the higher will be the cash reserves they want to maintain for any level of deposits.

The public's ratio of cash holdings to deposits partly reflects institutional factors, for example, whether firms pay wages by deposit, cheque, or cash. It also depends on the technology of payments, for example, the acceptance and use of cheques and debit cards. There is a questionable incentive to hold cash to make untraceable payments to evade taxes.

Review Questions 7, 8, 9 and 10

Credit cards are a temporary means of payment, a *money-substitute*, not money itself. A signed credit card slip cannot be used for further purchases. Soon, you have to settle your credit card account using money. Nevertheless, since credit cards allow people to carry less cash in their pocket, their widespread use reduces the ratio of cash to bank deposits. Debit cards, on the other hand, are a means of payment. When you use your card there is a direct transfer of funds on deposit between bank accounts. Unlike the use of a credit card, there is no further settlement required. Debit cards reduce the use of both cash and cheques, and reduce the ratio of cash holdings to deposits.

Figure 8.1 summarizes our discussion of the monetary base and the money supply. It shows the monetary base or stock of high-powered money, held either as cash reserves by the banks or used as cash in circulation. Since banks operate with fractional reserve ratios, we see that total deposits are much larger than the banks' cash reserves.

FIGURE 8.1 **The Monetary Base and the Money Supply**

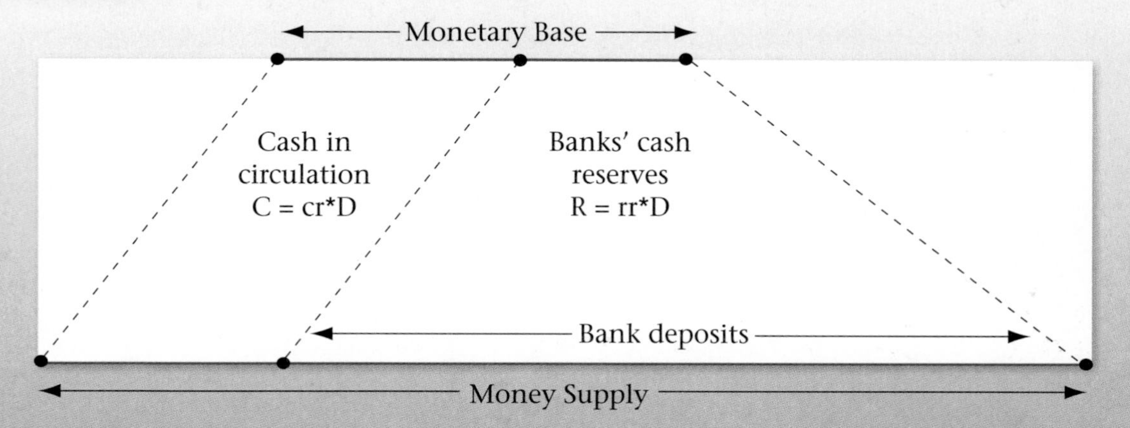

The money supply comprises currency in circulation and deposits at banks. The monetary base issued by the central bank is held either as currency in circulation or as banks' cash reserves. Since deposits are a multiple of banks' cash reserves, the money multiplier is greater than 1. The monetary base is "high-powered" money because part of it supports the larger stock of bank deposits created by the banks. These deposits are the major component of the money supply.

We can also write a simple money supply function that illustrates the determination of the money supply. The three variables we have discussed enter this function, namely:

1. **H**, the monetary base,
2. **cr**, the public's currency ratio, and
3. **rr**, the banks' reserve ratio.

Working with the money multiplier we derived previously as equation (8.5), where M is the money supply, we can write:

$$M = \frac{(1 + cr)}{(rr + cr)} \times H \tag{8.6}$$

The central bank's control of the monetary base, H, gives it control of the money supply, M, as long as cr and rr are constant.

Figure 8.2 uses a diagram to illustrate the money supply function and changes in the money supply. The line M_0 shows the size of the money supply for a given monetary base H_0 and the money multiplier $\frac{(1 + cr)}{(rr + cr)}$. The money supply in this diagram is vertical, because we assume cr and rr are not affected by the interest rate. M is therefore independent of the nominal interest rate i, which is measured on the vertical axis. This is the supply side of the *money market* with quantity measured on the horizontal axis and interest rate, which is analogous to price, on the vertical axis.

FIGURE 8.2 **The Money Supply Function**

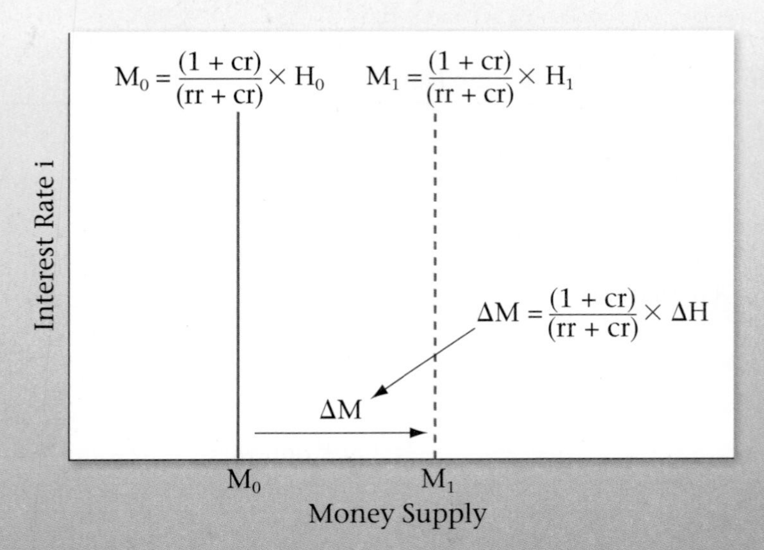

The monetary base H_0 and the money multiplier determine the money supply M_0. The vertical line in the diagram shows that this money supply is independent of the interest rate i, although we will see later that it is important to the determination of the interest rate. An increase in the monetary base, $\Delta M > 0$, increases the money supply according to the money supply multiplier as shown by the rightward shift from M_0 to M_0.

MONETARY POLICY

Our money supply function shows us how, if rr and cr are constant, the central bank's control of the monetary base gives it the power to change money supply and other financial conditions in the economy. If the central bank increases the monetary base, banks have larger cash reserves and increase their lending, offering favourable borrowing rates to attract new loans and create more deposits. In Figure 8.2 the increase in the monetary base to H_1 causes an increase in money supply by the change in H (ΔH), multiplied by the money multiplier. The money supply function shifts to the right to M_1. A decrease in the monetary base would shift the M function to the left, indicating a fall in the money supply.

Now, if the money supply and the terms on which loans are available from banks have effects on aggregate expenditure and aggregate demand, we have a policy link between central bank actions and the performance of the economy. The central bank can control the monetary base to change aggregate demand and reduce or eliminate recessionary and inflationary gaps. In Chapter 9 we will study the effects of money supply on financial asset prices, interest rates, and expenditures. Then, in Chapter 10, we will see how the Bank of Canada uses monetary policy to control output and inflation.

Review Questions 11 and 12

8.6 Measures of the Money Supply

The money supply is cash in circulation outside the banks, plus bank deposits, but which deposits and why only banks? We can think of a spectrum of liquidity. Cash, by definition, is completely liquid. Demand deposits (chequing accounts) are almost as liquid. Notice deposits (savings accounts) used to be less liquid, but now many banks offer automatic transfer between savings and chequing accounts when the latter run low. Savings deposits are now almost as liquid as chequing accounts.

Everybody used to be clear what a bank deposit was, and whose deposits counted toward the money supply. Financial deregulation blurred this distinction in Canada, the United States, the United Kingdom, and European countries. Now banks compete vigorously for mortgages, supermarket chains are in the banking business, and trust company and credit union deposits are widely accepted as means of payment. There is no longer a reason to exclude those deposits from measures of the money supply.

The Bank of Canada now publishes data on the monetary base in response to continuing changes in the types of bank deposits available to households and businesses. Advances in technology, financial deregulation, and competition in the financial services sector, which have led to more types of financial assets, make it easy for customers to substitute between those assets we include in narrow definitions of money supply and other assets. Once we leave the monetary base measure of money supply, there is no single measure of money that is clearly the means of payment.

Review Question 13

Table 8.5 shows the size of the money supply in Canada. The differences between the money supply as measured by these aggregates illustrates the difficulty in choosing a particular measure of the money supply.

Comparing money aggregates from one year to the next also shows the growth in the money supply and the change in its composition. All money aggregates increased, along with the monetary base, from 2005 to 2008. We would expect this from our money supply function. However, the percentage changes in M1B and M2 were different from the change in the monetary base. This suggests that the money multiplier was

TABLE 8.5 **The Money Supply in Canada in 2005 and 2008[1] ($ billions)**

	2005	2008	Change (%)
Monetary base H	46.6	53.2	14.2
Currency in circulation C	42.8	49.0	14.5
M1B = currency + chequable chartered bank deposits	310.6	382.5	23.1
M2 = M1B + notice and savings deposits in the banks	641.6	788.5	22.9
M2+ = M2 + deposits at other financial institutions	894.2	1,103.7	23.4

These measures of the money supply show clearly the importance of bank deposits as money. Currency in circulation is only about 7 percent of M2. Deposits account for the remaining 93 percent. The importance of bank deposits as money means that understanding of the operations of banks as sources of loans and deposits is the key to understanding the money supply function in the economy.

Note: [1] Seasonally adjusted February 2005 and February 2008.

Sources: Statistics Canada, CANSIM Table 176-0025, Series V37146, V37148, V41552795, V41552796, V41552798.

not constant. Something else must have changed to change the multiplier. What has happened to the desired reserve and currency ratios?

If you calculate cr and rr for M1B and M2 in each year, you will find they have declined. (In making the calculation, remember that the reserves of the banks are the monetary base not circulating as currency.) This would make the money multipliers larger. Then the increase in the monetary base, combined with an increase in multipliers, would result in changes in the money supply more than proportional to the change in the monetary base. Moreover, larger changes in cr and rr with respect to M1B than with respect to M2 are consistent with the larger growth we see in M1B than in M2.

Next

Now we have examined money, the banking system, and the size of the money supply, we have one important side of the *financial market* that will link money to expenditure and economic activity. This is the supply side of the market. In the next chapter, we will study the reasons why people wish to hold money balances. We also study how the portfolio choices people make between money and other assets create the demand for money balances. The interaction between the supply of money balances and the demand for money balances determines the prices of financial assets and interest rates. Interest rates in turn provide an important link between money, financial markets, and expenditures in markets for goods and services, both directly and through the foreign exchange rate.

SUMMARY

- **Money** has four functions: a **medium of exchange** or means of payment, a **store of value**, a **unit of account**, and a **standard of deferred payment**. The medium of exchange function distinguishes money from other assets.
- In a **barter economy**, trading is costly because there must be a double coincidence of wants. Money, a medium of exchange, reduces the costs of exchange and allows resources to be used for other things.
- A **token money** is a convertible claim on a commodity money. Because its monetary value greatly exceeds its production costs, token money economizes on the resource costs of transactions.
- **Fiat money** is money the government has declared **legal tender**. The **central bank** controls the supply of legal tender.
- **Banks create money** by making loans and creating deposits based on a **fractional cash reserve ratio, rr**. The banks' reserve ratio involves a trade-off between earnings and **bankers' risk**.
- Banks are **financial intermediaries**. Bank deposits, which can be transferred by cheque or debit card, provide a convenient means of payment. Bank services plus interest payments on deposits attract funds into the bank. Banks use these funds to make loans, purchase securities, and finance expenditures. The general acceptance of bank deposits as money, and well-developed financial markets, allow modern banks to operate with very low cash reserve ratios.
- The **monetary base H** is currency in circulation plus banks' cash reserves. The **money multiplier** is the ratio of a change in the money supply to the change in the monetary base that caused it, $\Delta M/\Delta H$. The money multiplier is larger (a) the smaller is the cash reserve ratio of the banks, rr, and (b) the smaller is the private sector's ratio of cash in circulation to deposits, cr.
- The **money supply** is currency in circulation plus bank deposits. The size of the money supply is determined by the monetary base, H, the banks' cash reserve ratio, rr, and the private sector's currency ratio, cr:

$$\mathbf{M} = \frac{(\mathbf{1} + \mathbf{cr})}{(\mathbf{rr} + \mathbf{cr})} \times \mathbf{H}$$

KEY TERMS

Medium of exchange *181*	Bank of Canada *186*
Barter economy *181*	Liquidity *187*
Unit of account *181*	Net interest income *189*
Store of value *182*	Currency ratio (cr) *189*
Token money *183*	Reserve ratio (rr) *190*
Legal tender *183*	Financial panic *193*
Bank reserves *183*	Commercial paper *193*
Fiat money *183*	Monetary base *194*
Credit money *183*	High-powered money (H) *194*
Money supply *183*	Money multiplier *195*
Financial intermediary *184*	

KEY EQUATIONS AND RELATIONS

Equations

Bank reserve holdings: $R = rrD$ **(8.1)** p. 195

Public currency holdings: $C = crD$ **(8.2)** p. 195

High-powered money (monetary base): $H = (rr + cr)D$ **(8.3)** p. 196

Money supply (currency plus deposits): $M = (1 + cr)D$ **(8.4)** p. 196

The money multiplier: $\frac{\Delta M}{\Delta H} = \frac{(1 + cr)}{(rr + cr)}$ **(8.5)** p. 196

The money supply function: $M = \frac{(1 + cr)}{(rr + cr)} \times H$ **(8.6)** p. 198

Relations

The Role of money: Money reduces transaction costs and facilitates specialization in production based on opportunities to trade.

Bank deposits as money: Public confidence in banks is required for bank deposits to be used as money.

Monetary base: The monetary base or high-powered money, H, used as reserves by the banking system and cash by the public comes from the central bank.

$$H = \text{cash} + \text{bank reserves}$$

Bank deposit creation: Profit-motivated banks holding fractional reserves create the bank deposit component of money supply.

Banking operations: Excess reserves → increased lending → increased deposits
Insufficient reserves → reduced lending → reduced deposits

Bank deposit creation: Deposit creation depends on:
Availability of monetary base, H,
$\Delta H \rightarrow \Delta D \rightarrow \Delta M$, and $\Delta M > \Delta H$ by the money supply multiplier

The public's currency ratio, cr,
$\uparrow cr \rightarrow \downarrow M$ as higher cash drains reduce cash reserves available to banks

The banks' reserve ratio, rr,
$\uparrow rr \rightarrow \downarrow M$ as higher reserve ratios reduce deposit and money supply multipliers

REVIEW QUESTIONS

Review Questions and answers are included in Connect at www.mcgrawhillconnect.ca.

1. What are the functions of money? What is money in Canada today? What is the money supply in Canada today? Are debit cards and credit cards money?

2. Since both central banks and commercial banks can create money, what is the key difference between a central bank, like the Bank of Canada, and the many commercial banks in the financial industry?

3. Do banks create money? Suppose the banks receive $100 cash from a new deposit of funds previously held outside the banking system. If banks operate with a 5 percent reserve ratio, use simple balance sheets to show by how much this new cash would affect lending and deposits of all banks in the system.

4. What is the "currency ratio"? If banks have a 10 percent reserve ratio and the public has a 10 percent currency ratio, how much lending and deposit creation can the banks undertake after they receive a new $1000 cash deposit? How much would the public's holding of cash increase? Would it be in the banks' interest to find ways to reduce the currency ratio? Why?

5. What protection does the Canadian Deposit Insurance Corporation provide for your money if your bank is unable to pay cash to its depositors?

6. Suppose a bank deposit of $100 is withdrawn from the banking system and held as cash. Would the banks' adjustment to this withdrawal destroy money? Would the money supply be changed? Explain your answers.

7. Define the *money multiplier* and explain how it might be used.

8. Suppose the banks in the banking system find it prudent to maintain holdings of cash equal to 10 percent of their deposit liabilities, and people find it convenient to hold cash balances equal to 15 percent.
   a. If the monetary base, the supply of high-powered money in the economy, is $1000, what is the size of the money supply?
   b. Suppose the monetary base decreased by $100, would the money change? If so, by how much would it change?

9. When people become concerned about political and economic stability, they often increase their use of cash and reduce their dependence on banks and bank deposits. Explain why and how the cash reserves of the banks and the public's currency ratio would be affected by this shift to using cash rather than bank deposits. What would happen to the money multiplier and the money supply?

10. Suppose a crisis in financial markets, like the collapse of the asset-backed commercial paper (ABCP) market in 2007 and 2008, increases the risk banks attach to lending and the non-bank public attaches to bank deposits. What are the implications for the desired reserve ratio, the currency ratio, the money supply multiplier, and the money supply?

11. Using a diagram, illustrate and explain the determinants of the position and slope of the money supply function assuming an initial monetary base of $1000, rr = 5 percent, and cr = 10 percent. If the monetary base were to increase by 10 percent, how would the money supply and the money supply function in your diagram change?

12. Suppose the currency ratio depends on the interest rate such that the non-bank public reduces their cash holdings relative to deposits (cr) as the interest rate rises. Use a diagram to illustrate what effect if any this condition would have on the money supply function.

13. If currency in circulation is $20 billion, bank deposits with chequing privileges are $120 billion, notice and savings deposits are $400 billion, deposits in financial institutions other than banks are $200 billion, and money market mutual funds are $300, what is M1B? What is M2? What is M2+?

14. *Internet* Visit the Bank of Canada's Web site, www.bankofcanada.ca/en/publication/pub_res.html#books, and examine James Powell's *A History of the Canadian Dollar*. Based on Powell's description of money in Canada before 1841, make a list of the different monies used in the colonies in that period. Why were playing cards used as money at times during this period? What is the origin of the name "dollar" for the monetary unit?

15. *Internet* Using Table E1– in the latest *Bank of Canada Banking and Financial Statistics* available on the Bank of Canada's Web site www.bankofcanada.ca, examine the data for the money supply measures M2 and M2+. What pattern of change or growth do you see in the money supply over the past five years?

16. *Internet* The Federal Deposit Insurance Corporation in the United States reports on bank failures at www.fdic.gov/bank/individual/failed/banklist.html. Visit their Web site and compare the numbers of failed banks in 2009 compared to numbers in earlier years. Does the recent pattern of failures suggest that the crisis in the financial system has passed?

CHAPTER 9

Financial Markets, Interest Rates, Foreign Exchange Rates, and Aggregate Demand

LEARNING OUTCOMES

By the end of this chapter you should understand:

1. Portfolio choices between money and other assets
2. Bond prices, yields, and interest rates
3. The demand for money balances
4. Financial market equilibrium and interest rates
5. Interest rates and foreign exchange rates
6. Interest rates, exchange rates, and aggregate demand
7. The monetary transmission mechanism

This chapter continues our study of the effects of money and financial markets on economic activity. In Chapter 8, we examined money and the supply of money created by the banking system. The *money supply* was defined as the non-bank public's holdings of currency and bank deposits. In this chapter, we will see that the non-bank public's holdings of money balances arise from decisions about the management of wealth.

Money balances are one asset in a *portfolio* of assets. People choose to hold some of their financial wealth as money and some in other financial assets. These choices create a demand for money balances, which we will examine in detail.

The demand for money balances and the supply of money balances form the money market. The equilibrium between supply and demand in the money market determines the interest rate. The interest rate has important effects on planned expenditure, aggregate demand, output, and employment directly and through its effect on the foreign exchange rate.

We start with a brief discussion of portfolio choice and the prices of financial assets.

9.1 Portfolio Choices between Money and Other Assets

A financial portfolio is a collection of financial assets. It might include money balances, bonds, equities, mortgages, and mutual funds. The structure of a portfolio, the proportion held in each type of asset, reflects two main characteristics of the assets involved:

1. The *returns* paid by different financial assets
2. The *risks* arising from changes in the market prices of assets

Wealth holders, and institutional portfolio managers for pension funds and insurance companies, like their portfolios to pay high returns with low risk. To achieve this, they hold mixed portfolios of money and other financial assets.

Suppose you win $10 million in a lottery. Now that you have wealth, what are you going to do with it? You will no doubt spend some and give some away. That is a wealth effect, but what about the balance of your winnings? You have to make a portfolio choice. Will you hold your wealth as money in the bank? Will you put your money in the stock market? Will you put your money in the bond market?

If you consult a financial planner, he or she will probably recommend a mixed portfolio made up of money, bonds, and equities. That recommendation will be based on your intention to increase your wealth and draw income from it while protecting it from losses in financial markets.

Money holdings are an important part of the portfolio. Money is the medium of exchange. It can be used directly to make payments for goods and services or to settle debts. Other assets, for example bonds, cannot be used as a means of payment. Furthermore, money has a fixed nominal price. It is a "safe asset." Wealth held as money does not rise or fall with the rise or fall in financial asset prices on stock and bond markets. However, money is exposed to the risk that inflation will lower its real purchasing power.

Other financial assets differ from money in three respects. First, they cannot be used as a means of payment. To use them to make a payment you would first have to sell them for money, at their current market price, and then use the money to make the payment. Second, they offer a return in the form of an interest payment, a dividend payment, or a rise in price that provides income to the portfolio holder. Third, because the prices of financial assets like bonds or stocks fluctuate daily on financial markets, these assets carry the risk that their values may decline significantly from time to time.

Portfolio management recognizes these differences between assets by trading some return for lower risk and greater convenience in the mix of assets held. Money in the portfolio offers the convenience of the means of payment, providing low risk but zero return. Other assets offer flow of interest and dividend income, and possible capital gains if asset prices rise, but the risk of capital loss if prices fall.

Review Question 1

This portfolio choice between money balances and other assets is the basis for our discussion of the demand for money balances in the remainder of this chapter.

9.2 Interest Rates, Bond Prices, and Yields

Before we can discuss the demand for money that comes from portfolio decisions, we need to understand the relationship between interest rates, bond coupons, the prices of financial assets, and yields on financial assets. To keep our discussion simple, we will assume only one type of financial asset, a bond. However, the prices and yields of other financial assets are related to interest rates in the same way as bond prices.

A **bond** is a financial contract that makes one or more fixed money payments at specific dates in the future.

The **interest rate** is the current market rate paid to lenders or charged to borrowers.

A **bond coupon** is the *annual* fixed money payment paid to a bond holder.

The **price of a marketable bond** is its current price in the bond market.

The **yield on a bond** is the return to a bond holder expressed as an annual percentage.

The **present value** is the *discounted* value of future payments.

Several concepts are important for our discussion. A **bond** is an asset that makes one or more *fixed money payments* to its holder each year until its maturity date. On its maturity date, it also repays its principal value.

The **interest rate** is the *current* market rate, expressed as a percentage, paid to lenders or charged to borrowers.

A **bond coupon** is the fixed money payment made *annually* to the holders of the bond from the date of issue until the date of maturity. The coupon rate is a fixed percentage of the principal value of the bond at the time of issue.

The **price of a marketable bond** is the current price at which it can be bought or sold on the open bond market at any time between its date of issue and its maturity date.

The **yield on a bond** is the return to a bond holder expressed as an annual percentage rate, which is a combination of the coupon payments and any change in the market price of the bond during the period in which it is held.

The ongoing and continuous purchases and sales of bonds on the bond market establish the equilibrium prices of bonds. At those prices, the *yields* on the bonds at that point in time are equal to the market rate of interest. Changes in bond prices with changing bond market conditions change yields and market interest rates. In late 2008, for example, uncertainty in financial markets led portfolio managers to shift to low-risk assets like Government of Canada bonds. This increased demand for bonds bid bond prices up, and yields on Government of Canada 1-to-3 year bonds fell from 3.22 percent in January 2008 to 1.11 percent in December 2008. In the same period, yields on 3-to-5 year bonds fell from 3.45 percent to 1.61 percent.

Consider an example that shows the relationship between bond coupons, current market interest rates, bond prices, and yields. Looking at the Department of Finance Web site, www.fin.gc.ca, I find listings for recent issues of Government of Canada bonds. Suppose one such bond is listed as:

Government of Canada 4.250 June 1, 2013

This is a marketable 4.25 percent bond with a maturity date of June 1, 2013. It promises to pay its holder $4.25 for each $100 of face value on June 1 each year until June 1, 2013. The $4.25 is the *coupon* value and $100 is the *principal* value. On June 1, 2013, the bond matures and pays $104.25, the coupon plus the principal.

The price of this bond today depends on the current market rate of interest. The price is the present value of the series of future payments the bond will make. The **present value** is the *discounted* value of future payments. It recognizes that money payments in the future are worth less than money payments today. To help understand present value, ask the following question: If someone offers to give you $1000, would you rather have it today or a year from today?

Notice that $1000 lent at an interest rate of 5 percent would give you a sum of:

$$\$1000 \times (1.05) = \$1050$$

one year from today. In the same way, the amount of money you need to lend today to have $1000 one year from today is:

$$\$M \times (1.05) = \$1000$$

$$\$M = \frac{\$1000}{(1.05)}$$

$$\$M = \$952.38$$

When the market rate of interest is 5 percent, $952.38 is the present value of $1000 to be received one year in the future.

Now consider the price of the 4.25 percent bond described above. Suppose you were to buy some of these bonds on June 1, 2010. Let's assume that the market rate of interest on that date is 4.25 percent. The price of the bond is then the present value of the future payments: $4.25 on June 1, 2011, $4.25 on June 1, 2012, and $104.25 on June 1, 2013. Payments to be received two years in the future are discounted twice, and three years in the future three times, to give:

$$PV = \frac{\$4.25}{(1.0425)} + \frac{\$4.25}{(1.0425)^2} + \frac{\$104.25}{(1.0425)^3}$$

$$PV = \$4.077 + \$3.911 + \$92.013$$

$$PV = \$100$$

If you paid $100 for each $100 of face value and held the bond to maturity, it would *yield* 4.25 percent, the current market rate of interest. We would say the bond is trading *at par* because the market price equals the face value.

However, suppose the *market rate of interest* when you want to buy this bond is 5 percent instead of the 4.25 percent. The present value of the payments promised by the bond would be:

$$PV = \frac{\$4.25}{(1.05)} + \frac{\$4.25}{(1.05)^2} + \frac{\$104.25}{(1.05)^3}$$

$$PV = \$4.048 + \$3.855 + \$90.055$$

$$PV = \$97.958$$

A higher current interest rate reduces the present value of the money payments the bond promises. The price of the bond falls and it trades *at a discount*. The yield on the bond—the present value of its coupon payment plus the **capital gain** as its price rises to par at maturity—gives a rate of return equal to the market interest rate of 5 percent.

The yield on a bond comes from its coupon plus any **capital gain or loss** from the decline in price between the date of purchase and the date of maturity.

Alternatively, if the market rate of interest were 3.5 percent, this 4.25 percent bond would trade at a premium. A lower interest rate would raise the bond's price until the capital loss from the decline in price at maturity offset the 4.25 percent coupon, to give a yield of 3.5 percent.

In general, because the future payments offered by bonds are fixed in dollar terms, the *prices of marketable bonds vary inversely to market rates of interest.* Rising interest rates mean falling bond prices, and falling interest rates mean rising bond prices. There are many types of bonds that differ by coupon, maturity date, frequency of future payments, and in other ways. However, the relationship between prices, yields, and interest rates remains the same. Because bond prices are the present value of future payments, prices and interest rates move in opposite directions.

Furthermore, the size of the change in the price of a bond as a result of a change in the interest rate depends on the bond's term to maturity. The prices of longer-term bonds are more volatile than those of shorter-term bonds. This is another source of risk to be considered by portfolio managers.

To illustrate the relationship between bond prices and term to maturity, calculate the price of a 4.25 coupon bond with 10 years to maturity rather than the 3 years in the example above, when the interest rate is 5 percent. Taking the present value as before gives a market price of:

$$PV = \frac{4.25}{1.05} + \frac{4.25}{(1.05)^2} \cdots\cdots + \frac{4.25}{(1.05)^9} + \frac{104.25}{(1.05)^{10}} = 94.36$$

This shows that a rise in the market interest rate of 0.75 percentage points lowers the price of the bond with 10 years to maturity by $5.64 or 5.64 percent. The same rise in the market rate lowered the price of the bond with 3 years to maturity by $2.042, just over 2 percent.

BOND MARKETS IN ACTION

Asset markets like the bond market are very active. Large volumes of bonds are bought and sold every business day. If portfolio managers see bond prices that offer yields higher than current market interest rates, they buy bonds. Buying makes prices rise and yields fall until yields and current interest rates are equal. Conversely, if bondholders find yields are lower than interest rates, they sell bonds, bond prices fall, and yields rise. Table 9.1 provides a sample of the information on bond prices and yields. The first three columns define the bond. The next two give current prices and yields.

A Government of Ontario bond with a 4.00 percent coupon is the first listed in Table 9.1. It matures on the 19th day of May 2009, about 12 months from the date of this quotation. The price is what sellers or buyers were willing to accept or pay for some of these outstanding bonds. The final column reports the yield to maturity from buying this bond in May 2008 and holding it until May 2009. These yields also reflect the market rate of interest for 12-month money on May 13, 2008.

All the bonds reported in the table are trading at a premium. Their market prices exceed $100 for $100 of principal value, and their yields to maturity are lower than their coupons. The coupons paid by the bonds reflect market interest rates at the time the bonds were issued. Market interest rates at those times were higher than on May 13, 2008. The borrowers had to offer higher coupons to sell bonds in the then current market.

The fall in Canadian interest rates over the past few years have been good for bondholders. As our calculation of bond prices tells us, falling interest rates raise bond prices. Bondholders enjoyed capital gains as the prices of their bonds rose, in addition to the interest income their bonds paid. We see these higher bond prices in the table.

Of course, market conditions can change. If interest rates were to rise from the 2008 levels, bond prices would fall. Bondholders would suffer capital losses as interest rates rose and bond prices fell. This is the *market risk* that comes with holding bonds and other marketable financial assets.

Review Questions 2, 3 and 4

Bonds are only one of the alternatives to money in a wealth portfolio. Application Box 9.1 describes some other assets, their prices and yields, in a bit more detail. To understand the demand for money balances and the operation of financial markets, we need to know how these financial assets, which are alternatives to money balances,

TABLE 9.1 **Examples of Bond Prices and Yields, May 13, 2008**

Issuer	Coupon	Maturity Date	Price	Yield
Ontario	4.00	2009/05/19	101.38	2.63
Scotiabank	5.30	2013/01/31	103.59	4.49
Quebec	4.50	2018/12/18	102.06	4.30

Source: Based on data originated by RBC Dominion Securities, May 13, 2008.

APPLICATION BOX 9.1

A Basic Guide to Financial Assets

There are three broad classes of financial assets that are bought and sold in financial markets. These are *bills*, *bonds*, and *equities*.

Bills are short-term financial assets that make no interest payment to the holder but do make specified cash payment on their maturity date. They trade at a discount. A government treasury bill or T-Bill is an example. Every second week the government sells T-Bills that promise to pay the buyer $100 for each $100 of face value on the date that is about three months in the future. The interest earned is the difference between the price paid and the face amount received at the maturity date.

Bonds are longer-term financial assets that pay a fixed money income payment each year and repay their face value on a fixed maturity date. Bonds are marketable, and trade on the bond market between their issue dates and maturity dates at prices determined by supply and demand. As with T-Bills, the return to the holder of a bond depends on the price paid for the bond. In this case, the calculation is more complex however, because it involves a fixed annual money payment and a fixed value at maturity.

Equities are shares in the ownership of the business. They give the holder the right to a share in the profits of the business, either in the form of dividend payments or in terms of the increase in the size of the business if profits are used for business expansion. The shares or stocks in publicly traded businesses can be bought and sold on stock markets like the Toronto Stock Exchange. The financial pages of major newspapers give you daily reports on stocks prices and stock markets. Shareholders' returns from their stock holdings depend on the combination of dividend income they receive and the changes in the market price of the shares they hold. Equity prices are the expected value of the future profits of business. Because expectations of future business performance are volatile, equity prices are volatile and therefore risky. Equities do however offer the prospect of higher long-term returns.

differ from money. The choice to hold money balances, regardless of motive, is a choice between money and other forms in which wealth could be held.

9.3 The Demand for Money Balances

The quantity of money M2 in Canada was 23 percent higher in 2008 than in 1998. Why did Canadian residents hold so much more money? We focus on three variables that affect the demand for money balances: interest rates, the price level, and real income.

MOTIVES FOR HOLDING MONEY

Money is a stock. It is the quantity of circulating currency and deposits *held* at any given time. Holding money is not the same as *spending* it. We hold money now to spend it later.

Money is the medium of exchange, for which it must also be a store of value. These two functions provide the reasons why people wish to hold money. People can hold their wealth in various forms—money, bills, bonds, equities, gold and property. The quantity of money people choose to hold is part of the *portfolio decision* they make about their wealth. They choose money instead of some other asset.

For simplicity, assume there are only two assets:

1. *Money*, which pays no interest income but serves as the medium of exchange
2. *Bonds*, which we use to stand for all other interest-bearing assets that are not directly a means of payment

As people earn income, they save and add to their wealth. How should people divide their wealth at any instant between money and bonds? That is the portfolio management question we introduced above.

The *cost* of holding money is the interest income given up by holding money rather than bonds. People hold money only if there is a *benefit* to offset the cost of interest income not earned. What is that benefit? It is the services provided by money.

THE TRANSACTIONS MOTIVE

If all transactions were perfectly synchronized, we would be paid at the same instant we did our spending. Except in that instant, we need hold no money at all. Otherwise, we need to hold money balances to cover the different timing of receipts and payments. The **transactions motive** for holding money reflects the fact that payments and receipts are not synchronized.

The **transactions motive** for holding money arises from the difference in the timing of payments and receipts.

Must we hold money between being paid—say, at the end of each month—and making purchases during the next month? We could put our monthly pay into interest-earning assets, to be resold later when we need to make a payment. We could also use credit cards to coordinate many payments at one point in time, the payment due date on the account. However, payment must still be made and every time we buy or sell assets there are brokerage and bank charges. And it takes an eagle eye to keep track of cash flow and judge the precise moment at which money is needed and assets must be sold. If small sums are involved, the interest income earned does not compensate for the brokerage fees and the time and effort. It is easier to hold some money as cash or bank balances accessible by debit card, to cover small regular expenditures, even though holding money involves the opportunity cost of interest income forgone.

How much money we need to hold depends on the value of transactions we later wish to make and the degree of synchronization of our payments and receipts. Money is a nominal variable, not a real variable. How much $100 buys depends on the price of goods and services. If all prices double, our receipts and our payments double in nominal terms. We need to hold twice as much nominal money to have the same real buying power. As a result, the demand for money is a *demand for real money* balances.

Real GDP is a good proxy for the total value of real transactions. We assume the demand for real money balances based on the transactions motive rises with real income. We also assume that the degree of synchronization of receipts and payments is constant over time. Thus we focus on real income as the main determinant of the demand for real transactions balances.

THE PRECAUTIONARY MOTIVE

We live in an uncertain world. Uncertainty about the timing of receipts and payments creates a **precautionary motive** for holding money.

The **precautionary motive** to hold money arises from uncertainty about the timing of receipts and payments.

Suppose your portfolio is mainly interest bearing bonds and you get by with a small amount of money. Walking down the street you see a great bargain in the store window, but have too little money to close the deal. By the time you sell some of your bonds for cash, the bargain is gone, snapped up by someone else. Alternatively, suppose you have an emergency need for cab fare as a result of car trouble. Bonds can't be used to pay the fare, even if you had access to them and could sell them for cash. Nor can you be sure your credit card will be accepted. You need money in spite of the opportunity cost it involves. The precautionary motive for holding money balances is a reflection of these unexpected opportunities or needs.

If uncertainty is roughly constant over time, the volume of transactions and the benefits from holding precautionary balances depend on real GDP. The higher real income is, the stronger will be the precautionary motive for holding money. But a rise in uncertainty or anxiety, perhaps as a result of political events or economic forecasts or instability in financial markets, increases the demand for money as precautionary balances. Increased confidence lowers the demand for money balances.

Review Question 5

THE ASSET MOTIVE

Now suppose money has been set aside to cover both usual and unexpected payments. Think of someone making the next portfolio decision, deciding how to divide wealth between money and bonds. At some future date that wealth may be spent. In the meantime, the aim is a good but safe return.

We have assumed just two asset choices for simplicity. One asset is money. It is the safe asset in the sense that its price is constant, $1 for $1, but it offers no yield or return. The other asset is bonds, which, on average, pay a positive return from a flow of interest income, but their prices change from day to day. Some days bond prices rise, and other days they fall, depending on conditions in the bond market. Bonds are risky. Sometimes they offer very high returns as their prices rise. At other times their prices fall and return is negative. How should people decide to divide their portfolios between these safe and risky assets?

Since people dislike risk, they will not put all their eggs in one basket. They will diversify their portfolios. As well as holding some risky bonds, to get the *higher expected return*, they will keep some of their wealth in the safe asset money. There is an **asset motive** for holding money, to reduce the risk of losses in the portfolio if bond prices fall. Wealth holders accept lower returns on their portfolios in exchange for lower risk.

The **asset motive** for holding money arises from the desire to reduce portfolio risk.

However, at higher interest rates the returns for holding more of the risky asset, bonds, are higher, and the opportunity cost of holding money balances is higher. This difference in returns and costs leads people to hold smaller money balances and more bonds in their portfolios at higher interest rates. They buy bonds, increasing bond holdings and reducing money balances. As a result, the demand for money balances is inversely related to the level of interest rates.

THE DEMAND FOR MONEY BALANCES: PRICES, REAL INCOME, AND INTEREST RATES

We can summarize the demand for money balances using Table 9.2 and a simple equation. Suppose we let the size of the real money balances people wish to hold for transactions and precautionary reasons be a fraction **k** of GDP. In Chapter 4 we defined nominal GDP as real GDP times the GDP deflator, P, to give nominal GDP = PY. Using this notation, the demand for *nominal* money balances for transactions and precautionary reasons is kPY, and the demand for *real balances* is kY, where k is a positive fraction. When real income changes, bringing with it a change in spending, the change in the demand for real money balances changes as determined by k.

TABLE 9.2 The Demand for Money

Quantity Demanded	Effect of a Rise in		
	Price Level	Real Income	Interest Rate
Nominal money	Rises in proportion	Rises	Falls
Real money	Unaffected	Rises	Falls

What is the value of **k** in Canada? In the first quarter of 2008, Canadians held money balances as measured by M1B of $386.6 billion. Nominal GDP in that quarter was $1559 billion measured at an annual rate. If we divide M1B holdings by GDP, we get k = 0.248, or about 25 percent of annual income. This value of k suggests that a rise in GDP of $100 will increase the demand for money balances by $25, measured in either nominal or real terms.

Changes in nominal interest rates change the size of the money balances people wish to hold, based on the asset motive. A rise in interest rates increases the opportunity cost of holding money balances rather than bonds. It may also create the expectation that interest rates in the future will fall back to previous levels. As a result, people will want to use some of their money balances to buy bonds, changing the mix of money and bonds in their wealth holdings. A fall in interest rates has the opposite effect.

The way people adjust their portfolios in response to changes in interest rates results in a negative relationship between the asset demand for money balances and the nominal interest rate. We can use the parameter **h** to measure the change in money balances in response to a change in interest rates. Then $h = \Delta L/\Delta i$, which is negative. If individual and institutional portfolio mangers' decisions are very sensitive to the current interest rates, h will be a large negative number. A small rise in interest rates will cause a large shift from money to bonds. Alternatively, if portfolio decisions are not at all sensitive to interest rate changes, h would be zero.

Putting these components of the demand for real money balances together gives the demand for money function, which is a demand to hold real money balances L:

$$\mathbf{L = kY - hi} \qquad \textbf{(9.1)}$$

Figure 9.1 shows the relationship between the demand for real money balances and the interest rate, drawn for a given level of real GDP, Y_0. This demand for money function has a negative slope that illustrates how people change their demand for money when interest rates change. The slope of the demand curve for money is $\mathbf{-1/h}$. The effect of a change in the interest rate is shown by a movement along the L function. A change in real income would require us to draw a new demand for money function, to the right of L_0 if Y increased, or to the left if Y decreased.

Review Question 6

THE RISE IN MONEY HOLDINGS FROM 1998 TO 2008

We began our discussion of the demand for money with the question: Why did Canadians hold larger money balances in 2008 than they held in 1998? We have identified three explanations: prices, real incomes, and nominal interest rates. Table 9.3 shows how these variables and money balances have changed over time.

FIGURE 9.1 **The Demand for Real Money Balances**

The demand for real money balances depends on real GDP and interest rates, according to the demand function:

$$L = kY - hi$$

If real GDP were Y_0 and the interest rate were zero, the demand for money would be kY_0 as shown on the horizontal axis. At higher interest rates the opportunity cost of holding money is higher because the expected return for holding bonds is positive. Point A shows the smaller money balances demanded at a positive interest rate i_1. The difference between kY_0 and L_1 measures the shift from money to bonds in portfolios. The slope of the demand function,

$$\frac{\Delta i}{\Delta L} = \frac{i_2 - i_1}{L_2 - L_1} = -\frac{1}{h}$$

shows how much the demand for money balances changes when interest rates change, moving along the L function. The position of the function is determined by k and real GDP, Y, which measure the demand for money based on real GDP. A change in either k or Y will shift the demand function.

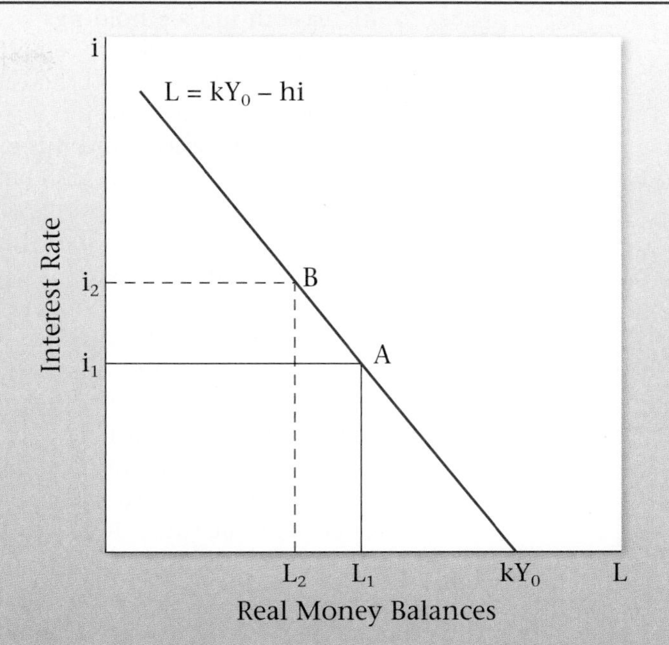

TABLE 9.3 **Holdings of M1B and M2 in Canada, 1998 and 2008**

	1998	2008
Index of:		
Nominal M1B	100	228.6
Nominal M2	100	176.6
Consumer prices	100	123.5
Real M1B	100	184.6
Real M2	100	143.0
Real GDP	100	146.5
Interest Rate Spread (%)		
(between 3–5-year bonds and bank deposits)	5.03	3.24

Source: Part of data is based on Statistics Canada CANSIM Database, http://cansim2.statcan.gc.ca, Table 380-0002 Series V1992067; Bank of Canada, 2009; and author's calculations.

Although nominal holdings of M1B and M2 rose by about 2.3 times and 1.8 times respectively, the price level rose by 23.5 percent between 1998 and 2008. Some of the increase in money holdings was necessary just to maintain the purchasing power of those money balances. Even allowing for that increase in price, the table shows that *real* money balances still increased by 1.8 times and 1.4 times. Real GDP in 2008 was 47 percent higher than in 1998. Higher real output and income raise the demand for real money balances, and this explains part of the increase in the holdings of M1B balances. But why did real M1B balances increase by more than the increase in GDP, as a constant value of k would suggest?

The answer lies, in part, in what happened to interest rates. The spread between the nominal interest rates paid on 3- to 5-year government bonds and the interest rate on the bank savings deposits included in M2 declined by about 2 percentage points, or about 40 percent. This reduced the opportunity cost of holding M1B balances rather than M2 balances or bonds. A lower cost of holding real M1B balances increased holdings of M1B by more than the increase in real GDP. The lower return on real M2 reduced the demand for M2 balances relative to both M1B and real GDP.

In terms of the money demand function in Figure 9.1, the increase in real GDP caused a shift in L to the right between 1998 and 2008, based on the parameter k. Over the same time, the decrease in interest rates caused a movement down the new L function, based on the parameter h, causing a further increase in holdings of money balances.

9.4 Financial Market Equilibrium and Interest Rates

Now we combine the money supply and the demand for money to show how financial market equilibrium determines the nominal interest rates. We have a *nominal* money supply from the monetary base and the money multiplier from Chapter 8, namely:

$$M = \frac{(1 + cr)}{(rr + cr)} \times H \tag{8.6}$$

The demand for money is a demand for *real* money balances as determined by real income and interest rates.

$$L = kY - hi \tag{9.1}$$

The **real money supply**, M/P, is the nominal money supply M divided by the price level P.

The **real money supply** is simply the nominal money supply M divided by the price level P, M/P, which measures its purchasing power in terms of goods and services.

The central bank, as the source of the monetary base H, controls the nominal money supply, as long as the currency ratio cr and the reserve ratio rr are constant. We will see how the central bank does this in the next chapter. As long as we keep our assumption that the price level is fixed, the central bank also controls the real money supply. (In later chapters, we allow the price level to change.) Changes in nominal money tend to lead eventually to changes in prices. However, the central bank can still control the real money supply in the short run—it can change M faster than prices P respond—but in the long run other forces determine real money M/P. For the moment, we continue to treat the price level as fixed.

Our discussion of the demand for money as a demand for real money balances is summarized above. The quantity of real money demanded rises when real income rises, but falls when nominal interest rates rise.

MONEY MARKET EQUILIBRIUM

Figure 9.2 combines the demand curve for real money balances from Figure 9.1 with the money supply function we saw in Figure 8.2 (page 198) into a money market diagram. The demand curve is drawn for a given level of real income, Y_0, and the supply curve for a given monetary base H_0. With a given price level, the central bank controls the supply of nominal and real money. The supply curve is vertical at $\frac{M_0}{P_0}$. Equilibrium in the money market is at E. At the interest rate i_0, the real money balances people wish to hold just equal the money supplied by the central bank and the banking system.

To see how this market operates, suppose the interest rate is i_1, lower than the equilibrium level i_0. There is excess demand for money in the amount AB in the diagram. People want to hold money balances equal to B at the interest rate i_0, but only A is available. How does the market adjust to remove this excess demand? The answer lies in our previous discussion of the portfolio decisions that distribute wealth between money holdings and bonds.

Consider the interaction between the bond and money markets. When portfolio managers want to restructure their holdings of bonds and money they do so by buying or selling bonds on the bond market. Their actions cannot change the supply of money balances that is fixed by the monetary base and the money supply multiplier. As a result, bond prices and interest rates change to maintain money market equilibrium.

In Figure 9.2 the excess demand for money at the interest rate i_1 will result in a rise in interest rates. With an excess demand for money, people sell bonds to adjust their money balances. There is an excess supply of bonds. Bond prices fall. Lower bond prices mean higher bond yields and interest rates, as you will recall from our earlier discussion of asset prices and yields. The higher interest rates reduce both the excess supply of bonds and the excess demand for money. The money market adjusts by *moving along* the L curve from B to E, as people want smaller money balances relative to their bond holdings at higher interest rates.

FIGURE 9.2 **Equilibrium in the Money Market**

The demand for real money balances L is drawn for a given level of real GDP. The higher the opportunity cost of holding money, as measured by the nominal interest rate, i, the lower will be the quantity of real balances demanded. The real money supply function M/P is vertical at M_0/P_0. Equilibrium in the money market is at point E, with the equilibrium interest rate i_0. At a lower interest rate, i_1, there is an excess demand for money balances in the amount AB. There must be a corresponding excess supply of bonds as people sell bonds to get money balances. In the diagram, the interest rate rises to i_0, its equilibrium level, and the market clears.

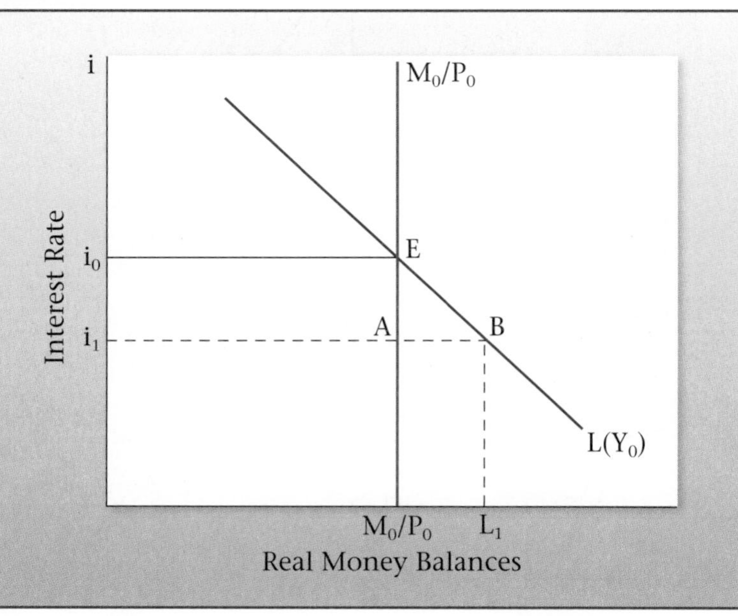

From now on, when we discuss adjustments in the money market caused by changes in either the demand for or supply of money balances, those adjustments involve trades in bonds that change bond prices and interest rates to maintain money market equilibrium.

Changes in Financial Market Equilibrium

A shift in either the money supply or money demand changes equilibrium in the money market (and the bond market). Interest rates move to restore equilibrium. Figure 9.3 gives examples.

A Fall in the Money Supply

Suppose the central bank lowers the monetary base and the money supply contracts. For a fixed price level, lower nominal money reduces the real money supply. Figure 9.3(a) shows this leftward shift in the money supply curve from M_0/P to M_1/P. The

FIGURE 9.3 **Changes in Equilibrium Interest Rates**

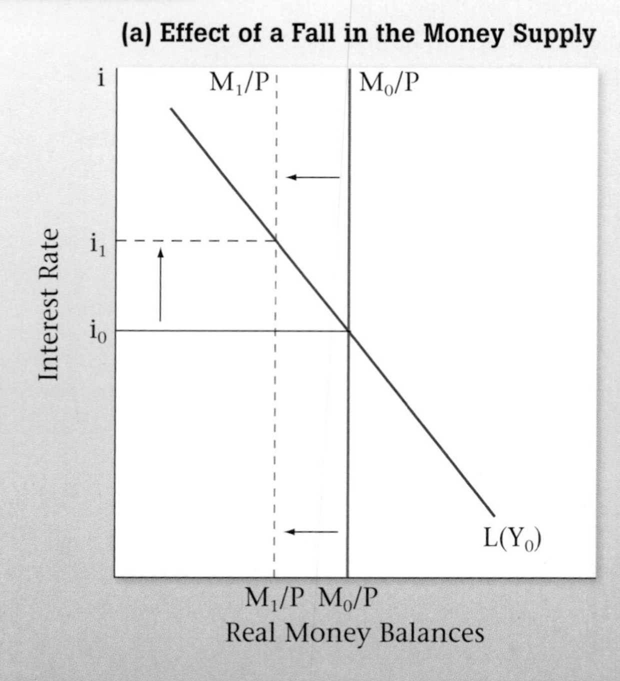

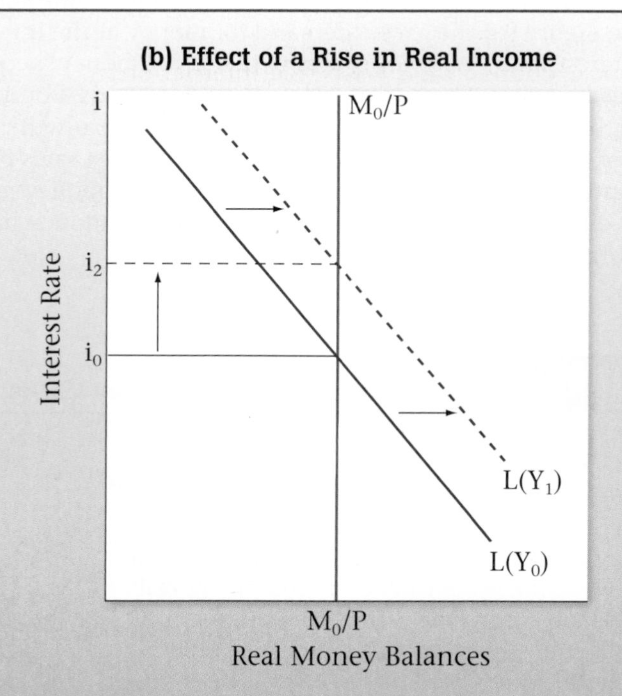

In panel (a), with given real income Y_0, $L(Y_0)$ is the demand for real money balances. A reduction in the real money supply from M_0/P to M_1/P moves the money supply function to the left. The excess demand for money at the initial interest rate i_0 leads people to sell bonds to get money balances. Bond prices fall, raising bond yields and interest rates and reducing the quantity of real money balances demanded along the L function. Figure 9.2 (page 215) showed this relationship. Equilibrium is restored at the higher interest rate i_1.

In panel (b), with a given real money supply, an increase in real GDP shifts the demand for real money balances to the right from $L(Y_1)$. Interest rates rise to a new equilibrium at i_2 as a result of bond sales that lower bond prices and raise yields. At i_2, the quantity of money balances demanded again equals the supply of balances.

equilibrium interest rate rises from i_0 to i_1 as people sell bonds. A higher interest rate reduces the demand for real money balances along the demand curve $L(Y_0)$, bringing demand into line with the reduced supply. Hence, a lower money supply raises equilibrium interest rates. Conversely, a rise in the money supply lowers the equilibrium interest rate.

A Rise in Real Income

Figure 9.3(b) shows real money demand $L(Y_0)$ for the real income Y_0. A rise in real income increases the demand for money balances at each interest rate, shifting the demand for money function from $L(Y_0)$ to $L(Y_1)$. The equilibrium interest rate rises as portfolio managers sell bonds in an attempt to increase their money holdings. The rise in the interest rate lowers the demand for real balances, moving along the money demand function $L(Y_1)$, and keeps demand for money equal to the unchanged supply. Conversely, a fall in real income would shift the demand for money to the left and reduce the equilibrium interest rate.

Review Questions 7 and 8

9.5 Interest Rates and Foreign Exchange Rates

The interest rates determined in the money market have important effects on the **foreign exchange rate**. With free international trade in financial assets, portfolio managers, having chosen to hold some part of their portfolios in bonds, have an additional choice. They can hold some bonds issued by domestic borrowers and some issued by foreign borrowers. They might, for example, hold some bonds issued by the Government of Canada, some issued by the United States Treasury and some issued by other governments. Similarly, residents of other countries can choose to include bonds issued by the Government of Canada in their holdings. These choices are made on the basis of the yields on bonds established by conditions in different national money and bond markets.

The **foreign exchange rate** is the domestic currency price of a unit of foreign currency.

To achieve the highest return on the bond portion of their portfolios, managers buy bonds that offer the highest rate of return for a given level of risk. If interest rates are constant in other financial markets, a rise in Canadian interest rates and bond yields makes Canadian bonds more attractive to both domestic and foreign bondholders. The demand for Canadian bonds increases. A fall in Canadian interest rates has the opposite effect.

Bonds are issued and priced in national currency. Most Government of Canada bonds are denominated in Canadian dollars. U.S. Treasury bonds are denominated in U.S. dollars, and bonds issued by European governments are denominated in euros. If Canadians want to purchase bonds on foreign bond markets they need foreign currency to make payment. Similarly, if residents of other countries want to purchase Canadian bonds they need Canadian dollars to make payment. These *foreign exchange* requirements for trading in financial assets are the same as those for trading in goods and services. The foreign exchange market is the market in which currencies of different countries are bought and sold and foreign exchange rates are determined.

Figure 9.4 shows both the domestic money and foreign exchange markets. The domestic money market is the same as in Figure 9.3. The foreign exchange market shows the supply and demand for foreign exchange, in this case of the U.S. dollar, and the exchange rate which is the Canadian dollar price of one U.S. dollar. The intersection of the supply and demand curves in the foreign exchange market determines the equilibrium foreign exchange rate.

FIGURE 9.4 **Interest Rates and Foreign Exchange Rates**

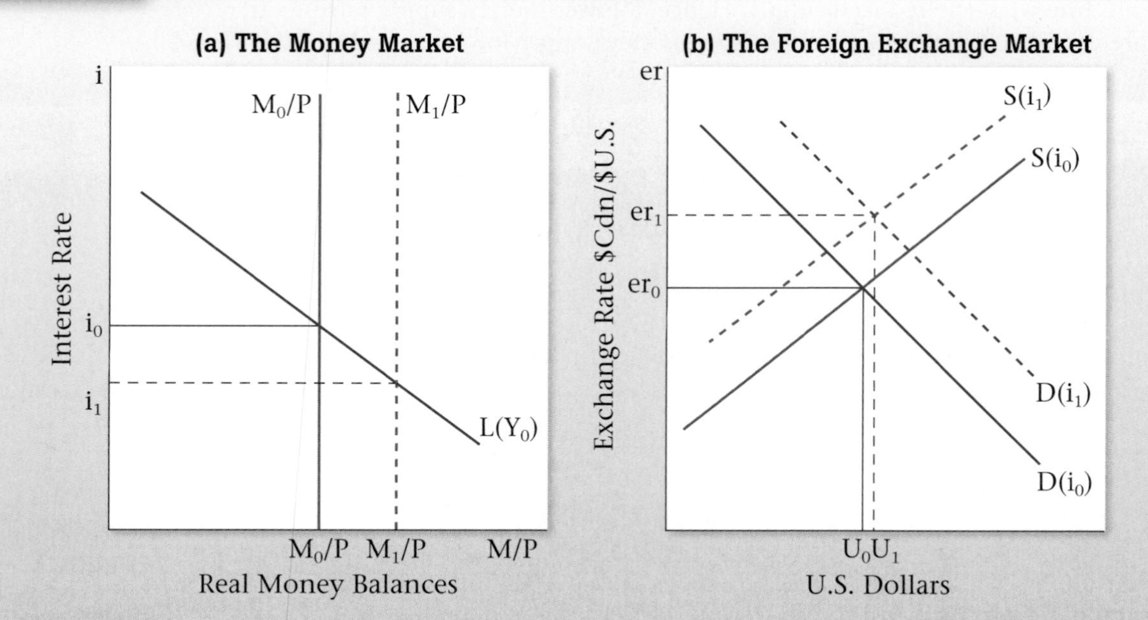

A change in the equilibrium interest rate in the money market causes a change in the equilibrium exchange rate.

The solid lines in the diagram show the domestic money market in panel (a) is in an initial equilibrium at i_0 with the demand for money $L(Y_0)$ equal to money supply M_0 /P. With interest rate i_0 the foreign exchange market in panel (b) is in equilibrium at the exchange rate er_0 based on the intersection of the supply of U.S. dollars $S(i_0)$ and the demand for U.S. dollars $D(i_0)$.

The dotted lines show the effect of an increase in money supply on the interest rate and the exchange rate. Increased money balances create excess money holdings and an increased demand for domestic bonds, raising bond prices and lowering domestic interest rates. With foreign interest rates constant, the yields on domestic bonds are reduced relative to yields on foreign bonds. Both Canadian and foreign bondholders shift their portfolios out of Canadian bonds into foreign bonds. The demand for U.S. dollars from Canadians wanting to buy U.S. bonds increases. The supply of U.S. dollars from residents of the U.S. wanting to buy Canadian bonds falls. The new supply and demand curves are $S(i_1)$ and $D(i_1)$. The exchange rate rises to a new equilibrium at er_1. It takes more Canadian dollars to buy one U.S. dollar.

The supply of U.S. dollars on the foreign exchange market comes from the export of goods, services, and financial assets to U.S. residents. Sales of lumber, potash, auto parts, BlackBerries, financial services, financial assets, and other exports generate receipts in U.S. dollars. Canadian exporters with costs denominated in Canadian dollars sell their U.S. dollar receipts on the Canadian foreign exchange market for Canadian dollars. This is the supply of U.S. dollars on the market.

In Figure 9.4(b) the upward sloping supply curve shows quantities of U.S. dollars coming to the market at different exchange rates, *all other things held constant.* It slopes upward because higher exchange rates lower the prices of Canadian goods and services in foreign markets. As a result, exports of goods and services, and total receipts from export sales increase, giving a positive slope.

The downward sloping demand curve is also drawn on the assumption that all things except the exchange rate are constant. It is derived from Canadian demand for imports of U.S. goods, services, and financial assets. A fall in the exchange rate lowers the Canadian dollar price of imported goods and services and increases Canadian expenditure on imports. As a result the demand curve for U.S. dollars is downward sloping.

The link between the foreign exchange rate and the money market comes from the interest rate. Demand and supply curves are drawn on the assumption that interest rates, among other things, are constant. This assumption determines the *positions* of the supply and demand curves in the foreign exchange market. However, if the domestic interest rate changes, the supply and demand curves in the foreign exchange market will shift and change the equilibrium exchange rate. Figure 9.4 gives an example.

The solid lines in Figure 9.4 give the initial equilibrium conditions in both the money market and the foreign exchange market. With interest rate i_0 in the money market, the supply and demand curves are $S(i_0)$ and $D(i_0)$ in the foreign exchange market. The intersection of the supply and demand curves determines the equilibrium exchange rate er_0. This exchange rate is the Canadian dollar price of a U.S. dollar. It was about \$1.02 Cdn = \$1.00 U.S. in mid-2008 but had risen to about \$1.25Cdn = \$1.00U.S. by early 2009 as a result of declines in energy and commodity prices.

A change in the domestic money market changes interest rates and the foreign exchange rate. The dotted lines in the diagram show the effect of an increase in the domestic money supply. Money and bond market adjustments to the increased money supply lower the interest rate from i_0 to i_1. At these lower interest rates domestic bond yields are lower relative to foreign bond yields than they were before. This provides the incentive for domestic portfolio managers to switch their purchases from domestic bonds to foreign (U.S.) bonds. To pay for foreign bonds they need foreign currency. The demand for U.S. dollars increases to $D(i_1)$ in panel (b) of the diagram.

Simultaneously, bond holders in the U.S. shift their purchases from the now relatively low-yield Canadian bonds to U.S. bonds. Lower exports of securities to the U.S. market reduce the supply of U.S. dollars to $S(i_1)$ in panel (b) of the diagram. This negative shift in supply combined with the positive shift in demand results in a rise in the exchange rate. If the exchange rate er_0 was \$1.02 Cdn = \$1.00 U.S., the exchange rate er_1 would be somewhat higher, say \$1.03 Cdn = \$1.00 U.S.

A decrease in the money supply or a change in the demand for money with a fixed money supply would affect the foreign exchange rate through the same linkages. Changes in domestic financial markets and foreign exchange markets happen simultaneously. With current communications and information technology these markets adjust very rapidly and continuously. The changes in interest rates and foreign exchange rates that result from changes in domestic money market conditions have important effects on aggregate expenditure and aggregate demand.

Review Question 9

9.6 Interest Rates, Exchange Rates, and Aggregate Demand

Bond prices, interest rates, and exchange rates determined in money and financial markets play a key role in our study of aggregate demand and output. Interest rates and exchange rates link changes in money and financial markets to the expenditure decisions that determine aggregate demand.

APPLICATION BOX 9.2

Nominal and Real Interest Rates

Both nominal and real interest rates play important roles in the economy. The **nominal** (or money) **interest rate** is the annual percentage of the principal of a loan that the borrower pays to the lender. It is determined by supply and demand conditions in money markets. The **real interest rate** is the nominal interest rate adjusted for annual changes in the price level (real interest rate = nominal interest rate minus the inflation rate). When the inflation rate is zero, nominal and real interest rates are equal.

Nominal interest rates and financial asset prices are linked. The present value calculation of asset prices uses the nominal rate for discounting. Nominal interest rates and asset prices vary inversely.

Nominal interest rates also affect nominal cash flows of both households and businesses. A rise in nominal rates on lines of credit or mortgages increases the current cash cost of that borrowing. A fall in nominal rates on lines of credit or mortgages releases current cash commitments.

Real interest rates determine the *real* cost of borrowing and the *real* return to lending.

A family borrows $200,000 for one year at a nominal interest rate of 5 percent to buy a house. At the end of the year they would owe the lender $200,000 plus $10,000 ($200,000 × 0.05) interest. Their nominal interest cost is $10,000. If the price level has been constant over the year, their nominal interest cost and their real interest cost are equal at 5 percent.

Suppose however that the price level is rising by 3 percent a year. The house bought today for $200,000 will sell for $206,000 one year from now. Borrowing at 5 percent to buy the house cost $10,000 but the rise in the price of the house by $6,000 offsets part of that cost. The real interest cost is $10,000 − $6,000 = $4,000. The real interest rate is 2 percent based on the nominal interest rate of 5 percent *minus* the change in the price level of 3 percent.

With inflation rates greater than zero, lenders' real interest earnings are less than nominal interest earnings. In the preceding example, the mortgage lender's real return was just 2 percent (5 percent − 3 percent inflation) because the $210,000 received at the end of the year had its purchasing power reduced to approximately $204,000 by the 3 percent rise in the price level.

Nominal and real interest rates affect expenditure decisions by their effects on asset prices, cash flows, and the real costs and returns involved in borrowing and lending.

The **transmission mechanism** links money, interest rates, and exchange rates through financial markets to output and employment and prices.

The impact of financial markets, interest rates, and exchange rates on aggregate expenditure, aggregate demand, and real output is described by the **transmission mechanism**. It has three important channels, namely:

1. the effect of interest rate changes on consumption expenditure,
2. the effect of interest rate changes on investment expenditure, and
3. the effect of interest rate changes on foreign exchange rates and net exports.

INTEREST RATES AND CONSUMPTION EXPENDITURE

Chapter 6 used a very simple consumption function, an upward-sloping straight line relating aggregate consumption to the disposable income of households. The slope of this line, the marginal propensity to consume, showed the change in consumption expenditure that would result from a change in disposable income. The vertical intercept of the consumption function showed autonomous consumption expenditure, the part not determined by disposable income. Changes in income moved households *along* the consumption function. Changes in autonomous consumption expenditure shifted the consumption function. How do interest rates affect autonomous consumption expenditure?

Household Wealth

Suppose real wealth, the purchasing power of financial assets held by households, rises because of a boom in financial markets. Households spend some of this new wealth on a new car. At each level of disposable income, consumption expenditure is higher. The entire consumption function shifts up when households' real wealth increases. This is another example of a **wealth effect**, similar to that we discussed earlier in Chapter 5.

The **wealth effect** is the change in the consumption function caused by a change in household real wealth.

Money and interest rates affect household wealth, and thus consumption expenditure and aggregate demand. First, money is a part of household financial portfolios and a component of household wealth. A higher real money supply adds directly to household wealth. Second, nominal interest rates affect household wealth indirectly. The price of financial assets, bonds, and company shares is the present value of the expected stream of interest and dividend payments. When interest rates fall, asset prices rise. Future income flows discounted at a lower rate have a higher present value.

From the earlier discussion of bond prices and yields, when market interest rates are 10 percent, a bond paying $2.50 each year forever is worth $25. New buyers pay $25 and get 10 percent return on their asset. If interest rates fall to 5 percent, bond prices rise to $50. Bondholders enjoy a capital gain, which increases their wealth. New buyers still get $2.50 each year, which is an annual return equal to the current market rate of 5 percent. A similar relationship exists for company share prices.

Changes in interest rates also have important effects on house prices by lowering the cost of financing, increasing the present values of rental incomes, and increasing demand for both owner occupied and rental housing. Until recently, and especially in the United States, households have used the increased market values and equity in their housing as collateral to raise funds for other expenditures by borrowing against their increased housing wealth. This sustained a strong boom in housing prices and consumer expenditures until the financial crisis starting in mid-2007 and growing through 2008. The collapse in financial markets and housing prices in late 2008 and into 2009 emerged as a major cause of the fall in U.S. consumption expenditure and the recession starting in 2008–09.

If changes in interest rates change real household wealth by changing nominal wealth by more than any concurrent change in the general price level, consumption expenditure is affected. We continue to assume a constant price level. Then, lower interest rates increase asset prices and household real wealth; consumption expenditure increases. Higher interest rates reduce asset prices and household real wealth; consumption expenditure declines. These changes in consumption *shift* the consumption function, the aggregate expenditure function, and the aggregate demand curve.

Application Box 9.3 reports on some recent research on the importance of wealth effects for consumption expenditure.

Durables and Consumer Credit

When spending exceeds disposable income, net wealth falls. People sell off assets or borrow money to finance their dissaving. A lot of borrowing is to finance *consumer durables*, household capital goods such as cars, televisions, and furniture. Buying a new car can

APPLICATION BOX 9.3

Wealth Effects

> "Our findings suggest that consumption does not respond significantly to a permanent increase in stock market wealth, while a permanent increase in housing wealth leads to a significant rise in consumption."

Summarizing recent academic research, Lise Pichette reported estimates of the wealth effects in Canada and the United States. These studies have found that one-dollar increases in non-human wealth lead to an increase in consumption within the range of 3 to 7 cents, although some estimates are much higher. Using Canadian data, Pichette found an average MPC from housing wealth of 5.7 cents per dollar. However, the effects of stock market wealth were small and statistically insignificant. Nonetheless, the changes in housing wealth have important impacts on consumption expenditure and aggregate demand.

Source: Lise Pichette, "Are Wealth Effects Important for Canada," *Bank of Canada Review*, Spring 2004, pp. 29–34. Bank of Canada, 2009.

cost most of a whole year's income. Financing is usually required, either by borrowing from a financial institution or by using wealth built up by past saving.

Money and interest rates affect consumer spending by affecting both the quantity of consumer financing available and the interest rate charged on it. An increase in the monetary base allows banks to extend more credit in the form of car loans and larger lines of credit. Assuming again a constant price level, lower nominal interest rates reduce the real cost of borrowing and allow households to take out bigger loans while still being able to meet the interest and repayments.

Thus, two forces—wealth effects, and availability and cost of credit—explain the effects of money on planned consumption expenditure. This is one part of the *transmission mechanism* through which money and interest rates affect expenditure. Operating through wealth effects and the supply and cost of credit, changes in money supply and interest rates *shift* the consumption function. We can recognize the effects of both income and interest rates on consumption by using an equation, namely:

$$C = (Y, i) \tag{9.2}$$

with a positive marginal propensity to consume out of national income, $0 < (\Delta C/\Delta Y) < 1$, and a negative relationship between consumption and interest rates, $\Delta C/\Delta i < 0$. When consumption expenditure is plotted relative to national income as in the 45° line diagrams of Chapters 6 and 7, a change in the interest rate *shifts the consumption function* but does not change its slope.

INVESTMENT EXPENDITURE

In earlier chapters we treated investment expenditure, including residential and non-residential construction, as autonomous, independent of current income. We now look more closely at what determines investment expenditure. We focus again on the interest rates determined in money and financial markets.

Investment spending is the purchase of currently produced fixed capital, which includes factories; houses; machinery and equipment; and inventories of raw materials, components, and finished goods. The share of investment in GDP fluctuates between

15 and 20 percent. Although the total change in inventories is quite small, this component of total investment is volatile and contributes significantly to changes in the total level of investment.

Public investment in buildings, roads, bridges, and machinery and equipment is a part of government expenditure G. We still treat government expenditure as part of fiscal policy. Thus, we assume that G is fixed at a level set by government, and focus here on private investment expenditure I.

Investment in Fixed Capital

Firms add to plant and equipment and increase their productive capacity when they expect profitable opportunities to expand output, or because they can reduce costs by using more capital-intensive and larger-scale production methods. TELUS needs new equipment because it is developing new products for data and voice transmission. Honda needs more assembly-line capacity to meet demand for its current and new fuel-efficient models. Wind energy and biofuel companies build new wind farms and ethanol plants to provide new sources of electricity and fuels.

In reaching an investment decision, the firm compares the value of the increase it expects in future profit with the current cost of financing investment. Will the investment yield enough extra revenue to pay back *with interest* the loan used to finance the investment, recover the cost, and leave a profit? Alternatively, if the project is funded internally out of retained earnings, will the investment yield at least as high a return as the funds could earn if lent to other businesses or government at current interest rates? The higher the market interest rate, the larger must be the expected return on new capital expenditures to match the finance or opportunity costs of funds used.

At any instant, there are many investment opportunities in the economy that private firms might undertake, but the expected rates of return or profitability for different projects are different. How does the expected profitability of a wind farm to produce electricity compare with a gas-fired electricity-generating plant? How does the expected profitability of fuel-cell cars compare with that of hybrid cars or plug-in electric cars? Does the expected profitability of organic farming justify setting up new organic farms or switching from conventional farming practices? Does the potential demand for bio-diesel provide profitable investment opportunities? If we think of different investment opportunities ranked in order of decreasing expected profitability, we can see how interest rates affect investment decisions. As interest rates fall, more and more projects have expected returns that match or exceed their costs of financing. Lower interest rates lead to higher investment expenditures, and vice versa.

Expectations of the profitability of investment projects relative to interest costs of financing depend on the stability of other underlying economic conditions. The sharp drops in crude oil and natural gas prices in late 2008 and early 2009 could call for rethinking alternative energy projects and alternative automobile design. Expenditures and expenditure plans are volatile when underlying conditions are volatile, even if interest and financing costs are stable or falling.

Inventory Investment

There are three reasons why firms want to hold inventories of raw materials, partly finished goods, and finished goods ready for sale. First, the firm may be betting on price changes. Sometimes firms hold large inventories of fuel, or commodities like sugar or base metals, believing it cheaper to buy now and hold rather than buying later when prices are expected to be higher. Similarly, firms may hold finished product off the market, hoping to get better prices later.

Second, production processes take time. A house cannot be built in a week or even several months. Large and complex machinery takes time to design and manufacture. Some inventories are simply goods in production.

Third, inventories help smooth costly adjustments in output and provide an immediate supply to customers. If demand for output rises sharply, plant capacity cannot be changed overnight. If demand exceeds current output, sellers would rather not disappoint potential customers. Car dealers hold inventories in part to help smooth the flow of production, and in part to be able to offer immediate delivery. Retail stores carry inventories so customers can buy what they want when they want it. As demand fluctuates, it can be more efficient to allow inventories of finished goods to fluctuate than to try to adjust production to volatile market conditions.

These benefits of holding inventories come with a cost. To the producer, unsold goods represent costs of labour, materials, and energy paid but not yet recovered from the sale of the product. These costs have to be financed, either by borrowing or tying up internal funds. Retailers have similar carrying costs for their inventories. Thus, interest rates are an important cost of holding inventories. If we assume prices are constant and interest rates rise, producers and retailers will want smaller inventories. Alternatively, if prices are rising, the difference between the nominal interest rate and the rate of inflation is the real cost of carrying inventories.

The **investment function**, $I = I(i)$, shows the level of planned investment expenditure at each interest rate.

The **investment function**, which relates planned investment expenditure to interest rates,

$$I = I(i) \tag{9.3}$$

is based on these explanations. The negative effect of interest rates in the investment function, $(\Delta I/\Delta i) < 0$, shows that higher interest rates cause lower levels of planned investment expenditure. But how sensitive are investment plans to financing costs? If these financing costs were not a large factor in the investment decision, $\Delta I/\Delta i$ would be small. A rise in the interest rate from i_0 to i_1 would still lower planned investment, but by only a small amount. Alternatively, a larger value for $\Delta I/\Delta i$ would mean that investment plans are sensitive to interest rates.

When plotted in a diagram, the slope of the investment function $I = I(i)$ is $-(\Delta i/\Delta I)$. The *position* of the investment function reflects the effect of all factors, other than interest rates, that affect investment decisions. The price of new capital equipment, optimism or pessimism about future markets and market growth, the introduction of new technologies embodied in newly available equipment, and many other factors underlie investment decisions. Changes in any of these conditions would *shift the I function* and change planned investment at every interest rate. Increased business confidence and expectations of stronger and larger markets shift the I curve to the right. Pessimism shifts it to the left.

The volatility of investment that causes business cycle fluctuations in output and national income comes from volatility in business profit expectations, rather than from interest rates. Changes in investment, either as a result of changes in interest rates or as a result of other factors, shift aggregate expenditure and work through the multiplier to change AD, output, and employment. The reaction of investment expenditure to changes in interest rates provides the important link in the monetary transmission mechanism but does not explain the volatility of investment expenditure we saw in Chapter 6.

Review Question 10

9.7 The Transmission Mechanism

We can now summarize and illustrate the relationships that transmit changes in money, financial markets, and interest rates to aggregate demand, output, and employment. There are four linkages in the transmission mechanism:

1. With prices constant, changes in money supply change interest rates.
2. Changes in interest rates change consumption expenditure through the wealth effect and the cost and availability of credit.
3. Changes in interest rates also cause changes in planned investment expenditure through the cost and availability of credit to finance the purchase of capital equipment and to carry inventories.
4. Changes in interest rates also cause changes in exchange rates, which change the price competitiveness and profitability of trade in goods and services.

Working through these linkages, the effects of changes in money and interest rates on aggregate demand and equilibrium real GDP is illustrated as follows:

$$\Delta M \rightarrow \Delta i \rightarrow \begin{pmatrix} \Delta C + \Delta I \\ \Delta er \rightarrow \Delta NX \end{pmatrix} \rightarrow \Delta AE \times \text{multiplier} \rightarrow \Delta AD \rightarrow \Delta Y$$

Figure 9.6 shows the transmission mechanism using four interrelated diagrams: (a) the money market, (b) interest rates and planned expenditure, (c) aggregate expenditure and equilibrium output, and (d) aggregate demand and supply, output, and prices. We continue to assume a constant price level, as the diagrams show. Changes in the money and financial sector affect aggregate demand and output, to add another dimension to our understanding of the sources of AD and fluctuations in A.

There are several key aspects to the linkages between money, interest rates, and expenditure. In the money market, the extent to which changes in money supply change interest rates depends on the slope of the demand curve for real money balances. A steep curve would show that portfolio managers do not react strongly to changes in market interest rates. It would take relatively large changes in rates to get them to hold higher money balances. Alternatively, if their decisions were very sensitive to the interest rates, the L function would be quite flat. The difference is important to the volatility of financial markets and interest rates, which in turn affect the volatility of expenditure.

The sensitivity of expenditure to interest rates and financial conditions is a second important aspect of the transmission mechanism. If the interest rate/expenditure function, the expenditure function in panel (b), is steep, changes in interest rates will have only small effects on expenditure, aggregate demand, and output. A flatter expenditure function has the opposite implication.

We saw in Chapter 7 that the slope of the aggregate expenditure function and its relationship to the multiplier was important to the built-in stability in the economy. Now, with financial markets in our model, we see that if the effect of money market disturbances on aggregate demand depends on the demand for money and the interest rate sensitivity of expenditure. Flat demand for money functions, together with steep interest rate and expenditure functions, reduce the impact of financial sector fluctuations on AD, output, and employment.

BUSINESS CYCLES, OUTPUT GAPS, AND POLICY ISSUES

The effect of money and financial markets on expenditure, output, and employment raises two issues for macroeconomic policy. First, fluctuations in money supply and

FIGURE 9.6 **The Monetary Transmission Mechanism**

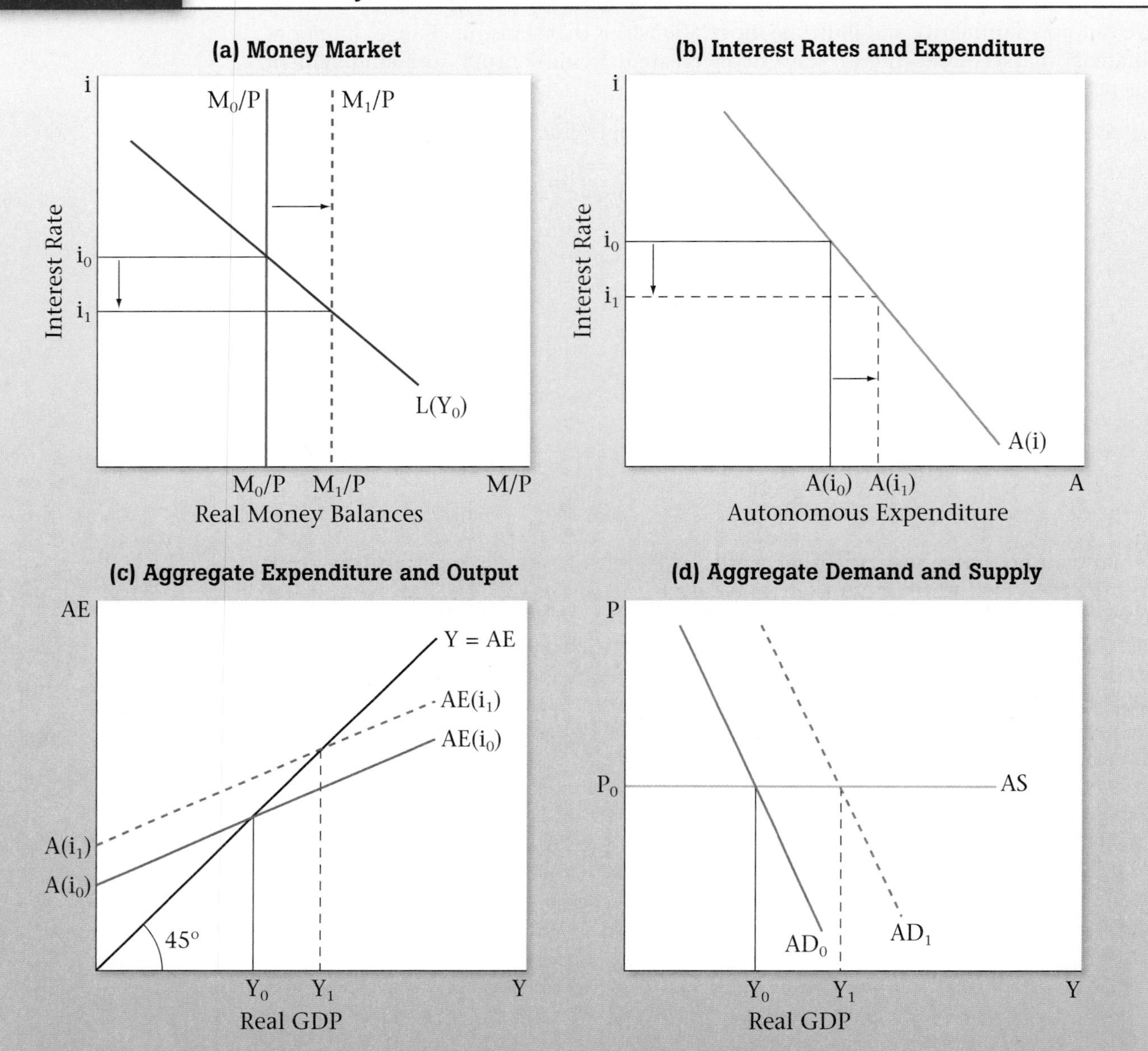

To see the transmission mechanism by which money and interest rates affect output and employment, *we start in the equilibrium based* on the solid lines in the diagrams. Panel (a) shows the equilibrium interest rate (i_0) determined by supply and demand in the money market. Panel (b) shows the level of consumption, investment, and net export expenditure determined by the interest rate i_1. Panel (c) shows equilibrium expenditure based on autonomous expenditure and the multiplier. In panel (d) this equilibrium expenditure places the AD curve at AD_1, giving the new equilibrium output Y_1 at the fixed price level P_0.

Now we increase the money supply, holding all other conditions constant, to see what happens to equilibrium output and income. The dotted lines in panels (a) to (d) illustrate the result. Interest rates fall in the money market, increasing sensitive autonomous expenditure along the function in A(i) in (b), shifting AE up in panel (c), and raising equilibrium expenditure and AD based on the multiplier.

An increase in money supply, or any other event that lowers interest rates, increases AD, output, and employment. A rise in interest rates would have the opposite effect.

financial conditions are an important source of business cycle fluctuations in output and employment. These effects are particularly strong and important when the small changes in money supply have big impacts on interest rates and expenditure. As we noted, a steep L function and a flat expenditure/interest rate function would create these conditions. Stabilization policy would then need to control and stabilize the money supply, a policy approach advocated by Monetarists, who see money supply disturbances as the major source of business cycles. If you fix money supply at M_0 in Figure 9.6, and the demand for money L(Y,i) and the interest rate/expenditure function are stable, you remove monetary disturbances as a source of business cycles.

This Monetarist approach to money and the financial sector concentrates on the "automatic" stabilization effects of money supply control. With the money supply fixed, any tendency for the economy to experience a recessionary or inflationary gap changes the demand for money, and interest rates change in an offsetting direction. A fall in real output that creates a recessionary gap reduces the demand for money L(Y, i) and, with a fixed money supply, interest rates fall to induce additional expenditure. An inflationary gap would produce an automatic rise in interest rates. The monetary sector automatically resists fluctuations in expenditure and output.

The second policy issue is the alternative to this approach. Discretionary monetary policy would attempt to manage money supply or interest rates or financial conditions more broadly. The objective would be to counter persistent autonomous expenditure and financial disturbances that create output gaps. The intent is to manage aggregate demand in an active way. In other words, if business cycles were caused by shifts and fluctuations in the interest rate/expenditure function in panel (b) of Figure 9.6, monetary policy would react by changing interest rates and money supply and move the economy along the new expenditure function to stabilize autonomous expenditure and aggregate demand. Keynesian and New-Keynesian economists advocate this active approach to policy in the money and financial sector, based on a different and broader view of the sources of business cycles in the economy.

Recent experience extends beyond these two policy concerns. A collapse in the financial sector on the supply side was a major cause of the recession of 2009. Banks and other financial institutions suffered losses on commercial paper asset holdings, and losses on other assets followed as energy and commodity prices dropped and expectations of business profits followed. Uncertainty on the part of many lenders about the quality of assets and the risks of lending reduced the availability of credit. Uncertainty on the part of households and businesses reduced their confidence in financial institutions. Although central banks worked to keep interest rates low and bank reserves strong, shifts in the availability of credit and the willingness to borrow shifted the A(i) curve in Figure 9.6 sharply to the left, expenditure fell, and AD shifted left, opening a strong recessionary gap.

Review Question 13

Next

In this chapter, we have made the link between money, interest rates, aggregate demand, and output in our model of the economy. We have also shown that monetary policy, working through the monetary transmission mechanism, provides a second policy channel, in addition to fiscal policy, which government might use to stabilize business cycle fluctuations. Chapter 10 studies in detail the monetary policy operations of central banks, including the Bank of Canada.

SUMMARY

- A **financial portfolio** is a mixed holding of money and other financial assets, such as bonds and equities, structured, to balance expected return and risk.
- The price of a financial asset that promises to make future payments is the **present value** of those payments. Because current interest rates are used to discount future payments and determine this present value, **bond prices and interest rates are inversely related.**
- The **demand for money**, L, is a demand for real money balances measured in terms of purchasing power over goods and services. It arises from the portfolio decisions people make about the form in which to hold their wealth. Holding money reduces the costs of making both routine and unexpected **transactions**. It also provides a **safe asset**, with a fixed nominal price, as a store of wealth. The cost of holding money is the **interest income** and potential capital gain sacrificed by not holding bonds.
- The quantity of real money demanded rises with real incomes, to finance higher transactions, and falls with higher nominal interest rates, the opportunity cost of holding money instead of bonds. The demand for money function is $\mathbf{L = kY - hi}$.
- The **interest rate**, **i**, is determined by supply and demand in the money market, together with supply and demand in the bond market. As people adjust the holdings of bonds and money in their wealth portfolios, bond prices and yields adjust to clear both bond and money markets simultaneously.
- Interest rates play a key role in the **transmission mechanism** that links money and financial markets to aggregate expenditure.
- Household consumption expenditure and business investment expenditure are dependent, in part, on interest rates. A higher interest rate reduces household **wealth** and increases the **finance costs** of borrowing. Lower wealth and higher finance costs reduce planned autonomous consumption, shifting the consumption function down. Lower interest rates have the opposite effect.
- Changes in interest rates lead to changes in **exchange rates** that change net exports. The international sector makes an additional link between money, interest rates, and expenditure.
- The **monetary transmission mechanism** links changes in money supply to changes in aggregate expenditure, aggregate demand, and output through interest rates and exchange rates.

KEY TERMS

KEY EQUATIONS AND RELATIONS

Equations

Demand for real money balances: $L = kY - hi$	**(9.1)**	p. 214
Consumption, income, and interest rates $C = (Y, i)$	**(9.2)**	p. 222
Investment and interest rates $I = I(i)$	**(9.3)**	p. 224
Net exports $NX = NX[Y, Y^*, P, P^*, er(i)...]$	**(9.4)**	p. 225

Relations

Financial asset prices and yields: Price of a financial asset = present value of expected future payments

When market interest rates rise: $i\uparrow \rightarrow PV\downarrow = \text{Asset } P\downarrow$
When market interest rates fall: $i\downarrow \rightarrow PV\uparrow = \text{Asset } P\uparrow$

Financial markets and interest rates: Trading in bond and money markets → bond prices → bond yields = market interest rates i.

↑ demand for bonds = ↓ demand for money → ↑ bond price↑ → ↓i
↓ demand for bonds = ↑ demand for money → ↓ bond price → ↑i

Financial portfolios: Financial portfolios combine holdings of money and bonds.

Financial wealth = money + bonds
Portfolio adjustments shift holdings between money and bonds.

Demand for money balances: Money holdings in a portfolio depend on nominal incomes and interest rates.

↑ money income → ↑ demand for money to finance expenditures = ↓ demand for bonds
↓ interest rates → ↓ demand for money = ↑ demand for bonds to earn higher returns

Money supply and interest rates: Changes in M supply disrupt financial market equilibrium → changes in interest rates.

↑ M → portfolio adjustment → ↑ demand for bonds → ↑ bond prices → ↓ i
↓ M → portfolio adjustment → ↓ demand for bonds → ↓ bond prices → ↑i

Interest rates and foreign exchange rates: Changes in domestic interest rates change the differential between domestic and foreign interest rate leading to changes in the exchange rate and net exports.

$$\uparrow i \rightarrow i \neq i^* \rightarrow \Delta S_{fe} + \Delta D_{fe} \rightarrow \Delta NX$$

Monetary transmission mechanism: Changes in money supply and interest rates change aggregate expenditure, aggregate demand, and equilibrium real GDP.

$$\uparrow M \rightarrow \downarrow i \rightarrow \uparrow (C + I + NX) = \uparrow AE \rightarrow \uparrow AD \rightarrow \uparrow Y$$
$$\downarrow M \rightarrow \uparrow i \rightarrow \downarrow (C + I + NX) = \downarrow AE \rightarrow \downarrow AD \rightarrow \downarrow Y$$

REVIEW QUESTIONS

Review Questions and answers are included in Connect at www.mcgrawhillconnect.ca.

1. Why do people hold money balances when they could hold bonds, which offer higher interest income?

2. If the current market interest rate is 3 percent and a bond promises a coupon of $3 each year in perpetuity (forever), what is the current market price of the bond?

3. Suppose you are holding a bond that will pay $5 each year for the next two years from today and mature two years from today.
   a. If current two-year market interest rates are 4 percent, what is the market price of your bond?
   b. If market interest rates rise tomorrow to 6 percent, what will be the market price of your bond?
   c. What is the "market risk" in holding bonds?

4. You are holding a cash balance that you want to place in the bond market for a period of three years. The market rate of interest on three year bonds today is 5.5 percent. Would you be willing to pay $1015 for a $1000 bond with a 6 percent coupon maturing three years from today? Explain your answer.

5. a. If employers who pay their employees monthly switched to paying them weekly, would the demand for money be affected? Explain why or why not?
   b. During recent years, interest rates on interest-paying financial assets have dropped sharply. Use your understanding of the demand for money balances to explain why and how this decline in interest rates would affect the demand for money balances, and, more specifically, the demand for M1B balances relative to M2 balances.

6. Draw a diagram to illustrate the relationship between the demand for real money balances and the interest rate when real GDP has a given value Y_0.
   a. Explain your choice of the intersection of your demand for money function with the horizontal axis, and your choice of the slope of the function.
   b. Using your diagram, illustrate and explain the quantity of real money balances demanded for a specific interest rate, say i_0. Pay particular attention to the underlying motives for holding these money balances.
   c. Suppose interest rates declined from your initial assumption of i_0 to a new lower rate i_1. Illustrate and explain the effect of the change in interest rates on the demand for money balances.
   d. Holding interest rates constant at either i_0 or i_1, suppose real GDP were to increase. Illustrate and explain the effect of the increase in real GDP on the demand function and the quantity of real money balances people hold.

7. Draw a diagram to illustrate equilibrium in the money market.
   a. Explain carefully what determines the slopes and positions of the demand and supply functions for real money balances in your diagram.
   b. Starting from your initial equilibrium, suppose real national income increased. Illustrate and explain how the money market would adjust to this change in economic conditions.
   c. How does the interest rate in the new equilibrium compare with the interest rate in the initial equilibrium?

8. Use a money market diagram to illustrate and explain the effects of an increase in the real money supply on equilibrium holdings of money balances, bond prices, and the equilibrium interest rate.

9. Draw a diagram to illustrate the foreign exchange market in which euros are bought with or sold for Canadian dollars, assuming the current exchange rate is $1.54Cdn = 1 euro. Starting from that equilibrium exchange rate, suppose Canadian interest rates fall relative to European rates. Using your foreign exchange market, show how the dollar–euro exchange rate would be affected.

10. Explain why and how a rise in interest rates would affect consumption expenditure plans by households and investment plans by business.

11. How would a rise in the exchange rate—the Canadian dollar price of foreign currencies—affect Canada's exports and imports?

12. Explain the linkages between interest rates and expenditure plans in the household, business, and net export sectors of the economy.

13. Construct a set of diagrams that shows the monetary transmission mechanism linking interest rates to aggregate demand and output. Using these diagrams, show and explain:
    a. How a reduction in the money supply would affect aggregate demand and output.
    b. Alternatively, how an increase in the precautionary demand for money balances caused by terrorist activity, or severe weather events, or an increase in uncertainty in general would affect aggregate demand and output. Assume the money supply is held constant.
    c. Alternatively, how an increase in autonomous investment expenditure and exports would affect interest rates, aggregate demand, and output.

14. *Internet* Visit the Bank of Canada's Web site, www.bankofcanada.ca, and follow the "Rates and Statistics" link to interest rates on Canadian bonds. You will find a set of charts reporting recent average yields on Government of Canada marketable bonds of different terms to maturity. Use those charts to answer the following questions.
    a. If you had bought a 3–5-year Government of Canada bond one year ago, what yield did it offer at that time?
    b. What is the latest reported yield on a 3–5-year Government of Canada bond?
    c. How has the price of 3–5-year bonds changed over the past year?
    d. Why are bonds considered risky assets, as compared with money, as a store of value in a portfolio?

CHAPTER 10

Central Banking and Monetary Policy

LEARNING OUTCOMES

By the end of this chapter you should understand:

1. Central banking and the Bank of Canada
2. Central banking operating techniques to control money supply and interest rates
3. Monetary policy targets and instruments in Canada
4. Monetary policy rules
5. The long-run neutrality of money
6. Monetary policy indicators

This chapter examines the role of the central bank. The central bank is responsible for monetary policy. Its monopoly control of the supply of cash, or monetary base, gives it a powerful influence in financial markets. Sometimes the central bank controls the monetary base to control the supply of money. Other times it controls short-term interest rates. In either case, central bank actions are designed to affect prices, output, and employment. They work through the transmission mechanism that links monetary policy to aggregate demand, as we discussed in the last chapter.

10.1 Central Banking and the Bank of Canada

A **central bank** conducts monetary policy using its control of monetary base and interest rates.

Today, every country of any size has a **central bank**. Some of these central banks, like the Bank of England, were private firms originally, in business for profit, but became concerned by financial market conditions and monetary policy. The focus of their business shifted. As governments became interested in monetary policy, central banking institutions were established in countries where none previously existed. The Federal

Reserve System, the United States central bank, was created under federal law in 1913. It is a system of 12 regional banks, each owned by the commercial banks that are its members. Canada's central bank, the Bank of Canada, was set up and started operations in 1935 as a privately owned institution, but was nationalized in 1938. In the United Kingdom, the Bank of England was founded as a private bank in 1694, acted as a central bank for many years, and was nationalized in 1947.

In every case, the important distinction between a private bank and a central bank is the purpose that drives the institution's operations. Private banks are profit-oriented businesses providing financial services to businesses and households. Central banks conduct their operations to influence the behaviour of other banks and intermediaries in the financial system. Profits are *not* the motive behind central banks' operations, although they do make profits. They also serve as banker to the government and to the banks. But their primary role and responsibility is to conduct **monetary policy**: to control the monetary base and interest rates, and perhaps the foreign exchange rate.

Monetary policy is central bank action to change money supply, interest rates, and exchange rates to change aggregate demand and economic performance.

The Bank of Canada is Canada's central bank. We can describe its operations, as we did with the commercial banks in the previous chapter, by looking at the Bank's balance sheet in Table 10.1.

Bank notes in circulation, the main component of the monetary base, are liabilities of the Bank of Canada. The total of notes in circulation is a result of two factors. The first of these is the Bank of Canada's decision about the appropriate size of the monetary base and the interest rate. The second is the demand for cash, relative to deposits, coming from the non-bank public and the banks. These are the banks' reserve ratio **(rr)**, and the public's cash ratio **(cr)** we saw in the last chapter.

Government securities are the main assets of the Bank. When the Bank of Canada buys these securities on the open financial market, it pays for them by issuing cash to the non-bank public, or by making deposits in the Bank of Canada for banks and other members of the Canadian Payments Association. Cash and deposits issued by the Bank of

TABLE 10.1 The Balance Sheet of the Bank of Canada, 2007 (Year-end, millions of dollars)

Assets		Liabilities	
Government of Canada securities		Notes in circulation	50,565
Treasury bills	20,281		
Government bonds of maturity		Deposits	
≤ 3 years	11,091	Government of Canada	1,970
> 3 years	18,269	Chartered banks and other members	502
		Canadian Payment Association	—
Advances to members of the			
Canadian Payments Association	1		
Securities from Resale Agreements	3,963	Foreign central banks	143
Foreign currency deposits	3	Foreign currency liabilities	—
Other assets	289	Other liabilities	717
Total	53,897	Total	53,897

Source: Bank of Canada Banking and Financial Statistics, April 2008, Table B1. Bank of Canada, 2009, and authors' calculations. Figures have been rounded.

Canada increase the monetary base. A larger monetary base allows the banks to expand their lending, according to the deposit multiplier we discussed in Chapter 8. As bank lending and deposits expand, both the banks and the public demand cash to meet their desired reserve, and currency ratios increase. The commercial banks meet these demands for cash by drawing Bank of Canada notes from their deposits in the Bank of Canada. These notes are in turn supplied to the banks' customers, over the counter or through automatic banking machines. It is the business of the Bank of Canada to supply a monetary base that is consistent with the Bank's monetary policy responsibility and objectives.

The Bank also has a responsibility to promote stability in financial markets. In the summer of 2007, a credit crisis arising in the asset-backed commercial paper and sub-prime mortgage markets in the United States created a significant increase in the demand for cash in the banking sector. Part of the Bank of Canada's response to the impact this had on Canadian financial markets was to provide short-term funds through "purchase and resale agreements." These are short-term transactions, usually 28 days, used to provide extra cash to the banks by buying some of the government securities they hold, with the agreement to sell them back at a specific date and price in the near future. The securities held at the end of 2007 as a result of these transactions are shown on the asset side of the Bank's balance sheet. The corresponding increase in cash is an increase in liabilities.

You will notice that the Bank of Canada's balance sheet differs from that of the commercial banks in a couple of important ways. The Bank of Canada does not have a cash reserve ratio. The Bank itself is the source of cash and can issue more on demand. The size of the Bank's balance sheet, measured as the total of either assets or liabilities, is the responsibility of the Governor of the Bank.

The current governor, Mark Carney, like governors before him, manages the Bank's balance sheet to implement monetary policy. He can expand the Bank's asset holdings and pay for that expansion by creating new Bank of Canada liabilities, which are additions to the monetary base. Alternatively, he can sell some of the Bank's assets, destroying an equal amount of liabilities and monetary base. No reserve requirements limit these operations. The management of the Bank's balance sheet and the monetary base depends on the wisdom and judgment of the Governor and management of the Bank. They work to get the monetary base and interest rates that are appropriate for the economy.

There is a further interesting difference between the commercial and central bank balance sheets. Private banks concentrate on their deposit base and loan operations. These are the main entries in their balance sheets and the source of their profits. The Bank of Canada, by contrast, does very little direct lending, and any it does is of very short duration. Indeed, in Table 10.1 we see that advances to members of the payments association, which are central bank loans, are just $1 million.

Nor does the Bank of Canada hold many deposits. It does not need deposits as a source of funds. Deposit facilities are provided to the commercial banks and other members of the Payments Association for their use in settling cheque-clearing balances among the banks, and to the Government of Canada. Cheques issued by the Government of Canada, like income tax refunds, Old Age Security payments, and Employment Insurance benefits, are drawn on the government's account in the Bank of Canada. This difference in the structure of operations again shows the difference between profit-oriented commercial banks and a central bank with responsibility for monetary policy.

Having the power to conduct monetary policy is one thing; how you use it is another. The Bank of Canada's responsibilities are set out in the *Bank of Canada Act*, the act of Parliament that established the Bank in 1934. According to the *Act*, the Bank is to conduct its policy in ways that support the economy by reducing fluctuations in output, prices, and employment while protecting the external value of the currency. In terms of our study of the economy, we can describe these goals of monetary policy as the pursuit of potential output and low, stable inflation rates.

Exactly how the Bank is to achieve those objectives has been, and continues to be, a topic for discussion and debate. Over the years, our understanding of what monetary policy can and cannot do has evolved, as have the Bank's interpretation of its mandate and the techniques it uses to conduct monetary policy. The Canadian economist Robert Mundell has been a major contributor to this work. His explanations of the transmission mechanism and the strength of monetary policy under different foreign exchange rate systems were recognized by his Nobel Prize in economics.

Review Questions 1, 2 and 3

Currently, the Bank works to maintain inflation within a target range of 1 percent to 3 percent, but that has not always been its explicit policy objective. Gordon Thiessen, a recent Governor of the Bank of Canada, provides an interesting overview of the evolution of monetary policy in Canada from the 1930s to the end of the 1990s.[1]

10.2 Central Bank Operating Techniques

The money supply—currency in circulation plus the deposits of the commercial or chartered banks—is partly a liability of the central bank (currency) and partly a liability of the commercial banks (deposits). In Chapter 8 we discussed the *monetary* base or high-powered money, **H**, supplied by the central bank. You will recall that the *money multiplier* ties the size of the money supply to the size of the monetary base. The money multiplier is larger when

(a) the reserve ratio (rr) banks hold is smaller, and

(b) the currency ratio (cr) the non-bank public wishes to hold is smaller.

If these two ratios are constant, the central bank can change the size of the money supply by changing the size of the monetary base.

In general, central banks have three main techniques for the control of the monetary base and the money supply. These are:

1. Establishing reserve requirements
2. Using open-market operations
3. Adjusting central bank lending rates

Not all central banks use all three techniques, but we will examine each of them. Later we will see that the Bank of Canada has some additional operating techniques it uses to influence interest rates in the short run.

In the financial crisis and deep recession of 2008–2009, central banks developed additional techniques to support the banking system, the availability of credit, and the money supply.

RESERVE REQUIREMENTS

In some cases, commercial banks operate under a legal **required reserve ratio**. They are required by law to hold cash reserves, and also central bank deposits not less than some specified percentage of their deposit liabilities.

A **required reserve ratio** is a legal minimum ratio of cash reserves to deposits.

[1] Thiessen, G., "Can a Bank Change?" *Bank of Canada Review*, Winter 2000/2001, pp. 35–46, available at www.bankofcanada.ca/en/speeches/2000/sp00-6.html.

Banks can hold more than the required reserves but not less. If their reserves fall below the required amount, they must borrow cash, from the central bank, to restore their required reserve ratio. Since a loan from the central bank carries an interest rate, usually higher than the market interest rate, borrowing imposes a cost on the bank and lowers profitability. Banks usually hold slightly larger reserves than required to avoid the costs of falling short.

A required reserve ratio is essentially a regulation used to give the central bank control of the money supply. The reserve ratio is a key determinant of the money multiplier. If a central bank has the power to change the commercial banks' required reserve ratio, it can use it to change the money supply. For a given monetary base, a rise in the required reserve ratio reduces the size of the money multiplier and the money supply. A reduction in the reserve ratio has the opposite effect.

However, required reserve ratios are blunt techniques for monetary control. Changes in reserve ratios simultaneously affect the reserve positions of all banks in a system and require large adjustments in financial markets. As a result, changes in reserve ratios are not widely used as techniques for money supply control.

Required reserve ratios are different in different national banking systems. In the United States, for example, the Federal Reserve is authorized to impose reserve requirements of 8 percent to 14 percent on chequable deposits, and up to 9 percent on non-personal time deposits. As of February 2002, the ratios were set at 10 percent for chequable deposits and 0 percent for time deposits. The European Central Bank also imposes reserve requirements. In early 2008, both India and China increased deposit reserve ratios on several occasions to limit monetary expansion in the face of rising inflation.

Until 1994, banks in Canada were subject to legal minimum reserve requirements. These have now been phased out, as have reserve requirements in many other countries. In Canada, the banks hold reserves made up of very small settlement balances in the Bank of Canada, in addition to their cash holdings. The banks decide the size of their reserve ratios based on their own assessments of their reserve needs, rather than a legal requirement. We will see later that reserve holdings, and the Bank of Canada's management of the available cash reserves, are important to the implementation of monetary policy in Canada.

The absence of legal reserve requirements in Canada means that reserve ratios in the banking system change from time to time. They may change as the banks change their outlook on financial conditions and their evaluation of banker's risk. These changes are linked to the profit motive of the banks rather than the control interests of the central bank. Whether they come from central bank action or commercial bank asset management, changes in the banks' reserve ratio change the money multiplier and the money supply.

OPEN MARKET OPERATIONS

An **open market operation** is a central bank purchase or sale of government securities in the open financial market.

Open market operations are the main technique used by central banks to manage the size of the monetary base. Whereas reserve requirements affect the money supply through control of the money multiplier, open market operations work directly on the monetary base. Since the money supply is the monetary base multiplied by the money multiplier, open market operations alter the money supply.

Central banks use open market operations to provide the monetary base needed to support the demand for money and the increase in the demand for money as the economy grows. If monetary policy is conducted by setting interest rates, as discussed later in the chapter, open market operations are passive. They provide the monetary base needed to meet the growing demand for money at the interest rate set by the central bank. An open market purchase makes a permanent addition to the central bank's assets and monetary base.

There are times when monetary policy is conducted through control of the money supply. If the money multiplier is constant, a central bank can control the size of the money supply by controlling the monetary base using open market operations. Open market purchases increase the monetary base and increased bank lending increase the money supply. Open market sales have the opposite effect.

In times of financial and economic crisis, as in 2008 and 2009, open market operations are used along with interest rate setting. High uncertainty in financial markets and falling demand in goods-and-services markets increase the demand for liquid cash balances. If interest rates are reduced close to zero without increasing lending and spending and asset demand, the central bank may undertake "quantitative easing," using open market purchase to increase the monetary base and offset a shortage of liquidity in the economy. This topic comes up again after we look at monetary policy in more normal times.

Table 10.2 illustrates an open market purchase and its effect on bank reserves and the money supply. To keep the example simple, we will assume the banks hold reserves

TABLE 10.2 **An Open Market Purchase and the Money Supply**

Central bank				Commercial banks			
Assets		Liabilities		Assets		Liabilities	
1. Open-market purchase of $100 million in government bonds							
Govt bond	+100	Cheque issued	+100	—no change—			
2. Pension fund deposits proceeds of bond sale in a commercial bank							
—no change—				Central bank cheque	+100	Pension fund deposit acct	+100
3. Central bank cheque clears giving commercial banks $100 million cash							
no change		Cheque o/s	−100	Central bank cheque	−100	no change	
		Cash issued	+100	Cash reserves	+100		
				(excess reserves	+95)		
4. Commercial banks increase lending and create new deposits based on new cash reserves							
—no change—				Loans	+1900	Deposits	+1900
5. Final effect of central bank open market purchase							
Govt bonds	+100	Cash issued (ΔH)	+100	Cash reserves	+100	Deposits	+2000
				Loans	+1900		
					+2000		
6. Change in money supply							
$\Delta M = \Delta H/rr = \$100/0.05 = \$2{,}000$							

equal to 5 percent of their deposits, rr = 0.05, but the public's currency ratio is zero, cr = 0. This means a simple money multiplier equal to $\frac{1}{rr} = \frac{1}{0.05} = 20$.

In the example, the central bank buys $100 million of government bonds on the open market. We'll assume a large pension fund sold these bonds, and received in payment a cheque for $100 million issued by the central bank. This transaction is recorded (as $100) under item 1 in the table.

Item 2 in the table records the pension fund's deposit of the central bank cheque in the commercial banking system. The commercial bank issues a deposit to the pension fund in return for the cheque drawn on the central bank.

The commercial bank does not want to hold the central bank cheque. It presents it for payment and receives, in this example, cash in the form of central bank notes. Cash is a reserve asset for the commercial bank. In item 3 in the table, the central bank has created new high-powered money, which has increased the cash reserves of the commercial bank by $100. The commercial bank now has new reserves of $100 against its increased deposit liabilities of $100. Based on its reserve ratio rr = 0.05, it has excess reserves of $95.

Excess reserves in the commercial banking system support an increase in lending and the creation of new bank deposits. Item 4 in the table shows the final results of this loan and deposit expansion, for the entire banking system. Based on a simple money multiplier of 20, we know that the increase in the monetary base in the form of new cash reserves by $100 will result in an increase in the money supply of $2000. Bank lending and deposit creation continue until total deposits have increased by $2000, based on an initial deposit of $100 and increased lending of $1900. Items 5 and 6 in the table show these final results.

In this example, an open-market purchase increased the monetary base and the money supply. The purchase was paid for by the creation of new high-powered money. An *open market sale* would have the opposite effect. The monetary base and the money supply would be reduced. An open market operation is a technique a central bank can use to shift the money supply function and affect equilibrium conditions in the money market.

Review Question 4

Open market operations are today the principal channel by which central banks, including the Bank of Canada, manage the *longer-term* growth of the monetary base.

THE BANK RATE

The **bank rate** is the interest rate the central bank charges on its loans to commercial banks.

The **bank rate** is the interest rate the central bank charges the commercial banks if the commercial banks borrow reserves. The bank rate or lending rate is set by central banks as a part of their monetary policy operations.

Suppose the banks think the minimum safe ratio of reserves to deposits is 5 percent. It does not matter whether this figure is a commercial judgement, as in Canada, or a legal requirement, as in the United States. Banks may also hold a little extra cash to cover day-to-day ups and downs in deposits and withdrawals, but maximum profit requires minimum cash holdings.

One way in which an individual bank can cover a shortage in its reserves is to borrow from other banks that have unexpected excess reserves. This creates a market for high-powered money or the monetary base. In Canada, this borrowing and lending takes place on an overnight basis—you borrow today and repay tomorrow, at the overnight interest rate. In the United States, the rate for similar lending and borrowing among banks is the federal funds rate.

If it happens that no other bank in the system has excess reserves to lend, a bank that is short of reserves borrows from the central bank. The interest rate charged is the *bank rate*, which is set higher than the overnight rate by the central bank, to encourage banks to borrow and lend reserves in the overnight market.

The bank rate is used in different ways by different central banks. There is a long tradition of using changes in the rate as a signal of changes in monetary policy. A cut in the bank rate signals the central bank's intention to increase the monetary base. A rise in the bank rate signals tighter monetary conditions. We will examine in detail the role the bank rate currently plays in Canada later in this chapter.

MONEY SUPPLY VERSUS INTEREST RATES

Control of the monetary base through open-market operations and stable desired reserve and cash ratios for the banks and the public give the central bank control of the money supply. This is easy in theory but not in practice.

There are several problems. Can the central bank control the monetary base precisely? The commercial banks can borrow from the central bank at the bank rate when they are short of reserves. Borrowings increase the monetary base. In more difficult financial market circumstances, like those of 2007 to 2009, orderly financial markets may call for large changes in the monetary base to offset demands for cash.

What is the size of the money multiplier? Are desired reserve ratios and cash ratios stable and predictable or do they fluctuate? If they fluctuate, the size of the money multiplier is difficult to predict. The money supply function may be unstable.

What money supply measure should the central bank control: H, M1B+, M2, M2+, or some other aggregate? Households and businesses can shift among the different deposits within these measures, and the banks are imaginative in developing new types of deposits.

In short, precise control of the money supply is difficult. Most central banks no longer try. Instead, they set interest rates. The television news and financial press report decisions by the central bank about interest rates, not decisions about money supply. The Bank of Canada and the United States Federal Reserve make regular announcements about their settings of the overnight rate and the federal funds rate, respectively.

Figure 10.1 shows the money market under two different conditions. In both cases we draw the demand for money function L(Y) for a given level of real GDP. If the central bank can control money supply, then, for a given level of prices, it fixes the money supply at M_0. The equilibrium interest rate is i_0. This is the case in panel (a) of the figure.

Alternatively, the central bank can fix the interest rate at i_0 and supply whatever money is needed to clear the market at this rate. In equilibrium, the central bank supplies exactly the quantity of money demanded at interest rate i_0. The quantity of money supplied is still M_0, but the money supply function is horizontal at the interest rate i_0.

Review Questions 5 and 6

The central bank can fix either the money supply or the interest rate but not both. If it fixes the money supply, it must accept the equilibrium interest rate implied by the demand for money. If it fixes the interest rate, it must accept the equilibrium money supply implied by the demand for money equation. Central banks now do the latter.

FIGURE 10.1 **Money Supply Control or Interest Rate Control**

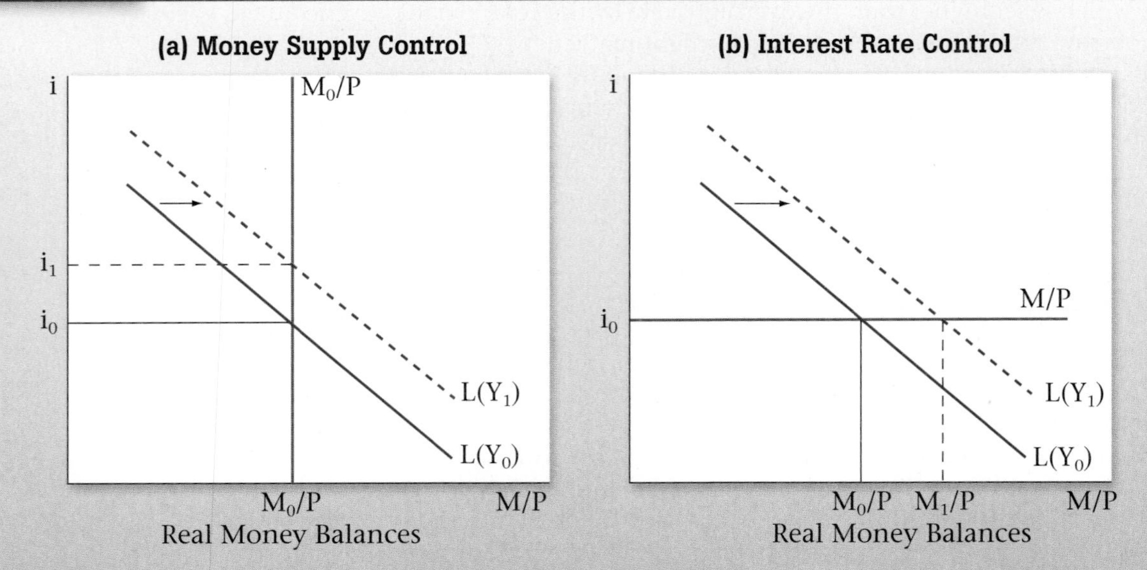

Both panel (a) and panel (b) start with a money supply M_0/P and a demand for money $L(Y_0)$, based on a given real GDP. In both panels the initial equilibrium interest rate is i_0.

In panel (a) we assume the central bank can fix the money supply at M_0/P, and the equilibrium interest rate is i_0. An increase in real GDP increases the demand for money from $L(Y_0)$ to $L(Y_1)$. With a fixed money supply, the interest rate rises to i_1. Alternatively, the central bank can control the money supply using interest rates, if the bank knows the demand for money. It would raise interest rates when real GDP increased, or lower them when real GDP fell. In either case, the interest rate is determined by the demand for money.

In panel (b) we assume the bank fixes the interest rate at i_0. To do this, it must supply whatever quantity of money is demanded at the interest rate it wishes to fix. An increase in real GDP that increases the demand for money from $L(Y_0)$ to $L(Y_1)$ results in an increase in the money supply from M_0/P to M_1/P. Now the money supply is determined by the demand for money.

10.3 Monetary Policy Targets and Instruments in Canada

A central bank can use the power it has over the monetary base and interest rates to pursue any one of three possible targets. It might

1. control the foreign exchange rate, or
2. control the money supply, or
3. control the inflation rate.

However, it must choose. Controlling one of these targets uses all the central bank's power, and it cannot pursue a second target at the same time. The central bank chooses among these targets based on its judgement as to which target will achieve the best results in terms of its broad monetary policy objective: to promote economic stability at potential output with low inflation. The Bank of Canada has conducted its monetary policy in terms of each of these targets at different times in the recent past.

From our discussion of the foreign exchange market in Chapter 9, we know that changes in interest rates will result in changes in the foreign exchange rate. Wealth holders shift their financial portfolios between assets of different countries based on differences in interest rates and bond yields between countries. Rather than allow private supply and demand in the foreign exchange market to set the exchange rate, the central bank can intervene to influence the rate. It buys or sells foreign exchange in the market, which changes the domestic monetary base until the difference between domestic and foreign interest rates is zero. To maintain a fixed **exchange rate target**, the central bank matches domestic interest rates to those set in the country to which it wishes to fix its exchange rate. In Canada, for example, to fix the exchange rate between the Canadian dollar and the U. S. dollar, the Bank of Canada would set its interest rate equal to that set by the Federal Reserve.[2]

With an **exchange rate target,** monetary policy maintains a fixed price for foreign currency in terms of domestic currency.

A central bank may choose to fix the exchange rate because it believes that is the best way to achieve the broader objectives of monetary policy. Canada operated with fixed exchange rates from 1962 to 1970. The Canadian-dollar price of the U. S. dollar was fixed at $1.075, and the Bank of Canada focused its monetary policy on that target. During the late 1950s and early 1960s, there was an intense debate over the monetary policy pursued by the Bank of Canada. Economic growth was slow, unemployment rates were high, and there was turmoil in financial markets. A fixed exchange rate was seen as the best solution to these economic problems. It essentially gave Canada the monetary policy of the United States, where economic performance had been stronger and more stable than in Canada. The fixed exchange rate target determined Canadian interest rates and money supply.

Rather than fixing the exchange rate, a central bank can choose to fix the size or growth rate of the domestic money supply. In Chapter 9 we discussed the money market in terms of a fixed money supply. However, central banks have found that the money multiplier, based on the desired reserve ratios of the banks and cash ratios of the public, is not stable enough to give them control of the money supply directly through their control of the monetary base. Instead, they set interest rates to get their target money supply from the demand for money. If money supply is above their target, they raise interest rates, reducing the demand for money until money holdings fall within their target range. They reduce interest rates if money holdings are less than their target.

In the 1970s, a sharp rise in inflation shifted the focus of monetary policy toward inflation control. At that time, developments in economic theory emphasized a strong link between money, money supply growth, and inflation. Central banks in many industrial countries shifted their focus to money supply control. Canada had dropped the fixed exchange rate target in 1970. In 1975, the Bank of Canada adopted **money supply targets** and used them until 1982 in an attempt to control inflation and promote a strong economy. By adjusting interest rates based on its understanding of the demand for money balances, the Bank was able to meet the targets for the growth in the money supply M1 that it set and revised from time to time.

With a **money supply target,** the central bank adjusts interest rates and the monetary base to control the nominal money supply.

However, controlling the money supply required wide fluctuations in interest rates and in the exchange rate. Financial markets did not like this volatility. More importantly, success in controlling M1 did not bring success in controlling inflation. The relationship between money supply, prices, and inflation turned out to be less stable than expected. The Bank abandoned its M1 control targets in 1982 and began a search for a better target for monetary policy.

In the early 1990s, the Bank of Canada and central banks in many other countries, including Australia, New Zealand, Sweden, the United Kingdom, and the European Union, decided to set explicit **inflation rate targets** for monetary policy. The Bank of

With an **inflation rate target,** the monetary policy aims to maintain an announced target inflation rate.

[2] We study different exchange rate policies in detail in Chapter 12.

APPLICATION BOX 10.1

The Costs of Inflation and the Benefits of Low Inflation

The Bank of Canada, as a background to its inflation target notes that:

"High inflation has many costs:

- Inflation erodes the value of money. When future prices are less predictable, sensible spending and saving plans are harder to make. People increasingly fear that their future purchasing power will decline and erode their standard of living.
- Inflation encourages investments that are speculative and take advantage of inflation rather than productive investment. It can also create the illusion of temporary financial success while masking fundamental economic problems.
- Businesses and households must spend more time, and money, protecting themselves from the effects of rising costs and prices. Businesses, workers, and investors respond to signs of inflation by pushing up prices, wages, and interest rates to protect themselves. This can lead to a "vicious circle" of rising inflation.
- Inflation can mean particular hardship for those whose incomes don't keep pace with the rising level of prices, especially people on fixed incomes such as senior citizens who are receiving pensions.

Low inflation has many benefits:

- Consumers and businesses are better able to make long-range plans because they know that their money is not losing its purchasing power year after year.
- Interest rates, both in nominal and real terms, are lower, encouraging investment to improve productivity and allowing businesses to prosper without raising prices.
- Sustained low inflation is self-reinforcing. Businesses and individuals do not react so quickly to short-term price pressures by seeking to raise prices and wages if they are confident that inflation is under long-term control. This contributes to keeping inflation low."

Source: Fact Sheets: "The Benefits of Low Inflation," http://bankofcanada.ca/en/backgrounders/bg-i2.html. Bank of Canada, 2009.

The **monetary policy instrument** is the monetary variable the central bank manipulates in pursuit of its policy target.

Review Question 7

Canada began to use the interest rate as its **monetary policy instrument**, and made changes in the interest rate, as necessary, to keep the Canadian inflation rate within a target range of 1 percent to 3 percent. The shifts to formal inflation targets for monetary policy in 1991, and the adjustment to that policy shift, were sources of a substantial policy debate in Canada. Inflation was reduced as planned, but with a deep and prolonged recession in real GDP and persistently high rates of unemployment. Sustained economic growth did not resume until the mid-1990s, and by most estimates, including those by the Bank of Canada, the recessionary GDP gap persisted until the end of the decade.[3] The Bank continues to focus on an inflation rate in the 1 percent to 3 percent range as its monetary policy target. The Bank's summary of the costs and benefits of inflation that lie behind its inflation targeting are discussed in Application Box 10.1.

[3] You can read about this debate in: D. Laidler, and Wm. Robson, *The Great Canadian Disinflation: The Economics and Politics of Monetary Policy in Canada 1988–1993* (Toronto: C.D. Howe Institute, 1993). P. Fortin, "The Great Canadian Slump," *Canadian Journal of Economics* 29, No. 4 (August 1996), pp. 1082–1092. C. Freedman and T. Macklem, "A Comment on the 'Great Canadian Slump'," *Canadian Journal of Economics* 31, No. 3 (August 1998), pp. 646–665.

BANK OF CANADA OPERATING TECHNIQUES

In Canada, the **overnight rate** is now the Bank of Canada's policy instrument. This is the interest rate that large financial institutions receive or pay on loans from one day until the next. The Bank implements monetary policy by setting a target for the overnight rate at the midpoint of an operating band that is plus or minus one-quarter of one percentage point, or 25 basis points, from the target rate.

The **overnight rate** is the interest rate large financial institutions receive or pay on loans from one day until the next.

The *bank rate* now marks the upper end of this operating band for the overnight rate. It is still the rate at which the Bank of Canada is willing to lend to the banks. The lower end of the operating band is the interest rate the Bank of Canada pays on deposits. Because the highest cost of borrowing cash is the bank rate, and the lowest return from lending cash is the deposit rate paid by the Bank of Canada, the rate on overnight borrowing and lending among the banks falls within the target range set by the Bank of Canada.

The Bank of Canada tells financial markets the direction in which it wants interest rates to move, by making changes to its target overnight rate and operating band. Changes in the target overnight rate lead to changes in interest rates banks offer to lenders and depositors. A lower target lowers bank lending rates, encouraging more borrowing by households and businesses and a corresponding expansion in the money supply. Figure 10.2 shows the operating band set by the Bank, and the overnight interest rate.

FIGURE 10.2 **The Bank of Canada Operating Band for the Overnight Rate**

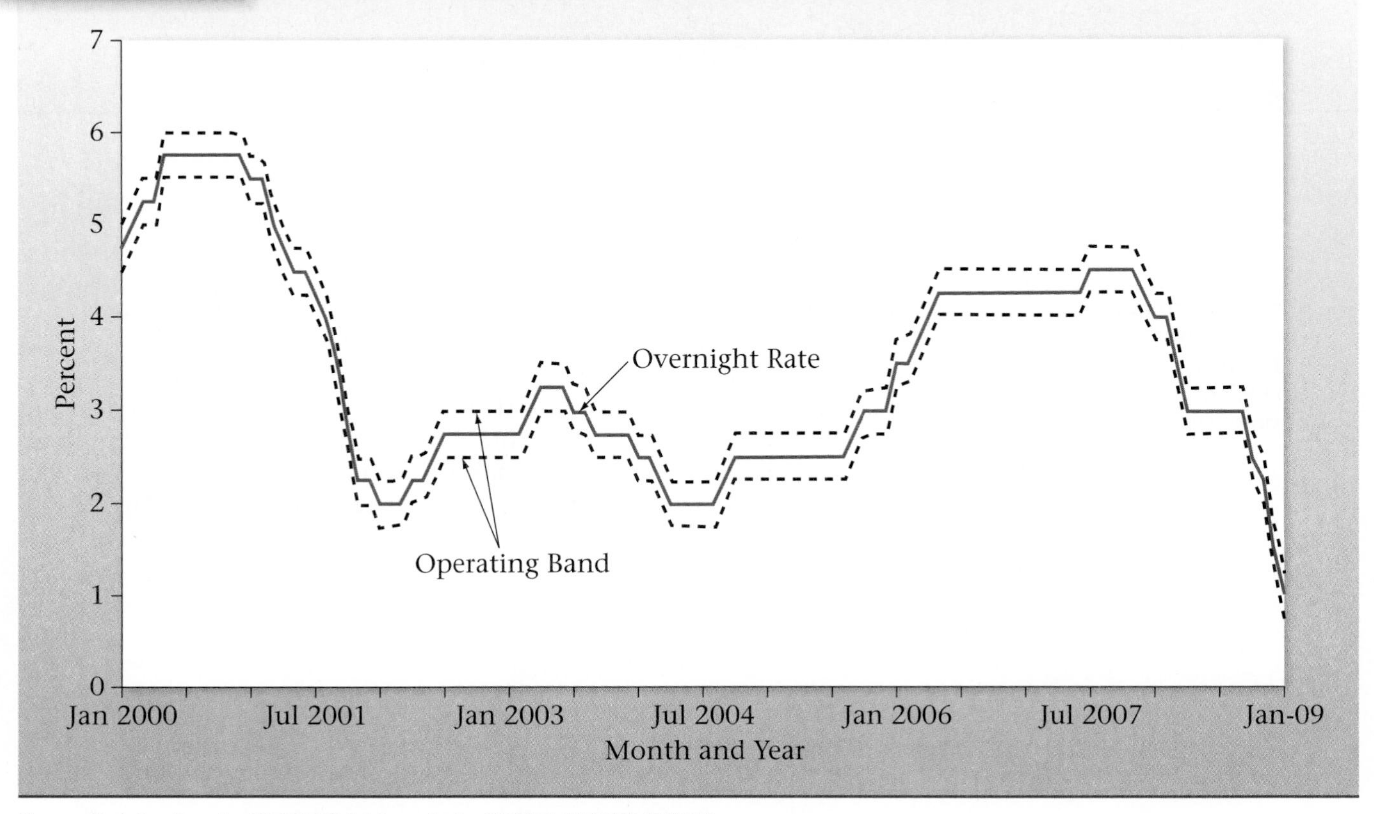

Source: Statistics Canada, CANSIM II database Series V39076, V39077, V39079.

FIGURE 10.3 **The Overnight Rate, Prime Rate and 5-Year Mortgage Rate**

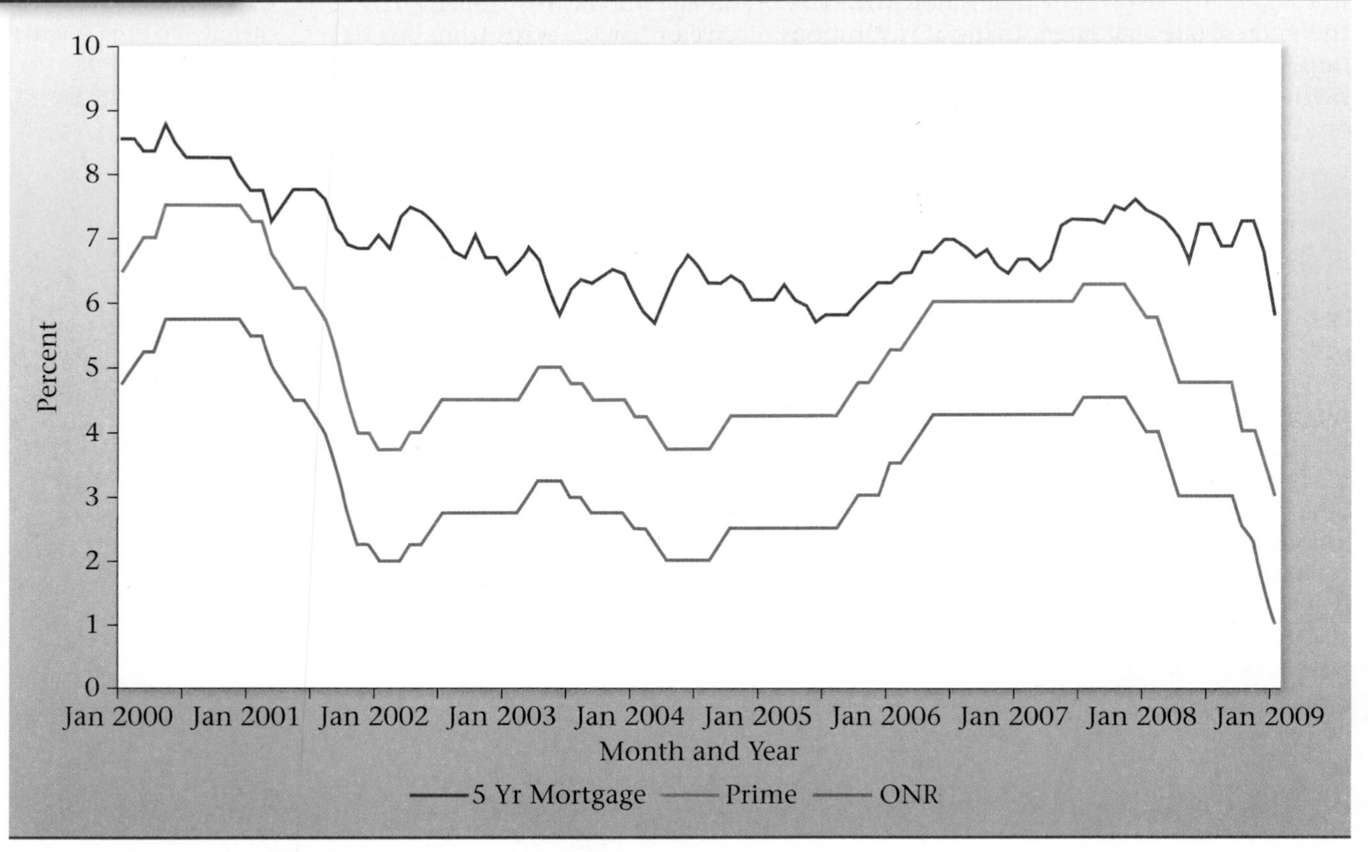

Source: Statistics Canada, CANSIM II Database, Series V39076, V122495, V122521.

The **prime lending rate** is the interest rate charged by banks on loans to their most credit worthy borrowers.

By setting the overnight interest rate the Bank has a direct impact on interest rates that are important to the monetary transmission mechanism. Banks respond to a rise in the overnight rate by raising their **prime lending rates**, the rates they charge on loans to their most credit-worthy borrowers. Rates on business and consumer lines of credit are also linked to the prime rate, and move up and down with it. The connection to mortgage rates is also strong and they move with the overnight rate, although the link is not quite as tight. These interest rates cover about two thirds of bank financing in Canada. This makes a strong link between the Bank of Canada's monetary policy action, expenditure, and aggregate demand. Figure 10.3 shows the relationship between changes in the setting of the overnight rate and other interest rates.

Other countries implement monetary policy by setting similar interest rates. The overnight rate set by the Bank of Canada is comparable to the United States Federal Reserve's target for the federal funds rate, and the Bank of England's two-week "repo rate," and the minimum bid rate for refinancing operations, the repo rate, set by the European Central Bank.

Institutional arrangements are the key to the Bank of Canada's use of the overnight rate as its policy instrument. The payments made by individuals and businesses, and their receipts, flow through the banking system. Some are small paper-based transactions that involve the writing of cheques on deposit accounts. Others, and indeed the majority, are transfers of large deposits between bank customers. On any day, an individual bank may take in more deposits through these transfers than it pays out, or pay out more than it takes in. Any difference in either case is settled using balances held on deposit at the Bank of Canada. Technology now allows for *same day settlement* of large-value transactions, and settlement balances can change quickly.

Chartered banks in Canada operate under a zero settlement balance requirement. This means that the balances they hold in their deposit accounts at the Bank of Canada cannot be less than zero at the end of the day. If a bank's account is overdrawn from making payments to other banks, it must borrow to cover the overdraft, either from another bank or from the Bank of Canada. Borrowing from other banks costs the *overnight rate*. Borrowing from the Bank of Canada costs the *bank rate*, which is set by the Bank of Canada one-quarter of a percentage point above the overnight rate. As a result, falling short of the zero-balance requirement imposes a cost on a bank, reducing its profitability, which it would like to avoid.

A positive settlement balance also imposes a cost. The Bank of Canada does pay interest on a positive balance in a bank's account, but it pays at its deposit rate. That rate is set one-quarter of one percentage point below the overnight rate. Not lending a positive balance to another bank at the overnight rate and accepting the Bank of Canada's *deposit rate* carries an opportunity cost a bank would prefer to avoid. This is a further incentive to maintain a zero settlement balance at the Bank of Canada.

This regulatory and institutional environment gives the Bank of Canada a framework for setting the interest rate to implement its monetary policy. The Bank makes eight scheduled announcements about its target for the overnight rate, and the operating band it is setting for the overnight rate. These announcements include a brief explanation of the economic conditions on which the Bank's rate-setting decision is based. Application Box 10.2 provides two examples. In the first example, the Bank raises its overnight rate to dampen aggregate demand and upward pressure on the inflation rate, which is already above the Bank's inflation target range. In the second example, the overnight rate target is reduced sharply to counter the effects of the growing international financial crisis and global recession by offering monetary stimulus.

SPECIAL PURCHASES AND SALES

To maintain the overnight interest rate within the target band, the Bank of Canada must intervene in the market to cover any shortages or remove any surpluses of funds that would push rates beyond its target. The Bank has two tools it uses for this purpose.

One tool is the **special purchase and resale agreement (SPRA)**. This is a transaction initiated by the Bank of Canada that puts cash into the system on a very short-term basis. It is used to maintain the target overnight rate, more specifically to offset upward pressure on the rate. In an SPRA, the Bank offers to buy Government of Canada securities from major financial institutions with an agreement to sell them back the next business day, at a predetermined price. The financial market gets an overnight injection of monetary base. The difference between the purchase and resale price determines the overnight interest rate on the transactions. Banks are willing to enter into these agreements with the Bank of Canada because they provide cash for the banks at rates of interest below what they would otherwise have to pay in the overnight market.

A Bank of Canada **SPRA** is a purchase of securities one day combined with an agreed resale of the securities the next day.

Alternatively, when the funds available in the overnight market put downward pressure on the overnight rate, the Bank has a second tool. A **sale and repurchase agreement (SRA)** is used to take cash out of the market overnight. In this case, the

A Bank of Canada **SRA** is a sale of securities one day combined with an agreed repurchase of the securities the next day.

APPLICATION BOX 10.2

Bank of Canada Announcements of Its Overnight Rate Target

FOR IMMEDIATE RELEASE
25 April 2006

Bank of Canada raises overnight rate target by 1/4 percentage point to 4 per cent

OTTAWA—The Bank of Canada today announced that it is raising its target for the overnight rate by one-quarter of one percentage point to 4 per cent. The operating band for the overnight rate is correspondingly increased, and the Bank Rate is now 4¼ per cent.

The global economy has been growing at a robust pace, exhibiting a little more momentum than had been anticipated. This global strength and the associated higher prices of many commodities, together with strong domestic demand in Canada, have produced solid growth in the Canadian economy. . . . All factors considered, the Canadian economy is judged to be operating at, or just above, its production capacity. High energy prices have kept total CPI inflation in Canada somewhat above the Bank's 2 per cent target. . . . Against this backdrop, the Bank decided to raise its target for the overnight rate.

In line with the Bank's outlook for the Canadian economy, some modest further increase in the policy interest rate may be required to keep aggregate supply and demand in balance and inflation on target over the medium term.

FOR IMMEDIATE RELEASE
20 January 2009

Bank of Canada lowers overnight rate target by 1/2 percentage point to 1 per cent

OTTAWA—The Bank of Canada today announced that it is lowering its target for the overnight rate by one-half of a percentage point to 1 per cent. The operating band for the overnight rate is correspondingly lowered, and the Bank Rate is now 1¼ per cent.

The outlook for the global economy has deteriorated since the Bank's December interest rate announcement, with the intensifying financial crisis spilling over into real economic activity. Heightened uncertainty is undermining business and household confidence worldwide and further eroding domestic demand. Major advanced economies, including Canada's, are now in recession and emerging-market economies are increasingly affected. Energy prices have fallen as a result of substantially weaker global demand.

Stabilization of the global financial system is a precondition for economic recovery. To that end, governments and central banks are taking bold and concerted policy actions. There are signs that these extraordinary measures are starting to gain traction, although it will take some time for financial conditions to normalize. In addition, considerable monetary and fiscal policy stimulus is being provided worldwide.

APPLICATION BOX 10.2 continued

Canadian exports are down sharply, and domestic demand is shrinking as a result of declines in real income, household wealth, and consumer and business confidence. Canada's economy is projected to contract through mid-2009, with real GDP dropping by 1.2 per cent this year on an annual average basis. As policy actions begin to take hold in Canada and globally, and with support from the past depreciation of the Canadian dollar, real GDP is expected to rebound, growing by 3.8 per cent in 2010.

A wider output gap through 2009 and modest decreases in housing prices should cause core CPI inflation to ease, bottoming at 1.1 per cent in the fourth quarter. Total CPI inflation is expected to dip below zero for two quarters in 2009, reflecting year-on-year drops in energy prices. With inflation expectations well-anchored, total and core inflation should return to the 2 per cent target in the first half of 2011 as the economy returns to potential.

Against this background, the Bank today lowered its policy rate by 50 basis points, bringing the cumulative monetary policy easing to 350 basis points since December 2007. Guided by Canada's inflation-targeting framework, the Bank will continue to monitor carefully economic and financial developments in judging to what extent further monetary stimulus will be required to achieve the 2 percent target over the medium term. Low, stable, and predictable inflation is the best contribution monetary policy can make to long-term economic growth and financial stability.

Bank of Canada Press Release, 25 April 2006, "Bank of Canada raises overnight rate target by 1/4 percentage point to 4 percent," http://www.bankofcanada.ca/en/fixed-dates/2006/rate_250406.html; and Bank of Canada Press Release, 20 January 2009, "Bank of Canada lowers overnight rate by 1/2 percentage point to 1 percent," http://www.bankofcanada.ca/en/fixed-dates/2009/rate_200109.html. Bank of Canada, 2009.

Bank of Canada offers to sell Government of Canada securities to major financial institutions with an agreement to buy them back at a predetermined price on the next business day. The difference in price is again the Bank's overnight rate on the transaction. Financial institutions are willing to make this transaction because it offers a return that is higher than they otherwise could get in the overnight market. From the Bank of Canada's point of view, it supports the overnight rate it has set by reducing the monetary base.

Figure 10.4 shows how this works. We start in equilibrium at E_0 with the demand for cash reserves just equal to the supply of monetary base at the overnight rate set by the Bank. Suppose a change in economic and financial circumstances causes a *temporary* increase in the demand for cash and settlement balances. The demand for monetary base shifts to the right to D_1. If the Bank took no action the overnight rate would rise to E_1 above the target the Bank has set. To prevent this, the Bank provides an overnight increase in the monetary base by buying securities on the agreement that it will sell them back the next business day. This is an SPRA. It gives a temporary increase in monetary base to MB_1 and reinforces the Bank's overnight rate. In the opposite case of a fall in the demand for monetary base, reducing the monetary base using an SRA would offset a drop in the demand for cash that put downward pressure on the overnight rate.

FIGURE 10.4 **Setting the Overnight Rate**

The Bank of Canada sets the overnight rate at the midpoint of its operating band. With monetary base MB_0 and demand for monetary base D_0, based on the demand for cash from the banks and the public, the overnight market is in equilibrium at the target overnight rate at E_0. A temporary increase in the demand for cash pushes the demand curve to D_1. If the Bank took no action the overnight rate would rise as shown at point E_1. To prevent this increase and maintain its target, the Bank makes SPRAs. It buys and holds securities until the next business day, paying for them by increasing the monetary base to MB_1. The overnight rate is maintained at E_2. Alternatively, a temporary decrease in the demand for cash would put downward pressure on the overnight rate, which the Bank would offset by using SRAs to reduce the monetary base.

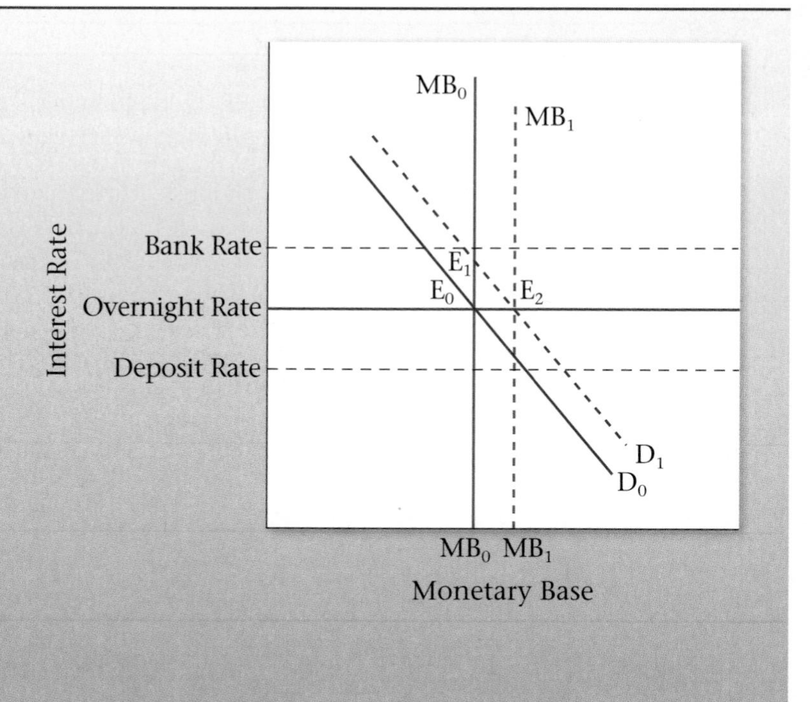

Figure 10.5 shows the pattern of Bank of Canada interventions in the overnight money market. Although these interventions occur daily, the data plotted in the graph are monthly averages of dollar amounts involved in those interventions. In the period covered by the graph, the Bank was reacting in the latter half of 2007 to upward pressure on the overnight rate. It provided overnight funds to the market using SPRAs: purchasing securities with the agreement to sell them back the next business day. Then, in the first half of 2008, the Bank used SRAs to maintain its overnight rate target by offsetting downward pressure on the rate. However, by mid-summer the developing financial crisis increased the demand for liquidity and concerns about a recession led to reductions in the overnight rate target supported by substantial SPRAs.

What if the increased demand for monetary base is permanent, not just a one-day event? In Chapter 8 we saw how the demand for monetary base comes from public demand and from bank demand for cash and reserve balances. Increases in nominal income increase the demand for money, including cash. Let's suppose the increased demand for monetary base we see in Figure 10.4 is permanent, the result of growth in the economy. Now, if the Bank of Canada wants to keep the overnight rate constant, it must make a permanent increase in the monetary base, not just an overnight increase. It will do this using the *open-market operations* we discussed earlier. An open-market purchase of government securities makes a lasting increase in the Bank of Canada's asset holdings, permanently increasing the monetary base.

While these operations by the Bank of Canada may seem quite complex, they have a simple effect. Like open-market operations, SPRAs and SRAs increase or decrease the monetary base. In this case, however, the buyers and sellers in the market are limited to a few major financial institutions rather than the full market. Furthermore, changes in the monetary base are very short-term, just one day. The objective is to set and control short-term interest rates, the *monetary policy instrument* used by the Bank of Canada.

Review Questions 8 and 9

FIGURE 10.5 **Bank of Canada Special Purchase and Resale Agreements (SPRAs) and Sale and Repurchase Agreements (SRAs)**

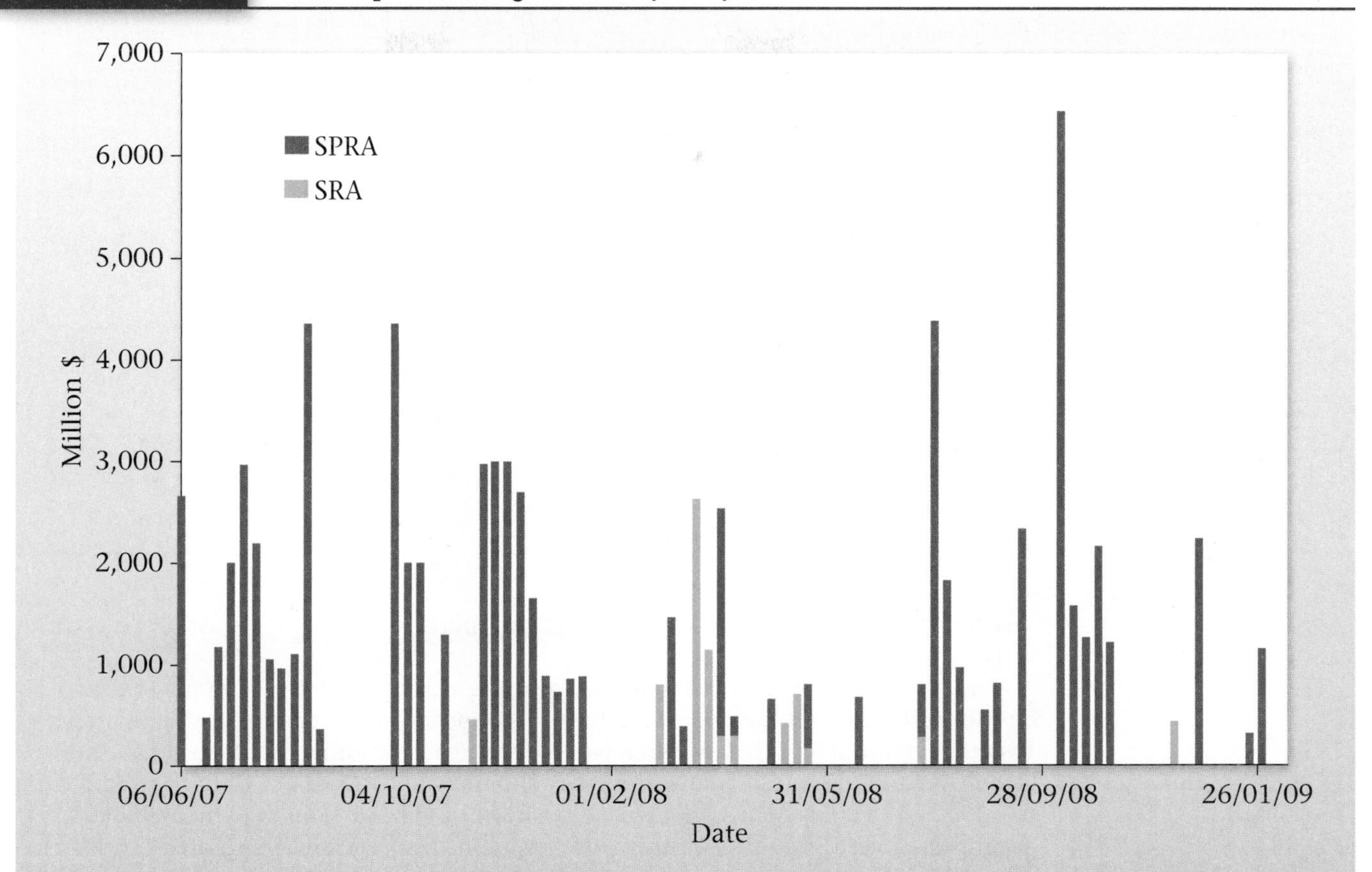

The Bank of Canada intervenes in the overnight money market to reinforce the operating band it has set for the overnight interest rate. Special purchase and resale agreements, SPRAs, provide overnight increases in the monetary base to offset upward pressure on the rate. Purchase and resale agreements make overnight reductions in the monetary base to offset downward pressure on the rate. The graph shows the Bank of Canada offsetting strong upward pressure on the rate using SPRAs in the summer and fall of 2007, and then using both SPRAs and SRAs to maintain its rate in early 2008, followed by large SPRAs later in the year as the financial crisis deepened.

Source: Statistics Canada, CANSIM II database Series V41838397, V41838399.

GOVERNMENT DEPOSIT ACCOUNTS

In Canada, the federal government holds some of its funds on deposit in the Bank of Canada and some in the commercial banks. The government also gives the Bank the authority to manage the distribution of its deposits between the central bank and the commercial banks. This arrangement provides another technique for short-term central bank management of the monetary base.

The Bank can increase the reserves of the commercial banks by transferring government deposits from the central bank to the commercial banks. The commercial banks then have increased government deposit liabilities and an equal increase in their reserve deposits in the Bank of Canada. Because their desired reserves increase by only a small fraction of their increased deposits, the commercial banks have excess

TABLE 10.3 **A Transfer of Government Deposits**

Central bank			Commercial banks			
Assets	Liabilities		Assets		Liabilities	
No change	Reserve deposits of banks	+10	Reserve deposits of banks	+10	Government deposits	+10
	Government deposits	−10				

In this example, the Bank of Canada has moved $10 in government funds from government accounts in the Bank of Canada (–10) and placed them on deposit in the commercial banks (+10). In payment for these increased deposit liabilities, the banks receive an increase in their reserve deposits in the Bank of Canada.

If the desired reserve ratio of the banks is 5 percent, the banks now have excess reserves of $9.50, which they will lend.

reserves. Bank lending and bank deposits can increase. Table 10.3 illustrates a transfer of government deposits.

A transfer of government deposits from the commercial banks to government accounts in the Bank of Canada would have the opposite effect. Commercial bank reserves would be reduced and they would have to reduce their lending and deposit liabilities.

Government deposit transfers were the main tool the Bank of Canada used during the 1990s to manage the cash reserve position of the banking system. The Bank was setting the overnight rate and using government deposit transfers to offset short-term pressure on its rate target. A change in the technology of the payments system in the late 1990s reduced the effectiveness of this technique. SPRA and SRA transactions replaced government deposits as the main tool of cash management.

The Bank does still manage government deposits, but the primary objective of that management has changed. Now government deposits are auctioned to the banks, and transfers play a minor role in offsetting the effects of government receipts and payments on the reserve positions of the commercial banks.

10.4 Monetary Policy Rules

We have seen that central banks use interest rates as the main tool of monetary policy. Now we need to examine how they decide to set and change the settings of interest rates. What lies behind the announcement of the overnight rate by the Bank of Canada or the setting of the federal funds rate in the United States? How are these interest rate decisions related to economic variables? Professor John Taylor of Stanford University found that most central banks, in fact, adjust interest rates in response to changes in two variables, output and inflation.

This finding was contentious. It implied monetary supply targets no longer played a role in decisions about interest rates. Instead, the interest rate was and is set based on expected inflation and expected output relative to the central bank's inflation target and the economy's potential output.

A central bank that follows a Taylor rule cares about output stability as well as price stability. However, as we know from our introduction to the aggregate demand and supply model in Chapter 5, deviations of output from potential output also tell us what will happen to prices. Booms leading to inflationary gaps push prices up and lead to inflation. Deflationary gaps tend to reduce inflation. Thus, a Taylor rule is also compatible with the interpretation that the central bank cares about prices and inflation, both now and in the future. It is hard to distinguish empirically between these two interpretations of why a Taylor rule is being followed.

Nevertheless, Taylor's claim that such a rule effectively describes central bank policy has been empirically verified for most of the leading central banks, including the U. S. Federal Reserve, the Bank of England, and the new European Central Bank. Taylor's insight is so widely used that it is called the **Taylor rule**.

The **Taylor rule** links central bank interest rate settings to inflation and output targets.

A TAYLOR RULE

We continue to assume prices are constant, so the inflation rate is zero for the first part of our study of policy rules. When prices are constant, monetary policy follows the output part of a Taylor rule. In simple algebra, the rule is:

$$i = i_0 + b(Y - Y_p) \quad \textbf{(10.1)}$$

When real output (Y) is at potential output (Y_p), the interest rate is set at i_0. This is the nominal and real interest rate under our assumption that prices are fixed. It is set by the central bank, based on the central bank's judgement about the interest rate required to support aggregate demand and equilibrium at potential output. Application Box 10.2 gave examples of the setting of i_0 and a change in that setting based on changed economic conditions. As you can see, according to this rule, when output *temporarily* exceeds Y_p, the central bank raises interest rates. At levels of output below Y_p, it lowers interest rates.

Figure 10.6 shows how this policy rule works. In panel (a), output is measured on the horizontal axis and interest rates on the vertical axis. A vertical line is drawn at the potential output level Y_p. The positively sloped line showing the central bank's reaction to fluctuations in output crosses the Y_p line at the interest rate i_0. If output were lower than Y_p, at Y_1 for example, the bank would lower interest rates to i_1 to provide some stimulus to aggregate expenditure.

Alternatively, for an output level Y_2, greater than Y_p, the central bank would raise interest rates to i_2 to reduce aggregate expenditure. This simple Taylor rule describes how the central bank sets its interest rate to achieve the target of equilibrium output at Y_p, and reacts to *temporary fluctuations* about Y_p.

Panel (b) shows the effect of the changes in interest rates on equilibrium output. We studied the transmission mechanism from interest rate changes to expenditure changes in Chapter 9. The central bank chooses the interest rate i_0 that gives aggregate expenditure $AE(i_0)$ and equilibrium output at Y_p.

If *short-run* economic conditions changed and autonomous expenditure declined, the AE line would shift down to $AE'(i_0)$. Y would fall to Y_1, which is less than Y_p. From the Taylor rule in panel (a), we see the reaction of the central bank. It lowers the interest rate to i_1. Lower interest rates work through the cost of and availability of finance, wealth effects, and exchange rate effects to increase expenditure. The AE line shifts back up to $AE'(i_1)$ to restore equilibrium at Y_p. By reacting to temporary changes in the state of the economy, the central bank attempts to stabilize output at Y_p.

A specific Taylor rule in Figure 10.6 sets an interest rate target i_0 based on an assessment of the *fundamental conditions* in the economy. It calls for changes in the interest

FIGURE 10.6 Interest Rates and Output with a Simple Taylor Rule

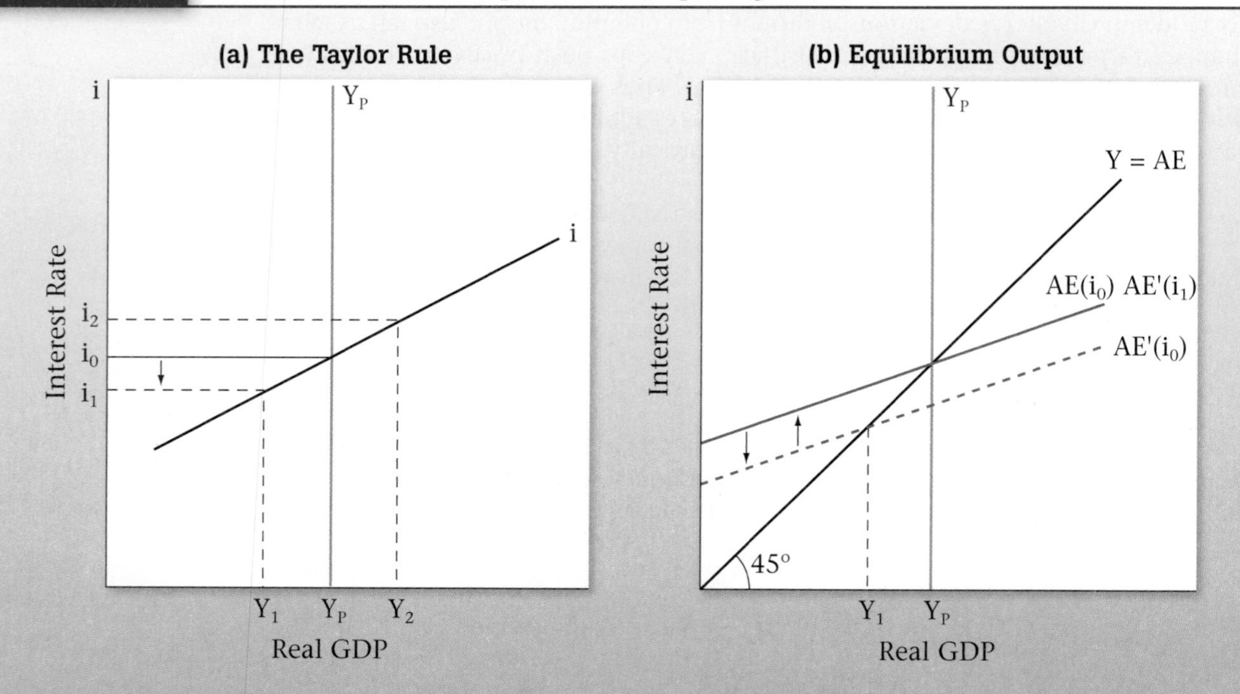

Panel (a): The central bank sets the interest rate i_0 consistent with Y_p. $Y > Y_p$ leads to $i > i_0$ and $Y < Y_p$ means $i < i_0$. The steeper the slope of the i line, the more the central bank is prepared to change interest rates in order to stabilize Y.

Panel (b): Fundamental economic conditions and the interest rate i_0 give equilibrium Y at Y_p. A fall in autonomous expenditure lowers Y. The central bank reacts by lowering interest rates to i_1, shifting AE back to its initial position and stabilizing output at Y_p.

rate in response to temporary fluctuations in those conditions. A more lasting change in economic conditions would need a different policy rule. The central bank would choose an interest rate target different from i_0, and appropriate to equilibrium at Y_p in the new conditions. A more expansionary monetary policy at each output level would mean a target rate lower than i_0. The policy rule line in panel (a) would *shift down* to cross the vertical line at Y_p at the new lower target rate. A more restrictive policy would *shift the line up*. Changes in the overnight rate in Canada or the federal funds rate in the United States are announced to tell financial markets of these changes in monetary policy.

POLICY RULES WHEN PRICES CHANGE

When we drop our assumption that prices are constant, the policy rules we have discussed are too simple. Central banks today, like the Bank of Canada, conduct their monetary policy by setting *inflation targets*. This does not mean that they ignore the level of output in the economy. Instead, inflationary and recessionary gaps are seen as important predictors of future inflation. We know this relationship from our brief discussion of the AD/AS model in Chapter 5. To recognize the current approach to monetary policy, we need to extend our monetary policy rule.

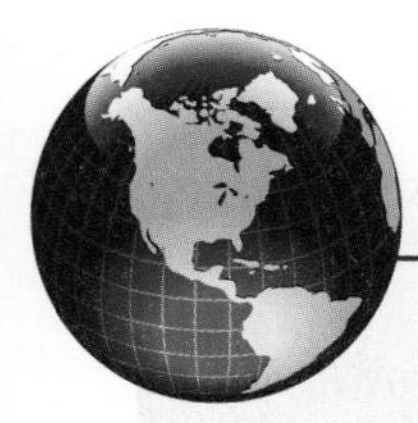

APPLICATION BOX 10.3

Empirical Estimates of Taylor Rules

Empirically, the interest rate decisions of central banks are explained quite well by Taylor rules, although central banks typically do not adjust interest rates as quickly as a simple rule predicts. Caution may reflect uncertainty about new data, which is often later revised, and uncertainty about the transmission mechanism of monetary policy, which evolves as the economic structure changes over time. The table shows estimates of interest rate responses to changes in inflation and output gaps in the United Kingdom, the United States, and Canada in the 1990s. Goodhart's results for the United Kingdom are based on a measure of the output gap. Mankiw estimates a Taylor rule for the United States, using the unemployment rate as an indicator of the output gap. Canadian estimates use the difference between the unemployment rate and the natural rate as a measure of the output gap.

Interest Rate Response to	United Kingdom	United States	Canada
1% more inflation	1.32	1.60	1.39
1% output gap	0.24	—	—
1% increase in unemployment	—	−1.60	−0.46

Sources: C. Goodhart, "Central Banks and Uncertainty," Bank of England Quarterly Bulletin (February 1999).
N. G. Mankiw, "Monetary Policy in the 1990s," Chapter 1 in J. Frankel and P. Orszag, eds. *American Economic Policy in the 1990s* (Cambridge: MIT Press, 2002).
D. Curtis, "Monetary Policy and Economic Activity in Canada in the 1990s," *Canadian Public Policy* (March 2005).

The central bank's policy for setting the interest rate could be described by the following equation, where π^* is the bank's target inflation rate:

$$i = i_0 + a(\pi - \pi^*) + b(Y - Y_P) \qquad (10.2)$$

As before, the central bank sets an interest rate i_0. This is the nominal interest rate the bank thinks is consistent with output at potential output and inflation at the target rate π^* under current conditions.

The Bank of Canada's current inflation target, for example, is 2 percent, the midpoint of a 1 percent to 3 percent range. If inflation rises above the target π^*, the central bank raises the nominal interest rate. The parameter "a" in the equation tells us by how much the nominal interest rate is changed in response to an inflation rate different from the bank's target.

Expenditure decisions depend on the interest rate. To stick to its inflation target, the bank must change the interest rate by changing the nominal interest rate by more than any change in inflation. This requires the parameter $a > 1$. A rise in inflation is then met by a rise in interest rates that is large enough to reduce expenditure and inflationary pressure.

By this rule, the central bank also reacts to any departure of output from potential output, as it did in our earlier study of the simple rule, equation (10.1). The parameter "b" measures how much the central bank would raise the interest rate in response to an inflationary gap, or lower it in response to a recessionary gap. Output stabilization requires that $b > 0$. Changing interest rates to offset an output gap is intended to stabilize output, but it will also work to offset any changes in the *future* inflation rate that would be caused by a persistent output gap. The size of the central bank's reactions, as measured by the parameters "a" and "b," are indications of the relative importance it attaches to inflation control and output stabilization.

Any change in economic conditions that the central bank thinks is *going to last for some time* will result in a change in its setting of i_0. The policy line in a diagram would shift up or down. Interest rates would then be higher or lower for all inflation rates and output gaps, depending on the change in i_0. The central bank would announce this change in the setting of its policy instrument, the overnight rate in Canada or the federal funds rate in the United States.

This approach to monetary policy has similarities to our earlier discussion of fiscal policy. In that case, we distinguished between automatic and discretionary policy. In the case of monetary policy, the discretionary component is the setting of the operating range for the overnight rate. These decisions are based on an evaluation of longer-term economic conditions relative to the target inflation rate. It positions the monetary policy line in a diagram in much the same way as the *structural budget balance* positions the government's BB line in Chapter 7. Short-term fluctuations in economic conditions result in short-term variations in the overnight rate—movements along the monetary policy line. This is similar to the automatic stabilization that comes from movements along the government's BB line as a result of fluctuations in output and income.

Review Questions 10, 11 and 12

There is, however, an important difference between monetary and fiscal policy. Monetary policy that uses the interest rate as the policy instrument provides strong automatic stabilization in response to money and financial market disturbances. Automatic stabilization in fiscal policy reduces the effects of fluctuations in autonomous expenditures.

MONETARY POLICY FOR "EXCEPTIONAL" TIMES

The financial crisis and recession of 2008–09 led to new and more intense monetary policy actions by central banks. Most continued with cuts to basic policy rates as their first response. The Federal Reserve in the United States lowered its federal funds rate, in steps, to a range of zero to 0.25 percent. The Bank of Canada followed, lowering its overnight rate setting to 0.5 percent by early March 2009. But these lower rates were not sufficient to stimulate borrowing and expenditure. Banks and other lenders were concerned by the increased risks of losses on their current lending and the risks involved in new lending. They had suffered losses on previous purchases of asset backed commercial paper and observed rising rates of bankruptcies across many business and consumer loan markets. Central banks needed additional policy responses to meet deep concerns in financial markets about risk and liquidity.

Two previously used techniques were introduced. The first was increased "moral suasion," an increase in communications with financial market participants to emphasize the central bank's longer-term support for markets and its actions to promote stability. More directly the banks were urged to maintain their lending operations. The second was "quantitative easing," and in the case of the U.S., an even more extensive "credit easing." "Quantitative easing" extends the use of open market operations described above. The central bank purchases a broader range of financial assets to expand its balance sheet to increase substantially the monetary base and cash positions of the banks. In other words, the objective is to increase the quantity of cash reserves in the banking system directly. A version of this policy action was used in Japan earlier in the decade after the Bank of Japan had lowered its borrowing rate to zero and wanted to provide further economic stimulus.

Open market operations usually involve central bank purchases of short-term government bonds. The U.S. Federal Reserve went beyond this, introducing three sets of policy tools:

1. lending to financial institutions,
2. providing liquidity directly to other key credit markets by buying highly rated commercial paper, and
3. buying longer-term securities, including mortgage backed securities.

Using these tools increases the size of the central bank's balance sheet and changes the structure of central bank asset holdings. The results are quantitative easing and **credit easing**. Quantitative easing is measured by the impact on the quantity of bank reserves. Credit easing is measured by the wider variety of loans and securities the central bank willingly holds on its balance sheet. A purchase of these assets puts cash directly into specific markets rather than feeding it through banks and bank lending. Both are intended to increase lending to businesses and households in times when very low, near zero, interest rates alone are not working.

Credit easing is the management of the central bank's assets designed to support lending in specific financial markets.

Figure 10.7 shows how quantitative easing affects the monetary base. In 10.7a, the cash component of the U.S. monetary base had quite a steady growth trend up until

FIGURE 10.7(a) **Currency Component of U.S. M1B Money Supply 2005 to 2009**

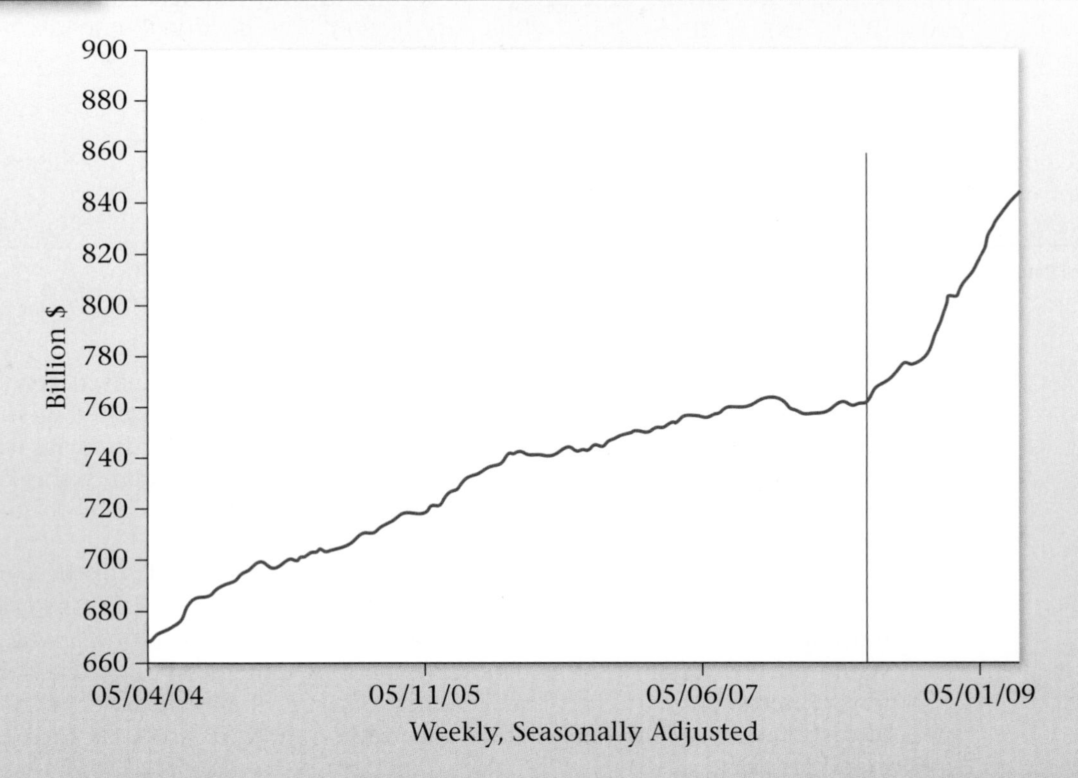

The large shift in the growth of the currency component of the monetary base and the money supply M1B illustrates the effect of "quantitative easing" by the U.S. Fed starting in mid-2007.

Source: Federal Reserve Bank of St. Louis, FRED database.

FIGURE 10.7(b) **Currency Component of Money Supply in Canada**

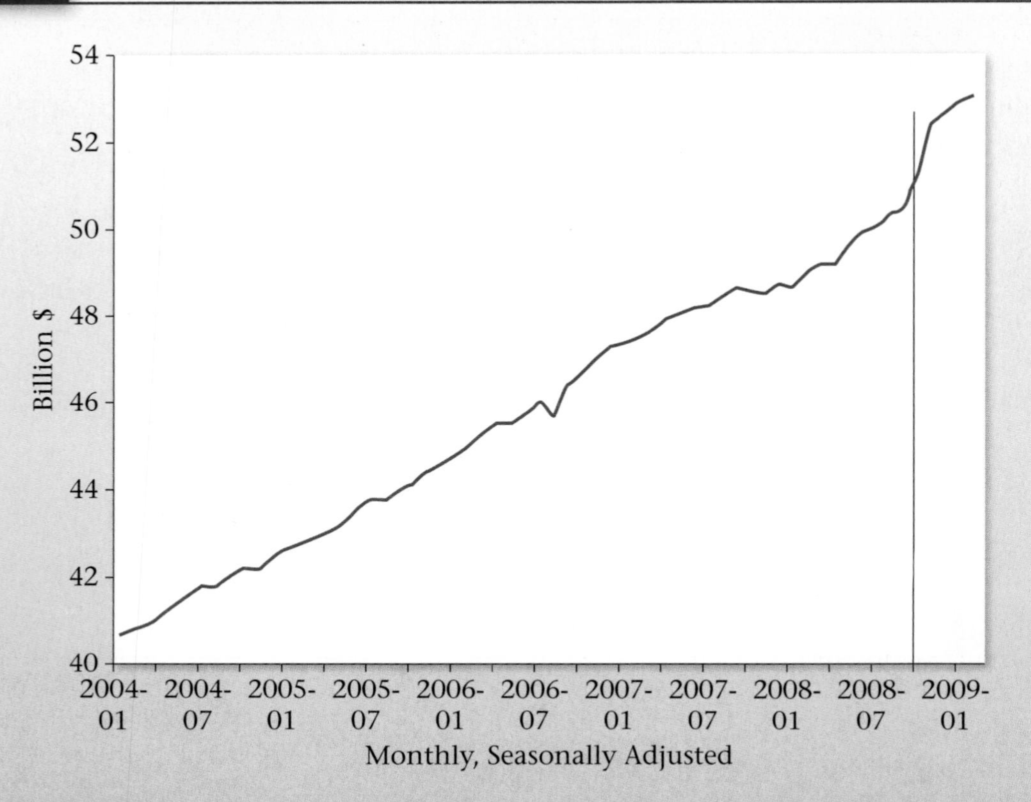

The growth in the currency component of the Canadian money supply accelerated in September 2008 as the Bank of Canada reacted to the growing financial crisis.

Source: Statisitcs Canada CANSIM Database Series V37148.

June 2007. Then, in spite of several reductions in the federal funds, down to the range of a zero to one-half percent rate, growth in cash stalled. Credit dried up in the face of the recession in output and growing risk and uncertainty in financial markets. The Fed's reaction through security purchases and growth in its balance sheet produced a strong upward shift in the quantity of cash in the banking and financial system, as shown in the graph.

Figure 10.7b shows the growth in cash balances in Canada for the same time period. Canada was slower to enter the recession and financial markets were somewhat more stable. The growth trend in the cash component of the monetary base was quite stable until the fall of 2008. Then the Bank of Canada's policy reactions through lower interest rates and increased lending to financial markets accelerated the growth of cash balances. Financial market uncertainty and increased risk increased the demand for cash.

Any credit easing for specific sectors that might lie behind the observed growth in the cash component of the monetary base is not shown by these data. That would call for an examination of the detailed changes in the asset side of the central bank's balance sheet.

10.5 The Long-Run Neutrality of Money

There is a long historic tradition of discussing money, economic activity, and prices based on the **equation of exchange**. In terms of real GDP, that equation is an identity, true by definition, namely:

The **equation of exchange** equates total money expenditure and nominal GDP.

$$MV \equiv PY \tag{10.3}$$

Suppose M is the money supply, V the velocity of circulation or the number of times a unit of money changes hands in a given time period, and P the flexible general price level like the GDP deflator, and Y real GDP. Then, by the equation of exchange, the total of expenditure, MV, is by definition equal to the money value of goods and services bought.

The equation of exchange is the foundation of the famous quantity theory of money, a theory of the price level or the inflation rate. Assume that V, the velocity of circulation of money is a constant, V_0. This velocity of circulation is just the inverse of the demand for money, L, based on the current financial structure and practice of making payments, without the effect of interest rates on that demand for money balances. This means V = 1/k, from the demand for money in Chapter 8.

Assume as well that the economy operates at the level of potential real GDP, Y_P. Further assume that the money supply is determined and firmly controlled by the central bank, which makes money supply exogenous. Based on these assumptions, the quantity theory of money says that the price level P is determined by the size of the money supply. This can be written as follows:

$$MV_0 = PY_P,$$

or restated as:

$$P = M \times \frac{V_0}{Y_P} \tag{10.4}$$

With (V_0/Y_P) a constant, a change in money supply M causes a change in P. If M doubles then P doubles. If M grows at 10 percent a year then P grows at 10 percent a year. The inflation rate is determined by the rate of growth of the money supply.

By this quantity theory of money and the price level, **money is neutral**. Changes in the money supply have no effect on the level of real output. Real output is constant at Y_p. Central bank or government control of the money supply gives the policy authorities control of the price level and the inflation rate.

The **neutrality of money** means monetary policy can set prices and inflation rates in the long run, but not output and employment.

Current approaches to monetary policy recognize that the conditions assumed by the quantity theory are not met in the short run. The demand for money is variable and thus the velocity of circulation is not constant. Real GDP and real GDP growth rates fluctuate about the trend of potential output. Prices in some markets are sticky and slow to adjust to changes in demand. The central bank's control of the money supply and the growth rate of the money supply are not precise. The quantity theory and the neutrality of money have important long-run implications but short-run conditions call for a different approach.

Monetary policy as described by the policy rule targets inflation by stabilizing output at potential output. In short time periods, prices tend to be sticky. This means that the central bank is able to change nominal interest rates more rapidly than prices change. Changes in the interest rates then change aggregate demand through the transmission mechanism we examined in Chapter 9.

FIGURE 10.8 **The Neutrality of Money**

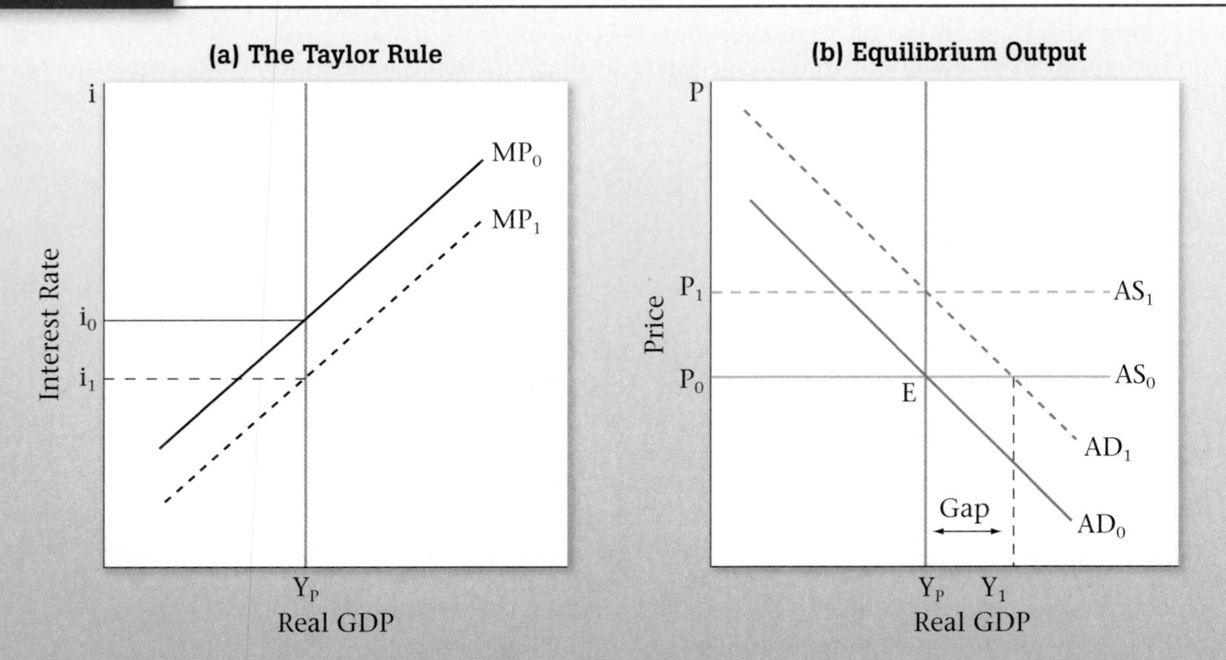

Monetary policy can change output in the short run but not in the long run. Starting at E in panel (b), with monetary policy MP_0 [as shown in panel (a)], output at Y_P, and price level P_0, the central bank lowers the interest rate from i_0 to i_1 [shown in panel (a)]. Lower interest rates shift AD_0 to the right to AD_1, creating an inflationary gap $Y_1 - Y_P$. A persistent inflationary gap means a rise in prices for the inputs to production, pushing costs up. The AS curve shifts up as P rises to P_1 and the inflationary gap is eliminated. Monetary policy has not produced a lasting increase in real output. Monetary policy is *neutral* in the long run.

Longer-term inflation targets are met by keeping actual output close to potential output. In an aggregate supply and demand model, prices or inflation rates change as a result of persistent recessionary or inflationary gaps. If monetary policy can reduce or eliminate the gaps by shifting the AD curve, it stabilizes both output and inflation.

What monetary policy cannot do is change *potential output*. This is the meaning of the long-run neutrality of money. Figure 10.8 provides an illustration. The economy starts with a monetary policy that sets the nominal and real interest rate i_0. The price level is constant, and the inflation rate is zero at the potential output at point E in the AD/AS diagram.

Now suppose the central bank decides it could raise output above Y_P and lower the unemployment rate below the natural rate u_n. The central bank sets the interest rate lower at i_1. According to the transmission mechanism, AD shifts to the right, creating an inflationary gap. The short-run effect of this shift to monetary expansion is, indeed, to increase output and employment and lower the unemployment rate.

If the inflationary gap created by expansionary monetary policy persists, AS will shift up. Low unemployment rates, high rates of utilization of plant and equipment, and strong demand for other inputs to production raise input prices and production costs, as we will discuss in more detail in Chapter 13. With strong demands for final output, higher costs result in higher prices. AS shifts up from AS_0 to AS_1. Rising prices move the economy up along AD_1 until output falls back to potential output. The only lasting effect of expansionary monetary policy is the higher price level P_1.

In the long run, money is neutral. Monetary policy can change the price level or the inflation rate in the long run, but it cannot change equilibrium output or employment. As a result, central banks set inflation targets for monetary policy, not output or employment targets.

Review Questions 13, 14, and 15

10.6 Monetary Policy Indicators

Policy rules describe how a central bank, like the Bank of Canada, would use interest rates to stabilize output, prices, and inflation in the economy. To see how the Bank's actions affect economic activity and inflation, we need some indicators of the expansionary or restrictive stance of monetary policy. These **monetary policy indicators** will allow us to go beyond the central bank's descriptions of its policy and observe the effects of its policy actions on monetary conditions in the economy.

Monetary policy indicators provide information about the stimulus or restraint coming from the central bank's policy.

Our earlier discussion of the monetary transmission mechanism suggests two monetary policy indicators, namely, *interest rates* and *exchange rates*. The central bank sets nominal interest rates, which have important effects on asset prices, cash flows, and expenditures. Interest rates are also important to expenditure decisions. Changes in nominal interest rates over time will show us how monetary policy has been implemented.

We have also mentioned briefly the foreign exchange rate and net exports. Because exchange rates change in part as a result of interest rate differences between countries, changes in the exchange rate provide an indicator of the thrust of domestic monetary policy relative to foreign monetary policy. Although in Canada it is important to recognize that commodity prices also have strong exchange rate effects.

The monetary transmission mechanism works through both interest rates and exchange rates. In setting its interest rates, a central bank in a small open economy needs to consider recent changes in the exchange rate. If economic conditions, or policies in other countries, have caused changes in the foreign exchange rate, those changes will affect expenditures and output in Canada.

The depreciation of the U. S. dollar in 2003 and 2006 is an important example. The corresponding appreciation of the Canadian dollar lowered import prices and reduced the profitability of exports. Without offsetting policy action, expenditure and output in Canada would fall. The Bank of Canada had to make a decision. Was the setting of its operating range for the overnight rate still consistent with its inflation target once the exchange rate had fallen? Should the Bank respond to the lower AD caused by the appreciation of the exchange rate by lowering its interest rate to provide some offsetting stimulus? If it were to respond, by how much should it lower interest rates? Clearly, the combined effect of interest rates and exchange rates is very important for monetary policy.

While interest rates and exchange rates provide important indicators of monetary policy, many economists and the Bank also regard the money supply or the rate of growth of the money supply as a policy indicator. Some suggest a monetary policy rule for money supply, which uses money supply as the central bank's policy instrument. We also know that the demand for nominal money balances depends on nominal income. Taking this into account, we can use the difference between the rate of growth on the money supply measure, M1B, and the rate of growth of nominal GDP as an indicator of the stance of monetary policy. M1B growth that exceeds growth in nominal GDP provides easier financial market conditions and suggests an expansionary policy stance.

The growth rates in the money aggregates M1B+ and real M2+, adjusted for inflation, provide alternative indicators of the effect of monetary policy. In the current policy context, the Bank of Canada sets the interest rates and the growth rates of money supply reflect the demand for money balances at those interest rates. Empirical research at the Bank and by other monetary economists has found that the growth in real M1B+ is a useful indicator of future growth in real GDP. Growth in real M2+ also provides a leading indicator of inflation. From these findings, an observed increase in the growth rates of these money aggregates indicates that the Bank's current policy is adding to aggregate demand.

Thus we have a set of monetary policy indicators: interest rates, exchange rates, and the growth rate in nominal and real measure of money supply. They come from our understanding of the way changes in monetary variables may affect expenditures, incomes, and prices and from our discussion of how monetary policy is designed and implemented.

Next

We have now completed our discussion of the basic expenditure and monetary structure of the economy under the assumption that the general price level is constant. In Chapter 11, we return to the aggregate demand and aggregate supply model we introduced in Chapter 5 to examine business cycles and fiscal and monetary policy in more detail.

SUMMARY

- **Central banks** operate to influence the behaviour of other banks and intermediaries in the financial system.
- A central bank conducts **monetary policy** through its control of the monetary base and interest rates. It is also banker to the government and to the commercial banks.
- The **Bank of Canada** is Canada's central bank. It is the source of the monetary base. It sets short-term interest rates, acts as banker to the commercial banks and the federal government, and is the lender of last resort to the banks.
- **Monetary policy** in Canada is the responsibility of the Bank of Canada. The Bank uses its control of the monetary base and interest rates to promote economic stability at potential output and a low stable inflation rate.
- Central banks have three main operating techniques: **reserve requirements imposed on commercial banks, open-market operations**, and **bank rate** setting. These techniques are used to manage the monetary base, the money multiplier, and interest rates.
- Central banks can implement **monetary policy through the monetary base and money supply control** or through **interest rate control**, but cannot do both simultaneously.
- In practice, the Bank cannot control money supply exactly. Thus, for most central banks, a short-term **interest rate is the instrument of monetary policy**.
- The Bank of Canada uses the **overnight interest rate as its policy instrument**, and an inflation rate of **1 percent to 3 percent as its policy target**.
- The Bank of Canada uses **SPRAs** and **SRAs** to intervene in the market for overnight funds and to reinforce its setting of the overnight interest rate.
- A **monetary policy rule** such as a Taylor rule for setting the interest rate provides a useful description of the way the central bank sets and adjusts its interest rate policy instrument.
- Changes in the central bank's policy instrument change nominal and real interest rates and change aggregate demand through the **transmission mechanism**, which includes wealth effects, cost of financing effects, and exchange rate effects on the components of aggregate expenditure.
- **Quantitative easing** is the use of central bank purchases of securities with the aim of increasing the monetary base to meet unusually high demands for liquid cash balances in times of financial and economic crisis.
- **Credit easing** is the increase in specific kinds of central bank asset holdings, commercial paper for

example, designed to provide liquidity and support lending in specific markets facing shortages of funds.

- In the short run, fixed or sticky prices allow the central bank to change real interest rates, real money supply, aggregate demand, and real output.
- **In the long run, when all prices are flexible, money is neutral.** The central bank can change nominal interest rates, prices, and inflation rates, but cannot change real interest rates or real output.

KEY TERMS

Central bank *234*
Monetary policy *235*
Required reserve ratio *237*
Open-market operation *238*
Bank rate *240*
Exchange rate target *243*
Money supply target *243*
Inflation rate target *243*
Monetary policy instrument *244*
Overnight rate *245*
Prime lending rate *246*
Special purchase and resale agreement (SPRA) *247*
Sale and repurchase agreement (SRA) *247*
Taylor rule *253*
Credit easing *257*
The equation of exchange *259*
Neutrality of money *259*
Monetary policy indicators *261*

KEY EQUATIONS AND RELATIONS

Equations

Taylor monetary policy rules:

Setting interest rates to stabilize output: $i = i_0 + b(Y - Y_p)$ **(10.1)** p. 253

Setting interest rates to stabilize inflation and output: $i = i_0 + a(\pi - \pi^*) + b(Y - Y_p)$ **(10.2)** p. 254

The Equation of Exchange: $MV \equiv PY$ **(10.3)** p. 259

The Quantity Theory of Money: $MV_0 = PY_P$, and

$$P = M \times \frac{V_0}{Y_P}$$ **(10.4)** p. 259

Relations

Central bank policy: Control of monetary base H gives central bank power to conduct monetary policy.

Changes in H lead to changes in M and i.
$\Delta H \rightarrow \Delta M + \Delta i$
$\uparrow H \rightarrow \uparrow M + \downarrow i$ and $\downarrow H \rightarrow \downarrow M + \uparrow i$

Open-market operations: Manage size of monetary base H

Open-market purchase → ↑H
Open-market sale → ↓H

Monetary policy targets: Central bank manages AD → equilibrium at target inflation π^* and Y_P

Monetary policy instrument: Bank of Canada uses a short-term interest rate as its policy instrument.

If $i \neq i^*$, then ΔH to get $i = i^*$

Operating techniques: Bank of Canada uses SPRAs and SRAs for day-to-day management of the monetary base to support its setting of i*.

$i > i^* \rightarrow$ SPRA $\rightarrow \uparrow H \rightarrow \uparrow i$
$i < i^* \rightarrow$ SRA $\rightarrow \downarrow H \rightarrow \downarrow i$

Operating techniques: Bank of Canada uses open market operations for longer-term management of the monetary base in support of its inflation rate target.

Policy rules: Interest rate policy rules explain central bank setting of the interest rate policy instrument to achieve a policy target of π^* at Y_P.

$i = i_0 + a(\pi - \pi^*) + b(Y - Y_P)$
If $(Y > Y_P) \rightarrow \uparrow i$ If $(Y < Y_P) \rightarrow \downarrow i$
If $(\pi > \pi^*) \rightarrow \uparrow i$ If $(\pi < \pi^*) \rightarrow \downarrow i$

Monetary policy effects: Changes in interest rates change aggregate expenditure and aggregate demand to stabilize short-run real output at potential output, and inflation at the longer-term inflation target.

Quantity theory of money and prices: With fixed velocity of circulation and real GDP, increases in the money supply cause proportionate increases in prices.

$$\Delta M/M \rightarrow \Delta P/P = \Delta M/M$$

Neutrality of money: In the long run, money is neutral. Monetary policy cannot change real output but can change prices and inflation.

$$\Delta M/M \rightarrow \Delta P/P + \Delta\pi \text{ in the long run}$$

REVIEW QUESTIONS

Review Questions and answers are included in Connect at www.mcgrawhillconnect.ca.

1. Explain carefully why a central bank does not operate to make a profit but a commercial bank does. What is the central bank's operating objective? What unique power does a central bank have that allows it to pursue its operating objective?
2. Explain carefully why a central bank's power to conduct monetary policy is based on its unique position as supplier of the monetary base.
3. Why would a change in the monetary base ΔH cause a change in the money supply?

4. a. Define an "open-market operation."
   b. Suppose a central bank buys $10 million on the open market. What effect does this have on the monetary base and the reserve position of the commercial banks?
   c. If the banks hold reserves equal to 2.5 percent of their deposit liabilities, and the public holds cash equal to 7.5 percent of their deposit holdings, describe the effect of this open-market transaction on:
      i. The money supply
      ii. The public's cash balances
      iii. The banks' reserve balances

5. Suppose the central bank decides to use its power to set interest rates. Use a money market diagram to show and explain what happens to the real money supply if real output increases and the central bank maintains a constant interest rate.

6. What are the bank rate, the overnight rate, the deposit rate, and the prime rate, and how are they related?

7. a. What is the Bank of Canada's monetary policy target?
   b. What monetary policy instrument does the Bank use to pursue this target?
   c. What do the Bank's procedures for implementing policy mean for its control over money supply?

8. Explain how the Bank of Canada operates to keep the overnight interest rate close to the midpoint of the operating band it sets for the rate.

9. Suppose the Bank of Canada sets its target for the overnight rate at 3.0 percent, with an operating band of 2.75 to 3.25 percent.
   a. Bank A finds it has $100 million more on deposit at the central bank than it needs to meet its overnight clearing balance requirement. What is the rate of interest it will earn by holding this central bank deposit overnight? What is the maximum rate it could earn by lending overnight to another bank?
   b. Bank B finds it has $75 million less than it needs to meet its overnight clearing balance requirement. Where can it borrow the funds it needs? What is the minimum rate it would have to pay to borrow overnight funds from another bank? What rate would it have to pay if no other bank is willing to lend?
   c. Explain why an overnight loan contract between Banks A and B would have an interest rate that falls within the central bank's operating band.

10. Use a diagram to show circumstances in the market for overnight funds that might lead the Bank of Canada to make an SRA. Why would the Bank use an SRA in this case rather than an open market operation?

11. Suppose a central bank decides to conduct monetary policy according to a Taylor rule for interest rates.
    a. How does it choose the basic setting for the interest rate within the rule?
    b. How would it respond to a rise in the unemployment rate?
    c. How would the bank react to an inflation rate higher than its target inflation rate?
    d. Why would the bank decide to change the basic setting of its interest rate?

12. Use diagrams to show and explain how monetary policy conducted according to a Taylor rule would stabilize real output at potential output.

13. The central bank wants to maintain inflation at a fixed target and to see the economy operating at potential output. It sets its overnight rate based on the following rule:
    $onr = 2.0 + 1.5(\pi - \pi^*) + 0.5[(Y - Y_P)/Y_P]*100$
    a. If the economy is operating at potential output and the inflation rate is at the Bank's target, π^*, what is the Bank's onr setting?
    b. Suppose a recession in a major trading partner lowers demand for domestic exports, lowers AD and lowers real income $Y = Y_P = 1000$ to $Y = 980$. How would the central bank respond?
    c. Alternatively, suppose a drop in labour productivity growth pushed the inflation rate up by 0.5 percent. How would the central bank respond?

14. Explain why, according to the Quantity Theory of Money, a ten-percent decrease in the money supply would result in a ten-percent decrease in the price level?

15. What does it mean to say that money is neutral in the short run but not in the long run?

16. *Internet* Visit the Bank of Canada's Web site, www.bankofcanada.ca, and look up the last two press releases that announced the Bank's setting of its key policy interest rate. What economic conditions led the Bank to change or maintain the setting of the overnight rate in each case?

17. *Internet* Visit the Bank of Canada's Web site, www.bankofcanada.ca, and examine the Bank's most recent estimates of the output gap. If the pattern of change you see in the output gap measure were to continue, what announcement would you expect the Bank to make about its setting of the overnight rate?

PART 5

Output, Inflation, and Monetary and Fiscal Policy

This Part extends our work in three important ways. First, we drop the assumption that the general price level is fixed, and derive the AD curve. This lets us examine how fiscal and monetary policy work to stabilize short-run business cycle fluctuations in output and prices, when there is some flexibility in output prices. That is the work of Chapter 11. Chapter 12 brings the international trade and financial sector, as well as foreign exchange rates, into the discussion of monetary and fiscal policies. Chapter 13 introduces price flexibility and inflation in both factor input prices and output prices on the aggregate supply side of the economy. This allows us to examine the economy's inflation rate, adjustment to changes in economic conditions, and longer-term fiscal and monetary policy issues.

CHAPTER 11

Monetary Policy and Fiscal Policy in the Short Run

LEARNING OUTCOMES

By the end of this chapter you should understand:

1. The relationship between prices, aggregate expenditure, and aggregate demand
2. The determinants of the slope and the position of the AD curve
3. The determinants of the slope and position of the short run AS curve
4. Short-run and long-run equilibrium output and price
5. The effects of fiscal policy on output, prices, and the public debt
6. The effects of monetary policy on output and prices in the short run
7. How monetary and fiscal policy interact
8. Recent monetary policy, fiscal policy, and economic conditions in Canada

The recession of 2009 was the most severe downturn in economic activity in thirty years. What caused the recession? How did it spread through the economy? Can governments take policy action to moderate a recession, reduce its duration, and support a speedy recovery? A carefully constructed macroeconomic model is needed to answer those questions.

This chapter draws together the material of the last five chapters to provide such a model. It integrates the study of expenditures, money, and financial markets, *when output prices are flexible,* to establish both the *position* and the *slope of the AD curve*. With flexible *output* prices, the downward-sloping AD curve and the upward-sloping AS curve combine to explain short-run equilibrium real GDP and the general price level, as well as business cycle fluctuations like the 2009 recession.

Fiscal policy and monetary policy provide two broad sets of tools that governments can use to manage aggregate demand, output, prices, and inflation. The short-run AD/AS model is used to study how changes in fiscal and monetary policy can be made to fight recessions and inflationary gaps. The recent performance of the Canadian economy under different monetary and fiscal policies provides interesting examples of macroeconomic policy in action.

We continue to work in the short run; the labour force, the stock of capital, and the state of technology are fixed, fixing potential output Y_P. The position of the short-run aggregate supply curve is based on Y_P, a given money wage rate, and a given rate of indirect taxes. With these conditions, fluctuations in aggregate demand or aggregate supply conditions cause the fluctuations in output, employment, and prices we often describe as business cycles. The economy moves to outputs and price levels that equate aggregate demand and supply.

11.1 Prices, Aggregate Expenditure, and Aggregate Demand

As seen in Chapter 5, aggregate demand is different from the market demand for an individual product or service. Aggregate demand explains how changes in the general price level, either the GDP deflator or the consumer price index, cause changes in aggregate expenditure. National accounts showed that this relationship is not based on changes in prices relative to income, as in the market for an individual product. Instead, we saw that the strongest links between the price level and aggregate expenditure come from financial markets, working through the monetary transmission mechanism we have studied in the last two chapters. Direct wealth effects on consumption and substitution effects on net exports may also provide some of the explanation for this relationship.

To explore this in more detail, suppose the central bank sets and controls the size of the nominal money supply, M_0. In our earlier study of the money market, we looked at the way the demand for real money balances and the supply of real money balances interact to determine the equilibrium interest rate. When the nominal money supply is fixed, a change in the price level changes the real money supply, M_0/P, disrupts the equilibrium in the money market, and causes a change in the interest rate and the foreign exchange rate.

We can see this relationship in the money market equilibrium condition from Chapter 9, namely:

$$\frac{M_0}{P} = L(Y, i) \tag{11.1}$$

The real money supply, measured in terms of the amount of goods and services it would buy, is the nominal money supply M_0 divided by the general price level P. The demand for real money balances is positively related to real GDP, Y, and negatively related to the nominal interest rate, i.

Figure 11.1 uses a money market diagram to show how a change in the price level affects interest rates. In the initial equilibrium, the central bank has set the nominal money supply at M_0, and conditions in the economy give a price level P_0. Real output or GDP is constant at Y_0. The money market is in equilibrium at the interest rate i_0.

FIGURE 11.1 **The Effect of Changes in the General Price Level on Interest Rates**

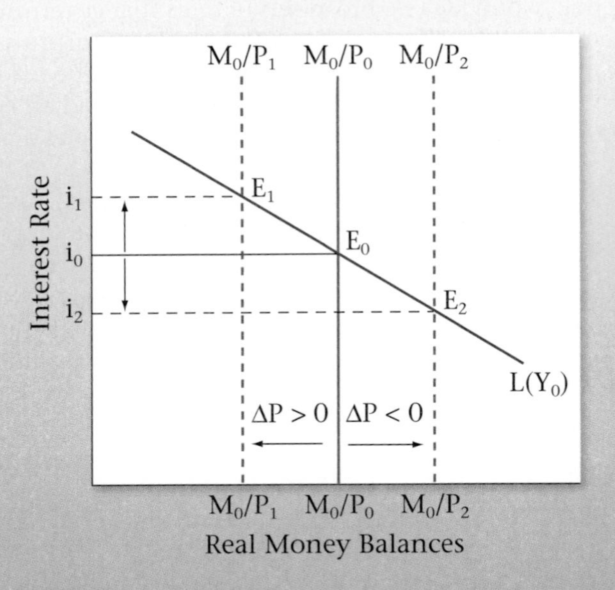

At E_0 the money market is in equilibrium. The demand for real money balances $L(Y_0)$ is equal to the supply of real money balances M_0/P_0 at the interest rate i_0. A rise in the general price level to $P_1 > P_0$ shifts the real money supply line left to M_0/P_1. Demand for real money balances at i_0 exceeds supply. Bond prices fall and yields rise until equilibrium is restored at E_1 at the higher interest rate i_1. A fall in the price level to P_2 has the opposite effect.

Changes in the price level change the real money supply, shifting the M_0/P line and disrupting the initial equilibrium. The real money supply line in the diagram shifts to the left if prices rise and to the right if they fall. Equilibrium is restored by a change in interest rates.

From the monetary transmission mechanism, we know that changes in interest rates will cause changes in aggregate expenditure. We will extend our discussion of the effect of changes in the price level, and make that linkage to expenditure and output, very shortly. First there is an interesting question to consider: How much do interest rates change as a result of a change in the price level? The answer is important for the effect of price changes on equilibrium output.

The demand for money determines the change in interest rates caused by the change in the price level and real money supply change. Figure 11.2 shows the importance of different demand conditions. The initial equilibrium is E_0, based on a nominal money supply M_0 and a price level P_0.

Two alternatives for the demand for money balances are shown. L_0 describes a demand for money that is very sensitive to interest rates. Small changes in interest rates result in relatively large shifts between money and bonds. This portfolio adjustment is a movement along the L_0 line. As a result, it takes only a small change in the interest rate to adjust to the change in the real money supply.

L_1 describes the opposite case. The demand for real money balances is not very sensitive to changes in interest rates. It takes a large change in interest rates to produce the portfolio adjustment required to restore equilibrium after a change in the real money supply.

FIGURE 11.2 **Changes in Interest Rates Under Different Demand Conditions**

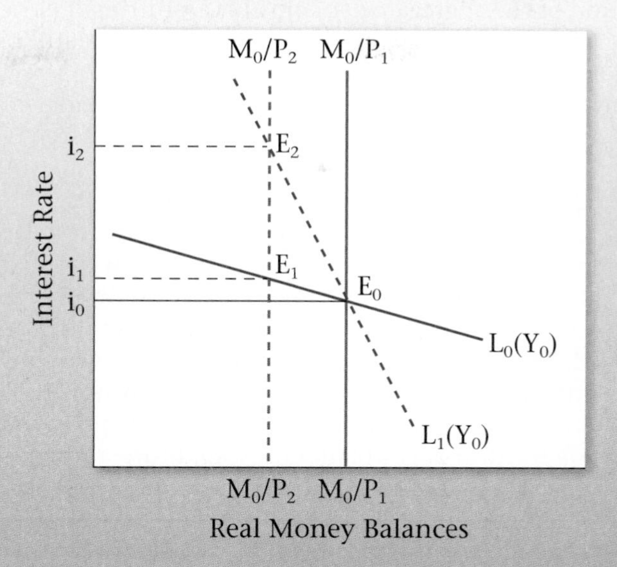

The lines L_0 and L_1 show two alternative demand conditions. L_0 tells us that small changes in interest rates cause large changes in holdings of bonds and money. By contrast, L_1 says it takes large changes in interest rates to get adjustments in the holdings of bonds and money balances. This difference is important in terms of the effects of a change in P on interest rates. A rise in P reduces the real money supply. If demand is L_0 the interest rate rises to i_1. Alternatively, if demand is L_1 the interest rate rises to i_2.

The difference between L_0 and L_1 is a reflection of different conditions in the money market. If financial markets offer lots of alternatives to money balances and portfolio managers can switch easily and at low cost, it is easy to make portfolio adjustments. If the real money supply falls, small increases in interest rates and yields on a range of financial assets make those assets more attractive than money balances. Portfolios adjust quickly from money to other assets. The L_0 curve describes this condition.

Alternatively, if portfolio managers have few alternatives to money and costs of financial transactions are high it is more difficult to make portfolio adjustments. Large differences between yields on financial assets and money balances are necessary to make portfolio adjustments worthwhile. The L_1 curve describes this condition.

In the diagram, the effect of a rise in P from P_1 to P_2 depends on which demand condition prevails in the money market. Along L_0, the responsiveness of the demand for money to the interest rate is high, and the rise in the interest rate is small, as shown by the new equilibrium E_1. Alternatively, if the responsiveness is low, L_1 is the demand for money and the new equilibrium is E_2. Changes in the price level cause much larger changes in interest rates. These differences are important because the interest rate changes are the link between changes in the price level and changes in aggregate expenditure.

Review Questions 1 and 2

Now we can derive an aggregate demand curve showing the relationship between the general price level and the equilibrium level of planned expenditure and output. To focus on this relationship, we assume that the nominal money supply is fixed by the central bank. We also assume that expenditures that are *not* related to interest rates and exchange rates are constant. Changes in any of these assumptions will change the position of the aggregate demand curve, shifting it either left or right.

Changes in the general price level change equilibrium expenditure and output through the monetary transmission mechanism. A rise in the price level lowers the real money supply. Interest rates rise in the money market and, if the exchange rate is flexible, the domestic currency appreciates and the foreign exchange rate—the Canadian dollar price of the U.S. dollar—falls.

Higher interest rates raise the costs of carrying the lines of credit outstanding to households and business, reducing their funds for other expenditures. Flexible mortgage rates have the same effect. The costs of new borrowing are similarly increased, and the fall in asset prices that comes with a rise in interest rates reduces household and business borrowing capacity. Domestic consumption and investment expenditure are reduced. The fall in the foreign exchange rate lowers import prices and reduces export competitiveness and profitability. Net exports fall. Through these linkages in the monetary transmission mechanism a higher price level, when the nominal money supply is fixed, reduces planned expenditure and equilibrium output. The economy *moves up to the left along* the AD curve.

A fall in the general price level would have the opposite effects on nominal and real interest rates and exchange rates, raising planned expenditure and equilibrium output. Again, a change in the price level moves the economy along the AD curve.

The linkages between changes in the general price level and changes in output can be summarized as follows, again using the Greek letter Δ to mean "change in":

$$\Delta P \rightarrow \Delta(M/P) \rightarrow \left\{ \begin{array}{c} \Delta i \rightarrow \Delta(C + I) \\ \Delta er \rightarrow \Delta NX \end{array} \right\} \rightarrow \Delta AE \rightarrow \Delta Y$$

Figure 11.3 shows this derivation of the aggregate demand curve by combining diagrams we have used before. Panel (a) shows money market equilibrium at E_0, based on an initial nominal money supply M_0, set by the central bank, and price level P_0. In panel (b), the interest rate i_0 determined in the money market results in a total of consumption, investment, and net export expenditure that is sensitive to the interest rate equal to $A(i_0)$. (In equilibrium, prices are constant, the inflation rate is zero, and therefore nominal interest rates equal real interest rates.) The net export part of this comes from exchange rate effects. Panel (c) shows the equilibrium level of aggregate expenditure and real output Y_0, based on autonomous expenditure, expenditure related to interest rates and exchange rates, and expenditure induced by the marginal propensities to consume and import and the marginal tax rate. These induced expenditures are the source of the multiplier studied in Chapters 6 and 7. The information in panels (a), (b), and (c), shows that when there is one general price level P_0, the corresponding equilibrium real output is Y_0. This combination is plotted in panel (d) at point G.

The aggregate demand curve describes what would happen to equilibrium real output if the general price level changed, everything else held constant. To show this, return to panel (a) in Figure 11.3 and assume the price level rises to P_1. This price increase reduces the real money supply and raises the interest rate to i_1. A corresponding higher interest rate i_1 reduces expenditure in panel (b), and this in turn lowers the AE curve in panel (c). The multiplier works to give a new equilibrium output Y_1. Plotting P_1, Y_1 in panel (d) gives point F. Alternatively, assuming a fall in the general price level to P_2, the same process would lead to P_2, Y_2, and point H in panel (d). G, F, and H are three points on the aggregate demand curve AD_0. The AD curve is the locus of equilibrium points based on Y = AE at different price levels.

Review Question 3

FIGURE 11.3 **Deriving the AD Curve Based on a Fixed Nominal Money Supply**

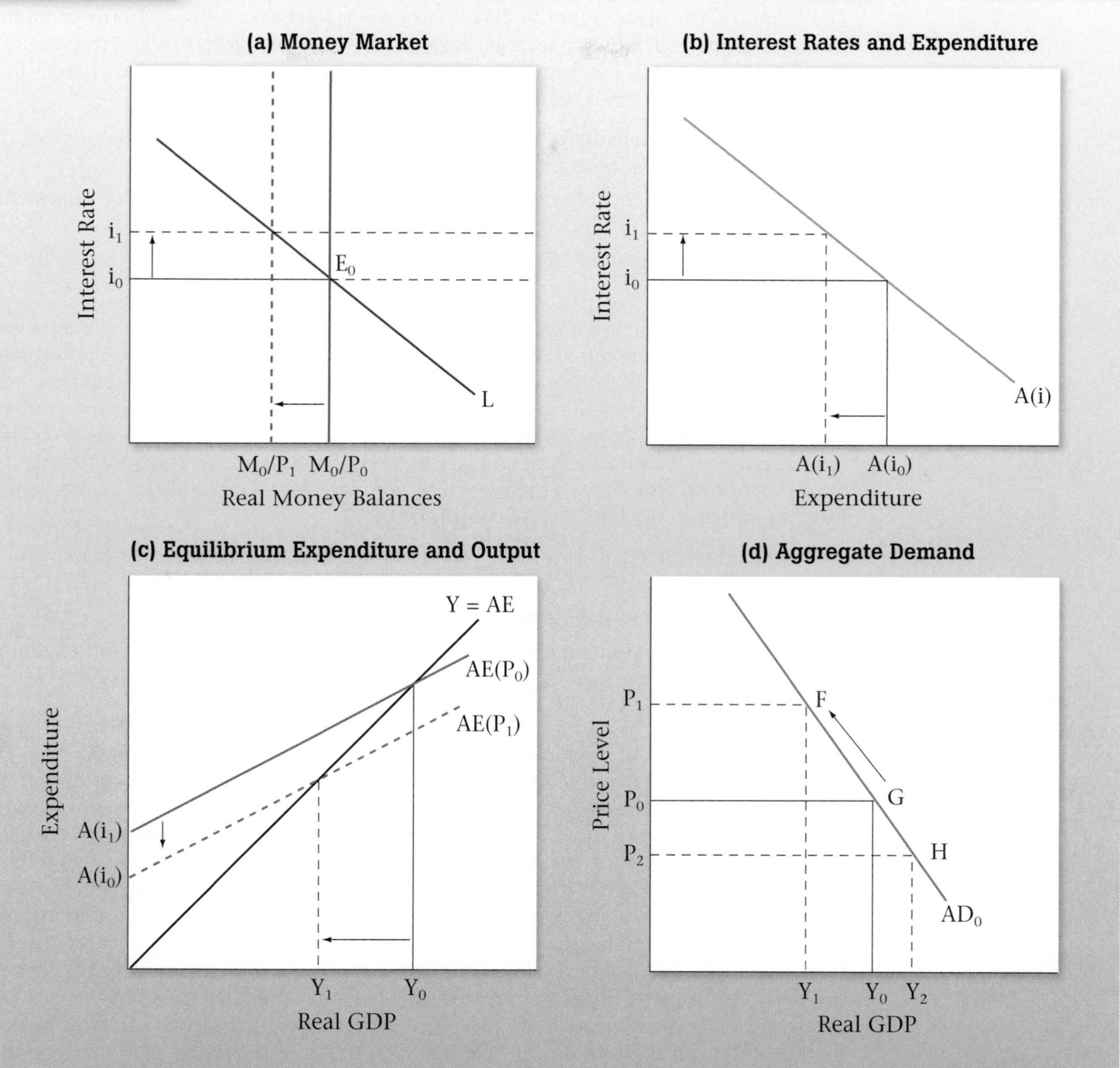

The AD curve is derived by introducing a change in the price level P in panel (a) and tracing the effects of that price increase on interest rates, expenditure in panel (b), and equilibrium output in panel (c) to find the combinations of P and Y labelled F, G, and H that lie on the AD curve in panel (d). Notice that the nominal money supply M_0, autonomous expenditure and the slope of the AE curve are all constant in the derivation of AD. Changes in P cause movements along AD, from G to F if prices rise, or from G to H if prices fall.

11.2 The Slope and Position of the AD Curve

The slope and the position of the AD curve describe a set of conditions in the economy. Changes in the general price level P cause *movements along the AD curve*. From the diagrams in Figure 11.3, the slope of AD, which describes the size of the change in Y caused by a change in P, is determined by *three economic relationships*:

1. The interest sensitivity of the demand for money as shown by the slope of the demand curve for money balances in panel (a)
2. The interest sensitivity of planned expenditure as shown by the slope of the A(i) curve in panel (b)
3. The size of the multiplier, which is determined by the slope of the AE line in panel (c)

You can experiment with the diagrams to see that, if the demand for money is very sensitive to interest rates, and if expenditure does not change much when interest rates change, and the expenditure multiplier is small, the AD curve will be steeply sloped. The effects of changes in the general price level P on equilibrium expenditure and output Y will be small. If conditions in the economy are the opposite of those described, the AD curve will be flatter, and changes in P will have large effects on Y.

The position and slope of the AD curve summarizes the material of Chapters 6 to 9 into one function. Its position is determined by:

1. Autonomous consumption, investment, and government and net export expenditures
2. The nominal money supply set by the central bank
3. The monetary transmission mechanism through interest rates and exchange rates, and
4. The multiplier

A change in any of these conditions results in a *shift* to a new AD curve.

The monetary transmission mechanism and the multiplier are also captured in the slope of the AD curve.

The AD curve is used as part of a model to analyze past macroeconomic performance and forecast future performance. It is important for providing an explanation of recessions like that of 2009 and in the policy responses available to governments. If we understand the internal workings of AD, we can see how changes in autonomous consumption, investment decisions, exports, government taxes and expenditures, interest rates, and other conditions affect output, employment, and incomes. All these expenditures in AD were involved in the 2009 recession and the later recovery. When AD is combined with the short-run AS curve, we can also see the effects of changing economic conditions on both output and price levels, and identify the roles for fiscal and monetary policy to stabilize output, employment, and prices.

Review Questions 3, 4, 5 and 6

11.3 Short-Run Aggregate Supply

The short-run aggregate supply (AS) curve defines a relationship between real GDP and the general price level. It is based on the following assumptions:

1. Prices of the factors of production, the money wage rates for labour in particular, are constant.

2. The stock of capital equipment, the buildings and equipment used in the production process, and the technology of production are constant.
3. The size of the labour force is constant but the level of employment is variable.
4. The rates of indirect taxation imposed by governments are held constant, and
5. The prices of key raw material inputs, which are determined in international markets like the market for crude oil, are constant.

These conditions determine the *position* of the AS curve. If the price level is constant, as assumed in earlier chapters, the AS curve is a horizontal line.

If the price level is not constant, but positively linked to the level of real GDP, the short-run AS curve is upward sloping. The steepness of its slope is a measure of the flexibility or stickiness of the general price level. This degree of price flexibility reflects the underlying structure of industry in the aggregate economy, production costs, and the way output and price decisions are made.

The determinants of the slope and position of the short-run aggregate supply curve were explained in Chapter 5. Based on the income approach to measuring GDP and the GDP deflator, the relationship between output and the general price level on the supply side of the economy depends on what happens to unit costs (factor cost per unit of output) as output increases or decreases. In the short run, with constant factor prices, unit costs and prices depend on factor productivity as output changes. The largest component of factor cost is labour cost (about 70 percent), based on its share of factor income in national accounts. If labour productivity measured by output per hour worked decreases as employment and output increase and the money wage rate is constant, unit labour costs and unit factor costs of production rise.

The change in the general price level when real GDP and unit labour cost change depends on the structure of industry and producer price and output decisions. Chapter 5 examined these relationships. The result was a positively sloped short-run AS based on the assumption that unit costs rise as output and employment increase in at least some sectors of the economy. Figure 11.4 illustrates the AS curve.

The AS curve in Figure 11.4 shows the relationship between the output of goods and services, real GDP, and the general price level, all other conditions held constant. Point A on the curve AS_0 is drawn for a given level of money wage rates w_0. Point P_0Y_0 on AS_0 reflects unit costs at output Y_0 and producer decisions with respect to output at that price.

If output were higher at Y_1 producers' unit costs would be higher because factor productivity is lower at that higher output. A higher price, P_1, would be required to cover costs and make producers willing to supply goods and services. With everything but price and output held constant, movements along the upward-sloping AS curve show the prices producers would need in order to supply different aggregate outputs as measured by real GDP.

A change in any of the conditions underlying AS_0 would shift the aggregate supply curve. The money wage rate is a key factor driving shifts in AS because wages are the largest component of costs in GDP. But changes in indirect taxes like the GST, PST, or HST, or changes in commodity prices like the price of energy will also shift the AS curves. In Figure 11.4 the aggregate supply curve AS_1 is drawn based on a money wage rate w_1 greater than the wage rate w_0 underlying AS_0. A higher money wage rate means higher unit labour costs at every level of output. A higher price is necessary at every output if producers are to cover their costs. At output Y_0, for example, producers now need P_2 to cover the increase in unit labour costs and maintain their profits.

FIGURE 11.4 **The Short-Run Aggregate Supply Curve**

The aggregate supply curve AS_0 shows the relationship between aggregate output and the general price level when everything except output and price, including the money wage rate, are held constant. Its positive slope reflects the increases in costs as productivity falls when employment and output increase. An increase in the money wage rate increases costs at every level of output. Producers need higher prices to continue to produce that same output at wage rate w_1 as they were willing to produce when the money wage rate was w_0. The AS curve shifts up to show the effect of the higher money wage rate.

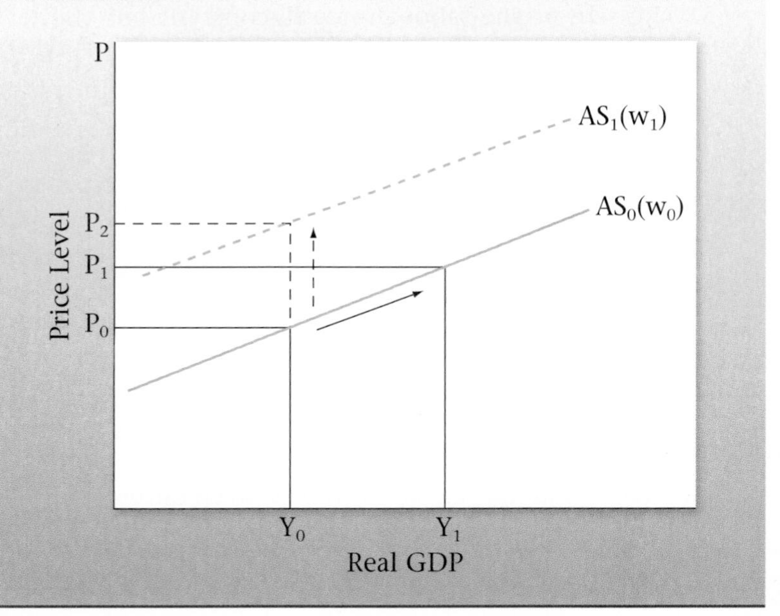

11.4 Short-Run Equilibrium Output and Prices

Figure 11.5 shows short-run equilibrium real GDP and prices determined by aggregate demand and short-run aggregate supply. The aggregate demand curve is based on a given nominal money supply set by the central bank, planned private sector and government expenditures, and a multiplier. The aggregate supply curve is based on a given stock of capital, a given supply of labour, a given state of technology, and fixed prices for factor inputs. The intersection of the aggregate demand and supply curves gives a combination of real GDP and price level P_0Y_0, at which planned expenditures and outputs are equal. There is a corresponding level of employment.

CHANGES IN SHORT-RUN EQUILIBRIUM

This AD/AS framework provides a useful way to study how the economy reacts to changes in economic conditions. Some changes affect AD, others affect AS, and some more complex events affect both AD and AS. In all cases, the AD/AS model shows how changes in economic conditions change output, employment, and the price level. An economy that experiences a series of disturbances to AD and AS, both positive and negative, over time goes through business cycles. Real GDP and unemployment rates fluctuate around potential GDP and the natural unemployment rate.

AD Shocks

Changes in autonomous expenditure shift the AD curve, as we have seen in earlier chapters. These might be changes in investment expenditure as a result of changes in business expectations of future markets, or changes in exports as a result of events in other countries, or changes in household expenditure plans. Regardless of the cause, a

FIGURE 11.5 **Short-Run Equilibrium Output and Price**

Aggregate demand, AD, and short-run aggregate supply, AS, together determine short-run equilibrium real GDP and the price level. A particular AD curve reflects a particular set of planned expenditures by all sectors of the economy. The short-run AS curve is based on fixed factor prices, fixed capital stock and technology and a given labour supply. Changes in the conditions underlying AD or AS will shift the curves and change short-run equilibrium output and price level.

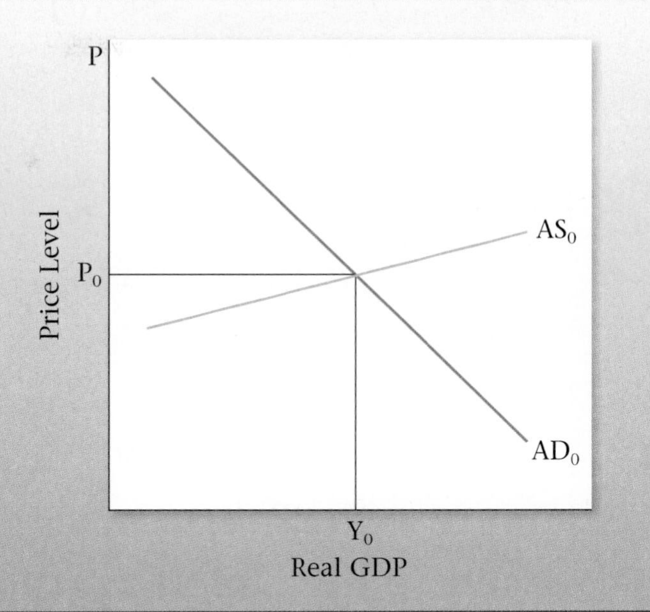

change in autonomous expenditure shifts AD, horizontally, by the expenditure change times the multiplier. In the short-run AD and AS model, real output and the price level both change in the same direction in response to an AD shock. In the recession of 2009, for example, falling investment, consumption, and exports reduced AD and output and employment dropped on an international scale.

AS Shocks

Changes in production costs and indirect taxes shift the AS curve. Although we assume *factor prices are constant* in the short run, commodity prices are not. Changes in the prices of base metals like steel, copper, and nickel come from international market conditions. Large international increases in energy and commodity prices in 2008 and the precipitous declines in 2009 provide a clear example of the volatility in prices of these inputs. The same applies to the prices of sugar, cocoa, coffee, and cereal grains. Producers of products and services that contain these commodities experience changes in their costs as commodity prices fluctuate. They pass these changes along to buyers through the pricing of their outputs. Rising commodity prices raise costs and push the AS curve up. Falling commodity prices pull the AS curve down.

Changes in the price of crude oil have been the most visible and widely reported of these supply shocks in recent years. As consumers, we see the effects of fluctuating oil prices in the price of gasoline at the pump and the costs of home heating oil. Higher oil and gas prices also affect production and distribution costs across the economy. The costs of petroleum-based feedstocks, which are raw material inputs to many of the products we buy, fluctuate. Transportation costs rise as fuel costs go up, and fall as fuel costs fall. Persistently higher crude oil prices eventually work their way into the market prices of goods and services as producers price to recover their costs. The AS curve shifts up as a result, the equilibrium price level rises, and real GDP falls.

FIGURE 11.6 **Short-Run Equilibrium with Aggregate Demand and Supply Shocks**

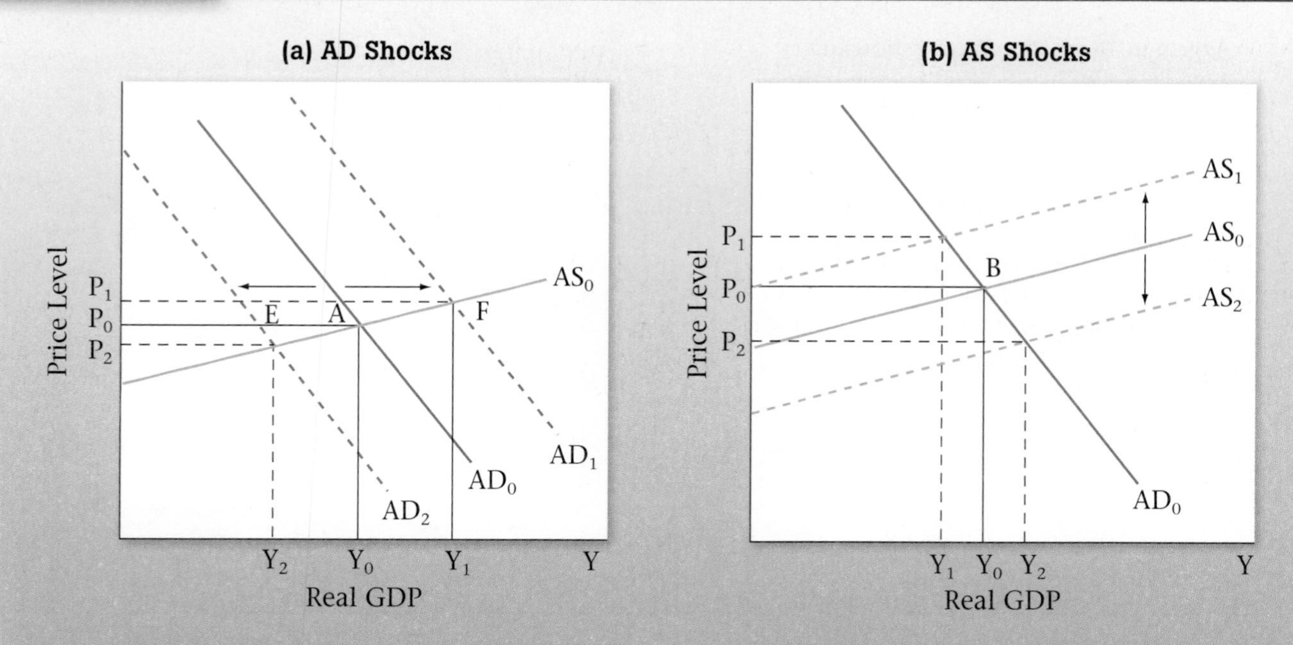

When demand shocks shift AD right and left, short-run equilibrium output and the price level move up and down together.

When supply shocks shift AS up and down, short-run equilibrium output and the price level move in opposite directions. A negative shock shifts AS up, raising P and reducing Y. A positive shock has the opposite effects.

From the national accounts we know that market prices include indirect taxes in addition to factor costs. If governments change the indirect tax rate, raising or lowering sales and excise taxes, market prices change in the same direction. Producers and sellers will continue to supply the same output only if they can collect the increased tax they must remit to governments through an increase in price. An increase in an indirect tax, like the GST or the tax on gasoline, or a provincial retail sales tax, shifts AS up by the amount of the tax increase at each level of output. GST cuts introduced by the Conservative government in 2006 and 2008 shift AS down.

The effects of AS shocks on short-run equilibrium output and price are different from the effects of AD shocks. A negative AS shock shifts the short-run AS upwards. Equilibrium real output falls and prices increase. A positive AS shock lowers prices and increases real output.

AD and AS Shocks Compared

Figure 11.6 illustrates the effects of aggregate demand and supply shocks on real output and prices. In the left-hand panel, the initial short-run equilibrium is at point A, with price level P_0 and real output Y_0. Aggregate demand shocks—for example, increases or decreases in investment expenditures—shift AD right and left between AD_1 and AD_2. The equilibrium output and price level fluctuate up and down as a result.

The addition of the upward sloping short-run AS curve reduces the effects of AD fluctuations on output, compared with our analysis of earlier chapters, where the AS was horizontal. The size of the shift in AD is exactly the same, but the change in equilibrium output is smaller. Price changes cause some offsetting changes in expenditure and reduce the impact on equilibrium output. AD shifts between E and F at P_0, but equilibrium output fluctuates by the smaller amount Y_2 to Y_1, because the price level increases from P_0 to P_1 and reduces some planned expenditure. Furthermore, notice that the steeper the slope of AS the smaller will be the variation in Y for given variations in AD, and the larger will be the variation in the price level.

In the right-hand panel of Figure 11.6, the initial short-run equilibrium is at B with price level P_0 and real output Y_0. Aggregate supply shocks—for example, large variations in the price of crude oil—shift AS up, if crude oil prices increase, or down when they decrease. Short-run equilibrium output and prices fluctuate. A rise in crude oil prices reduces output and raises the price level. A fall in crude price does the opposite. Notice that the slope of the AD curve determines the size of the variations in Y as a result of shifts in the AS curve.

Often the world is not as simple as these examples suggest. AD and AS may both move, making predictions of the outcome more challenging. In 2007 and 2008 rising energy and commodity prices raised costs and pushed that AS curve up. At the same time commodity prices and easy credit conditions provided stimulus to investment expenditure in resource development, residential construction, and consumption. AD shifted to the right. Canada and many other countries experienced strong growth and pressure on inflation.

After mid-2008 conditions changed, first in financial and credit markets and then in energy and commodity markets. The availability of credit collapsed with the financial crisis. Residential construction, especially in the U.S., collapsed, taking with it the demand for building materials and machinery. Falling demand for energy reduced energy prices by more than 50 percent. Investment in energy and commodity production dropped sharply and, with declines in both incomes and access to credit, consumption expenditure fell. Declines in export markets impacted strongly on countries like Canada with high shares of exports in AD. AS shifted down, AD to the left, but the drop in AD overshadowed any stimulus from lower prices on the AS side. The recession was international in scope.

Review Questions 8 and 9

SHORT-RUN EQUILIBRIUM AND ECONOMIC PERFORMANCE

The aggregate demand and supply model offers explanations of short-run real GDP and prices, which are also linked to changes in employment and unemployment rates. But it does not provide enough information for us to evaluate either the performance of the economy or the need for economic policy. We need to re-introduce *the benchmarks of potential output and the natural unemployment rat*e we used in earlier chapters to judge performance and policy needs.

Figure 11.7 introduces the level of potential output into the short-run AD/AS model. It is important to recall from Chapter 5 that potential output is independent of short-run economic conditions. It is determined by the stock of capital, the state of technology, and the size of the labour supply when all factor-input markets are in equilibrium. The unemployment rate is then equal to the natural unemployment rate.

Short-run equilibrium output may or may not equal potential output. Indeed, it is useful to think of fluctuations in short-run output, i.e., business cycles, as fluctuations in actual output around potential output that create recessionary and inflationary gaps. Factor prices that are sticky in the short run allow for these output and

FIGURE 11.7 **Short-Run Equilibrium versus Potential Output**

Short-run equilibrium output and price depend mainly on AD conditions. With AD_0 the economy operates at potential output Y_P, the natural unemployment rate u_n, the price level P_0 and the inflation rate zero. Stronger demand AD_1 means higher real output, higher price, and lower unemployment with an inflationary gap $Y_1 - Y_P$. Weaker demand AD_2 means lower output, lower price, and higher unemployment with a recessionary gap $Y_P - Y_2$. Fluctuations in AD, between AD_1 and AD_2, cause business cycle fluctuations in real output and employment.

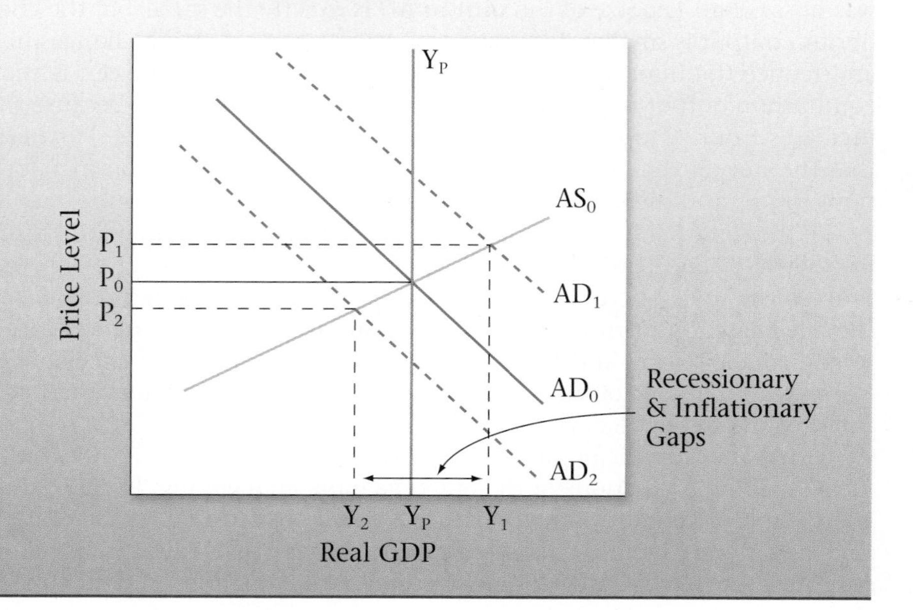

employment fluctuations, which mean unemployment rates fluctuate around the natural rate. Figure 11.7 shows the effects of different short-run demand conditions on output and prices.

The differences between short-run equilibrium output and potential output may be persistent. Different expert forecasts in 2008 and 2009 about the depth and duration of the recession illustrate the range of speculation about the adjustment process. In the short run, the prices of factor inputs, especially money wage rates, are fixed. Weak AD as a result of business pessimism and reduced investment, or a fall in exports, may last for months. The recessionary gap and labour market disequilibrium at Y_2, for example, means high unemployment rates. Some employees have been laid off by their employers, and new jobs are scarce as fewer businesses are hiring. Money wage rate cuts in industries under high stress, like parts of the auto industry in 2009, are possible but unusual, and in any case the average wage rate across all occupations is slow to adjust. Total levels of employment fall. Lost employment and output reduce incomes and standards of living, with those who have lost jobs and those trying to find their first jobs most seriously affected. There are people willing to work for the current money and real wage rate who cannot find employment.

In the short run, with very slow adjustment in factor prices like money wage rates, the economy does not have a built-in mechanism to adjust to the weakness in demand. The short-run price flexibility in the AS curve has offset some of the weakness in demand, but it is not enough to maintain output at Y_P. Further price adjustments may take many months or even years. Contracts fixing money wage rates and some output prices often extend years into the future.

Government monetary and fiscal policies offer solutions to these short-run fluctuations in output, employment, and prices. Monetary and fiscal policies have some built-in stabilization effects through interest rate flexibility and tax and transfer programs. These moderate the effects of the changes in economic conditions but do not offset them completely. *Discretionary* monetary and fiscal policy actions are needed to change aggregate demand to offset short-run departures from potential output and reduce the costs to society.

11.5 The Effects of Fiscal Policy on AD

Fiscal policy, which we discussed in Chapter 7, is demand management policy. Taxes, transfer payments, and government expenditures on goods and services are the tools of fiscal policy. They influence aggregate expenditure, equilibrium output, and aggregate demand through disposable income and consumption expenditure, and directly through government expenditures. The net tax rate, determined by the government's tax and transfer programs, also affects the size of the expenditure multiplier. Changes in tax rates, transfer rates, and government expenditures shift the AD curve.

FISCAL POLICY OBJECTIVES AND INSTRUMENTS

We can look at fiscal policy design and action in a way that is similar to our treatment of monetary policy. The government has two broad fiscal policy objectives or targets that are important for aggregate demand. It wants

1. stable aggregate demand consistent with full employment and potential output, and
2. to control the debt ratio.

The debt ratio is the size of the public (government) debt relative to GDP. The government's budget balance is *the instrument of fiscal policy.* It changes the budget balance by changing its net tax and expenditure programs to shift the AD curve and try to get equilibrium at potential output, or to control its budget balance and debt.

However, the fiscal policy objectives are interdependent. Changes in the budget designed to manage aggregate demand also have effects on the government's debt. At times the size of government debt relative to GDP may constrain the government's use of expansionary fiscal policy. At other times, fiscal policy and budget changes aimed at deficit and debt control can reduce aggregate demand, even though a recessionary gap would call for fiscal stimulus. We look at fiscal policies in terms of each of these objectives.

Fiscal Policy and Aggregate Demand

Figure 11.8 shows the effects of fiscal policy on aggregate demand. The AD curve in panel (a) includes the government fiscal program defined by the budget function BB_0. You will recall from Chapter 7 that $BB = tY - G$. The budget function BB_0 comes from the policy decision to set a specific net tax rate of t_0 and expenditure level G_0. This budget function is shown in panel (b). Government expenditures are part of the autonomous expenditure that positions the AD_0 curve. Net taxes are reflected in the slope of AD_0 through their effect on the expenditure multiplier. We start at P_0 and Y_p and the structural budget balance SBB_0.

To see the use of fiscal policies to manage AD and stabilize real GDP, consider a fall in autonomous consumption, investment, or exports that shifts AD to the left to AD_1.

FIGURE 11.8 **Fiscal Policy and Aggregate Demand**

AD_0 includes the government expenditure, net tax rate, and interest payments on the public debt in the fiscal plan BB_0.

Starting from P_0, Y_p, a fall in autonomous expenditure shifts AD left to AD_1. Income and output fall to Y_1. Automatic stabilizers reduce the budget balance to $BB(Y_1)$.

If lower autonomous expenditure persists, the government reacts with discretionary fiscal policy shifting BB_0 to BB_1, indicated by the fall in the structural budget balance. This fiscal stimulus shifts AD back to AD_0 and Y back to Y_p.

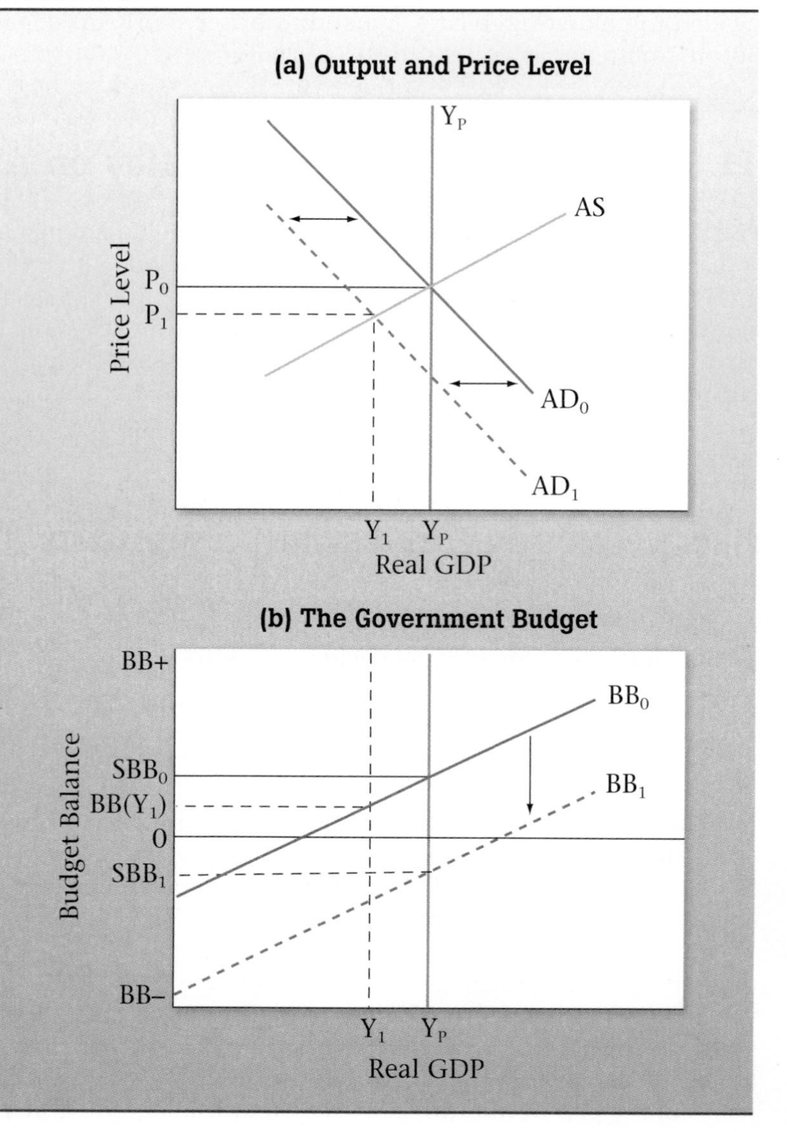

The recession of 2009 is a good example. National income and output falls to Y_1. The net tax system provides some automatic stabilization, indicated by the movement along the budget function BB_0 to the budget balance $BB(Y_1)$, but does not prevent the recessionary gap. The short-run equilibrium in the absence of discretionary policy is P_1Y_1.

If this lower expenditure, output, and income persist, the Minister of Finance may use discretionary fiscal policy, an *increase in expenditure or a cut in taxes*, or both, to stimulate the economy. An increase in G, for example, shifts the policy BB function down as the structural budget balance SBB_0 is reduced to SBB_1. Thus it gives fiscal stimulus to AD. The increased government expenditure working through the multiplier eventually shifts AD back to AD_0, restoring output to Y_p at P_0. Fiscal policy has been used to manage aggregate demand when the fiscal policy target is Y_p.

As an alternative to increased expenditure, the government could add fiscal stimulus to increase AD and close the recessionary gap by cutting the net tax rate. The slope of the BB function would be reduced by a cut in t, to give the reduction in the structural balance required to shift AD to the right. The increase in AD would come from increases in both disposable income and the multiplier.

This example is based on a fall in autonomous expenditure that reduced AD and created a recessionary gap. The opposite conditions also call for discretionary fiscal policy if Y_P is the policy objective. Starting from a short-run equilibrium at Y_P, a strong increase in exports would create an inflationary gap, $Y > Y_P$. Automatic stabilizers would limit, but not eliminate, the gap. Fiscal restraint, from expenditure cuts or tax increases, would be required to reduce AD and eliminate the gap. In terms of the diagram, the budget function would shift up and the structural budget balance would be increased.

Review Questions 10 and 11

Discretionary fiscal policy can provide either fiscal stimulus or restraint by changing government expenditure, the net tax rate, or both. An interesting policy question is whether it is better to implement fiscal policy through government expenditure changes, or tax changes, or a combination of changes in expenditure and tax rates. This was an important part of the often heated political debates in both Canada and the U.S. when the federal governments were designing fiscal stimulus packages to fight the 2009 recession. Those debates reflected differences in political philosophy, differences in opinions about the relative strengths of tax changes and expenditure changes for fiscal stimulus, and different ideas about the best structure of tax and expenditure changes.

FISCAL POLICY AND THE PUBLIC DEBT

To see the importance of the public debt to the design of fiscal policy, we need to elaborate on the government budget function used above. That function, $BB = tY - G$, does not explicitly recognize the interest payments the government must make on its outstanding public debt. But these interest payments cannot be changed as a part of *current* fiscal policy. They are fixed by the current size of the debt and the interest rates on outstanding government bonds. Both are the results of financing past deficits.

Recognizing these interest payments explicitly, because they are not fiscal policy tools, extends the government budget function to give

$$BB = tY - G - iPD \tag{11.2}$$

where PD is the total of government bonds outstanding, and i is the weighted average of the interest rates on those bonds set at the date of issue. The product of the two (iPD) is the annual **interest on the public debt** paid by government to bond holders.

Interest on the public debt (iPD) is the annual interest paid on the outstanding public debt.

The government's **primary budget balance** excludes these interest payments. It is the balance between current net revenues and current expenditures on goods and services. This means it includes the two key components of government fiscal policy, namely, the net tax rate, t, and expenditure on goods and services, G. The primary budget balance function is then:

The **primary budget balance (PBB)** excludes interest payments on the public debt.

$$PBB = tY - G \tag{11.3}$$

The corresponding **structural primary budget balance** function is

$$SPBB = tY_p - G \tag{11.4}$$

The **structural primary budget balance (SPBB)** is the primary balance at Y_P.

which gives the primary budget balance measured at potential output. Changes in fiscal policy are changes in t and G. They shift the primary budget function and change the structural primary balance.

We can also separate the automatic and discretionary dimensions of fiscal policy in the budget function. Using the primary and structural primary budgets, and recognizing the effects of fluctuations in GDP, gives:

$$\mathbf{BB = SPBB_0 + t_0(Y - Y_p) - iPD} \tag{11.5}$$

The Minister of Finance sets the net tax rate t_0 and government expenditure G_0 that yield a primary budget balance at potential output, $SPBB_0$. Setting the SPBB is the discretionary component of fiscal policy. Its setting is based on an evaluation of economic conditions relative to the full employment/stable debt-ratio targets.

The net tax rate t_0 in the budget also gives the automatic fiscal policy reaction to fluctuations in Y relative to Y_p. Notice that if real GDP exceeds potential GDP, $(Y > Y_p)$, the primary budget balance will exceed the structural primary balance. Alternatively, a recessionary gap $(Y < Y_p)$ reduces the primary budget balance, reducing the change in disposable income relative to the change in GDP, and reducing the size of the recessionary gap.

Data in Table 11.1 on federal government balances in Canada for three years illustrate these budget concepts. The overall budget BB and the structural budget SBB were in deficit in 1995 and in surplus in 2000 and 2007, but in each year the primary budget PBB was a surplus. In 1995 the primary surplus was not sufficient to cover the interest payments on the public debt, causing the deficit in BB. Primary surpluses exceeded interest payment required on the public debt in 2000 and 2007 resulting in overall budget surpluses. The public debt declined by the amount of the surplus.

Changes in the structural primary budget balances SPBB indicate changes in fiscal policy. From 1995 to 2000 the rise in the structural primary balance suggests restrictive fiscal policy. Cuts in government expenditure and increases in net tax rates increased the balance by about $50 billion. The change from 2000 to 2007 indicates the opposite policy stance of higher expenditure and lower net tax rates and a drop in the structural primary surplus.

The cyclical balance measures the impact of the state of the economy on the budget. This is the difference between the actual balance and the structural balance caused by the difference between actual GDP and estimated potential GDP. In 1995, a recessionary gap resulted in actual balances lower than structural balances and thus a cyclical deficit.

TABLE 11.1 Federal Government Budget Balances in Canada 2000, 2004, 2007 (millions of dollars)

	1995	2000	2007
Actual balance ($BB = tY - G - iPD$)	−31,700	20,028	15,387
Structural balance ($SBB = tY_p - G - iPD$)	−26,496	13,949	15,397
Interest on public debt (iPD)	44,381	42,390	27,244
Primary balance ($PBB = tY - G$)	12,651	62,418	42,631
Structural primary balance ($SPBB = tY_p - G$)	17,885	56,339	42,621
Cyclical balance ($BB - SBB$)	−5204	6,079	−10

Source: Fiscal Reference Tables 2008, Table 45, Finance Canada, 2008. Reproduced with the permission of the Minister of Public Works and Government Services, 2009.

In 2000, a strong economy and an inflationary gap created a cyclical surplus. The very small cyclical deficit in 2007 means the economy was operating very close to its potential, with just a very small recessionary gap.

BUDGET BALANCES AND OUTSTANDING DEBT

The *current* outstanding public debt PD, and the interest rate on that debt, are not under the control of the minister. They are the result of past budget balances and financing. However, they are important to the *overall* budget balance and the setting of fiscal policy. One year's budget balance shows up in the next year's public debt. In terms of a simple equation, the change in the outstanding public debt is directly linked to the budget balance as follows:

$$\Delta PD = -BB \qquad (11.6)$$

An overall budget surplus, BB > 0, reduces the public debt outstanding in the next year. A budget deficit, BB < 0, increases it.

If the most important target for fiscal policy is to *fix the size of the public debt,* then the actual primary budget balance PBB must be a surplus equal to iPD, the interest costs of carrying the outstanding debt. The overall budget is then balanced, BB = PBB −iPD = 0. However, departures from BB = 0, as a result of either automatic or discretionary fiscal stimulus, will change both the size of the debt and the primary budget balance needed to control the size of the debt.

To illustrate the relationship between budget balances and outstanding debt, consider the finances of a household. Suppose a household with no debt has monthly money income (revenue) just equal to its expenditure. The household budget is balanced at the end of the month, and outstanding debt is still zero.

The following month, this household decides to spend more than its income to buy a holiday, or some home entertainment equipment, or something else it wants. Expenditure exceeds revenue. The budget is in deficit. The household must borrow, incur a debt, to finance its deficit, let's say $1000. It decides to carry this balance on its credit card. Its outstanding debt is now greater than zero, $1000, equal to its budget deficit.

In the following month, to keep its outstanding debt from growing, the household must pay at least the interest on its credit card balance at, say, 1.5 percent per month (an annual rate of 19.6 percent) on $1000, or $15. To make this payment, its *primary* budget balance, income minus current expenditures, must have a surplus of $15. It pays this $15 against its credit card interest charge. Now the *overall* household budget is balanced, income minus expenditures minus interest payments on debt equals zero. Its outstanding debt at month-end is constant at $1000. To fix the size of its debt, the household must *cut its current expenditures* from the level they were at before it went into debt. If it does not cut expenditures (or increase income) but just continues with current expenditures equal to current income, its overall budget balance is a deficit, less than zero, and the household's outstanding debt will grow at the rate of 1.5 percent per month compounded, or about 19.6 percent a year. Alternatively, a household budget surplus will allow the household to reduce its outstanding debt.

These same conditions affect the government's finances. To keep its outstanding debt constant, it must at least pay the interest on the outstanding debt. If the government increases expenditure or reduces revenue and incurs an overall budget deficit, its debt will increase, the interest payments on the debt will increase, and an increase in the primary budget surplus will be required to stabilize the debt. The room for fiscal stimulus may be limited by the size of the debt.

APPLICATION BOX 11.1

Canada's Debt Ratio Reduction Target

The Government of Canada's 2008 budget confirmed a debt reduction target for fiscal policy established in 2005, and reported recent progress.

"Since coming into office, the Government has already reduced the federal debt by $27.4 billion. With planned debt reduction over the budget-planning period of $13.8 billion, and planned debt reduction of $3 billion per year for 2010–11 to 2012–13, total debt reduction by the Government will be more than $50 billion.

This will allow the Government to meet its commitment to reduce the debt-to-GDP ratio to 25 per cent by 2011–12, three years ahead of the original target date. It also furthers the objective, as a country, to eliminate total government net debt by 2021."

Source: Canada, Department of Finance, *The Budget Plan 2008*, Chapter 3, Ottawa, February 26, 2008. www.budget.gc.ca/2008/plan/chap3a-eng.asp#debt. Reproduced with the permission of the Minister of Public Works and Government Services, 2009.

On the other hand, budget surpluses automatically reduce the government's outstanding debt as some borrowings mature and are not refinanced. The interest costs of carrying the debt are reduced, and the primary surplus needed to stabilize the debt is smaller. There is room for new fiscal policy initiatives and fiscal stimulus.

However, if the most important target of fiscal policy is Y_p, pursuit of this target can conflict with the target of debt control. This is not a problem when economic conditions call for discretionary fiscal restraint. The increase in the budget balance that provides fiscal restraint also helps to control the size or the increase in the public debt. *However, when economic conditions call for fiscal stimulus, as in the recession in Canada in 2009, the reduction in the budget balance that provides stimulus will conflict with attempts to control or reduce the public debt. The government must then choose between its policy targets.*

Review Question 12

Conversely, if the fiscal policy target is to reduce the public debt, an increase in the structural primary budget balance is required. Expenditure cuts or tax increases, or a combination of the two, are required. The effect is a reduction in aggregate demand, output, and employment. There is a conflict between the Y_P target and the debt target.

Application Box 11.1 reports on the debt ratio target for Canadian fiscal policy by the federal government in 2008. However, the move to fiscal stimulus to fight the 2009 recession created a large overall budget deficit. The Minister of Finance announced that the focus on the budget balance and debt reduction would be delayed for some time. As we will see later in this chapter, except for the recession of 2009, debt reduction has been a major fiscal policy target in Canada for the past 20 years.

11.6 The Effects of Monetary Policy on AD

Monetary policy is also a demand management tool. It affects the position of the AD curve. A change in the money supply will shift the AD curve. The central bank can react to short-run weakness in AD by increasing the money supply, either directly using open-market purchases to expand the monetary base, or indirectly lowering interest rates and providing increased cash and reserves demanded at lower interest rates. In either case, the bank's policy action lowers interest rates and works through the transmission mechanism to change AD.

Our construction of the AD curve is based on the nominal money supply as the central bank's policy instrument. The equilibrium inflation rate is zero. As a result, the bank's policy objective is equilibrium at Y_P. To pursue that objective, it reacts to short-run differences between actual and potential output by setting the nominal money supply as follows:

$$M = M_0 - \gamma(Y - Y_P) \tag{11.7}$$

This is a monetary policy rule like the Taylor rule in Chapter 10, but in terms of a different policy instrument. It describes how a central bank uses its control of the money supply to implement policy. The nominal money supply rather than the nominal interest rate is the policy instrument. It is used here because the AD curve derived earlier in the chapter is based on a fixed nominal money supply combined with a variable general price level.

M_0 is the central bank's setting of the money supply that it thinks will result in equilibrium at Y_P and price level P_0. It reflects the bank's view about the levels of autonomous expenditures and the multiplier. In Figure 11.9, these conditions, and the money supply M_0, give AD_0 and equilibrium at P_0Y_P.

If a persistent short-run increase in investment or exports increased AD to AD_1, equilibrium real output and prices would increase as in Figure 11.9. The result would be $Y > Y_P$, an inflationary gap. The central bank's monetary policy response would

FIGURE 11.9 **Monetary Policy and Potential Output**

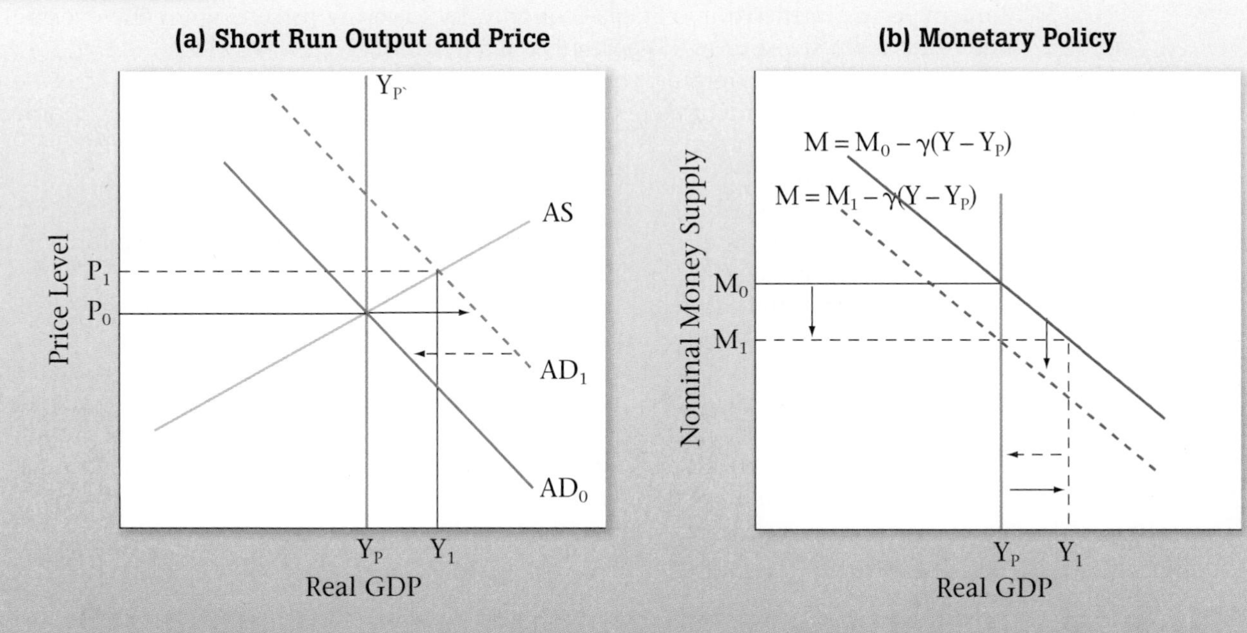

Start with equilibrium output Y_P, price P_0, and the Bank's money supply setting M_0. A rise in aggregate expenditure, for example an increase in NX or I, shifts AD to AD_1. The Bank's initial response is to lower M to M_1, moving along the policy function. Notice that the slope of this function is $-\gamma$. If the Bank sees this as a persistent shift in AD, which it expects will result in higher P if it does not change its policy, it changes its policy stance. As a result, it chooses a new lower setting for its money supply instrument M_1. This new monetary policy reaction shifts AD_1 back to AD_0, working through the monetary transmission mechanism.

be to lower the nominal money supply. Equation (11.7) describes this initial change in the monetary policy instrument by the parameter γ. The size of the change in the money supply described by γ is based on the bank's research and experience with the monetary transmission mechanism. The objective is to stabilize AD and output at Y_P and P_0.

Figure 11.9 shows how this approach to monetary policy works. The position of the AD curve in the left-hand diagram depends on the central bank's setting of the nominal money supply M_0 in the right-hand diagram. The slope of the monetary policy reaction function $\Delta M/\Delta Y$ is $-\gamma$, which describes the bank's reaction to temporary or transient changes in equilibrium Y. The initial short-run equilibrium is P_0,Y_P, based on autonomous expenditures and the nominal money supply M_0.

A short-run increase in autonomous expenditure shifts AD to AD_1, raising equilibrium income above Y_P and pushing price up to P_1. The bank's initial reaction to this increase in AD is to reduce the money supply from M_0 to M_1, *moving along its policy function* in panel (b) of Figure 11.9. Failure to react would result in output persistently greater than potential output and inflationary gap, and upward pressure on wage rates, costs, and the price level.

Reducing the money supply is a restrictive monetary policy. It raises nominal and real interest rates, reducing expenditure and shifting AD back to AD_0. This meets the bank's policy target of $Y = Y_P$. *If the underlying conditions continue*, the bank will make M_1 its new setting for the money supply, giving the new monetary policy reaction function $M = M_1 - \gamma(Y - Y_P)$.

A sharp fall in expenditure would call for the opposite policy response. In the fall of 2008 and winter of 2009, the Bank of Canada reacted to serious weakness in demand, coming from the earlier appreciation of the Canadian dollar and financial and housing crisis in the United States economy, by lowering its setting for the overnight interest rate, in steps, from 4.0 percent to 0.5 percent.

In terms of the diagrams, the AD curve was shifting to the left as exports, consumption, and investment were declining. Reducing the interest rate setting required an increase in monetary base to meet the demand for money balances at the lower interest rates. This monetary stimulus was intended to increase expenditure and shift AD to the right. In announcing the final change in its rate setting, the Bank predicted that inflation would rise to a level consistent with a return to potential output and the Bank's inflation target of 2 percent by mid 2010.

Review Question 13

Although the environment in which the Bank of Canada conducts monetary policy, and its instruments and operating techniques, are different from what we have used here, the principle is the same. The Bank of Canada's inflation target requires demand management to keep the economy close to potential output. The Bank of Canada uses the short-term interest rate as its policy instrument, but that means it must provide a monetary base consistent with equilibrium in the overnight market at that rate. The result is a nominal money supply consistent with equilibrium at Y_P.

11.7 Interactions between Monetary and Fiscal Policy

Although both monetary policy and fiscal policy can change aggregate demand, the two policies are not interchangeable. They affect aggregate demand through different routes and have different implications for the composition of aggregate demand. Furthermore, they may at times reinforce one another, or conflict. The *mix* of monetary and fiscal policy is important.

There are two ways to increase AD. First, there is expansionary fiscal policy, with high government expenditure and low tax rates resulting in structural budget deficits. If this leads to high aggregate demand, perhaps exceeding Y_p at P_0, tight monetary policy is needed to keep income in check. The central bank must reduce the money supply to raise interest rates and reduce aggregate demand. In this case, the mix of easy fiscal policy and tight monetary policy means that some private expenditure on consumption, investment, and net exports is **crowded out** by high interest rates and a low exchange rate. Government expenditure is a larger share of national income, and private expenditure is a smaller share.

Crowding out is the reduction in private expenditures caused by a rise in interest rates if autonomous expenditure increases when the money supply is held constant.

An alternative mix is tight fiscal policy and easy monetary policy. Aggregate demand still gives income at Y_p, but the underlying conditions are quite different. The central bank can set a lower interest rate, and the government's budget balance is higher. The lower interest rate and higher exchange rate support higher private-sector spending to offset the restraint in government expenditure. With easier monetary policy and tighter fiscal policy, the share of private expenditure is higher and the share of government expenditure is lower. With lower interest rates, there is less crowding out of private expenditure.

Of course, easy monetary policy and easy fiscal policy together can be strongly expansionary. That is the policy mix used to fight the recession of 2009. Conversely, tight monetary policy and tight fiscal policy are highly restrictive. The challenge is to get the mix of policy that is consistent with the central bank's inflation target, the government's potential output and debt ratio targets, and society's preferred mix of public and private services.

Suppose, however, that the target of monetary policy and fiscal policy is not Y_p. The target of monetary policy is, instead, an inflation rate π^* lower than the current inflation rate, and the target of fiscal policy is a ratio of public debt to GDP lower than the current ratio. Aggregate demand effects are not the primary policy focus of these policy targets. Both policies will be restrictive and, to the extent that restrictive monetary policy reduces AD, it will make the fiscal policy target of debt ratio reduction more elusive. We see some of this in the Canadian experience with monetary and fiscal policy in the 1990s.

Review Question 14

11.8 Recent Economic Performance and Policy in Canada

Major changes in monetary and fiscal policy in Canada in the last 20 years were both interesting and controversial. They occurred at the same time as Canada moved to free trade with the United States, through the Free Trade Agreement (FTA), and subsequently with Mexico, in the North American Free Trade Agreement (NAFTA). There was also a major change in sales taxes resulting in the introduction of the GST. Most importantly for the discussion of this chapter, debt control emerged as the main target for fiscal policy, and inflation targets as the main focus of monetary policy. Each of these policy changes and their impacts on the economy generated a lot of public debate.

Table 11.2 provides a record of economic performance and policy in Canada from 1985 to 2008. The data, except for the latest period, are five-year averages of economic performance indicators and policy indicators. Economic performance indicators are in the first four rows of the table, monetary and fiscal policy indicators in rows five and six.

The first two five-year periods in the table, 1985–1989 and 1990–1994, cover approximately the terms of the Progressive Conservative government of Prime Minister Brian Mulroney. The Honourable Michael Wilson was Minister of Finance for most of

TABLE 11.2 **Economic Performance and Macroeconomic Policy in Canada 1985 to 2008**

	1985–1989	1990–1994	1995–1999	2000–2004	2005–2008
1. Output gap (%)	0.88	−2.20	−0.86	0.42	0.83
2. Unemployment rate (%)	8.91	10.33	8.89	7.31	6.28
3. Inflation rate (%)	4.30	2.62	1.62	2.43	2.03
4. Public debt/GDP (%)	53.20	64.90	71.10	52.00	37.10
5. Real overnight rate (%)	5.30	4.89	3.20	1.03	1.66
6. Structural primary budget balance ($ billions)	−8.78	6.56	42.68	51.25	33.79

Sources: Part of data is based on Statistics Canada CANSIM Database, http://cansim2.statcan.gc.ca, Table 326-0022 Series V41690914 and Table 380-0001 Series V498074; Bank of Canada, Rates and Statistics, Monetary Policy Indicators, Indicators of Capacity and Inflation Pressures for Canada, bankofcanada.ca/en/rates/indinf/product_data_en.html; *Fiscal Reference Tables 2007*, Tables 14 and 45, Finance Canada, 2007. Reproduced with the permission of the Minister of Public Works and Government Services Canada, 2009.

this time period. George Bouey was the Governor of the Bank of Canada until 1987. John Crow was Governor from 1987 to 1994.

The Liberal governments of Prime Ministers Jean Chrétien and Paul Martin held power in the period from 1995 to 2005. The Honourable Paul Martin was Minister of Finance for most of this time, followed by the Honourable John Manley and the Honourable Ralph Goodale. Gordon Thiessen was Governor of the Bank of Canada from 1994 to 2001, David Dodge from 2001 to 2008.

The current Conservative government of Prime Minister Stephen Harper took office in early 2006. The Honourable James Flaherty is the current Minister of Finance. Mark Carney, was appointed Governor of the Bank of Canada, succeeding David Dodge, in 2008.

1985 to 1989

Although the economy was strong in the 1985 to 1989 period, operating slightly above the level of potential output as indicated by the output gap, despite the high unemployment rate, there were two important policy issues:

1. a large government budget deficit and a growing ratio of public debt to GDP
2. an inflation rate in the 4 percent range, and rising

Fiscal policy shifted from fighting a recession in the early 1980s to focus on the first of these problems. Finance Minister Wilson introduced fiscal restraint aimed, first, at eliminating the deficit in the primary budget balance. His longer-term objective was to eliminate growth in the debt ratio, which would require a substantial reduction in the total budget deficit. Tax increases and expenditure controls eliminated the structural primary budget deficit by the end of the period. The effect on aggregate demand was negative, but the objective was deficit and debt control, not income stabilization.

Both components of this policy package were criticized. Tax increases, it was argued, increased an already excessive tax burden and threatened economic growth and international competitiveness. Furthermore, they supported an increase in the size of government relative to the total economy. Selective expenditure controls were seen to reduce government's role in environmental protection, support for research, the defence budget, and support for other sectors of the economy thought to be worthy of government support. Perhaps most importantly, the shift in policy was not sufficient to eliminate the deficit and stop the growth in public debt.

Monetary policy shifted during this period to focus primarily on inflation. After the Bank of Canada had spent several years searching for a monetary policy strategy, Governor Crow, in 1987, named price stability as the target for monetary policy. Short-term interest rates were adopted as the main policy instrument. The decline in real short-term rates in 1986 and 1987, which had supported aggregate demand as fiscal policy shifted to debt control, was reversed. Rates rose sharply as the Bank's focus shifted to inflation. This added restrictive monetary policy to the fiscal restraint coming from the government's budget adjustments. Aggregate demand was reduced substantially.

During this period, although the economy operated, on average, with a small positive output gap, output greater than potential output, adding monetary restraint to fiscal restraint reduced aggregate demand sufficiently to push output below potential output at the end of the period.

1990 to 1994

Deficit reduction together with debt and inflation control continued as the major policy targets in the early 1990s.

The effects of the restrictive policies of the 1985 to 1989 period are shown clearly in the performance indicators of 1990 to 1994. The reduction in aggregate demand created a large negative output gap. The economy operated well below potential output. Employment declined and the unemployment rate rose sharply. The economy was in a policy-induced recession. Professor Pierre Fortin called it the "great Canadian slump."

Monetary policy in this period was firmly and formally focused on inflation. The Governor of the Bank and the Minister of Finance had signed an agreement in 1991, establishing clear targets for reductions in the inflation rate. The credibility of the Bank's monetary policy rested on meeting those targets, and an extremely tight monetary policy was implemented. Inflation rates did fall sharply, more than called for by the new inflation targets. Although the real overnight interest was a bit lower on average in this period than in the earlier period, monetary policy was strongly restrictive. Rates rose sharply in 1990 and again in 1992, holding aggregate demand down, until inflation had dropped below the targets initially set.

Fiscal policy was less successful. Although successive budget adjustments raised the primary structural budget into a surplus, the debt ratio rose persistently. This was partly a result of the automatic stabilization built into budget programs as monetary restraint pushed the economy into recession. Part was a result of the increased interest rates and interest costs on the public debt. Actual budget balances moved further into deficit. The debt ratio rose to an average 65 percent of GDP. There was clearly no room for fiscal stimulus to AD to address the recession.

1995 to 1999

The 1995 to 1999 period was a time of easing monetary conditions and large, restrictive fiscal adjustments. Lower inflation rates and persistently high unemployment rates allowed an easing of monetary policy, consistent with the inflation target of 2 percent. Easier monetary conditions, indicated by the lower real short-term interest rates, supported an expansion in aggregate demand and real output.

Fiscal policy, on the other hand, was highly restrictive. The debt and debt ratio had risen strongly, raising questions about longer-term financial stability. Finance Minister

Martin focused on control and reduction of the debt ratio by setting overall budget deficit targets, and aiming ultimately for budget surpluses. Cuts to government expenditures and transfers raised the primary structural budget surplus from under $6 billion to $43 billion. This was a large upward shift in the government's budget function. It pushed the aggregate demand curve to the left, raising the output gap in the first years of the period.

However, most of the fiscal adjustment was made in those first years of the period. From then on a stable budget function with consistent surpluses, combined with the easing of monetary policy and strong export growth, raised aggregate demand. The economic recovery eliminated the output gap by the end of the period. Unemployment fell while inflation remained within the target range set by monetary policy. Although the debt ratio was higher on average in this period than in the previous five years, it was declining strongly.

This period provides an example of the economy's response to a combination of easing monetary conditions and restrictive fiscal policy, supported by strong export growth. The result was the aggregate demand condition needed for the economy to return to potential output.

2000 to 2004

Low unemployment rates, stable inflation rates, and declining debt ratios illustrate strong economic performance in this time period. The output gap and the unemployment rate indicate an economy working, on average, at full employment and potential output. Inflation was slightly above the target of 2 percent but well within the 1 percent to 3 percent target band set by the Bank. The federal government's primary budget surplus was higher than in the previous period, and the debt ratio declined significantly. In short, there was a mix of monetary and fiscal policy that supported aggregate demand at just the right level.

The focus of economic policy was unchanged. The inflation target of 2 percent for monetary policy was renewed and extended. Ministers of Finance reaffirmed their commitment to funding federal government programs within the context of a balanced budget. The debt ratio continued as an important fiscal policy objective. After several informal announcements, the Minister of Finance set a target for the debt ratio at 25 percent of GDP by the year 2012.

The economy's performance was quite remarkable, given the events of the period. It began with considerable anxiety over the start of the new millennium and "Y2K" concerns. Volatility in financial markets lowered major stock market indexes like the Toronto S&P/TSX by more than 40 percent from the peak of 11,248 in mid-2000 to the trough of 6250 in late 2002. International terrorist activity, including the 9/11 2001 attack on the World Trade Center in New York, disrupted international trade and travel, with negative effects on business and consumer confidence and expectations. The United States went to war, first in Afghanistan and then with Iraq. Crude oil prices rose significantly. These events would lower aggregate demand and restrict aggregate supply. Output and employment would decline without a policy response.

Monetary policy in Canada and other countries played a major stabilizing role. Interest rates were reduced to levels not seen in many years. In Canada, real overnight rates averaged just over 1 percent. This monetary policy response was sufficient to maintain aggregate demand, output, and employment at approximately full employment levels. It established an economic and policy environment in which government could begin to reverse some of the cuts made to major social programs made in the 1990s, reduce tax rates, and continue to control and reduce the public debt.

2005 to 2008

Strong economic performance continued from 2005 to the summer of 2007, before concerns about financial market problems originating in the United States sub-prime mortgage market emerged. High energy and commodity prices had already caused a substantial appreciation of the Canadian dollar relative to the U.S. dollar, shifting the strength of economic growth and performance from the central to the western provinces. A strong domestic currency combined with high oil prices and collapsing U.S. housing markets caused difficult times for Canadian manufacturers based on export markets. The full consequences of these conditions lie in the future.

Before this shift in international and domestic economic conditions, the growth and stability of economic performance and policy established in the earlier period continued. By the Bank of Canada's estimate, there was a small positive output gap and the unemployment rate continued to decline. Despite this demand pressure, and rising oil and commodity prices, an inflation rate of just over 2 percent was lower on average than in the 2000–2004 period, and very close to the Bank of Canada's target. Strong federal government finances continued the previous string of overall budget surpluses and continued to reduce the public debt ratio toward the target of 25 percent set by the Minister of Finance.

Monetary and fiscal policy contributed to this strong, stable performance. In response to the positive output gap, and its implications for rising inflation, the Bank of Canada raised its setting of the overnight interest rate, progressively, from 2.0 percent in mid 2004 to 4.25 percent by late 2007. Success with public debt and debt ratio reductions provide room for some fiscal stimulus, partly in the form of tax relief, that lowered the structural primary surplus substantially from its levels in the earlier period. This fiscal stimulus was unwarranted in terms of the strong underlying growth of the economy, the output gap, and the bank's concerns about inflation. Nevertheless the economic fundamentals were strong.

In early 2008, conditions were much more uncertain. U.S. economic performance has weakened substantially, primarily in the important consumer spending sector as a result of the financial difficulties with household mortgages and finances. Crude oil prices had risen dramatically, spreading cost increases across most sectors of the economy. Growth in Canadian exports slowed in 2007 and export sales declined absolutely in the fourth quarter of 2007 and the first quarter of 2008. Real GDP declined in the first quarter of 2008, based on initial reports. In short there was uncertainty about economic performance in the next few years.

The 2009 Recession

By early 2009, a recession was well underway. Preliminary data for Canada in Table 11.3 for the period up to the first quarter illustrate the changing state of the economy.

The slowdown in output growth which started in late 2007 persisted in the first three quarters of 2008 until the recession hit in the fourth quarter and gathered force in the first quarter of 2009. Rising output gaps accompanied the slowdown and recession in growth, ending a long run of small positive output gaps and steady economic performance. The unemployment rate rose as output growth declined until it was two percentage points higher in the first quarter of 2009 than it had been in the first quarter of 2008 and based on monthly data was continuing to rise.

Commodity prices and consumer price inflation rates were an important dimension of this economic performance. Dramatic increases in energy and other commodity prices in early 2008 contributed to a rise in the inflation rate until the third quarter of

TABLE 11.3 **Selected Economic Indicators of 2008 and 2009 (% or annual % change as indicated, quarterly seasonally adjusted data)**

	2008Q1	2008Q2	2008Q3	2008Q4	2009Q1
Real GDP %Δ	−0.5	0.6	1.0	−1.2	−6.5
Output gap %	0.9	0.6	0.2	−1.1	−3.5
Unemployment rate %	6.1	6.1	6.4	7.6	8.0
Inflation rate %	1.5	3.0	3.3	1.2	1.4
Commodity prices %Δ	52.4	92.1	−26.5	−78.8	−46.6
Overnight interest rate %	3.5	3.0	3.0	1.5	0.5

Source: Bank of Canada Banking and Financial Statistics, April 2009, Tables A1, A2, and H8, Bank of Canada, 2009; and author's calculations.

2008. Then falling demand and output precipitated a collapse in commodity prices and inflation, perhaps most evident to consumers as the decline in the pump price of gasoline by more than 50 percent. The effect on the Canadian dollar value of energy exports was severe and caused sharp cutbacks in energy exploration and development expenditures.

The government responded with monetary stimulus by mid 2008 but fiscal stimulus was delayed. Even in the fourth quarter of 2008, the federal government was reluctant to introduce significant fiscal stimulus. In its November 2008 Fiscal Statement it announced plans for balanced budgets over the following five years, starting with a small surplus in 2008–09. However, the budget of January 2009 brought fiscal stimulus with projected deficits in excess of $30 billion in 2009–10 and 2010–11.

As the data show clearly, the state of the economy and the focus of economic policy have changed dramatically.

Next

Now we have studied how aggregate expenditure and aggregate demand determine output and employment. We have also seen how monetary and fiscal policy might be used to manage aggregate demand and offset fluctuations in output, employment, and price. Chapter 12 extends this discussion by looking in more detail at international trade and finance. The design and effectiveness of monetary and fiscal policies to manage aggregate demand depend importantly on the exchange rate policy a country adopts.

SUMMARY

- **Aggregate demand (AD)** is the relationship between the general price level, and equilibrium real GDP.
- Aggregate demand integrates the explanation of **equilibrium aggregate expenditure**, the money and financial markets, monetary policy, and fiscal policy into a price/output function.
- In the *traditional approach* to aggregate demand, the central bank conducts monetary policy, using its control and setting of the **money supply** as the

policy instrument. Changes in the general price level change the real money supply and real expenditure through the monetary transmission mechanism.

- The slope and position of the aggregate demand curve describe economic conditions in the economy and the setting of economic policy. Money market conditions, the response of expenditure to changes in interest rates, and the expenditure multiplier determine the **slope of AD.** Autonomous expenditures and the expenditure multiplier determine the **position of AD.** Changes in autonomous expenditures cause business cycles by shifting the AD curve.
- **Short-run aggregate supply (AS)** defines the relationship between the economy's output (GDP) and the price level when factor prices, particularly wage rates, are constant but output prices are flexible. With constant money wage rates, the AS curve is upward sloping if labour productivity—output per worker—declines as employment and output increase, raising labour cost per unit of output.
- AD and AS determine **short-run equilibrium** real GDP and price.
- **Monetary policy** is a **demand management** tool. The central bank uses its control of the monetary base and interest rates to create AD conditions consistent with potential output and the bank's inflation target.
- **Fiscal policy** is a **demand management** tool. The Minister of Finance has both output and debt stabilization targets. Changes in fiscal policy change structural budget balances and change the slope and position of the AD curve. At times, the income stabilization and debt control objectives will conflict.
- The **mix of monetary and fiscal policy** is important to the effects they have on AD and on the structure of national income and output.
- **Indicators of monetary and fiscal policy** show that in the past 25 years, until the recession of 2009, Canadian fiscal policy was primarily concerned with control and *reduction of the public debt.* Monetary policy focused initially on meeting an *inflation target.* Once that target was achieved, the Bank of Canada worked to maintain it by setting interest rates to keep aggregate demand and real GDP close to potential output.

KEY TERMS

KEY EQUATIONS AND RELATIONS

Equations

Money market equilibrium: $\frac{M_0}{P} = L(Y, i)$ **(11.1)** p. 269

The government budget function: $BB = tY - G - iPD$ **(11.2)** p. 283

The government primary budget function: $PBB = tY - G$ **(11.3)** p. 283

The government structural primary budget function: $SPBB = tY_P - G$ **(11.4)** p. 283

Structural primary, cyclical, and debt interest in the budget function:

$$BB = SPBB_0 + t_0(Y - Y_P) - iPD$$ **(11.5)** p. 284

The change in the public debt: $\Delta PD = -BB$ (11.6) p. 285

Central bank monetary policy function: $M = M_0 - \gamma(Y - Y_P)$ (11.7) p. 287

Relations

Aggregate demand AD: A change in the price level has interest rate, wealth, and substitution effects that change aggregate expenditure and equilibrium real GDP.

$$\Delta P \rightarrow \Delta M/P \rightarrow \Delta i + \Delta \text{wealth} + \Delta \text{relative prices} \rightarrow \Delta AE \rightarrow \Delta Y$$

Aggregate demand: $\frac{\Delta Y}{\Delta P} < 0$

Short run aggregate supply AS: With fixed money wage rates, a fall in labour productivity as employment and output increase raises labour cost per unit of output and increases prices.

$$\Delta Y \rightarrow \Delta N \rightarrow \Delta(Y/N) \rightarrow \Delta(wN/Y) \rightarrow \Delta P$$

Short run aggregate supply: $\frac{\Delta Y}{\Delta P} > 0$

Short-run equilibrium: Short-run equilibrium real GDP and price are determined by AD = AS.

Business cycles: Short-run fluctuations in AD and AS cause recessionary and inflationary gaps.

AD shocks: $\uparrow A \rightarrow \uparrow AE \rightarrow \uparrow AD \rightarrow \uparrow Y + \uparrow P$

$\downarrow A \rightarrow \downarrow AE \rightarrow \downarrow AD \rightarrow \downarrow Y + \downarrow P$

AS Shocks: $\uparrow$costs or indirect taxes $\rightarrow \uparrow P \rightarrow \downarrow Y$

$\downarrow$costs or indirect taxes $\rightarrow \downarrow P \rightarrow \uparrow Y$

Fiscal policy: Changes in government budget balance to change AD and stabilize Y at Y_P.

$Y < Y_P \rightarrow \uparrow G \text{ or } \downarrow t \rightarrow \uparrow AD \rightarrow \uparrow Y \rightarrow Y_P$

$Y > Y_P \rightarrow \downarrow G \text{ or } \uparrow t \rightarrow \downarrow AD \rightarrow \downarrow Y \rightarrow Y_P$

Automatic fiscal stabilization from the net tax system: $T = tY$

$\Delta Y \rightarrow \Delta T \rightarrow \downarrow \text{multiplier} \rightarrow \downarrow \Delta Y$

Monetary policy: Sets i and M to manage AD and stabilize Y at Y_P and longer term π at π^*.

If $Y \neq Y_P$ then $\Delta i \rightarrow \Delta Y \rightarrow Y_P$

If $\pi \neq \pi^*$ then $\Delta i \rightarrow \Delta Y \rightarrow \pi = \pi^*$ at Y_P

REVIEW QUESTIONS

Review Questions and answers are included in Connect at www.mcgrawhillconnect.ca.

1. Define aggregate demand and explain the difference between an aggregate demand function and an aggregate expenditure function.
2. From national accounts: GDP at market price by expenditure ≡ GDP by incomes plus capital consumption and net indirect taxes.

$$P(C + I + G + X - Z) \equiv W + BI + CCA + T_{IN}$$

Using this national accounting identity, explain why an increase in the general price level (P) does not make goods and services more expensive relative to money incomes in the economy.

3. Suppose the central bank conducts monetary policy by controlling the nominal money supply.
   a. Use a money-market diagram to show how changes in the general price level (P) would affect the equilibrium interest rate.
   b. Use a 45°-line diagram to show how changes in expenditure caused by the changes in interest rates in (a) would change equilibrium real GDP.
   c. Combining the results from parts (a) and (b), construct an AD curve that shows combinations of real GDP and the general price level when autonomous expenditures and money supply are constant.

4. Under what demand for money conditions and interest rate/expenditure conditions would changes in the general price level cause large changes in aggregate expenditure and equilibrium real GDP? Illustrate these conditions in diagrams.

5. Do you agree that a flatter AE curve (a lower value for the slope) would result in a steeper AD curve? Explain why.

6. Consider a numerical example of an AD curve when the central bank sets the money supply:

   $AE = 100 + 0.5Y + 0.2(M/P)$ and

   $M = 500$

   where AE is planned aggregate expenditure, Y is real GDP, M is the nominal money supply, and P is the general price level.
   a. Suppose the nominal money supply M = 500. Find and write the AE function for each of the price levels 1.0, 2.0, and 2.5.
   b. Explain why a change in the price level changes planned aggregate expenditure.
   c. Based on the equilibrium condition Y = AE, what is the equilibrium level of planned expenditure at each price level? Plot these combinations of P and Y in a diagram and draw the AD curve.
   d. Suppose an increase in investment increased autonomous expenditure by 25. Plot the new AD curve in your diagram.

7. Consider a numerical example of a short run aggregate supply curve (AS) for an economy in which producers are price setters as follows:

   $P = 100 + 1.5 \times W/(Y/N)$.

   Assume the money wage rate W = \$1000, and labour productivity (Y/N) declines as employment and output increase according to:

   $Y/N = 200 - 10N$.

   This gives the following values: Y = 360, Y/N = 180; Y = 640, Y/N = 160; Y = 840, Y/N = 140.
   a. Calculate the price level P for each income level given, and plot the resulting AS curve in a diagram.
   b. Explain the reason for the change in the price level as real output Y increases and the economy moves along the AS curve.
   c. Suppose the money wage rate increased by 10 percent from \$1000 to \$1100. Recalculate the price levels for incomes of Y = 360, 640 and 840 and plot this AS curve in the same diagram used in part (a).
   d. What effect does a change in money wage rates have on the AS curve? Why?

8. When short run AD/AS equilibrium is disrupted, the patterns of change in real GDP and the price level PGDP indicate whether the source of the disruption is a demand shock or a supply shock. Do you agree or disagree? Use a diagram to illustrate and explain your answer.

9. An economy has the following aggregate demand and short-run aggregate supply conditions:

   AD: $Y = 1000 - 30P$

   AS: $Y = 500P - 6950$
   a. Plot the AD and AS functions in a diagram.
   b. What are the equilibrium values for real GDP and the price level?
   c. If potential output is $Y_P = 650$, what type of output gap, if any, do you observe?
   d. Suppose research reveals that the aggregate expenditure function underlying the AD curve has a slope $[c(1 - t) - z] = 0.5$. What change, if any, in the expenditure component of fiscal policy would be needed to eliminate any observed output gap?

10. Draw an AD/AS diagram to illustrate an economy in short run equilibrium at potential output Y_P.

a. Using your diagram illustrate and explain the effect of a fall in international demand for the economy's manufactured exports. What type of output gap, if any, is caused by the fall in exports?
b. Use a government budget function to show how the output gap affects the government's budget balance.
c. Illustrate the difference, if any, between the actual budget balance and the structural budget balance in a diagram.
d. If the Finance Minister's fiscal policy objective is equilibrium at potential output, what fiscal policy changes would you recommend?
e. Suppose your recommendation is accepted and implemented and eliminates the recessionary gap. Show the new budget function that includes your policy recommendation, and show the actual and structural balances that result.

11. Draw an AD/AS diagram to illustrate an economy in short run equilibrium at potential output Y_P.
   a. Using your diagram illustrate the effect of an increase in international energy and commodity prices that raises costs of production and distribution across the economy. What sort of output gap, if any, is caused by the increase in energy and commodity prices?
   b. How do the changes in equilibrium real GDP and the price level in this case differ from the changes observed in question 9, above?
   c. Can a change in fiscal or monetary policy restore equilibrium at Y_P at the price level P_0 that existed before the change in energy and commodity prices? Explain why or why not.

12. Suppose the government's total budget balance this year, including its interest payments on the public debt, is zero (BB = 0).
   a. If the public debt this year is $100 billion, how much will the debt be next year?
   b. If the economy experiences a recessionary gap next year, and no fiscal policy changes are made, will the government's budget balance next year be zero, positive, or negative? Explain why and illustrate with a diagram of the budget function.
   c. Will the public debt the following year be equal to, less than, or greater than $100 billion?
   d. Suppose the government makes a change in the budget designed to stabilize the public debt at the level you predict in (c). What change in the budget is required?
   e. How will the change in the budget needed to stabilize the public debt affect AD and the recessionary gap?

13. Suppose the central bank uses the money supply as its policy instrument. It finds, based on its research, that planned autonomous investment and exports have increased and are expected to stay at new and higher levels for the foreseeable future.
   a. Use a diagram to show the bank's setting of the money supply that supported AD conditions and short-run equilibrium at Y_p, and a constant price level before the increase in autonomous expenditure.
   b. If the increase in autonomous expenditure persists as expected, show in a diagram how short-run equilibrium conditions would be changed.
   c. What change, if any, would you expect the bank to make in its setting of the money supply in reaction to these new equilibrium conditions?
   d. If the bank did change its money supply setting, in response to this equilibrium, how would this change the AD conditions in your diagram?

14. Suppose the government, which has been operating with a balanced budget, decides to reduce the size of the outstanding public debt.
   a. What change in the government's structural budget balances would you predict?
   b. Use a diagram of the government's budget function to show the change in fiscal policy required to lower the public debt.
   c. What effect, if any, would you expect this change in fiscal policy to have on AD? Use an AD diagram to illustrate your answer.
   d. If the central bank wanted to offset the effects of the change in fiscal policy and maintain its output target Y_p, what change would it make in the setting of its money supply and interest rates? Show the effects of the change in monetary policy in your diagram.

15. *Internet* The Government of Canada has recently emphasized public debt control and reduction as goals of its budgetary and fiscal policy. To provide information, it issues a regular Debt Management Report, which is available at www.fin.gc.ca. Examine the introductory section of the most recent version of this report, and those for earlier years, and make a summary report on the effectiveness of this policy program.

16. *Internet* Most large financial institutions and investment firms issue reports based on the economic research conducted by their staff economists. One example of this range of information and content is the site provided by BMO Nesbitt Burns at: www.bmonesbittburns.com/economics/publications.asp. Visit this site and examine recent editions of the weekly publication "Focus." What are the main current topics and concerns discussed in these publications?

CHAPTER 12

The Balance of Payments, Exchange Rates, Monetary Policy, and Fiscal Policy

LEARNING OUTCOMES

By the end of this chapter you should understand:

1. The balance of payments accounts
2. The balance of payments and international indebtedness
3. The foreign exchange market
4. Flexible exchange rates and fixed exchange rates
5. Monetary and fiscal policy under flexible exchange rates
6. Monetary and fiscal policy under fixed exchange rates
7. The European Monetary System and the Euro

In 1999 the Canadian economist Robert Mundell won the Nobel Prize in Economics for his work on the importance of exchange rate policy for the effectiveness of monetary and fiscal policies as tools to manage aggregate demand. Mundell showed for a small open economy like Canada, with a high degree of international capital mobility, that:

- with *flexible* exchange rates monetary policy is a powerful demand management tool, but fiscal policy is weak, and
- with *fixed* exchange rates monetary policy is ineffective as a demand management tool, but fiscal policy is strong.

In this chapter we study the foreign exchange market, flexible and fixed exchange rates and the reasons why different exchange rate policies affect the design and effectiveness of monetary and fiscal policy.

12.1 The Balance of Payments

The **balance of payments accounts** provide the background to supply and demand in the foreign exchange market. They record transactions between residents of one country and the rest of the world that involve payments in different national currencies. Taking the Canadian economy as the domestic economy and the United States as the "rest of the world," all transactions that give rise to an inflow of U.S. dollars to Canada are entered as credits in the Canadian balance of payments. Transactions requiring payments in U.S. dollars are debits, entered with a minus sign. Table 12.1 shows the actual Canadian balance of payments accounts in 2008.

The **balance of payments accounts** record transactions between residents of one country and the rest of the world.

The **current account** of the balance of payments records international flows of goods, services, and transfer payments. The merchandise trade is exports and imports of goods, things like cars and car parts, steel, wheat, and electronic equipment. Non-merchandise trade measures exports and imports of services like travel, banking and financial services, transportation, and tourism. The total of merchandise and non-merchandise trade is the trade balance we have seen as *net exports* in our earlier study of planned expenditure and aggregate demand.

The **current account** records trade in goods, services, and transfer payments.

However, the trade balance is not the same thing as the current account of the balance of payments. There are also flows of investment income in the form of interest payments, dividends and reinvested earnings, and transfer payments between countries as a result of government programs like foreign aid, and private receipts and payments. The flows of investment income are what create the difference between GDP and GNP we saw in Chapter 4.

TABLE 12.1 The Canadian Balance of Payments, 2008 ($CDN billions)

	Exports (receipts)	Imports (payments)	Balance
1. Current account			
Merchandise Trade (goods)	489.5	442.8	46.7
Non–merchandise trade (services)	68.0	90.5	−22.5
Investment income, Transfers etc.	69.3	83.3	−14.0
			10.2
2. Capital account			
Investment:			
Foreign in Canada	89.2	—	89.2
Canada in foreign countries	—	100.1	−100.1
			−10.9
3. Statistical discrepancy			−0.6
4. Change in official international reserves			−1.6
5. Balance of payments (1 + 2 + 3 − 4)			0

Source: Bank of Canada Banking and Financial Statistics, April 2009, Tables J1 and J2, Bank of Canada, 2009.

Table 12.1 shows Canada had a trade surplus in goods in 2008, offset partly by deficits on trade in services and other transactions. Combining the trade in goods, services, and other transfers, the current account balance of the balance of payments was $10.2 billion in surplus.

A current account surplus means that a country's foreign income exceeds its foreign spending. A current account deficit would mean that its foreign spending exceeds its foreign income. These surpluses and deficits are saving and dissaving, and lead to the purchase or sale of foreign assets.

The **capital account** records purchases and sales of real and financial assets.

The capital account of the balance of payments records international purchases and sales of real and financial assets. Table 12.1 shows a net capital outflow of $11.2 billion in 2008. The payments made by Canadians buying foreign physical and financial assets exceeded the inflow of receipts from foreigners buying Canadian assets. A capital account deficit was the result.

The **change in official international reserves** is the change in the Government of Canada's foreign currency balances.

A government's holdings of foreign currencies are in its official international reserves account. These balances are like investments in foreign countries because they show the government's holdings of foreign assets. An increase in the official reserves is like a payment item in the capital account of the balance of payments. The **change in official international reserves** in Table 12.1 records the increase or decrease in the Government of Canada's holdings of foreign currency balances. Because Canada maintains a flexible exchange rate annual changes in international reserves are small. As we will see later when discussing different exchange rate policies, countries that adopt fixed exchange rates often experience large changes in their foreign currency reserves in defence of the exchange rate they have set.

The **balance of payments** is the sum of the balances in current accounts and capital accounts, minus the change in the holdings of official reserves.

The **balance of payments** is the sum of the balances in current and capital accounts minus the change in the official international reserves account. In Table 12.1, this balance is shown as the sum of accounts $(1 + 2 + 3 - 4)$. If all items in the accounts were measured correctly, the balance would be zero. To recognize this, a statistical discrepancy adjustment is made, as shown in the table, to account for any errors in the measurement of other items.

A simple numerical example helps to illustrate the Balance of Payments identity, which by definition gives total receipts minus total payments equal to zero. Suppose, measured accurately with no statistical discrepancy, the balance on current account (CA) is a deficit, a net payment of -5, and the balance on capital account (KA) is a surplus, a net receipt of $+3$. Then by addition:

Balance on current account (CA) + Balance on capital account (KA) = Change in international reserves (ΔOR).

Using the numbers in the example:

$$CA + KA = \Delta OR$$
$$-5 + 3 = -2.$$

Payments exceed receipts by 2 and are financed by a decline in official reserves.

Recognizing that the change in official reserves is a payment to cover the shortfall between receipts and payments, and putting all net payments on the left hand side of the identity gives:

$$CA + KA - \Delta OR = 0$$
$$-5 + 3 + 2 = 0.$$

Now the balance of payments is zero. Line 5 in Table 12.1 shows the balance in the balance of payments in the same way.

The balance of payments shows the net flow of money to the country when individuals, firms, and governments make the transactions they wish to make under existing market conditions. It is in surplus (deficit) when there is a net inflow (outflow) of money. It takes account of the transactions that individuals wish to make in importing and exporting and in buying and selling foreign assets, and the transactions that governments wish to make in the form of foreign aid, maintaining foreign embassies, military spending abroad, and so on.

Review Question 1

The record of the change in official reserves is always of equal magnitude to the sum of the balances on the current and capital account, if there is no statistical discrepancy in the measurements. As a result, the *balance of payments always balances,* but the state of the individual accounts underlying that overall balance needs further study.

DETERMINANTS OF THE CURRENT ACCOUNT

The exports and imports of goods and services are the largest components of the current account. As we discussed in Chapter 9, trade in goods and services is based, in part, on the price of domestic goods and services relative to foreign goods and services. Three factors determine the prices of foreign goods relative to domestic goods namely:

1. The domestic price level, P_{CDN}
2. The foreign currency price of imports, P_{US}, in the case of imports from the U.S.,
3. The **nominal exchange rate**, er, the domestic currency price of foreign currency.

The **nominal exchange rate (er)** is the domestic currency price of a unit of foreign currency.

The **real exchange rate**, which combines these three factors, measures international price competitiveness. For example, the real exchange rate between Canada and the United States would be:

The **real exchange rate** is the relative price of goods and services from different countries measured in a common currency.

$$\textbf{Real exchange rate} = \frac{er \times P_{US}}{P_{CDN}} \qquad (12.1)$$

where the nominal exchange rate **er** is the Canadian dollar price of the U.S. dollar and P_{US} and P_{CDN} are general price levels as measured, for example, by GDP deflators or consumer price indexes. It measures the price of United States goods and services in Canadian dollars *relative to* Canadian goods and services in Canadian dollars.

Consider the following example:

- The nominal exchange rate er = $1.25Cdn/$1U.S.
- The GDP deflator for Canada is 121.3, on the base year 2002.
- The GDP deflator for the U.S. is 110.4, on the base year 2002.

Then the real exchange rate, which gives the price of U.S. goods in Canadian dollars relative to the price of Canadian goods in Canadian dollars is:

$$\textbf{Real exchange rate} = \frac{er \times P_{US}}{P_{CDN}} = \frac{1.25 \times 110.4}{121.3} = 1.138$$

U.S. goods and services are about 14 percent more expensive than Canadian goods and services, on average, when both are priced in Canadian dollars.

Holding all other things constant, a rise in the real exchange rate makes imports more expensive relative to competing domestic goods and services and reduces expenditure on imports. From equation 12.1, a rise in the nominal exchange rate, or in foreign prices raises the real exchange rate and lowers imports. Conversely, a fall in the nominal exchange rate or foreign prices lowers the real exchange rate and increases imports.

Purchasing power parity (PPP) means a real exchange rate equal to one.

Purchasing power parity (PPP) describes the long run equilibrium value of the real exchange rate. That value is one. It means that nominal exchange rates adjust to the value required to make imports of goods and services equal to exports of goods and services and net exports are zero.

Although economic conditions are seldom tranquil long enough for nominal exchange rates to adjust to the values required for a real exchange rate of one, purchasing power parity is still useful for understanding changes in nominal rates over time. For example, if inflation rates differ between trading partners, purchasing power parity predicts a depreciation of the currency of the country with the higher inflation rate. In terms of equation 12.1, a rise in the domestic price level P_{CDN} relative to the foreign price level P_{US} calls for a rise in er to maintain a constant real exchange rate. Alternatively, differences in productivity growth rates among countries, by affecting the way domestic price levels change over time, call for offsetting changes in nominal exchange rates to maintain the real exchange rate.

Review Question 2

EXPORTS

Chapter 6 assumed that demand for exports was autonomous and given. We now recognize that the demand for Canadian exports depends on two things. First, since Canadian exports are imports by the rest of the world, higher income in other countries leads to higher Canadian exports. Second, the higher is the Canadian *real exchange rate,* the greater is Canadian competitiveness and export profitability, and the larger are Canadian exports.

Exports respond quickly to changes in world income, but changes in competitiveness affect exports more slowly. Exporters may be unsure if the change in competitiveness is temporary or permanent. If they believe it to be temporary, they may change their profit margins but leave the price of their goods in foreign currency unaffected. Car manufacturers do not change the U.S. dollar prices of the cars they assemble in Canada and sell in the United States with each change in the exchange rate. The profit margins on those sales vary when exchange rates change.

Even when this means losses in the short run, it may be cheaper in the long run than temporarily repricing product or withdrawing from these markets and having to spend large sums on advertising and marketing to win back market share when competitiveness improves again. But if competitiveness fails to improve and the real exchange rate remains low, firms will gradually conclude that they should quit the exporting business. These are the sorts of decisions faced by many Canadian manufacturing firms in the last few years as the strong rise in the Canadian dollar relative to the U.S. dollar (the fall in er) has lowered the real exchange rate substantially. The recession of 2009 further complicated the situation as the decline in U.S. GDP and U.S. demand for Canadian exports more than offset the improvements in competitiveness provided by the rise in the nominal and real exchange rate.

IMPORTS

The higher domestic income is, the larger will be import demand, as we recognized with the marginal propensity to import in Chapter 6 . But import demand is also larger when the real exchange rate is lower, which makes foreign goods and services cheaper relative to Canadian goods and services when both are measured in Canadian dollars. Again, in practice, imports respond more quickly to changes in domestic income than to changes in the real exchange rate. However, if sustained, a fall in the real exchange rate eventually raises imports. The costs of travel and shopping in foreign countries are reduced and foreign products are offered for sale in Canada at lower Canadian dollar prices. The experience of 2007 and early 2008, when the Canadian dollar appreciated strongly as the U.S. dollar weakened internationally illustrates this exchange rate effect on international travel and import prices.

There are three things of major importance to the balance in current account, namely:

1. Incomes at home and abroad, Y_{CDN} and Y_f,
2. Prices at home and abroad, P_{CDN} and P_f, and
3. The nominal exchange rate, er.

These can be summarized in export and import functions. For exports, we can write:

$$X = X(Y_f, P_f, P_{CDN}, er) \tag{12.2}$$

and for imports:

$$Z = Z(Y_{CDN}, P_f, P_{CDN}, er) \tag{12.3}$$

In each case, Y_{CDN} and Y_f are incomes in home and foreign countries, P_{CDN} and P_f are price levels, and er is the nominal exchange rate, the Canadian dollar price of the U.S. dollar. When we come to look at the foreign exchange market, it will be helpful to see that the incomes and prices that determine exports and imports also determine supply and demand in the foreign exchange market.

Furthermore, we can use equations (12.2) and (12.3) to derive the net export function $NX = X - Z$ we included in aggregate expenditure in Chapter 6.

By subtraction, we have:

$$NX = NX(\underset{-}{Y_{CDN}}, \underset{+}{Y_f}, \underset{+}{P_f}, \underset{-}{P_{CDN}}, \underset{+}{er}) \tag{12.4}$$

For this function, the +/− sign under each variable indicates the effect an increase in that variable would have on our net exports and our balance in current account. When we plotted the net export function in Chapter 6, we put particular emphasis on the relationship between national income and net exports. The marginal propensity to import meant that an *increase* in real GDP, Y_{CDN} in this case, *increased* Z and *reduced* NX. The net export function has a *negative slope* with respect to domestic national income, but *shifts if foreign* national income changes. That's why we have the negative sign (−) under Y_{CDN} and the positive sign (+) under Y_f in equation (12.4).

Review Questions 3, 4, 5 and 6

OTHER ITEMS IN THE CURRENT ACCOUNT

Foreign aid and spending on military bases and action abroad are matters of government policy. The net flow of interest, dividend, and profit income between countries arises because residents of one country hold assets in another. The size of this net flow of income depends on the pattern of international asset holding and on the level of interest rate, profits, and dividends at home and abroad and the currencies in which assets are denominated.

THE CAPITAL ACCOUNT

Inflows and outflows in the capital account reflect sales and purchases of foreign assets. These flows have become increasingly important. Computers and electronic communications make it as easy for a Canadian resident to buy and sell stocks and bonds in the financial markets of New York or London as in Toronto. Moreover, controls on international capital flows have gradually been dismantled with globalization and financial integration.

The world's financial markets now have two crucial features. First, capital account restrictions have been abolished for capital flows between advanced countries. Funds can move freely from one country to another in search of the highest *rate of return.* Second, trillions of dollars are internationally footloose, capable of being switched between countries and currencies when assets with similar degrees of risk are expected to offer different rates of return in different countries and currencies.

Perfect capital mobility means very small differences in expected returns cause very large international flows of funds.

This is the age of **perfect capital mobility** when small differences in expected returns trigger very large flows of funds from country to country. Indeed, the stock of international funds is now so huge that capital flows could swamp the typical current account flows from exports and imports.

In international asset markets, capital gains or losses arise not merely from changes in the domestic price of an asset, but also from changes in exchange rates while temporarily holding foreign assets. Table 12.2 provides an example. Suppose you can invest $1000 Canadian for a year. Canadian one-year interest rates are 4 percent. In the United States one-year rates are 5 percent. The higher United States rates look attractive. If you keep your funds in Canadian dollars, row 1 shows that you will have $1040 at the end of the year. Can you do better by buying a United States asset?

Row 2 shows what happens if you convert $1000CDN into U.S. dollars at an initial exchange rate of $1.03 CDN/$1U.S. You have $970.87U.S. to invest at the United States interest rate of 5 percent. You get $1019.41U.S. at the end of one year. You would be ahead *if the exchange rate remained constant.* $1019.41U.S. is $1050CDN, a return of 5 percent, as you would expect.

Suppose, however, the exchange rate changes while your funds are out of the country. Let's say the Canadian dollar appreciates by 2 percent during the year, lowering the exchange rate to $1.009CDN/$1U.S. Your $1019.41U.S. now buys $1028.50CDN. You get 1 percent more interest from holding the United States asset instead of the Canadian asset, but you suffer a capital loss of 2 percent by temporarily holding U.S. dollars, whose value relative to Canadian dollars fell by 2 percent in that year.

In this example, you end up with about $1028.50CDN if you lend in U.S. dollars. The Canadian dollar appreciated by more than 1 percent, the difference between Canadian and United States interest rates. As a result, the capital loss from the exchange

TABLE 12.2 Returns from Lending $1000 for a Year

$1000 Lent in	Interest Rate (%)		Exchange rate ($CDN/$U.S.)		Final Asset Value	
	Canada	United States	Initial	Final	$CDN	$U.S.
Canada	4.0				1040	
United States		5.0	1.03	1.009	1028.50	1019.41

rate while holding U.S. dollars outweighed the gain on interest. This was the experience of many portfolios in 2008 as the Canadian dollar appreciated strongly and the exchange rate fell. The total return on lending in U.S. dollars was lower than the return in Canadian dollars.

Conversely, if the Canadian dollar depreciated against the U.S. dollar while you were holding your United States asset, your total return would be higher than the 1 percent interest rate differential. You would get a gain on the exchange rate when you converted back to Canadian dollars. This was the experience of portfolios holding assets denominated in U.S. dollars as the Canadian dollar depreciated over the period from May 2008 to March 2009, raising the nominal exchange rate from er = 0.9994 to er = 1.2645. The exchange rate movement provided a 26.5% annual return, in terms of Canadian dollars, to portfolios holding U.S. dollar assets.

Equation 12.5 summarizes this important result. The total return on temporarily lending in a foreign currency is the interest paid on assets in that currency plus any capital gain (or minus any capital loss) arising from the depreciation (appreciation) of the domestic currency during the period.

Return on asset	=	Return on foreign asset	=	Foreign interest rate +/− % increase/% decrease in nominal exchange rate (er)

$$\textbf{Total return on foreign asset} = i_f + \%\Delta er \qquad (12.5)$$

When the *total return* expected from holding a foreign asset according to equation 12.5 is equal to the domestic rate of interest, we have the **interest parity** condition. Any interest rate differential between countries is offset by an expected change in the exchange rate.

Interest parity occurs when *expected* exchange rate changes offset interest rate differentials between countries.

With near perfect capital mobility, there is a vast capital *outflow* if the expected net return to foreign lending exceeds the total return on domestic lending. There is a huge capital inflow if the expected return on domestic lending exceeds the return on foreign lending. As a result, with no barriers to capital mobility, expected total returns are the same in assets of different currencies.

Three things determine the direction and size of the net capital flow that appears as the balance in the capital account in the balance of payments, namely: the difference between domestic and foreign interest rates, the current nominal exchange rate, and the nominal exchange rate expected in the future.

$$CF = CF\left(i - i_f, \left({}^{er^e}/_{er} - 1\right)\right) \qquad (12.6)$$

Equation (12.6) summarizes this relationship. The net capital flow depends positively on the differential between domestic and foreign nominal interest rates ($i - i_f$). A rise in domestic rates relative to foreign rates would attract a flow of funds into the domestic financial market. A fall in domestic rates would push the flow toward foreign financial markets, assuming in both cases that the exchange rate is not expected to change in an offsetting direction.

Alternatively, assuming the interest rate differential is constant, the capital flow depends negatively on the expected rate of depreciation of the domestic currency suggested by [$(er^e/er) - 1$]. An expectation that the domestic currency will depreciate (a rise in er^e) will increase the returns from holding foreign assets and lead to a net capital outflow ($CF < 0$). An expected appreciation would reduce expected returns on foreign assets. These capital flows have important effects on the supply and demand for foreign exchange on the foreign exchange market.

Review Questions 7, 8, 9 and 10

12.2 The Balance of Payments and International Indebtedness

The structure of the balance of payments matters despite the fact that the balance of payments always balances. In Table 12.1 the Canadian Balance of Payments involved a small surplus on current account and an offsetting small deficit on capital account. This capital account balance reflected larger investment by Canadians in foreign countries than by foreign countries in Canada. As a result, Canada's international indebtedness declined, as it had done in the recent past. Furthermore, from 2000 to 2008 the proportion of Canadian public debt held by non-residents declined from approximately 22 percent to 13 percent of outstanding debt.

The recent experience in other countries has been quite different. In the United States, strong economic growth until 2008 and a large government budget deficit have been accompanied by a large current account deficit in the balance of payments. The U.S. follows a flexible exchange rate policy and does not intervene through an official reserves account to offset this deficit. International capital flows from foreign sales of U.S. dollar bonds and other private capital assets, including the asset-backed commercial paper at the centre of the financial crisis in 2008–09, produce an offsetting capital account surplus. However, the result is an ongoing accumulation of U.S. assets held in foreign countries and a rise in U.S. international indebtedness. Foreign holdings of U.S. federal government bonds increased from approximately $1.0 trillion dollars or 18 percent of outstanding debt in 2000 to $2.3 trillion dollars or 25 percent of outstanding debt in 2007.

In the international context, a large current account deficit matched by a capital account surplus in the U.S. implies the opposite situation in other countries. Some must have a current account surplus, based on strong net exports of goods and services, and a capital account deficit from imports of U.S. and other foreign debt. China is the most notable example. Its current account surplus increased from 21 billion U.S.$ in 2000 to 250 billion U.S.$ in 2006, the latest year for which data are reported by the World Bank.

China has a fixed foreign exchange rate in terms of the U.S. dollar. As we will discuss in more detail below, when a country with a fixed exchange rate has a current account surplus not offset by a capital account deficit, the official reserves account must accumulate the difference. In China's case, official foreign reserve account holdings have been increasing strongly in recent years. The State Administration for Foreign Exchange, People's Republic of China, reported foreign reserve currency holdings increased from 165.6 billion U.S.$ in 2000 and 1,528 billion U.S.$ at the end of 2007.

The implications of large changes in international indebtedness like those illustrated by these recent conditions raise difficult questions for future adjustments in trade patterns and exchange rates. The decline in the international value of the U.S. dollar in recent years is one part of this adjustment. But there are larger questions about the exchange rate setting by China and the fiscal deficit in the U.S., in addition to the longer-term impacts of strong growth in the Chinese and Indian economies.

12.3 The Foreign Exchange Market

The foreign exchange market is the market in which the currencies of different countries are bought and sold and the prices of currencies, the foreign exchange rates, are established. Consider the market for U.S. dollars as foreign currency. The sources of supply and demand for foreign exchange are shown by the balance of payments in

Table 12.1. Exports of goods, services, and financial assets generate receipts in foreign currencies that are sold in the foreign exchange market for Canadian dollars. Imports of goods, services, and securities must be paid for in foreign currencies. The demand for foreign exchange is derived from this demand for imports. Without intervention by governments, demand and supply determine the exchange rate, as, for example, $er_0 = 1.16$ in Figure 12.1.

The exchange rate $er_0 = \$1.16$ is what it costs in Canadian dollars to buy each U.S. dollar you want for your winter reading week break in Florida. Alternatively, if you as an exporter of lumber to the U.S. market receive $1000U.S. for every 1000 board feet of 2x4's you sell to U.S. builders, your Canadian dollar revenue to cover your Canadian costs is $1160.

If the price of goods in U.S. markets is constant, a lower exchange rate er_1; say, $er_1 = 1.15$, *other things constant,* by lowering the price and raising the quantity of Canadian imports, must raise the demand for U.S. dollars. In Figure 12.1, the demand curve for U.S. dollars D_0 *slopes downwards.* More U.S. dollars are demanded to buy more imports at a lower CDN$/U.S.$ exchange rate.

The U.S. dollars supplied on the foreign exchange market are the receipts from the export of goods, services, and securities to U.S. residents. From our discussion of the current and capital accounts of the balance of payments, exports of goods and services depend on foreign income, the relative prices of domestic and foreign goods and services, and the exchange rate. Net exports of securities depend on the difference between domestic and foreign interest rates, for given expectations of the future exchange rate.

In Figure 12.1, the supply curve shows the quantities of U.S. dollars that would come to the market at different exchange rates, er, *all other things constant.* It slopes upward because a higher CDN$/U.S.$ exchange rate ($er > \$1.16$) *lowers* the prices of Canadian goods and services to U.S. buyers. As a result, United States residents buy more Canadian exports and total export receipts rise. The quantity of U.S. dollars

FIGURE 12.1 **The Foreign Exchange Market**

S_0 shows the supply of U.S.$ from the sale of Canadian goods, services, and securities to other countries. D_0 is the demand for U.S.$ by Canadians wishing to buy U.S. goods, services, and securities. The equilibrium exchange rate is er_0 Canadian dollars per U.S. dollar. For example, $er_0 = \$1.16$CDN. Any change in tastes, incomes, or interest rates would shift S or D or both S and D, and change the equilibrium exchange rate.

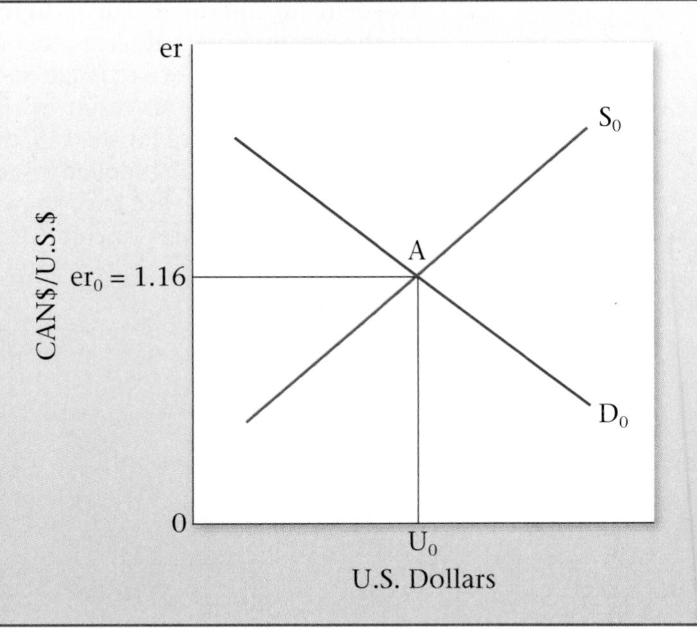

coming onto the foreign exchange market increases as we move up the supply curve. The supply curve has a *positive slope.*

Figure 12.1 assumes that the demand for Canadian exports and the Canadian demand for imports are price elastic. Price increases caused by changes in the exchange rate reduce total revenue. Price reductions caused by changes in the exchange rate increase total revenue. These conditions give the slopes shown for the supply and demand curves.

At the equilibrium exchange rate er_0, the quantities of U.S. dollars supplied and demanded are equal. In terms of the balance of payments, the balance is zero. Receipts equal payments.

In practice, as seen in Table 12.2, the balance of payments is recorded in domestic currency. However, the equality of receipts and payments still holds. Both are easily converted to Canadian dollars by multiplying the U.S. dollar amounts by the exchange rate. In terms of Figure 12.1, multiplying U_0 on the horizontal axis by the exchange rate er_0 on the vertical axis gives the area of the rectangle er_0AU_0O, the Canadian dollar value of total receipts or total payments recorded in the balance of payments.

What would change the equilibrium in Figure 12.1? A change in any of the factors we have held constant in order to draw the supply and demand curves will shift one or the other or both curves. We see this in both the net export and capital flow functions. A rise in United States income would increase U.S. imports from Canada and shift the supply of foreign exchange to the right. As we discussed in Chapter 9, a change in interest rates in Canada or the United States would change the trade in financial assets and affect both the supply curve and the demand curve. In short, a change in any market condition other than the exchange rate er will change supply and demand conditions in the market. The exchange rate will then change to a new equilibrium. Figure 12.2 and 12.3 provide examples.

THE EFFECT OF A RECESSION IN THE U.S. ECONOMY ON THE EXCHANGE RATE

The demand and supply curves in the foreign exchange market of Figure 12.2 are drawn on the assumption that tastes, incomes, prices of goods and services, interest rates, and expectations of future exchange rates are constant. The flows of payments and receipts under these conditions result in the equilibrium exchange rate er_0. This would be a Canadian dollar price for the U.S. dollar of, for example, $1.16. From the United States perspective, a Canadian dollar costs a United States resident about $0.86U.S.

Now suppose, as occurred in early 2008 and 2009, a recession in the United States lowers United States real income. United States imports fall, based on the U.S. marginal propensity to import. United States imports are Canadian exports, and the U.S. dollar receipts of Canadian exporters are reduced. The recession and difficult household financial conditions reduce U.S. residential construction and Canadian lumber exports decline. Recession also reduces travel by U.S. residents, and the Canadian tourism industry suffers a decline in bookings and receipts. If expenditures on new cars in the United States are reduced, Canadian auto industry sales to the United States market are reduced. In the balance of payments, the balance on trade in goods and services falls, and in the foreign exchange market *the supply of U.S. dollars on the market is reduced.*

Review Question 11

The supply curve in Figure 12.2 shifts leftward to S_1. At the initial exchange rate er_0, the demand for U.S. dollars exceeds the supply, putting upward pressure on the exchange rate. In terms of the balance of payments, the excess demand for U.S. dollars represents a balance of payments deficit. In the example shown here, the exchange rate rises to restore equilibrium in the foreign exchange market and the balance of payments.

FIGURE 12.2 **The Exchange Rate Effect of a Recession in the U.S.**

A recession in the U.S. reduces Canadian exports to the U.S. and reduces the supply of foreign exchange from S_0 to S_1. At the initial exchange rate er_0 there is an excess demand for U.S. dollars in the amount AB and a corresponding balance of payments deficit. As a result, the exchange rate increases to er_1. Changes in import and export revenues restore equilibrium in the market for foreign exchange and the balance of payments at C.

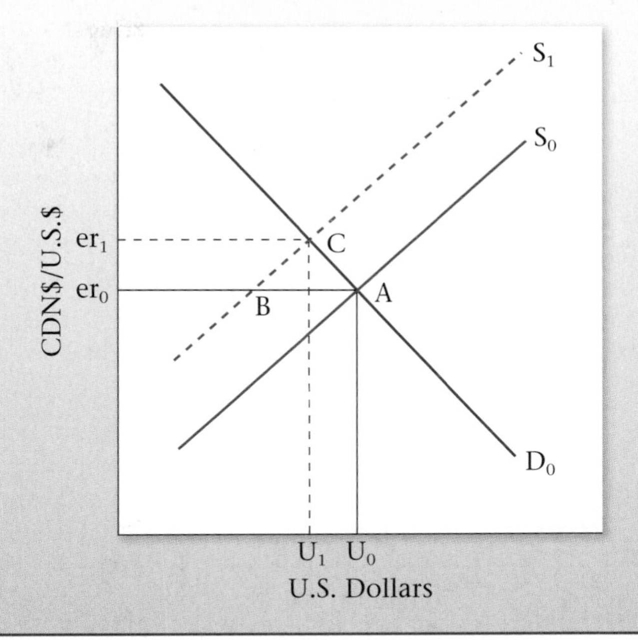

A higher price for the U.S. dollar reduces Canadian imports and increases the Canadian dollar receipts of Canadian exporters. The Canadian balance of payments effects of the U.S. recession are offset by the exchange rate change.

The rise in the exchange rate in this case is a **depreciation** of the Canadian dollar and a corresponding **appreciation** of the U.S. dollar.

The Canadian dollar **depreciates,** falls in external value, when the CDN$/U.S.$ exchange rate rises.

The Canadian dollar **appreciates,** increases in external value, when the CDN$/U.S.$ exchange rate falls.

Before the recession of 2009, Canadian experience was the opposite of this example. High GDP growth rates in the U.S. and Asia created very strong international demand for Canadian commodities and crude oil at high international prices. Strong oil and commodity exports increased the supply of foreign currencies on the Canadian foreign exchange market. The Canadian dollar *appreciated* strongly, with the exchange rate falling from $1.57CDN/$1U.S. in 2002 to an average of $0.9994 CDN/$1U.S. in May of 2008, a fall of about 60 percent over the six year period. Exchange rate changes led to a restructuring of both exports and imports to maintain equilibrium in the balance of payments as Canada's international trade changed dramatically.

THE EFFECT OF A FALL IN FOREIGN INTEREST RATES ON THE FOREIGN EXCHANGE RATE

In the previous example a change in foreign income and the supply of foreign exchange disrupted the equilibrium in the foreign exchange market and changed the exchange rate. As an alternative to that example, consider the effects of a cut in foreign interest rates.

In Figure 12.3 the foreign exchange market is in equilibrium, initially at an exchange rate er_0. A fall in foreign interest rates, other things constant, disrupts this equilibrium. Now lower foreign rates make domestic (Canadian) bonds more attractive to foreign portfolios than they were previously. The demand for domestic bonds rises. The supply of U.S. dollars on the market to pay for these bond exports increases, shifting S_0

FIGURE 12.3 **The Effect of a Cut in Foreign Interest Rates**

A cut in foreign interest rates increases the supply of U.S. dollars on the foreign exchange market and reduces the demand as domestic and foreign portfolios shift to the purchase of domestic rather than foreign bonds. The fall in the nominal exchange rate to er_1 lowers the real exchange rate and reduces net exports to offset the increased net capital flow and maintain balance of payments and exchange rate equilibrium.

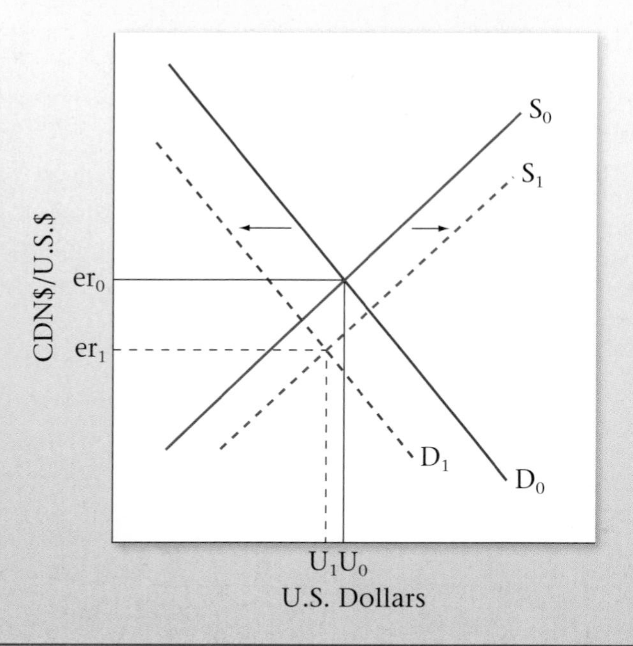

to S_1 in the diagram. At the same time, the attractiveness of foreign bonds for domestic portfolios is reduced, reducing the demand for U.S. dollars to pay for them. The demand curve shifts from D_0 to D_1. The equilibrium exchange rate falls to er_1.

In balance of payments terms the net capital inflow, the balance on capital account, is increased. The change in the exchange rate causes an offsetting change in the current account that restores equilibrium in the foreign exchange market and the balance of payments. A lower nominal exchange rate lowers the real exchange rate. Imports are now cheaper and exports, priced internationally in U.S. dollars, are less profitable. Export receipts are reduced. As we saw in Chapter 9, changes in the exchange rate are one channel by which changes in financial conditions impact AD and equilibrium GDP.

Figures 12.2 and 12.3 provide two examples of adjustments in the foreign exchange rate. The underlying assumption is that exchange rates are flexible and allow the market to adjust freely and quickly to changing circumstances. However, there are alternative exchange rate arrangements. To understand how the foreign exchange rate operates in different countries, we need to consider the different *exchange rate policies* governments can adopt. These result in different foreign exchange rate regimes, different ways that the balance of payments adjusts to change, and different roles for monetary and fiscal policies.

12.4 Flexible Exchange Rates and Fixed Exchange Rates

An **exchange rate regime** describes how exchange rates are determined.

To grasp the basics of **exchange rate regimes**, we focus on two extreme forms that have been adopted to handle international transactions in the world economy: *flexible exchange rates and fixed exchange rates.*

FLOATING OR FLEXIBLE RATES

In a **floating or flexible exchange rate** regime, the exchange rate is allowed to find its equilibrium level on the foreign exchange market *without central bank intervention.*

Supply and demand determine the equilibrium **floating** or **flexible exchange rate.**

Figures 12.2 and 12.3 showed the exchange rates that would result if rates adjusted flexibly and freely in response to changes in demand and supply. The central bank *did not intervene* to fix or adjust the rate. The rise in the demand for U.S. dollars would result in a rise in the exchange rate to clear the foreign exchange market and maintain the balance of payments. Alternatively, the fall in demand would result in a fall in the exchange rate. The Bank of Canada would not intervene in either case. The holdings of official foreign exchange reserves and the domestic money supply would not be affected by foreign exchange market adjustments.

The alternative is a fixed exchange rate. In this regime, the central bank intervenes in the foreign exchange market to offset the effects of fluctuations in supply and demand and maintain a constant exchange rate.

How do countries choose between fixed and floating exchange rates? Obviously, there is not one answer for all countries or we would not see different exchange rate regimes today. With flexible rates, the foreign exchange market sets the exchange rate, and monetary policy is available to pursue other targets. One the other hand, fixed exchange rates, which we look at next, require central bank intervention. Monetary policy is aimed at the exchange rate.

The importance a country attaches to an *independent monetary policy* is one very important factor in the choice of an exchange rate regime. Another is the size and volatility of the international trade sector of the economy. A flexible exchange rate provides some automatic adjustment and stabilization in times of change in net exports or net capital flows.

FIXED EXCHANGE RATES

In a **fixed exchange rate** regime, governments intervene actively through their central banks to maintain convertibility of their currency into other currencies at a fixed exchange rate. A currency is **convertible** if the central bank will buy or sell as much of the foreign currency as people wish to trade at a fixed exchange rate.

A **fixed exchange rate** means the exchange rate does not change as a result of changes in market conditions.

A currency is **convertible** if the central bank will buy or sell unlimited quantities at a fixed exchange rate.

In Figure 12.4, suppose the exchange rate is *fixed at* er_1 . This would be a free market equilibrium at A if the supply curve for U.S. dollars is S_1 and the demand curve for U.S. dollars is D_1. The central bank does not need to buy or sell U.S. dollars. The market is in equilibrium and clears by itself at the fixed rate.

Suppose demand for U.S. dollars shifts from D_1 to D_2. Canadians want to spend more time in Florida to escape the long, cold Canadian winter. They need more U.S. dollars to finance their expenditures in the United States. The free market equilibrium would be at B, and the exchange rate would rise if the Bank of Canada took no action. However, at a fixed exchange rate $er_{1;}$ there is an excess demand for U.S. dollars equal to AC. To peg the exchange rate, the Bank of Canada sells U.S. dollars from the **official exchange reserves** in the amount AC. The supply of U.S. dollars on the market is then the "market" supply represented by S_1 plus the amount AC supplied by the Bank of Canada. The payment the Bank receives in Canadian dollars is the amount ($er_1 \times$ AC), which *reduces the monetary base* by that amount, just like an open market sale of government bonds. The exchange rate target drives the Bank's monetary policy.

Official exchange reserves are government foreign currency holdings managed by the central bank.

What if the demand for U.S. dollars falls to D_3? The market equilibrium would be at D. At the exchange rate at er_1 there is an excess supply of U.S. dollars EA. To defend

FIGURE 12.4 **Central Bank Intervention to Fix the Exchange Rate**

Suppose the exchange rate is fixed at er_1. When demand for US dollars is D_2 there is excess demand AC. The Bank of Canada intervenes by supplying AC US dollars from *official reserve* holdings in exchange for Canadian dollars. If demand were D_3 there is an excess supply of US dollars EA, which the Bank of Canada buys with Canadian dollars and adds to foreign exchange reserves. To fix the exchange rate at er_1 the Bank must be prepared to buy or sell foreign exchange to offset any excess supply or demand at that rate.

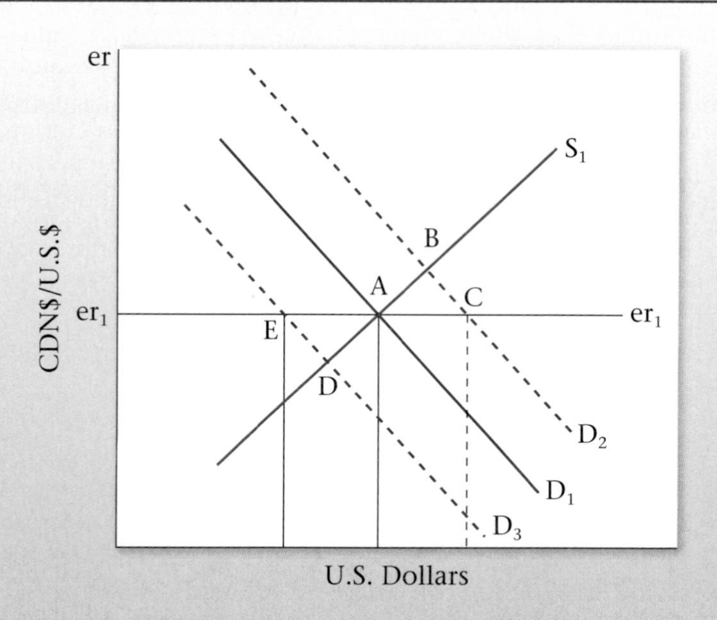

the peg, the Bank of Canada would have to buy EA U.S. dollars, reducing the supply of U.S. dollars on the market to meet the "unofficial" demand. The Bank of Canada's purchase would be added to foreign exchange reserves. The Bank would pay for these U.S. dollars by *creating more monetary base*, as in the case of an open market purchase of government securities. In either case, maintaining a fixed exchange rate requires **central bank intervention** in the foreign currency market. The central bank's monetary policy is committed to the exchange rate target.

The **central bank intervenes** by buying or selling foreign currency to fix the exchange rate.

When the demand schedule is D_2, foreign exchange reserves are running down. When the demand schedule is D_3, foreign exchange reserves are increasing. If the demand for U.S. dollars fluctuates between D_2 and D_3, the Bank of Canada can sustain and stabilize the exchange rate in the long run.

However, if the demand for U.S. dollars is, on average, D_2, the foreign exchange reserves are steadily declining to support the exchange rate er_1, and the monetary base is falling as well. In this case, the Canadian dollar is overvalued at er_1; or, in other words, er_1 is too low a price for the U.S. dollar. A higher er is required for long-run equilibrium in the foreign exchange market and the balance of payments. As reserves start to run out, the government may try to borrow foreign exchange reserves from other countries and the International Monetary Fund (IMF), an international body that exists primarily to lend to countries in short-term difficulties.

Review Question 12

At best, this is only a temporary solution. Unless the demand for U.S. dollars decreases, or the supply increases in the longer term, it is necessary to **devalue** the Canadian dollar. If a fixed exchange rate is to be maintained, the official rate must be reset at a higher domestic currency price for foreign currency.

A **devaluation (revaluation)** is a reduction (increase) in the international value of the domestic currency.

The earlier discussion of the recent rise in China's foreign exchange holdings provides a good example of the defence of an undervalued currency. With the yuan at its current fixed rate relative to U.S. dollars and other currencies, China has a large current account surplus that is not offset by a capital account deficit. Balance of payments equilibrium requires ongoing intervention by the Chinese central bank to buy foreign exchange and add to official reserve holdings. Buying foreign exchange adds to the monetary base and money supply, raising concerns about inflation. The Bank has responded in part with a small revaluation of the yuan and in part with an increase in the reserve requirements for Chinese banks. Neither of these adjustments has been sufficient to change the situation fundamentally and growth in official foreign exchange reserves continues.

Of course, it is not necessary to adopt the extreme regimes of pure or clean floating on the one hand and perfectly fixed exchange rates on the other hand. *Dirty or managed floating* is used to offset large and rapid shifts in supply or demand schedules in the short run. The intent is to smooth the adjustment as the exchange rate is gradually allowed to find its equilibrium level in response to longer-term changes.

THE CANADIAN DOLLAR, 1990 TO 2008

The Canadian government adopted a flexible exchange rate policy in 1970, after approximately 10 years of fixed exchange rates. Figure 12.5 compares nominal and real exchange rates since 1990. The *real exchange rate* measures the price of U.S. goods and services *relative to* Canadian goods and services in Canadian dollars. The United States GDP deflator (P_{GDPUS}) provides a measure of U.S. prices, and the Canadian GDP deflator (P_{GDPCAN}) provides the corresponding measure of Canadian prices. Nominal exchange rates (er) are Canadian dollar prices of the U.S. dollar. Using the same formula used earlier:

$$\textbf{The real exchange rate} = \frac{er \times P_{GDPUS}}{P_{GDPCAN}}. \qquad (12.1)$$

To make comparisons between nominal and real exchange rates easier, both are expressed and plotted as index numbers from 1990 base values of 100.

A rise in real exchange rates indicates a rise in the price of U.S. goods and services relative to Canadian goods and services, and an increase in Canadian competitiveness. The Canadian dollar appreciated strongly in the late 1980s and 1990, lowering the price of the U.S. dollar and the real exchange rate in the period before the data in the figure. A tight Canadian monetary policy was introduced in the late 1980s to fight inflation. The prospect of high interest rates for some time to come, and strong commodity prices, led to a sharp fall in the nominal exchange rate. This is the background to the movements in exchange rates seen in Figure 12.5.

From that point, we see in the figure that nominal and real exchange rates rose over the period 1991 to 1994. Success with inflation control meant that further increases in interest rates were unlikely and some decline was expected. Most of the change in the real exchange rate came from the rise in the nominal rate. However, lower inflation rates in Canada than in the United States in this period also contributed to the rise in the real rate. The *difference* between the real and nominal rates we see in Figure 12.5 comes from this difference in inflation rates. The result of the changes in nominal rates and the differential in inflation rates was an improvement in Canadian competitiveness, which contributed to the recovery from the persistent recession of the early 1990s.

After 1994, the exchange rates were stable until the foreign exchange crisis in Southeast Asia in 1997. Declines in export markets and international prices for Canadian commodity exports, and a general shift in international preference toward

FIGURE 12.5 **Canadian Nominal and Real Exchange Rates 1990 to 2009**

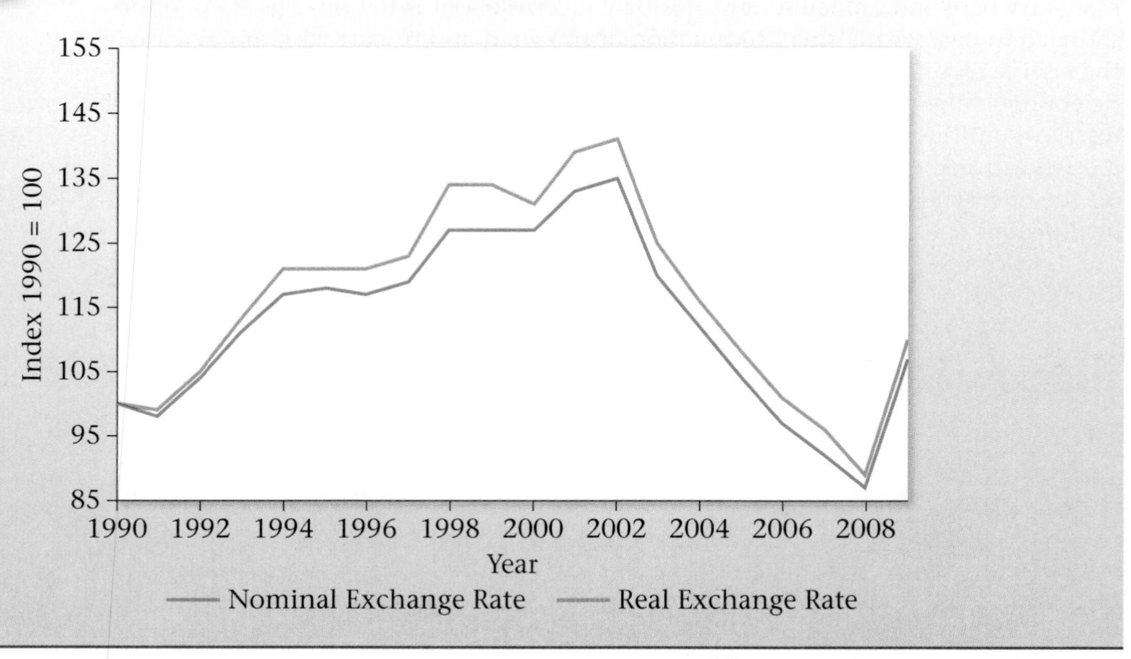

Source: Part of data is based on Statistics Canada CANSIM Database, http://cansim2.statcan.gc.ca, Table 380-0003, Series V1997759, Bank of Canada, 2009; Federal Reserve Bank of St. Louis, FRED Database; and authors' calculations.

U.S. dollar assets, resulted in a sharp rise in the nominal and real exchange rates. Once again, a higher inflation rate in the United States pushed the real exchange rate up relative to the nominal rate. Canadian competitiveness increased again and, in combination with strong growth in the U.S. economy at the end of the 1990s, led to an export boom in Canada.

In 2002 and 2003, the nominal exchange rate dropped sharply. Higher interest rates in Canada than in the United States and a further strong rise in prices and demand for Canadian commodity exports led to a strong appreciation in the currency. The Canadian dollar price of the U.S. dollar fell from about \$1.57 in the autumn of 2002 to \$1.018 on average in 2008, having been as low as \$0.999 in May 2008. The competitiveness and profitability of Canadian exports were sharply reduced, as shown by the fall in the real exchange rate from 2002 to 2007. In early 2008, Canadian exporters, especially in the manufacturing sector, were continuing to adjust to a sharp change in their competitive position and export receipts.

Overall, the period from 1990 to 2008 is unique in terms of the strong trends in exchange rates as seen in Figure 12.5. In earlier time periods, exchange rates had moved in both directions. In the 1980s, for example, the exchange rate started the decade at \$1.16, rose to \$1.39 by 1986, and then fell to \$1.19 in 1989. Although we don't have a calculation of the real exchange rate over this period, Figure 12.5 shows that movements in the nominal rates account for most of the movements in real exchange rates. International capital flows in response to international interest rate differentials and exchange rate expectations caused most of the short-term movements in nominal rates. As we have seen, the effect of monetary policy on nominal exchange rates is an important part of the monetary policy transmission mechanism. It played an important role in the Canadian fight against inflation in the early 1990s and in the export-led boom of the late 1990s.

More recently, increases in energy and commodity prices drove exchange rates lower, from 2002 until 2008. Then the financial crisis, the recession, and sharp drops in energy and commodity prices led to a rise in the exchange rate from $1.02CDN/$1.00U.S. in May 2008 to $1.27CDN/$1.00U.S. in April 2009.

Review Question 13

12.5 Monetary and Fiscal Policy with Flexible Exchange Rates

In a closed economy with slow wage and price adjustments, monetary and fiscal policies are important tools for aggregate demand management in the short run. Things are different in open economies with high international capital mobility. With flexible exchange rates, monetary policy is powerful. It works through both interest rate and exchange rate linkages in the transmission mechanism, not just the interest rate linkages of the closed economy. By contrast, the effects of fiscal policy on aggregate demand are reduced. In the absence of supporting monetary policy, fiscal expansions crowd out private sector expenditures through both interest rate and exchange rate linkages.

As we will see later, fixed exchange rates have the opposite implications for policy effectiveness. The power of fiscal policy is enhanced, but monetary policy is almost powerless. As a result, the first important step in the design of macroeconomic policy in the open economy is the choice of an exchange rate regime.

MONETARY POLICY

With flexible exchange rates, monetary policy causes changes in both interest rates and exchange rates. Equation 12.6 makes the link between the exchange rate and changes in domestic interest rates when exchange rates are flexible. Given the exchange rate expected in the long run, higher interest rates in the short to medium run cause a capital inflow, an increased supply of foreign exchange on the foreign exchange market, which lowers the exchange rate, er.

Conversely, lower domestic interest rates relative to international rates cause a rise in the exchange rate, er.

As a result, current monetary policy and expected future monetary policies have strong effects on the nominal exchange rate and the international competitiveness of the domestic economy. Changing current interest rates for a short time will have only small exchange rate effects. However, a credible change in monetary policy for a sustained period will cause a large and persistent change in current exchange rates. This can have large short-run effects on the real economy.

As we discussed briefly in Chapter 9, in an open economy with flexible exchange rates, monetary policy affects aggregate demand not just through the effects of interest rates on consumption and investment. Changing interest rates, by changing the exchange rate, also change the international competitiveness of exports and imports. Net exports change in the same direction as domestic expenditure, increasing the impact of interest changes on aggregate demand. Lower interest rates boost domestic expenditure, raise the exchange rate, and increase net exports. Higher interest rates reduce domestic expenditure, lower the exchange rate, and reduce net exports. With linkages through both domestic and international components of expenditure, monetary policy is more powerful under flexible exchange rates than in a closed economy.

Canada and a number of other countries conduct monetary policy in terms of a target for the domestic inflation rate. A flexible exchange rate policy is essential for the monetary policy independence and power required to pursue that target. Application Box 12.1 provides more detail on the Bank of Canada's approach to monetary policy.

APPLICATION BOX 12.1

Bank of Canada Monetary Policy

The Bank of Canada's monetary policy is designed and implemented within a flexible exchange rate framework. On its Web site www.bankofcanada.ca, the Bank provides the following description of its monetary policy and its effects on demand and inflation.

A. The framework:

Canada's monetary policy is built on a framework consisting of two key components:

1. Flexible exchange rate
2. Inflation rate target

B. The transmission mechanism: A chain of consequences

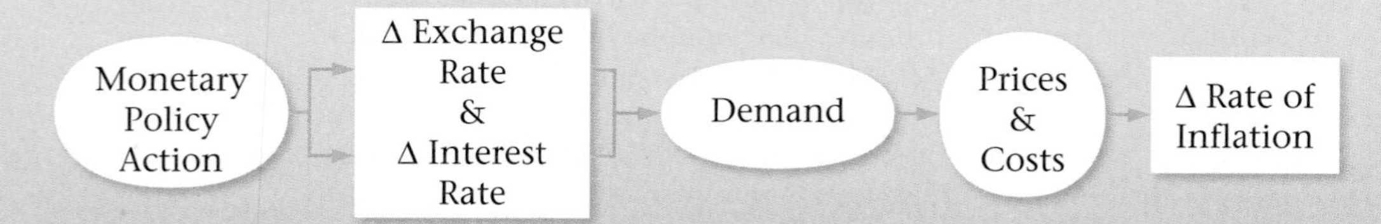

Interest rates and exchange rates are the key linkages between monetary policy actions, aggregate demand and inflation rate targets. If you follow the Monetary Policy link on the Bank of Canada's Web page you will find a more extensive discussion of how monetary policy works under the flexible exchange rate regime.

Source: www.bankofcanada.ca/en/monetary/monetary_main.html. Bank of Canada, 2009.

FISCAL POLICY

With flexible exchange rates, but without monetary policy accommodation or support, the effect of interest rate changes on exchange rates and competitiveness *undermines* the power of fiscal policy to manage aggregate demand.

Suppose the government undertakes a fiscal expansion, raising government expenditures or lowering taxes or some combination of the two. Aggregate demand increases. When monetary policy targets an inflation rate based on either an interest rate rule or a money supply rule, the expansion in demand caused by fiscal policy changes the economic conditions on which the central bank's policy had been set and induces the bank to raise interest rates. The higher interest rates cause a net capital inflow and an increased supply of foreign exchange on the foreign exchange market, and the nominal exchange rate falls. A fall in the nominal foreign exchange rate lowers the real exchange rate. International price competitiveness as measured by the real exchange rate is reduced and net exports fall. Monetary policy dominates fiscal policy.

Recent Canadian experience provides an example. In the 2005-to-2007 period, the federal government provided fiscal stimulus through tax cuts and expenditure increases. The primary structural budget balance fell from an average 3.4 percent of potential GDP for 2002 to 2004 to 2.6 percent for 2005 to 2007. At the same time the Bank of Canada's estimates showed the economy operating with a small but persistent inflationary gap. The inflation rate was in the upper level of the Bank's target range. The Bank responded to strong current and expected demand, coming from both the government and private sector, by raising its overnight rate in steps from 2.5 percent in late 2005 to 4.5 percent by mid-2007 to defend its inflation target. The inflationary gap and inflation were contained as higher interest rates and lower exchange rates limited the growth of aggregate demand, including that coming from fiscal stimulus.

In a closed economy, fiscal expansions that push up interest rates cause partial **crowding out** of private expenditure by reducing consumption and investment. In an open economy with flexible exchange rates the crowding out mechanism is stronger. Fiscal expansion causes both a rise in interest rates and a fall in the exchange rate. Both domestic expenditure and net exports are reduced. The extended crowding out through the change in exchange rates and net exports when exchange rates are flexible reduces the power of fiscal policy to manage aggregate demand in the short run.

However, if control or reduction of the debt ratio is the prime target of fiscal policy, the flexible exchange rate is helpful. If the government raises tax rates or cuts expenditures to raise its structural budget balance and reduce the debt ratio, lower interest rates and a rising exchange rate provide some offsetting "crowding in" through both domestic expenditure and net exports. The limited aggregate demand effects of fiscal policy under flexible exchange rates facilitate control of the government's budget balance and debt ratio.

Review Question 14

POLICY CO-ORDINATION

This analysis of the policy implications of flexible rate regimes leads to a clear recommendation for policy co-ordination. Flexible exchange rates provide the framework for effective monetary policy focused on a medium term inflation target. The exchange rate regime enhances the power of monetary policy to moderate business cycle fluctuations and the output gaps they create. Stabilizing the economy at or close to potential output avoids the cumulative inflationary or recessionary pressures that would push inflation rates away for the monetary policy target. Monetary policy is then the demand management tool.

Fiscal policy is not an effective demand management tool when exchange rates are flexible. Its impacts on aggregate demand are limited by crowding out and dominated by monetary policy. However, this does enhance the power of fiscal policy to pursue deficit control and debt ratio control. The effects of fiscal restraint aimed at improved public finances are moderated by a monetary policy focused on an inflation target in a flexible exchange rate regime.

The Canadian experience with economic policy and performance described in Chapter 11 (in particular, Table 11.2) provides an excellent example of this sort of coordinated policy. Starting in 1995 the federal government introduced a policy of strong fiscal adjustment through restraint aimed at reducing the public debt-to-GDP ratio. The structural primary budget balance was increased through expenditure cuts and tax increases. At the same time, monetary policy was aimed at maintaining inflation within the 1–3 percent target band, which required monetary stimulus. The nominal and real overnight interest rate was reduced. Economic growth recovered from the recession of the early 1990s to eliminate the recessionary gap and, in the process, lowered the unemployment rate from more than 9 percent to less than 7 percent. A combination of fiscal restraint and monetary stimulus moved the economy to potential output with stable inflation and a falling ratio of public debt to GDP.

Policy responses to the recession of 2009 also involved strong policy co-ordination, both domestic and international. Monetary policy was the first line response, with central banks in most industrial countries lowering their interest rate to or close to the zero lower bound. Some countries, like the U.S., then went further to provide quantitative and credit easing through general and selective open market operations. Fiscal stimulus added to these highly accommodative monetary conditions. Central bank commitments, like those in both the U.S. and Canada to maintain policy rates at their minimum for periods as long as a year or more eliminated concerns about fiscal crowding out.

Co-ordinating the focus of both monetary policy and fiscal policy was designed to stimulate aggregate demand and restore growth in real GDP. In a time of deep recession, high indebtedness, and high uncertainty even very low interest rates won't induce households and business to take on more debt to build more houses or factories. There is already an excess supply of productive capacity and housing. Monetary conditions can support an expansion in expenditure but cannot trigger it.

Fiscal policy, by contrast, can add directly to expenditure and aggregate demand, especially expenditure on infrastructure, education, research, and similar public investments. Tax cuts are likely to have smaller expenditure effects if only because the recipients have marginal propensities to spend that are less than one. Nonetheless, there is an important debate about whether expenditure increases or tax cuts should be used for fiscal stimulus, and which will have the larger and more desirable effect.

With this policy coordination there is no cause for concern about crowding out. Central banks were not concerned about the effects of increased aggregate demand on inflation rates and their inflation targets. Quite the opposite, like the Bank of Canada they hoped to raise inflation to their target. Fiscal expansion will not induce higher interest rates or lower exchange rates.

12.6 Monetary and Fiscal Policy under Fixed Exchange Rates

MONETARY POLICY

If a country adopts a fixed exchange rate policy, *the exchange rate is the target of monetary policy*. Monetary policy cannot pursue an inflation target or an output target at the same time as it pursues an exchange rate target. Nor can it set either interest rates or money supply growth rates independently.

With a fixed exchange rate, interest rates must be set as needed to maintain the exchange rate when capital mobility is high. Indeed, the higher international capital mobility is, the less is the scope for independent monetary policy. This is what we mean when we say fixed exchange rates eliminate monetary policy sovereignty. The central bank cannot follow an independent monetary policy.

FISCAL POLICY WITH FIXED EXCHANGE RATES

A fixed exchange rate and perfect capital mobility undermine the scope for monetary policy, but maintain the effectiveness of fiscal policy.

In a closed economy, in the short run, fiscal expansion raises output. Under a Taylor rule, *as long as output is less than potential output*, the central bank supports the increase in output by maintaining interest rates and increasing the money supply as output expands. However, at outputs equal to or greater than potential output, central banks raise interest rates to crowd out the effect of fiscal expansion.

In an open economy with fixed exchange rates, monetary policy adjusts passively to keep the interest rate fixed in order to defend the exchange rate. Interest rates do not change to support fiscal policy or moderate the effect of fiscal policy. Hence, any fall in domestic demand can be offset by a fiscal expansion to help restore potential output. If the change in domestic demand is the only reason that the current account balance departed from equilibrium, this fiscal expansion will also restore the current account balance.

Review Question 8

APPLICATION BOX 12.2

Robert Mundell's Model

Robert Mundell's innovative contribution to open economy macroeconomics came initially from his analysis of the controversy over monetary policy and exchange rates in Canada in the late 1950s. He was the first person to realize that international capital mobility and the choice of exchange rate regimes had powerful implications for the effectiveness of monetary and fiscal policies. He subsequently showed what it would be like for a small open economy to try to hang on to monetary policy sovereignty when international capital mobility was high. Openness in product and factor markets may create powerful pressures for monetary unions.

The diagrams below show an economy with a fixed exchange rate. On the left, the money market has an interest rate set to match the foreign interest rate i*. The money supply function is horizontal at this interest rate, and the real money supply is determined by the demand for money. There is inflation in the economy, with the result that the fixed real money supply we see in the diagram means that the growth rate of the nominal money supply equals the rate of inflation.

On the right, aggregate demand and supply show an economy in equilibrium at potential output Y_p and an inflation rate π_0. With a fixed exchange rate, interest rates cannot be set to target domestic inflation according to a Taylor rule, with the result that the price elasticity in AD comes from the effect of inflation on real exchange rates and net exports.

Any attempt to change domestic interest rates from i* causes an immediate capital inflow or outflow until money supply and interest rates are restored to M_0 and i*. For a small open economy with a fixed exchange rate, monetary policy is powerless. It cannot change aggregate demand.

A fiscal expansion shifts AD to AD_1, raising real output to Y_1, inflation to π_1 and the demand for money to L_1. Since interest rates cannot rise to dampen the expansion, monetary policy is forced to create additional money supply to accommodate the extra demand for money when output and inflation rise. Fiscal policy has strong short-run effects on output because there is no crowding out through interest rate and exchange rate changes. However, if the economy starts at potential output, as in this illustration, the fiscal expansion creates an inflationary gap. Rising domestic prices reduce competitiveness, net exports, and output. If this takes too long to adjust the economy to potential output at π_0, a shift to fiscal restraint must shift AD back to AD_0.

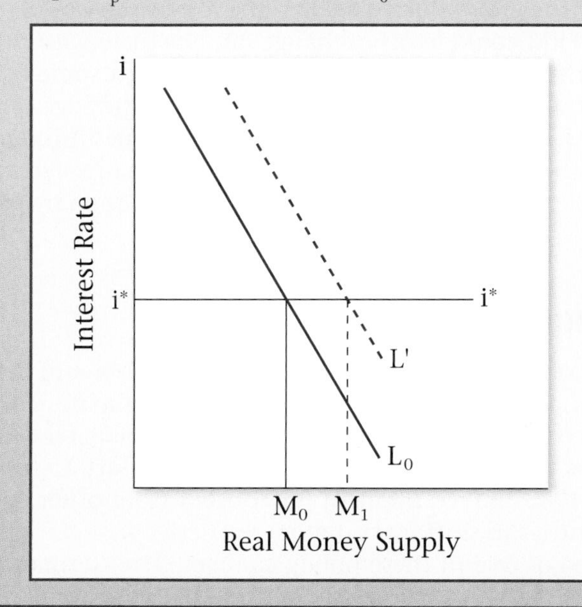

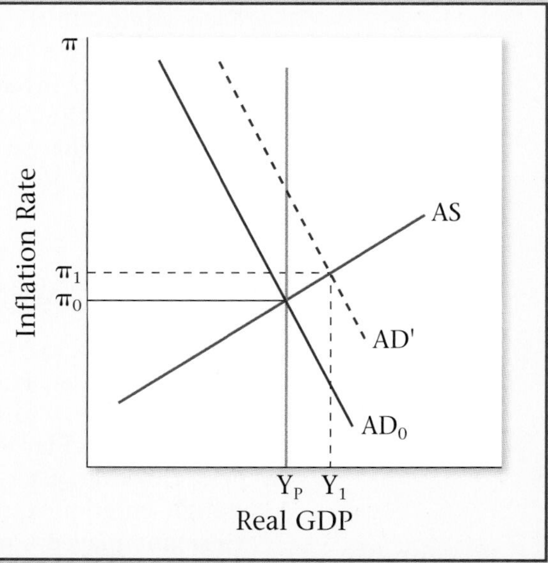

Fiscal policy is potentially an important stabilization policy under fixed exchange rates. It helps to compensate for the fact that monetary policy can no longer be used. Automatic fiscal stabilizers play this role. Discretionary changes in government spending or taxes are useful only if fiscal policy can react quickly to temporary shocks. In some political systems, such as in Canada this is feasible. In others such as in the United States, where Congress and the President may be from different parties and budget decisions are more protracted, rapid changes in fiscal policy are more difficult.

In times of prolonged recession, discretionary fiscal policy can contribute importantly to a return to potential output. With interest rates tied to the exchange rate, financing a fiscal expansion does not push rates up to crowd out private sector expenditure; nor does the recovery of the economy result in rising rates. Indeed, fiscal policy is the only effective domestic demand management tool available.

Review Question 15

12.7 The European Monetary System and the Euro

The evolution of exchange rate policy that resulted in the adoption of the euro bank notes and coins in January 2002 illustrates the links between exchange rate policy, domestic policy co-ordination, and international policy co-ordination.

In 1979, members of the European Community set up the European Monetary System (EMS), a system of monetary and exchange rate co-operation in Western Europe. This system had three aspects. First, it established a European Currency Unit (ECU) made up of a weighted blend of different national currencies as a unit of account for transactions among EU governments. This ECU eventually became the euro.

Second, member governments agreed to lend each other foreign exchange reserves. The purpose was to make central banks more important relative to speculators. This was to provide the central banks with access to sufficient reserves to offset speculation against individual currencies. Unfortunately, it did not really work because the funds controlled by speculators were also growing rapidly.

Third, the Exchange Rate Mechanism (ERM) set a fixed nominal exchange rate for each country against each of the other ERM countries. Exchange rates were fixed within the ERM, but collectively the group floated against the rest of the world.

Each country in the ERM could let its exchange rate fluctuate within a band of +/−2.25 percent of the parities it had agreed to defend, although some countries were later allowed a somewhat wider band. When the currency hit the edge of the band, all central banks in the ERM countries were supposed to intervene in foreign exchange markets to try to defend the parity. Realignments of fixed exchange rates against partner countries were possible, but had to be unanimously agreed upon by participants of the ERM.

THE ERM IN PRACTICE

Did the fixed rates of ERM provide effective policy co-ordination and financial discipline? At the outset, France and Italy were high inflation countries compared with Germany. Were they forced into policy convergence? Not immediately, as old policies continued and regular exchange rate realignments were necessary to fix up competitiveness. However, after 1983 the requirement for consent from other countries pressured high inflation countries to shift toward more restrictive monetary policies.

Germany played a major role in these policy changes. The German central bank (the Bundesbank) set interest rates that protected price stability in Germany. Starting in the mid-1980s, Germany made it harder for high inflation countries to get regular devaluations. Without them, high inflation countries had to reduce inflation or face trend deteriorations in their competitiveness. They chose austerity and disinflation.

This European experience provides an excellent example of the way fixed exchange rates force countries to co-ordinate and give up monetary policy sovereignty. Germany set interest rates as required for German economic conditions. Other ERM countries adopted German interest rates in order to keep exchange rates pegged within the ERM. The credibility of these policies was enhanced because Germany might block any devaluation needed if inflationary policies re-emerged.

FROM THE ERM TO THE EURO

The longer-term survival of the ERM was based on a convergence of national policies on low inflation. But the shorter-term survival was a result of two key features of the system.

First, with a band of +/−2.25 percent, there were periods in which national exchange rates were effectively floating. High inflation countries could start with exchange rates at the bottom of the band that gradually depreciated towards the top, just as if they were floating. This would accommodate a significantly higher inflation rate for some time. Then, as they approached the top of the band, devaluation followed, moving the band up, and the inflation differential could continue.

Second, most countries initially had controls preventing big capital account flows. These allowed fixed nominal exchange rate parties to co-exist with interest rate differentials because capital could not move freely between countries. However, after 1987, countries committed to a removal of capital controls, and then highly mobile capital required that all countries have the same interest rate. Germany set the single interest rate from then on.

This policy co-ordination did not prevent further exchange rate crises. After a period of five years without any currency realignments, several exchange rates appeared overvalued. Agreement could not be reached, and a period of intense speculation followed, eventually forcing some countries out of the ERM while others devalued but remained inside.

Nevertheless, during this period, the Maastricht treaty was signed in 1991. The heart of this treaty was the creation of a single European currency, the euro. This common currency would facilitate trade and financial transactions among European countries by eliminating foreign exchange transactions. It would also give Europe as an entity a single currency for international transactions and a potentially larger role in international finance. In 2008, the euro was the currency of 15 EU countries: Austria, Belgium, Germany, Greece, Spain, France, Ireland, Italy, Luxembourg, the Netherlands, Portugal, Finland, Greece, Slovenia, Cyprus and Malta.

A common currency required co-ordination of national monetary and fiscal policies. The Maastricht treaty set price stability as a key goal for monetary policy and imposed restrictions on fiscal policies. Targets for government budget deficits were set at 3 percent of GDP, together with a gross public debt ratio target of 60 percent.

A common currency also required a single central bank. The European Central Bank was established to conduct monetary policy for the euro countries. It operates very much the same way any other central bank would. The ECB's monetary policy objective is to maintain price stability. To this end, it aims at inflation rates of below, but close to, 2 percent over the medium term. As the sole issuer of banknotes and bank reserves in the euro area, it is the monopoly supplier of the monetary base. This allows ECB to manage the liquidity situation in the money market and influence money market interest rates.

This recent evolution from a set of national currencies through a period of fixed exchange rates to a common currency in Europe provides an interesting example of the way different exchange rates operate and the implications of adopting a common currency.

Review Question 16

Next

This chapter extended the discussion of short-run macroeconomic performance and policy by covering in more detail the importance of international trade, capital flows, and exchange rates for the design and co-ordination of monetary and fiscal policies. The next step in the analysis of the macro economy drops the assumption that the equilibrium price level is constant to examine two topics: the inflation rate and the economy's adjustment over time from short-run equilibrium to long-run equilibrium at potential output with a stable, positive inflation rate.

SUMMARY

- The **balance of payments** records transactions between residents of one country and the rest of the world. The **current account** shows the trade balance plus net international transfer payments, which are largely income earned on holdings of foreign assets. The **capital account** shows net purchases and sales of foreign assets. The balance of payments is the sum of the current and capital account balances.
- The trade in goods and services recorded in the current account is **net exports**, based on tastes, incomes, and the real exchange rate, which measures the price of foreign goods and services relative to the price of domestic goods and services.
- The **trade in financial assets** recorded in the capital account is based on the total return expected from holding foreign rather than domestic assets.
- The total return on holdings of foreign assets depends on the interest rate differential between countries and the change in the exchange rate during the period in which assets are held. **Perfect international capital mobility** means that an enormous quantity of funds shifts between currencies when the perceived rate of return differs across currencies.
- The **interest parity** condition says that, when capital mobility is perfect, the interest rate differential across countries should be offset by expected exchange rate changes, so that the total expected return is equated across currencies.
- The **foreign exchange market** is the market in which currencies of different countries are bought and sold and foreign exchange rates are established. The **exchange rate** is the price at which one currency trades for another. It can be expressed either as the domestic currency price of foreign currency or as the foreign currency price of domestic currency.
- The **demand for foreign currency** on the foreign exchange market arises from imports of goods and services and purchases of foreign assets. The **supply of foreign currency** on the foreign exchange market arises from exports of goods and services and sales of domestic assets to foreigners.
- Under a **fixed exchange rate regime**, a balance of payments surplus or deficit must be matched by an offsetting quantity of **official financing**. The central bank intervenes in the foreign exchange market to offset any excess demand or supply of foreign exchange at the fixed rate.
- Intervention reduces **foreign currency reserves** when there is excess demand in the market and increases reserves when there is an excess supply.

- Under **floating or flexible exchange rates**, supply and demand in the foreign exchange market change the exchange rate as necessary for a current account balance that offsets a capital account balance. As a result, the balance of payments is zero and no official intervention is involved.
- The **choice between fixed and floating exchange rate regimes** reflects a country's assessment of the importance of an independent monetary policy, the volatility and robustness of flexible rates in the face of nominal and real shocks, and the financial discipline that may come with fixed rates.
- **Flexible exchange rates** increase the effectiveness of monetary policy as a tool to manage aggregate demand in pursuit of inflation and stabilization targets. The effectiveness of fiscal policy for demand management is reduced, but pursuit of deficit and debt ratio control may be enhanced.
- Monetary policy sovereignty is lost when **fixed exchange rates** are adopted. Monetary policy cannot effectively pursue domestic inflation or output targets. However, the effectiveness of fiscal policy as a demand management tool is enhanced.
- The **European Monetary System** provides a recent example of requirements for international policy co-ordination that led eventually to a common currency, the euro, and to the European Central Bank.

KEY TERMS

Balance of payments accounts *301*
Current account *301*
Capital account *302*
Change in official international reserves *302*
Balance of payments *302*
Nominal exchange rate *303*
Real exchange rate *303*
Purchasing power parity *304*
Perfect capital mobility *306*
Interest parity *307*
Depreciates *312*
Appreciates *312*
Exchange rate regime *312*
Floating exchange rate *313*
Flexible exchange rate *313*
Fixed exchange rate *313*
Convertible currency *313*
Official exchange reserves *313*
Central bank intervention *314*
Devaluation *314*
Revaluation *314*

KEY EQUATIONS AND RELATIONS

Equations

Real exchange rate $= \dfrac{er \times P_{US}}{P_{CDN}}$	**(12.1)**	p. 303
Export function: $X = X(Y_f, P_f, P_{CDN}, er)$	**(12.2)**	p. 305
Import funtion: $Z = Z(Y_{CDN}, P_f, P_{CDN}, er)$	**(12.3)**	p. 305
Net export function: $NX = NX(\underset{-}{Y_{CDN}}, \underset{+}{Y_f}, \underset{+}{P_f}, \underset{-}{P_{CDN}}, \underset{+}{er})$	**(12.4)**	p. 305
Total return on foreign asset $= i_f + \% \Delta er$	**(12.5)**	p. 307
Net capital flow function: $CF = CF\left(i - i_f, \left({}^{er^e}/_{er} - 1\right)\right)$	**(12.6)**	p. 307

Relations

Balance of payments equilibrium: Current account + capital account − Δ official reserves ≡ 0

Receipts and payments recorded in balance of payments → supply and demand in foreign exchange markets

Interest rate parity condition:

Domestic interest rate = foreign interest rate + expected rate of exchange-rate depreciation

Flexible exchange rates → independent domestic monetary policy

Fixed exchange rates → loss of monetary policy sovereignty → international policy co-ordination

A common currency → policy co-ordination + supranational central bank

REVIEW QUESTIONS

Review Questions and answers are included in Connect at www.mcgrawhillconnect.ca.

1. Suppose a country has a current account surplus of $20 billion, but a capital account deficit of $18 billion.
   a. Is its balance of payments in deficit or surplus? Why?
   b. What change in official exchange reserves would you see? Why?
   c. Is the central bank buying or selling foreign currency?
   d. What effect does the central bank's foreign currency purchase or sale have on the monetary base? Explain why.

2. Suppose the initial exchange rate is $1.20CDN for $1.00U.S. After 10 years, the United States price level has risen from 100 to 200, and the Canadian price level has risen from 100 to 175. Which country experienced the higher inflation rate? What nominal exchange rate would preserve the initial real exchange rate? Which currency depreciated?

3. What are the main determinants of a country's exports?

4. In the year 2000, Canadian exports of goods and services, measured in constant 2002 dollars, were $487.9 billion. In 2001, exports declined to $473.5 billion, then further to $468.4 billion in 2003. Based on the determinants of exports you identified in question 2, how would you explain the decline in Canadian exports?

5. What are the main determinants of a country's imports?

6. How would you explain the rise in Canada's imports from $446 billion 2002 dollars in 2003 to $545 billion in 2006?

7. Suppose portfolio managers shift some of the assets under their control out of Canadian government securities and into United States government securities. Explain how this portfolio shift would affect the capital account of the Canadian balance of payments.

8. Suppose Canadian interest rates rise by 1 percent and United States interest rates are unchanged. If nothing else changes, what effect would this change in Canadian interest rates have on capital flows between Canada and the United States?

9. Explain the "interest parity condition." If Canadian interest rates are higher than United States interest rates, what changes would you predict in the international value of the Canadian dollar? Explain why.

10. Suppose natural gas and crude oil prices were to drop sharply and expectations were they would remain low. What would you predict would happen to the Canadian exchange rate? Base on your prediction, would you hold your financial wealth in Canadian dollars or U.S. dollars? Explain why.

11. Using a diagram, illustrate and explain, in terms of the balance of payments and the determinants of exports, imports, and capital flows:
    a. The sources of the demand for foreign exchange and the demand curve for foreign exchange.
    b. The sources of the supply of foreign exchange and the supply curve for foreign exchange.
    c. The equilibrium exchange rate.

12. Draw a foreign exchange market diagram. In your diagram, show equilibrium with a flexible or floating exchange rate. Now, suppose the country shown in your diagrams experiences a sharp decline in world demand for its exports.
    a. How does the decline in exports affect the foreign exchange rate?
    b. How do exports and imports change to give balance of payments equilibrium at the new equilibrium exchange rate?
    c. What are the effects on the holdings of official reserves? Explain why.

13. Draw a foreign exchange market diagram to show equilibrium with a fixed exchange rate.
    a. How does the decline in exports affect the current account balance and conditions in the foreign exchange market when the exchange rate is fixed?
    b. In your diagram show the amount of the purchase or sale of foreign exchange reserves required if the central bank defends the fixed exchange rate.
    c. What are the effects on the holdings of official reserves and the monetary base?

14. Why do economists argue that monetary policy is more powerful and fiscal policy is weak when a country has a flexible exchange rate regime?

15. Illustrate and explain why the choice of a fixed exchange rate makes fiscal policy a more powerful tool for demand management. What happens to the domestic money supply when the government increases its expenditures on goods and services?

16. If floating exchange rates are so great, why did 15 EU countries join a monetary union from 1999 and 2008, and why do some economists advocate a fixed exchange rate or even a monetary union between Canada and the United States?

17. Why are the following statements wrong?
    a. Countries with lower inflation rates gain international competitiveness.
    b. Floating exchange rates make sure that exports and imports always balance.
    c. Fixed exchange rate regimes prevent necessary changes in competitiveness.
    d. Canadian interest rates are high. This means the Canadian dollar will appreciate for the next few months.

18. *Internet* Visit the Bank of Canada's Web site at www.bankofcanada.ca/en/exchange.htm and follow the link to the *Summary, CDN$/U.S.$ closing*. Compare the latest closing exchange rate to the closing rates in the past 12 months, and to the historic high and low values. Has the Canadian dollar appreciated or depreciated over the past 12 months? How does the dollar stand in the most recent report compared with its historic range since 1949?

19. *Internet* Visit the Department of Finance Web site, www.fin.gc.ca, and select the link to the Media Room and News Releases. Examine the changes reported in Canada's International Reserves as reported for the past three months. What do the reported changes in reserves mean for the state of the combined balances on current and capital accounts of the balance of payments in those months? What pressures on the Canadian dollar exchange rate do these changes suggest?

CHAPTER 13

Aggregate Supply, Inflation, and Adjustments to Shocks

LEARNING OUTCOMES

By the end of this chapter you should understand:

1. Aggregate supply and potential output
2. Inflation and aggregate demand
3. The equilibrium inflation rate
4. Labour markets and wage rates
5. The Phillips curve and money wage rate changes
6. Wages rates and short-run aggregate supply
7. The adjustment from short-run equilibrium to potential output
8. The effects of shifts in aggregate supply
9. The role of monetary policy

Why worry about inflation? The inflation rate in Canada over the last 15 years has averaged just about 2.2 percent a year. Indeed, in the recession of 2009, the recessionary gap resulted in inflation close to zero percent for a year or so, leaving prices of goods and services in 2010 about the same on average as in 2009. Inflation does not seem to be a matter of great importance.

However, the Bank of Canada and most other central banks make the control of inflation the prime target of their monetary policies. They set *inflation rate targets* and adjust their monetary policy instruments—short-term interest rates—to achieve those targets over the medium term.

The importance of inflation and policies to control inflation comes from the effects of compounding over time. An inflation rate like the annual 2.2 percent in Canada means that goods and services that cost consumers $100 in 1994 cost about $139 in 2009. If inflation is maintained at about 2.2 percent a year, and you accept a job today at an annual salary of $45,000, about the average annual earnings in Canada in early 2009, 20 years later your annual income would need to be about $70,000, just to give you the same purchasing power you had in 2009. If you hope that your standard of living will increase over time, say by a modest 1.0 percent a year, your annual salary after 20 years would have to be about $85,000. Even low inflation rates have large cumulative effects over time.

Alternatively, if starting in 2009 your income were constant at $45,000 over a period of 20 years and annual inflation averaged 2.2 percent, your purchasing power would decline to the equivalent of about $29,000. Your standard of living would be reduced by about one third. This is the unhappy experience of those on fixed incomes or pensions even when inflation rates are quite low.

To bring inflation into our study we derive an aggregate demand relationship between the inflation rate and equilibrium aggregate expenditure. This aggregate demand function, together with the long-run aggregate supply defined by potential output, determines the equilibrium inflation rate. In the short run, fluctuations in both aggregate demand and aggregate supply cause short-run changes in output and inflation. A more detailed examination of short-run aggregate supply uncovers the economy's potential to adjust to offset these economic shocks.

To bring inflation into our study of the economy, we now turn to the aggregate supply side of the economy in more detail and derive an aggregate demand relationship between the inflation rate and equilibrium aggregate expenditure. Aggregate demand and aggregate supply together determine equilibrium output and the inflation rate.

13.1 Aggregate Supply and Potential Output

To study aggregate supply, we find it useful to work with different time horizons. The short run is a time period in which *factor prices*, like money wage rates paid to labour, are *fixed*, and output prices are sticky and slow to change. The positively sloped short-run aggregate supply curves in Chapter 11, showing the supply side relationship between *price* and real GDP, were built on the assumption that money wage rates and other factor prices were constant and prices were slow to change.

Over longer time periods, wages and prices become increasingly flexible. When there is sufficient time, *fully flexible wages and prices* adjust to give equilibrium in all markets, and the economy operates at *potential output*, Y_P. This longer-term flexibility in wages and prices is fundamental to the economy's internal capacity to adjust and to eliminate output gaps. Then, in long-run equilibrium, employment is provided to all who wish to work at the equilibrium wage rate, capital equipment is employed to full efficiency, and production is based on the best available technology.

Over a still longer time period, the size of the labour force changes, investment results in changes in the factories and equipment, which are the physical capital stock, and human skills and knowledge and technology advance to improve the efficiency of production processes. These changes produce *growth in potential output* as the economy's capacity to produce goods and services increases.

We will examine economic growth in the next chapter, Chapter 14. Our focus in this chapter is on *output, inflation, and the economy's adjustment* to equilibrium at Y_P, potential output, through changes in wage rates and other factor prices, when wage rates and prices are flexible and changing over time.

No matter what time frame we use, the economy's output depends on the level of technology, the quantities of factor inputs (labour, capital, land, energy, entrepreneurship) to production, and the efficiency with which resources and technology are used. A simple **production function** defines the relationship between outputs and labour and capital inputs to production as follows:

The **production function** determines output based on technology and inputs of labour and capital.

$$Y = A \times F(N, K) \tag{13.1}$$

In this equation, Y is real GDP, **A** is the state of technology, and **N** and **K** are inputs of labour and capital, respectively, used in the production process.

The notation **F**(. . .) tells us that the size of output as measured by real GDP depends on the amount of labour and capital used in the production process. More labour and more capital used means more output. An improvement in technology would make **A** larger, and increase the output produced by any given amount of labour and capital employed. This would be an increase in **productivity**.

Productivity is output per unit of input.

Potential output is determined by the current state of technology, A_0, the current stock of capital, K_0, and the *equilibrium* level of employment, N_F. In terms of the simple production function, this means:

$$Y_P = A_0 \times F(N_F, K_0)$$

The short-run fluctuations in output we studied in earlier chapters are linked to differences between actual labour input **N** and the "full employment" labour input N_F. Unemployment rates fluctuate as a result of these changes in output and employment.

Money illusion is the confusion of nominal (money) and real variables.

If wages and prices are flexible, how does inflation, a continuous rise in the price level (and a corresponding increase in money wage rates), affect the incentives producers have to supply more goods and services? The answer depends on the state of **money illusion**, the confusion of nominal (money) and real variables.

The **real wage rate** is the quantity of goods and services the money wage rate will buy.

Thinking in *real terms*, producers compare the **real wage rate** (the money wage rate w divided by the price level P) with the real output of another unit of labour employed. Similarly, workers compare real take-home pay (the purchasing power of their money wage in terms of goods and services) with the disutility of sacrificing more leisure to work more. If wage rates and output prices both double, real wage rates are unaffected. Neither producers nor workers would change their behaviour. In the absence of money illusion, aggregate supply is unaffected by pure inflation, since everything nominal, measured in money terms, rises in the same proportion.

FIGURE 13.1 **The Vertical LAS Schedule at Potential Output**

With flexible wages and prices, aggregate supply equals potential output, whatever the inflation rate. The LAS curve is vertical. In the long run economic growth raises potential output from Y_{p0} to Y_{p1}. The LAS shifts to the right from LAS_0 to LAS_1.

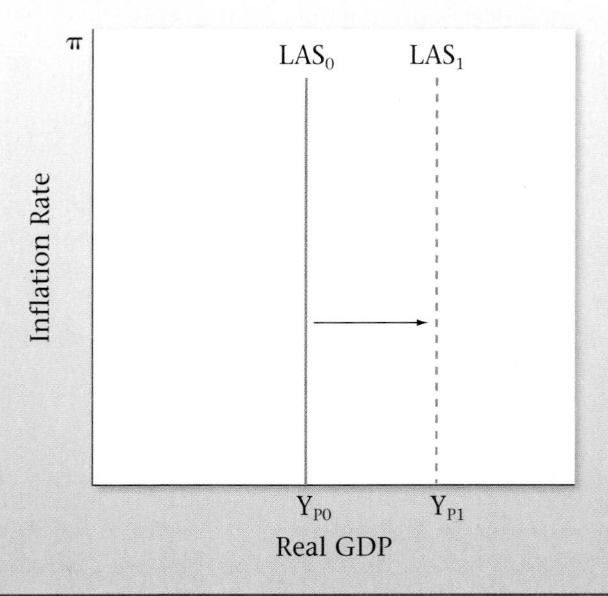

With enough time for flexibility in wages and prices, and in the absence of money illusion, the long-run aggregate supply curve, LAS, is vertical at potential output, as shown in Figure 13.1. Equilibrium output is independent of the inflation rate, which is measured on the vertical axis.

Review Question 1

Better technology, more capital, or greater labour supply raise potential output, shifting the vertical LAS curve from LAS_0 to LAS_1 in Figure 13.1. This is economic growth, a topic we take up in the next chapter. For now, the key observation is that, for any given level of potential output, changes in the general price level or the inflation rate do not have any permanent effect on the real output producers want to supply.

13.2 Inflation and Aggregate Demand

The aggregate demand curve comes from the monetary policy of the central bank. In Chapter 11, the aggregate demand curve was derived from changes in the general *price level* relative to a *fixed money supply* set by central bank monetary policy. Changes in the general price level changed the real money supply, causing changes in interest rates and asset prices. These worked through the monetary transmission mechanism to change equilibrium aggregate expenditure and move the economy along an AD curve. That is the traditional approach to AD in a price level–output model.

When central banks set *interest rates* to control the *inflation rate* based on an inflation rate target, the derivation of the AD curve is based on this alternative monetary policy. The link between the inflation rate and aggregate expenditure still comes through interest rates and the monetary transmission mechanism. The effects of changes in the inflation rate on interest rates come directly from monetary policy reactions rather than passing first through the money market. The basic mechanics of the model are not different, but using this approach to monetary policy and the inflation rate adds to the realism of the analysis.

Simple forms of this aggregate demand model are based on two familiar relationships. The first relationship is the monetary transmission mechanism as in the traditional approach to AD. Aggregate expenditure is determined by autonomous expenditure, expenditure that is sensitive to interest rates, and a multiplier. However, when the model includes inflation, the distinction between the nominal and the **real interest** (r) rate is important (see Application Box 9.2 in Chapter 9).

The **real interest rate** is the nominal interest rate minus the rate of inflation

The real interest rate is the nominal interest rate minus the rate of inflation:

$$r = i - \pi \quad (13.2)$$

It measures the cost of borrowing or the return to lending in terms of the quantities of goods and services that can be bought in the future. Suppose you borrow $1000 today at an annual nominal (market) interest rate of 5 percent when the annual inflation rate is 2 percent. You pay $1050 ($1000 × 1.05) to retire the loan one year from today. The nominal cost of borrowing is $50. But the $1050 you pay to retire the loan one year from today buys only about $1030 ($1050/1.02) worth of goods and services. The real cost in terms of goods and services is $30. The real interest rate is 3 percent.

Alternatively, a one-year bond priced to give a nominal annual yield of 1.5 percent provides a real annual yield of – 0.5 percent if the inflation rate is 2 percent. At the end of one year the buyer of the bond receives $101.50 for each $100 paid to purchase the bond, but it costs $102 to buy what $100 bought one year earlier. The real interest rate is negative. It is not attractive to lend but it is to borrow.

When inflation is included in the model, the real interest rate differs from the nominal rate and it is the real interest rate that affects expenditure decisions. The expenditure part of the model has two basic relationships, which are familiar from earlier chapters. The first is the aggregate expenditure function:

$$AE = A_0 - vr + [c(1 - t) - z]Y \quad (13.3)$$

where A_0 is autonomous expenditure, v measures the impact of a change in the real interest rate, **r**, on expenditure, and $[c(1 - t) - z]$ is the marginal propensity to spend. Using the equilibrium expenditure condition $Y = AE$ gives:

$$Y = A_0 - vr + [c(1 - t) - z]Y$$

$$Y = \frac{A_0 - vr}{1 - c(1 - t) + z} \quad (13.4)$$

In a basic 45° diagram, $(A_0 - vr)$ is the vertical intercept of the aggregate expenditure line, $[c(1 - t) - z]$ is its slope, and $1/[1 - c(1 - t) + z]$ is the multiplier. This relationship is the same as the one we saw in the traditional approach to AD, but with the real interest rate explicitly included in the expenditure function.

The second relationship is between inflation and the real interest rate based on the monetary policy of the central bank. The central bank sets an inflation rate target based on actual output at potential output, and reacts to an increase in the inflation rate by raising short-term interest rates, like the overnight rate in Canada or the federal funds rate in the United States, by enough to raise real interest rates. This gives

$$r = r_0 + \beta(\pi - \pi^*) \quad (13.5)$$

where r is the real interest rate, π is the inflation rate, π^* is the central bank's inflation rate target, and β is a positive parameter that measures the central bank's response to a change in the inflation rate. The monetary policy objective is to keep inflation from rising or falling farther and ultimately to bring it back to the target value π^*.

If equilibrium expenditure output, equation (13.4), and the central bank policy reaction function, equation (13.5), are combined, the result is an aggregate demand curve,

$$Y = \frac{A_0 - v[r_0 + \beta(\pi - \pi^*)]}{1 - c(1 - t) + z} \quad (13.6)$$

This aggregate demand curve differs from the traditional P, Y aggregate demand curve by relating real output and inflation, π and Y. It is consistent with current observations that central banks implement monetary policy by setting interest rates, not money supply. Similarly, positive inflation rates describe current experience better than the zero inflation rates that underlie the traditional approach to aggregate demand.

A numerical example illustrates this AD curve. Suppose

$$AE = 200 + 0.5Y - 10r$$

and the central bank has an inflation target $\pi^* = 1.0$ percent. The bank thinks a real interest rate of 2.0 percent is needed for equilibrium at potential output. It sets interest rates as:

$$r = 2.0 + 1.5(\pi - 1)$$

Then,

$$AE = 200 + 0.5Y - 10[2.0 + 1.5(\pi - 1.0)]$$
$$AE = 195 - 15\pi + 0.5Y$$

and using the equilibrium condition Y = AE gives the AD curve:

$$Y = \frac{195 - 15\pi}{(1 - 0.5)} = 390 - 30\pi$$

The aggregate demand curve AD_π gives the negative relationship between the inflation rate and equilibrium real GDP. When the inflation rate is equal to the monetary policy target of 1 percent, the equilibrium level of real GDP and demand is 360. If the inflation rate were to rise to 1.5 percent, which exceeds the target, the bank's reaction would be to raise real interest rates. This would lower equilibrium aggregate expenditure and real GDP to 345, moving up along the AD_π curve. A fall in inflation from the target would bring the opposite reaction.

Figure 13.2 gives a diagrammatic illustration of the derivation of the AD_π curve. Monetary policy is described by a Taylor type rule or reaction function as presented earlier in Chapter 10, with the central bank inflation target and the interest rate as the policy instrument. The bank reacts to fluctuations in the inflation rate with offsetting changes in the interest rate. The interest rate changes alter equilibrium expenditure through the monetary transmission mechanism. The result is a negatively sloped AD curve in π, Y space.

Changes in the inflation rate, other things constant, move the economy along the AD function.

Changes in autonomous expenditures *not* caused by changes in interest rates (ΔA_0), like changes in autonomous consumption, investment, exports, or government expenditure would shift the AD function by amounts driven by the multiplier. Similarly, a change in monetary policy made by changing r_0, in response to a change in economic fundamentals would shift the AD function. The recession of 2009 brought a sharp drop in Canadian exports and a shift in AD to the left. The Bank of Canada lowered its setting for the overnight interest rate in steps from 4.75 percent to 0.25 percent to offset some of this drop in AD.

Review Question 2

13.3 The Equilibrium Inflation Rate

When wages and prices are flexible, and there is no money illusion, Figure 13.3 shows the aggregate demand curve AD_0 and the vertical long-run aggregate supply curve LAS_0. Output is at potential output, and the *inflation rate*, π_0^*, is determined by aggregate demand. At point A there is equilibrium in all markets: for output, money, and labour.

The labour market is in equilibrium anywhere on the LAS line, since the economy is at potential output and full employment. Point A is also on the aggregate demand curve, which reflects autonomous expenditure, fiscal policy, and the monetary policy of the central bank. Aggregate demand for goods and services equals the actual output of goods and services.

WHAT DETERMINES THE INFLATION RATE?

From the diagram, we can see that the equilibrium inflation rate π_0^* reflects the position of the AD and LAS curves. We have already discussed the conditions that

FIGURE 13.2 **The Aggregate Demand Curve with Inflation**

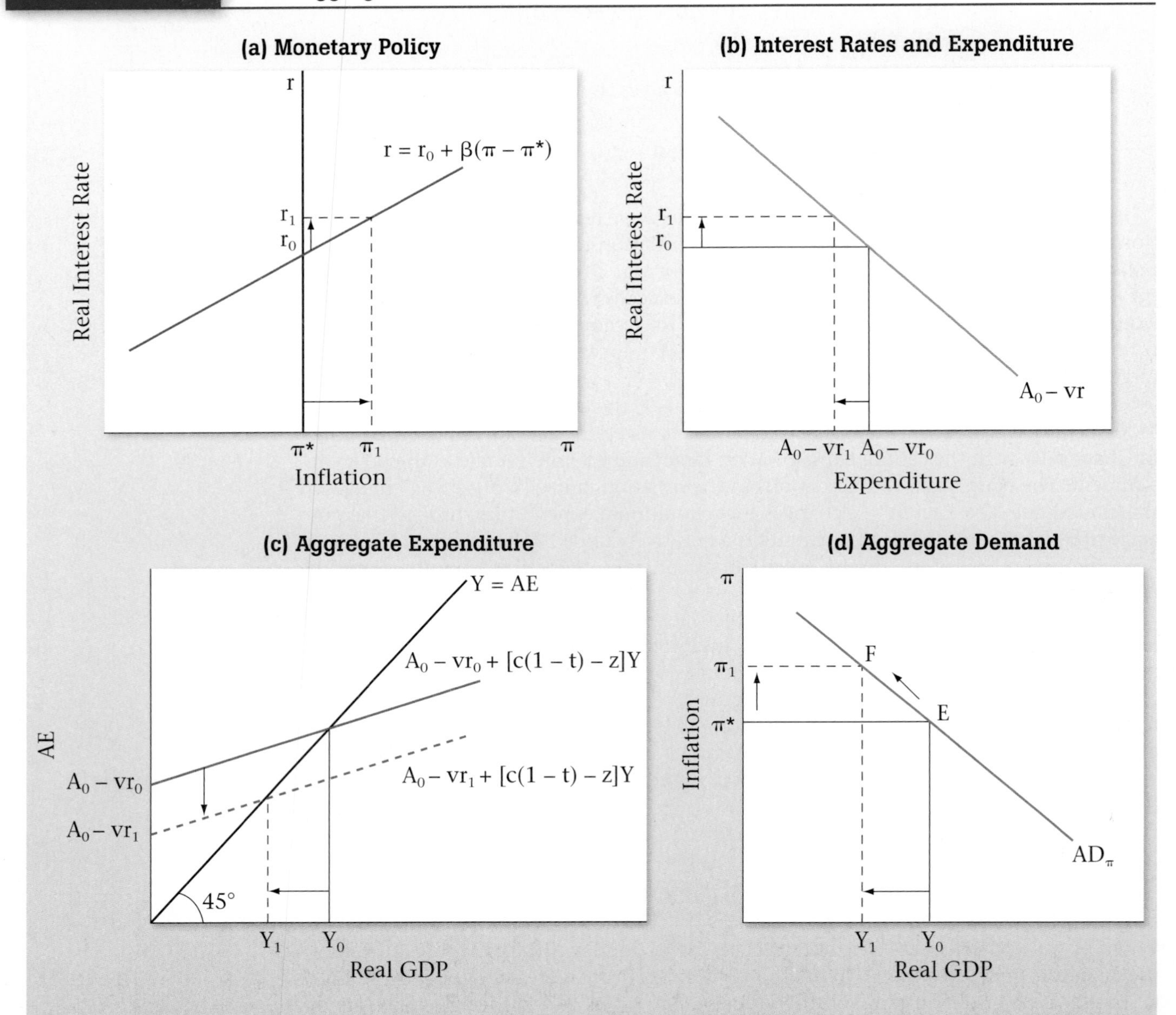

The AD_π curve shows all equilibrium combinations of real GDP and inflation for one set of economic conditions. Starting in panel (a), with the inflation rate at the bank's target π^*, the real interest rate is r_0, by the bank's monetary policy rule. In panel (b) with r_0, planned autonomous expenditure is $A_0 - vr_0$. In panel (c), autonomous expenditure $A_0 - vr_0$ and the multiplier, given the marginal propensities to consume and import and the marginal tax rate, equilibrium aggregate expenditure is Y_0. Point E in Panel (d) plots the equilibrium combination π^*, Y_0. This is one point on the AD curve.

Suppose the inflation rate increases from π^* to π_1, all other conditions hold constant. The central bank reacts in panel (a) by raising its interest rate to r_1. The higher real interest rate reduces expenditure in panel (b), which reduces equilibrium aggregate expenditure in panel (c) to Y_1 to give a second equilibrium combination π_1, Y_1 plotted at point F in panel (d). A change in the inflation rate, all other things constant, moves the economy along the AD curve.

FIGURE 13.3 **The Equilibrium Inflation Rate**

With potential output at LAS_0 and aggregate demand AD_0, equilibrium is at point A with an inflation rate π_0* and real output Y_P. Different AD conditions as with AD_1 give a different equilibrium inflation rate. At point B output is still Y_P, but the inflation rate is zero.

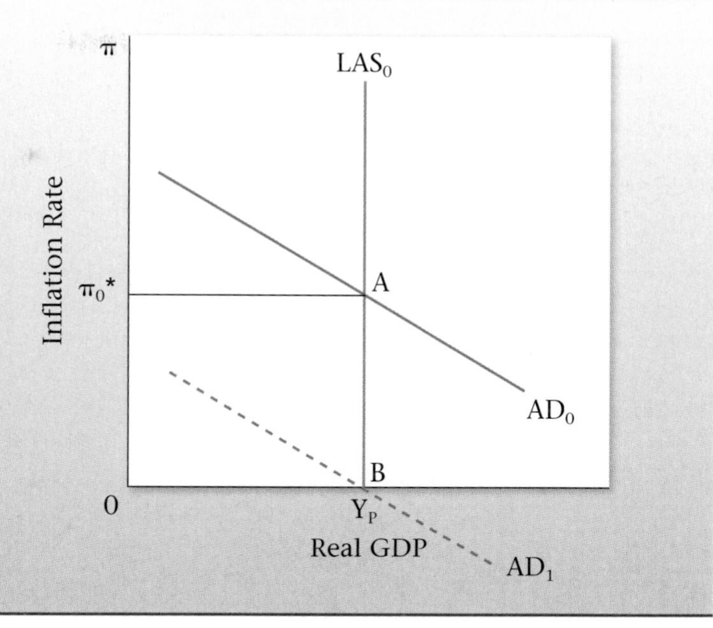

determine LAS at Y_P. The position of the AD curve reflects the interest rate and money supply set by the monetary policy of the central bank.

If monetary policy is directed to a constant equilibrium price level, as seen in previous chapters, the equilibrium inflation rate is zero. This is shown in Figure 13.3 by the aggregate demand curve AD_1. Point B shows equilibrium at output Y_P and the inflation rate $\pi = 0$.

However, central banks don't set zero inflation targets for monetary policy. As we have seen, some, including the Bank of Canada, set explicit low inflation rate targets. Others, including the United States Federal Reserve, work to implicit inflation rate targets that are also positive and low. There has been and still is a lot of discussion among economists about the appropriate level of the inflation rate target. The Bank of Canada's 2 percent target represents a current consensus on the issue.

The AD_0 curve in Figure 13.3 is based on a monetary policy inflation target of π_0*. In setting its inflation target, the central bank recognizes that *money is neutral* when wages and prices are flexible and there is no money illusion. This means that the central bank cannot influence potential output, but it can determine the equilibrium inflation rate. It sets the interest rate and accepts growth in the money supply consistent with its inflation target. A rate of inflation, $(P_t - P_{t-1})/P_{t-1}$, greater than zero means the rate of growth of the money supply, $(M_t - M_{t-1})/M_{t-1}$, is greater than zero. This puts the AD curve at AD_0, and keeps it there as inflation raises the price level at the target rate.

A Demand Shock

The aggregate demand curve reflects aggregate expenditure plans, including the effects of interest rates on expenditure. Suppose aggregate expenditure increases as a result of an increase in autonomous exports or investment or government expenditures. Figure 13.4 shows what happens.

FIGURE 13.4 **Equilibrium Inflation and a Demand Shock**

A rise in aggregate demand from AD_0 to AD_2 violates the central bank's inflation target. The central bank reacts by raising its interest rate and reducing money supply sufficiently to raise real interest rates and shift AD back to AD_0.

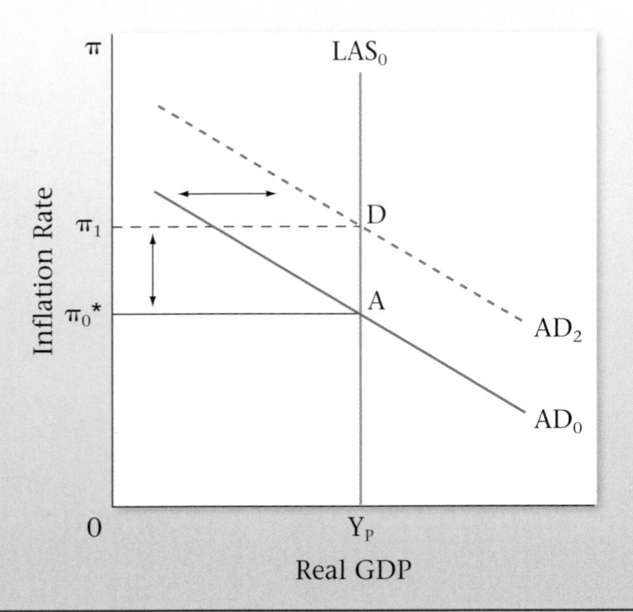

Beginning from equilibrium at A and keeping supply fixed at Y_P and LAS_0, a shift in AD from AD_0 to AD_2 appears to lead to a new equilibrium at point D. But we must think about how monetary policy responds.

Facing a permanent demand change but no change in potential output, the central bank can continue to hit its inflation target π_0* only by tightening monetary policy to offset the demand shock. In full equilibrium at Y_P at LAS_0, aggregate demand must not change. By raising its interest rate setting above r_0 , the central bank uses monetary policy to offset fully the demand shock. AD_2 shifts back down to AD_0. Equilibrium remains at A and inflation at π_0*.

There is another interesting way to look at Figure 13.4. Suppose the rise in aggregate demand comes from monetary policy, an increase in the inflation target from π_0* to π_1*. With a higher inflation target, the central bank can relax its interest rate setting and control of money supply growth accordingly. Interest rates fall, growth in the money supply increases, and the AD line shifts out. Equilibrium moves from A to D.

In this new equilibrium, the equilibrium inflation rate is higher because the central bank has set a higher inflation target. Real output is unchanged. The real money supply M/P will also be constant. Since prices grow at the inflation rate π_1*, the nominal money supply must also grow to accommodate the demand for money as price levels rise. This is consistent with the long-run neutrality of money and the long-term relationship between nominal money supply growth and inflation. *Monetarists* argue that, in a model with full wage and price flexibility and no money illusion, nominal money supply growth causes inflation but not growth in output or employment.

A Supply Shock

Supply shocks may be beneficial, as with technical progress, or adverse if natural disasters, or climate shifts, or political events like armed conflict result in a loss of productive

FIGURE 13.5 **A Change in Potential Output**

A rise in potential output shifts LAS_0 to LAS_1. If the central bank takes no action, the equilibrium inflation rate would fall. The central bank does react to the increase in Y_P by lowering interest rates and expanding money supply. It provides the monetary conditions required for AD_2 and its inflation target π_0*. Equilibrium is at point F.

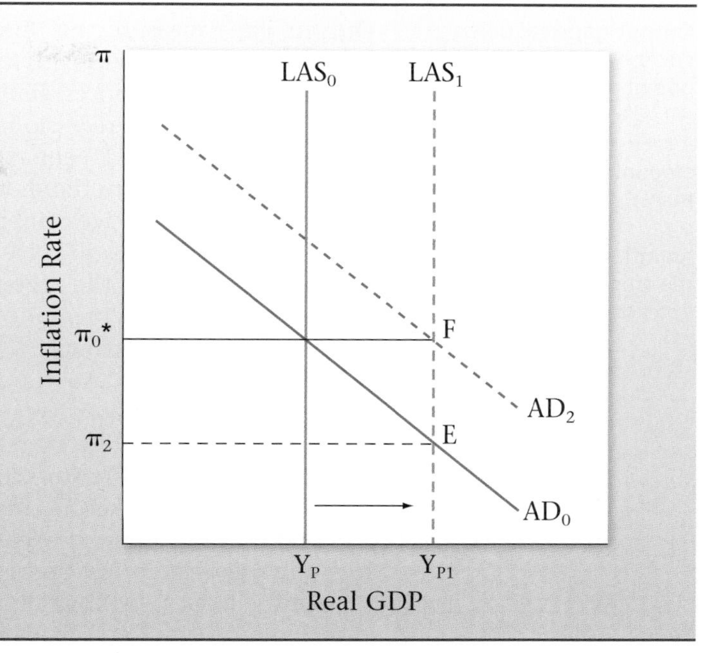

capacity. The Bank of Canada has recently lowered its estimate of potential output as a result of the loss of productive capacity caused by business failures in the recession of 2009. Nonetheless, looking forward to the post-recession period, suppose new technology raises potential output. In Figure 13.5, the LAS line shifts to the right from LAS_0 at Y_P to LAS_1 at Y_{P1}. For a given aggregate demand curve, it appears that inflation falls to π_2 and a new equilibrium at point E.

However, the central bank still has the inflation target π_0*. As a result it responds to this supply shock with monetary stimulus, reducing interest rates. Lower interest rates and higher real output raise the demand for money. To make the lower interest rate compatible with money market equilibrium, the central bank must supply more money. Aggregate demand is increased to AD_2. The new equilibrium is at F, with higher real GDP and the same equilibrium inflation rate π_0* the central bank has set.

These examples illustrate the equilibrium conditions when wages and prices are fully flexible, there is no money illusion, and the central bank sets an inflation rate target for monetary policy. Equilibrium output is potential output, and equilibrium inflation is set and determined by monetary policy.

But the price and wage adjustments assumed by this equilibrium take time. Until the adjustment is complete, output and inflation may not be at the equilibrium values we have discussed in this section. The rest of this chapter studies the adjustment process by which the economy responds to disturbances that push it away from potential output. To see the transition from short-run equilibrium to long-run equilibrium at potential output we return to a study of the short-run aggregate supply curve we have used in earlier chapters, starting with the behaviour of money wage rates.

Review Questions 3 and 4

13.4 Labour Markets and Wage Rates

Output gaps are differences between actual and potential real GDP.

A **recessionary gap** is the amount by which Y is less than Y_p.

An **inflationary gap** is the amount by which Y exceeds Y_p.

Output gaps measure the differences between actual output and potential output. Equilibrium in the model with full flexible wages and prices assumes that changes in wage rates, and changes in prices, eliminate output gaps. If actual real GDP at Y_a is less than potential GDP, there is a **recessionary gap** equal to $Y_a - Y_P < 0$. Alternatively, if actual real GDP Y_b is greater than potential GDP, there is an **inflationary gap** equal to $Y_b - Y_P > 0$.

The transition from the short-run model of the economy to the long-run recognizes the time it takes for wages and prices to adjust to changes in demand, output, and employment. Slow wage and price adjustments result in GDP gaps. Wages are the largest costs of production in the aggregate economy. The Canadian National Accounts data in Table 4.5 show employment income in Canada was more than 60 percent of factor costs of production in 2008. Sluggish wage adjustment is the main cause of slow adjustment of prices and output to equilibrium at potential output. But why are wages slow to adjust to changes in economic activity?

For both firms and workers, a job is often a long-term commitment. For the firm, it is costly to hire and fire workers. Firing entails a redundancy payment and the loss of the expertise the worker has built up on the job. Hiring entails advertising, interviewing, and training a new worker in the special features of the job. Firms are reluctant to hire and fire workers just because of short-term fluctuations in demand.

For the worker, looking for a new job costs time and effort, and throws away experience, seniority, and the high wages justified by the high productivity that comes from having mastered a particular job in a particular firm. Like firms, workers care about long-term arrangements. Firms and workers reach an understanding about pay and conditions in the medium term, including how to handle fluctuations in the firm's output in the short run.

ADJUSTING LABOUR INPUT

A firm and its workers have explicit or implicit labour contracts, specifying working conditions. These include normal hours, overtime requirements, regular wages, and pay schedules for overtime work. The firm then *sets the number of hours* within the limits of these conditions, depending on how much output it wishes to make in a particular week. Labour input is variable, but not the wage rate.

When demand falls and inventories increase beyond planned levels and a firm has to cut its output, does it change hours or workers? Given the costs of hiring and firing, the firm initially reduces hours of work. Overtime ends, and factories close early. If demand does not recover, or declines further, firms start to lay off workers.

Conversely, in a boom, a firm makes its existing workforce work overtime. Then it recalls employees previously laid off, and seeks temporary workers to supplement its longer-term labour force. Only when the firm is sure that higher sales will be sustained does it hire new permanent workers.

WAGE ADJUSTMENT

Wage rates are *not* set in a daily auction in which the equilibrium wage clears the market for labour. Firms and workers both gain from longer-term understandings. This mutual commitment partly insulates the firm and its workforce from temporary conditions in the labour market. Nor can the firm and its workforce spend every day haggling. Bargaining is costly, using up valuable time that workers and managers could use to produce output. Although there are regular meetings to deal with minor grievances, the costs of bargaining about the firm's general wage structure mean that such negotiations are undertaken only infrequently. In Canada and the United States, wage agreements often cover periods of three or more years.

Bargaining costs mean wage rates change only at discrete but overlapping intervals. Some contracts are currently under negotiation, while other agreements reached at earlier dates remain in effect. Immediate wage adjustment to demand fluctuations is ruled out. At best, firms must wait until the next scheduled date for a revision in the wage structure. In practice, complete wage rate adjustment is unlikely to take place even then.

Even when unemployment rises, it may have a limited impact on wages. Long-term co-operation between a firm and its workers matters more than the short-term gains from forcing wage rates down a bit. The reputation of the firm as a good employer affects its ability to attract and retain its skilled workers in the long term.

If workers dislike fluctuations in wage rates, the firm may smooth out wage fluctuations to keep workers happy. Compared with operating with more flexible wages, the firm loses out when demand is low but gains when demand is high. Firms and workers may reach an implicit understanding that wage rates do not fall a lot in slumps or rise a lot in booms.

13.5 The Phillips Curve and Money Wage Rate Changes

Wage flexibility or wage rigidity is very important for the size and duration of short-run fluctuations in real GDP and employment. When wages and prices are rigid and slow to change, the short run AS curve has a low slope. Fluctuations in aggregate demand cause short-run fluctuations in output with little effect on rates of wage and price inflation. According to Okun's Law, these fluctuations in output cause fluctuations in employment and unemployment rates. A fall in AD reduces output and employment in the short run as producers cut back output in order to stop the unwanted increase in inventories. A rise in AD has the opposite effect. In both cases, the short-run response to a change in AD is a change in output and employment.

Alternatively, if wage rates and prices are very flexible, changes in AD have much smaller effects on real GDP and employment. In this case the short run AS curve has a steep slope. Most of the impact of demand fluctuations is on the rates of wage and price inflation. The important question then is: What are the relationships across the economy between average rates of increase in money wage rates, inflation rates, rates of unemployment and output gaps? Put another way, what are the dynamics of the labour market? Consider the simple labour market diagram in Figure 13.6.

The diagram shows a very short run market for labour services based on the *rate of increase* in money wage rates measured on the vertical axis and the level of real GDP (Y) on the horizontal axis, given an expected inflation rate π^*. The shape of labour supply curve N_S shows fixed *rates of wage increases* in the current time period, up to the level of full employment N_F, based on agreements and decisions made in the recent past. This is consistent with empirical observations in labour markets. Even at the end of February 2009, with the recession underway, the annual increase in average hourly earnings excluding overtime was 4.1 percent, and private sector wage settlements averaged rates of increase of 3.0 percent. Some industries like the auto industry were facing absolute cuts to money wage rates but the economy-wide average wage rate was still increasing.

The downward-sloping demand for labour curve N_D is based on the current output level and would shift if output changed. However, business would be willing to hire more labour at lower rates of wage increase given the expected inflation rate and all other things constant.

FIGURE 13.6 **Wage Rate Adjustments in a Simple Labour Market**

Initially the labour market is in equilibrium at full employment N_F with money wage rates increasing at the annual rate ω_0.

A recession like that of 2009 creates a recessionary gap by lowering aggregate demand and output from Y_P to Y_1. Faced with lower demand for output, businesses cut output to prevent a sharp rise in inventories. Reduced output means a reduced demand for labour and the demand for labour shifts to $N_{D(Y1)}$. The result is employment at N_1 and an unemployment rate $(N_F - N_1)/N_P$, but rates of wage increase ω_0 established in the recent past are not immediately affected.

However, the recessionary gap and the unemployment rate put downward pressure on rates of inflation and rates of wage increase. It takes time for these pressures to reduce rates of increases in wages, illustrated by the downward shift in N_S to ω_1, and move the economy gradually back to potential output and full employment

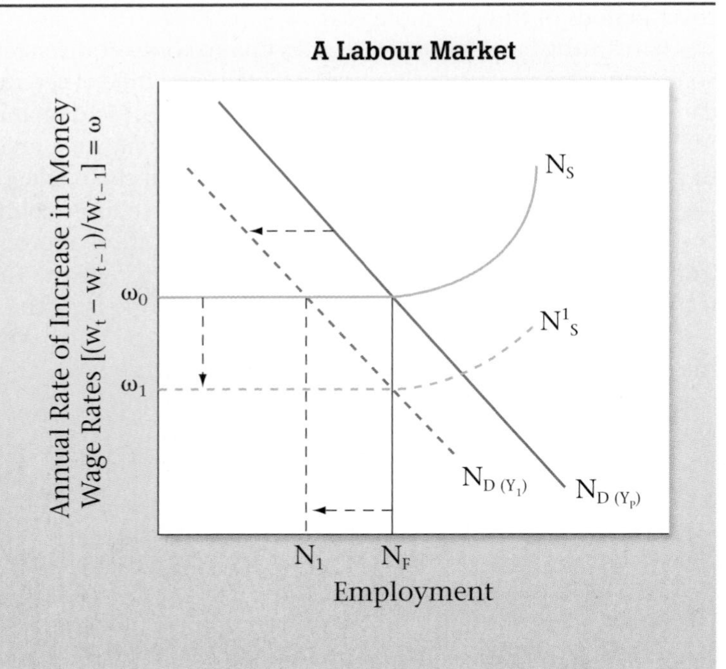

Initially, the labour market and the economy are in equilibrium. The economy is at potential output (Y_P) with full employment (N_F). Inflation of π^* per annum is expected and money wage rates, based on wage settings in the recent past, are increasing at $\omega_0 = \pi^*$ per annum.

A demand shock like the recession of 2009 creates a recessionary gap and reduces the demand for labour. In the diagram N_D shifts to the left, employment falls, and the unemployment rate rises. These conditions put downward pressure on prices and wage rates, but it takes time for prices and wage rates to adjust. Given sufficient time and otherwise tranquil economic conditions, the dynamics of the labour market and product pricing would reduce the rate of increase in wages and prices. This would mean a slow downward transition of the N_S curve until the rate of increase in average wage rates ω, and the rate of inflation π reached ω_1. The Phillips curve offers a description of the labour market dynamics involved.

The **Phillips curve** is the relationship between output gaps and employment rates and changes in the *rate of change* in money wage rates.

The **Phillips curve** is one of the most famous relationships in post-war macroeconomics. In 1958, Professor Phillips of the London School of Economics found a strong statistical relationship between wage rate changes and annual unemployment in the United Kingdom.[1] Similar relationships were found in other countries.

Conditions in labour markets and the adjustment of labour markets to disequilibria as in Figure 13.6 lie behind the Phillips curve. Changes in employment, and unemployment rates that reflect disequilibrium in labour markets cause changes in the *rate of increase* in money wage rates. Wage rate adjustment moves the market back toward equilibrium. The short-run Phillips curve describes this relationship between wage rate increases and differences between the unemployment rate and the natural unemployment rate.

[1] A. W. H. Phillips, "The Relationship Between Unemployment and the Rate of Change in Money Wage Rates in the UK, 1861–1957," *Economica*, NS 25(2) (1958), pp. 283–99.

FIGURE 13.7 **The Phillips Curves**

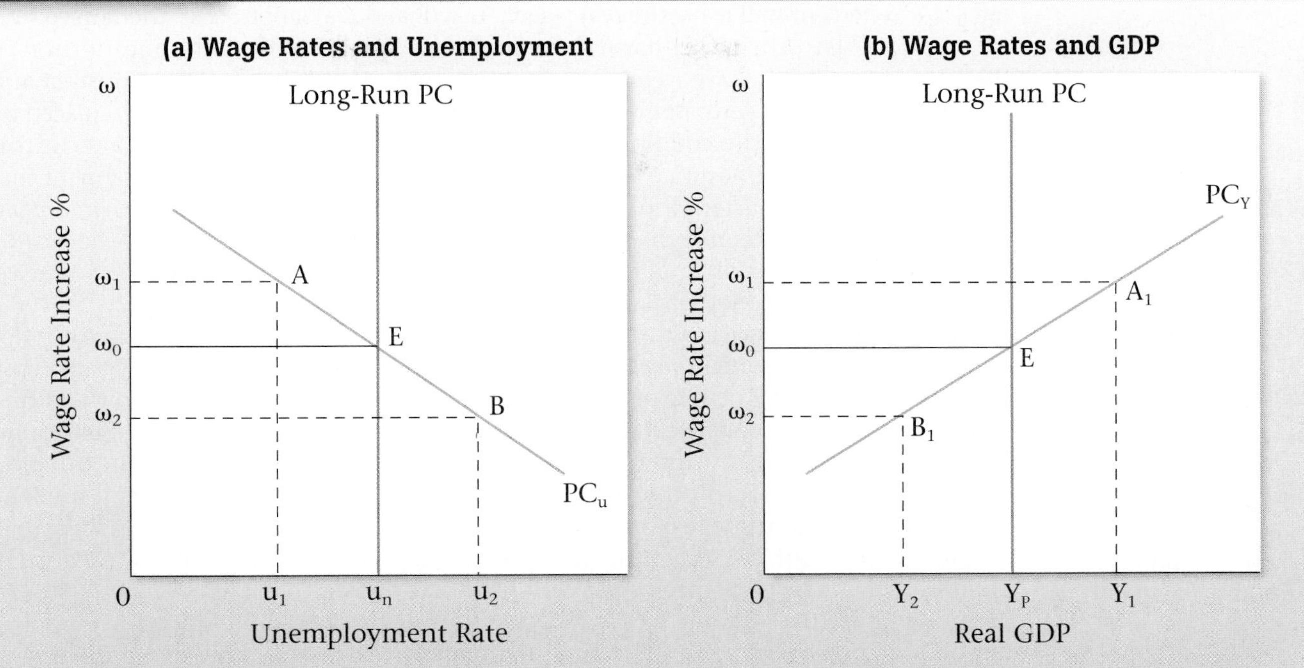

The Phillips curves show the relationships between unemployment rates and output levels and *rates of change* in money wages. In the short run, money wages adjust slowly to changes in unemployment rates. At points E, the economy is at the natural unemployment rate and potential output. Money wage rates are increasing at $\omega_0 = \pi_0$, the rate needed to maintain the real wage for equilibrium at potential output. At points A and A_1 unemployment rates are lower than the natural rate, output is above potential output and money wage rates are increasing at ω_1. At points B and B_1 high unemployment and a recessionary gap are reducing the rate of increase in money wage rates. When the economy has enough time to adjust all wages and prices, it operates at u_n and Y_P and wage rates increase at the expected rate of inflation along the vertical Phillips curve at Y_P.

Furthermore, because fluctuations in output and employment are tied together in the short run as described by Okun's law, the Phillips curve relationship also shows the relationship between GDP gaps and the rate of increase in money wage rates. Recessionary gaps reduce the rates at which wages rise. Inflationary gaps increase the rates at which wages rise.

Figure 13.7 shows Phillips curves for

1. Wage rate increases and unemployment
2. Wage rate increases and real GDP

At point E in each diagram, the unemployment rate is the natural rate u_n, and the economy is at potential output Y_P. The *rate of increase in wage rates*, ω, is

$$\omega = \frac{w_t - w_{t-1}}{w_{t-1}} = \frac{\Delta w}{w_{t-1}} \tag{13.7}$$

where w_t is the money wage rate in the current year and w_{t-1} is the money wage rate in the previous year, and is shown as ω_0 at point E. Because the economy is at potential output and the labour market is in equilibrium at E, the increase in wages ω_0 must equal the expected inflation rate π^e_0 to give the equilibrium *real wage rate*. If, for example, workers and firms correctly anticipate inflation of $\pi^e = 5$ percent, an increase in money wage rates $\omega = 5$ percent will leave the real wage rate w/P and real labour cost unchanged.

We have used the term "natural unemployment rate" to describe equilibrium in the labour market while we were assuming the equilibrium price level was constant and the inflation rate was zero. But the zero inflation assumption has now been replaced by the assumption that the equilibrium rate of inflation is positive and constant. In this context it will be more accurate to think in terms of the equilibrium unemployment that is consistent with a constant inflation. The **NAIRU**, *the non-accelerating inflation rate of unemployment*, is that unemployment rate. Any unemployment rate other than the NAIRU indicates labour market disequilibrium and corresponding pressure to increase or decrease the *rate of change* of money wage rates and the rate of inflation.

The **NAIRU** is the unemployment rate at which the rate of inflation in wages and prices is constant.

The **expected inflation rate** is the inflation rate people think will occur in the future.

Review Questions 6, 7 and 8

This **expected inflation rate** π^e is what people think will happen to the rate of price change in the future when they evaluate the purchasing power of the money wages they will receive. π^e is also the rate of inflation that employers think will occur in the future when they commit to a particular rate increase in money wages. The expected rate of inflation might be simply the inflation rate of the previous year, or it might be the inflation rate people expect, based on the policy announcements of the government and the forecasts of the financial press or some combination of these factors. At the present time, in Canada this would be something like 2 percent a year, based on the Bank of Canada's policy target and its track record in meeting that target over the past 18 years.

We will use here a value $\pi^e_0 = \pi^*_0$, the central bank's inflation target, to simplify our discussion. This is the equilibrium inflation rate we defined earlier in our discussion of AD and Y_P. We want to see how the wage rates and inflation rates in the economy are affected if the economy is not at Y_P and the unemployment rate is not u_n, or the NAIRU, and therefore real GDP is not at potential GDP. Points A and B in the diagrams of Figure 13.7 illustrate these conditions

At points A and A_1 in Figure 13.7, the unemployment rate is below the full employment or NAIRU. There is excess demand in the labour market as producers wish to hire more people than wish to work for current real wage rates. Actual output is greater than potential output. The economy is not in equilibrium at Y_P. The Phillips curve tells us that this situation causes an *increase* in the rate at which money wages are rising from ω_0 to ω_1. If, for example, the inflation rate π_0 had been 2 percent and money wage rates had been rising by $\omega_0 = 2$ percent a year, they will begin to rise at a higher rate, say 2.5 or 3.0 percent a year.

Points B and B_1 in Figure 13.7 show the opposite economic circumstances, which correspond to the labour market conditions during the recession shown in Figure 13.6. The unemployment rate is above the natural rate. There is excess supply in the labour market. Real GDP is less than potential GDP, and there is a recessionary gap. Low demand for goods and services, and, correspondingly, reduced demand for labour inputs, slow the rate of growth in wages and prices. In Figure 13.7, the unemployment rate u_2 and the recessionary gap $Y_2 - Y_P$ result in a lower rate of increase in wages ω_2.

The *slope of the Phillips curve* shows us how a change in the unemployment rate changes the rate at which wages increase. It reflects the flexibility of wages and prices in the economy and the slope of the short run AS curve. We usually see that wages and prices adjust slowly to changes in economic conditions. In most industries, wage rates are set for periods of several months or years by agreement or normal practice. Similarly, many producers of goods and services set their prices and fees and adjust them periodically, not continuously. As a result, we can draw the short-run Phillips curve with a low slope, or even as a horizontal line, to reflect the short-run stability in the rate of increase in wages. The corresponding short-run AS curve has a low slope or is horizontal. However, if wage

APPLICATION BOX 13.1

Phillips Curves in Canada and the United States

The Phillips curve can be expressed as a relationship between inflation and unemployment, or as a relationship between output gaps and inflation. We have seen that higher unemployment rates result in lower or negative inflation rates. Okun's Law tells us that higher unemployment rates occur in times of negative (recessionary) output gaps. Then real GDP is less than potential GDP. Conversely, low unemployment rates mean positive (inflationary)

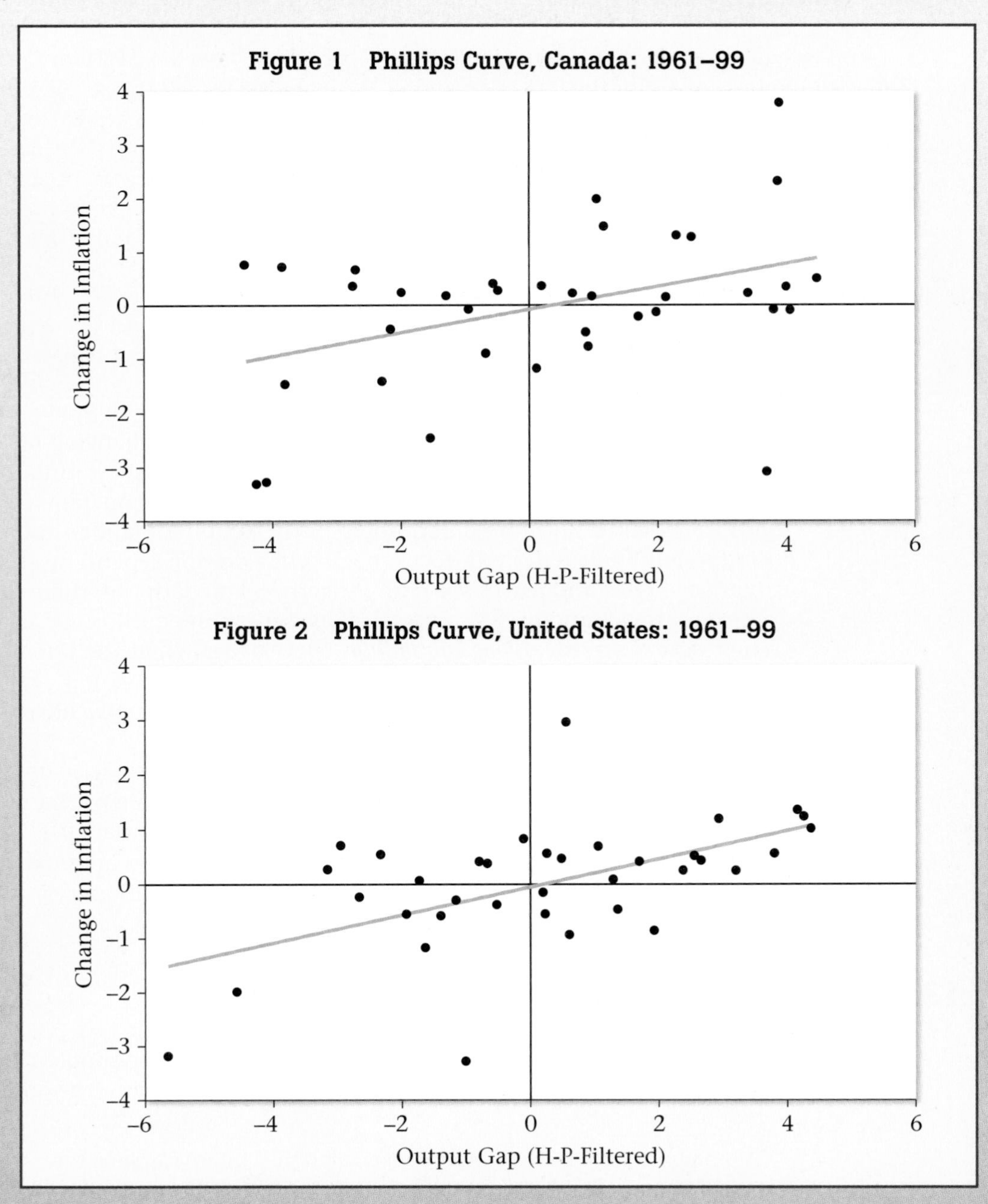

APPLICATION BOX 13.1 continued

output gaps as real GDP exceeds potential GDP. Using these relationships, the Phillips curve tells us that when real GDP rises above potential GDP, the positive output gap will increase in the rate of wage increases and the inflation rate, and vice versa. The question of interest then is: Does the Canadian economy operate in this way?

Paul Beaudry and Matthew Doyle[2] have examined Phillips curves for the Canadian and United States economies in a recent paper. They considered the following simple Phillips curve:

$$\Delta\pi = \alpha + \beta \times (\text{output gap})$$

In this equation, $\Delta\pi$ is a change in the inflation rate, α is a constant, and β measures by how much the inflation rate would change as a result of an output gap. The argument of the Phillips curve is that β is a positive number. A positive output gap will increase the inflation rate, and a negative output gap will reduce the inflation rate.

Figures 1 and 2 plot scatter diagrams of the data on inflation and output gaps for Canada and the United States from 1961 to 1999. Each figure also includes a regression line that illustrates the statistical relationship between inflation and output gaps for each country. The slopes of the lines are 0.214 for Canada and 0.256 for the United States. These are the values for β in the equation. They tell us that a positive output gap of 1 percent would increase the inflation rate by 0.214 percent points in Canada or by 0.256 percent points in the United States. Negative output gaps would have the opposite effect.

These findings mean the Phillips curve is a useful explanation of the way output gaps and unemployment rates affect inflation rates in Canada.

rates and prices were extremely flexible and continuously changing, we would show that condition with a steep short-run Phillips curve and a steep short-run AS curve.

Given enough time to adjust, however, the economy operates at potential output and the NAIRU. Both are determined by the supply of labour and capital inputs to production and the state of technology. They do not depend on inflation, provided that wage rates and prices are rising together. Furthermore, there is enough time to adjust all wages and prices to values consistent with equilibrium at potential output. The result is a vertical *long-run Phillips* curve as shown at the unemployment rate u_n and output Y_p, in Figure 13.7. The corresponding long-run aggregate supply curve LAS is vertical. It shows there is no long-run trade-off between wage rate increases and levels of employment and real output.

The key relationship illustrated by the Phillips curve is the adjustment process in the labour market whereby unemployment affects the rate of change of money wage rates. Sometimes real GDP grows more slowly than potential GDP, a recessionary gap develops, unemployment rates rise, and wage rate increases are smaller. At other times, real GDP grows more rapidly than potential GDP, an inflationary gap develops, unemployment rates fall, and wage rate increases are larger.

13.6 Wage Rates and Short-Run Aggregate Supply

Now we can extend our discussion of short-run aggregate supply from Chapter 11 to include the rate of inflation. The underlying explanations for the position and slope of

[2] P. Beaudry and M. Doyle, "What Happened to the Phillips Curve in the 1990s in Canada," Bank of Canada, *Price Stability and the Long-Run Target for Monetary Policy* (Proceedings of a seminar held by the Bank of Canada, June 2000), pp. 51–82. Also available from the Bank of Canada's Web site, www.bankofcanada.ca.

FIGURE 13.8 **Short-Run Aggregate Supply**

The short-run aggregate supply curve AS_0 is based on a particular rate of nominal wage growth set in the past. If inflation is equal to expected inflation and that rate of nominal wage growth, the economy is at A, in equilibrium at Y_p and π^e_0. If inflation is higher than π^e_0 some producers find prices for their products are higher than they expected and raise output. The economy moves along AS_0 to B. An inflation rate lower than π_0 would move the economy to point C. As long as the rate of increase in nominal wages remains as it was set in the past, the economy moves along one AS curve.

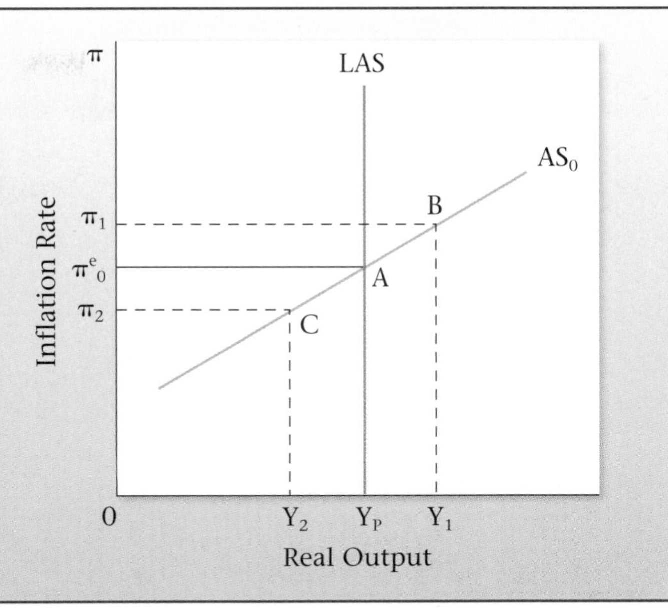

the short-run aggregate supply curve remain the same, but the underlying wage rates and prices are rising continuously over time.

In Figure 13.8, the economy is at potential output at A. In the short run, firms in the economy inherit a given rate of nominal wage growth (ω_0 equal to π^e_0 shown in the figure) based on past wage rate negotiations and contracts. These negotiations anticipated remaining in full employment equilibrium at point A with inflation rate π^e_0. By keeping up with inflation, nominal wage growth is *expected* to maintain the real wage rate required for labour market equilibrium. There would be no GDP gap, and the unemployment rate would then be the NAIRU.

If inflation exceeds the expected inflation rate π^e_0, producers see prices for their output rising faster than the money wage rates they have to pay. The real labour costs of production are falling. If this higher inflation had been foreseen when wages were negotiated, the agreed rate of increase in nominal wage rates would have been higher. However, prices are now rising faster than costs. Producers take advantage of their good luck by supplying more output at higher profit. They can afford to pay overtime to ensure that their workforce co-operates, and may also take on extra temporary staff. In Figure 13.8, for example, the economy moves along the short-run aggregate supply curve to point B, and the inflationary gap opens as Y_1 exceeds Y_p. The unemployment rate is lower than the NAIRU.

Review Questions 9 and 10

Conversely, if the inflation rate is less than π_0, the real wage rate and labour costs of production are higher than when the rate of increase in nominal wages was agreed. Since labour is now more costly and profits are squeezed, producers cut back their output. The economy moves back down the short-run aggregate supply curve from A to C, and a recessionary gap occurs with Y less than Y_p.

When there is not enough time to renegotiate the rate of increase in money wage rates, the economy operates on one short-run aggregate supply curve. But, as *time passes*, money wage rates can be renegotiated as can supply contract prices. If a recessionary gap persists and unemployment rates exceed the NAIRU, the *rate of increase* in wages falls. This is the relationship we observed in the Phillips curve. With lower rates of increase in

FIGURE 13.9 **Shifts in Short-Run Aggregate Supply**

A persistent GDP gap leads to a new negotiated rate of increase in money wage rates and a shift in the SAS curve. In this example the recessionary gap $Y_0 - Y_P$ leads to a lower rate of increase in money wage rates and SAS shifts down to SAS_1. A persistent inflationary gap would cause an upward shift in SAS.

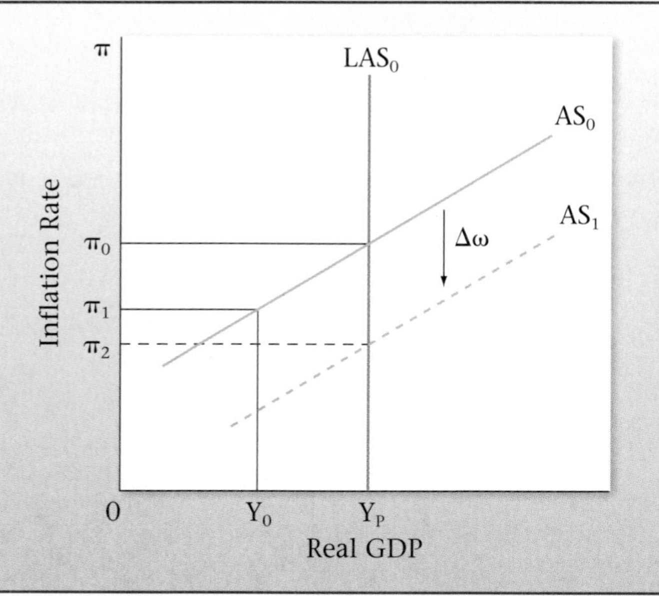

money wages, labour costs of production increase more slowly, and producers do not need to raise output prices so quickly. The new expected rate of inflation and the equal rate of increase in money wage rates give a new short-run aggregate supply curve. Figure 13.9 shows this change.

A persistent inflationary gap with Y greater than Y_p and the inflation rate higher than expected will lead, in time, to an upward shift in the short-run aggregate supply curve. The inflationary gap means strong demand for labour from producers, higher profits, and pressure for larger increases in money wage rates. As the Philips curve predicts, labour negotiations lead to higher agreed rates of wage increase. We see this change in expected inflation and the equivalent increase in nominal wage growth as an upward shift in AS. You can illustrate it by drawing a higher AS curve in Figure 13.9.

These short-run aggregate supply curves give a realistic picture of the way the economy reacts to fluctuations in AD. Because the short-run aggregate supply schedule is quite flat, a shift in aggregate demand leads mainly to changes in output and employment in the short run without much effect on inflation rates. This is because of the sluggish response of wage rates to changes in economic conditions. But persistent GDP gaps lead gradually to changes in wage rate growth. Changes in the rate at which wage rates increase shift the AS curve. These wage rate adjustments and their impact on inflation rates move the economy toward its long-run equilibrium.

Review Questions 11 and 12

13.7 The Adjustment from Short-Run Output to Potential Output

We now consider how demand or supply shocks that move the economy away from potential output trigger an *adjustment process*. In combining the AD and AS curves, we are assuming the market for goods and services clears even in the short run, but the labour market takes longer to adjust. Short-run aggregate supply gradually changes over time as wage rate growth adjusts to the unemployment rate and restores full employment at potential output, placing the economy eventually at potential output.

However, sluggish wage rate changes mean the adjustment process takes time. If aggregate demand for goods and services falls, firms reduce output and employment. A recessionary gap opens, and unemployment rates rise. Since wages do not fall at once, there is involuntary unemployment. Employment, like output, is demand determined in the short run. Application Box 13.2 shows recent output gaps in Canada and the United States.

Figure 13.10 shows a fall in aggregate demand as a leftward shift in the AD schedule. A decline in exports or investment or government expenditure, or a change in the inflation target set for monetary policy, would have this effect on AD. Before this change, the economy was in equilibrium at full employment and potential output at E_0.

In the short run, the leftward shift in AD causes a move from E_0 to E_1. Since producers cannot cut costs per unit of output by very much, they reduce output to Y_1 and unemployment increases. At E_1 the goods market clears. It is a point on both the AS and AD curves. Inflation has fallen a little because market demand is weak, and output has fallen a lot. With inflation lower than what was expected and built into nominal wage agreements, *real wage rates rise* despite the fall in output. Firms adjust employment by laying off some workers. The drop in AD creates a recessionary gap, with an unemployment rate higher than the natural rate.

Now let's assume that the central bank does not react immediately to this change in AD and its effect on the bank's inflation target. It continues to hold the interest rates it thought was appropriate for the inflation rate π_0 and allows financial markets to determine nominal money supply. There is no active policy intervention.

FIGURE 13.10 **Adjustment to a Change in AD**

A fall in aggregate demand shifts AD_0 to AD_1. Short-run equilibrium is at E_1 with lower output and inflation and a recessionary gap of $Y_1 - Y_p$. The adjustment to these short-run economic conditions comes from the reaction of wage rates to the recessionary gap. Over time, rates of increase in wage rates are negotiated down and the AS shifts down with them. AS_1 shows one step in this adjustment process. From the diagram we see that if AD were to stay at AD_1, the adjustment process would continue until the recessionary gap was eliminated and equilibrium was at E_3 with $Y = Y_p$ and inflation rate π_3.

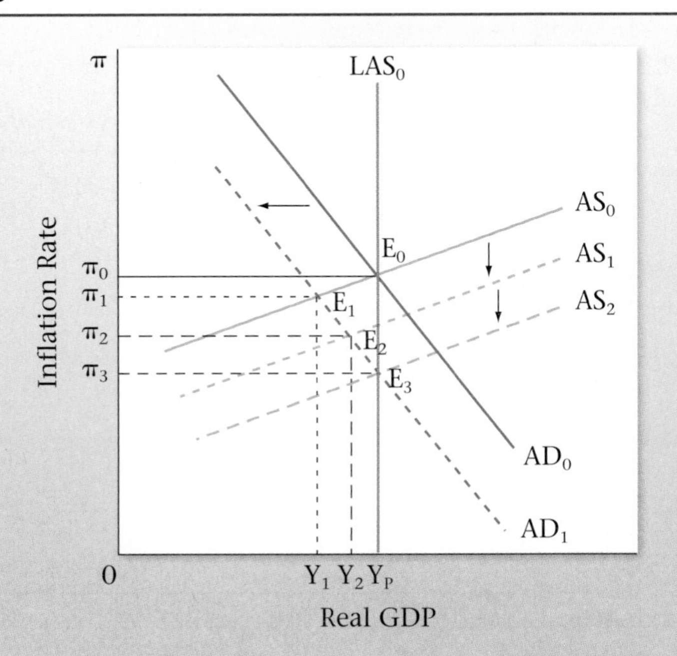

APPLICATION BOX 13.2

Output Gaps in Canada and the United States 1985 to 2009

The output gap is the percentage deviation of real GDP from potential GDP. Actual output is (relatively) easy to measure by national accounts methods. Potential GDP is more difficult, and we rely on estimates made by government agencies or international organizations as well as private scholars. The chart below shows estimates for Canada and the United States. Positive gaps are inflationary gaps that correspond to booms in the economy. Negative gaps are recessionary gaps indicating recessions.

The figure shows the recession of the early 1990s in both countries and the different patterns of recovery from that recession. In Canada in particular the shift in the Bank of Canada's focus to explicit inflation targets came in early 1991, and preceded the recession.

Although the Canadian economy seemed to recover from the 1991 recession by mid-1993, a second recessionary gap developed and lasted until the end of the decade. By contrast, the United States economy enjoyed a sustained recovery after 1991, which led ultimately to a large inflationary gap by the end of the decade.

The experiences of the economies were different again in the next decade. The Canadian economy has been remarkably stable, fluctuating between small recessionary and inflationary gaps with a small recessionary gap on average. By contrast, the United States economy shifted from a strong inflationary gap in 2000 to a large recessionary gap in late 2003 following the collapse of equity markets and the distruptions that followed the terrorist attacks of 9/11, 2001.

The most recent data show the large recessionary gaps in both countries created by the recession of 2009.

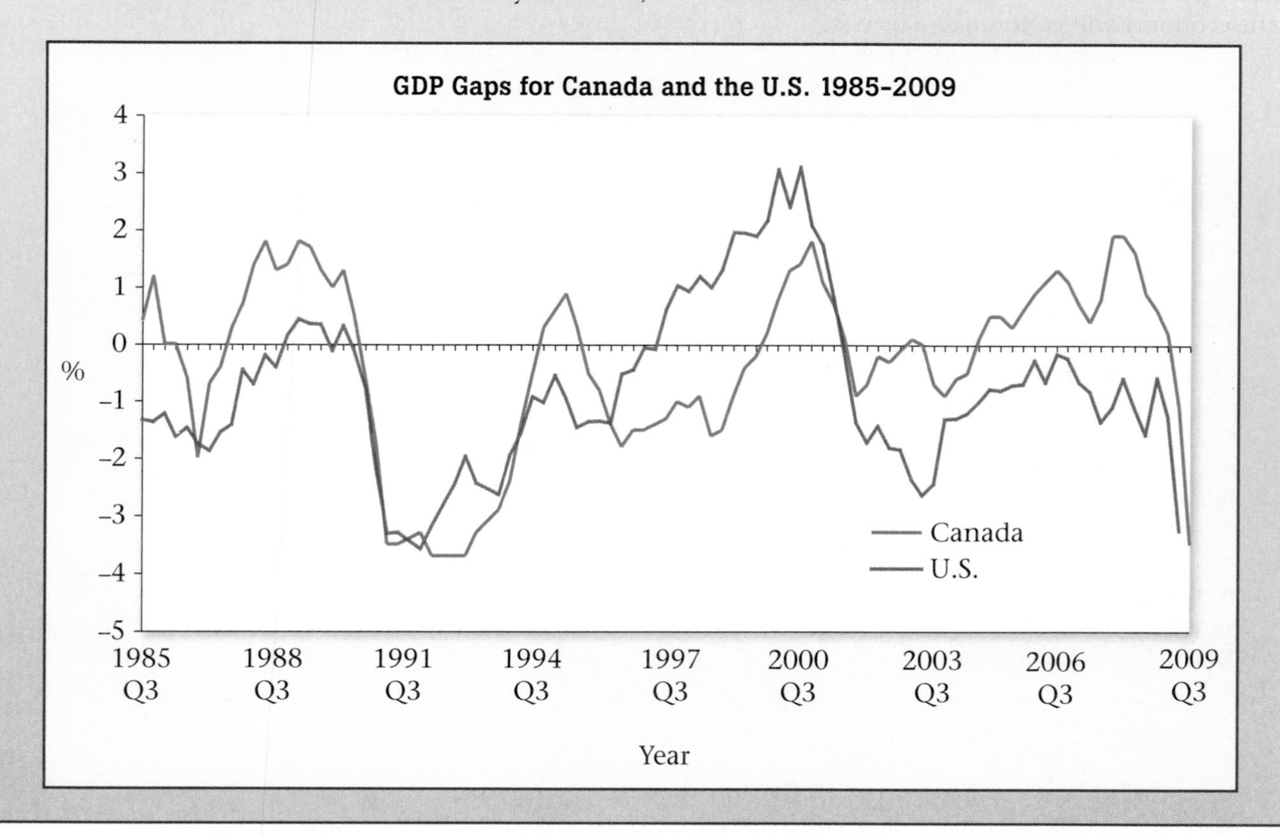

Source: http://bankofcanada.ca/en/rates/indinf/product_data_en.html, Bank of Canada, 2009; and Federal Reserve Bank of St. Louis, FRED database.

In the medium run, the recessionary gap and higher unemployment start to reduce wage rate growth in accordance with the Phillips curve. Lower wage rate growth shifts AS down, and firms move along this lower short-run aggregate supply curve AS_1. The goods market now clears at E_2. Output and employment recover a bit, but some unemployment persists. When output and the inflation rate fall, real interest rates fall, moving the economy along AD_1 to E_2.

Eventually, given enough time and no further disturbances, the adjustment process is complete. Wage growth and inflation fall to π_3. The short-run aggregate supply curve is AS_2 in Figure 13.10. The economy is in full equilibrium at E_3 on LAS_0, AS_2, and AD_1. Output is at Y_P, and the labour market is in equilibrium at the natural unemployment rate.

In the real world, adjustments to changes in aggregate demand come from the effects of GDP gaps and unemployment on the wage agreements negotiated, formally and informally, in labour markets. A recessionary gap like that in Figure 13.10 pushes wage rate *increases* down, lowers inflation, and allows monetary policy to support an increase in demand along the AD curve. An inflationary gap results in the opposite process. Wage rate increases rise, inflation rises, and unchanged monetary policy results in higher real interest rates to reduce AD. In both cases, the eventual changes in wage rate agreements together with the reaction of monetary policy to changes in inflation rates move the economy, over time, from short-run to long-run equilibrium. But, as we can see from Application Box 13.2, output gaps, particularly recessionary gaps, can persist for substantial periods of time.

This adjustment process has important implications for the inflation targets set by monetary policy. It means that, if the inflation target is cut, shifting the AD curve to the left, the economy will go through a recession, and perhaps a prolonged recession, while money wage rate agreements are renegotiated to reflect the new inflation target. The time required for this adjustment is linked in a very important way to the independence and the credibility of the central bank. Canadian experience in the 1990s provides an interesting example. We have seen the persistent recessionary gaps during this period in Canada as the Bank of Canada worked toward its inflation target of 2 percent.

Review Questions 13 and 14

13.8 Shifts in Aggregate Supply

A PERMANENT AGGREGATE SUPPLY SHOCK

Potential output and long-run aggregate supply grow over time. This growth comes from a combination of growth in the labour force, growth in capital stock, and improvements in technology. We will study the growth process in more detail in Chapter 14. For now we want to consider how the economy would adjust to growth in potential output.

Suppose the age distribution of the population following a "baby boom," and then the echo from that boom, leads to a short period of rapid growth in the labour force. As this new labour force finds employment, the output of the economy grows. If these new members of the labour force bring new levels of skills and education to their work, the technology of production is improved. Employers will install new capital equipment for these new employees. The economy's capacity to produce goods and services, its potential output, is larger. The long-run aggregate supply curve in Figure 13.11 shifts to the right.

The economy's potential output has increased. Both LAS and AS have shifted to the right, but AD is still at AD_0. Short-run equilibrium means a recessionary gap equal to $Y_1 - Y_{P_1}$. This gap will put downward pressure on the growth of wage rates, and start the adjustment to equilibrium at Y_{P_1} and lower inflation π_2, unless there is some shift

FIGURE 13.11 **A Permanent Increase in Aggregate Supply**

An increase in potential output shifts LAS_0 and AS_0 to the right to LAS_1 and AS_1. The economy moves in the short run from E_1 to E_2, if the central bank just maintains money supply growth. The internal adjustment process starts in response to the recessionary gap, and AS will shift down as growth in money wage rates falls and inflation rates fall. However, movement along AD_0 does not meet the central bank's inflation target at LAS_1. The bank lowers its interest rate setting and allows faster growth in money supply to shift AD to AD_1 and give equilibrium at E_3.

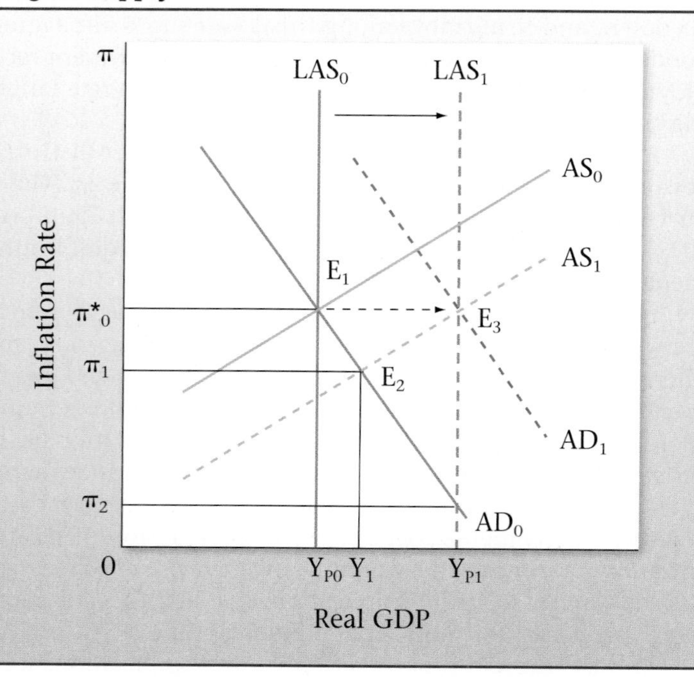

in AD. If the central bank is committed to the inflation target π^*_0, it will provide the monetary stimulus needed to shift AD to AD_1, and ease the adjustment to the new level of potential output.

A TEMPORARY SUPPLY SHOCK

A temporary supply shock leaves potential output unchanged. It does not shift the vertical LAS curve, but it does shift the AS curve. Although the AS curve is *mainly* influenced by the inherited nominal wage rates, it is also affected by other input prices. Suppose a temporary increase in oil and other commodity prices makes firms charge higher prices at any level of output. Figure 13.12 shows a shift upwards in short-run supply from AS_0 to AS_1. The new short-run equilibrium is at E_1. Inflation rises but output and employment fall, as real money supply decreases and real interest rates rise as a result of higher inflation relative to money supply growth.

Review Question 15

If the central bank maintains its inflation target π^*_0, lower output and employment at E_1 will gradually reduce nominal wage growth, shifting AS_1 back to AS_0. The economy gradually moves down the AD curve, back to the original equilibrium at E. The supply shock has produced a recession and higher inflation that persist until wage rate growth and inflation adjust to the new conditions.

There is another possible outcome. When the rise in oil and commodity prices makes AS shift up, it is possible to avoid the period of low output—the recession—as the economy moves along AD. A change in monetary policy can shift AD up enough to pass through E_2. Output can quickly return to potential output, but only because the inflation target has been loosened. However, if the supply shock is temporary and AS later shifts back to the original inflation target, the temporary increase in inflation

FIGURE 13.12 **A Temporary Supply Shock**

Higher oil and commodity prices force firms to raise prices to cover increased costs. AS shifts up to AS_1, and short-run equilibrium is at E_1. Higher inflation reduces aggregate demand along AD. Once oil and commodity prices stabilize, the economy will adjust as the recessionary gap reduces the growth in wage rates and SAS drifts back down to restore equilibrium at E.

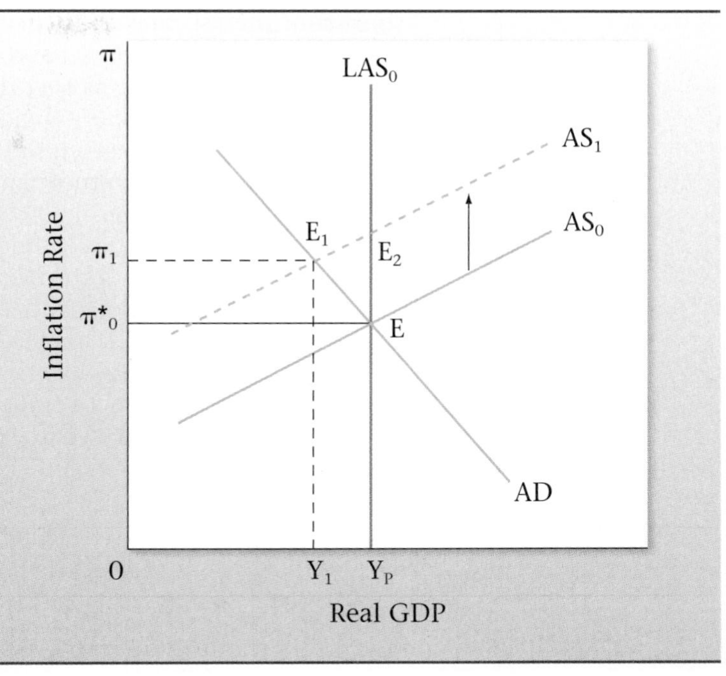

may be acceptable. Indeed, many central banks monitor **core inflation**, inflation that excludes the effects of food and energy prices, when setting monetary policy for longer-term inflation targets.

Core inflation is inflation that excludes changes in the volatile prices of food and energy.

A central bank caring a lot about output stability may be prepared to accommodate short-run supply shocks, even if this means higher short-run inflation. A central bank caring more about inflation control will not accommodate temporary supply shocks.

It matters whether the supply shock is temporary or permanent. If potential output is permanently affected, aggregate demand must eventually change with the change in potential output. Once a supply shock is diagnosed as permanent, it should be accommodated.

13.9 The Role for Monetary Policy

We have used a *monetary policy rule* to describe how monetary policy is conducted. The policy rule describes the central bank's setting of the interest rate, based on the bank's inflation and output targets. The aggregate demand curve embodies an assumption about the form of the monetary policy rule, whether explicit or only implicit.

The way the economy adjusts to GDP gaps reflects the monetary policy rule. Traditional approaches to adjustment, like those we have studied in earlier chapters, are based on money supply rules. They assume the central bank sets the nominal money supply, or the growth in nominal money supply at a particular value. Monetary policy is passive and does not respond to output gaps. The adjustment process comes from changes in the real money supply caused by changes in prices and inflation rates.

However, modern central banks conduct monetary policy in an active and continuous way as described by an interest rate rule. They set inflation targets. They use short-run interest rates as their policy instruments. Equation 13.5 is an example of such a rule. Central banks set and change short-term interest rates from time to time as required to hit their targets over the longer term.

If you visit the Bank of Canada's Web site, www.bankofcanada.ca, you will see the Bank's inflation control target, the current inflation rate based on total CPI, and the core inflation rate, reported on the home page. Below these data, the Bank reports the current target it has set for the overnight interest rate, its policy instrument. The Bank changes the setting of this interest rate to change the stance of its monetary policy. You will also find, under "Upcoming Events," the next scheduled date for the interest rate announcement.

The Bank's explanation of how its monetary policy works is given under the Monetary Policy link on the bank's home page under the topic "How Monetary Policy Works," www.bankofcanada.ca/en/monetary_mod/index.html. The Bank uses a clear set of graphic models to illustrate the motives for monetary policy action, the changes in the policy instrument, and the impact of those changes on expenditure, output, and inflation.

Figure 13.13 shows how monetary policy responses like those made by the Bank of Canada react to shocks to aggregate demand and aggregate supply. The policy objective is the target inflation rate at Y_P, but the role monetary policy can play depends on the type of shocks the economy experiences.

FIGURE 13.13 **Monetary Policy and Temporary AD and AS Shocks**

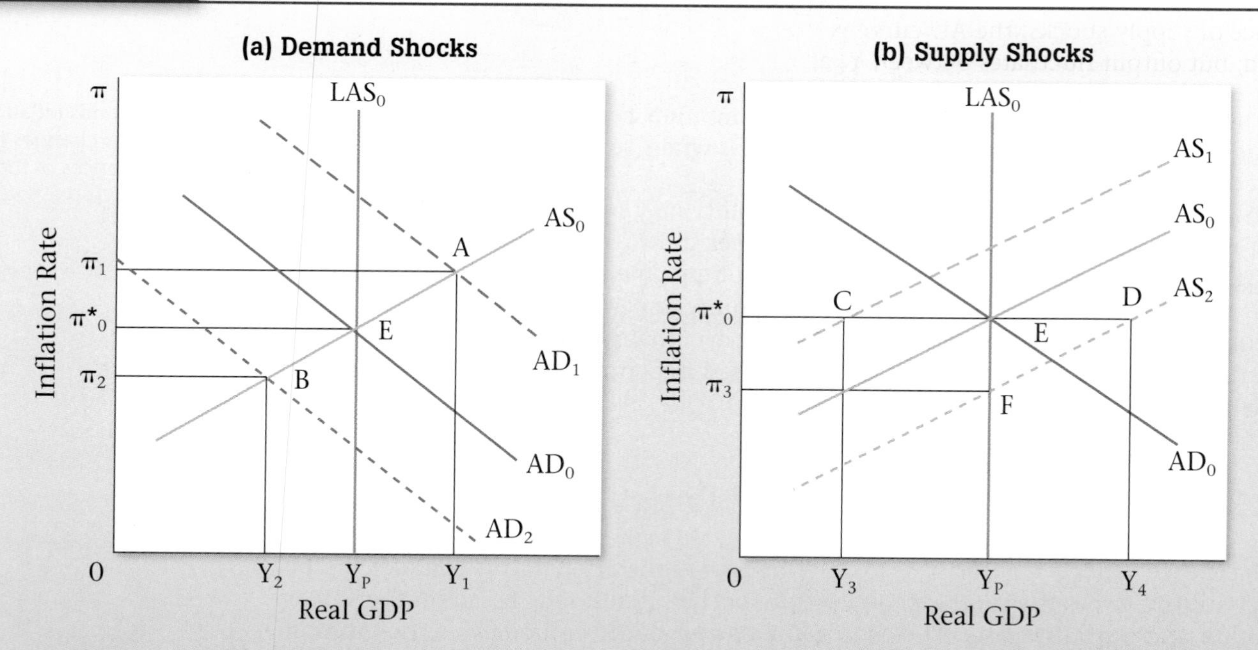

(a) Positive and negative AD shocks shift AD to AD_1 and AD_2 creating inflationary and recessionary gaps in the absence of monetary policy reaction. If the central bank reacts to the departures from its inflation rate target π^*_0 by changing its interest rate, it offsets the AD shock, stabilizing inflation at π^*_0 and output at Y_P.

(b) Supply shocks shift AS between AS_1 and AS_2. If monetary policy sets interest rates to stabilize inflation at π^*_0, output fluctuates between Y_3 and Y_4. Monetary policy cannot stabilize both inflation and output in the face of supply shocks.

In part (a) of the diagram, the only shocks are demand shocks *not* caused by monetary policy. If demand is high, AD_1, the economy moves along its short-run aggregate supply curve to point A. If demand is low, AD_2, the economy moves along the AS_0 curve to point B.

Suppose the central bank quickly diagnoses that an expansionary demand shock has occurred, based on the change in the inflation rate. It could set a higher interest rate to tighten monetary policy and shift AD_1 back to AD_0. Similarly, it could set a lower interest rate to loosen monetary policy whenever it thinks AD would otherwise be AD_2. Since the economy remains at E, both inflation and output are stabilized. Indeed, *when all shocks to the economy are demand shocks, stabilizing inflation also stabilizes output.*

It is easy for the central bank to tell where inflation is relative to its target inflation rate. Price indexes and inflation rates are reported monthly. It is harder to estimate the level of potential output, which can change over time. In this sense, an inflation target is easier to implement than the policy rule we used in Chapter 11, which required estimates of how output differs from potential output. This is part of the modern case for using inflation targeting as the longer-term target for monetary policy, and interest rates as the policy instrument. When all shocks to the economy are demand shocks, it works perfectly.

Suppose, instead, that all shocks are supply side shocks as illustrated in part (b) of Figure 13.13. If the average level of short-run supply is AS_0, but supply conditions fluctuate between AS_1 and AS_2, on average, output is at Y_P, and inflation is on target at π^*_0.

If monetary policy is very aggressive in setting interest rates to stabilize inflation in the face of supply shocks, the AD curve is effectively horizontal at π^*_0. Inflation is stabilized, but output fluctuates between Y_3 and Y_4 as AS fluctuates between AS_1 and AS_2, giving equilibrium at C and D. Unlike the case of demand shocks, it is no longer possible to stabilize both inflation and output.

Alternatively, if monetary policy works aggressively to stabilize output at Y_P, the cost is big fluctuations in the inflation rate. The AD curve is effectively vertical at Y_P. An increase in AS to AS_2 brings a big rise in real interest rates to reduce AD to equilibrium at point F. With increased supply and reduced demand, inflation, π, is temporarily low, relative to the growth in wage rates, and firms cut output back to Y_P. In the opposite case, an upward shift in AS would result in a fall in interest rates, to increase AD and maintain output at Y_P with an inflation rate greater then π^*_0.

Review Questions 16, 17 and 18

TRADE-OFFS IN MONETARY POLICY OBJECTIVES

Part (b) of Figure 13.13 implies that it may be a bad idea either to stabilize inflation at π^*_0 (and accept big fluctuations in Y) or to stabilize output at Y_P (and accept big fluctuations in π). Monetary policy faces a trade-off when supply shocks are the causes of fluctuations in output and inflation.

This trade-off does not arise for demand shocks. By fully offsetting demand shocks, the central bank stabilizes both output and inflation rates. In reality, the central bank faces both demand and supply shocks, and cannot always diagnose which is which. It must choose a monetary policy rule that gives reasonable outcomes under both kinds of disturbances.

The *Taylor rule* provides an example. When rapid diagnosis of shocks is difficult, monetary policy follows a middle course between what is required for demand shocks and what is required for supply shocks. When this is done, interest rates are changed in response to deviations of both output and inflation from their equilibrium and target levels. This is accomplished by setting nominal interest rates, the central bank's policy instrument, in accordance with a Taylor rule, as follows:

$$i = i_0 + a(\pi - \pi^*_0) + b(Y - Y_p) \qquad a > 0, b > 0 \tag{13.8}$$

As we saw in Chapter 10, empirically, almost every central bank's behaviour can be represented as a Taylor rule. Now you understand why. It is a smart response when facing both supply and demand shocks.

FLEXIBLE INFLATION TARGETING

However, central banks do not admit to following a Taylor rule. Many, including the Bank of Canada, pursue explicit *inflation targets* but not output or unemployment rate targets. Others, like the United States Federal Reserve, are explicitly charged with stabilizing both inflation and output. Yet, empirically, almost all central banks act as if they care about both output and inflation. Why not openly acknowledge it?

There are four possible answers. One is the inability of the central bank to affect potential output, so that it must make output a subsidiary goal of monetary policy in the short run. Indeed, monetary policy may create short-run output gaps in order to achieve its longer-term inflation targets.

Another answer is that admitting to caring about output would somehow jeopardize the central bank's ability to fight inflation. This is an important issue of credibility. It underlies the effect inflation targets have on *expectations* about inflation, which are important to inflation rate stability.

A third is that we are pretty ignorant about the growth path of potential output, which is not directly observable. If inflation tends to rise when actual output exceeds potential output, and to fall when actual output falls short of potential output, it may be better to target inflation, which at least can be easily measured. This argument has some force if central banks are to be held accountable for their policy actions and outcomes.

A fourth answer is that flexible inflation targeting still allows a temporary role for output stabilization. The eventual commitment to hitting the inflation target is not flexible, but how quickly the target is achieved is flexible.

The key to successful flexible inflation targeting is that any concerns about output stabilization lead only to *temporary* changes in inflation and interest rates. Credible central banks can partially offset a shock today while promising to reverse the change in interest rates once the shock is over. They cut interest rates when they predict the demand will otherwise fall short of potential output, but make it clear that future interest rate adjustments will prevent demand in excess of potential output. With no sustained policy boost to demand, there is no reason for people to expect or fear future inflation in excess of the bank's longer-term target.

However, weak central banks that lack credibility may cause panic by easing monetary policy today. People worry that they will not be tough enough later to reverse that demand expansion. Foreseeing sustained expansion, inflation increases. This insight places credibility centre stage, where it belongs. It also highlights the importance of the credibility the Bank of Canada has earned by its success in meeting inflation targets since 1991.

This completes an important part of our work on macroeconomic theory and policy. We now have a full aggregate demand and aggregate supply model that allows us to examine and understand short-run business cycle fluctuations in output, employment, and inflation, and the role of policy, particularly monetary policy, in reducing those fluctuations. We have also studied the importance of wage rate and price flexibility to the economy's adjustment to potential output, even in the absence of policy intervention. In general, we have a model that explains short-run fluctuations about a longer-term

APPLICATION BOX 13.3

AD and AS in Canada 1994 to 2007

The chart shows inflation rates and real GDP in Canada in each year from 1994 to 2007. Each point represents an intersection of aggregate demand and short-run aggregate supply curves, some of which are also shown.

The rightward shift in the short-run aggregate supply curves reflects the growth in potential GDP in Canada over the last ten years.

The small changes in inflation rates from year to year suggest that short-run supply conditions were quite stable. Aggregate demand grew faster than potential output and aggregate supply. As a result, the unemployment rate declined over the period, as reported earlier in Table 11.2, as Okun's Law predicts.

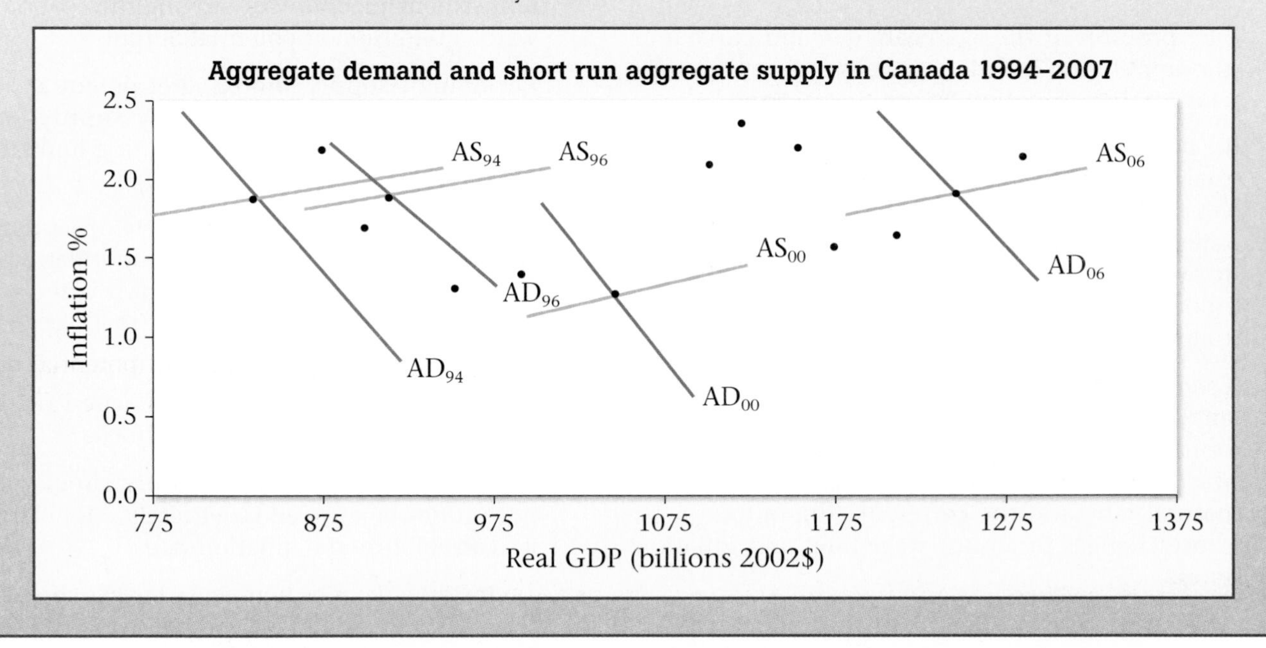

Source: Adapted from Statistics Canada CANSIM Database Table 380-0002 Series V1992067 and Table 326-0022 Series V41690926. Retrieved on Department of Finance Canada Website, Fiscal Reference Tables 15 and 45, September 2008, http://www.fin.gc.ca/frt-trf/2008/frt08_e.pdf; and Bank of Canada Banking and Financial Statistics, June 2008, Tables H2 and H8. Bank of Canada, 2009.

equilibrium level of real output. This model describes an economy that tends to equilibrium at potential output with an inflation rate determined by monetary policy. Application Box 13.3 shows how the AD–AS model we have developed could be used to explain recent real GDP and inflation in the Canadian economy.

Review Question 19

Next

This chapter extended the macroeconomic model to include inflation and the adjustments in rates of wage increase and rates of inflation that work toward the elimination of output gaps. Such wage and price adjustment is time consuming, particularly in times of recessionary gaps, confirming the roles of monetary policy as the main policy tool for aggregate demand management aimed at an inflation rate target. However, the growth in potential GDP over time has yet to be discussed. This is done in Chapter 14.

SUMMARY

- Potential **output, Y_p,** is the output of goods and services when wage rates and prices are fully flexible, there is no money illusion, and all markets are in equilibrium.
- The **long-run aggregate supply curve, LAS,** is vertical at potential output. The economy is operating at full employment.
- The **equilibrium inflation rate** is determined by the intersection of the aggregate demand curve and the vertical long-run aggregate supply curve.
- The position of the aggregate demand curve and the equilibrium inflation rate depend on the **monetary policy target** set by the central bank.
- In **labour markets**, implicit and explicit contractual relationships between employers and employees limit the short-run flexibility of money wage rates. Employers and employees prefer adjustments to levels of employment in response to fluctuations in demand for output before adjustments are made to money wage rates.
- Over time, persistent changes in aggregate demand and output do result in changes to the *rate of growth* of money wage rates. **Phillips curves** describe the ways that unemployment rates that differ from the natural rate, and the corresponding output gaps, cause changes in money wage rates and inflation rates.
- The **short-run aggregate supply curve, AS,** is drawn on the assumption of a **rate of growth of money wage rates** determined mainly by decisions in the recent past, which reflects recent labour market conditions.
- Changes in the rate of growth of money wage rates, as a result of persistent GDP gaps, **shift the short-run aggregate supply curve**. A recessionary gap lowers the rate of money wage growth and shifts AS down. An inflationary gap increases the rate of money wage rate growth and shifts AS up. In either case, **the change in wage rate growth is the key adjustment mechanism** moving the economy toward equilibrium at potential output.
- **Permanent supply shocks** alter potential output and equilibrium AS. **Temporary supply shocks** shift the short-run supply curve for a limited time period.
- **Monetary policy** could completely offset **demand shocks**, stabilizing both output and inflation—if it were applied immediately and if effects were instant.
- **Monetary policy** must choose between output stability and inflation rate stability when the economy faces a **temporary supply shock**.
- The effect of a **permanent supply shock** on output cannot be escaped indefinitely. Monetary policy can stabilize the inflation rate.
- **Taylor rules** describe how central banks choose their settings for interest rates in response to deviations in both inflation rates and output from targets.

KEY TERMS

KEY EQUATIONS AND RELATIONS

Equations

The aggregate production function: $Y = A \times (F(N, K)$	(13.1)	p. 329
The real interest rate: $r = i - \pi$	(13.2)	p. 331
Aggregate expenditure: $AE = A_0 - vr + [c(1 - t) - z]Y$	(13.3)	p. 332
Equilibrium real GDP: $Y = \dfrac{A_0 - vr}{[1 - c(1 - t) + z]}$	(13.4)	p. 332
Monetary policy function: $r = r_0 + \beta(\pi - \pi^*)$	(13.5)	p. 332
Aggregate demand: $Y = \dfrac{A_0 - v[r_0 + \beta(\pi - \pi^*)]}{[1 - c(1 - t) + z]}$	(13.6)	p. 332
The rate of change in money wage rates: $\omega = \dfrac{w_t - w_{t-1}}{w_{t-1}} = \dfrac{\Delta w}{w_{t-1}}$	(13.7)	p. 341
A Taylor rule for monetary policy: $i = i_0 + a(\pi - \pi_0^*) + b(Y - Y_P)$	(13.8)	p. 354

Relations

Long-run equilibrium: With fully flexible wages and prices, long-run equilibrium real GDP is equal to potential GDP, $Y = Y_P$

A change in long-run equilibrium comes from ΔY_P.

Neutrality of money: The long-run equilibrium inflation rate is determined by monetary policy.

$\pi > 0$ requires $\dfrac{\Delta M}{M} > 0$

Inflation targets: Central bank inflation target leads to stabilization of Y at Y_P.

$\pi \neq \pi^* \rightarrow \Delta i \rightarrow \Delta AD \rightarrow \Delta Y \rightarrow Y_P$

Business cycles: Short-run fluctuations in AD and AS cause business cycles in real GDP and create recessionary and inflationary gaps.

AD shocks $\rightarrow$ Y and π move in the same direction
AS shocks $\rightarrow$ Y and π move in opposite directions

Self-adjustment to Y_P: Persistent output gaps cause offsetting AS adjustments if wage rates and prices are flexible.

By the Phillips curve:
$Y < Y_P \rightarrow \downarrow$wage rate increase $\rightarrow \downarrow$cost increases $\rightarrow \downarrow\pi + \uparrow Y$
$Y > Y_P \rightarrow \uparrow$wage rate increase $\rightarrow \uparrow$cost increases $\rightarrow \uparrow\pi + \downarrow Y$

Monetary policy's role: Stickiness or slow adjustment in wage rate increases and inflation in times of output gaps create a role for monetary policy to offset the costs of output gaps.

Persistent output gaps and inflation rates that differ from the central bank's target rate call for:

$\Delta i \rightarrow \Delta AD \rightarrow \Delta Y + \Delta\pi \rightarrow Y_p + \pi^*$

REVIEW QUESTIONS

Review Questions and answers are included in Connect at www.mcgrawhillconnect.ca.

1. Define potential output. Draw a diagram that shows an AS curve that represents potential output, and explain what determines its position and slope. Why is potential output not affected by changes in the inflation rate?

2. Suppose the central bank's monetary policy sets the real interest rate according to the function:
   $r = 3.0 + 2.0(\pi - \pi^*)$ with $\pi^* = 4.0$,
   and aggregate expenditure is the sum of:
   $C = 200 + 0.75Y$
   $I = 85 - 2r$
   $G = 100$
   $NX = 50 - 0.15Y - 3r$
   a. What is the equation for the AD curve?
   b. Plot the AD curve in a diagram, not necessarily to scale, that shows the horizontal intercept and slope of the curve.

3. Use a diagram to illustrate the equilibrium inflation rate. In this diagram, show how a permanent increase in export demand would affect the equilibrium inflation rate, if the central bank did not change its monetary policy. If the central bank did react to this change in the equilibrium inflation rate to defend its inflation target, what change in the interest rate setting and money supply growth would you observe? How would this change in the interest rate setting affect AD and the composition of AD?

4. If careful research estimates potential output Y_p at 1000, and the AD function is as derived in question 2, what is the equilibrium inflation rate? What interest rate must the central bank set to defend its inflation target?

5. Suppose opportunities for investing in high tech applications boost aggregate demand in the short run, but aggregate supply in the long run. Using AS and AD curves starting in equilibrium at potential output, show why output might rise without much of an increase in inflation.

6. Why are wages slow to adjust to changes in economic activity?

7. Explain the position of the Phillips curve in terms of the rate of wage increase when the economy is at potential output and the natural unemployment rate. What determines the slope of the Phillips curve?

8. Using a Phillips curve, illustrate and explain how GDP gaps would affect the rate of increase in money wages and prices.

9. What is the difference between a short-run aggregate supply curve (AS), and a long run aggregate supply curve (LAS) at potential output?

10. In a diagram, draw an aggregate supply curve at potential output (LAS), and a short-run aggregate supply curve (AS). When the economy is in full equilibrium, why do these aggregate supply curves intersect at the inflation rate π^*_0 and output Y_p? What is the inherited rate of increase of money wage rates in your diagram?

11. Starting from a point at the intersection of the LAS and AS curves, show and explain what would happen to output in the short run if the inflation rate declined. What determines the slope of the AS curve?

12. Suppose a new round of labour negotiations results in a higher average rate of increase in money wage rates for the next three years. Illustrate and explain how this would affect short-run aggregate supply conditions and the AS curve.

13. Draw an aggregate supply and demand curve diagram to show an economy in short-run equilibrium at potential output. Suppose a wide-spread recession reduces incomes in foreign countries, leading to reduced demand for exports. Illustrate and explain how this would affect the short-run equilibrium conditions in your diagram.

14. If the short run effects of the change in exports in question 13 were persistent, and there were no discretionary monetary or fiscal policy reactions, would the economy return to an equilibrium at potential output on its own? Use an AD/AS/Y_P diagram to illustrate and explain your answer.

15. In the latter part of 2007 and the first half of 2008 international prices for crude oil and commodities increased dramatically. What is your prediction of the effect of these developments on AD, AS, and short run equilibrium output and inflation?

16. Suppose an economy in equilibrium at potential output experiences a large increase in investment expenditure to develop existing and new energy supplies and sources. Use an AD/AS/LAS diagram to show and explain the effect of this change in demand on short-run equilibrium conditions. What monetary policy action would be required to restore equilibrium at potential output and the target inflation rate?

17. Suppose the central bank reacted to maintain its target inflation rate in the face of a permanent increase in government expenditure on health care not financed by increased tax rates, at a time when the economy was operating at potential output. Use an AD/AS/LAS diagram to show the effects of the increased government expenditure and the reaction by the central bank. What is crowding out?

18. In recent years the federal government reduced the GST from 7 percent to 5 percent. Use an AD/AS/LAS diagram to illustrate and explain the effects of this tax change on equilibrium output and inflation. If the economy was in equilibrium at potential output and the target inflation rate before the tax cut, what monetary policy action, if any, would be required to maintain those equilibrium conditions after the tax cut?

19. Strong demand for crude oil raises the price of oil for several years, but then new supply from both conventional and non-conventional energy sources and new energy technologies stabilize oil prices. Show how the economy is affected under the following alternative approaches to monetary policy:
    a. fixed interest rate
    b. a Taylor rule
    c. flexible inflation targeting
    d. a nominal money supply growth target

20. Visit the Bank of Canada's Web site www.bankofcanada.ca/en/backgrounders and summarize the Bank's views on the costs of high inflation and the benefits of low inflation. What current and target rates of inflation and overnight interest rate target does the bank report on its homepage?

PART 6

Growth Theory and International Trade Theory

This Part of the text covers two important additional topics. Chapter 14 provides an introduction to theories of economic growth. It is focused on the growth in potential GDP over longer periods of time. Earlier chapters concentrated on the short-run business cycle fluctuations of real GDP relative to potential GDP, but growth in potential GDP is the source of the improvements in standards of living that short-run stabilization policies try to protect. Chapter 15 covers the theory of international trade that explains the flows of goods and services exports and imports—important components of aggregate demand in a small open economy like Canada. It also examines international trade policies designed to influence those trade flows.

CHAPTER 14

Economic Growth

LEARNING OUTCOMES

By the end of this chapter you should understand:

1. The pattern of economic growth across countries
2. The growth and sources of growth in potential output
3. The growth and sources of growth in real GDP per worker
4. Technology and growth in per capita output
5. Neoclassical growth theory and the convergence hypothesis
6. Recent growth studies and policy issues

Economists have always been fascinated by economic growth and the theory of economic growth. In 1798, Thomas Malthus' *First Essay on Population* predicted that output growth would be far outstripped by population growth, causing starvation and the end of population growth. This was the origin of the notion of economics as a "dismal science." Some countries are still stuck in a Malthusian trap. Others broke through to sustained growth and prosperity. We will examine how they did it.

By the end of the 1960s, economists had worked out theories of economic growth. One of these theories, the neoclassical growth model, yielded many insights but had one central failing. It left little room for government policy to make a difference to the long-run growth rate. Later work has addressed this limitation.

In the mid-1980s, a simple insight spawned a new approach, in which long-run growth is also affected by private behaviour and government policy. We briefly explain both the neoclassical growth theory and this new approach.

14.1 The Pattern of Economic Growth across Countries

Economic growth is the annual percentage change in real GDP or per capita real GDP.

Recall, from Chapter 4, that the growth rate of a variable is its percentage change over time. To define **economic growth** we must specify both the variable to measure and the period over which to measure it. Table 14.1 uses percentage changes in real GDP and real GDP per person over periods of one year to measure annual rates of economic growth.

Annual real GDP measures the total output of final goods and services in the economy for one-year periods. As a result, the annual rate of growth in real GDP is the change in the size of the total economy. But, as we also discussed in Chapter 4, increases in the size of the total economy may not reflect changes in standards of living or welfare. To get an indication of how these grow or stagnate we need to look at growth in real GDP per person. Growth in real GDP can raise standards of living only if it exceeds the growth in population, providing, on average, more goods and services to the average individual.

Over the period 1950 to 2004, Canadian real GDP grew 7.5-fold, and income per person increased more than threefold. On average, we are richer today than our grandparents were, but not as rich as our grandchildren will be. Table 14.1 and 14.2 show these long-term trends were even more dramatic in some other countries. In Japan, for example, real GDP grew more than 17-fold and real GDP per person increased more than 11-fold. Growth in China has been even more dramatic.

These observations raise three questions.

1. What is long-term growth?
2. What are the causes or sources of growth?
3. Can economic policies affect growth?

We will focus mainly on industrial countries, but growth or lack of it in poor countries is also an extremely important issue for the economics of development. To see other interesting dimensions of growth compared across many more countries over longer time periods, visit the Web site www.gapminder.org

TABLE 14.1 Growth in Real GDP and Per Capita Real GDP in Selected OECD Countries 1950 to 2004 (Based on purchasing power parity, 2000 U.S. $)

	Ratio of Real GDP in 2004 to 1950	Annual Growth Rate (%)	Ratio Real GDP Per Capita in 2004 to 1950	Annual Growth Rate (%)
Canada	7.6	3.9	3.3	2.2
United States	6.1	3.4	3.2	2.2
United Kingdom	3.8	2.5	3.1	2.2
Japan	17.8	5.6	11.7	4.7
Sweden	4.2	2.7	3.3	2.3
Spain	11.1	4.6	7.7	3.9
France	5.9	3.4	4.1	2.7
Australia	7.7	3.9	3.2	2.2

Source: Based on data from the Groningen Growth and Development Centre and the Conference Board, *Total Economy Database*, January 2005, http://www.ggdc.net.

TABLE 14.2 Growth in Real GDP and Per Capita Real GDP in Newly Industrialized Countries 1970–2006 (In 1990 U.S. $)

Country	Ratio Real GDP 2006 to 1970	Annual Growth Rate (%)	Ratio Per Cap 2006 to 1970	Annual Growth Rate (%)
Hong Kong	9.3	6.5	5.1	4.7
Indonesia	8.0	6.0	4.2	4.1
Malaysia	11.5	7.1	4.8	4.5
Rep of Korea	11.0	6.9	7.3	5.7
Singapore	13.2	7.5	6.2	5.3
Thailand	8.5	6.2	5.0	4.7
China	20.9	8.9	13.2	7.5
India	6.2	5.2	2.9	3.1

Source: United Nations Statistical Division, National Accounts Main Aggregates Database, August 2007 and author's calculations. http//:unstats.un.org/unsd/snaama/SelectionCountry.asp

GDP AND ECONOMIC OUTPUT

Because real GDP measures final output of goods and services, it omits output not bought and sold, which may be important to economic welfare and standards of living. It also suffers from two big omissions, leisure and externalities such as pollution and congestion.

In most industrial countries, average hours of work have fallen significantly since 1950. In choosing to work fewer hours, people reveal that the extra leisure is worth at least as much as the extra goods they could have bought by working longer. As a result, GDP understates the true economic output of the economy. Conversely, the output of pollution reduces the net welfare that the economy is producing, and ideally should be subtracted from GDP. If the value of leisure rose more slowly than measured output, and the cost of pollution rose more rapidly, true growth rates including these factors would be lower than those recorded in Tables 14.1 and 14.2.

GDP AND HAPPINESS

Even with an accurate and comprehensive measure of real GDP, two problems remain. First, do we care about total GDP or GDP per capita? Tables 14.1 and 14.2 tells us that, although real GDP grew more quickly in Canada and Australia than in France from 1950 to 2004, France had faster growth in real GDP per person. As a result, the ratio of GDP per person in 2004 to 1950 in France was higher than in Canada or Sweden, suggesting a larger improvement in the standard of living in France than in the other two countries.

This observation reveals a further important aspect of economic growth, whether measured in terms of total GDP or per capita GDP. *Small differences in annual growth rates result in large changes over time.* Total GDP in Spain grew at an average rate of 4.6 percent as compared with 3.9 percent in Canada, a difference of 0.7 percentage points. But Spanish GDP in 2004 was 11 times its 1950 value, whereas Canadian GDP in 2004 was only 7.6 times its 1950 value. Similarly, the rate of growth of per capita

GDP in China at 7.5 percent exceeded the growth rate of *per capita* GDP in the Republic of Korea by 1.8 percentage points, with the result that *per capita* GDP in China increased thirteenfold while that in Korea increased by just over sevenfold. Looked at in another way, small differences in the annual rate of growth of per capita real GDP have large cumulative effects on standards of living.

Review Questions 1 and 2

14.2 Growth in Potential Output

In the last two chapters we saw how the economy fluctuates around potential GDP when wages and prices are sticky and slow to adjust. We also saw that, given a time period long enough to allow for complete adjustment in wages and prices, the economy would move to a long-run equilibrium at potential output. Now we move to a third time horizon, the **very long run**, a time frame in which wages *and* prices are fully flexible, and the labour force, the stock of capital equipment, and the technology used in production can change. In this time frame, output fluctuations around potential output are swamped by the growth of potential output itself.

The **very long run** is the time required for changes to occur in the stock of capital, the size of the labour force, and the technology of production.

The aggregate production function we used in Chapter 13 described the links between inputs to production and real GDP produced. Recall that, for the whole economy, Y is real GDP produced by using inputs of labour (N) and capital (K). The function F tells us how much we get out of particular amounts of labour and capital used in the production process.

$$Y = A \times F(N, K) \qquad (14.1)$$

The function F(. . .) does not change, but changes in N and K cause changes in output Y. We also capture technical progress or improvements in technology separately through A, which measures the state of technology at any date. As technology improves, A increases and we get more real GDP from the same inputs of labour and capital. A 10 percent increase in A gives 10 percent more real GDP from the same inputs of labour and capital. We describe this as an increase in productivity because outputs per worker and per machine increase. A is often called **total factor productivity (TFP)**.

Total factor productivity (TFP) is output relative to the combined inputs of both labour and capital, the total factor inputs to production.

Actual real GDP is the output produced at any time based on the actual inputs of capital and labour. In terms of our production function, we would show this by writing:

$$Y_t = A_t \times F(N_t, K_t) \qquad (14.2)$$

In this equation, Y_t is real GDP in year t, A_t is determined by the current state of technology, and K_t and N_t measure the actual use of capital and labour in year t.

Potential output is the real GDP produced when labour and capital are employed at equilibrium rates using the best available technology. To recognize this, we write a specific production function:

$$Y_P = A_t \times F(N_F, K_0) \qquad (14.3)$$

Y_P is potential output produced by operating plants and machinery at their designed capacity (K_0) and using the full employment equilibrium supply of labour services (N_F). A_t is the state of knowledge and technology used in the production process and reflected in the productivity of labour and capital.

Any *growth* in the potential output of goods and services then comes from *growth* in labour inputs to production, capital inputs to production, and *changes* in factor productivity as a result of new and improved technology.

Growth accounting measures the sources of growth in real GDP. From the production function, it follows that:

Growth accounting measures the contributions of labour, capital, and technology to growth in output.

Growth in Real GDP	=	Effect of Growth in Total Factor Productivity	+	Effect of Growth in Labour Inputs	+	Effect of Growth in Capital Inputs

The way that growth in capital and labour affects the growth in total output can be measured by the incomes they receive. The income approach to the measurement of net domestic product and GDP identifies these incomes. Table 14.3 (page 366) provides data on GDP in Canada in 2008. From that data we see that employment income was about two-thirds of net domestic income. This is close to the longer-term average of employment income in net domestic product, and it shows where the measure comes from. Labour's average contribution to and share of national income, measured over time periods of many years, is approximately two-thirds of national income. Capital's contribution and share is the remaining one-third of national income.

The growth in potential GDP over time can then be expressed as the growth in total factor productivity plus the *weighted sum* of the growth in the capital and labour inputs to production as follows:

$$\frac{\Delta Y_P}{Y_P} = \frac{\Delta A}{A} + 2/3\left(\frac{\Delta N}{N}\right) + 1/3\left(\frac{\Delta K}{K}\right) \tag{14.4}$$

The weights 2/3 and 1/3 applied to growth in labour and capital inputs are based on their shares in national income. They determine the rate of growth in real GDP as a result of growth in the inputs of capital and labour. By these weights, a 10 percent increase in labour input, capital and technology held constant, would result in an increase in real GDP of 2/3 × 10 percent, which is 6.6 percent. Similarly, a 10 percent increase in capital input would result in a 1/3 × 10 percent increase in real GDP.

The increase in productivity from improvements in technology cannot be seen and measured directly. As a result, growth accounting classifies these effects as a *residual*. The difference between the growth in real GDP and the weighted sum of the growth in labour and capital inputs is called the **Solow residual**, named after Professor Robert Solow, whose work on growth theory was recognized with a Nobel Prize. The Solow Residual is a measure of the contribution to growth made by improvements in the technology of production that raise the productivity of both labour and capital.

The **Solow residual** is the growth in real GDP or per capita real GDP not caused by growth in factor inputs, but attributed to improved technology.

The Solow residual measured by $\Delta A/A$ is found by rearranging the growth accounting equation (14.4) as follows:

$$\frac{\Delta A}{A} = \frac{\Delta Y}{Y} - 2/3\left(\frac{\Delta N}{N}\right) - 1/3\left(\frac{\Delta K}{K}\right) \tag{14.5}$$

The numerical example in Table 14.3 illustrates the procedure. It assumes we know the growth rates of real GDP, capital stock, and employment, measured as annual percentage changes.

The calculation made using growth accounting shows that the increased productivity of both labour and capital resulting from improvements in technology was the source of 2.1 percent of the 5.0 percent growth in real GDP in our example.

TABLE 14.3 **An Example of Growth Accounting**

Observed growth rates:	$\Delta Y/Y$	$\Delta N/N$	$\Delta K/K$
	5.0	2.4	3.9

Calculating the Solow residual by equation (14.5):

$$(\Delta A/A) = 5.0 - 2/3(2.4) - 1/3(3.9)$$
$$(\Delta A/A) = 5.0 - 1.6 - 1.3$$
$$(\Delta A/A) = 2.1$$

Source: Canadian Social Research Links, www.canadiansocialresearch.net/stats.htm, various tables.

Table 14.4 shows the results of some research at the Bank of Canada on the sources of growth in real GDP and potential GDP in Canada over the period 1950 to 1996 and projections for future growth in potential GDP. The contributions of capital and labour inputs are weighted as in the simple example above. Growth in actual and potential real GDP are the result of growth in factor inputs and the growth in productivity coming from improvements in the technology of production.

We can see that growth in real GDP and potential GDP declined over the 1950 to 1996 period. This slowdown was partly a result of a slowdown in the growth of population, and labour and capital inputs to production. But starting in the 1970s there was also a slowdown in productivity growth, which reduced the rate of growth of output per worker. We will look at this slowdown in productivity in more detail later in this

TABLE 14.4 **Sources of Growth in Real GDP and Potential GDP in Canada 1950 to 1996 with Projections to 2021 (Annual average percentage change)**

	Real GDP	Total Factor Productivity	Labour Input	Capital Input	Estimated Potential GDP
	$\Delta Y/Y$	$\Delta A/A$	$\Delta N/N$	$\Delta K/K$	$\Delta Y_P/Y_P$
1950 – 1960	4.6	1.8	1.2	6.1	—
1960 – 1970	5.2	2.2	2.1	4.8	5.2
1970 – 1980	4.6	1.5	2.6	4.1	4.4
1980 – 1990	2.9	0.7	1.7	3.3	2.9
1990 – 1996	1.5	0.4	0.4	2.5	2.1
Projections:					
1996 – 2001	—	1.3	1.7	1.7	3.0
2001 – 2011	—	1.2	1.2	1.2	2.4
2011 – 2021	—	1.2	0.5	0.5	1.7

Source: J. Kuszczak and R. Dion, "Potential Output Growth: Some Long-Term Projections." *Bank of Canada Review*, Winter 1997–1998, pp. 43–59, Tables 1 and 5. Bank of Canada, 2009.

chapter. It had important implications for the standard of living in many countries, including Canada. Some further research on productivity growth in Canada by the Centre for the Study of Standards of Living, www.csls.ca, and at the Bank of Canada has uncovered another productivity slowdown in Canada relative to the United States after the year 2000, which is a current source of concern.

Review Question 3 and 4

The *projections* for growth in potential output in the table are based on simple assumptions about growth in total factor productivity, labour force, and capital stock. Productivity grows at 1.2 percent a year. Declining growth rates in population and labour input after 1996 result in forecasts of declining growth rates in potential GDP.

14.3 Growth in Per Capita GDP

Growth in potential GDP measures the increase in the size of the economy, but it does not tell us what is happening to per capita GDP and *standards of living*. To discover the sources of growth in per capita GDP and improvements in standards of living, we need to study the production function in more detail. Then we can use growth accounting to uncover the sources of past growth in per capita GDP.

Consider the same production function we have used for total GDP:

$$Y = A \times F(N, K) \quad (14.1)$$

Again, we will assume that Y will grow by two-thirds of the growth in labour input and one-third the growth in capital input. If, for example, labour force growth increases employment by 10 percent, with fixed capital stock, K, and technology, A, GDP will increase by 6.67 percent. You can make a similar calculation for the effects of growth in the capital stock. The weights 2/3 and 1/3 are the *elasticities* of output with respect to the inputs of labour and capital.

FACTOR CONTRIBUTIONS AND SCALE ECONOMIES

The increase in total output when an additional unit of a factor (labour or capital) is used in the production process, and other inputs are held constant, is the **marginal product** of that added factor. The production functions widely used in economics have *diminishing marginal productivity*. As more and more workers are employed using a fixed number of machines, each additional worker adds less and less to total output. The marginal product of labour, $\Delta Y/\Delta N$, falls. Furthermore, because each additional input of labour adds less to total output than the unit before it, output per worker, Y/N, also falls.

The **marginal product** of a factor is the change in total output caused by a change of one unit in the input of that factor to production.

It is often assumed that production involves *constant returns to scale*. Instead of increasing just one input to production, suppose all inputs are increased together, in the same proportions. Labour and capital inputs might both be doubled, for example. Then, if output increases in exactly the same proportions as inputs have increased, there are constant returns to scale.

The production functions used in growth accounting have these properties. Consider the following example. Holding technology constant at $A = 1$ to simplify matters, we can write:

$$Y = N^{2/3} \times K^{1/3} \quad (14.6)$$

using the weights we have used in growth accounting to measure the contributions of labour and capital to output, based on their shares in national income, as the exponents

TABLE 14.5 **Outputs and Changes in Outputs When Factor Inputs Change**

Production Function: $Y = N^{2/3} \times K^{1/3}$

Labour Input (N)	Capital Input (K)	Output (Y)	%ΔN	%ΔK	%ΔY
50	20	36.8	—	—	—
55	20	39.3	10.0	0	6.6
55	22	40.5	0	10.0	3.3
60.5	24.2	44.6	10.0	10.0	10.0

on labour and capital inputs. Table 14.5 gives numerical examples of the way this production function works.

The first row of the table shows that a labour input of 50 units combined with a capital input of 20 units gives output $Y = 50^{2/3} \times 20^{1/3} = 36.8$ units. The next three rows illustrate the underlying diminishing returns and constant returns to scale in this production process. An increase of either labour input of 10 percent or capital input of 10 percent with the other input constant increases output, but by less than 10 percent in each case. Because output grows by less than the growth of the input in each case, output per worker or per unit of capital falls.

However, when only one input grows, output per unit of the factor held constant rises. In the second row of the table, capital input is constant when labour input grows. More labour inputs increase total output and output per unit of capital. Similarly, in the third row an increase in capital input increases labour productivity.

The fourth row of the table shows constant returns to scale. When labour and capital inputs both increase by the same proportion, 10 percent in this example, output increases by the same proportion, 10 percent. As a result, output per worker and output per unit of capital are constant. In terms of economic growth, equal growth rates of labour force and capital stock make total GDP grow at that same rate, but leave *per capita* GDP unchanged.

To see the sources of growth in *per capita* GDP, we can manipulate the production function and apply growth accounting. To get per capita GDP, simply divide both sides of the production function (14.6) by N to give output per worker as follows:

$$\mathbf{Y = A \times N^{2/3} \times K^{1/3}} \qquad \mathbf{(14.6)}$$

$$Y/N = A \times (N^{2/3} \times K^{1/3})/N$$

$$Y/N = A \times (N^{1/3} \times K^{1/3}) = A \times (K/N)^{1/3}$$

To make the notation a bit neater, we can use lower case letters to indicate output per worker ($y = Y/N$) and capital per worker ($k = K/N$). This gives:

$$\mathbf{y = A \times k^{1/3}} \qquad \mathbf{(14.7)}$$

Table 14.6 shows the important properties of this *per worker production function.* Part (a) of the table assumes constant technology at $A = 1$, and shows the effects of increasing the capital stock used in production. With labour input held constant, the

TABLE 14.6 **An Output per Worker Production Function: $y = A \times k^{1/3}$**

	Labour Input (N) (1)	Capital Input (K) (2)	Capital/ Labour (k = K/N) (3)	Output/ Worker ($y = A \times k^{1/3}$) (4)	Δ(Output/ Worker) (Δy) (5)
(a) Assume A = 1					
(i)	100	500	5	1.71	—
(ii)	100	600	6	1.82	0.11
(iii)	100	700	7	1.91	0.09
(iv)	100	800	8	2.00	0.09
(v)	100	900	9	2.08	0.08
(vi)	100	1000	10	2.15	0.07
(b) Assume A = 1.10					
(i)	100	500	5	1.88	—
(ii)	100	600	6	2.00	0.12
(iii)	100	700	7	2.10	0.10
(iv)	100	800	8	2.20	0.10
(v)	100	900	9	2.29	0.09
(vi)	100	1000	10	2.37	0.08

capital/labour ratio (k) in column (3) rises from 5 to 10. Output per worker in column (4) rises as a result from 1.71 to 2.15. However, the important observations are in column (5). Increased capital inputs yield smaller and smaller increases in output per worker. There is a limit to the increases in per capita output and standards of living that can be achieved by increasing capital stock.

Although the table does not show it, increases in labour input with capital stock held constant also reduce output per worker. In row (a) (i), for example, if labour input were 110 and capital input 500, then k would be 4.55 and y would be 1.67 rather than 1.71. *Population and labour force growth need to be matched by growth in the capital stock to maintain standards of living.*

Part (b) of the table shows the effect of a one-time increase in productivity by 10 percent based on improved technology. In column (4), output per worker increases by 10 percent, compared with the levels in part (a) of the table. Furthermore, the changes in output per worker given by increased capital inputs are also 10 percent higher. Improved technology does not eliminate the pattern of decline in output per worker in column (5), but it does make the change in output per worker 10 percent higher in each case. This means that continuing increases in productivity based on new technologies can provide *sustained* increases in per capita output and standards of living.

Figure 14.1 shows these production relations in a diagram. The ratio of capital stock to labour, k, is measured on the horizontal axis. Output per worker, y, is measured on the vertical axis. Two per-worker production functions are used to distinguish between the effects of increases in capital stock and the effects of improvements in technology.

FIGURE 14.1 **The Effects of Increases in the Capital Labour Ratio and Improvements in Technology on Output per Worker**

An increase in the capital to labour ratio from k_1 to k_2 raises output per worker from y_1 to y_2. The shape of the production function shows that further increases in k will give further but smaller increases in y. A change in technology shifts the production function up as y increases at every k. The *combined effects* of an increase in k and an increase in A are increased output per worker from y_1 to y_3.

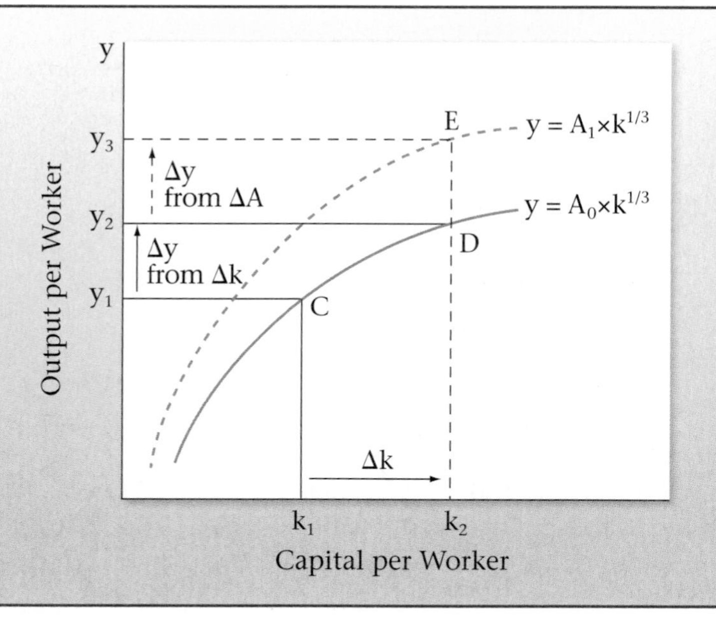

The declining slopes of both production functions illustrate the diminishing returns that lead to the declining changes in output per worker as the capital/labour ratio increases. For example, starting at point C, an increase in the ratio of capital to labour moves the economy along the production function to point D. Output per worker increases at a decreasing rate. This shows that increased capital to labour ratios can increase output per worker until diminishing returns set in and limit sustained increases in output per worker.

Review Question 5

An improvement in technology that increases productivity shifts the production function up. At capital to labour ratio k_2, for example, the increased productivity moves the economy from D to E as output per worker rises from y_2 to y_3. This shows us that growth in per capita output, moving from y_1 to y_3, points C to E in Figure 14.1,is a result of both the growth in the capital to labour ratio and improvements in productivity.

Once again, growth accounting allows us to sort out the effects of these two factors on growth in output per worker and per capita GDP. Table 14.7 uses recent Canadian experience as an example.

The first three columns of the table give data on real GDP, employment, and real capital stock for four years over the 1990 to 2005 period. Columns (4) and (5) use these data to calculate the output per worker and capital per worker that we see in our per-worker production function. The growth in output per worker and the growth in capital per worker are reported in columns (6) and (7) as the percentage changes over the five-year periods.

Growth accounting divides the sources of growth in output per worker between increases in capital per worker and increases in productivity based on improvements in technology. From the production function, we know that an increase in the capital/labour ratio increases output per worker by a factor of 1/3. Column (8) in the table reports this weighted contribution of the increase in capital per worker to the increase we see in output per worker. Subtracting these contributions from the increases in output

TABLE 14.7 **Sources of Growth in Per-Worker GDP in Canada, 1990 to 2005**

	Real GDP Y (bill $97) (1)	Employment N (millions) (2)	Capital Stock K (bill $97) (3)	Real GDP per Worker Y/N = y (000 $97) (4)	Capital per Worker K/N (000 $97) (5)	Growth in Y/N %Δy (6)	Growth in K/N %Δk (7)	Contribution from Δk = %Δk/3 (8) = (7)/3	Solow Residual %ΔA (9)=(6)–(8)
1990	762	13.07	1,308	58.30	100.07	—	—	—	—
1995	832	13.27	1,450	62.69	109.27	7.5	9.2	3.1	4.4
2000	1,020	14.76	1,560	69.11	105.69	10.2	–3.3	–1.1	11.3
2005	1,158	16.18	1,873	71.56	115.76	3.5	9.5	3.2	0.3

Source: Adapted from Statistics Canada CANSIM Database Table 380-0002 Series V1992067, Table 031-0002 Series V4419841, and Table 282-0087 Series V2062811, and author's calculations.

per worker gives the Solow residual, column (9), which again is a measure of the effect of improvements in technology on output per worker.

Canadian experience over the 1990 to 2005 period provides three different and interesting examples of growth in GDP per worker. In the first five years, 1990 to 1995, there was very little growth in employment but substantial growth in capital stock. As a result, the capital to labour ratio, k, increased by 9.2 percent and accounted for 3.1 percentage points, or 41 percent of the 7.5 percent growth in real GDP per worker. Improved technology as measured by the Solow residual contributed the other 4.4 percentage points.

By contrast, employment and capital stock both grew strongly from 1995 to 2000, but employment growth (11.2 percent) exceeded capital stock growth (7.6 percent). As a result, the growth in the capital to labour ratio was negative, −3.3 percent. Nevertheless, output per worker grew more in the second period, up 10.2 percent. Productivity gains from improved technology, again measured by the Solow residual, were the major source of strong growth in GDP per worker.

The decline in the capital to labour ratio in the 1995 to 2000 period appears to have reduced the growth in output per worker in the 2000 to 2005 period. Even though capital stock increased by about 20 percent and employment grew by just 9.6 percent, output per worker increased by only 3.5 percent over the period. The Solow residual in column (9) shows a very small contribution to growth in output per worker from improved technology.

Thinking of these experiences in terms of the production functions in Figure 14.1 illustrates the differences between sub-periods. From 1900 to 1995, the economy moved to the right along the production function as k grew by 9.2 per cent, for example, from C to D in the diagram. This provided a 3.1 percent increase in y, as from y_1 to y_2. Improved technology shifted the production function up to further increase output per worker from y_2 to y_3 at point E in the diagram. In the next period, 1995 to 2000, the movement along the production function was in the opposite direction, to the left from E, as k declined. However, a very strong effect from improved technology as measured by the Solow residual of 11.3 percent shifted the production function upward (not shown in the diagram) and sustained the growth in output per worker at 10.2 percent.

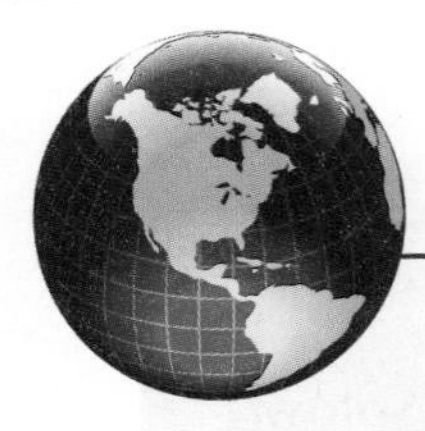

APPLICATION BOX 14.1

Causes of Recent Weakness in Productivity Growth

The following introduction to a recent study of the slowdown in productivity in Canada shows the important role productivity growth plays in improving standards of living. The full article is available from the Centre for the Study of Living Standards Web site at the address given below.

An Analysis of the Causes of Weak Labour Productivity Growth in Canada since 2000

Jean Francois Arsenault and Andrew Sharpe,
Centre for the Study of Living Standards

Since 2000 Gross Domestic Product (GDP) growth in Canada and the United States has followed a similar path. Business sector GDP growth averaged 2.5 percent per year between 2000 and 2007 compared to 2.6 percent in the United States. The similarity of GDP growth, however, obscures the emergence of a 1.6 percentage point gap in labour productivity growth since 2000. Between 1973 and 2000, business sector labour productivity, defined as output per hour worked, grew at similar rates in Canada and the United states, averaging 1.55 percent and 1.71 percent per year respectively, a 0.16 percentage point difference. The growth rate difference widened significantly in the post 2000 period, with labour productivity growth in the United States (2.60 percent per year) more than two and a half times larger than in Canada (0.95 percent per year)........"

The authors argue that this situation is temporary, arising largely from the structural adjustment of the economy from a surplus labour to a labour shortage economy. They find that weak productivity growth is concentrated in the goods sector of the economy, which faced most of the adjustment. Part of the adjustment in this sector was linked to the steady rise in the international value of the Canadian dollar. The result was an extended period of declining output in manufacturing, making productivity increases more difficult to achieve. They note there is some recent evidence of a turnaround in this experience based on preliminary estimates for the 2005 to 2007 period.

Source: International Productivity Monitor/Observateur international de la productivité, Number 16, Spring 2008, Centre for the Study of Living Standards, 111 Sparks Street, Suite 500, Ottawa, Ontario, Canada K1P 5B5, www.csls.ca.

By contrast, the economy experienced a sharp slowdown in productivity growth in the 2000 to 2005 period. Even though capital per worker did grow strongly in this five-year period, output per worker grew by only 3.5 percent. The Solow residual shows a very weak contribution by improvements in technology to the growth in productivity. This slowdown in productivity has raised concerns about future improvements in standards of living and calls for government action to address this decline in productivity growth and the lower rate of productivity growth in Canada than in the United States.

These examples and our discussion of the nature and sources of growth emphasize two key aspects of the growth process. One aspect is the growth in the stock of capital, which comes from the flow of savings and investment in the economy. The other is changing technical knowledge and technology of production. These are the keys to sustained growth in total output and standards of living, but their sources are more obscure than the sources of growth in capital stock. Indeed, pessimism about the fate of society was based on both the inadequacy of investment and stagnant technology.

14.4 Technology and Growth in Output per Worker

Advances in knowledge based on research and development and experience are the key to sustained rates of productivity growth and improvements in standards of living.

TECHNICAL KNOWLEDGE

At any given time, society has a stock of technical knowledge about ways in which goods and services can be produced. Some of this knowledge is written down in books and blueprints, but much is reflected in working practices learned by hard experience. Technical advances come through **invention**, the discovery of new knowledge, and **innovation**, the incorporation of new knowledge into actual production techniques.

Invention is the discovery of new knowledge.

Innovation incorporates new knowledge into production techniques.

Major inventions can lead to spectacular increases in technical knowledge. The wheel, the steam engine, electrical generation, and the modern computer are examples. Technical progress in agriculture has also been dramatic. Industrial societies began only when productivity improvements based on advances in mechanized power, in crop science, and in animal husbandry freed some of the workforce to produce industrial goods without leaving people short of food. The replacement of animal power by machines, the development of fertilizers, drainage, and irrigation, and new hybrid seeds all played a large part in improving agricultural technology and productivity and enabling economic growth.

To introduce new ideas and methods to actual production, innovation often requires investment in new machines. Without investment, bullocks and horses cannot be transformed into tractors, even once the know-how for building tractors is available. Major new inventions thus lead to waves of investment and innovation as the ideas are put into practice. The mid-nineteenth century was the age of the train, and the mid-twentieth century the age of the car. We are now in the age of the microchip. These technologies allowed those of us in industrial countries to avoid the limits on improvements in standards of living created by the declining marginal productivity of capital per worker.

Investment in human capital can matter as much as physical capital. It brings advances in knowledge and experience to production processes. With practice, workers get better at doing a particular job. The most famous example is the Horndal effect, named after a Swedish steelworks built during 1835–36, and kept in the same condition for the next 15 years. With no change in the plant or size of the labour force, output per worker nevertheless rose by 2 percent a year. Eventually, however, as skills become mastered, further productivity increases are harder to attain.

RESEARCH AND DEVELOPMENT

What determines the amount of invention and innovation that is so important to improved standards of living? Some new ideas are the product of intellectual curiosity or frustration: There must be a better way to do this! But, like most activities, the output of new ideas depends to a large extent on the amount of resources devoted to looking for them, which in turn depends on the cost of tying up resources in this way, and the prospective benefits from success. Some research activities take place in university departments, usually funded at least in part by government, but a lot of research is privately funded through the money firms devote to research and development (R&D).

APPLICATION BOX 14.2

Economic Structure, Technology, and Prosperity

Estimates of historical standards of living, measured by per capita income, suggest a significant change originating in the U.K. and North America starting in about 1750–1800. For several centuries before then, per capita income in those areas was roughly constant at a subsistence level, about equal to that of today's poorer African countries.[1]

The shift to growth in per capita income and standards of living involved several concurrent developments first observed in the U.K. after about 1750 and continuing thereafter. The agricultural revolution brought scientific knowledge to agriculture and, with changes in land ownership, began to shift the agricultural production function, increasing productivity. Steam power technology based on mineral fuel replaced waterpower and animal power. Investment and ongoing technical development spread steam technology over a wide range of industries, including coal mining, textiles, metalworking, and transportation. Increased agricultural productivity allowed a shift in labour from agriculture to industry, and in population from rural to urban.[2] Industrialization was underway.

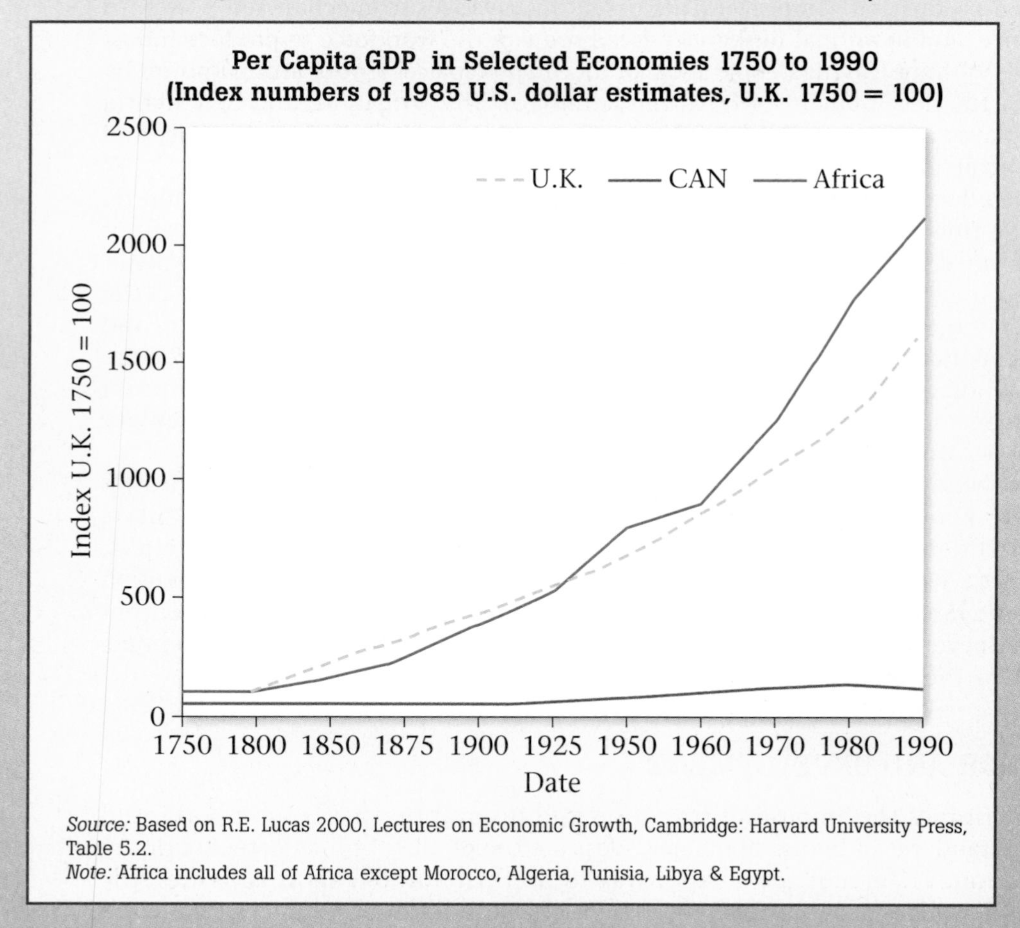

Source: Based on R.E. Lucas 2000. Lectures on Economic Growth, Cambridge: Harvard University Press, Table 5.2.
Note: Africa includes all of Africa except Morocco, Algeria, Tunisia, Libya & Egypt.

[1]Based on data in by R.E.Lucas, 2002, *Lectures on Economic Growth*. Cambridge: Harvard University Press, 2002. Table 5.2

[2] Peter Mathias, 2001, *The First Industrial Nation*, London: Routledge. Chapter 5 provides a detailed description of the links between structural change, technology, and innovation.

APPLICATION BOX 14.2 continued

Other inventions and technological changes followed these early beginnings with similar evolutions in economic structure. Telegraph and telephone, electric power, steel, automobiles, aircraft, and microchips all changed technology, increasing productivity and expanding economic capacity. Economic structure shifted from primary production to manufacturing to services, from rural to urban populations, and to increasing international trade. Productivity and standards of living improved dramatically in countries involved in this process, but not in others, as illustrated by a time-series plot of indexes of per capita income.

The outcome of research is risky. Research workers never know whether or not they will find anything useful. Research is like a risky investment project. The funds are committed before benefits, if any, start to accrue, but there is an important difference. Suppose you spend a lot of money developing a better mousetrap. When you succeed, everyone copies your new mousetrap; the price is bid down, and you never recoup your initial investment. In such a world, there would be little incentive to undertake R&D.

If the invention becomes widely available, society gets the benefit but the original developer does not; there is an externality. Private and social gains do not coincide, and the price mechanism does not provide the correct incentives. Society tries to get around this market failure in two ways. First, it grants *patents* to private inventors and innovators, legal monopolies for a fixed period of time that allow successful research projects to repay investment in R&D by temporarily charging higher prices than the cost of production alone. Second, government subsidizes a good deal of basic research in its own laboratories, in universities, and in private industry.

Review Question 6 and 7

14.5 Neoclassical Growth Theory and the Convergence Hypothesis

Now we look in more detail at the links between output growth, factor accumulation, and technical progress. Our production function again provides the framework for our discussion. We have seen that growth in output and in output per worker comes from growth in the inputs of labour and capital, changes in the ratio of capital to labour, and changes in the technology of production. Where does growth in capital and the ratio of capital to labour come from? In other words, what is the theory of economic growth? How does the theory of growth explain the *growth in productivity* as measured by *output per worker*?

Post-war theories of economic growth date back to work in the 1940s by Roy Harrod in England and Evesy Domar in the United States. In the late 1950s, Bob Solow of MIT assembled the nuts and bolts of neoclassical growth theory, the basis of most empirical work ever since. The Solow residual in growth accounting is an example.

The theory is *neoclassical* because it does not ask how actual output gets to potential output. Over a long enough period, the only question of interest is what is happening to potential output itself, and why. Neoclassical growth theory simply assumes that actual and potential output are equal.

In this long run, labour and capital grow. Usually equilibrium means that things are not changing. Now we apply equilibrium, not to levels, but to growth rates and ratios. The *steady state* is the long-run equilibrium in growth theory. Along the **steady-state** path, output, capital, and labour grow at the same rate. As a result, with constant returns to scale, capital per worker and output per worker are constant.

In the **steady state**, output, capital, and labour grow at the same rate.

FIGURE 14.2 **Steady-State Neoclassical Growth**

The line nk shows the investment per worker that maintains the ratio of capital per worker as the labour force grows. The per worker production function y = F(k) shows output per worker and the diminishing returns to increasing capital/labour ratios. sy is both saving and investment per worker. At E the economy is in a steady state. Investment sy = nk as needed to keep k constant at k*. Per worker output is constant at y* while total output and capital stock grow at the rate of labour force growth n. At any $k \neq k^*$, such as k_1, $sy \neq nk$, and k changes, moving the economy toward k* and E.

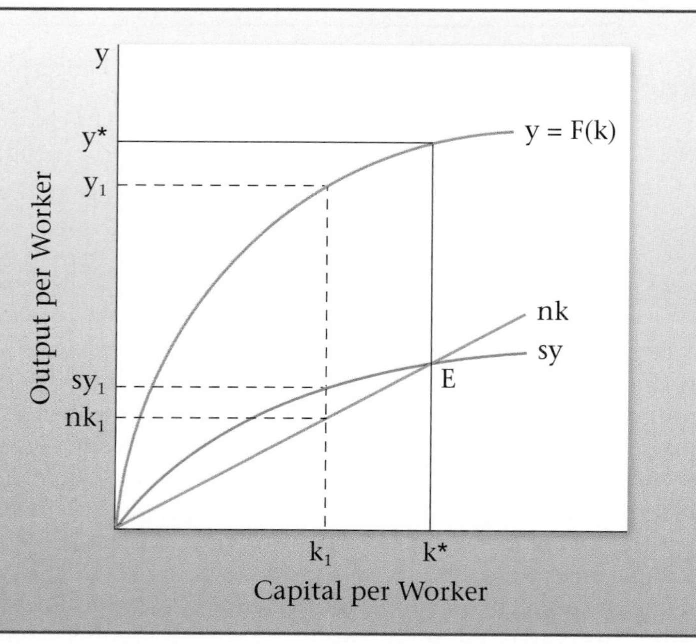

Assume that the population and labour force grow at a constant rate, n. To keep things simple, we also assume a constant fraction, s, of income is saved; the rest is consumed. Investment, which results in capital formation, is the part of output not consumed. Therefore, savings determine investment. We also ignore the rate of depreciation of the capital stock. Investment first widens and then deepens capital. In a growing economy, **capital-widening** extends existing capital per worker to new workers entering the labour force. **Capital-deepening** raises capital per worker for all workers.

Capital widening extends capital to workers entering the labour force.

Capital deepening raises the capital/worker ratio.

To keep capital per worker constant, we need more investment per worker the faster is the growth in the labour force, $\Delta N/N = n$ (extra workers for whom capital must be provided), and the higher the ratio of capital to labour. If capital stock grows faster than the labour force, more capital per worker is added to production, k increases, and output per worker, y, increases. But, as we have seen earlier, increasing capital per worker raises output per worker with diminishing returns. Since a constant fraction, s, of output is saved and invested, the rate of growth of the capital stock declines as income increases.

In the steady state, capital per worker is constant. As a result, investment per worker, sy, must equal nk, the growth in capital stock per worker needed to keep capital per worker constant by increasing the capital stock at the same rate as the labour force. Point E in Figure 14.2 shows the steady-state condition:

$$sy = nk \tag{14.8}$$

Let us define k* as the capital/labour ratio where this condition is met.

Figure 14.2 also shows what happens if the economy is not in the steady state. If capital per worker is less than k*, at k_1, for example, we see that per worker saving and investment sy_1 exceed nk_1, the investment required to keep capital growing with labour. Indeed, for any k less than k* the line sy is above the line nk. So, capital per worker rises and output per worker rises, moving toward the steady state. Conversely, to the right of k*, sy lies below nk. Capital per worker and output per worker fall back toward k* and y*.

The theory says and the diagram shows that, whatever level of capital and output per worker the economy starts with, it gradually *converges* to the (unique) steady state.

Consider a numerical example that illustrates the steady state condition. Suppose output per worker by the per worker production function is $y = k^{1/2}$. Assume that the saving in this economy, based on the propensity to save is $s = 0.1y$, and the labour force grows at the rate of 2 percent a year ($n = 0.02$). What are the steady state values for capital stock per worker and output per worker?

From the production function and the savings function, saving per worker, which is the increase in capital stock, is:

$$s = 0.1y, \text{ so}$$
$$s = 0.1k^{1/2}$$

A constant ratio of capital per worker as the number of workers grows by 2 percent a year ($\Delta N/N = 0.02$) requires a growth of capital stock equal to 2 percent a year:

$$\Delta K/K = 0.02, \text{ and therefore requires}$$

$$s = 0.02k$$

Equating actual saving with that required to maintain the ratio of capital per worker gives:

$$0.1k^{1/2} = 0.02k$$
$$0.1 = 0.02k^{1/2}$$
$$k^{1/2} = 0.1/0.02 = 5$$
$$k = 25,$$

the ratio of capital per worker in the steady state.

From the production function $y = k^{1/2}$, output per worker is 5.0, savings and investment per worker are 0.5, which gives a rate of growth of capital equal to $0.5/25 = 0.02$ that matches the rate of growth of the labour force. Capital stock per worker and output per worker are constant while labour force, capital stock, and output all grow by 2 percent a year. The economy is in a steady state.

Now suppose that capital per worker was less than the steady state value, say $k = 20$ rather than $k = 25$. Would the economy adjust toward the steady state with a higher ratio of capital to labour? The adjustment would require growth in capital per worker greater than the growth in labour force. Based on $k = 20$:

$$y = 20^{1/2} = 4.47.$$

Then saving per worker is:

$$sy = 0.1(4.47) = 0.447$$

With labour force growing at 2 percent a year, a constant capital-to-labour ratio requires growth in capital equal to nk:

$$0.02k = 0.02(20) = 0.4$$

However, savings and investment at the current level of income is 0.447, with the result that capital stock per worker and output per worker are growing toward the steady state values determined above. Furthermore, growth in total output is higher than the growth in labour force and higher than it will be in the steady state. Economies with ratios of

TABLE 14.8 **Annual Growth Rates of Per Capita Real GDP (Average annual % Δ based on PPP 2000 U.S. $)**

	Canada	U.S.	U.K.	Japan	Sweden	Spain	France	Australia
1950–1973	2.85	2.08	2.43	8.09	3.08	5.66	4.05	2.45
1974–1979	2.63	2.02	1.54	2.40	1.48	2.86	2.24	1.79
1980–1990	1.45	1.96	2.06	3.30	1.69	2.64	1.74	1.65
1991–2007	1.69	1.92	2.03	1.31	1.68	2.45	1.30	2.36

Source: Groningen Growth and Development Centre and the Conference Board, *Total Economy Database,* January 2005.

Review Question 8

capital per worker and output per worker less than their steady state values tend to grow faster than those with the same characteristics that are at or closer to their steady states.

GROWTH IN THE OECD

The Organization for Economic Co-operation and Development is a club of the world's richest countries, from industrial giants like the United States and Japan to smaller countries like New Zealand, Ireland, and Turkey. Table 14.8 shows growth rates for a selection of these countries since 1950.

Productivity growth as measured by growth in per capita real GDP slowed sharply after 1973 in all OECD countries. Several explanations were put forward. Some stressed the rise in the power of trade unions, which enjoyed greater legal protection in the 1970s. If this explanation is correct, the supply side reforms of the late 1980s should have led to high productivity growth from the 1990s on. There is little evidence of this among the countries in Table 14.8.

The year 1973 was also the year of the first oil price shock, when real oil prices quadrupled. This had two effects. First, it diverted R&D to long-term efforts to find alternative energy saving technologies. These efforts take decades to pay off and raise actual productivity. Second, higher energy prices made much of the capital stock obsolete overnight. Energy guzzling factories were closed. The world lost part of its capital stock, which reduced output per worker. In practice, scrapping took a long time, and was given renewed impetus by another sharp rise in oil prices in 1980 to 1981. That is why its effects were drawn out over such a long period. Similarly, the dramatic increases in energy and commodity prices after 2006 are seen as one important factor contributing to the 2009 international recession. Although the recession produced a sharp initial collapse in these prices, they recovered strongly in the second quarter of 2009, and will continue to affect future growth patterns.

Having noted the differences in growth rates across time periods, we now examine differences across countries. One sheds light on the other. The fact that OECD-country growth rates move together across sub-periods shows that many aspects of growth are external to individual countries. Technical progress diffuses across countries quickly, wherever it originates. Countries are increasingly dependent on the same global economy.

Even so, growth rates differ markedly across countries. Can neoclassical growth theory explain why? First, it suggests that, if countries have access to the same technology, differences in *total* output growth should reflect differences in labour-force

FIGURE 14.3 **Average Annual Growth in Per Capita Real GDP 1950 to 2004 versus Average Per Capita GDP 1950-55**

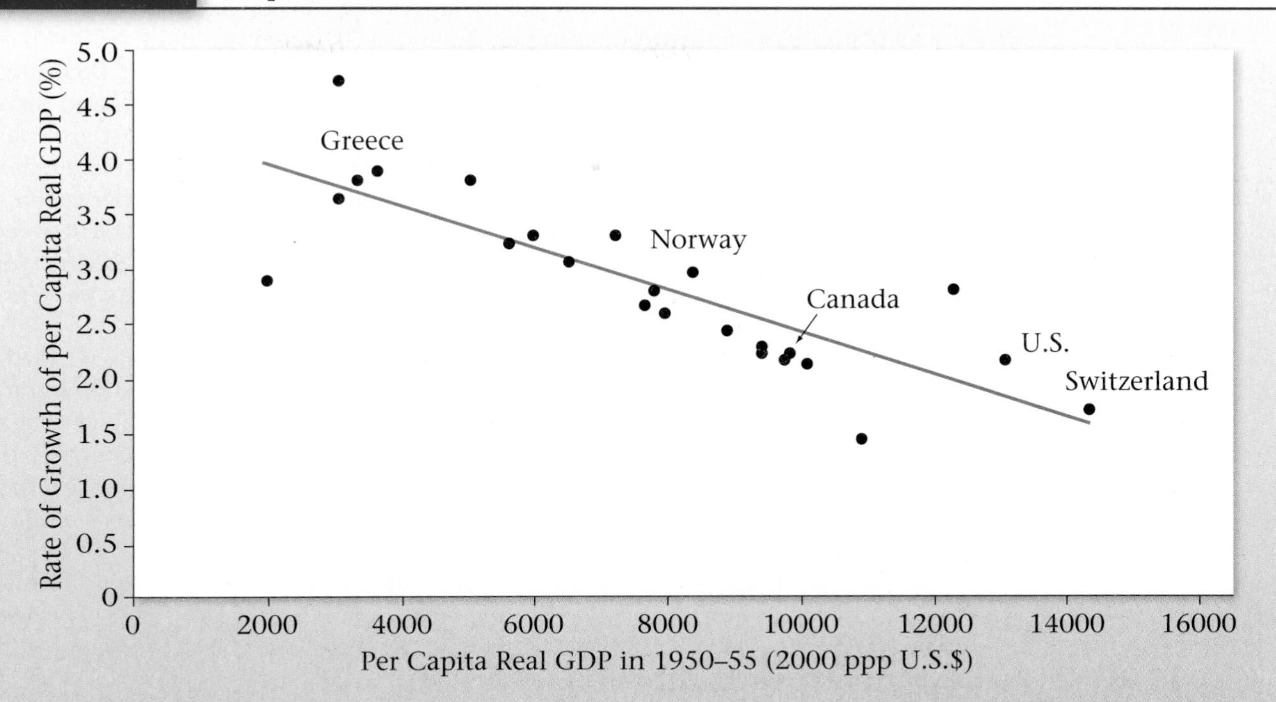

For OECD countries, average rates of growth in per capita real GDP over the 1950 to 2004 period were inversely related to levels of per capita real GDP at the beginning of the 1950 to 2000 period. As a result the differences between per capita incomes in lower income countries and higher income countries were reduced, as the convergence hypothesis predicts.

Source: Groningen Growth and Development Centre and The Conference Board, Total Economy Database, January 2005, http://www.ggdc.net

growth, and differences in growth in *per capita output* should reflect differences in capital to labour ratios. In terms of Figure 14.2, the further a country is below the steady-state capital to labour ratio (i.e., k*), the faster will be the growth in capital per worker and in output per worker.

This property of the neoclassical growth model leads to the convergence hypothesis. The **convergence hypothesis** asserts that countries with lower per capita incomes grow more quickly than average, while countries with higher per capita incomes grow more slowly, with the result that per capita incomes tend to *converge across countries*. This explanation of convergence is based purely on the adjustment to the steady state through different country rates of investment and capital accumulation, starting from different initial capital to labour ratios.

The **convergence hypothesis:** Higher rates of growth in lower per capita income countries than in higher per capita income countries leads to the convergence of per capita incomes across countries.

A second explanation for convergence operates through a different channel. It introduces changes in technology, which, as we have seen from growth accounting, are an important source of growth in output per worker. Suppose that high per capita income countries have human and physical capital to undertake R&D, and that it is in these countries that technical progress is made. However, once discovered, new ideas and technologies are soon spread to other countries. Since lower-income countries do not have to use their own resources to make technical breakthroughs, they can devote scarce investment resources to capital that embodies the latest technology from other countries. By using the slipstream from the higher-income countries, they can grow faster as their technology catches up.

Figure 14.3 provides some evidence in support of the convergence hypothesis. It shows a scatter plot of growth rates in per capita real GDP over the 1950 to 2004 period compared with average levels of per capita GDP in 1950 to 1955 for OECD countries. For convergence, we need an inverse relationship between income levels and income growth rates. Countries with lower incomes at the start of the period must grow faster than countries with higher incomes. This is the pattern observed in the data, as the downward-sloping line in the diagram illustrates. Countries with lower per capita real GDP in 1950 to 1955, like Greece, had higher average growth rates in real GDP over the 1950 to 2000 period than did high-income countries like the United States and Switzerland. Canada and Norway were in the middle of the OECD group, in terms of initial income and income growth.

Unfortunately, not all countries are members of the "convergence club." Growth in per capita real GDP depends on growth in the ratio of capital to labour and on improvements in technology. Many low-income countries do not have incomes high enough to support the levels of investment necessary to raise their capital stock more quickly than their labour force grows. They may also lack the basic infrastructure, education levels, and institutional frameworks needed to adopt better production technologies. As a result, the two key sources of growth identified by the neoclassical growth model are not available. The gap between high-income and low-income countries tends to widen, not diminish.

Review Question 9

14.6 Recent Growth Studies and Policy Issues

Solow's neoclassical growth theory and the basic growth accounting methodology based on it leave a large part of aggregate growth and productivity growth in the Solow Residual. Growth in employment and capital stock, and the relationship between them, play important roles in aggregate growth and labour productivity growth, but the effects of changes in the characteristics of labour and the composition of capital stock reside in the total factor productivity estimates of the Solow residual. This residual captures changes in technology along with other undefined factors.

Recent work on productivity growth still uses the growth accounting methodology, but focused on particular sectors of the economy and with extensions designed to unpack some things previously left in the residual. These include, in particular, investment in different components of the capital stock and changes in the composition and quality of labour.

Increases in capital per worker or per hour of work—capital deepening—continues to be important, but increases in capital stock are disaggregated into investment into several categories such as:

Information and communications technology,
Machinery and equipment, and
Physical structures.

Changes in educational qualifications, gender structure, and age structure are used as indicators of changes in the composition and quality of the labour force. To the extent that these measures of change in characteristics and structure affect productivity, less remains in the residual. More importantly, these are areas in which policies to support education, training, and labour force participation could affect productivity growth. Table 14.9 gives an example of some recent results based on this approach.

TABLE 14.9 **Canadian Business Sector: Labour Productivity Growth, 1974 to 2005 (Percent per year)**

	1974–96	1997–2000	2000–05
Labour productivity	1.4	3.0	1.0
Capital deepening	1.1	1.0	0.7
Info & communications Technology (ICT)	0.4	0.7	0.3
Non – ICT	0.7	0.4	0.4
Labour quality	0.4	0.4	0.4
Total factor productivity	0.0	1.6	– 0.1

Source: R. Dion, "Interpreting Canada's Productivity Performance in the Past Decade: Lessons from Recent Research." *Bank of Canada Review*, Summer 2007. Bank of Canada, 2009.

The results in the table show clearly the increase in the information, communications, and technology components of the capital stock. Particularly in the 1997 to 2000 period, the increase in capital per unit of labour input was the largest part of capital deepening. This is also the period of strongest growth in labour productivity and the largest increase in total factor productivity. The latter captures the effects of improved technology embodied in the new capital stock.

The estimated contributions of changes in labour quality to labour productivity growth provide an interesting refinement of the growth accounting methodology. Ignoring this change, as the simple accounting process did in Section 14.3, leaves the contribution of changes in the structure and characteristics of the labour force in the residual measure of total factor productivity. The results in the table extract and quantify this important source of productivity growth.

Changes in the structure of investment and in the quality of labour are both areas in which public policy plays a role. Government tax policy can be designed to encourage producers to direct investment to areas like communications and information technology. Some of this investment has effects confined to specific industries. Other parts create and strengthen national capacity and efficiency that is widely available and used by business and households, for example high-speed internet service and expanded wireless service and capacity. Educational policy and other human resource policies contribute to the quality, adaptability, and mobility of the labour force.

ENDOGENOUS GROWTH THEORY

Another interesting strand of work makes more fundamental changes in growth theory. The simple neoclassical growth theory made economic growth depend on **exogenous variables**, the rate of population growth, the saving rate, and the rate of capital accumulation, whose values are determined outside the growth model. The subsequent work on catch-up and convergence makes technical progress respond to economic and political factors. But it would be nice to have a stronger link between economic behaviour and the rate of economic growth. We want to make *growth endogenous*, or determined within our model. **Endogenous growth** implies that the steady-state growth rate is affected by economic behaviour and economic policy.

The original insight is due to Professor Paul Romer of the University of Chicago. Saving, investment, and capital accumulation lie at the heart of growth. In neoclassical

An **exogenous variable** has a value determined outside the model.

Neoclassical growth theory is exogenous growth theory.

Endogenous growth is growth determined within the model.

FIGURE 14.4 **A Simple Exogenous Growth Model**

The aggregate production function y = Ak has constant returns to capital per worker. The saving rate, s, exceeds the rate of labour force growth, n, increasing the ratio of capital per worker. As a result output per worker y grows continuously without encountering diminishing returns. A rise in the saving rate or a fall in the rate of growth of the labour force would increase the growth rate of output per worker.

Alternatively if s < n, (not shown in the diagram) capital stock would not grow as fast as the labour force, reducing the capital labour ratio and the rate of growth of output per worker would be negative.

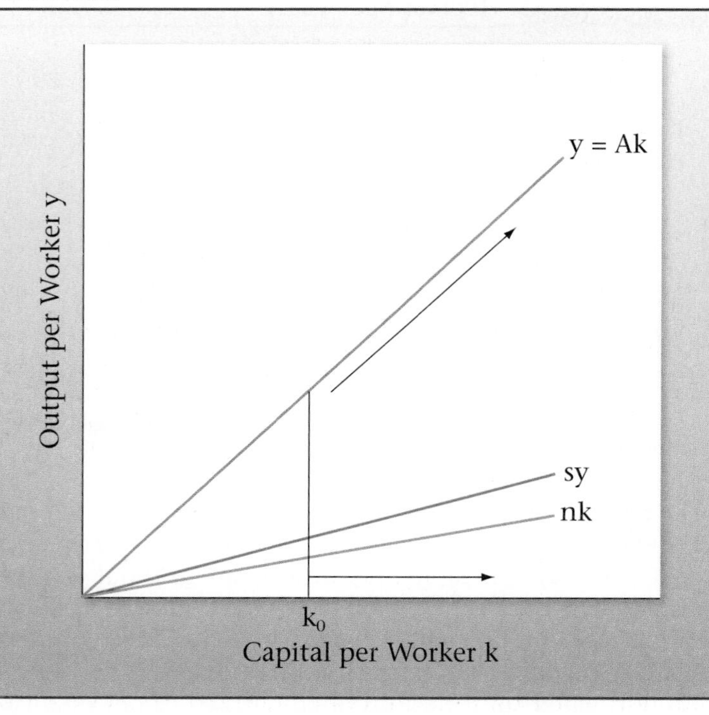

theory, applying more and more capital to a given growth path for population runs into the diminishing marginal product of capital. It cannot be the source of permanent growth in output per worker and per capita GDP.

We know there must be diminishing returns to capital alone at the level of individual firms; otherwise, one firm would get more and more capital, steadily become more productive, and gradually take over the entire world! Because diminishing returns to capital hold at the level of the firm, economists have assumed they held also at the level of the economy.

Romer's insight was the possibility that there are significant externalities to capital. When Telus or Rogers invests in better communications equipment, other firms can do things previously impossible. The insight also applies to human capital. Training and experience in one firm has beneficial effects for others. The results in Table 14.9 capture some of this, but it goes farther.

While the production function of each individual firm exhibits diminishing returns from its own capital input, it also depends on capital of other firms. No firm, acting in isolation, would wish to raise its capital without limit. But, when all firms expand together, the economy as a whole may face *constant returns* to aggregate capital.

Consider the following simple example of the aggregate economy. Per worker output, y, is proportional to capital per worker, k. To isolate the role of accumulation, suppose there is *no technical progress*. Each new unit of capital is identical to all previously existing units. Then suppose we have

$$y = A \times k, \tag{14.9}$$

where A is constant and the exponent on k is 1 instead of the 1/3 in our neoclassical model. This gives constant returns, as a 10 percent increase in k gives a 10 percent increase in y. Figure 14.4 illustrates this simple model.

Constant returns to raising the aggregate capital to labour ratio in the economy allows an escape from the key growth limitation in the neoclassical theory. It makes growth endogenous and dependent upon parameters that could be influenced by private behaviour or public policy.

In the neoclassical model, without technical progress, steady-state growth in total output is always n, the rate of population and labour force growth, and growth in per capita output is zero. These results hold whatever the saving rate s, or the level of productivity A. However, with constant returns to rising capital to labour ratios, any policy that succeeded in raising the saving rate s would permanently raise the growth rate. Similarly, any policy achieving a one-time rise in the level of A, for example, greater workplace efficiency, would permanently raise the growth rate of k. Since $y = A \times k$, this would mean permanently faster output growth.

Not only can government policy affect growth in this framework, government intervention may also increase efficiency. In the simple Romer model outlined above, there are externalities to capital accumulation: Individual firms neglect the fact that, in raising their capital, they also increase the efficiency of other firms' capital. Government subsidies to investment might offset this externality and increase investment.

Note, also, that endogenous growth models explain why growth rates in different countries might be permanently different. This may explain why convergence does not take place, even over long periods of time, and why some countries remain permanently poor. If output per worker and per capita is too low to provide more than a minimal standard of living there is no room for saving and investment to increase the capital stock as fast as the population is increasing. Capital–labour ratios decline and output does not grow enough to maintain living standards. Some countries stagnate and others suffer increasing poverty.

While endogenous growth theory is an exciting development, it also has its critics. Most criticisms boil down to one key point. Why should there be exactly constant returns in the aggregate from accumulating one factor of production? With diminishing returns, we return to the Solow model where long-run growth is exogenous. With increasing returns, the economy would not settle on a steady-state growth path but on ever more rapid expansion of output and capital stock. We know this is not happening. So, for endogenous growth, only *constant returns* will do. Some people think this seems just too good to be true.

Furthermore, the production function $y = Ak$ implies, from the growth accounting perspective, that the share of capital income in national income is 100 percent while that of labour income is zero. By contrast, an examination of national accounts over time reveals a remarkably constant distribution of national income between labour income and non-labour income, with the share of labour income about two-thirds of national income. This does not support the argument for a constant returns aggregate production function.

Review Question 10

There is a way to reconcile the new growth theory with the neoclassical growth theory. This could be accomplished by combining the neoclassical per worker production function of Figure 14.1 with the new growth theory function of Figure 14.4. Figure 14.5 illustrates this. The basic neoclassical growth theory treats all labour and capital as homogenous inputs. Each new input is the same as all existing inputs. Marginal productivities of labour and capital are diminishing. Technological change is exogenous.

New growth theory emphasizes the roles of research and development, innovation, education and "learning by doing" as sources of improved technology and productivity. Research, development, and innovation come from decisions to invest in new knowledge and to apply it to production processes. Education comes from decisions to invest in human capital. Learning by doing is a natural outcome of employment experience. All these are ongoing processes, although they may be pursued unevenly over time as economic conditions and economic policies change.

FIGURE 14.5 **Growth Theory with Technology Embodied in Capital and Labour**

The Y = Ak line traces the locus of changes in per worker output over time as a result of growth in the ratio of capital per worker. Increases in capital per worker reflect growth in the capital stock greater than the growth in the labour force. New additions to the capital stock and to the labour force *embody* new technology based on ongoing discovery, innovation, education, and learning from the experience of others already in the labour force. As a result, increases in capital per worker bring with them improvements in technology that shift the production function $y = Ak^{1/3}$ up and offset the diminishing returns to capital per worker. The economy appears to grow along the y = Ak line based on increases in both k and A.

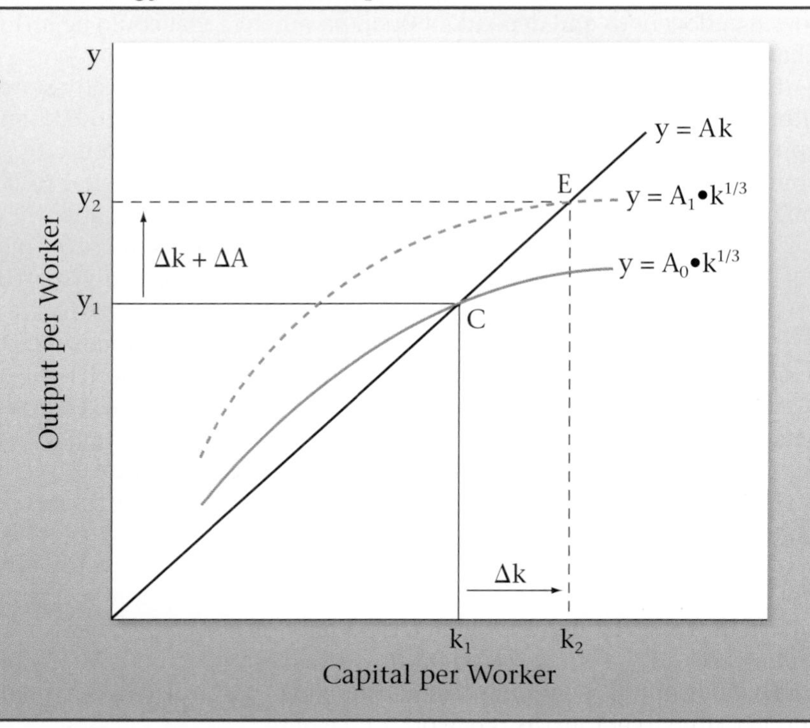

As a result, increases in the stock of capital and the level of employment always embody new technology and knowledge. There is no separation between increases in the capital to labour ratio and the state of technology, as in the basic neoclassical model. In Figure 14.5, the per worker production function shifts up as capital per worker increases because the new capital stock and new employees bring new technology to the production process. As k increases from k_1 to k_2 the economy moves from C to E. These points also appear as two points on the y = Ak function because the embodied technological improvements offset otherwise diminishing returns.

Recent studies of the sources of productivity growth based on growth accounting are consistent with this approach to reconciling neoclassical and new growth theory. The findings reported in Table 14.9 above show the contributions to productivity growth made by different types of capital equipment and changes in labour force structure. These changes in "technology" are made integral parts of the growth in capital stock and employment rather than left as exogenous residuals.

THE COSTS OF GROWTH

Can the benefits of economic growth be outweighed by its costs? Pollution, congestion, and a hectic lifestyle are a high price to pay for more cars, washing machines, video games, and iPods.

Since GDP is an imperfect measure of the true economic value of goods and services produced by the economy, there is no presumption we should want to maximize the growth of measured GDP. Without government intervention, a free market economy produces too much pollution. But the elimination of all pollution is also wasteful.

Society should undertake activities accompanied by pollution up to the point at which the marginal net benefit of the goods produced equals the marginal pollution cost imposed on society. Government intervention, through pollution taxes or regulation of environmental standards, can move the economy towards a more efficient allocation of resources and a higher standard of living, broadly defined.

The full implementation of such a policy would (optimally) reduce growth of measured GDP to below the rate when there is no restriction on pollution and congestion. This is the most sensible way in which to approach the problem. It tackles the issues directly.

In contrast, the "zero growth" solution is a blunt instrument. It fails to distinguish between measured outputs accompanied by social costs, and measured outputs without additional social costs. It does not provide the correct incentives, and may result in neglecting the pollution and congestion already coming from the "fixed" output. Thus, when there is already too much pollution, congestion, environmental damage, or stress, the best solution is to provide incentives that directly reduce these phenomena. Restricting growth in measured output is a crude alternative.

Some problems might evaporate if economists and statisticians measure true GDP more accurately, including the "quality of life" activities (clean air, environmental beauty, etc.) that yield consumption benefits but at present are omitted from measured GDP. Voters and commentators assess government performance against measurable statistics. A better measure of GDP might remove perceived conflicts between measured output and the quality of life.

This is also a good way to address "sustainable" growth. Mediterranean and Caribbean beauty spots become concrete jungles of hotels and bars; once the environment is spoiled, upmarket tourists move on somewhere else. An economist's advice, however, is not to abandon being a tourist destination, but to keep track of environmental depreciation and engage only in activities that show a clear return after the cost of environmental damage. Embodying these costs in actual charges also provides the market incentive to look after the environment.

Review Questions 11 and 12

No matter how complete the framework, the assessment of the desirable growth rate will always be a normative question hinging on the value judgements of the assessor. Switching resources from consumption, however defined, to investment will nearly always reduce the welfare of people today but allow greater welfare for people tomorrow. The priority attached to satisfying wants of people at different points in time is always a challenging value judgement.

Next

We have now studied the performance and policy issues in the macro economy in terms of business cycle fluctuations, the stabilization role of government, and the sources of economic growth, all of which are linked to the standard of living.

There is, however, an important topic that remains. International trade in goods and services is important to both the level of aggregate economic activity as measured by real GDP and the standard of living as measured by per capita real GDP. International trade theory explains the underlying incentives for international trade, the impacts of international trade on efficiency and living standards, and the policies that might be directed at international trade flows. Chapter 15 deals with these topics.

SUMMARY

- **Economic growth** is the percentage annual increase in real GDP or per capita real GDP. It is an imperfect measure of the rate of increase of economic well-being because of the limitations of the measurement of GDP.
- When all markets have had time to adjust to equilibrium, economic growth measures the **growth in potential output.** For most countries, the strong growth trend in potential GDP swamps the short-run business cycle fluctuations in GDP.
- A **comparison of growth rates across countries** shows wide **variations in country growth rates** for total real GDP and per capita real GDP. It also shows that **small differences in annual growth rates have large cumulative effects** on real and per capita real GDP over time.
- Growth in potential output has **three main sources**, namely, growth in labour force, growth in capital stock, and improvements in productivity as a result of technical change. **Growth accounting** provides a way of measuring the contribution of each of these sources to overall growth. Different growth rates among countries reflect differences in one or more of these sources of growth.
- Recent research on the **growth of Canada's potential GDP** found that the contribution of productivity growth from technology declined in the 1980s and early 1990s and again from 2000 to 2005.
- Growth in *per capita real GDP* has **two main sources**, namely, growth in the *ratio* of capital to labour in the production process, and improvements in technology. Growth accounting provides a way of measuring the sources of growth in per capita real GDP.
- **Sustained growth in per capita real GDP**, in a neoclassical model of growth, depends on improvements in technology to overcome the diminishing returns to increases in the capital to labour ratio.
- **Neoclassical growth theory** argues that, in the absence of technological change, a country will adjust to a steady-state rate of growth in total real GDP equal to the rate of growth of population. In this steady state, a positive rate of growth in per capita real GDP depends on the rate of growth of productivity based on technological change.
- The **convergence hypothesis** based on the neoclassical growth model says that similar countries will tend to move toward and converge upon the same level of per capita real GDP. This means that countries with relatively low per capita real GDP will experience faster growth in per capita real GDP than countries with relatively high per capita real GDP. The experience of OECD countries since 1950 provides some evidence in support of the convergence hypothesis.
- Recent work on **new or endogenous growth theory** suggests that positive externalities from the growth in a country's capital stock may offset the tendency toward diminishing returns to capital, and allow sustained growth in per capita real GDP based on a country's saving rate and rate of technology-based productivity growth. This argument gives an important role for policies that might change the rate of saving and investment.
- Although growth in per capita real GDP may improve well-being or standards of living, growth also has costs. More output means more **pollution and congestion.**
- The costs of growth create a role for **government policy intervention through pollution taxes, regulation, and environmental standards** to move the economy toward a more efficient allocation of resources and a higher standard of living, broadly defined, even if that reduces the growth rate of measured real GDP.

KEY TERMS

KEY EQUATIONS AND RELATIONS

Equations

The aggregate production function: $Y = A \times F(N, K)$	**(14.1)**	p. 364
Real GDP at time t: $Y_t = A_0 \times F(N_t, K_t)$	**(14.2)**	p. 364
Potential GDP: $Y_P = A_0 \times F(N_F, K_0)$	**(14.3)**	p. 364
Growth accounting equation: $\Delta Y_P/Y_P = \Delta A/A + {}^2\!/_3(\Delta N/N) + {}^1\!/_3(\Delta K/K)$	**(14.4)**	p. 365
The Solow residual: $\Delta A/A = \Delta Y/Y - {}^2\!/_3(\Delta N/N) - {}^1\!/_3(\Delta K/K)$	**(14.5)**	p. 365
An explicit aggregate production function: $Y = N^{2/3} \times K^{1/3}$	**(14.6)**	p. 367
Real GDP per worker: $y = A \times k^{1/3}$	**(14.7)**	p. 368
Steady-state neoclassical growth: $sy = nk$	**(14.8)**	p. 376
Per capita real GDP with constant returns: $y = A \times k$	**(14.9)**	p. 382

Relations

Sources of growth: Growth in labour and capital inputs and changes in technology

Diminishing marginal productivity: Growth in one input to production, with other inputs constant, results in output growth at a declining rate.

Constant returns to scale: Growth in labour and capital inputs at equal rates results in constant output growth at the same rate.

Productivity growth: Growth in output per unit of input

Technology and technical knowledge: Known methods and techniques used to organize and combine inputs to produce output

Exogenous growth theory: Explains growth by conditions external to the model

Convergence hypothesis: Countries with the same savings rates, labour force growth rates, and technology will have the same steady-state output per worker and the same rate of growth in total output and output per worker.

Endogenous growth theory: Explains growth by conditions internal to the growth model

REVIEW QUESTIONS

Review Questions and answers are included in Connect at www.mcgrawhillconnect.ca.

1. a. What is the distinction between growth in potential GDP and growth in per capita real GDP?
   b. Why is this distinction important to an evaluation of the relationship between economic growth and growth in standards of living?
   c. Which grows more rapidly, potential GDP or per capita real GDP?

2. Consider two countries with the same level of potential GDP, say $100 billion, today. Suppose potential GDP grows at an annual rate of 3.5 percent (0.035) in one country and 3.25 percent (0.0325) in the second country. Based on this information:
   a. What do you predict for the percentage difference in potential GDP between the two countries 10 years in the future?
   b. 20 years in the future?
   [Note that the growth rates will compound to determine real GDP according to the following formula: $Y_t = Y_0(1 + \text{growth rate})^t$.]

3. Suppose you have the following information about an economy:
   Average annual rates of growth from 1998 to 2008:

i. Potential GDP	3.5%
ii. Labour force	2.1%
iii. Capital stock	3.0%

   Share of labour income in national income: 2/3
   Using growth accounting, find the contributions to the annual growth in potential GDP that came from:
   a. Growth in labour force
   b. Growth in capital stock
   c. Improved productivity as measured by the Solow residual.

4. If technology were constant while labour force grew at a rate of 2.5 percent a year, capital stock grew at 1.5 percent per year, and the share of labour income in national income was 70 percent, how fast would potential GDP grow?

5. Suppose you have the following information for two economies:

	Country A	Country B
Average annual growth rates: i. Labour force	2.5%	4.0%
ii. Capital stock	3.5%	3.5%
Labour income/national income:	2/3	2/3

   a. Assuming a constant state of technology, which of these two countries will have the faster rate of growth in total real GDP?
   b. Which of the two countries will have the faster rate of growth in per capita real GDP?
   c. What differences, if any, do you see in the growth rates of the capital to labour ratios in the two countries?
   d. Explain the reasons for the differences in growth rates you have found?

6. In Wonderland, labour force and capital stock both grow at the rate of 2.5 percent a year but technology is constant.
   a. At what rate will potential GDP grow?
   b. At what rate will per capita GDP grow?
   c. If improvements in technology increased total factor productivity by 1.5 percent a year, how fast would per capita real GDP grow?

7. a. Why do economists emphasize that improvements in technology are the key to improvements in standards of living?
   b. Using a diagram that shows the relationship between capital per worker and output per worker, illustrate and explain why growth in capital per worker cannot provide sustained growth in output per worker and standards of living.
   c. In the diagram in (b), show how an improvement in productivity coming from improved technology could provide sustained increases in standards of living.

8. Suppose an economy has the following conditions:

   Per worker GDP: $y = k^{1/3}$
   Savings per worker: $s = 0.2y$
   Population and labour force growth: $n = 0.05$

   a. What is the steady-state level of output per worker, y?
   b. What is the rate of growth of *total* GDP required for the steady state?
   c. If savings increased to $s_1 = 0.25y$, what new steady-state output would result?
   d. What is the rate of growth of total GDP required for the new steady state?
   e. Use a diagram to show the steady-state output per worker in (a) and in (c).

9. a. Explain the convergence hypothesis.
   b. Why does the convergence hypothesis anticipate faster growth in standards of living in the lower per capita income OECD countries than in the higher per capita income OECD countries?
   c. Does the convergence hypothesis offer hope for improved standards of living in poor African countries? Why or why not?

10. a. What is the key difference between the neoclassical (exogenous) theory of growth and the new "endogenous" theory of growth?
    b. Would government policy that encouraged a higher rate of saving result in a higher sustained rate of growth in output per worker according to the:
       i. Neoclassical growth theory? Explain why.
       ii. Endogenous growth theory? Explain why.

11. a. If economic growth is accompanied by pollution and congestion, would you favour a "zero growth" policy?
    b. How would you define "zero growth" in a country with a growing population and labour force?
    c. Do policies that limit and regulate pollution and congestion offer a better alternative to zero growth policies? Explain why or why not.

12. Critically evaluate the following statements, based on the sources of growth identified by growth theories.
    a. Since the earth's resources are limited, growth cannot continue forever.
    b. If we would only save more, we'd enjoy faster improvements in our standard of living.
    c. Because growth has pollution and congestion costs, zero economic growth is the key to improved standards of living.

13. *Internet* The *International Productivity Monitor,* Number 10, Spring 2005, published by the Centre for the Study of Living Standards, contains a paper by Dirk Pilat, "Canada's Productivity Performance in International Perspective." You can download this paper at http://www.csls.ca/ipm/10/pilat-e.pdf. Page 31 of Pilat's paper provides a table that compares the contributions to GDP growth in a selection of industrial countries in the time periods 1990 to 1995 and 1995 to 2002. Examine the data in that table, and consider Canada's productivity performance as measured by the Solow residual (MPF) relative to the other countries in each time period.
    a. Which countries had higher productivity growth than Canada from 1990 to 1995?
    b. Which had higher productivity growth than Canada from 1995 to 2002?
    c. In which countries did productivity growth improve between 1990–1995 and 1995–2002?
    d. What are the implications of these different productivity performances for the pattern of living standards among these countries?

14. *Internet* The Gapminder Web site offers a rich selection of data on economic growth and its relationship to different measures of standard of living. Visit the Web site

at http://www.gapminder.org/ and click on the graphs available in Gapminder World. You can choose the variables you wish to compare and plot on the axes of the graph provided. Suppose you plot life expectancy on the vertical axis and real income per capita on the horizontal axis and then run the time sequence.

a. What relationship do you see between growth in real income per person and life expectancy over the time period provided?
b. Which countries had the highest and lowest life expectancy, respectively, in 2006?
c. How does life expectancy in China compare with that in Canada in 1960?
d. In 2006?

(Note: you can choose a year using the time slide and identify individual country data by placing your cursor on the dot that represents that country).

CHAPTER 15

International Trade

LEARNING OUTCOMES

By the end of this chapter you should understand:

1. Patterns of international trade
2. Trade issues for Canada and the world
3. Comparative advantage and the gains from trade
4. Intra-industry trade: two-way trade in the same product
5. The gains and losses from trade
6. The economics of tariffs, subsidies, and quotas
7. Good and bad arguments for tariffs
8. Current trade policies and institutions

International trade is part of daily life. Canadians drink French, Australian, and Californian wine; Americans drive Korean and Japanese cars run on gasoline and diesel derived from Canadian crude oil; the world eats Canadian wheat; China exports manufactured goods to virtually anywhere we can think of.

As consumers we love the choice and variety of products that trade offers. We further benefit from lower prices than would prevail in a world of protectionism. At the same time there is a constant chorus of voices calling for protection from trade: Manufacturers are threatened by more competition from Asia; dairy farmers cry out against the imports of cheese, poultry, beef, and dairy products; even the service sector is concerned about offshore competition from call centres and designers of all sorts. In this world of competing views it is vital to understand how trade has the potential to improve the well-being of economies.

This chapter examines the theory of international trade, trade flows, and trade policy: who trades with whom, in what commodities, and why. In general, countries trade with one another because they can buy foreign products at a lower price than it costs to make them at home. International trade reflects specialization and exchange, which in turn improve living standards. It is cost differences between countries rather than technological differences that drive trade: In principle, Canada could supply Toronto with olives and oranges grown in Nunavut greenhouses. But it makes more sense to import them from Greece and Florida.

Trade between Canada and other countries differs from trade between Halifax and Vancouver in at least two ways.

First, because international trade crosses national boundaries, governments can monitor this trade and treat it differently. The ability to monitor international trade in goods and services is essential if those products are to be treated differently from domestically supplied products. Second, international trade may involve the use of different national currencies. A Canadian buyer of French wine pays in Canadian dollars, but the French vineyard worker is paid in euros. International trade involves international payments. Foreign exchange rates—the price of one national currency in terms of other national currencies—are part and parcel of international transactions. Exchange rates are one factor in determining national competitiveness in international markets.

15.1 Trade Patterns

THE WORLD ECONOMY

Every international transaction has both a buyer and a seller. One country's imports are another country's exports. To establish how much trade occurs, we can measure either the total value of exports by all countries or the total value of imports. Table 15.1 shows world trade in total and by region in 2007.

World trade has grown rapidly since 1950, at an average annual rate of 7.5 percent by volume. It has thus become ever more important to national economies. Between 1990 and 2006, Canadian exports of goods and services as a fraction of GDP rose from 26 to 35 percent, and imports rose from 25 to 34 percent. Canada is now a very open economy. Smaller economies are typically more open than large economies—Belgium

TABLE 15.1 **World Trade in Goods and Services by Region in 2007, in billions $U.S.**

	Exports			Imports		
Region	Goods	Services	Total	Goods	Services	Total
World	13,950	3,292	17,242	14,244	3,086	17,330
North America	1,854	536	2,390	2,707	1,461	4,168
Latin America	499	92	591	456	99	555
Europe	5,772	1,703	7,475	6,061	1,461	7,522
Africa	424	78	502	359	102	461
Asia	4,131	739	4,870	3,804	102	3,906

Source: World Trade Organization, International Trade Statistics 2008. www.wto.org/english/res_e/statis_e/statis_e.htm.

is more open than the United States—because large economies have a sufficient variety of resources to supply much of an individual country's needs. The European Union is similar, in population terms, to the United States, but it is composed of many distinct economies. Some European economies are similar in size to individual American states. But trade between California and New York is not international, whereas trade between Italy and the Netherlands is. Details of trade growth for selected countries, as measured by trade as percent of GDP, are shown in Table 15.2.

Because our economy is increasingly open to international trade, events in other countries affect our daily lives much more than they did 20 years ago. The conditions in international markets for basic commodities and energy affect all nations, both importers and exporters.

DEVELOPED AND LESS DEVELOPED ECONOMIES

Table 15.3 breaks the world's economies into developed, developing, and in-transition groups. The industrial or developed countries or regions include Western Europe, North America, Japan, Australia, and New Zealand—the rich countries with a disproportionate share of world income. The developing economies and economies in transition make up the less developed countries (LDCs)—ranging from the very poor African countries to the nearly rich, such as Brazil. The developed economies are clearly dominant in world trade, despite the rise of globalization and high economic growth in many lower-income Asian economies.

THE COMMODITY COMPOSITION OF TRADE

In rich countries, the service sector accounts for most of GDP. While international trade in services is growing rapidly, it still forms a relatively small part of total world trade. Trade in goods—merchandise trade—remains dominant, partly because many countries import goods, add a little value, and re-export them. While the value added from such import–export activity may make just a small contribution to GDP, the gross flows of imports and exports can still be large relative to GDP. By importing goods,

TABLE 15.2 **Trade in Goods and Services as a Percentage of GDP**

	1990	2000	2006
Canada	26	43	35
Belgium	69	83	86
Netherlands	55	67	70
United Kingdom	25	29	30
France	22	28	28
Italy	19	27	28
United States	10	13	14
Japan	10	10	16

Source: Based on Country Statistical Profiles, under Others from OECD. Stat Extracts, http://stats.oecd.org.

TABLE 15.3 **Structure of World Exports by Origin**

	1993	2000	2007
Total Goods Exports			
World (billion U.S.$)	3,774	6,456	13,833
Developed economies (%)	71	66	59
Developing economies (%)	27	31	37
Economies in transition (%)	2	3	4
Total Exports of Services			
World (billion U.S.$)	998	1,527	3,337
Developed economies (%)	79	76	73
Developing economies (%)	21	23	26
Economies in transition (%)	0	1	1

Source: "Structure of World Exports," *UNCTAD Handbook of Statistics 2008,* © United Nations, 2009. Reproduced with permission.

adding some value, and re-exporting, it is even possible for the value of exports to exceed the value of GDP itself.

World trade has evolved rapidly in recent years. Table 15.3 shows changes in the pattern of world trade flows. From 1998 to 2007, as world trade expanded, developing economies and economies in transition gained a larger share of that expanding trade. Developed countries' shares of exports declined correspondingly, but they continue to be the origin of the largest part of world exports in both product categories.

Tables 15.4 and 15.5 show the patterns of Canadian trade in goods between 2005 and 2007. The United States is Canada's major trading partner, buying over 75 percent of Canadian exports and supplying more than 50 percent of Canadian imports. The change in the trade pattern over time reflects ongoing changes in trade flows relative to GDP as noted in Table 15.2, changes in exchange rates, and developments in export and import markets. Canadian exports as a percentage of GDP declined between 2005 and 2007 and the pattern of trade shifted from the United States to other export markets and sources of imports. In part this shift reflected the strong, continuous appreciation of the Canadian dollar, particularly with respect to the U.S. dollar after 2002 and to a much lesser degree with respect to other currencies. This made exporting to the U.S., where the proceeds are received in U.S. dollars, less profitable and reduced the domestic currency value of imports from the U.S. The rise of Asian markets for Canadian exports and as sources of imports added to this shift in trade patterns.

Although exports of resource-based products only account for about 35 percent of total exports, Canada is often thought of as a resource-based economy. This is in part because manufactured products account for almost 80 percent of U.S. and European exports but less than 60 percent of Canadian exports. Asia concentrates heavily on exports of manufactured goods—Canada buys lots of products from Sony, Canon, Toshiba, and Daewoo. Nevertheless, Canada has important export strength in machinery, equipment, and automotive products.

TABLE 15.4 **Canada's Trade Patterns, 2005 and 2007**

	Goods Exports by Destination (%)		Goods Imports by Source (%)	
	2005	2007	2005	2007
United States	82.1	76.9	66.1	54.2
Japan	2.3	2.2	2.8	3.8
United Kingdom	2.1	3.1	2.4	2.8
Other EU economies	3.3	5.2	7.6	9.3
Other OECD economies[1]	3.3	4.3	6.1	9.1
Others[2]	6.4	8.4	15.3	20.8
Total	100.0	100.0	100.0	100.0

[1] OECD, excluding United States, Japan, United Kingdom, and other EU economies.
[2] Economies not included in the EU or the OECD.

Source: Adapted from Statistics Canada CANSIM Database, http://cansim2.statcan.gc.ca, Tables 228-0001 and 228-0002.

Changes in energy and commodity prices have important effects on the composition of Canadian exports over time. From 2005 to 2008, the years reported in Table 15.5, the indexes of energy prices, commodity food prices, and industrial raw material prices increased by 41 percent, 42 percent, and 32 percent respectively. These commodity price changes are reflected in the increased shares of energy, agricultural products, and industrial materials in Canadian goods exports. The sharp declines in these prices in the international recession of 2008–09 moderated this development.

Review Question 1

TABLE 15.5 **Composition of Canadian Goods Exports in Percentages, 2005 and 2008**

	2005	2008
Agriculture and fishing	7.2	8.1
Energy	23.1	29.6
Forestry	7.6	5.3
Industrial goods and materials	18.0	24.0
Machinery and equipment	20.2	18.0
Automotive products	20.1	11.4
Other consumer goods	3.7	3.7
Total	100.0	100.0

Source: Adapted from Statistics Canada CANSIM Database, http://cansim2.statcan.gc.ca, Table 376-0007.

15.2 Trade Issues for Canada and the World

Tables 15.1 to 15.5 set out the facts. World trade has grown faster than world income, and is increasingly important. Half of all international trade is between rich, industrial countries, which are also the main export markets for LDCs. A fifth of world trade is in primary products, the rest in manufactures and services. These facts help explain some of the key issues in world trade.

Agricultural Protection

Farmers in rich countries not only receive agricultural subsidies, such as those through the EU Common Agricultural Policy, but also enjoy protection behind tariffs and quotas on imported farm products. Such barriers hurt the consumer. Furthermore, LDCs complain that exclusion of their exports from the richest markets not only reduces the quantities they can sell; it also forces prices down when all their supply must be absorbed in the remaining world markets to which they have access.

Outsourcing of Manufacturing to LDCs

LDCs want to make their own manufactured goods and export them to the industrial countries. Brazil, Mexico, China, and Korea already have major manufacturing industries. But exports to industrial countries have led to complaints in the latter that jobs are being threatened by competition from cheap foreign labour. In many sectors, producers in Asia are undercutting established firms in North America and Europe. Outsourcing of service jobs has also begun: Call centres in Mumbai and software developers in Bangalore are now competing effectively with "on-shore" suppliers of these services in developed economies. Should such global outsourcing and subcontracting be restricted somehow to prevent job losses in North America and Western Europe, or should rich countries take advantage of low production costs in Asia?

Trade or Aid?

Aid from developed economies is frequently seen as a means of helping LDCs develop. Yet lower barriers against the import of goods and services from LDCs would likely have a far greater impact on their well-being. LDCs see their voice in international organizations such as the World Trade Organization as being weak. These economies believe that rich countries, acting according to their own self-interest, largely dictate the evolution of trade practices and the reduction of barriers to trade. They feel pressured to dismantle their own tariffs and allow in foreign investors, while rich countries remain reluctant to address LDC concerns. By raising the demand for LDC exports, the reduction of agricultural protection in rich countries might do more to help than the entire program of foreign aid.

Expansion of the European Union

The Balkans and Turkey are the modern-day meeting ground between East and West—the region where the former Ottoman and Hapsburg empires faced off. Today the countries in this area want to join the EU—but not just to secure easier access for their goods to Europe. While trade is about mobility, mobility concerns people as well as goods and services, and the EU grants freedom of movement to all its members' citizens. Expansion, therefore, involves greater freedom, not only for goods and services to

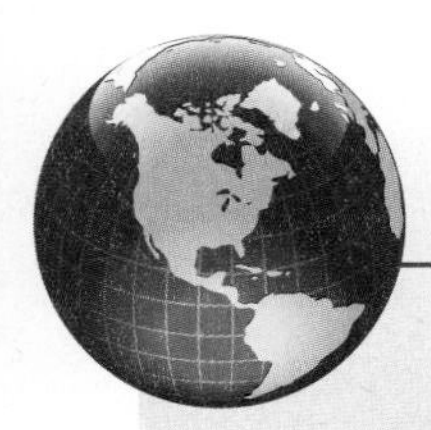

APPLICATION BOX 15.1

Primary Products and LDC Revenues

Many primary products, such as coffee, cocoa and sugar, and raw materials, such as metals, are produced in relatively low-income countries. On a very long-time scale, the prices of such products have not kept up with the prices of most other traded goods, and this has meant lower revenues for the economies that produce them.

A second problem is that the revenues from such products are highly volatile and strongly correlated with the business cycle. For a dramatic illustration of how volatile these prices can be, go to the IMF Web site and search under data/statistics. The address is: www.imf.org.

flow between the constituent economies, but also for people. Cultural readiness is as much an issue as cheaper goods and bigger markets.

North American Free Trade

Canada signed the Free Trade Agreement with the U.S. in 1988, for implementation in 1989, and signed a further North American Free Trade Agreement (NAFTA) that included Mexico, which came into force in 1994. While these treaties garnered much attention and opposition in all of the economies in question, they in fact represented a continuation of the post-war trend in the reduction of trade barriers between the economies. By the 1990s tariffs were already very low. NAFTA aimed at eliminating the remaining obstacles, and also implementing a dispute resolution mechanism.

15.3 Comparative and Absolute Advantage

Trade is beneficial when there are international differences in the opportunity costs of goods. The opportunity cost of a good is the quantity of another good or service given up in order to have one more unit of the good in question. To illustrate its importance in international trade, consider the following example: A closed economy with given resources can make solar panels or plywood sheets. The more resources used to make solar panels, the fewer resources can be used to make plywood. The opportunity cost of a solar panel is the number of plywood sheets sacrificed (not produced) by the resources used to make that solar panel rather than plywood.

Opportunity costs in this context tell us about *relative costs* of producing different goods. International differences in relative production costs are a prime determinant of trade, and they give rise to the **law of comparative advantage.** This law states that countries specialize in producing and exporting the goods they produce at lower *relative cost* than other countries.

By the **law of comparative advantage,** countries specialize in the production and export of products they produce at lower *relative cost* than other countries.

Opportunity, or relative, costs tend to differ across countries—frequently for reasons of technology—and these differences can give rise to trade. Our two countries, Canada and the United States, *both* produce plywood and solar panels. To keep things simple, we will assume that labour is the only input to production, that there are constant returns to scale, and that goods are sold at cost. Table 15.6 shows the assumed production costs. It takes 42 hours of Canadian labour to make a solar panel and 6 hours to make a sheet of plywood. In the United States, labour is more productive. It

TABLE 15.6 **Production Costs in Canada and the United States**

	Canada	United States
Unit Labour Requirement		
Solar panel	42 hours	30 hours
Plywood	6 hours	5 hours
Wage per hour	$10Cdn	$10U.S.
Unit Cost		
Solar panel	$420CDN	$300U.S.
Plywood	$60CDN	$50U.S.

Review Question 2

The **law of absolute advantage** states that, if one economy uses fewer inputs than another economy to produce a good or service, then that economy has an absolute advantage in its production.

takes 30 hours to make a solar panel and 5 hours to make a sheet of plywood. Workers earn $10 per hour in their own currency; correspondingly, the selling prices of the goods are as given in the final two rows of the table.

Canadian unit labour requirements are *absolutely* higher for *both* goods than those in the United States. But Canadian labour is *relatively* more productive in plywood than in solar panels. It takes 7/5 times as much labour to produce a solar panel in Canada as it does in the United States, but only 6/5 times as much labour to make plywood in Canada, compared with the time in the United States (note that 7/5 = 42/30). These *relative productivity differences* are the basis for specialization and international trade. In this example, the United States has an **absolute advantage** in the production of both goods because it uses less labour to produce each than Canada does.

THE GAINS FROM TRADE

In order to illustrate how comparative advantage is key to international trade, let us push the example further. Let each economy have 210 units of labour and consider the production possibility frontier (PPF) for each. The PPF, as we described in Chapter 1, defines the combinations of goods that can be produced when an economy uses all of its productive resources. The United States and Canadian PPFs are given in Figure 15.1. If the United States uses all of its labour to produce solar panels, it can produce seven of them (210/30 = 7), or it could produce 42 sheets of plywood (210/5 = 42). These are the intercept values in the figure. By the same reasoning, Canada could produce 5 solar panels or 35 sheets of plywood. This PPF is linear, rather than concave as in Chapter 1, to keep the example uncomplicated. Its linearity reflects the fact that the opportunity cost is the same regardless of the quantities produced. The U.S. PPF lies completely outside the Canadian PPF, and since each economy has the same resources, it follows that the U.S. has an absolute advantage in producing each good. Nonetheless, trade can still benefit both Canada and the United States. Here is why.

Let the United States specialize completely in the good where it has the comparative advantage, and let Canada do the same. Hence, the United States will produce 7 solar panels and Canada will produce 35 sheets of plywood. Having specialized in producing solar panels, but wishing to consume both goods, the United States now wishes to trade solar panels for plywood. If it can trade with Canada at the rate at which

FIGURE 15.1 **Comparative Advantage**

Each economy has 210 hours of labour. Canada requires 42 hours to produce a solar panel, the U.S. requires 30. Canada needs 6 hours to produce a sheet of plywood, the U.S. needs 5. These requirements define each country's production possibility frontier. If each economy specializes where it has a comparative advantage, Canada produces plywood and the U.S. solar panels. The U.S. and Canadian consumption possibility frontiers are drawn on the assumption that each can trade at the other country's rate of product transformation.

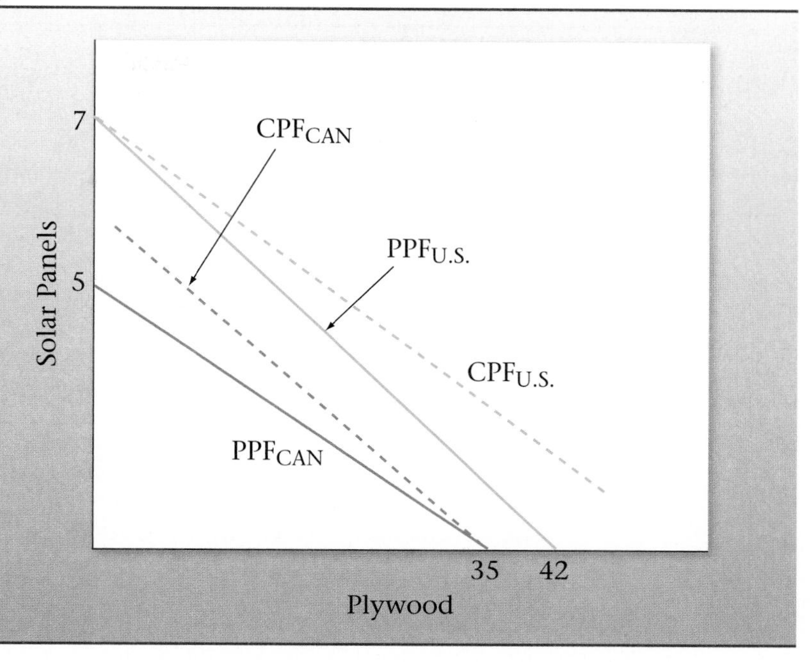

Canada can transform solar panels into plywood (5/35 = 1/7), then it could consume *outside* its PPF. The consumption possibilities that this trading gives rise to form the U.S. *consumption* possibility frontier, CPF_{US}. The horizontal intercept is 49, since the assumed trading rate is 1 to 7. If the United States can trade at this rate, it can clearly increase its consumption relative to the no-trade situation where its consumption possibilities coincide with its PPF.

We can develop an exactly similar case for Canada. It could consume on a consumption frontier outside of its PPF by trading with the United States at the rate at which the United States can turn one good into the other (1/6 in this case). So Canada's CPF extends upward from the intersection of its PPF with the horizontal axis, and outside its PPF, as illustrated in the figure.

Of course, we cannot simultaneously have each country trade with the other at two different trading rates. Accordingly, if they trade at a rate between 1/6 and 1/7, say 1/6.5, there is scope for each country to gain in the sense that each could attain a CPF outside its own PPF. At such a rate of exchange, this means that Canada is really just sacrificing 6.5 sheets of plywood for one solar panel, rather than 7 as when no trade took place. The no-trade scenario is called *autarky.*

EXCHANGE RATES

What we have shown here is that there exists a *potential for gain*, not that gains are actually realized. Such gains depend upon markets, not economic planners, and countries trade with each other using different currencies which themselves have a market. The rate at which one currency trades for another is the exchange rate. Citizens of Canada buy U.S. goods if these goods sell more cheaply in Canada than Canadian-produced goods, not because the United States may have a comparative advantage. To illustrate the possibilities, consider three separate cases.

APPLICATION BOX 15.2

The One Hundred Mile Diet

In 2005 two young British Columbians embarked on what has famously become known as the "one hundred mile diet"—a challenge to eat and drink only products grown within this distance of their home. They succeeded in doing this for a whole year, wrote a book on their experience and went on to produce a TV series. They were convinced that such a project is good for humanity, partly because they wrapped up ideas on organic farming and environmentally friendly practices in the same message.

Reflect now on the implications of this superficially attractive program: If North Americans were to espouse this diet, it would effectively result in the closing down of the mid-west of the Continent. From Saskatchewan to Kansas, we are endowed with grain-producing land that is the envy of the planet. But since most of this terrain is not within 100 miles of any big cities, these deluded advocates are proposing that we close up the production of grains and cereals exactly in those locations where such production is extraordinarily efficient. Should we sacrifice grains and cereals completely in this hemisphere, or just cultivate them on a hillside close to home, even if the resulting cultivation were to be more labour and fuel intensive? Should we produce olives in greenhouses in Edmonton rather than importing them from the Mediterranean, or simply stop eating them? Should we sacrifice wine and beer in North Battleford because insufficient grapes and hops are grown locally?

Would production in temperate climates really save more energy than the current practice of shipping vegetables and fruits from a distance—particularly when there are returns to scale associated with their distribution?

The one hundred mile diet is based on precepts that are contrary to the norms of the gains from trade. In its extreme the philosophy proposes that food exports be halted—and that the world's great natural endowments of land, water, and sun be allowed to lie fallow. Where would that leave a hungry world?

1. *Exchange rate is $1CDN = $1U.S.* In this case, Canadians would have an incentive to purchase both goods from the United States, because each is cheaper *in Canada* than the Canadian-produced counterpart. United States solar panels would sell for $300CDN and plywood would sell for $50CDN.
2. *Exchange rate is $1CDN = $0.80U.S., i.e. $1U.S. = $1.25CDN.* In this case, Canadian plywood sells for $48 in the United States ($60CDN × 0.8 = $48U.S.) and therefore is cheaper than U.S. plywood in the United States. Hence, this good would be exported. By the same reasoning, solar panels from the United States sell at $375CDN in Canada ($375CDN = $300U.S./0.8) and therefore would be imported by Canadians.
3. *Exchange rate is $1CDN = $0.60U.S., i.e. $1U.S.= $1.67CDN.* In this case, Canadian plywood sells for $36U.S. in the United States and solar panels sell for $252U.S. Consequently, Canada would export both goods, because they would each be cheaper than American goods in the United States.

Comparative advantage has the *potential* to generate trade and improve the consumption possibilities of trading economies. These are the *gains from trade*. Only when opportunity costs are the same in both countries are there no gains to be reaped. *What actually happens* to trade flows depends critically upon the exchange rate, as is clear from the foregoing example, and many different factors influence this rate in the foreign exchange market. However, it should be obvious that it would be impossible for one country to import all of its goods and produce none—economies must generate income in order to pay for their purchases. Trade is a two-way or multi-way affair.

Review Questions 3, 4, and 5

The principle of comparative advantage still holds with many goods, rather than just two, even though we have followed our normal practice of developing arguments in two dimensions in order to use geometric explanations. Additionally, the principle of comparative advantage has many applications in everyday life, as we saw in Chapter 1. Suppose two students share an apartment. One is faster at both making dinner *and* vacuuming. If tasks are allocated according to absolute advantage, the slower student does nothing. However, the total work gets done faster if each student does the task at which he or she is relatively good.

OTHER REASONS FOR COMPARATIVE ADVANTAGE

In the example we developed above, the reason for comparative advantage was that the factors of production were operating at different levels of efficiency, or were using different technologies. There are other reasons for comparative advantage; one is different factor endowments, another is returns to scale.

Factor Endowments

Some goods demand a lot of some factors of production and little of others. Wheat requires land, clothing requires workers, and aluminum requires power. We say that wheat production is *land intensive*, that aluminum production is *power intensive*, that research and development is *skill intensive*, that auto manufacture is *capital intensive*. Consequently, if a country is well endowed with some particular factors of production, it is to be expected that it will specialize in producing goods that use those inputs. A relatively abundant supply or endowment of one factor of production tends to make the cost of using that factor relatively cheap. It is relatively less expensive to produce clothing in Hong Kong and wheat in Canada than the other way around. This explains why Canada's Prairies produce wheat, why Quebec produces aluminum, why Asia produces apparel, and why California produces movies.

Thus, even if countries have access to the same knowledge and technologies, goods and services prices may still differ on account of different factor endowments, thereby giving rise to trade. But factor endowments are not static, particularly in the modern era. Globalization means that the communications revolution, coupled with freer and easier movement of capital, has changed comparative advantage. Ireland, which once specialized heavily in agricultural products and exports to the United Kingdom, now finds itself exporting medical equipment, computer components, and pharmaceuticals. Ireland was well endowed with labour skills in the 1970s, and the free flow of capital meant that Ireland's comparative advantage in trade changed radically from agriculture to knowledge-based products. The world is no longer static; comparative advantage can change, and this can both create and eliminate jobs and traditional ways of life.

Returns to Scale

Increasing returns to scale and the resulting falling costs as firm size increases can result in oligopoly or even monopoly market structures. Increasing returns are evident in the world market place as well as the domestic marketplace. Witness the small number of aircraft manufacturers—Airbus and Boeing are the only two manufacturers of large

Intra-industry trade is two-way international trade in products produced within the same industry.

Intra-firm trade is two-way trade in international products produced within the same firm.

aircraft. Large fixed costs—in the form of research, design, and development—or large capital outlays frequently result in decreasing unit costs, and the world marketplace can be supplied at a lower cost if some specialization can take place.

But trade patterns are more subtle than this. In North America, we observe that Canadian auto plants produce different models than their counterparts in the U.S. Canada exports some models of a given manufacturer to the United States and imports other models. This is the phenomenon of **intra-industry trade** and **intra-firm trade**.

15.4 Intra-Industry Trade

We observe large volumes of trade in goods and services that lie *within* the same general product category. This intra-industry trade is evident in, for example, automobiles, office equipment, and telecommunications.

In addition to scale economies, intra-industry trade reflects the preference of consumers for a wide choice of brands; consumers do not all want the same car, or the same software, or the same furnishings. The tendency to specialize in a particular variety of a product, to which demand for diversity and the possibility of scale economies give rise, is limited by transport costs: Intra-industry trade between Canada and the United States is larger than intra-industry trade between Canada and Japan.

Data on world trading patterns suggest that, as a general principle, the more commodities are *undifferentiated* (e.g., fuel and steel) the more trade patterns reflect comparative advantage based on relative resource abundance. As we move towards finished manufactures, product differentiation and variety become more important and comparative advantage based on factor endowments becomes less dominant in determining trade patterns.

Table 15.7 provides more detail on the importance of intra-industry trade flows among countries. For Canada, this trade is as large a share of manufacturing exports as it is in the major European countries. By contrast, intra-industry trade is much less important between Australia and New Zealand, which are further removed geographically from other industrial economies.

TABLE 15.7 **Manufacturing Intra-Industry Trade as a Percentage of Total Manufacturing Trade**

Average for Years	1988–1991	1992–1995	1996–2000
Canada	73.5	74.7	76.2
United States	63.5	65.3	68.5
France	75.9	77.6	77.5
Germany	67.1	72.0	72.0
United Kingdom	70.1	73.1	73.7
Ireland	58.6	57.2	54.6
Japan	37.6	40.8	47.6
New Zealand	37.2	38.4	40.6
Norway	40.0	37.5	37.1
Australia	28.6	29.8	29.8

Source: OECD, Economic Outlook, 71, Chapter VI: "Intra-Industry and Intra-Firm Trade and the Internationalisation of Production." www.oecd.org/dataoecd/6/18/2752923.pdf.

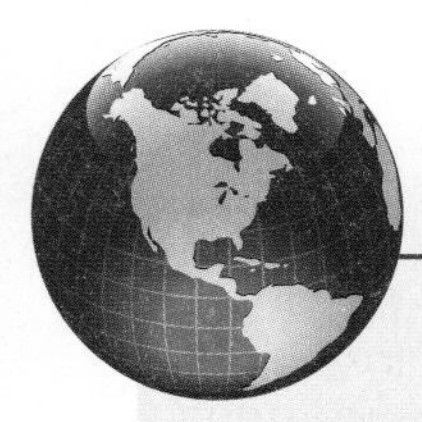

APPLICATION BOX 15.3

Paul Krugman and Intra-Industry Trade

Paul Krugman was awarded the 2008 Nobel Prize in Economics. The prize recognized his work since the late 1970s on new theories that integrated economies of scale, product diversity, and imperfect competition to explain patterns of foreign trade among developed industrial countries.

As the Royal Swedish Academy of Sciences pointed out:

> "[Krugman's] model can be used to show that foreign trade will arise not only between countries that are *different* (as in traditional theory), but also between countries that are identical in terms of access to technology and factor endowments. Moreover, it can be demonstrated that extensive *intra-industry* trade will occur........ This allows each country to take effective advantage of economies of scale, thereby implying that consumers worldwide benefit from greater welfare due to lower prices and greater product diversity......."[1]

Krugman's explanation of trade in differentiated manufactured products is now seen as an important complement to the earlier, traditional theories of international trade.

You can read more about Professor Krugman's Nobel Prize and his work at: http://nobelprize.org/nobel_prizes/economics/laureates/2008/press.html

[1] Information for the public: The prize in Economic Sciences 2008, The Royal Swedish Academy of Sciences: www.kva.se.

15.5 Does Everyone Gain from Trade?

Whatever underlying production structures are responsible for trade, countries are better off with trade than without it because they can buy some goods more cheaply or buy a wider variety of goods. Although trade is beneficial in aggregate, this is no guarantee that trade makes *everyone* better off. Current concerns about globalization arise because there are losers, too. Here are two examples of the conflicts to which international trade gives rise.

REFRIGERATION

At the end of the nineteenth century, the invention of refrigeration enabled Argentina to supply frozen meat to the world market. Argentina's meat exports, non-existent in 1900, rose to 400,000 tons a year by 1913. The United States, with beef exports of 150,000 tons in 1890, had virtually stopped exporting beef by 1913.

Who gained and who lost in this early example of globalization? Argentina's economy was transformed. Owners of cattle and land gained; other land users lost out because higher demand bid up land rents. Argentine consumers found their steaks becoming dearer as meat was shipped abroad. Argentina's GDP rose, but the gain from trade was not equally distributed. Some people in Argentina were worse off, while in Europe and the United States cheaper beef made consumers better off, but beef producers lost out because beef prices fell. *As a whole,* the world economy gained, and in principle the gainers could have compensated the losers and still had something left over. But, in practice, gainers rarely compensate losers. Some people do lose out. In this example, the losers were beef producers elsewhere in the world, and other land users in Argentina.

THE U.K. AUTO INDUSTRY

A second example is the United Kingdom's auto industry. As recently as 1971, imports were only 15 percent of that market, while 35 percent of U.K. output was exported—the U.K. was thus a net auto exporter. Since 1971, U.K. automakers have lost market share to foreign imports, which now exceed 60 percent. Exports recovered in the 1990s, in part because companies like Nissan, Honda, and Toyota established plants in the U.K. to produce for the EU market.

U.K. buyers and foreign exporters benefited from the rise in U.K. imports of cheaper, and perhaps better-made, foreign cars. But U.K. producers had a very tough time, and the British government faced pressure to restrict imports to prevent further job losses in the industry. Restricting car imports would help the British auto industry, but raise prices to British buyers. Should government please producers or consumers?

These are just two examples of the general move towards globalized production, where reduced transportation costs, easier communications, and freer movement of financial and physical capital have seen countless manufacturing patterns in the developed world turned upside down. A common trait of this process is that while most consumers gain from reduced costs and greater product variety, particular sectors and their employees take the hit. We now analyze the costs and benefits of tariffs and other types of trade restrictions.

15.6 The Economics of Tariffs, Quotas, and Subsidies

A **tariff** is a tax imposed on imports.

A **quota** is a limitation on the quantity of an import.

A **non-tariff barrier** can take a variety of forms, but product content and standards are the most frequent forms.

A **subsidy** is a transfer from the government to a domestic producer in order to reduce the producer's supply price.

The most common form of trade restriction is an import **tariff** or duty. An import tariff is a tax imposed on imports. There also exist **quotas**, which are quantitative restrictions on imports; other **non-tariff barriers**, such as product content requirements; and **subsidies**. By raising the domestic price of imports, a tariff helps domestic producers but hurts domestic consumers. Quotas and other non-tariff barriers have similar impacts.

MARKETS AND TARIFFS

Figure 15.2 describes how tariffs operate. We can think of this as the wine market—a market that is heavily taxed in Canada. The world price of Cabernet Sauvignon is $10 per bottle, and this is shown by the horizontal supply curve at that price. It is horizontal because we assume that the world can supply us with any amount we wish to buy at the same price. The Canadian demand for this wine is given by the demand curve D, and Canadian suppliers have a supply curve given by S (Canadian Cabernet is assumed to be of the same quality as the imported variety in this example). At a price of $10, Canadian consumers wish to buy Q_D litres, and domestic producers wish to supply Q_S litres. The gap between domestic supply Q_S and domestic demand Q_D is filled by imports. This is the *free trade equilibrium*.

If the government now imposes a 20 percent tariff on imported wines, foreign wine sells for $12 a bottle, inclusive of the tariff. The tariff raises the domestic "tariff-inclusive" price above the world price, and this shifts the supply of this wine upwards. By raising wine prices in the domestic market, the tariff protects domestic producers by raising the domestic price at which imports become competitive. Those domestic suppliers who were previously not quite competitive at a global price of $10 are now competitive. At the new equilibrium, domestic producers supply the amount Q_S' and imports fall to the amount $(Q_D' - Q_S')$. Imports fall and are partly displaced by domestic producers who supply at prices between $10 and $12.

FIGURE 15.2 **The Effect of a Tariff**

At a world price of \$10 the domestic quantity demanded is given by Q_D. Of this amount Q_S is supplied by domestic producers and the remainder by foreign producers. A tariff increases the world price to \$12. This reduces demand to Q_D', and the domestic component of supply increases to Q_S'. Of the total loss in consumer surplus (LFGJ), tariff revenue equals EFHI, increased surplus for domestic suppliers equals LECJ, and the deadweight loss is therefore the sum of the triangular areas A and B.

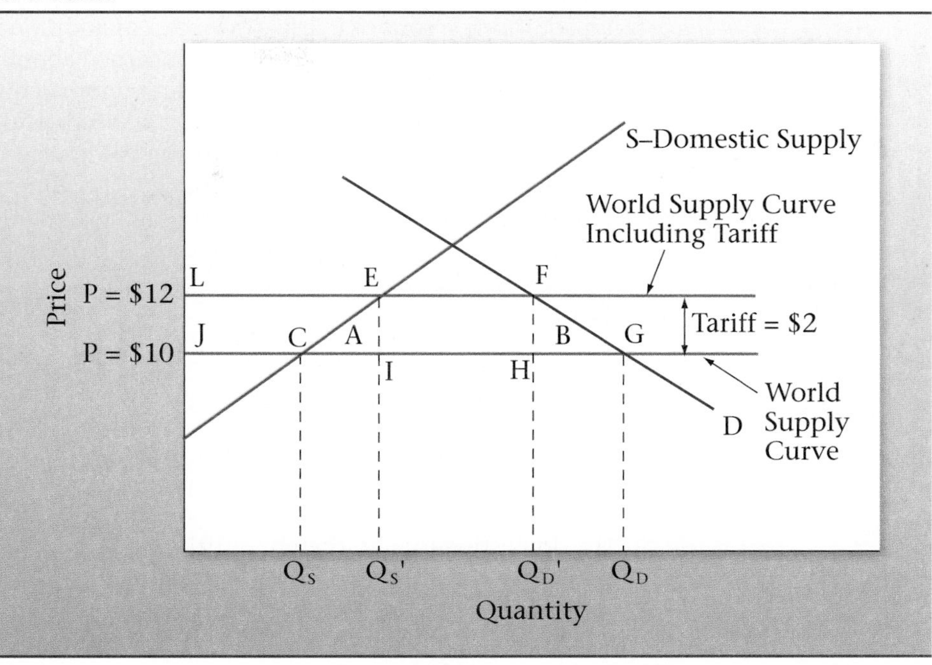

The higher price also moves consumers up their demand curve from G to F. The total quantity demanded falls from Q_D to Q_D'. For consumers, the tariff is a tax. Figure 15.2 shows the combined effect of higher domestic production but lower domestic consumption. Imports fall both because total consumption falls and because domestic suppliers can displace imports under the protective tariff. In Chapters 4 and 5 we illustrated how the impact of a tax imposition depends upon the elasticities of supply and demand in the market: The more elastic is the demand curve, the more a given tariff reduces imports. In contrast, if it is inelastic the quantity of imports declines less.

COSTS AND BENEFITS OF A TARIFF

The costs of a tariff come from the higher price to consumers, but this is partly offset by the tariff revenue that goes to the government. This tariff revenue is a benefit and can be redistributed to consumers or spent on goods from which consumers derive a benefit. But there are also efficiency costs associated with tariffs—deadweight losses, as we call them. These are the real costs of the tariff, and they arise because the marginal cost of production does not equal the marginal benefit to the consumer. Let us see how these concepts apply with the help of Figure 15.2.

Consumer surplus is the area under the demand curve and above the equilibrium market price. It represents the total amount consumers would have been willing to pay for the product but did not have to pay at the equilibrium price. It is a measure of consumer welfare. The tariff raises the market price and reduces this consumer surplus by the amount LFGJ. This area measures by how much domestic consumers are worse off as a result of the price increase caused by the tariff. But this is not the net loss for the whole domestic economy, because the government obtains some tax revenue and domestic producers get more revenue and profit.

Government revenue is the revenue from the domestic sales of imports. Since the quantity of imports is ($Q_D' - Q_S'$), tax revenue is EFHI. Then, domestic producers obtain an additional profit of LECJ—the excess of additional revenue per bottle over their cost per additional bottle. If we are not concerned about who gains and who loses, it is clear that there is a net loss to the domestic economy equal to the areas A and B.

The area B is the standard measure of deadweight loss. At the quantity Q_D', the cost of an additional bottle is less than the value placed on it by consumers; and, by not having those additional bottles supplied, consumers forgo a potential gain. The area A tells us that when supply by domestic higher-cost producers is increased, and supply of lower-cost foreign producers is reduced, the corresponding resources are not being used efficiently. The sum of the areas A and B is therefore the total deadweight loss of the tariff.

Review Questions 6, 7, and 8

PRODUCTION SUBSIDIES

Figure 15.3 illustrates the effect of a subsidy to a supplier. As in Figure 15.2, the amount Q_D is demanded in the free trade equilibrium and, of this, Q_S is supplied domestically. With a subsidy per unit of output sold, the government can reduce the supply cost of the domestic supplier, thereby shifting the supply curve downward from S to S'. In this illustration, the total quantity demanded remains at Q_D, but the domestic share increases to Q_S'.

Review Question 9

The new equilibrium represents a misallocation of resources. When domestic output increases from Q_S to Q_S', a low-cost international producer is being replaced by a higher cost domestic supplier; the domestic supply curve S lies above the international supply curve P in this range of output.

FIGURE 15.3 **The Impact of a Subsidy**

With a world supply price of P, a domestic supply curve S, and a domestic demand D, the amount Q_D is purchased. Of this, Q_S is supplied domestically and ($Q_D - Q_S$) by foreign suppliers. A per-unit subsidy to domestic suppliers shifts their supply curve to S', and ultimately increases their market share to Q_S'.

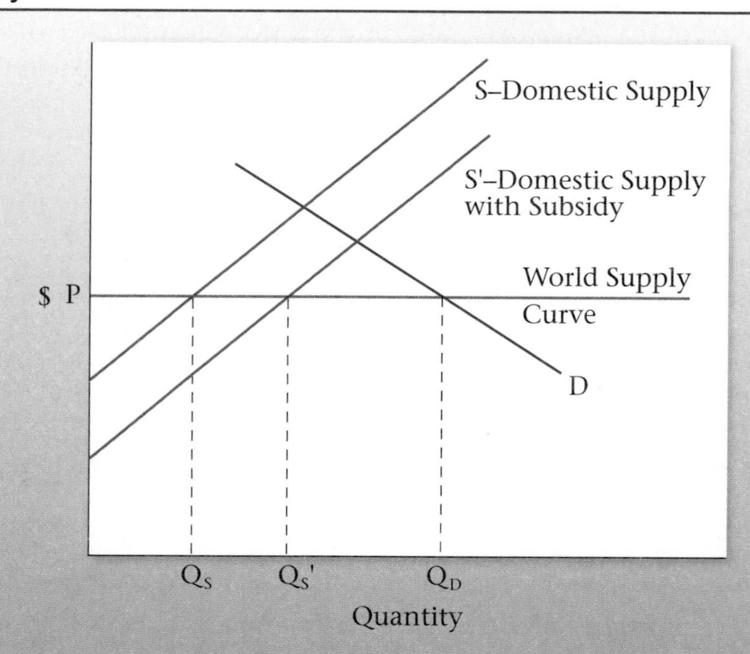

QUOTAS

A quota is a limit placed upon the amount of a good that can be imported. Consider Figure 15.4, where again there is a domestic supply curve coupled with a world price of P, and suppose that, rather than imposing a tariff, the government imposes a quota that restricts imports to a physical amount denoted by the distance *quota* on the quantity axis. The supply curve facing domestic consumers then has several segments to it. First it has the segment RC, reflecting the fact that domestic suppliers are competitive with world suppliers up to the amount C. Beyond this output, world suppliers can supply at a price of P, whereas domestic suppliers cannot. Therefore the supply curve becomes horizontal, but only *up to the amount permitted under the quota*—the quantity CU corresponding to *quota*. Beyond this amount, international supply is not available and therefore additional amounts are supplied by the (higher cost) domestic suppliers. Hence the supply curve to domestic buyers becomes the supply curve from the domestic suppliers once again.

The resulting supply curve yields an equilibrium quantity Q_D'. There are several features to note about this equilibrium. First, the quota pushes the domestic price above the world price because low-cost international suppliers are partially supplanted by higher-cost domestic suppliers. Second, if the quota is chosen "appropriately," the same domestic market price could exist under the quota as under the tariff in Figure 15.3. Third, in contrast to the tariff case, the government obtains no tax revenue from the quotas. Fourth, there are inefficiencies associated with the equilibrium at Q_D': consumers lose the amount $PGTP_{dom}$ in surplus. Against this, suppliers gain $PUTP_{dom}$ (domestic suppliers gain the amount $PCWP_{dom}$ + UYT, which represents the excess of market price over their "willingness to supply" price; the holders of the quota can import at a price P and sell at P_{dom}, and therefore gain a surplus equal to CUYW). Therefore the deadweight loss of the quota is the area UTG—the difference between the loss in consumer surplus and the gain in supplier surplus.

Review Question 10

FIGURE 15.4 **The Impact of a Quota**

At a world price of P, plus a quota on international supply limited to <u>quota</u>, the supply curve to the domestic market becomes RCUV. This has three segments: the first is made up of domestic suppliers who can supply at or below the world price; the second is composed of the import quota and the third by those domestic suppliers who supply the domestic market at a price above the world price, because some foreign, lower-price, suppliers are excluded by the quota. The quota equilibrium is thus at T, with price P_{dom} and quantity traded Q'_D, whereas the free-trade equilibrium is at G. Of the amount Q'_D, <u>quota</u> is supplied by foreign suppliers and the remainder by domestic suppliers. The quota increases the price in the domestic market. The holders of the quota earn a rent because they can import the good for P and sell it domestically for more than this amount.

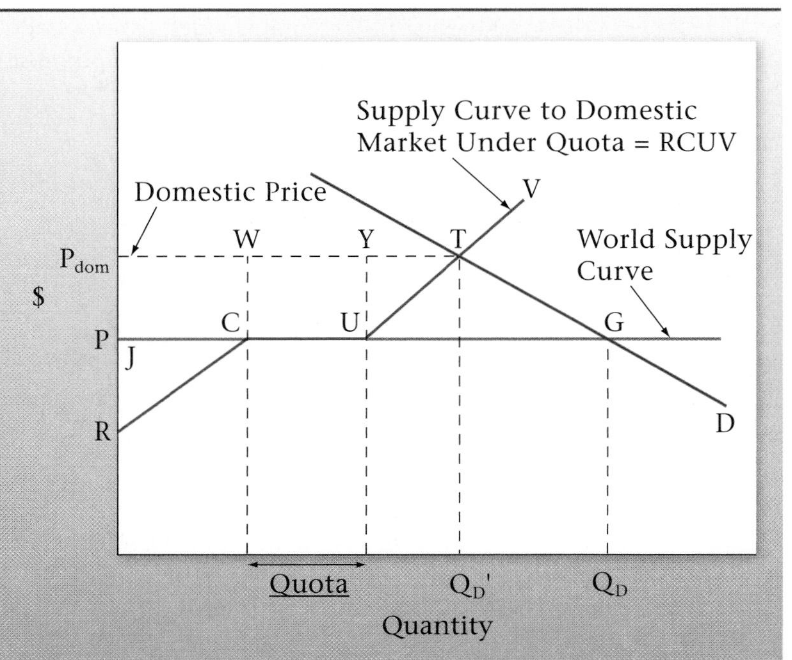

APPLICATION BOX 15.4

Cheese Quota in Canada

In 1978 the federal government set a cheese import quota for Canada at just over 20,000 tonnes. This quota was implemented initially to protect the interests of domestic suppliers. Despite a strong growth in population and income in the intervening decades, the import quota has remained unchanged. The result is a price for cheese that is considerably higher than it would otherwise be. The quotas are owned by individuals and companies who have the right to import cheese. The quotas are also traded among importers, at a price. Importers wishing to import cheese beyond their available quota pay a tariff of about 250 percent. So, while the consumer is the undoubted loser in this game, who gains?

First the suppliers gain—as illustrated in Figure 15.4—Canadian consumers are required to pay high-cost domestic producers who displace lower-cost producers from overseas. Second, the holders of the quotas gain. With the increase in demand for cheese that comes with higher incomes, the domestic price increases over time and this in turn makes an individual quota more valuable.

15.7 Good and Bad Arguments for Protection

Should tariffs or quotas ever be imposed? Should subsidies ever be granted? Most popular arguments for restricting trade through tariffs, quotas, non-tariff barriers, and subsidies are bad arguments. A very small number of these arguments have a solid foundation—but they are not the popular arguments, as we shall see.

POPULAR (MOSTLY BAD) ARGUMENTS FOR RESTRICTING TRADE

The fundamental characteristic of trade is that, by specialization, economies can increase their consumption potential, and most limitations on trade reduce that potential.

Infant Industries

A common argument for a tariff is that it allows infant industries to get started, particularly if *learning by doing* is involved. In this instance, only by actually producing do firms learn how to reduce costs and become efficient international competitors. A tariff may provide protection to such industries, it is frequently proposed, until they master the business and can compete with more experienced foreign suppliers.

Investment in new industries should be made only if they are viable in the long run; the long-run benefit must outweigh the initial losses during the period when the infant industry is a higher-cost "learner." But, if the industry is such a good idea in the long run, society should begin by asking why private firms cannot borrow the money to see them through the early period when they are losing out to more efficient foreign firms. If private lenders are not prepared to invest or lend, should the government be willing to step in? Does the government know more than the private sector about long-term investment returns?

The classical problem with the infant industry argument is that the protected industries do not have a sufficient incentive to grow up. A protection measure that is initially intended to be temporary can become permanent because of the job losses associated with a cessation of the protection to an industry that fails to become internationally competitive.

Way of Life

Throughout its existence, the EU has subsidized small farmers in a variety of ways: tariffs against imports, production subsidies, and quotas. Ostensibly this menu of policies has been aimed at protecting a traditional way of life, or at least permitting a gentle adaptation to a more open world market. But these measures have led to overproduction in the form of the "butter mountain," the "wine lake," etc., and have made it very difficult for international producers to compete on the world market—the prices of their products are forced down as a result of overproduction by inefficient small-scale European farmers.

Is the "way of life" argument so valid that it can justify not only excessive inefficient production to the detriment of domestic consumers, but also damaging impacts on the impoverished nations of the world who are seeking to export to such protected markets?

Defence

In this case, most nations believe that they do not want to be dependent upon other countries to supply them with the means of defence in times of conflict. Supporting this industry is based on a somewhat different argument. Societies are in effect saying that the market supply and demand curves do not accurately reflect social costs and values, and therefore deadweight loss and efficiency arguments are not applicable.

Cost of Generating Revenue

In the eighteenth century, most government revenue came from tariffs. Administratively, it was the simplest tax to collect, and today this is still true in some developing countries. But in modern economies with sophisticated accounting and administration, the administrative costs of raising revenue through tariffs are not lower than the cost of raising revenue through income taxes or taxes on expenditure. The need to raise revenue on imported, rather than domestically produced, commodities is therefore not a justification for tariffs in modern economies.

Cheap Foreign Labour

Home producers frequently argue that tariffs are needed to protect them from cheap foreign labour. Yet the whole point of trade is to exploit international differences in relative prices of different goods. If the domestic economy is relatively well endowed with capital, it benefits from trade precisely because its exports of capital-intensive goods allow it to purchase more labour-intensive goods from abroad than would be obtained by diverting domestic resources to produce labour-intensive goods.

As technology and relative factor endowments change over time, countries' comparative advantages alter. In the nineteenth century, Britain exported Lancashire textiles all over the world. But textile production is relatively labour intensive. Once Southeast Asian countries acquired the technology, it was inevitable that their relatively abundant labour endowment would give them a comparative advantage in producing textiles. New technology frequently gives a country a temporary advantage in particular products. As time passes, other countries acquire the technology and relative factor endowments and relative factor costs evolve and change.

In the long run, the economy as a whole will benefit by recognizing that comparative advantage has changed, and by transferring production to the industries in which it now has a comparative advantage. Of course, in the short run, the adjustment may be painful. Workers lose their jobs and must start over in sectors where they don't have years of experience and acquired skills.

Strategic Tariffs and Subsidies

In international trade, strategic rivalry may exist between giant firms or "national champions" of different countries, or between governments acting on their behalf. For example, we see that Europe favours Airbus through subsidy policies, and the United States favours Boeing. It is sometimes proposed that the imposition of a tariff (or the provision of a subsidy) may deter foreigners from attempting a price war to force domestic producers out of the industry, or may even prevent foreign producers from entering the industry in the first place.

This argument should be viewed with considerable caution. If it is attractive for one country to impose tariffs or to subsidize their national suppliers for this purpose, it may be attractive for foreigners to do the same. If we then create market conditions where little trade takes place, domestic suppliers obtain a monopoly status and no longer face effective competition from foreigners. All countries suffer in this outcome.

SUSTAINABLE ARGUMENTS FOR RESTRICTING TRADE

Dumping

Dumping occurs when foreign producers sell at prices below their marginal production cost, either by making losses or with the assistance of government subsidies. Domestic producers say this is unfair, and demand a tariff to protect them from foreign competition. This was the basis of the softwood lumber dispute between Canada and the United States some years ago, when American lumber producers argued that Canadian producers had an unfair advantage on account of low "stumpage fees" set by governments on crown lands. This long-running dispute was resolved in 2006.

When foreign producers are willing to sell at prices below cost, we might welcome this practice. If we knew they would supply cheap goods indefinitely, we should say thank you, close down our more expensive industry, and put our resources to work elsewhere. To this extent, dumping is a non-argument for a tariff. However, foreign producers may be engaged in predatory pricing, designed to drive our producers out of the industry. Once foreigners achieve monopoly power in world markets, the consequences for our economy may be unfavourable. In this instance it is wise for a domestic government to resist.

Optimal Tariffs

In our analysis to date we have assumed that the world can supply goods at a constant price. But what would happen if, in fact, the supply from the rest of the world is upward sloping? For example, if one country is a very big importer, the world price may respond to changes in purchases by that economy. Think of the American or Chinese demand for copper or oil; these are very big economies, and the scale of their purchases impacts world prices.

In this case, the analysis becomes more subtle, because, in demanding more imports, the economy raises the price it has to pay on the quantity *already being imported*. Under free trade, each individual buys imports until the benefit *to the individual* equals the price he or she pays.

APPLICATION BOX 15.5

The Byrd Amendment

The Byrd Amendment is a clause in a trade bill passed in 2000 by the United States Congress. It specifies that the revenues from tariffs levied on foreign suppliers who "dump" or who are improperly subsidized at home can be distributed to those firms in the United States that suffer from the dumping and also register a complaint with United States authorities.

The World Trade Organization has ruled this amendment as illegal under WTO rules. The amendment encourages firms who are subject to strong competition to "cry foul," and initiate dubious claims on the hope that they may thereby gain.

See: http://www.dfait-maeci.gc.ca/tna-nac/disp/byrdback-en.asp.

However, when individual producers in China import more copper, they bid up the price for other Chinese importers; they inflict a higher price on other importers. Therefore, the collective cost of those marginal imports exceeds the price, which is to say that the social cost of that import exceeds its benefit: There are too many imports. Society can therefore gain by restricting imports until the benefit of the last import equals its social cost. A tariff that performs this task is called an *optimal tariff.*

SO WHY DO WE HAVE TRADE BARRIERS?

From the foregoing discussion, we can see that valid arguments favouring tariffs and trade restrictions in general are few in number. If this is so, why are barriers still so popular? The answer is to be found in the fact that *benefits from barriers are concentrated and costs are diffuse.*

A tariff on a particular commodity, or a quota, helps a particular industry. The Canada–U.S. softwood lumber dispute forms a good example. It is relatively easy for firms and workers in an industry to organize effective political pressure on a single issue that they see as central to their livelihood. Such pressure can be generated through a trade union representing workers or an association representing producers. But if a tariff or quota is imposed as a result of successful lobbying on the part of interest groups, the cost in terms of higher consumer prices (in this case for newly constructed homes) is borne by a much larger and more diverse group of people. Organization to rally governments in their favour is more difficult for the latter group because the benefits to individual organizers are much smaller, and the beneficiaries are widespread.

As a result, politicians heed the vociferous well-organized group lobbying for tariff protection, especially if they are geographically concentrated in an area where, by voting together, they have a significant effect on the outcome of the next election. This type of outcome is what we frequently describe as resulting from the forces of **political economy:** Political forces dominate in the formation of economic policy that may not be in keeping with efficient resource allocation principles. Indeed this regionally defined concentration of interest goes a long way to explaining agricultural protection: Any political candidate in a rural area that speaks to the interests of consumers nationwide, rather than the interests of local farmers, severely compromises her chances of being elected.

Political economy outcomes result from political forces dominating efficient resource allocation arguments.

15.8 Institutions Governing Trade

In the nineteenth century, world trade grew rapidly, in part because the leading trading nation at the time—the United Kingdom—pursued a vigorous policy of free trade. In contrast, U.S. tariffs averaged about 50 percent, although they had fallen to around 30 percent in the early 1920s. As the industrial economies went into the Great Depression of the late 1920s and 1930s, there was pressure to protect domestic jobs by keeping out imports. Tariffs in the United States returned to around 50 percent, and the United Kingdom abandoned the policy of free trade that had been pursued for nearly a century. The combination of world recession and increasing tariffs led to a disastrous slump in the volume of world trade, further exacerbated by World War II.

THE WTO AND GATT

After World War II, there was a collective determination to see world trade restored. Bodies such as the International Monetary Fund and the World Bank were set up, and many countries signed the General Agreement on Tariffs and Trade (GATT), a commitment to reduce tariffs successively and dismantle trade restrictions.

Under successive rounds of GATT, tariffs fell steadily. By 1960, United States tariffs were only one-fifth their level at the outbreak of the War. In the United Kingdom, the system of wartime quotas on imports had been dismantled by the mid-1950s, after which tariffs were reduced by nearly half in the ensuing 25 years. Europe as a whole moved toward an enlarged European Union in which tariffs between member countries have been abolished. By the late 1980s, Canada's tariffs had been reduced to about one-quarter of their immediate post-World War II level.

Review Questions 11 and 12

The GATT Secretariat, now called the World Trade Organization (WTO), aims both to dismantle existing protection that reduces efficiency and to extend trade liberalization to more and more countries. Tariff levels throughout the world are now as low as they have ever been, and trade liberalization has been an engine of growth for many economies. The consequence has been a substantial growth in world trade.

NAFTA AND THE EU

In North America, recent trade policy has led to a free trade area that covers the flow of trade between Canada, the United States, and Mexico. The Canada/United States free trade agreement (FTA) of 1989 expanded in 1994 to include Mexico in the North American Free Trade Agreement (NAFTA). The objective in both cases was to institute free trade between these countries in most goods and services. This meant the elimination of tariffs over a period of years and the reduction or removal of non-tariff barriers to trade, with a few exceptions in specific products and cultural industries. We have seen evidence of the success of these agreements in Tables 15.2 and 15.4. Canadian exports have grown to 40 percent of GDP, and trade with the United States accounts for the lion's share of Canadian trade flows.

The European Union was formed after World War II, with the prime objective of bringing about a greater degree of *political* integration in Europe. Two world wars had laid waste to their economies and social fabric. Closer economic ties and greater trade were seen as the means of achieving this integration. The Union was called the "Common Market" for much of its existence. The Union originally had six member states, but as of 2009 the number is 27, with several other candidate countries in the process of application, most notably Turkey. The European Union (EU) has a secretariat and parliament in Bruxelles. You can find more about the EU at http://europa.eu.

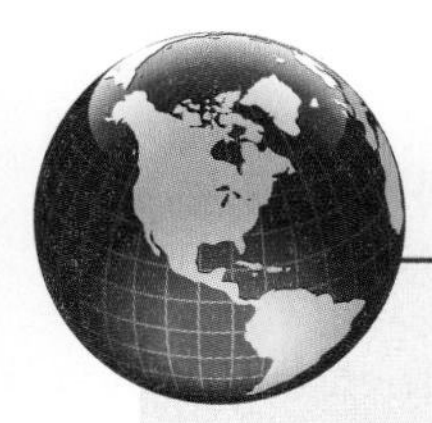

APPLICATION BOX 15.6

The National Policy of J. A. MacDonald

In Canada, tariffs were the main source of government revenues, both before and after Confederation in 1867 and up to World War I. They provided "incidental protection" for domestic manufacturing. After the 1878 federal election, tariffs were an important part of the National Policy introduced by the government of Sir John A. MacDonald. The broad objective was to create a Canadian nation based on east-west trade and growth.

This National Policy had several dimensions. Initially, to support domestic manufacturing, it increased tariff protection on foreign manufactured goods, but lowered tariffs on raw materials and intermediate goods used in local manufacturing activity. The profitability of domestic manufacturing improved. But on a broader scale, tariff protection, railway promotion, Western settlement, harbour development, and transport subsidies to support the export of Canadian products were intended to support *national* economic development. Although "reciprocity agreements" with the United States removed duties on commodities for a time, tariff protection for manufactures was maintained until the GATT negotiations of the post–World War II era.

Many smaller and less well-known "free trade areas" have the same development objectives as the larger organizations. The ASEAN Free Trade Area in Southeast Asia (www.asean.org) covers five countries: Brunei-Darussalam, Indonesia, Malaysia, Singapore, and Thailand. The South Cone Free Trade Area (MERCOSUR) in South America (www.mercosur.int) includes Argentina, Brazil, Paraguay, and Uruguay, with Bolivia and Chile as associate members. In Central America, the US-DR-CAFTA (www.caftaintelligencecenter.com) covers trade among six Central American countries and the United States. Most free trade areas are actively seeking new member states.

SUMMARY

- **World trade has grown rapidly** over the past forty years, and is dominated by the **developed countries**. Primary commodities are 35 percent of Canada's exports; the rest is trade in manufactures and services.
- Countries trade because they can buy goods more cheaply from other countries. Differences in costs reflect differences in **technology** and **factor endowments. Scale economies** also lead to international specialization.
- Countries have a **comparative advantage** in the goods they can produce **relatively** cheaply. When countries specialize in production based on international differences in opportunity costs, international trade leads to a **pure gain** for the world economy.
- The **law of absolute advantage** states that if one economy uses fewer inputs than another economy to produce a good or service, then that economy has an absolute advantage in its production.
- When technology diffuses quickly among countries, **relative factor endowments** are the main source of differences in opportunity costs. Countries then produce and export goods that use inputs in which they are relatively well endowed.
- **Intra-industry trade** occurs because of scale economies, product variety, and consumer demand for product variety. The gain from this trade is lower costs and a greater variety of products.
- While comparative advantage determines the potential gains to trade, the **exchange rate** will

determine the actual flows of trade between economies, because this determines the prices at which goods are actually sold.

- Although international trade can benefit the world as a whole, trade usually **hurts some groups** of people and **benefits others**, unless the gainers compensate the losers.
- A **tariff** is a tax on imports. By raising the domestic price, it reduces consumption and raises domestic production. A **quota** is a limit on the quantity of a good or service that can be imported. **Subsidies** are designed to increase the share of trade by domestic producers. **Non-tariff barriers** include import content rules and other regulations that hinder imports.
- A tariff leads to **inefficiencies** or **deadweight losses**; first by increasing the price to consumers above the marginal cost of production, and second by encouraging higher-cost domestic production at the expense of lower-cost foreign production.
- Most **popular arguments against trade liberalization are contrary to economic reasoning**. A very small number have substance—those dealing with **dumping** (and the subsequent possibility of foreign monopoly power) and the **optimal tariff.** In the presence of an upward-sloping world supply curve, an optimal tariff would reduce the quantity of the imported good to a point where its marginal cost equalled its marginal benefit.
- Tariffs and other non-tariff barriers have fallen greatly since World War II under **GATT** and the **WTO**. The **NAFTA** and the **EU** aim to reduce trade barriers, and the latter aims additionally to increase political integration in Europe.
- Trade protection is usually costly to society, yet governments often adopt it as a result of concentrated political pressure. The **benefits of a tariff are usually concentrated** among few individuals who, therefore, have an incentive to lobby for tariffs. In contrast, the **costs are widely dispersed** and the affected individuals have less of an incentive to fight these tariffs.
- **Political economy outcomes** result from political forces dominating efficient resource allocation arguments.

KEY TERMS

Law of comparative advantage *397*
Law of absolute advantage *398*
Intra-industry trade *402*
Intra-firm trade *402*
Tariff *404*
Quota *404*
Non-tariff barrier *404*
Subsidy *404*
Political economy outcomes *411*

REVIEW QUESTIONS

Review Questions and answers are included in Connect at www.mcgrawhillconnect.ca.

1. From the statistics presented in Tables 15.1, 15.2, and 15.3:
   a. Which region of the world had the largest flows of exports and imports among countries? Explain why.
   b. Which countries experienced the largest growth in the share of imports in GDP between 1988 and 2005? What changes in trade policy do you think would help to explain these changes?
   c. From 1980 to 2003, which group of countries enjoyed the largest increase in their share of world exports of manufactures and of world exports of commodities and fuels? Why?
2. Explain carefully the difference between "absolute advantage" and "comparative advantage" to someone who has not had the pleasure of studying trade theory. Is it possible that a country with an absolute *disadvantage* in all its industries might

still export goods to other countries? Explain the reasoning for your answer.

3. The following table shows the labour input requirements to produce a bushel of wheat and a litre of wine in two countries, Northland and Southland, on the assumption of constant cost production technology.

Labour Requirements per Unit Produced

	Northland	Southland
Per bushel of wheat	1	3
Per litre of wine	2	4

   a. Which country has an absolute advantage in the production of both wheat and wine?
   b. What is the opportunity cost of wheat in each country? Of wine?
   c. Describe and explain the pattern of comparative advantage that you find.
   d. Suppose the country with a comparative advantage in wine reduces wheat production by one bushel and reallocates the labour involved to wine production. How much additional wine does it produce?
   e. Which country, if either, gains from this change in production and trade, and what is the gain?
   f. If the country with the comparative advantage in wheat reduced wine production enough to increase wheat production by one bushel, how much wine could it get by selling the additional bushel of wheat to the other country at that country's opportunity cost?

4. Suppose wage rates in Northland are $10 and in Southland are €8. What are the costs of producing wheat and wine in each country?

5. Canada and the United States can produce two goods, xylophones and yogurt. Each good can be produced with labour alone. Canada requires 60 hours to produce a ton of yogurt and 6 hours to produce a xylophone. The United States requires 40 hours to produce the ton of yogurt and 5 hours to produce a xylophone.
   a. Describe the state of absolute advantage between these economies in producing goods.
   b. In which good does Canada have a comparative advantage? Does this mean the United States has a comparative advantage in the other good?
   c. Draw the production possibility frontier for each economy to scale on a diagram, assuming that each economy has an endowment of 240 hours of labour.
   d. On the same diagram, draw Canada's consumption possibility frontier on the assumption that it can trade with the United States at the United States rate of transformation. Do the same for the United States under the assumption that it can trade at Canada's rate of transformation.

6. Define intra-industry trade. Consider three products: wine, cars, and newsprint. Which of these products would you expect to have high levels of intra-industry trade? Explain why.

7. The domestic demand for bicycles is given by $P = 36 - 0.3Q$. The foreign supply is given by $P = 18$ and domestic supply by $P = 16 + 0.4Q$.
   a. Illustrate the market equilibrium on a diagram, and compute the amounts supplied by domestic and foreign suppliers.
   b. If the government now imposes a tariff of $6 per unit on the foreign good, illustrate the impact geometrically, and compute the new quantities supplied by domestic and foreign producers.
   c. In the diagram, illustrate the area representing tariff revenue and compute its value.

8. In question 7 above, illustrate the deadweight losses associated with the imposition of the tariff, and compute the amounts. Compute the additional amount of profit made by the domestic producer as a result of the tariff. [Go back to Figure 15.2 (page 366) and estimate the value of the area LECJ.]

9. The domestic demand for office printers is given by $P = 40 - 0.2Q$. The supply of domestic producers is given by $P = 12 + 0.1Q$, and international supply by $P = 20$.
   a. Illustrate this market geometrically.
   b. Compute total demand and the amounts supplied by domestic and foreign suppliers.

c. If the government gives a production subsidy of $2 per unit to domestic suppliers in order to increase their competitiveness, calculate the new amounts supplied by domestic and foreign producers. [*Hint:* The domestic supply curve becomes $P = 10 + 0.1Q$].
d. Compute the cost to the government of this scheme.

10. The domestic demand for turnips is given by $P = 128 - (1/2)Q$. The market supply of domestic suppliers is given by $P = 12 + (1/4)Q$, and the world price is $32 per bushel.
    a. First graph this market and then solve for the equilibrium quantity purchased.
    b. How much of the quantity traded will be produced domestically and how much will be imported?
    c. Assume now that a quota of 76 units is put in place. Illustrate the resulting market equilibrium graphically.
    d. Can you figure out the domestic price of turnips and the associated quantity traded with the quota in place? Hint: you could shrink the demand curve in toward the origin by the amount of the quota and equate the result with the domestic supply curve.

11. "Large countries gain proportionately more from trade than small countries." Is this statement true or false? Explain why.

12. *Internet* Visit the Statistics Canada Web site www.statcan.gc.ca and search for the latest information on Canada's imports from and exports to China. Has the volume of this trade changed in recent years? Has the recent global recession affected this bilateral trade?

13. *Internet* On your favourite Internet search engine, enter "sugar quotas" and see if you can establish the impact of these trade restrictions in the U.S. on producers from less developed economies.

Glossary

An **AD/AS model** is a framework used to explain the behaviour of real output and prices in the national economy. (95)

Aggregate demand is **planned aggregate expenditure** on final goods and services at different price levels, all other conditions remaining constant. (95)

Aggregate expenditure (AE) is the sum of planned expenditure in the economy. (120)

The **aggregate expenditure function** is the relationship between planned expenditure in the total economy and real national income or GDP. (128)

Aggregate Supply is the output of final goods and services businesses would produce at different price levels, all other conditions held constant. (96)

The Canadian dollar **appreciates**, increases in external value, when the CDN$/U.S.$ exchange rate falls. (312)

The **asset motive** for holding money arises from the desire to reduce portfolio risk. (211)

Automatic stabilizers reduce fluctuations in GDP caused by autonomous expenditure shocks. (164)

Autonomous expenditure is expenditure not related to current income. (122)

The **balance of payments** is the sum of the balances in current accounts and capital accounts, minus the change in the holdings of official reserves. (302)

The **balance of payments accounts** record transactions between residents of one country and the rest of the world. (301)

The **Bank of Canada** is Canada's central bank. (186)

The **bank rate** is the interest rate the central bank charges on its loans to commercial banks. (240)

Bank reserves are the cash held by the bank to meet possible withdrawals by depositors. (183)

A **barter economy** has no medium of exchange. Goods trade directly for goods. (181)

A **behavioural law** is a sensible theoretical relationship that has been supported by data for a long period of time. (22)

A **bond** is a financial contract that makes one or more fixed money payments at specific dates in the future. (206)

A **bond coupon** is the *annual* fixed money payment paid to a bond holder. (206)

The **budget function** gives the budget balance at each level of income. (158)

Business and investment income (BI) is the sum of profit, interest, investment, and business income. (81)

The **business cycle** is the short-term fluctuation of actual real GDP. (104)

The **capital account** records purchases and sales of real and financial assets. (302)

Capital Consumption Allowance (CCA) measures depreciation of the capital stock. (82)

Capital deepening raises the capital/worker ratio. (376)

A rise (fall) in the price of an asset between its date of purchase and its date of sale generates a **capital gain (loss)** to the holder of the asset. (207)

Capital widening extends capital to workers entering the labour force. (376)

A **central bank** conducts monetary policy using its control of monetary base and interest rates. (234)

The **central bank intervenes** by buying or selling foreign currency to fix the exchange rate. (314)

The **change in official international reserves** is the change in the Government of Canada's foreign currency balances. (302)

The **circular flow diagram** shows how real resources and money payments flow between households and businesses. (75)

In a **command economy,** a government planning office decides what, how, and for whom goods and services will be produced. (10)

Short-term 30-day and 60-day notes designed to pay buyers the interest income generated by bundled accounts receivable and loans of different types during the term to maturity are called **commercial paper.** (193)

Comparative advantage signifies an ability to supply a product at a lower relative cost than a competitor can. (10)

Comparative static analysis compares an initial equilibrium with a new equilibrium, where the difference is due to a change in one of the other things that lie behind the supply and demand curves. (49)

Complementary goods: If a price reduction for one good increases the demand for a second good, the second good is a complement to the first. (44)

The **Consumer Price Index (CPI)** compares the cost of living in one year to the cost of living in a base year. (68)

Consumption expenditure (C) is spending by households on currently produced final goods and services. (79)

The **consumption function** explains consumption expenditure at each level of disposable income. (121)

The **convergence hypothesis** Higher rates of growth in lower per capita income countries than in higher per capita income countries leads to the convergence of per capita incomes across countries. (379)

A currency is **convertible** if the central bank will buy or sell unlimited quantities at a fixed exchange rate. (313)

Core inflation is inflation that excludes changes in the volatile prices of food and energy. (351)

Credit easing is the management of the central bank's assets designed to support lending in specific financial markets. (257)

Credit money is the debt of a private business or individual. (183)

Cross-section data record the behaviour of economic variables across different individuals or groups at a point in time. (23)

Crowding out is the reduction in private expenditures caused by a rise in interest rates if autonomous expenditure increases when the money supply is held constant. (289)

The **currency ratio (cr)** is the ratio of cash balances to deposit balances. (189)

The **current account** records trade in goods, services, and transfer payments. (301)

Cyclical unemployment would be eliminated by higher levels of economic activity. (70)

Data are pieces of evidence about behaviour. (22)

The **debt ratio** is the ratio of public debt to GDP. The net debt ratio is the ratio of net public debt to GDP. (170)

The **deflation rate** is the percentage decrease in the consumer price index. (27)

Demand is the quantity of a good or service that buyers wish to purchase at each possible price, with all other influences on demand remaining unchanged. (40)

The **demand curve** shows the relation between price and quantity demanded, holding other things constant. (42)

The Canadian dollar **depreciates**, falls in external value, when the CDN$/U.S.$ exchange rate rises. (312)

A **devaluation (revaluation)** is a reduction (increase) in the international value of a domestic currency. (314)

Discretionary fiscal policies change net tax rates and government expenditure to offset autonomous expenditure shocks and stabilize aggregate expenditure and output. (164)

Disposable income (YD) is national income minus net taxes. (151)

Econometrics is the science of examining and quantifying relationships between economic variables. (29)

Economic equity is concerned with the distribution of well-being among members of the economy. (13)

Economic growth is the annual percentage change in real GDP or per capita real GDP. (362)

Economics is the study of how society decides to allocate scarce resources in determining what, how, and for whom to produce goods and services. (2)

Employment is the number of adults employed full-time and part-time and self-employed. (68)

Employment income (W) is the sum of all wages, salaries, and benefits paid to labour. (81)

The **employment rate** is the percentage of the population15 years of age and over that is employed. (70)

Endogenous growth is growth determined within the model. (381)

The **equation of exchange** equates total money expenditure and nominal GDP. (259)

The **equilibrium** or **natural unemployment rate** is the unemployment rate when the economy is at potential output Y_P. (107)

The **equilibrium price** clears the market. It is the price at which the quantity demanded equals the quantity supplied. (41)

Equilibrium real GDP means planned expenditure equals current output and provides business revenues that cover costs including expected profit. (101)

Excess demand exists when the quantity demanded exceeds the quantity supplied at the going price. (41)

Excess supply exists when the quantity supplied exceeds the quantity demanded at the going price. (41)

An **exchange rate regime** describes how exchange rates are determined. (312)

With an **exchange rate target** monetary policy maintains a fixed price for foreign currency in terms of domestic currency. (243)

An **exogenous variable** has a value determined outside the model. (381)

The **expected inflation rate** is the inflation rate people think will occur in the future. (342)

Exports, X, are domestic goods and services sold to residents of other countries. (126)

Fiat money is the money the government has declared as legal tender. (183)

Final goods and services are purchased by the ultimate user. (78)

A **financial intermediary** is a business that specializes in bringing borrowers and lenders together. (184)

In a **financial panic,** people lose confidence in banks and rush to withdraw cash. (193)

Fiscal policy is government expenditure and tax changes designed to influence AD. (112)

A **fixed exchange rate** means the exchange rate does not change as a result of changes in market conditions. (313)

Supply and demand determine the equilibrium **floating** or **flexible exchange rate.** (313)

The **foreign exchange rate** is the domestic currency price of a unit of foreign currency. (217)

A **free market** is one in which governments do not intervene significantly. (11)

GDP at basic price = Net Domestic Income + Capital Consumption Allowance. (82)

GDP at market price = Net Domestic Income + Capital Consumption Allowance + Net Indirect Tax. (82)

The **GDP deflator** is an index of current prices relative to base year prices. (85)

The **government budget** reports government revenues and expenditures. (157)

Government expenditure (G) is government spending on currently produced final goods and services. (79)

Growth accounting measures the contributions of labour, capital, and technology to growth in output. (365)

Imports (Z) are our purchases of goods and services produced by other countries.

An **index number** expresses data relative to a given base value. (25)

Induced expenditure is expenditure determined by national income. (122)

An **inferior good** is one whose demand falls in response to higher incomes. (45)

Inflation is a persistent rise in the general price level. (68)

The **inflation rate** is the annual percentage change in the price level. (68)

With an **inflation rate target**, the monetary policy aims to maintain an announced target inflation rate. (243)

An **inflationary gap** is a measure of the amount by which actual GDP is greater than potential GDP. (104)

Innovation incorporates new knowledge into production techniques. (373)

The **intercept** is the height of the line when the variable on the horizontal axis has a zero value. (31)

Interest and investment income is income earned from financial assets. (81)

Interest on the public debt (iPD) is the annual interest paid on the outstanding public debt. (283)

Interest parity occurs when *expected* exchange rate changes offset interest rate differentials between countries. (307)

The **interest rate** is the current market rate paid to lenders or charged to borrowers. (206)

The **interest rate effect** is the change in expenditures when interest rates change. (97)

Intermediate inputs are services, materials, and components purchased from other businesses and used in the production of final goods. (78)

Intra-firm trade is two-way trade in international products produced within the same firm. (402)

Intra-industry trade is two-way international trade in products produced within the same industry. (402)

Invention is the discovery of new knowledge. (373)

Investment (I) is expenditure by business on currently produced final goods and services. (79)

Investment expenditure (I) is business expenditure on current output to add to physical capital (factories and machinery) and to inventories. (124)

The **investment function, I = I(i)**, shows the level of planned investment expenditure at each interest rate. (224)

The **invisible hand** is the assertion that the individual pursuit of self-interest within free markets will allocate resources efficiently from society's viewpoint. (11)

The **labour force** is those adults employed plus those not employed but actively looking for work. (68)

The **law of absolute advantage** states that, if one economy uses fewer inputs than another economy to produce a good or service, then that economy has an absolute advantage in its production. (398)

By the **law of comparative advantage,** countries specialize in the production and export of products they produce at lower *relative cost* than other countries. (397)

Legal tender is the money that by law must be accepted as a means of payment. (183)
Liquidity is the cheapness, speed, and certainty with which asset values can be converted into cash. (187)
Longitudinal data follow the same individuals or units over time. (25)
Macroeconomics is the study of the behaviour and performance of the whole economy as a system, and the total output of goods and services. (17)
The **marginal product** of a factor is the change in total output caused by a change of one unit in the input of that factor to production. (367)
The **marginal propensity to consume (MPC)** is the change in consumption expenditure caused by a change in income. (122)
The **marginal propensity to save (MPS)** is the change in saving caused by a change in income. (122)
The **marginal propensity to import (MPZ)** is the change in imports caused by a change in national income. (127)
The **market demand curve** is obtained by summing individual demand curves horizontally. (58)
Markets are institutions that bring together buyers and sellers of goods and services. (10)
Money is the **medium of exchange** used to make payments. (181)
Microeconomics analyzes individual decisions at the household and firm level. (16)
A **mixed economy** is one where goods and services are supplied by both the private sector and the government. (11)
A **model** is a formalization of the essential elements of a theory and is a deliberate simplification of reality. (22)
The **monetary base** or stock of **high-powered money (H)** is the notes and coins in circulation plus the cash held by the banks. (194)
Monetary policy: changes in interest rates and money supply designed to influence AD. (112)
Monetary policy indicators provide information about the stimulus or restraint coming from the central bank's policy. (261)
The **monetary policy instrument** is the monetary variable the central bank manipulates in pursuit of its policy target. (244)
The **money supply** is the stock of medium of exchange in circulation. (183)
Money illusion is the confusion of nominal (money) and real variables. (330)
The **money multiplier** is the change in the money supply caused by a change in the monetary base or stock of high-powered money. (195)
The **money supply** is the stock of medium of exchange in circulation. (183)
With a **money supply target,** the central bank adjusts interest rates and the monetary base to control the nominal money supply. (243)
The **multiplier ($\Delta Y/\Delta A$)** is the ratio of the change in equilibrium income Y to the change in autonomous expenditure A that caused it. (136)
The **NAIRU** is the unemployment rate at which the rate of inflation in wages and prices is constant. (342)
The **natural unemployment rate** reflects structural unemployment. (70)
Neoclassical growth theory is exogenous growth theory. (381)
Net Domestic Income (NDI) is the total income earned by factors of production. (81)
Net exports (NX) are the difference between exports and imports. (80)
Net indirect taxes (T_{IN}) are sales and excise taxes minus subsidies. (82)
Net interest income is the excess loan interest earned over deposit interest paid. (189)
The **net public debt** is the difference between the government's total debt and its financial assets. (170)
Net taxes ($NT = T_d - T_r$) are taxes minus transfer payments. (151)
The **neutrality of money** means monetary policy can set prices and inflation rates in the long run, but not output and employment. (259)
The **nominal exchange rate (er)** is the domestic currency price of a unit of foreign currency. (303)
Nominal GDP measures the output of final goods and services, the money incomes generated by the production of that output, and expenditure on the sale of that output in a specific time period. (77)
The **nominal price index** reflects the dollar price of a good or service, without reference to the consumer price index. (27)
A **non-tariff barrier** can take a variety of forms, but product content and standards are the most frequent forms. (404)
A **normal good** is one whose demand increases in response to higher incomes. (45)
Normative economics offers recommendations that incorporate value judgements. (12)
Official exchange reserves are government foreign currency holdings managed by the central bank. (313)
Okun's Law: Changes in unemployment rates result from differences between the growth rate of Y and the growth rate of Y_P. (107)
An **open market operation** is a central bank purchase or sale of government securities in the open financial market. (238)
The **opportunity cost** is the quantity of other goods or services that must be sacrificed to get an increment in the first good. (7)
Output gaps are differences between actual and potential real GDP. (338)
The **overnight rate** is the interest rate large financial institutions receive or pay on loans from one day until the next. (245)
The **participation rate** is the percent of the population that is either working or unemployed. (68)
Per capita real GDP is real GDP per person. (87)
Percentage change = (difference in values)/ base value × 100. (25)
Perfect capital mobility means very small differences in expected returns cause very large international flows of funds. (306)
The **Phillips curve** is the relationship between output gaps and employment rates and changes in the *rate of change* in money wage rates. (340)
Political economy outcomes result from political forces dominating efficient resource allocation arguments. (411)
Positive economics studies objective or scientific explanations of how the economy functions. (12)
Potential output is the output the economy can produce on an ongoing basis with current labour, capital, and technology without putting continuous upward pressure on prices. (102)
The **precautionary motive** to hold money arises from uncertainty about the timing of receipts and payments. (210)
The **present value** is the *discounted* value of future payments. (206)
Price controls are government rules or laws that inhibit the formation of market-determined prices. (54)
A **price index** is a measure of the price level in one year compared with prices in a base year. (68)
The **price level** in the economy is a measure of the average prices of all goods and services produced. (68)
The **price of a marketable bond** is its current price in the bond market. (206)

The **primary budget balance (PBB)** excludes interest payments on the public debt. (283)

The **prime lending rate** is the interest rate charged by banks on loans to their most credit worthy borrowers. (246)

Production efficiency means that the economy's resources are being fully utilized. (7)

The **production function** determines output based on technology and inputs of labour and capital. (329)

The **production possibility frontier (PPF)** shows, for each output of one good, the maximum amount of the other that can be produced with given resources and a given state of technology. (6)

Productivity is output per unit of input. (330)

Profit and business income is the sum of corporate profit and small business income. (81)

The **public debt (PD)** is the outstanding stock of government bonds issued to finance government budget deficits. (168)

Purchasing power parity (PPP) means a real exchange rate equal to one. (304)

Quantity demanded refers to the amount purchased at a particular price. (41)

Quantity supplied refers to the amount supplied at a particular price. (41)

A **quota** is a limitation on the quantity of an import. (404)

The **rate of growth** in real GDP is the annual percentage change in real GDP. (67)

The **real exchange rate** is the relative price of goods and services from different countries measured in a common currency. (303)

Real GDP measures the quantity of final goods and services produced by the economy in a specified time period and the real incomes generated by that production. (67)

The **real interest rate** is the nominal interest rate minus the rate of inflation. (331)

The **real money supply,** M/P, is the nominal money supply M divided by the price level P. (214)

The **real price index** for a product is its nominal price index divided by the consumer price index, scaled by 100. (27)

The **real wage rate** is the quantity of goods and services the money wage rate will buy. (330)

A **recession** is a decline in economic activity, often defined as two consecutive quarters of negative growth in real GDP. (73)

A **recessionary gap** is a measure of the amount by which actual GDP is less than potential GDP. (104)

A **regression line** represents the average relationship between two variables in a scatter diagram. (30)

A **required reserve ratio** is a legal minimum ratio of cash reserves to deposits. (237)

The **reserve ratio (rr)** is the ratio of cash reserves to deposit liabilities held by banks. (190)

The **saving function** shows planned saving at each level of income. (123)

A **scatter diagram** plots pairs of values simultaneously observed for two variables. (29)

In the **short run**, factor prices, supplies of factors of production, and technology are fixed by assumption. (95)

Short-run equilibrium output: Aggregate expenditure equals current output. (129)

The **short side** dominates, at prices other than the equilibrium price. (42)

The **slope** of the line is the ratio of the vertical distance divided by the horizontal distance for any segment of the line. (31)

The **Solow residual** is the growth in real GDP or per capita real GDP not caused by growth in factor inputs, but attributed to improved technology. (365)

A Bank of Canada **SPRA** is a purchase of securities one day combined with an agreed resale of the securities the next day. (247)

A Bank of Canada **SRA** is a sale of securities one day combined with an agreed repurchase of the securities the next day. (247)

In the **steady state**, output, capital, and labour grow at the same rate. (375)

A **store of value** carries purchasing power forward in time for future purchases. (182)

The **structural budget balance (SBB)** is the budget balance at potential output. (163)

The **structural primary budget balance (SPBB)** is the primary balance at Y_P. (283)

Structural unemployment comes from labour market structures and institutions. (70)

A **subsidy** is a transfer from the government to a domestic producer in order to reduce the producer's supply price. (404)

Substitute goods: If a price reduction for one good reduces the demand for a second good, the second good is a substitute for the first. (44)

The **substitution effect** is the change in net exports when relative national prices change. (97)

Supply is the quantity of a good or service that sellers are willing to sell at each possible price, with all other influences on supply remaining unchanged. (40)

The **supply curve** shows the relation between price and quantity supplied, holding other things constant. (42)

A **tariff** is a tax imposed on imports. (404)

The **Taylor rule** links central bank interest rate settings to inflation and output targets. (253)

A **theory** is a logical view of how the world and its parts work. (21)

A **time series** is a sequence of measurements at different points in time. (23)

Token money is a convertible claim on a commodity money. (183)

Total factor productivity (TFP) is output relative to the combined inputs of both labour and capital, the total factor inputs to production. (364)

The **transactions motive** for holding money arises from the difference in the timing of payments and receipts. (210)

The **transmission mechanism** links money, interest rates, and exchange rates through financial markets to output and employment and prices. (220)

Unemployment is the number of adults not working but actively looking for work. (68)

The **unemployment rate** is the percentage of the total labour force that is not employed but is actively looking for employment. (69)

A **unit of account** is the unit in which prices are quoted and accounts are kept. (181)

Value added is the difference between the market value of the output of the business and the cost of inputs purchased from other businesses. (77)

The **very long run** is the time required for changes to occur in the stock of capital, the size of the labour force, and the technology of production. (364)

The **wealth effect** is the change in the consumption function caused by a change in household real wealth. (221)

The **yield on a bond** is the return to a bond holder expressed as an annual percentage. (206)

Index

f indicates a figure
n indicates a footnote
t indicates a table
bold-faced numbers indicate the term is bold-faced in the text

N

O

P